PETER NORTON'S®

Introduction to Computers

FOURTH EDITION

Mc Graw Hill Glencoe McGraw-Hill

New York, New York   Columbus, Ohio   Woodland Hills, California   Peoria, Illinois

Library of Congress Cataloging-in-Publication Data

Norton, Peter, 1943—
   [Introduction to computers]
   Peter Norton's introduction to computers.—4th ed.
    p. cm.
   Includes index.
   ISBN 0-07-821058-5
   1. Computers. 2. Computer software. I. Title.
QA76.5.N6818   2000
004—dc21   00-034045
                             CIP

Glencoe/McGraw-Hill

A Division of The **McGraw·Hill** *Companies*

Send all inquiries to:

Glencoe/McGraw-Hill
8787 Orion Place
Columbus, OH 43240-4027

ISBN: 0-07-821058-5

1 2 3 4 5 6 7 8 9   083   04 03 02 01 00

About Peter Norton

Acclaimed computer software entrepreneur Peter Norton is active in civic and philanthropic affairs. He serves on the boards of several scholastic and cultural institutions and currently devotes much of his time to philanthropy.

Raised in Seattle, Washington, Mr. Norton made his mark in the computer industry as a programmer and businessman. *Norton Utilities*™, *Norton AntiVirus*™, and other utility programs are installed on millions of computers worldwide. He is also a best-selling author of computer books.

Mr. Norton sold his PC-software business to Symantec Corporation in 1990 but continues to write and speak on computers, helping millions of people better understand information technology. He and his family currently reside in Santa Monica, California.

Editorial Consultant

Tim Huddleston

Academic Reviewers

Teresa Beatty
ECPI College of Technology

Bill Boroski
Trident Technical College

J. Timothy Dunigan
West Virginia University

Lynn Dee Eason
Sault College

Terry A. Felke
William Rainey Harper College

Mary Hanson
Northwest Technical College

Patrick A. T. Kelly
Mount Royal College

Ron Lenhart
Mohave Community College

Jan L. McDanolds
Hamilton College

Alex Morgan
West Valley College

Cindi A. Nadelman
Naugatuck Valley Community College

Mava F. Norton
Lee University

Ronny Richardson
Southern Polytechnic State University

Annette Sarrazine
College of Lake County

Melissa L. Stoneburner
Moraine Valley Community College
College of DuPage

Wilson E. "Bill" Stroud
Joliet Junior College

Jacqueline Wall
Chaffey College

Technical Reviewers

Barbara Bouton
Bill Brandon
Emmett Dulaney
Kurt Hampe
Drew Heywood
Molly E. Holzschlag
Steve Probst

Acknowledgments

Others who contributed to the content and development of this project: Sue Coons, Robert Goldhamer, Cynthia Karrasch, Marianne L'Abbate, Elliot Linzer, Purple Monkey Studios, Charles A. Schuler, and Tom White.

Special thanks goes to the individuals at Glencoe/McGraw-Hill whose dedication and hard work made this project possible.

Foreword to the Student

Why Study Computer Technology?

The computer is a truly amazing machine. Few tools can help you perform so many different tasks. Whether you want to track an investment, publish a newsletter, design a building, or practice landing an F14 on the deck of an aircraft carrier, you can use a computer to do it. Equally amazing is the fact that the computer has taken on a role in nearly every aspect of our lives, for example:

◆ Tiny embedded computers control our alarm clocks, entertainment centers, and home appliances.

◆ Today's automobiles could not even start, let alone run efficiently, without embedded computer systems.

◆ In the United States, more than half of all homes now have at least one personal computer, and the majority of those are connected to the Internet.

◆ An estimated ten million people now work from home instead of commuting to a traditional workplace, thanks to PC and networking technologies.

◆ People use e-mail for personal communications nearly ten times as often as ordinary mail, and nearly five times more often than the telephone.

◆ People do an ever-increasing amount of shopping online. During the Christmas season of 1999, an estimated seven billion dollars worth of retail business was conducted over the World Wide Web.

◆ Routine, daily tasks are affected by computer technologies such as banking at automated teller machines, talking over digital telephone networks, and paying for groceries with the help of computerized cashiers.

Here are just a few personal benefits you can enjoy by developing a mastery of computers:

◆ **Improved Employment Prospects.** Computer-related skills are essential in many careers. And this does not apply only to programmers. Whether you plan a career in automotive mechanics, nursing, journalism, or archaeology, computer skills will make you more attractive to prospective employers.

◆ **Skills That Span Different Aspects of Life.** Many people find their computer skills valuable regardless of the setting—at home, work, school, or play. Your computer education's usefulness will not be limited simply to your work.

◆ **Greater Self-Sufficiency.** Those who truly understand computers know that they are tools—nothing more or less. We do not give up control of our lives to computer systems; rather, we use them to suit our needs. By knowing how to use computers, you can actually be a more self-sufficient person, whether you use computers for research, communications, or time-management.

◆ **A Foundation of Knowledge for a Lifetime of Learning.** Basic computing principles have not changed over the past few years, and will be valid well into the future. By mastering fundamental concepts and terminology, you will develop a strong base that will support your learning for years to come.

Regardless of your reasons for taking this course, you are wise to do so. The knowledge and skills you gain should pay dividends in the future, as computers become even more common at home and at work.

VISUAL ESSAY: COMPUTERS IN OUR LIVES

A Millions of people use handheld computers to manage their schedules, send e-mail and faxes, create documents, and more.

B Using 3-D CAD tools, designers can create photorealistic three-dimensional renderings of a finished building's interior and exterior. These capabilities enable the designer and client to visualize the completed project before the first shovel of dirt has been turned.

C Factories use computerized robotic arms to do physical work that is hazardous or highly repetitive.

D Computers have become a creative tool for musicians. The Musical Instrument Digital Interface (MIDI) allows different electronic instruments to be connected to one another, as well as to computers.

E The military is often at the forefront of technology. This man is using an Airborne Warning and Aircraft Control (AWAC) system to track the in-flight progress of missiles and jets. The military also uses computers to keep track of one of the largest payroll and human-resource management systems in the world.

F Perhaps no area of science has benefited more from computer technology—or contributed more to its growth—than the space program.

G Many movies and television productions now use motion-capture technology to enable computer-generated characters to move realistically. Special sensors are attached to an actor, who moves in a tightly choreographed way. Movements are recorded by a computer. The data can then be assigned to the corresponding parts of a digital character's body, so that its movements exactly mimic the actor's movements.

Brief Table of Contents

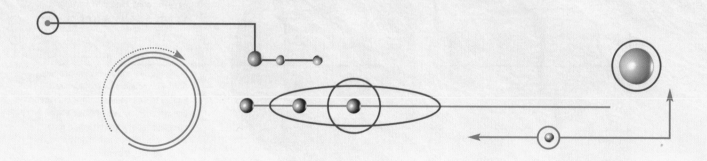

Table of Contents

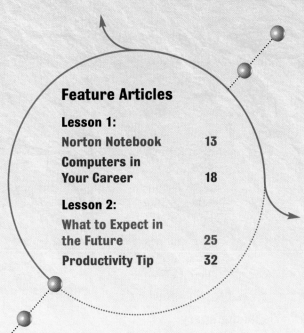

Unit 2: Interacting With Your Computer 40

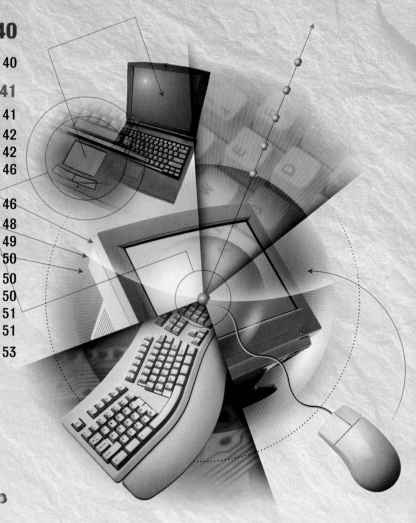

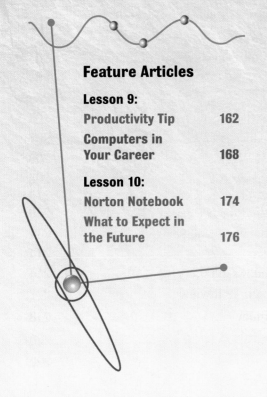

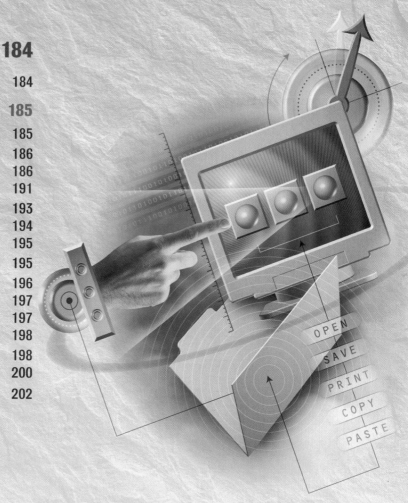

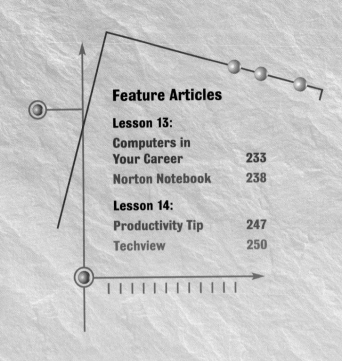

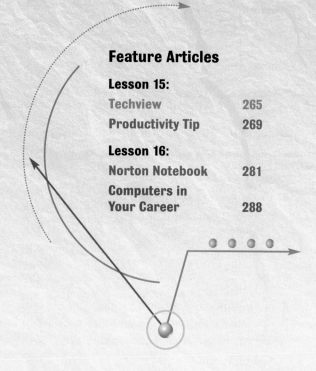

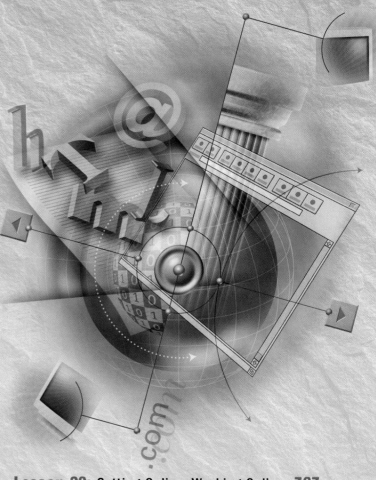

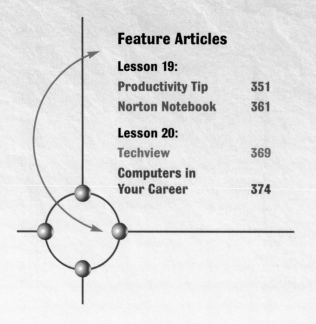

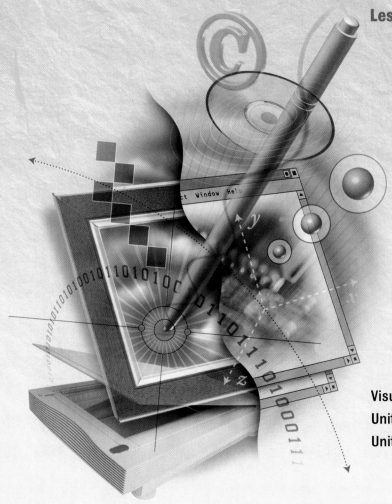

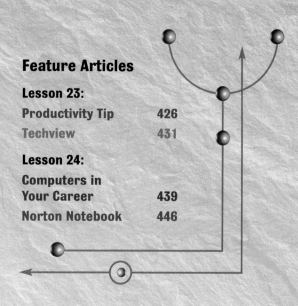

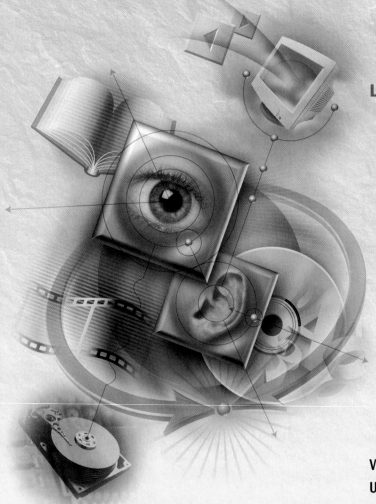

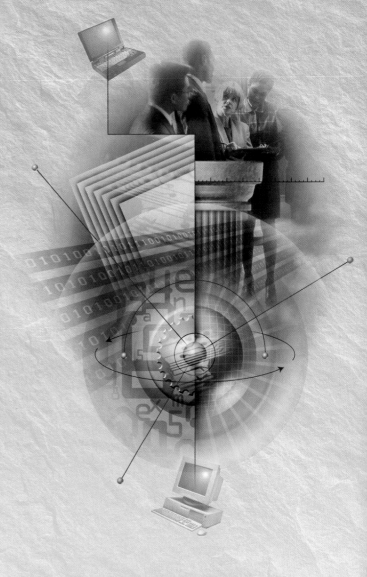

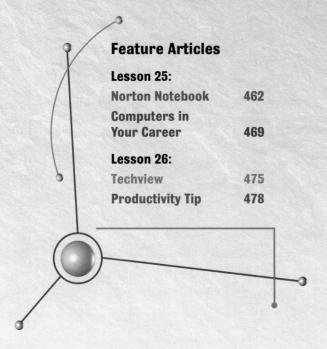

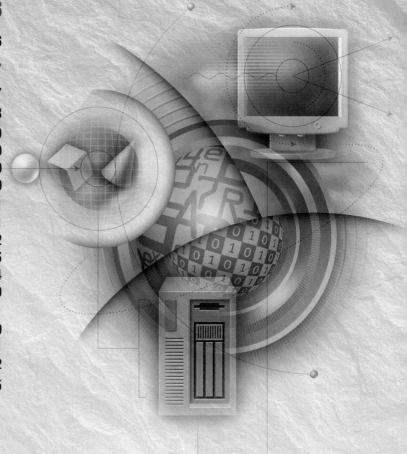

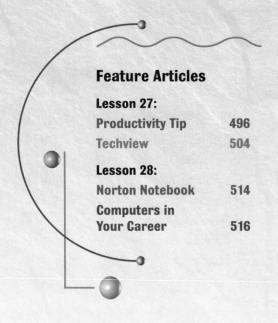

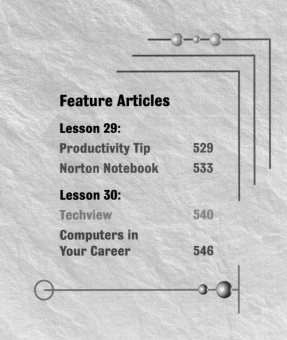

Feature Articles

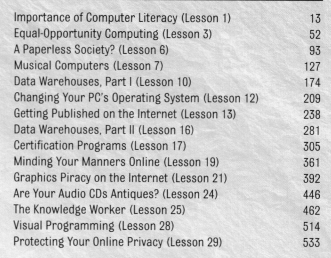

PRODUCTIVITY Tip

Techview

WHAT TO EXPECT IN THE FUTURE

Prerequisites

What You Should Know Before Using This Book

This book assumes that you have never used a computer before, or that your computer experience has been very brief. If so, you may need to learn some basic computer skills before proceeding with this course. This section introduces basic skills, using illustrations to help you recognize and remember the hardware or software involved in each skill. Some of these skills are covered in greater detail in other units of this book. In such cases, you will find references that point you to more information.

Equipment Required for This Book's Exercises

◆ A personal computer
◆ A keyboard
◆ A two-button mouse

◆ Windows 95, 98, 2000, or NT
◆ An Internet connection
◆ A Web browser

TURNING THE COMPUTER ON AND OFF

As simple as it may sound, there is a right way to turn a computer's power on and off. If you perform either of these tasks incorrectly, you may damage its components or cause problems for the operating system, programs, or data files.

Turning On the Computer

1. Before turning on your computer, make sure that all the necessary cables (such as the mouse, keyboard, printer, etc.) are connected to the system unit. Also make sure that the system's power cords are connected to an appropriate power source.

2. Make sure that there are no diskettes in the computer's diskette drive, unless you must boot the system from a diskette. (The term *booting* means starting the computer.) If you must boot the system from a diskette, ask your instructor for specific directions.

3. Find the On/Off switch on each attached device (the monitor, printer, etc.), and place it in the ON position. A device's power switch may not be on the front panel. If not, check the sides and back.

4. Find the On/Off switch on the computer's system unit—its main box, into which all other components are plugged—and place it in the ON position.

   Most computers take a minute or two to start. Your computer may display messages during the start-up process. If one of these messages prompts you to perform an action (such as providing a network user ID and password), ask your instructor for directions. After the computer has started, the Windows desktop will appear on your screen. (See the sample desktop on the following page.)

The start-up process is explained in greater detail in Lesson 1, "An Overview of the Computer System."

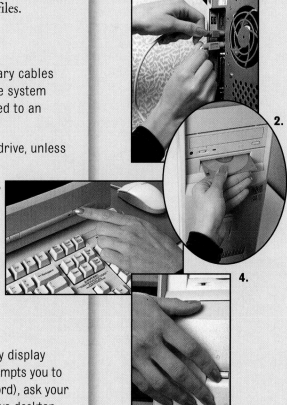

Turning Off the Computer

For more information on Windows and other operating systems, see Unit 6, "The Operating System and User Interface."

In Windows-based systems, it is critical that you shut down properly, as described here. Windows creates many temporary files on your computer's hard disk when running. By shutting down properly, you give Windows the chance to erase those temporary files and do other "housekeeping" tasks. If you simply turn off your computer while Windows or other programs are running, you can cause harm to your system.

1.

1. Remove any disks from the diskette and CD-ROM drive, and make sure that all data is saved and all running programs are closed. (For help with saving data and closing programs, see your instructor.)

2. Using your mouse pointer, click the Start button, which is located on the taskbar. The Start menu will appear. On the Start menu, click Shut Down. The Shut Down Windows dialog box will appear.

3. In the Shut Down Windows dialog box, select the Shut Down option; then click the OK button.

The background is called the desktop.

Icons are pictures that represent programs, files, disks, and other resources on your computer.

You use the mouse pointer to access resources by clicking icons and commands.

Taskbar

Click the Start button to open the Start menu.

Click Shut Down to turn off the computer.

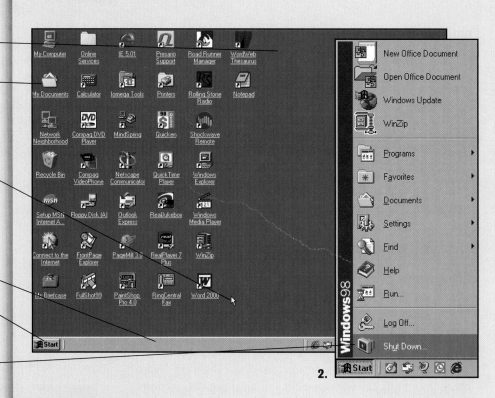

2.

Windows will begin the shut-down process. Windows may display a message telling you that it is shutting down. Then it may display the message "It is now safe to turn off your computer." When this message appears, turn off the power to your system unit, monitor, and printer.

In some newer computers, the system unit will power down automatically after Windows shuts down. If your computer provides this feature, you need to turn off only your monitor and other devices.

3.

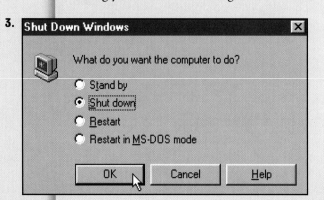

USING THE KEYBOARD

A. If you know how to type, then you can easily use a computer keyboard. The keyboard contains all the alphanumeric keys found on a typewriter, plus some keys that perform special functions.

B. In Windows, the Enter key performs two primary functions. First, it lets you create paragraph ("hard") returns in application programs such as word processors. Second, when a dialog box is open, pressing Enter is like clicking the OK button. This accepts your input and closes the dialog box.

C. The Shift, Ctrl (control), and Alt (alternate) keys are called modifier keys. You use them in combination with other keys to issue commands. In many programs, for example, pressing Ctrl+S (hold the Ctrl key down while pressing the S key) saves the open document to disk. Used with all the alphanumeric and function keys, the modifier keys let you issue hundreds of commands.

D. In Windows programs, the Esc (escape) key performs one universal function. That is, you can use it to cancel a command before it executes. When a dialog box is open, pressing Esc is like clicking the Cancel button. This closes the dialog box and ignores any changes you made in the dialog box.

E. Depending on the program you are using, the function keys may serve a variety of purposes or none at all. Function keys generally provide shortcuts to program features or commands. In many Windows programs, for example, you can press F1 to launch the online help system.

F. In any Windows application, a blinking bar—called the cursor, or the insertion point—shows you where the next character will appear as you type. You can use the cursor-movement keys to move the cursor to different positions. As their arrows indicate, these keys let you move the cursor up, down, left, and right.

G. The Delete key erases characters to the right of the cursor. The Backspace key erases characters to the left of the cursor. In many applications, the Home and End keys let you move the cursor to the beginning or end of a line, or farther when used with a modifier key. Page Up and Page Down let you scroll quickly through a document, moving back or ahead one screen at a time.

The keyboard is covered in detail in Lesson 3, "Standard Methods of Input."

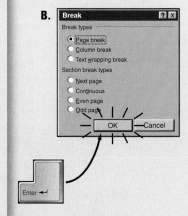

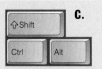

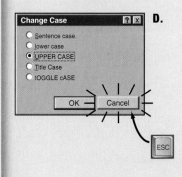

F. I am what I am. | — Cursor (or insertion point)

— Cursor-movement keys

Backspace key

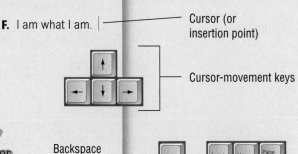

USING THE MOUSE

The mouse makes your computer easy to use. In fact, Windows and Windows-based programs are mouse-oriented, meaning their features and commands are designed for use with a mouse.

The mouse is covered in greater detail in Lesson 3, "Standard Methods of Input."

A. This book assumes that you are using a standard two-button mouse. Usually, the mouse's left button is the primary button. You press ("click") it to select commands and perform other tasks. The right button opens special "shortcut menus," whose contents vary according to the program you are using.

A.

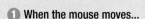

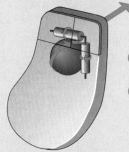

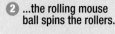

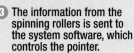

B. You use the mouse to move a graphical pointer around on the screen. This process is called pointing.

B.

C. The pointer is controlled by the mouse's motions across your desktop's surface. When you push the mouse forward (away from you), the pointer moves up on the screen. When you pull the mouse backward (toward you), the pointer moves down. When you move the mouse to the left or right, or diagonally, the pointer moves to the left, right, or diagonally on the screen.

C.

1 When the mouse moves...

2 ...the rolling mouse ball spins the rollers.

3 The information from the spinning rollers is sent to the system software, which controls the pointer.

D. To click an object, such as an icon, point to it on the screen, then quickly press and release the left mouse button one time. Generally, clicking an object selects it, or tells Windows that you want to do something with the object.

E. To double-click an object, point to it on the screen, then quickly press and release the left mouse button twice. Generally, double-clicking an object selects and activates the object. For example, when you double-click a program's icon on the desktop, the program launches so you can use it.

F. To right-click an object, point to it on the screen, then quickly press and release the right mouse button one time. Generally, right-clicking an object opens a shortcut menu that provides options for working with the object.

G. You can use the mouse to move objects around on the screen. For example, you can move an icon to a different location on the Windows desktop. This procedure is often called drag-and-drop editing. To drag an object, point to it, press and hold down the left mouse button, drag the object to the desired location, then release the mouse button.

"click"

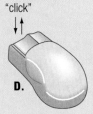

D.

"click click"

E.

"click"

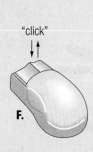

F.

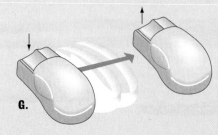

G.

USING YOUR BROWSER AND THE WORLD WIDE WEB

This book features many Internet-related discussions, as well as exercises and review questions that require you to use the World Wide Web ("the Web"). This section is designed to help you learn the basic steps required for using a browser and navigating the Web.

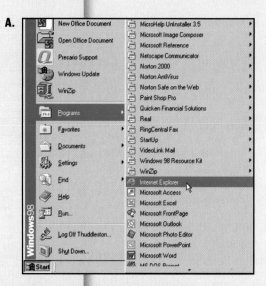

A.

A. To launch your browser, click the Start button on the Windows taskbar. When the Start menu opens, point to Programs. When the Programs menu opens, find the name of your browser and click it. Your browser will open on your screen.

B. A Web browser is software that enables you to view specially formatted Web pages. This illustration shows Netscape Navigator and names some of the the browser's most important tools.

Menu bar
Toolbar
Bookmarks list
Location/Address bar

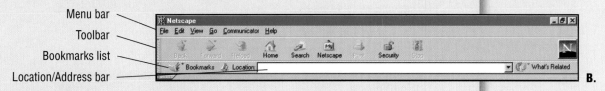

B.

C. You navigate the Web by moving from one Web page to another. A Web page is a document formatted with Hypertext Markup Language (HTML) tags. (A Web site is a collection of related Web pages.) Every Web page has a unique address called a uniform resource locator, or URL (pronounced as spelled: U-R-L). When you provide a URL for the browser, the browser loads that URL's page onto your PC.

C.

http://www.glencoe.com/

D. To navigate to a Web page, type a URL in the Location bar; then press Enter. For example, to go to the White House Web site, click in the Location (or Address) bar and type **http://www.whitehouse.gov/**. Then press Enter.

D.

Type a URL in the Location bar; then press Enter.

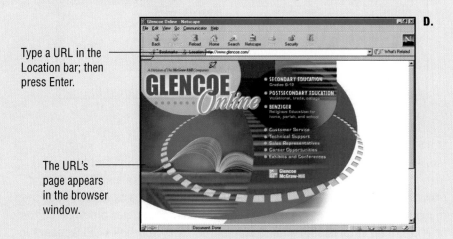

The URL's page appears in the browser window.

E. A hyperlink is simply a part of the Web page that is linked to a URL. When text has a hyperlink assigned to it, you can click it and "jump" from your present location to the URL specified by the hyperlink. Hyperlinked text looks different from normal text in a Web page; it is usually underlined, but can be formatted in any number of ways. When your mouse pointer touches hyperlinked text, the hyperlink's URL appears in the browser's status bar, and the pointer changes shape to resemble a hand with a pointing index finger (see page xxviii).

Unit 10, "The Internet and Online Resources," provides a detailed look at many aspects of the Internet.

E.

The mouse pointer is resting on hyper-linked text.

If you click the hyperlink, the browser will open the page with the URL shown on the status bar.

F.

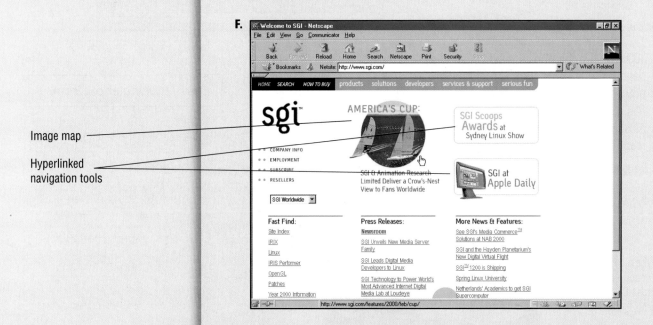

Image map

Hyperlinked navigation tools

F. Many Web pages provide pictures or graphical buttons—called navigation tools—that direct you to different pages, making it easier to find the information you need. Another popular tool is the image map, a single image that provides multiple hyperlinks. You can click on different parts of the image map to jump to different pages. When your mouse pointer touches a navigation tool or image map, it turns into a hand pointer, and the hyperlink's URL appears in the status bar of your browser.

G. The Back and Forward buttons return you to recently viewed pages, similar to flipping through a magazine. The Back button returns you to the previously opened Web page. After you use the Back button, you can click Forward to move forward again, returning to the last page you opened before you went back.

G.

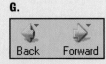

H. If you have saved any bookmarks to pages you have visited earlier, you can open the Bookmarks (or Favorites) list, select a bookmark, and quickly return to that page.

I. When you type URLs into the Location bar, your browser saves them, creating a history list for the current session. You can choose a URL from this list and return to a previously opened page without having to use the Back button or any other tools.

J. To close your browser, open the File menu and choose Close. You also can close the browser by clicking the Close button on the title bar. It may be necessary to close your Internet connection, too.

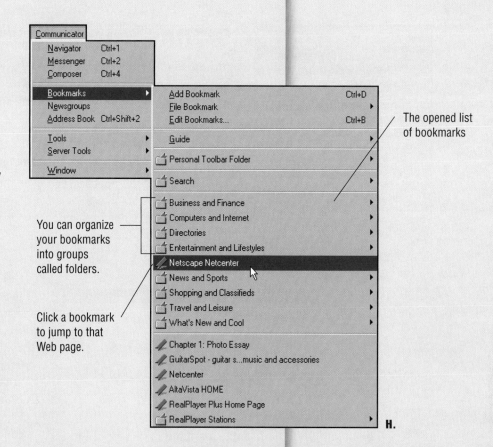

The opened list of bookmarks

You can organize your bookmarks into groups called folders.

Click a bookmark to jump to that Web page.

H.

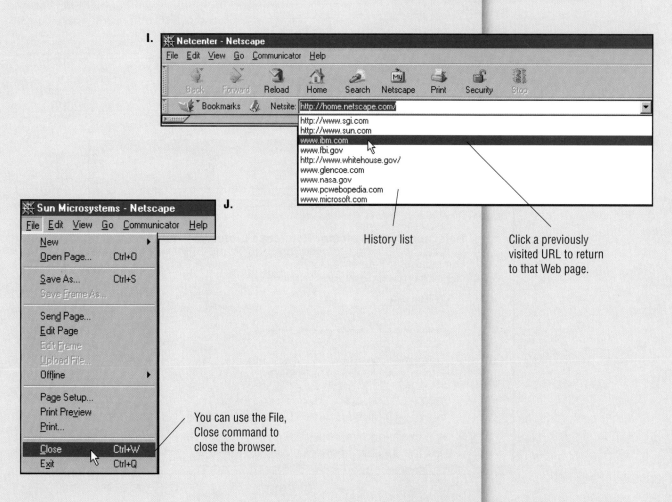

I.

History list

Click a previously visited URL to return to that Web page.

J.

You can use the File, Close command to close the browser.

1.

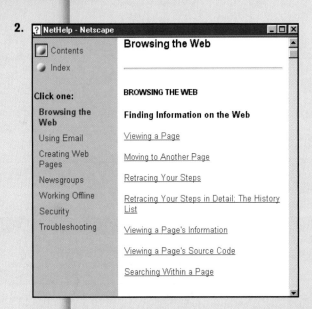

GETTING HELP WITH YOUR BROWSER

Although most browsers are easy to use, you may need help at some point. Newer browsers provide comprehensive Help systems, which can answer many of your questions about browsing and the World Wide Web.

1. Open the browser's Help menu, then choose Contents. (Depending on your browser, this option may be called Help Contents, Contents and Index, or something similar.)

2. A Help dialog box appears, listing all the topics for which help or information are available. Look through the list of topics and choose the one that matches your interest. When you are done, click the Close button on the window's title bar.

To get help from your browser maker's Web site, open your browser's Help menu and look for an option that leads you to the product's Web site. (In Netscape Navigator, you can get Web-based help information by clicking the Reference Library, Release Notes, or Product Information and Support options. In Microsoft Internet Explorer, click the Online Support option.) The resulting Web page will provide access to a knowledgebase of questions and answers, lists of frequently asked questions, links to help topics, and methods for getting in-depth technical support.

2.

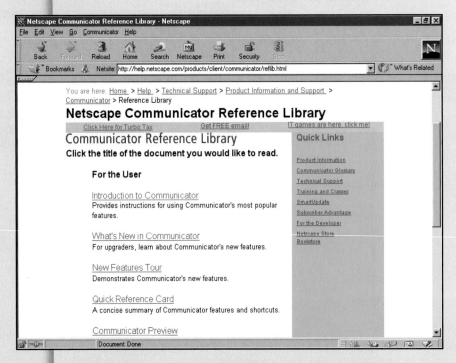

PETER NORTON'S®
Introduction
to Computers

FOURTH EDITION

Glencoe McGraw-Hill

New York, New York   Columbus, Ohio   Woodland Hills, California   Peoria, Illinois

UNIT 1

The Amazing Computer

UNIT OBJECTIVES

Identify the parts of a computer system.

Identify the two main categories of software.

Name three examples of software from each category.

List five types of computers.

UNIT CONTENTS

This unit contains the following lessons:

An Overview of the Computer System

OVERVIEW:
Dissecting the Ultimate Machine

Have you ever watched an incredible scene in a movie, or seen a drawing that looked so realistic you thought it was a photograph? Afterward, were you amazed to learn that it was done on a computer? If so, you are certainly not alone. We are endlessly surprised by the feats accomplished with the help of computers, and we marvel at their complexity. For this reason, many people assume that computers must be difficult to understand and difficult to use. Most of us do not realize, however, that computers are basically simple devices, and all computers have a great deal in common. Most computers—from the biggest to the smallest—operate on the same fundamental principles. They are all fabricated from the same basic types of components, and they all need instructions to make them run.

As a first step toward understanding and learning to use computers, this lesson gives you a peek at these fascinating machines. You will learn about the types of hardware that all computer systems use, and the types of software that make them run. You will also see that without a user—someone like you—a computer system is not really complete.

OBJECTIVES

- List the four parts of a computer system.
- Identify four types of computer hardware.
- List five units of measure for computer memory and storage.
- Provide two examples of input and output devices.
- Name and describe three types of storage devices.
- Differentiate the two main categories of computer software.
- List four specific types of application software.

THE PARTS OF A COMPUTER SYSTEM

What is a computer? In general terms, a **computer** is an electronic device used to process data, converting the data into information that is useful to people. Any computer—regardless of its type—is controlled by programmed instructions, which give the machine a purpose and tell it what to do.

Computers come in many varieties, including the personal computer, tiny computers built into appliances and automobiles, and mainframe machines used by many people simultaneously to run a business. Despite their differences in size and use, all these computers are part of a system. A complete **computer system** consists of four parts: hardware, software, people, and data (see Figure 1.1).

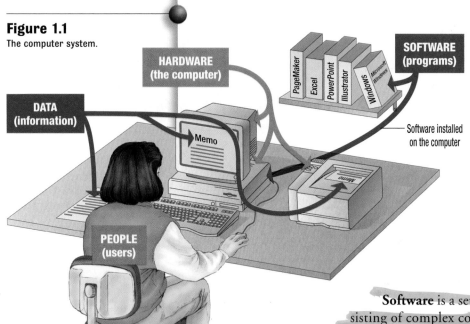

Figure 1.1
The computer system.

The mechanical devices that make up the computer are called **hardware.** In other words, hardware is any part of the computer you can touch. Hardware consists of interconnected electronic devices that you can use to control the computer's operation, input, and output. (The generic term **device** refers to any piece of hardware.)

Software is a set of electronic instructions consisting of complex codes (also known as **programs**) that make the computer perform tasks. In other words, software tells the computer what to do. Some programs exist primarily for the computer's use and help the computer perform and manage its own tasks. Other types of programs exist primarily for the user and enable the computer to perform tasks, such as creating documents or drawing pictures.

People are the computer operators, also known as **users.** It can be argued that some computer systems are complete without a person's involvement; however, no computer is totally autonomous. Even if a computer can do its job without a person sitting in front of it, people still design, build, program, and repair computer systems. This lack of autonomy is especially true of personal computer systems, which are the focus of this book and which are designed specifically for use by people.

Data consists of raw facts, which the computer stores and reads in the form of numbers. The computer manipulates data according to the instructions contained in the software and then forwards it for use by people or another computer. Data can consist of letters, numbers, sounds, or images. No matter what kind of data is entered into a computer, however, the computer converts it to numbers. Consequently, computerized data is **digital,** meaning that it has been reduced to digits, or numbers. (In Unit 4, "Processing Data," you will learn how the binary numbering system enables a computer to represent data.)

Within the computer, data is organized into files. A computer **file** is simply a set of data or program instructions that has been given a name. A file that the user

can open and use is often called a **document.** Although many people think of documents simply as text, a computer document can include many kinds of data. For example, a computer document can be a text file (such as a letter), a group of numbers (such as a budget), a video clip (which includes images and sounds), or any combination of these items. Programs are organized into files as well, but because programs are not considered data, they are not document files.

LOOKING INSIDE THE MACHINE

The computer itself—the hardware—has many parts, but the critical components fall into one of four categories (see Figure 1.2):

1. Processor   **3.** Input and output devices

2. Memory   **4.** Storage

While any type of computer system contains these four types of hardware, this book focuses on these types from the perspective of the personal computer.

The Processor

The procedure that transforms raw data into useful information is called **processing.** To perform this transformation, the computer uses two components: the processor and memory.

The **processor** is like the brain of the computer in the way that it organizes and carries out instructions that come from either the user or the software. In a personal computer, the processor usually consists of one or more **microprocessors** (sometimes called "chips"), which are slivers of silicon or other material etched with many tiny electronic circuits. To process data, the computer passes electricity through the circuits to complete an instruction.

As shown in Figure 1.3, the microprocessor is plugged into the computer's motherboard. The **motherboard** is a rigid rectangular card containing the circuitry that connects the processor to the other hardware. The motherboard is an example of a **circuit board.** In most personal computers, many internal devices—such as video cards, sound cards, disk controllers, and other devices—are housed on their own smaller circuit boards, which attach to the motherboard. Newer microprocessors are large and complex

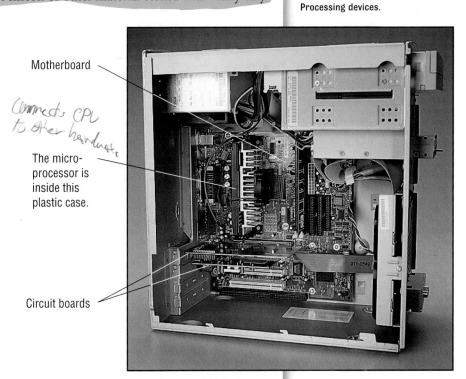

Figure 1.2
Types of hardware devices.

OUTPUT

MEMORY

INPUT AND OUTPUT

PROCESSOR

STORAGE

INPUT

Figure 1.3
Processing devices.

Motherboard

The microprocessor is inside this plastic case.

Circuit boards

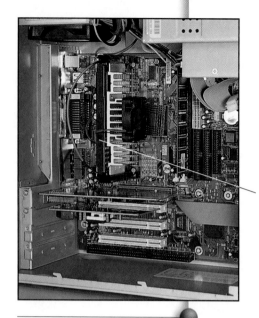

Central processing unit

enough to require their own dedicated circuit boards, which plug into a special slot in the motherboard. (Older microprocessors were single chips.) You can think of the motherboard as the master circuit board in a computer. Note, however, that in newer personal computers, some devices are built directly onto the motherboard instead of attaching to it as a separate circuit board. This development promises to make computers smaller, faster, and less expensive.

A personal computer's processor is usually a single chip or a set of chips contained on a circuit board. In some powerful computers, the processor consists of many chips and the circuit boards on which they are mounted. In either case, the term **central processing unit (CPU)** refers to a computer's processor (see Figures 1.4 and 1.5). People often refer to computer systems by the type of CPU they contain. A Pentium system, for example, uses a Pentium-class microprocessor as its CPU.

Figure 1.4

The CPUs of modern personal computers are small, considering the amount of processing power they provide. Early PC microprocessors were not much larger than a thumbnail. Processors such as Intel's Pentium III are somewhat larger.

Memory

Memory is like an electronic scratch pad inside the computer. When you launch a program, it is loaded into and run from memory. Data used by the program is also loaded into memory for fast access. As you enter new data into the computer, it is also stored in memory—but only temporarily. The most common type of memory is called **random access memory,** or **RAM** (see Figures 1.5 and 1.6). As a result, the term *memory* is commonly used to mean RAM. (It is also sometimes called read/write memory.) Data is both written to and read from this memory.

NORTON ONLINE

Visit **www.glencoe.com/norton/online/** for more information on **computer processors.**

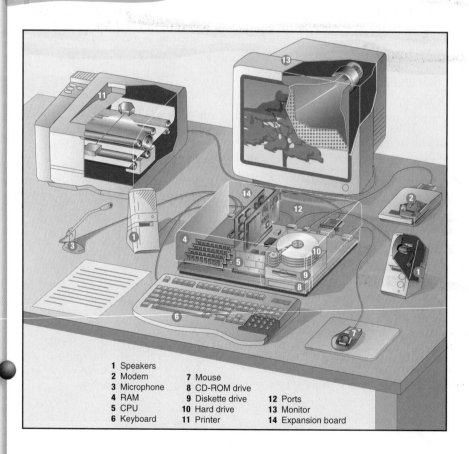

Figure 1.5

Most personal computer systems include the types of hardware components shown here.

1 Speakers		
2 Modem	7 Mouse	
3 Microphone	8 CD-ROM drive	
4 RAM	9 Diskette drive	12 Ports
5 CPU	10 Hard drive	13 Monitor
6 Keyboard	11 Printer	14 Expansion board

Perhaps the most important thing to remember about RAM is that it is volatile, so it needs a constant supply of power. When you turn off a computer, everything in RAM disappears. As you will soon learn, this is why you frequently have to save your data files to a storage device.

One of the most important factors affecting the speed and power of a computer is the amount of RAM it has. Generally, the more RAM a computer has, the more it can do and the faster it can perform certain tasks. The most common measurement unit for describing a computer's memory is the **byte**—the amount of memory it takes to store a single character, such as a letter of the alphabet or a numeral. When people talk about memory, the numbers are often so large that it is useful to use terms such as **kilobyte, megabyte, gigabyte,** and **terabyte** to describe the values (see Table 1.1).

NORTON ONLINE

Visit **www.glencoe.com/norton/online/** for more information on **RAM**.

Table 1.1	Units of Measure for Computer Memory and Storage			
Unit	**Abbreviation**	**Pronounced**	**Approximate Value (bytes)**	**Actual Value (bytes)**
Kilobyte	KB	KILL-uh-bite	1,000	1,024
Megabyte	MB	MEHG-uh-bite	1,000,000 (1 million)	1,048,576
Gigabyte	GB	GIG-uh-bite	1,000,000,000 (1 billion)	1,073,741,824
Terabyte	TB	TERR-uh-bite	1,000,000,000,000 (1 trillion)	1,099,511,627,776

Today's personal computers commonly have from 64 to 128 million bytes of memory (or 64 to 128 MB). Newer systems seldom have less than 64 MB. Newer generations of PCs feature more RAM than previous generations did because newer versions of operating systems and application software require ever-increasing amounts of RAM to operate efficiently. Adding RAM is a relatively inexpensive way to boost a system's overall performance. As a rule of thumb, the more RAM a computer has, the better. Note, too, that it is usually possible to add more RAM to a standard computer; some newer systems can be upgraded to nearly 1 GB of RAM. (You will learn more about the various types of RAM and other kinds of computer memory in Lesson 7, "Transforming Data into Information.")

Input and Output Devices

Computers would be useless if they did not provide interaction with users. They could not receive instructions or deliver the results of their work. **Input devices** accept data and instructions from the user or from another computer system (such as a computer on the Internet). **Output devices** return processed data back to the user or to another computer system.

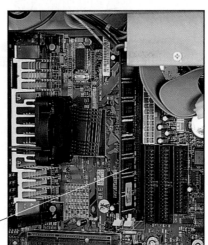

RAM

Figure 1.6
Random access memory (RAM).

Input Devices -

The most common input device is the **keyboard,** which accepts letters, numbers, and commands from the user. Another popular input device is the **mouse,** which lets you select options from on-screen menus. You use a mouse by moving it across a flat surface and pressing its buttons. Other popular input devices are **trackballs, touchpads, joysticks, scanners, digital cameras,** and **microphones.** A keyboard, mouse, and microphone are illustrated in Figure 1.7.

The mouse, trackball, and touchpad enable you to draw or point on the screen. The joystick is especially well suited for playing fast-moving video games. A scanner can copy a printed page of text or a graphic into the computer's memory, eliminating the time-consuming step of typing input or creating an image from scratch. Digital cameras record live images that can be viewed and edited on the computer. A microphone or CD player attached to the computer enables you to add the sound of a voice or a music selection.

The function of an output device is to present processed data to the user. The most common output devices are the display screen, known as the **monitor,** and the **printer.** The computer sends output to the monitor when the user needs only to see the output. It sends output to the printer when the user needs a paper copy— also called a "hard copy." Just as computers can accept sound as input, they can use stereo speakers or headphones as output devices to produce sound. A monitor, printer, and speakers are illustrated in Figure 1.8.

Some types of hardware can act as both input and output devices. One example is the **touch screen,** a type of monitor that displays text or icons you can touch. Touch screens are popular in museums and libraries, where they help direct people to specific areas. In bookstores and music stores, touch screens enable customers to locate an item quickly without wandering the aisles or searching through card catalogs. Touch screens are even used in gambling casinos, where they provide a fun and non-mechanical interface to slot machines. When you touch the screen, special sensors detect the touch, then the computer calculates the point on the screen where you placed your finger. Depending on the location of the touch, the computer responds by displaying new data.

The most common types of devices that can perform both input and output are **communications devices,** which connect one computer to another—a process known as networking. Among the many kinds of communications devices, the most common are modems, which enable computers to communicate through telephone lines or cable television systems, and network interface cards (NICs), which let users connect a group of computers to share data and devices. (You will learn more about networking and communications devices in Unit 9, "Networks and Data Communications.")

Storage

A computer can function with only processing, memory, input, and output devices. To be really useful, however, it also needs a place to keep program files and related data when it is not using them. The purpose of **storage** is to hold data.

Figure 1.7
The keyboard, mouse, and microphone are common input devices. Most new computers come equipped with these three devices.

Keyboard

Microphone   Mouse

NORTON
ONLINE

Visit **www.glencoe.com/norton/online/** for more information on **input and output devices** of all types.

Monitor

Printer

Speakers

Figure 1.8
The monitor, printer, and speakers are common output devices. Most new computers come equipped with a monitor and speakers. A printer is usually added to the computer system, at extra cost, although you can purchase complete systems that feature a printer.

Think of storage as an electronic file cabinet and RAM as an electronic worktable. When you need to work with a program or a set of data, the computer locates it in the file cabinet and puts a copy on the table. After you have finished working with the program or data, you put it back into the file cabinet. If you make changes to data while working on it, the changed data replaces the original data in the file cabinet (unless you put it in a different place in storage). There are three major distinctions between storage and memory:

A. There is more room in storage than in memory, just as there is more room in a file cabinet than there is on a tabletop.

B. Contents are retained in storage when the computer is turned off, whereas the programs or the data you put into memory disappear when you shut down the computer.

C. Storage is very slow compared to memory, but it is much cheaper than memory.

Remember the distinction between storage and memory. Their functions are similar, but they work in different ways. Novice computer users often use the term *memory* when they actually mean *storage* or *disk*. This mistake can cause confusion.

The most common storage medium is the **magnetic disk.** A disk is a round, flat object that spins around its center. **Read/write heads,** which are similar to the heads of a tape recorder or VCR, are used to read data from the disk or write data onto the disk. Depending on the type of disk, the read/write heads may float just above the disk's surface or may actually touch the disk.

The device that holds a disk is called a **disk drive.** Some disks are built into the drive and are not meant to be removed; other kinds of drives enable you to remove and replace disks. Most personal computers have at least one nonremovable **hard disk** (or **hard drive**). In addition, there is also a **diskette drive,** which allows you to use removable **diskettes.** A hard disk can store far more data than a diskette can, so the hard disk serves as the computer's primary filing cabinet. Diskettes are used to load new programs or data onto the hard disk, trade data with other users, and make backup copies of the data on the hard disk.

Because you can remove diskettes from a computer, they are encased in a plastic or vinyl cover to protect them from fingerprints and dust. Because the cover used in

NORTON
ONLINE

Visit **www.glencoe.com/norton/online/** for information on **storage**.

early diskettes was thin, the diskette was flimsy, or "floppy." As a result, they came to be called **floppy disks** (see Figure 1.9).

The **CD-ROM drive** is the most common type of storage device after the hard and diskette drives (see Figure 1.10). **Compact disks (CDs)** are a type of optical storage device, identical to audio CDs, that can store about 74 minutes of audio or 650 MB of data, or about 450 times as much information as a diskette. The type used in computers is called **Compact Disk Read-Only Memory (CD-ROM).** The name implies that you cannot change the information on the disk, just as you cannot record over an audio CD.

If you purchase a **CD-Recordable (CD-R)** drive, you have the option of creating your own CDs. A CD-R drive can write data to and read data from a compact disk. To use a CD-R drive, you must use a special CD-R disk, which can be written on only once, or a **CD-ReWritable (CD-RW)** disk, which can be written to multiple times, like a floppy disk.

An increasingly popular data storage technology is the **Digital Versatile Disk** or **Digital Video Disk (DVD),** which is revolutionizing home entertainment. Using sophisticated compression technologies, a single DVD (which is the same size as a standard compact disk) can store an entire full-length movie. DVDs can hold a minimum of 4.7 GB of data and as much as 17 GB. Future DVD technologies promise much higher storage capacities on a single disk. DVD drives can also locate data on the disk much faster than standard CD-ROM drives.

DVDs require a special player (see Figure 1.11). The new players, however, can play audio, data, and DVD disks, freeing the user from the necessity of purchasing different players for each type of disk. DVD drives are now standard equipment on many new personal computers. Users not only install programs and data from their standard CDs, but they can also watch movies on their PCs by using a DVD.

Other types of storage devices include **tape drives, optical drives, removable hard drives,** and many others. (You will learn more about these and other types of storage devices in Unit 5, "Storing Information in a Computer.")

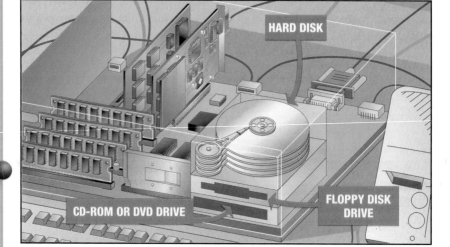

HARD DISK

CD-ROM OR DVD DRIVE

FLOPPY DISK DRIVE

Figure 1.11
DVD players are now standard on many PCs and are found in many home entertainment centers.

Self Check

Answer the following questions by filling in the blank(s).

1. A(n) _____ is an electronic device used to process data.

2. There is more room in storage than in _____ in a computer.

3. A device that holds a disk is called a(n) _____ .

SOFTWARE: BRINGING THE MACHINE TO LIFE

Computers are general-purpose machines. This means that a computer can be applied to many different types of tasks. Whether you need to write a report, draw a magazine illustration, edit videotape, manage a network, or play a chess game with someone on the other side of the world, a computer can help you do it.

Of course, the computer itself—the hardware—cannot do any of these things. The ingredient that enables a computer to perform a specific task is software, which consists of electronic instructions. These instructions tell the machine's physical components what to do; without them, a computer could not do anything at all. It would just be a box of metal and plastic.

As you saw earlier in this lesson, a set of instructions that drives a computer to perform specific tasks is called a program. When a computer uses a particular program, it is said to be **running** or **executing** that program. This section introduces you to the two main categories of software, and explains the purpose of each kind.

Although the array of available programs is vast and varied, most software falls into two major categories: **system software** and **application software** (see Figure 1.12). One major type of system software, the **operating system,** tells the computer how to use its own components. Examples of operating systems include Windows 2000, Windows NT, the Macintosh Operating System, UNIX, Linux OS/2, and DOS.

Application software tells the computer how to accomplish specific tasks, such as word processing or drawing, for the user. Examples of popular application programs are Microsoft Word, CorelDRAW, AutoCAD, and Netscape Navigator.

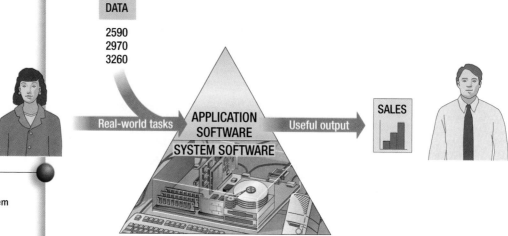

Figure 1.12
Application software and system software.

Operating Systems

When you turn on a computer, it goes through several steps to prepare itself for use. The first step is called the **power-on self test (POST).** The computer identifies the devices attached to it, identifies the amount of memory available, and does a quick check to see whether the memory is functioning properly. This routine is initiated by a part of the system software located in **read-only memory (ROM),** a chip that contains brief, permanent instructions for starting the computer.

Next, the computer looks for an operating system, which is usually stored on the hard disk. The operating system tells the computer how to interact with the user and how to use devices such as the disk drives, keyboard, and monitor. When it finds the operating system, the computer loads a portion of it into memory. (The portion loaded includes essential commands that the computer needs to perform basic operations. It also includes the user interface and instructions that enable the computer to find other commands and operating system elements on disk when needed.) Because the operating system is necessary for controlling the computer's most basic functions, it continues to run until the computer is turned off.

After the computer finds and runs the operating system, it is ready to accept commands from an input device—usually the keyboard or a mouse—or from a program. At this point, the user can issue commands to the computer. A command might, for example, list the programs stored on the computer's disk or make the computer run one of those programs. Table 1.2 on page 14 shows the process the computer follows at startup. (You will learn more about operating systems in Unit 6, "The Operating System and User Interface.")

NORTON
ONLINE

Visit **www.glencoe.com/norton/online/** for more information on **operating systems.**

Norton Notebook

IMPORTANCE OF COMPUTER LITERACY

Today, computers are no longer specialized tools used only by scientists or engineers. They do not hum behind sealed, glass walls in climate-controlled environments. Computer systems are everywhere—in places you cannot see or would not expect to find them. They are a fact of life, a common thread that ties together our education, work, and home life.

With computers touching nearly every facet of our lives, the issue of computer literacy becomes important. But what is computer literacy, and why is it so crucial? Why should you spend your time and energy studying books like this one, and becoming "computer literate"?

Technically, to be "literate" in a subject means to have knowledge of that subject. You understand its basic terms and concepts. As an example, consider driving a car. If you have a driver's license, then you are literate in driving-related terms and you understand the rules of the road. You were not born with such knowledge or abilities, but it may be hard to imagine living without them today.

Someday, perhaps sooner than you think, you may not be able to imagine living without computer skills. Consider the fact that computers are an essential part of business today, whether you are an auto mechanic or a surgeon, a journalist or an airline pilot. Like the cars that take us to work each day, we rely on computers more with each passing year. If you do not use a computer regularly, chances are great that you will soon.

How will you benefit from computer literacy?

- **Increased Employability.** If you have basic computer knowledge along with specific job skills, employers will consider you more trainable in and adaptable to the computerized work environment.

- **Greater Earnings Potential.** As you increase your computer skills, you become a more valuable worker, especially if you focus on high-tech skills such as programming, network administration, or hardware maintenance. However, you do not have to become a computer expert to increase your

Computers are becoming increasingly important tools in all types of workplaces, from offices to factories.

earnings. Skills that involve application of the computer to specific tasks (such as desktop publishing or database management) are highly valued.

- **Greater Access to Resources.** Computers are incredible learning tools, especially when you have access to data on CD-ROMs or the Internet. You can use a PC to access vast knowledgebases on almost any topic, search archives of information dating back decades, and even take online courses for credit.

- **Greater Control of Assets.** Using the power of the Internet and only a little knowledge of computers, you can manage your personal finances and indulge your interests in ways that were not possible just a few years ago. Online banking and investing give you control of every dollar you earn. Online shopping makes it easier than ever to spend your money, too. New technologies enable you to monitor your entire household via a PC—to set your air conditioner or alarm clock, start your coffee maker or sprinklers, and activate your alarm system.

Because of the growth of computer technologies, we now live in an information society—where information is considered to be an extremely valuable commodity. Those who control important information, or who simply know how to access and use it, are key players in the information-based economy. Computer literacy and the skills you can build with that literacy are essential to success in this society, not just in our working lives, but in the way we learn, manage our finances, and improve our standard of living.

NORTON ONLINE

Visit **www.glencoe.com/norton/online/** for more information on **computer literacy**.

Table 1.2	The Startup Process	
Step	Source of Instruction	Type of Instruction
1	ROM	System self-check
2	Hard disk	System software loaded into memory
3	User	Controls hardware by issuing operating system commands or loads an application from a disk

Application Software

The operating system exists mostly for the benefit of the computer. Other programs are required to make the computer useful for people. Programs that help people accomplish specific tasks are referred to as application software. Application software has been written to do almost every task imaginable, from word processing to selecting a college to attend. A special type of application software, called utility software, helps you to fine-tune the performance of a computer, prevent unwanted actions, or perform special, system-related tasks such as checking for viruses or sending a fax.

Thousands of applications are available for many purposes and for people of all ages. Here are some of the major categories of these applications:

◆ Word processing software for creating text-based documents such as newsletters or brochures

◆ Spreadsheets for creating numeric-based documents such as budgets or balance sheets

◆ Database management software for building and manipulating large sets of data

◆ Presentation programs for creating and presenting electronic slide shows

◆ Graphics programs for designing illustrations or manipulating photographs, movies, or animation

◆ Multimedia authoring applications for building digital movies that incorporate sound, video, animation, and interactive features

◆ Entertainment and education software, many of which are interactive multimedia events

◆ Web design tools and Web browsers, and other Internet applications such as newsreaders and e-mail programs

◆ Utilities that make the computer system easier to use or that perform highly specialized functions

◆ Games, some of which are for a single player and many of which can be played by several people over a network or the Internet

◆ Programming languages, such as C++, Visual Basic, and Java, which allow the user to create new applications

◆ Networking and communication software that let computers connect to one another and exchange data

You will learn about different types of application software in later units.

NORTON
ONLINE

Visit **www.glencoe.com/norton/online/** for information on all kinds of **application software.**

VISUAL ESSAY: SOFTWARE MAKES THE SYSTEM USEFUL

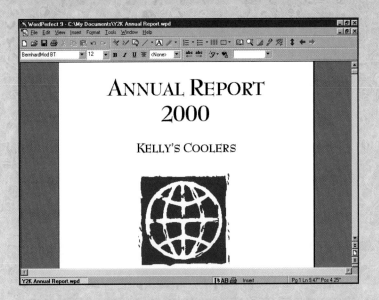

Word processing software is designed for creating documents that consist primarily of text. New word processors also let you include graphics and sounds in your documents, and they provide sophisticated layout features that enable you to create brochures, newsletters, business documents, and more.

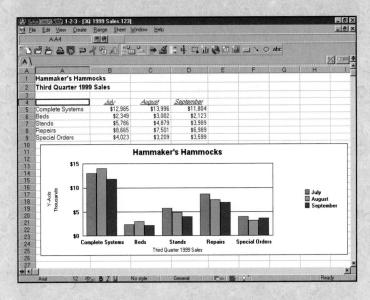

Spreadsheet programs are designed to work with numbers and are used in business to create budgets, payrolls, and analytical documents. Your document can contain text, numbers, and formulas for calculating numbers. Spreadsheet programs also let you create colorful charts from your data.

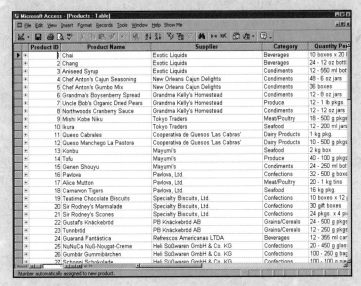

This screen shows a database of products sold by a company. Database management software makes it easy to reorganize data. For example, you can rearrange this list by product names or by categories. Large companies and government agencies use enormous databases containing millions of lines of information about people, products, and more.

Graphics software lets you create and edit images of all types. Some graphics programs are specially designed to work with electronic photographs, while others excel at manipulating line drawings or text. Such programs are essential in document design, Web site design, multimedia authoring, and game and movie production.

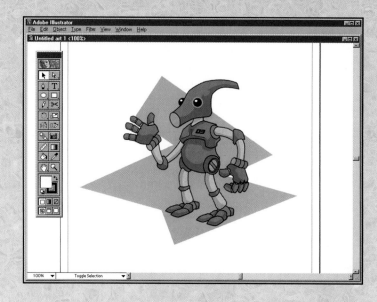

Presentation software is most often used for creating sales presentations, although it can be effective for any type of electronic slide show.

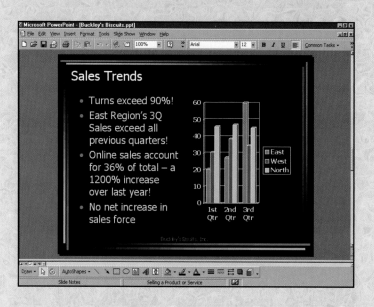

Using a Web-page design program, you can create colorful documents for publication on the World Wide Web. These programs enable you to add different fonts, graphics, and hyperlinks to your Web pages.

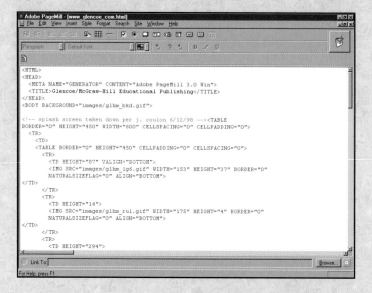

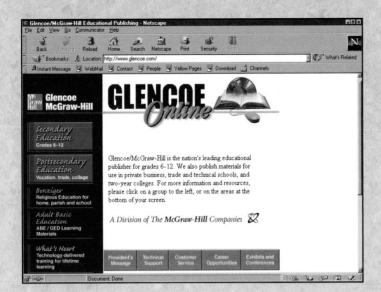

Web browsers have quickly become one of the most commonly used—and important—types of application software. Using a Web browser and an Internet connection, you can view documents (called "Web pages") from around the world.

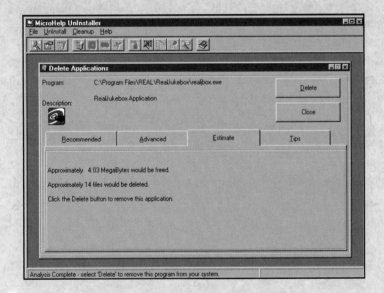

There are hundreds of utility programs available for personal computers. This one is an "uninstaller" program, which completely removes installed programs and their associated files from a hard disk.

Multimedia programs can feature content stored on a disk (such as a CD-ROM-based encyclopedia) or "streaming" data received over the Internet. The application shown here can play many types of audio and video files from a disk or the Internet.

COMPUTERS
in your career

Computer Knowledge Opens Doors

Although there are still many professions that do not rely on computers, they are becoming fewer all the time. Remember that computers do not necessarily take the form of a PC, so there is a good chance that your career path will bring you in contact with some type of computer. Whether it is a supercomputer (described in Lesson 2) or a bar code reader, an automated machining tool or a telephone switchboard, many of the tools in today's workplace use computer technology.

So it is important to have a basic understanding of computer technology, which is what this book is about. Regardless of your career choice, you can benefit from a knowledge of computer hardware and software, and how these components function together. Even if your job does not require you to work directly with a computer, this knowledge may help you to envision new ways of using computers in your work, resulting in a more productive work environment. This can also lead to career advancement opportunities.

If you think this case is being overstated, and that computers are not being used that much, consider this: computers are popping up in places and professions that may seem unlikely. The following list presents some examples:

◆ **Restaurant and Grocery Store Managers.** Restaurants, grocery stores, and retail outlet managers use computer systems of all kinds—from handheld units to mainframes—to monitor inventories, track transactions, and manage product pricing. Store managers frequently use portable devices to check stock levels and to change prices. These devices can be networked with a single store's computer system or a chain's wide area network.

◆ **Courier Dispatchers.** Courier services of all types use computerized terminals to help dispatchers schedule deliveries, locate pickup and drop-off points, generate invoices, and track the location of packages. Such systems are used by cross-town delivery services and by national carriers such as Federal Express.

◆ **Construction Managers.** Construction managers and estimators use specialized software to analyze construction documents and to calculate the amount of materials and time required to complete a job. These computerized tools—which often read information directly from disk files provided by the architect—help contractors manage costs and make competitive bids. On the job site, construction workers use computerized measuring devices and laser beams to calculate precise measurements quickly. Field managers and laborers alike routinely use portable computers to check plans and other construction documents or to manage inventories of materials.

◆ **Automotive Mechanics.** Automotive mechanics and technicians use computer systems to measure vehicle performance, diagnose mechanical problems, and determine maintenance or repair strategies. These systems are sometimes networked to regional or national databases of automotive information.

Each of the following units in this textbook features a discussion of computers in the professional world. Each discussion focuses on the type of technology introduced in that unit, and is designed to help you understand how that particular technology is used in one or more professions.

Computers are now used in a surprising variety of workplaces, including places where you might not expect to find them.

LESSON QUIZ

True/False

Answer the following questions by circling True or False.

True   False   **1.** A complete computer system has two parts: hardware and software.

True   False   **2.** In a personal computer, the processor consists of one or more microprocessors.

True   False   **3.** The keyboard and monitor are examples of output devices.

True   False   **4.** The purpose of a storage device is to hold data.

True   False   **5.** When a computer is using a program, it is said to be processing that program.

Multiple Choice

Circle the word or phrase that best completes each sentence.

1. _____ is a set of electronic instructions that tells the computer what to do.
   A. Software   **B.** A program   **C.** Both A and B

2. The most common type of computer memory is called _____ .
   A. storage   **B.** RAM   **C.** neither A nor B

3. A _____ can perform both input and output functions.
   A. trackball   **B.** monitor   **C.** communications device

4. One major type of system software is called _____ .
   A. a program   **B.** application software   **C.** operating system software

5. _____ programs are used to create numeric-based documents such as budgets or balance sheets.
   A. Word processing   **B.** Presentation   **C.** Spreadsheet

LESSON LABS

Complete the following exercises as directed by your instructor.

1. Using a computer, label each external device you can identify.

2. With your instructor's help, remove the cover from a computer. Make a diagram of the computer's internal components and label as many of them as you can. Can you find the motherboard, RAM, and processor? What other components can you identify?

3. With your instructor's help, turn on a computer and watch the screen carefully as the system starts up. What do you see? Does the PC provide information about itself during the startup process? If so, what types of information can you gather about the system? Can you tell how much memory it has? What operating system does it use, and what is the version of that operating system?

The Shapes of Computers Today

OBJECTIVES

- List the five most common types of computer systems.
- Identify two unique features of supercomputers.
- Describe a typical use for mainframe computers.
- Differentiate workstations from personal computers.
- Identify four types of personal computers.

OVERVIEW:
A Computer for Every Job

Computers come in many different sizes and ranges of power, and different types of computer systems have varying capabilities. Basically, today's computer systems fall into one of the following categories:

- ► Supercomputers
- ► Mainframe computers
- ► Minicomputers, or midrange computers
- ► Workstations
- ► Microcomputers, or personal computers

All of these computers can be connected to form networks of computers, but each individual computer, whether or not it is on a network, falls into one of these five categories. As you will see, some of these categories—especially microcomputers—can be divided into subcategories, some of which are growing rapidly enough to become major categories in their own right.

SUPERCOMPUTERS

Supercomputers are the most powerful computers made, and physically they are some of the largest (see Figure 2.1). These systems are built to process huge amounts of data, and the fastest supercomputers can perform more than 1 trillion calculations per second. Some supercomputers—such as the Cray T90 system—can house thousands of processors. This speed and power make supercomputers ideal for handling large and highly complex problems that require extreme calculating power.

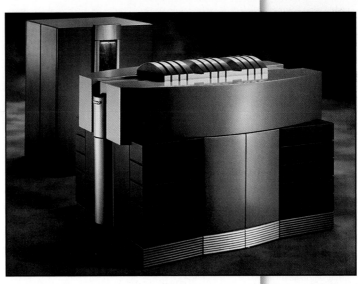

Figure 2.1
Supercomputers are the most powerful computers made. This supercomputer is the Cray T90.

Scientists and engineers frequently build models of complex processes, then simulate the processes on a supercomputer. These computers help analyze and forecast global weather patterns, for example, while shedding light on related issues such as pollution, global warming, and the depletion of the earth's ozone layer. Nuclear scientists use supercomputers to create and analyze models of nuclear fission and fusion, predicting the actions and reactions of millions of atoms as they interact.

Supercomputers are also being used to map the human genome, or DNA structure. The Human Genome Project, for example, uses supercomputing resources around the world in the hope of discovering all the human genes. Scientists estimate there are from 80,000 to 100,000 human genes, made up of more than 3 billion chemical bases. If printed, the human DNA sequence would fill about 200,000 pages.

Supercomputers can cost tens of millions of dollars and consume enough electricity to power dozens of homes. They are often housed in protective rooms with special cooling systems, power protection, and other security features. Because of their size and cost, supercomputers are relatively rare, used only by large corporations, universities, and government agencies that can afford them. Supercomputing resources are often shared to give researchers access to these precious machines.

Visit **www.glencoe.com/norton/online/** for information on **supercomputers**.

MAINFRAME COMPUTERS

The largest type of computer in common use is the mainframe. **Mainframe computers** are used in large organizations like insurance companies and banks where many people need frequent access to the same data, which is usually organized into one or more huge databases (see Figure 2.2 on page 22).

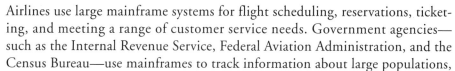

Figure 2.2

A powerful mainframe system can support the processing and output needs of thousands of users spread over a wide geographic area.

Airlines use large mainframe systems for flight scheduling, reservations, ticketing, and meeting a range of customer service needs. Government agencies—such as the Internal Revenue Service, Federal Aviation Administration, and the Census Bureau—use mainframes to track information about large populations, individual tax records, payroll, and more. Many large grocery and retail chains interconnect their stores with a mainframe, which immediately registers every sale, oversees stock, and manages inventory levels.

Mainframes are being used more and more as specialized servers on the World Wide Web, enabling companies to offer secure transactions with customers over the Internet. If you purchase an airline ticket over the Web, for example, there is a good chance your transaction is being handled by a mainframe system. In this type of application, the mainframe system may be referred to as an enterprise server or an electronic commerce (e-commerce) server.

NORTON ONLINE

Visit www.glencoe.com/norton/online/ for more information on **mainframe computers**.

In a traditional mainframe environment, each user works at a computer terminal. A **terminal** is a monitor and a keyboard (and sometimes a pointing device, such as a mouse) wired to the mainframe. There are basically two types of terminals used with mainframe systems. A dumb terminal does not have its own CPU or storage devices; these components are housed in the mainframe's system unit and are shared by all users. Each dumb terminal is simply an **input/output (I/O) device** that functions as a window into a computer located somewhere else. An intelligent terminal, on the other hand, has its own processor and can perform some processing operations. Intelligent terminals, however, do not usually provide any storage.

Figure 2.3

This IBM S/390 is the heart of many mainframe computer systems.

Many enterprises are now connecting personal computers and personal computer networks to their mainframe systems. This connection gives users access to mainframe data and services and also enables them to take advantage of local storage and processing, as well as other features of the PC or network.

A mainframe system can house an enormous volume of data, containing literally billions of records. Large mainframe systems can handle the input and output requirements of several thousand terminals. The largest IBM S/390 mainframe, for example, can support 50,000 users simultaneously while executing more than 1,600,000,000 instructions per second (see Figure 2.3).

Depending on their size, capabilities, and the number of users they must support, mainframe systems can cover a huge price range. Mainframe systems start at around $30,000; extensive mainframes can cost several million dollars.

It used to be common for mainframe computers to occupy entire rooms or even an entire floor of a high-rise building. Typically, they were placed inside glass offices with special air conditioning to keep them cool and on raised floors to accommodate all the wiring needed to connect the system. This setup is not used much anymore. Today, a typical mainframe computer looks like an unimposing file cabinet—or a row of file cabinets—although it may still require a somewhat controlled environment.

MINICOMPUTERS

First released in the 1960s, **minicomputers** got their name because of their small size compared to other computers of the day. The capabilities of a minicomputer are somewhere between mainframes and personal computers. (For this reason, minicomputers are increasingly being called midrange computers.) Like mainframes, minicomputers can handle much more input and output than personal computers can. Although some "minis" are designed for a single user, most are designed to handle multiple terminals. The most powerful minicomputers can serve the input and output needs of hundreds of users at a time.

Minicomputers, such as the one shown in Figure 2.4, are commonly used as servers in network environments that handle the data-sharing needs of other computers on the network. Dozens or hundreds of personal computers can be connected to a network with a minicomputer acting as a server. Like mainframes, midrange computers are used more and more as Web servers, handling thousands of transactions per day. Single-user minicomputers are commonly applied to sophisticated design tasks, such as animation and video editing. Minicomputers cost anywhere from $18,000 to $500,000 and are ideal for many organizations and companies that cannot afford or do not need a mainframe system.

Figure 2.4
The HP 3000 is a midrange computer used by medium- and large-size businesses.

NORTON
ONLINE

Visit **www.glencoe.com/norton/online/** for information on **minicomputers**.

Answer the following questions by filling in the blank(s).

1. The fastest supercomputers can perform _____ calculations per second.

2. A(n) _____ is simply an input/output (I/O) device that connects to a mainframe computer system.

3. Minicomputers are referred to more and more as _____ .

WORKSTATIONS

Somewhere between multi-user midrange computers and personal computers are **workstations.** Workstations are specialized, single-user computers with many of the features of a personal computer but with the processing power of a minicomputer (see Figure 2.5). These powerful machines are popular among scientists, engineers, graphic artists, animators, and programmers—users who need a great deal of number-crunching power. Workstations typically use advanced processors and feature more RAM and storage capacity than personal computers. Workstations often have large, high-resolution monitors and accelerated graphics-handling capabilities, making them perfect for advanced design, modeling, animation, and video editing. Although workstations are often found in single-user applications, they are more and more often used as servers on personal computer networks and as Web servers.

Until a few years ago, the term *workstation* implied certain differences in terms of chip design and operating system, making it distinct from a personal computer. (The term *workstation* is also used to describe a single computer on a network. In this context, a workstation is usually a personal computer.) Today, the differences between minicomputers, workstations, and personal computers are becoming blurred. Low-end minicomputers and high-end workstations are now similar in features and capabilities. The same is true for low-end workstations and high-end personal computers.

Figure 2.5
Although it looks like a personal computer, this system is actually a powerful Ultra 60 workstation from Sun Microsystems.

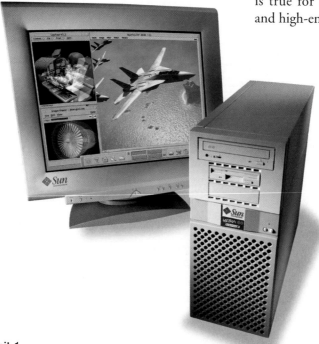

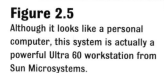

Visit **www.glencoe.com/norton/online/** for information on **workstations.**

FUTURE

Molecule-Sized Computers?

Personal computing devices are getting smaller all the time. In fact, new types of limited-function handheld devices are not much larger than a credit card. These devices offer personal information management features by storing date book and contact information for their users. At some point, however, devices of that size (or even smaller) may offer the same computational power and features as today's most powerful desktop PCs.

But how small can computers be? Researchers are already answering that question, developing complete computer systems not much larger than a match head and chemical-based transistors so tiny that they function on the molecular level.

A Web Server on a Chip

In the summer of 1999, a graduate student at the University of Massachusetts announced that he had created a complete computer system not much larger than a match head—and for less than a dollar. H. Shrikumar's invention uses 512 bytes of program ROM and 16 bytes of RAM in a standard microprocessor chip. It can store enough data and instructions to host a complete Web server which connects directly to the Internet. You can visit the Web site at **http://enablery.org/iPic**. The pages on this Web site are all served directly from this tiny computer.

Shrikumar's creation—named iPic—was not the first tiny microcomputer, but it proved that small computing devices can be made affordably and with enough power to perform various applications. For example, a mass-produced version of iPic (or a similar system) can be placed inside many kinds of appliances, enabling them to be connected by a network and accessed through the Internet.

Shrikumar envisions a home or workplace where all electronic appliances are networked together and all are controlled through a customized Web page. In his vision, a homeowner can open the Web page in a browser and make selections that turn lights on or off, set timers, adjust the home's temperature, activate security systems, set the VCR to record a program, and perform many other tasks. Because the iPic is so small and cheap,

it is easy to imagine a house filled with networked appliances that are remotely controlled via a handheld device, such as a PDA with an Internet connection.

Dress Yourself in Processors

Meantime, researchers at Hewlett-Packard Research Laboratories and the University of California at Los Angeles announced breakthroughs that may give the term *microcomputer* an entirely new meaning. In these systems, still in the theoretical stages, basic computer components are created from special chemical compounds rather than silicon and metal. The potential result is computers the size of molecules. Scientists foresee "stitching"

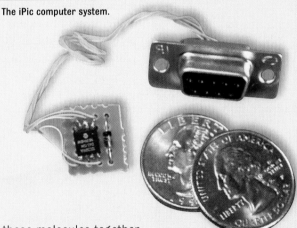

The iPic computer system.

these molecules together to create supercomputers that can sit in the palm of your hand. Computerized "fabrics" may someday be incorporated into clothing. Computers, in theory, could become part of anything. Such computers could take innumerable forms, and they could perform countless functions. Huge warehouses of data could be stored digitally in a device the size of a shoebox, with any byte instantly available.

Molecular-scale computer systems will not materialize soon, probably not for decades. Nonetheless, their promise is exciting, especially when you consider that a molecular computer—containing billions of molecules—could be more powerful than all the computers currently running put together.

MICROCOMPUTERS, OR PERSONAL COMPUTERS

The terms **microcomputer** and **personal computer** are interchangeable, but **PC**—which stands for *personal computer*—sometimes has a more specific meaning. In 1981, IBM called its first microcomputer the IBM-PC. Within a few years, many companies were copying the IBM design, creating "clones" or "compatibles" that were meant to function like the original. For this reason, the term *PC* has come to mean the family of computers that includes IBMs and IBM-compatibles. The vast majority of microcomputers sold today are part of this family. The Apple Macintosh computer, however, is neither an IBM nor a compatible. It is another family of microcomputers, made by Apple Computer. So it is accurate to say that a Macintosh such as the iMac (see Figure 2.6), is a personal computer. Even so, some people consider it misleading to refer to the "Mac" as a PC. This book uses the term *PC* as a simple abbreviation for *personal computer,* referring to both IBM-compatible models and Apple's Macintosh line.

One source of the PC's popularity is the rate at which improvements are made in its technology. Microprocessors, memory chips, and storage devices make continual gains in speed and capacity, while physical size and price remain stable—or in some cases are reduced. For example, compared to the typical PC of ten years ago, a machine of the same

Figure 2.6
The iMac is one of the more recent lines of personal computers from Apple.

price today will have about ten times as much RAM, about 100 times more storage capacity, and a microprocessor at least 100 times as fast. What's more, many analysts believe that this pace of change will continue for another 10 or 20 years.

One result of increasing PC power is that the differences among mainframes, minis, and microcomputers are not as great as they once were. In fact, the processing power of PCs often rivals that of current mainframes. Mainframes are still popular because they can handle the input and output needs of many users at once, so they are still the right choice for the massive databases that many people need to use at the same time. Another reason for the continued popularity of mainframe systems is their reliability. Mainframes are known for their robustness and ability to handle tremendous loads without failing.

NORTON
ONLINE

Visit **www.glencoe.com/norton/online/** for more information on **personal computers**.

The microcomputer category has grown tremendously in the past decade. There are now several specific types of microcomputers, each with its own capabilities, features, and purposes. Within each subcategory of microcomputer, you can find dozens or even hundreds of unique systems. This range of options makes the microcomputer "the computer for the masses" and explains why so many systems have appeared in offices, homes, briefcases, and even pockets over the past few years. Microcomputers include the following types:

◆ Desktop models, including tower models

◆ Notebook computers, also called laptop computers

◆ Network computers

◆ Handheld personal computers (H/PCs) of all types

Desktop Models

The first style of personal computer introduced was the desktop model (see Figure 2.7). In common usage, the term *desktop system* means a full-size computer that is small enough to be used at a desk but too big to carry around. Traditionally, a desktop computer's main case (called the system unit) is horizontally oriented, meaning it can lie flat on a desk or table.

A variation of the desktop system is the tower model, where the system unit sits vertically and has more space for devices. Because of its design, the system unit is often placed on the floor to preserve desk space, allowing more room to place external components, such as removable disk drives or scanners, on the desktop.

Figure 2.7
Two common designs for PCs are shown here. The more traditional desktop model features a horizontally oriented system unit, on top of which many users place the monitor. Vertically oriented tower models have become the more popular style of desktop system.

Tower models have become increasingly popular in recent years—so much so that some PC makers have stopped offering horizontally oriented desktop systems.

Personal computers can cost anywhere from $600 to $7500, depending on the capabilities and capacity. The most popular models cost between $1000 and $3000. The tremendous growth and potential of the PC market has brought many manufacturers into this arena.

Notebook Computers, or Laptop Computers

Notebook computers, as their name implies, approximate the shape of an 8.5- by 11-inch notebook and can fit inside a briefcase easily (see Figure 2.8). Also called **laptop computers,** they can operate on alternating (plug-in) current or special batteries. Notebooks are fully functional microcomputers; the people who use them need the power of a full-size PC wherever they go.

Some notebook systems are designed to be plugged into a **docking station** (also called an expansion base, as shown in Figure 2.9), which may include a large monitor, a full-size keyboard and mouse, or other devices such as an additional hard drive or backup tape unit. Docking stations also provide additional ports that enable the notebook computer to be connected to different devices in the same manner as a desktop system. Some expansion bases also feature built-in networking cards so one is not required in the notebook computer.

Because of their size, notebook computers often feature a smaller display, less memory, and less storage space than a full-size PC. The most expensive notebooks, however, can be configured with just as much memory and storage space as a desktop system. Notebook systems are also available with the same processing power as the most powerful full-size PCs. Also because of their size, notebook computers tend to be more expensive than comparably equipped desktop computers. Depending on its features, a fully equipped notebook computer can cost between $500 and $5000.

Figure 2.8
A notebook computer. When a notebook computer is not being used, the top folds down, and in some models the keyboard collapses. The whole computer becomes about the size of a thick pad of paper.

Figure 2.9
A notebook computer plugged into a docking station.

Visit **www.glencoe.com/norton/online/** for more information on **notebook** and **laptop** computers.

Network Computers (NCs)

In some situations, a user does not need all the power and features provided by a personal computer. If you want to use only the Internet, for example, or if your job involves data entry, then you may not need the processing power, memory, and storage capacity of a fully equipped PC. In this instance a **network computer (NC)** becomes useful.

A network computer is a less powerful version of a personal computer, with minimal processing power, memory, and storage. (Some types of network computers provide no storage at all.) Network computers are designed to be connected to a network, a corporate intranet, or to the Internet. The NC relies on the network for software and data storage and may even use the network's server to perform some processing tasks.

In the mid-1990s, the concept of network computers became popular among some PC manufacturers, who pronounced the NC as the future of computing. However, no single NC standard emerged as various hardware and software makers fought to command this new market. As a result, several variations on the network computer quickly became available, and consumers almost immediately became confused about their differences and special purposes. While network computers have gained some market share in business, they have not succeeded to the extent their makers anticipated.

In business, variations of the network computer are thin clients, diskless workstations, Windows terminals, and NetPCs. Some network computers are designed to be connected only to the Internet or to an intranet. These devices are sometimes called Internet PCs, Internet boxes, Internet appliances, or set-top boxes. In home settings, some network computers do not even include a monitor; instead, they connect to the user's television, which serves as the output device.

A popular example of a home-based network computer is WebTV, which enables the user to connect a television to the Internet and enjoy both standard television programming and Internet services (see Figure 2.10). The WebTV service uses a special set-top box to connect to the Internet and provides a set of simple controls to enable the user to navigate the Internet, send e-mail, and perform other tasks on the network while watching television.

Figure 2.10
The WebTV service is a network computer in the home.

Many large companies have adopted network computers for their users because they have a lower **total cost of ownership (TCO)** than standard personal computers. NCs are cheaper to purchase, operate, and maintain than normal PCs. Because most users' systems are connected to a company network anyway, users can take advantage of the network server's speed and storage capacity and can often access the Internet through the company's network connection.

In corporate settings, network computers such as the Sun JavaStation (see Figure 2.11 on page 30), offer several other advantages:

Figure 2.11
The Sun JavaStation is one type of network computer.

◆ **Enhanced Data Security.** Because NCs have no floppy disk drive or CD-ROM drive, it is impossible for users to install programs or copy data files directly to or from a network computer. This feature enhances the security of sensitive business data and prevents users from filling disks with unneeded programs.

◆ **Reduced Threat of Viruses.** Because individual users cannot install files at the NC, there is little risk that users will introduce computer viruses into the network by copying files from infected disks.

◆ **Centralized Software.** It is less expensive to purchase software for network computers because software must be installed only on the server rather than on each individual NC. Some types of NCs can store and run an operating system and applications locally but not to the extent that a full-fledged PC can. Thus, software costs are greatly reduced.

◆ **Limited Upgrades.** A large company no longer must individually upgrade the operating systems and applications in thousands of PCs every two or three years.

Handheld Personal Computers (H/PCs)

Since the mid-1990s, many new types of small personal computing devices have been introduced, and all fall under the category of **handheld personal computers (H/PCs).** These tiny systems are also called **palmtop computers.** A handheld PC can be any sort of computer that fits in the user's hand, such as a(n):

◆ Personal digital assistant (PDA)

◆ Cellular telephone with Internet, e-mail, and fax capabilities

◆ H/PC Pro device

As shown in Figure 2.12, many H/PCs look like miniature notebook computers, with small displays and keyboards, but are much smaller than even the tiniest full-featured notebook PC. (Some of these systems are not much larger than a checkbook.) This type of H/PC is sometimes called a mini-notebook computer. Most H/PC systems do not provide disks, but memory can be added through PC cards or other means. Software is abundant for these devices, most of which are Internet-capable and can connect to a full-size computer to exchange data.

Personal Digital Assistants (PDAs)

Personal digital assistants (PDAs) are among the smallest of portable computers. Often, they are no larger than a small appointment book, but they are much less powerful than notebook or desktop computers. PDAs are normally used for special applications, such as taking notes, displaying telephone numbers and addresses, and keeping track of dates or agendas. Many PDAs can be connected to larger computers to exchange data.

NORTON ONLINE

Visit **www.glencoe.com/norton/online/** for more information on **H/PCs.**

Most PDAs come with an **electronic pen** that lets the user write on a touch-sensitive screen. (These systems are sometimes called **pen-based organizers.**) Even though they do not include real keyboards, some of these devices provide a graphical keyboard that appears on the screen; you type by tapping the desired keys with the unit's pen. Depending on the model, PDAs may include the following features:

◆ Built-in microphone and speaker, enabling the user to record speech digitally

◆ Personal information management (PIM) software

◆ Miniaturized versions of personal productivity applications

◆ Internet, fax, or e-mail software

Cellular Phones

Some new cellular phones are doubling as miniature PCs (see Figure 2.13). Advanced cellular devices combine analog and digital cell-phone service with e-mail capabilities. Such phones enable the user to check and send e-mail and faxes over the phone. They offer features not normally found on a phone, such as personal organizers or access to the Web. Some models even break in half to reveal a miniature keyboard.

H/PC Pro Devices

Probably the most curious new development in handheld technology is the **H/PC Pro** family of devices. These systems are larger than PDAs or miniature notebooks, but they are not quite as large as typical notebook PCs, with features somewhere between the two. For example, H/PC Pro systems boast nearly full-size keyboards and color displays. They can run more types of miniaturized applications than their smaller counterparts, but those applications still do not provide the features of normal desktop software. H/PC Pro units offer long battery life and instant-on access (features still missing from many laptop systems), but they do not include disks. Although they will gain speed and storage capacity quickly, H/PC Pro systems offer very limited RAM and relatively slow processor speeds.

Figure 2.12
Many popular H/PC systems, like the HP Jornada, provide a wide variety of software packages and communications capabilities packed into a tiny shell.

Figure 2.13
Some new-generation cellular phones rival computers in their features. This cellular phone, by Nokia, provides an organizer, e-mail, and other features. It even has a built-in keyboard.

PRODUCTIVITY Tip

Choosing the Right Tool for the Job

Buying a computer is a lot like buying a car because there are so many models and options from which to choose! Before deciding which computer is best for you, identify the type of work for which you want to use the computer.

Depending on your job, you may not need to use a computer much. A handheld system is great if you want to:

◆ **Manage Your Schedule on a Daily or Hourly Basis.** Handheld computers are popular for their calendar and schedule-management capabilities, which enable you to set appointments, track projects, and record special events.

◆ **Manage a List of Contacts.** If you need to stay in touch with many people and travel frequently, personal digital assistants provide several contact-management features.

◆ **Make Notes on the Fly.** Some H/PCs feature small keyboards, which are handy for tapping out quick notes. Others feature electronic pens, which enable the user to "write" directly on the display screen. Many newer handheld systems also provide a built-in microphone, so you can record notes digitally.

◆ **Send Faxes and E-Mail.** Most popular H/PCs have fax and e-mail capabilities and a port that lets them exchange data with a PC.

Laptop computers enable you to work almost anywhere.

If your job requires you to travel but you still need a full-featured computer, then consider a laptop or notebook computer. This option is the best choice if you want to:

◆ **Carry Your Data With You.** If you need to take presentations on the road or keep up with daily work while traveling, portable PCs are ideal. Laptop systems offer nearly as much RAM and storage capacity as desktop models. Many portables have built-in CD-ROM drives; others accept plug-in CD-ROM and hard drives, which can greatly increase their capacity.

◆ **Be Able to Work Anywhere.** Portable PCs run on either rechargeable batteries or standard current.

◆ **Communicate and Share Data From Any Location.** Most portable computers have built-in modems or slots for plugging in a modem.

If you work in one place and need to perform various tasks, a desktop computer is the best choice. Choose a desktop computer if you want to:

◆ **Work With Graphics-Intensive or Desktop Publishing Applications.** Complex graphics and page-layout programs require a great deal of system resources, and a desktop system's large monitor reduces eye fatigue. Desktop models also can accept many different types of pointing devices that can make graphics work easier.

　◆ **Design or Use Multimedia Products.** Even though many portable computers have multimedia features, you can get the most for your money with a desktop system. Large screens make multimedia programs easier to see, and stereo-style speakers optimize sound quality.

　◆ **Set Up Complex Hardware Configurations.** A desktop computer can support multiple peripherals—including printers, sound and video sources, and various external devices—at the same time. If you want to swap video or audio cards easily, increase RAM, or perform other configuration tasks, a desktop system will provide many options.

LESSON QUIZ

True/False

Answer the following questions by circling True or False.

True   False   **1.** Supercomputers have no more real processing power than today's personal computers.

True   False   **2.** Mainframe computers are almost obsolete thanks to the World Wide Web.

True   False   **3.** Another name for minicomputer is midrange computer.

True   False   **4.** Workstations are specialized, single-user computers with many features of a PC and the power of a minicomputer.

True   False   **5.** Even the most expensive notebook computers cannot offer the same processing power as a full-sized PC.

Multiple Choice

Circle the word or phrase that best completes each sentence.

1. Because of their size and cost, _____ are relatively rare.

   A. supercomputers   **B.** mainframes   **C.** both A and B

2. _____ computers are sometimes called enterprise servers.

   A. Workstation   **B.** Mainframe   **C.** Network

3. Both IBM-compatible computers and Macintosh computers can be called _____ .

   A. set-top boxes   **B.** personal computers   **C.** network computers

4. A _____ is a less powerful version of a PC, designed especially for use on a network.

   A. handheld computer   **B.** cellular phone   **C.** network computer

5. A _____ is an example of a handheld computer.

   A. personal digital assistant   **B.** thin client   **C.** neither A nor B

LESSON LABS

Complete the following exercises as directed by your instructor.

1. What type of computer system do you use in class or in the lab? How much can you tell about the system by looking at it? List as much information as you can about the computer. Is it a desktop or tower model? Is it an IBM-compatible or a Macintosh computer? What brand is it? What are the model and serial numbers? What external devices does it have? Is it connected to a network or a printer?

2. What kind of software is installed on your computer? To find out, all you have to do is turn on your computer. After it starts, you should see a collection of icons—small pictures that represent the programs and other items on the computer's disks. List the icons that appear on your screen and the names of the software programs they represent.

VISUAL SUMMARY

LESSON 1: An Overview of the Computer System

The Parts of a Computer System

- A computer is an electronic device used to process data, converting it into information that is useful to people.

- A complete computer system includes hardware, software, data, and people.

- Hardware consists of electronic devices, the parts you can see.

- Software, also known as programs, consists of organized sets of instructions for controlling the computer.

- Data consists of text, numbers, sounds, and images that the computer can manipulate.

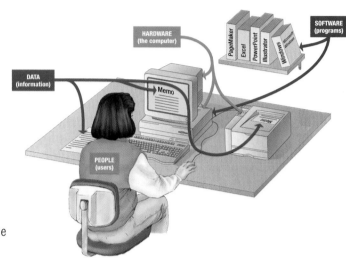

Looking Inside the Machine

- The hardware, or physical components, of a computer consists of a processor, memory, input and output (I/O) devices, and storage.

- The processing function is divided between the processor and memory.

- The processor, or CPU, is the brain of the machine.

- Memory holds data and program instructions as the CPU works with them.

- The most common units of measure for memory are the byte, kilobyte, megabyte, gigabyte, and terabyte.

- The role of input is to provide data from the user or another source.

- The function of output is to present processed data to the user or to another computer.

- Communications devices perform both input and output functions, allowing computers to share information.

- Storage devices hold data not currently being used by the CPU.

Software: Bringing the Machine to Life

- Programs are electronic instructions that tell the computer how to accomplish certain tasks.

- When a computer is using a particular program, it is said to be running or executing the program.

- The operating system tells the computer how to interact with the user and how to use the hardware devices attached to the computer.

- Application software tells the computer how to accomplish tasks the user requires.

- Some important kinds of application software are word processing programs, spreadsheets, database management software, presentation programs, graphics programs, multimedia authoring applications, entertainment and education software, Web design tools and Web browsers, Internet applications, utilities, and networking and communications software.

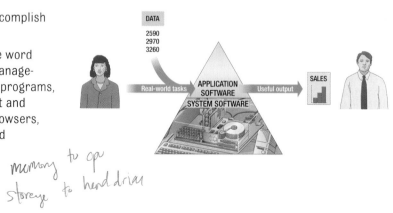

LESSON 2: The Shapes of Computers Today

Supercomputers *universities, large businesses*

20 ■ Supercomputers are the most powerful computers in terms of processing. They are useful for problems requiring complex calculations.

21 ■ Because of their size and expense, supercomputers are relatively rare. They are typically used by large organizations such as universities, government agencies, and very large businesses.

Mainframe Computers *e-commerce servers*

22 ■ Mainframe computers, which generally have many terminals or PCs connected to them, handle massive amounts of input, output, and storage.

23 ■ Mainframe computers are commonly used in corporations and government agencies, but they are also used as e-commerce servers, handling transactions over the Internet.

Minicomputers *network servers / intranet / internet servers*

24 ■ Minicomputers are smaller than mainframes but larger than microcomputers. They usually have multiple terminals.

25 ■ Minicomputers are used more and more often as network servers and Internet servers.

Workstations *used by engineers, scientists, graphic artists*

26 ■ Workstations are powerful single-user computers that are used by engineers, scientists, and graphic artists. Like minicomputers, workstations are often used as network and Internet servers.

Microcomputers, or Personal Computers *PC*

27 ■ Microcomputers are more commonly known as personal computers. The term *PC* often denotes microcomputers that are either IBM-PCs or compatibles. The term can also refer to personal computers made by other manufacturers, such as Apple.

28 ■ Desktop computers are the most common type of personal computer. *desktop, notebook handheld*

29 ■ Notebook computers (laptops) are used by people who need portable computing power outside the office or away from home.

30 ■ Handheld personal computers are the smallest computing devices. They lack the power of a desktop or notebook PC, but they offer specialized features for users who need only limited functions and small size.

UNIT REVIEW

KEY TERMS

After completing this unit, you should be able to define the following terms.

application software, *12*
byte, *7*
CD-Recordable (CD-R), *10*
CD-ReWritable (CD-RW), *10*
CD-ROM drive, *10*
central processing unit (CPU), *6*
circuit board, *5*
communications device, *8*
Compact disk (CD), *10*
Compact Disk Read-Only Memory
   (CD-ROM), *10*
computer, *4*
computer system, *4*
data, *4*
device, *4*
digital, *4*
digital camera, *8*
Digital Versatile Disk (DVD), *10*
Digital Video Disk (DVD), *10*
disk drive, *9*
diskette, *9*
diskette drive, *9*
docking station, *28*
document, *5*
electronic pen, *31*
executing, *11*
file, *4*
floppy disk, *10*

gigabyte (GB), *7*
handheld personal computer (H/PC), *30*
hard disk, *9*
hard drive, *9*
hardware, *4*
H/PC Pro, *31*
input device, *7*
input/output (I/O) device, *22*
joystick, *8*
keyboard, *8*
kilobyte (KB), *7*
laptop computer, *28*
magnetic disk, *9*
mainframe computer, *21*
megabyte (MB), *7*
memory, *6*
microcomputer, *26*
microphone, *8*
microprocessor, *5*
minicomputer, *23*
monitor, *8*
motherboard, *5*
mouse, *8*
network computer (NC), *28*
notebook computer, *28*
operating system, *12*
optical drive, *10*
output device, *7*

palmtop computer, *30*
pen-based organizer, *31*
personal computer (PC), *26*
personal digital assistant (PDA), *30*
power-on self test (POST), *12*
printer, *8*
processing, *5*
processor, *5*
program, *4*
random access memory (RAM), *6*
read-only memory (ROM), *12*
read/write head, *9*
removable hard drive, *10*
running, *11*
scanner, *8*
software, *4*
storage, *8*
supercomputer, *21*
system software, *12*
tape drive, *10*
terabyte (TB), *7*
terminal, *22*
total cost of ownership (TCO), *29*
touchpad, *8*
touch screen, *8*
trackball, *8*
user, *4*
workstation, *24*

KEY TERMS QUIZ

Fill in each blank with one of the terms listed under Key Terms.

1. The expense of purchasing, operating, and maintaining a computer system is known as
_____ .

2. Electronic instructions that tell the hardware what to do are known as _____ .

3. A(n) _____ is a powerful single-user computer usually used by scientists, engineers, graphic artists, animators, or programmers.

4. Portable computers that can fit easily inside a briefcase are called
_____ .

5. A hard disk may also be referred to as a(n) _____ .

6. A(n) _____ is a device that holds a disk.

7. The term _____ refers to the combination of hardware, software, data, and people.

8. A keyboard and screen that are wired to a mainframe are known as a(n) _____ .

9. A(n) _____ is a set of data or program instructions that has been given a name.

10. The generic term _____ refers to a piece of hardware.

REVIEW QUESTIONS

In your own words, briefly answer the following questions.

1. List the four key components of a computer system.

2. For each of the following devices, describe the type of component it is and briefly describe its function within a computer system:

   - Mouse

   - Monitor

   - Hard disk

3. List the three major distinctions between storage and memory.

4. Computers fall into five categories. List them.

5. Which type of computer provides a user with mobility as well as essentially the same processing capabilities as a desktop personal computer?

6. Name the two major categories of software.

7. What happens during the first step of a computer's startup process?

8. What does application software do?

9. What is the difference between a "file" and a "document" in a computer?

10. What are the five values used to describe a computer's memory or storage capacity, and approximately how much data does each value represent?

DISCUSSION QUESTIONS

As directed by your instructor, discuss the following questions in class or in groups.

1. Home computers are used more extensively than ever for tasks such as banking, investing, shopping, and communicating. Do you see this as having a positive or a negative impact on our society and economy? Do you plan to use a computer in these ways? Why?

2. Describe your experience with computers so far. Have you worked with (or played with) computers before? If so, why? Has your past experience with computers influenced your decision to study them?

 ETHICAL ISSUES
Computer skills can make a difference in a person's employability. With this thought in mind, discuss the following questions in class.

1. A factory is buying computerized systems and robots to handle many tasks, meaning fewer laborers will be needed. The company needs people to run the new equipment but wants to hire new workers who already have computer skills. Is the company obligated to keep the workers with no computer skills and train them to use the equipment? Are workers obligated to learn these new skills if they want to keep their jobs?

2. You are a skilled drafter with 15 years of experience. You have always done your drafting work using traditional methods (pen and paper). Now you want to move to a different city and have sent résumés to several drafting firms there. You learn, however, that none of those firms will consider you for employment because you have no experience drafting on a computer. Is this fair? Why? What would you do?

UNIT LABS

You and the Computer

Complete the following exercises using a computer in your classroom, lab, or home. No other materials are needed.

1. **Explore Your Disk.** Once you are familiar with your computer's hardware, it is time to see the folders and files that reside on its hard disk. To see what is on your disk, take these steps:

   A. Click the Start button on the Windows taskbar to open the Start menu.

   B. On the Start menu, point to Programs. The Programs submenu will appear.

   C. Move the mouse pointer up or down the Programs submenu until you find Windows Explorer.

   D. Click Windows Explorer. The Exploring window will open.

   E. The left pane of the Exploring window lists the drives and folders on your system. Click any icon and its contents will appear in the right pane of the Exploring window.

   F. Close the Exploring window by clicking the Close button (with an **X** on it) in the top righthand corner.

2. **Get Some Help.** If you do not know how to perform a task on your computer, turn to its online help system for answers and assistance. (You will access application help later.) For now, browse your operating system's help system to learn more about your computer:

   A. Click the Start button on the Windows taskbar to open the Start menu.

   B. On the Start menu, click Help. The Windows Help window will appear.

   C. Click the Contents tab to see the categories of help topics. Click any category (with a closed book icon) to see which topics it contains.

   D. Click a topic (identified by a question mark). Its contents will open in the window's right pane.

   E. Click the Index tab to see an alphabetical list of all the terms covered by the help system. To see the help information associated with a term, click the term, then click Display.

   F. Click the Search tab to search for help on a specific topic. In the text box, type a term (such as **print**), then click List Topics. When the topics appear in the list box, double-click on a topic to view its information. Search for help on these terms:

   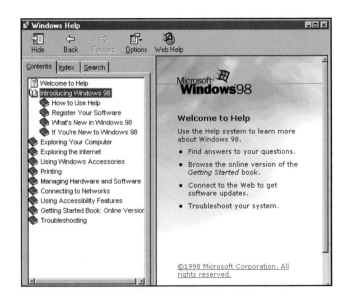

   - Finding documents

   - Copying files

   - Shutting down

   G. Close the help window by clicking the Close button (with an **X** on it) in the top righthand corner.

Internet Labs

To complete the following exercises, you need a computer with an Internet connection and a Web browser. (For more information on using these tools, see "Prerequisites" at the front of this textbook.)

1. **What's Out There?** A search engine is a special Web site that helps you find information on the Internet. Popular search engines include About.Com (**http://www.about.com/**), Alta Vista (**http://www.altavista.com/**), Excite (**http://www.excite.com/**), WebCrawler (**http://www.webcrawler.com/**), and Yahoo! (**http://www.yahoo.com/**). Follow these directions to visit a search engine site and look up information on the Web:

   A. Connect to the Internet and launch your Web browser.

   B. Click in the browser's Address box (it may be called the Location box), and type the address of the search engine you want to visit, such as **http://www.yahoo.com/**.

   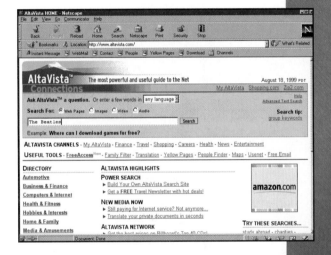

   C. When the search engine's Web page opens, click in the search box and type a topic that you want information on. You can type multiple words and sometimes questions in a search engine's search box. Press Enter.

   D. If the search engine finds any Web pages relating to the specified topic, it displays links to them. Click one of the provided links to visit that page. After you read the page, click your browser's Back button to return to the search page.

   E. Search for information on the following topics: supercomputers, the Beatles, and Greenpeace.

2. **Pick a Favorite.** To add the Web site to your browser's Favorites list, take these steps:

   A. In your Web browser, return to the home page of a site you like (for example, **http://www.usatoday.com/**).

   B. On your browser's toolbar, click the Favorites (or Bookmarks) button. From the menu that appears, click Add Favorite (or Add Bookmark).

   C. Click the Favorites (or Bookmarks) button again and look at the menu. The new page appears in the list. The next time you want to visit this page, select its name from this menu.

IBE Labs

If you have the Interactive Browser Edition (IBE) CD-ROM for this textbook, you may complete the following interactive exercises using the instructions provided in the IBE.

1. **Matching.** Play this game of matching key terms with their definitions.

2. **Labeling.** Drag-and-drop pieces of a puzzle to "build" a computer system.

3. **Association Game.** Challenge your understanding of computer software by arranging information correctly in a table.

4. **Mouse Practice.** Develop your ability to use the mouse by practicing pointing, clicking, double-clicking, and dragging.

UNIT 2

Interacting With Your Computer

UNIT CONTENTS

This unit contains the following lessons:

Standard Methods of Input

OVERVIEW:
The Keyboard and the Mouse

If the CPU is the brain of the computer, then the input devices are its eyes and ears. From the user's point of view, input devices are just as important as the CPU—more so, in fact. After you have purchased and set up the computer, you can take the CPU for granted because you interact directly with input devices (more so than with output devices, which are covered in Unit 3) and only indirectly with the CPU. Your ability to use input devices is critical to your overall success with the whole system.

An input device does exactly what its name suggests; it enables you to input information and commands into the computer. The most commonly used input devices are the keyboard and mouse. In fact, if you buy a new personal computer today, it will include a keyboard and mouse unless you specify otherwise. As you will see, many other types of input devices are available, including variations of the mouse and specialized "alternative" input devices such as microphones and scanners.

This lesson introduces you to the keyboard and mouse. You will learn the importance of these devices, the way the computer accepts input from them, and the many tasks they enable you to perform on your PC.

OBJECTIVES

- Identify the five key groups on a standard computer keyboard.
- Name six special-purpose keys found on all standard computer keyboards.
- List the five steps a computer follows when accepting input from a keyboard.
- Describe the purpose of a mouse and the role it plays in computing.
- Identify the five essential techniques for using a mouse.
- Identify three common variants of the mouse.

THE KEYBOARD

The keyboard was one of the first peripherals to be used with computers, and it is still the primary input device for entering text and numbers. A relatively simple device, a standard keyboard includes about 100 keys, each of which sends a different signal to the CPU.

If you have not used a computer keyboard or a typewriter, you will learn quickly that you can use a computer much more effectively if you know how to type. The skill of typing, or **keyboarding,** as it is often called today, implies the ability to enter text by using all ten fingers—and without having to look at the keys. Certainly, you can use a computer without being able to type, and many people do. Some people claim that when computers can understand handwriting and speech, typing will become unnecessary. But for now and the foreseeable future, keyboarding remains the most common way to enter text and other data into a computer.

The Standard Keyboard Layout

Keyboards for personal computers come in many styles. The various models differ in size, shape, and feel, but except for a few special-purpose keys, most keyboards are laid out almost identically. Among IBM-compatible computers, the most common keyboard layout is the IBM Enhanced Keyboard. It has 101 keys arranged in five groups, as shown in Figure 3.1. In Macintosh computers, the keyboard layout is close to the IBM Enhanced Keyboard, but there are a few differences.

The Alphanumeric Keys

The **alphanumeric keys**—the parts of the keyboard that look like a typewriter—are arranged the same way on almost every keyboard. Sometimes this common arrangement is called the **QWERTY** layout because the first six keys on the top row of letters are Q, W, E, R, T, and Y.

For decades, many expert typists have supported a different arrangement for alphanumeric keys called the DVORAK keyboard. This keyboard layout (designed in the 1930s by a teacher named August Dvorak) places the most commonly used letters in the middle row of keys, making them easier to reach. Special DVORAK keyboards are available for computer systems but they are not standard equipment. A few keyboard manufacturers now offer keyboards that can be switched from QWERTY to DVORAK configurations.

Along with the keys that produce letters and numbers, the alphanumeric key group includes a few additional keys, with specific functions. These keys are similar to those found on a typewriter:

◆ **Tab.** The Tab key moves you to predefined tab stops in many application programs (such as word processors). In dialog boxes, you can press Tab to move from one option or field to another.

◆ **Caps Lock.** As the name implies, this key lets you "lock" the alphabet keys so they produce only capital letters. Caps Lock does not affect the numeric keys or the keys that produce punctuation or special characters.

◆ **Backspace.** This key enables you to erase characters you have just typed. For example, in a word processing program you can press Backspace to "back over" an incorrect character and delete it.

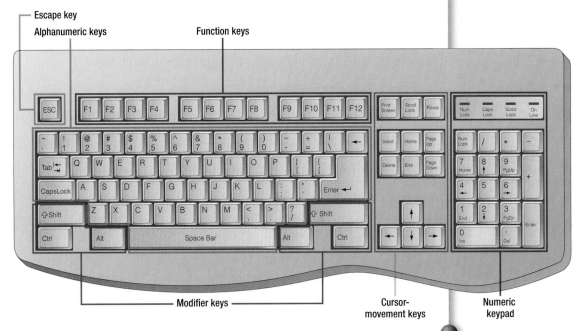

Figure 3.1
This is the standard keyboard layout found in IBM-compatible PCs.

◆ **Enter.** The Enter key (labeled "Return" on some keyboards) lets you finalize data entry in many types of application programs. You can also use Enter to choose commands and options in many programs and at various places in an operating system's interface.

The Modifier Keys

A keyboard's **modifier keys** are so named because they are used to modify the input of other keys. You press another key while holding down one of the modifier keys. On a PC, the modifier keys are as follows:

◆ **Shift.** A computer's Shift keys have the same function as a typewriter's Shift keys; when pressed in conjunction with an alphanumeric key, Shift forces the computer to output a capital letter or symbol. Shift also acts as a modifier key on some programs. In most word processors you can press Shift along with various cursor-movement keys to select text for editing.

◆ **Ctrl.** This key (labeled with an abbreviation of the word *control*) produces different results depending on the program you are using. In many Windows-based programs, Ctrl-key combinations provide shortcuts for menu commands. For example, the Ctrl-key combination Ctrl+O enables you to open a new file.

◆ **Alt.** This key (called the Alternate key) operates like the Ctrl key, except that it produces a different set of results. In Windows-based programs, Alt-key combinations enable you to navigate menus and dialog boxes without using a mouse.

Macintosh computers also use Shift and Ctrl keys, and they function in much the same manner as their IBM-compatible counterparts. Macintosh systems also offer two additional modifier keys (see Figure 3.2 on page 44):

◆ **Command.** The Command key (sometimes called the Apple key) functions like the IBM-compatible PC's Alt key in many programs. Depending on the computer's age, this key may be labeled with a symbol that resembles a four-leaf clover, a picture of an apple, or both.

◆ **Option or Alt/Option.** This button lets you change quickly the function of other designated keys on the keyboard.

The Numeric Keypad

The **numeric keypad,** usually located on the right side of the keyboard, looks like an adding machine, with its ten digits and mathematical operators (+, -, *, and /). The numeric keypad also features a Num Lock key, which works like the Caps Lock key in the alphanumeric key group, to force the numeric keys to input numbers. When Num Lock is deactivated, the numeric keypad's keys perform cursor-movement control and other functions.

The Function Keys

The fourth part of the keyboard consists of the **function keys.** The function keys (F1, F2, and so on) are usually arranged in a row along the top of the keyboard. They allow you to input commands without typing long strings of characters or navigating menus or dialog boxes. Each function key's purpose depends on the program you are using. For example, in most programs, F1 is the help key. When you press it, a special window appears to display information about the program you are using. Most IBM-compatible keyboards have 12 function keys; most Macintosh systems have 15.

The Cursor-Movement Keys

The fifth part of the keyboard is the set of **cursor-movement keys.** They let you move around the screen. In many programs and operating systems there is a mark on the screen where the characters you type will be entered. This mark, called the **cursor** or **insertion point,** can appear on the screen as a small box, a vertical line, or some other symbol that indicates your place in a document or command line. Figure 3.3 shows a cursor in a document that is being edited in a desktop publishing program called FrameMaker.

Most keyboards include the following standard cursor-movement keys:

◆ **Arrow Keys.** Each of these four keys is labeled by an arrow pointing in a specific direction. The arrow keys move the cursor up or down a single line, or left or right one character space. Depending on the program you are using, you may be able to use the Shift and/or Ctrl keys to modify the arrow keys' behavior—for example, to move a greater distance or to select text for editing.

◆ **Home/End.** Depending on the program you are using, you may be able to press Home to move the cursor to the beginning of a line, and End to move to the end of a line. Used in conjunction with modifier keys, Home and End may move the cursor greater distances.

◆ **Page Up/Page Down.** These keys are sometimes abbreviated as PgUp and PgDn. Typically, they let you "flip" through a document, screen by screen, like turning the pages of a book. Press Page Up to jump to the previous screen; press Page Down to jump to the next. Their functions may be affected by modifier keys, depending on the program you are running.

Special-Purpose Keys

In addition to the five groups of keys described earlier, all IBM-compatible keyboards feature six special-purpose keys, each of which performs a specialized function.

Figure 3.2
A Macintosh keyboard.

Option key   Command keys

◆ **Insert.** Although it is included in the cursor-movement keys, Insert does not really control the cursor's movement. Insert may be used to switch a program from "insert mode" (where text is inserted into the document at the cursor) to "overtype mode" (where new text is typed over existing text), and vice versa. Like other keys, the function of Insert depends on the program and may be affected by using the modifier keys.

◆ **Delete.** As its name implies, Delete is used to delete characters from a document. Used alone, Delete removes a single character at a time at the cursor's location. In conjunction with modifier keys and depending on the program you are using, Delete may be able to remove multiple characters of text. The Delete and Backspace keys function in opposite ways. Delete erases characters to the right of the cursor, and Backspace erases characters to the left of the cursor.

◆ **Esc.** This key's function depends on your program or operating environment. Typically, the Esc key is used to "back up" one level in a multilevel environment.

◆ **Print Screen.** This key allows the user to capture whatever is shown on the screen as an image. The image can then be printed, pasted into a document, or manipulated in various ways by the software.

◆ **Scroll Lock.** Despite its name, the Scroll Lock key does not necessarily make the screen's contents scroll. Its purpose may vary with the operating system and application in use. Usually, this key controls the functions of the cursor-movement keys. With some programs, Scroll Lock causes the cursor to remain stationary on the screen, and the document's contents move around it. When Scroll Lock is turned off, the cursor moves normally. This key does not function at all in some programs.

◆ **Pause.** In some programs, the Pause key can be used to stop a command in progress.

Since 1996, nearly all IBM-compatible keyboards include two additional special-purpose keys designed to work with Windows operating systems (see Figure 3.4).

◆ **Start.** This key, which features the Windows logo (and is sometimes called the Windows logo key), opens the Start menu in the Windows 95, 98, 2000, and NT operating systems on most computers. Pressing this key is the same as clicking the Start button on the Windows taskbar. On many systems, this key can be programmed to perform other tasks.

◆ **Shortcut.** This key, which features an image of a menu, opens an on-screen shortcut menu in Windows-based application programs. Pressing this key is the same as right-clicking within a Windows application window (described later in this lesson). Because it can be programmed to open a specific application instantly, this key is sometimes called the Application key.

Figure 3.3
The cursor shows where the next letter typed on the keyboard will appear.

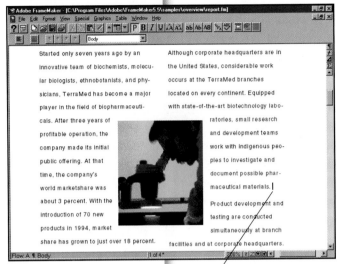

The cursor

Figure 3.4
These two keys are appearing more frequently on new-model keyboards sold with Windows-based computers.

Start key   Shortcut key

Ergonomic and Specialty Keyboards

Many variations have been made on the standard keyboard, primarily for the sake of comfort and the reduction of repetitive stress injuries. People who type a great deal are susceptible to arm and hand fatigue and strain. New, ergonomically correct keyboards can help reduce those problems.

Ergonomically correct keyboards are designed to help the user's hands stay positioned correctly, reducing bending and strain. As shown in Figure 3.5, an ergonomic keyboard may be curved in some way, or it may be broken into two separate sections so the user can place them most comfortably on the desktop. (Ergonomics, correct posture and hand position, and specially designed input devices are covered in detail in Unit 15, "Living With Computers.")

How the Computer Accepts Input From the Keyboard

You might think the keyboard simply sends the letter of a pressed key to the computer—after all, that is what appears to happen. Actually, the process is more complex than that, as shown in Figure 3.6.

A tiny computer chip, called the **keyboard controller,** notes that a key has been pressed. The keyboard controller places a code into part of its memory, called the **keyboard buffer,** indicating which key was pressed. (A buffer is a temporary storage area that holds data until it can be processed.) This code is called the key's **scan code.** The keyboard controller then signals the computer's system software that something has happened at the keyboard. It does not specify what has occurred, just that something has.

The signal the keyboard sends to the computer is a special kind of message called an **interrupt request.** (An interrupt is a signal; it notifies a program that an event has occurred.) The keyboard controller sends an interrupt request to the system software when it receives a complete keystroke. For example, if you type the letter *r,* the controller immediately issues an interrupt request. If you hold down the Shift key before typing the letter *R,* the controller waits until the whole key combination has been entered.

Figure 3.6
How input is received from the keyboard.

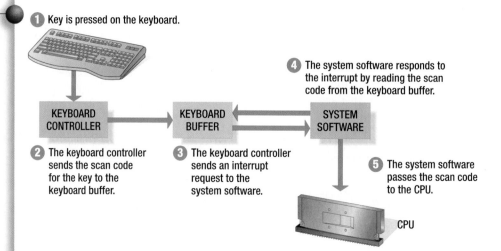

1. Key is pressed on the keyboard.

2. The keyboard controller sends the scan code for the key to the keyboard buffer.

3. The keyboard controller sends an interrupt request to the system software.

4. The system software responds to the interrupt by reading the scan code from the keyboard buffer.

5. The system software passes the scan code to the CPU.

KEYBOARD CONTROLLER

KEYBOARD BUFFER

SYSTEM SOFTWARE

CPU

PRODUCTIVITY Tip

Working Faster With Keyboard Shortcuts

In the 1980s, as programmers began packing more features into PC software, they also developed ways for users to issue an ever-increasing number of commands. Software packages came with long lists of commands, all of which had to be entered at the keyboard. (These lists preceded the acceptance of the mouse by PC users.) As a result, the computer keyboard rapidly became valuable real estate.

Programmers began devising keyboard shortcuts. These enable users to issue commands quickly by typing a short combination of keystrokes. Keyboard shortcuts involve using a modifier key (such as Ctrl on the PC or Command on the Macintosh) along with one or more alphanumeric keys. To print a document in many applications, for example, the user can press Ctrl+P on a PC or ⌘+P on a Macintosh.

Function keys also became important. The F1 key, for example, became the universal way to access online help. IBM-compatible computer keyboards originally had ten function keys; eventually that number was expanded to twelve keys. Macintosh computers eventually included fifteen function keys.

Another common type of keyboard shortcut involves pressing the Alt key to access a program's menu systems. When running any Windows program, you can press Alt to activate the menu bar, and then press a highlighted letter in a menu's name to open that menu.

Still, a keyboard can hold only so many keys, and the lists of keyboard shortcuts started to become unmanageable. A single program could use dozens of "hotkeys," as these shortcuts were called. If you used several programs you had to learn different shortcuts for each one.

The Common User Access (CUA) standard led to the standardization of many commonly used hotkeys across different programs and environments. CUA dictated that different programs use many of the same hotkeys, thus making them easier to remember; for example:

Windows	Mac	Function
CTRL+N	⌘+N	Open the New file dialog box
CTRL+O	⌘+O	Open the Open file dialog box
CTRL+Z	⌘+Z	Undo an earlier command
CTRL+F	⌘+F	Open the Find dialog box

These are some of the shortcut keys available in Microsoft Word 2000.

Press	To
CTRL+SHIFT+ SPACEBAR	Create a nonbreaking space
CTRL+HYPHEN	Create a nonbreaking hyphen
CTRL+B	Make letters bold
CTRL+I	Make letters italic
CTRL+U	Make letters underline
CTRL+SHIFT+<	Decrease font size
CTRL+SHIFT+>	Increase font size
CTRL+Q	Remove paragraph formatting
CTRL+SPACEBAR	Remove character formatting
CTRL+C	Copy the selected text or object
CTRL+X	Cut the selected text or object
CTRL+V	Paste text or an object
CTRL+Z	Undo the last action
CTRL+Y	Redo the last action

Despite such standards, pointing devices (such as the mouse) came along none too soon for hotkey-weary computer users. Microsoft Windows and the Macintosh operating system gained popularity because of their easy-to-use, mouse-oriented graphical interfaces, and even DOS-based programs began using toolbars, pull-down menus, and dialog boxes. This made commands easier to issue because users could select them visually from menus and dialog boxes by operating the mouse. Emphasis rapidly began shifting away from the keyboard to the screen; today, many users of popular programs probably cannot tell you what their function keys do!

Pointing, however, can slow you down. As menus and dialog boxes become increasingly crowded, commands can be hard to find and their locations can be as difficult to remember as keyboard shortcuts.

Many computer users are overcoming these problems by using a combination of keyboard shortcuts and a pointing device. You use one hand to issue many basic shortcuts (such as Ctrl+P, Ctrl+S, and others) or to launch macros. A macro is a series of commands that a program memorizes for you. Macros enable you to issue an entire set of commands in just a few keystrokes. These techniques minimize keystrokes and leave a hand free to use a pointing device.

When the system software receives an interrupt request, it evaluates the request to determine the appropriate response. When a keypress has occurred, the system reads the memory location in the keyboard buffer that contains the scan code of the key that was pressed. It then passes the key's scan code to the CPU.

The keyboard buffer can store many keystrokes at one time. This capability is necessary because some time elapses between the pressing of a key and the computer's reading of that key from the keyboard buffer. With the keystrokes stored in a buffer, the program can react to them when it is convenient.

In many newer systems, the keyboard controller handles input from the computer's mouse and stores settings for both the keyboard and the mouse. One keyboard setting, **repeat rate,** determines how long you must hold down an alphanumeric key before the keyboard will repeat the character and how rapidly the character is retyped as long as you press the key. You can set the repeat rate to suit your typing abilities. (You will learn how to check your keyboard's repeat rate in the lab exercises at the end of this unit.)

Self Check

Answer the following questions by filling in the blank(s).

1. The _____ and _____ keyboard layouts are so called because of the first six keys in the top row of letter keys.

2. The _____ key works as part of the alphanumeric keys (as in a typewriter) but also functions as a modifier key.

3. When you press a key on the keyboard, a(n) _____ tells the computer which key was pressed.

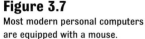

NORTON
ONLINE

Visit **www.glencoe.com/norton/online/** for more information on **mice**.

THE MOUSE

If you bought a PC in the early 1980s, a keyboard would probably have been the only input device that came with it. Today, all new PCs come with a **pointing device** as standard equipment, as shown in Figure 3.7. If the computer is a desktop or tower model, the pointing device is usually a mouse. A mouse is an input device that rolls around on a flat surface (usually on a desk or keyboard tray) and controls the pointer. The **pointer** is an on-screen object, usually an arrow, that is used to select text; access menus; and interact with programs, files, or data that appear on the screen. Figure 3.8 shows an example of a pointer in a program window.

The mouse first gained widespread recognition when it was packaged with the Apple Macintosh computer in 1984. Initially, some users scoffed at this simple tool, but it quickly became apparent that the

Figure 3.7
Most modern personal computers are equipped with a mouse.

Mouse

mouse is convenient for certain types of input. For example, a mouse lets you position the cursor anywhere on the screen quickly and easily without having to use the cursor-movement keys. You simply move the pointer to the on-screen position you want, press the mouse button, and the cursor appears at the preselected position.

The advantages of the mouse are so numerous that it changed the entire personal computing industry. Although the Macintosh operating system was the first widely available system to take advantage of the mouse, the tool's popularity grew rapidly. By the late 1980s, IBM-compatible PCs were quickly adopting the mouse as a secondary input device.

Instead of forcing you to type or issue commands from the keyboard, the mouse and mouse-based operating systems let you choose commands from easy-to-use menus and dialog boxes. The result is a much more intuitive way to use computers. Instead of remembering obscure command names, users can figure out (sometimes pretty easily) where commands and options are located.

A mouse also allows you to create graphics such as lines, curves, and freehand shapes, on the screen. With this new capability, the mouse helped establish the computer as a versatile tool for graphic designers, starting what has since become a revolution in the graphic design field.

Using the Mouse

You use a mouse to point to a location on the screen. Push the mouse forward across your desk, and the pointer moves up; push the mouse to the left, and the pointer moves to the left. To point to an object or location on the screen, you simply use the mouse to place the pointer on top of the object or location.

Everything you do with a mouse you accomplish by combining pointing with four other techniques: clicking, double-clicking, dragging, and right-clicking. Clicking, double-clicking, and dragging are illustrated in Figure 3.9.

Clicking something with the mouse means to move the pointer to the item on the screen and to press and release the mouse button once. **Double-clicking** an item means to point to it with the mouse pointer and then press and release the mouse button twice in rapid succession. **Dragging** an item means to position the mouse pointer over the item, press the mouse button, and hold it down as you move the mouse. As you move the pointer, the item is "dragged" along with it. You can then drop the item in a new position on the screen. This technique is called **drag-and-drop editing.**

With Macintosh computers, most mice have only one button (see Figure 3.10 on page 50). With IBM-compatible computers, most mice have two buttons, but clicking, double-clicking, and dragging are usually carried out with the left mouse button. (In multibutton mice, one button must be designated as the "primary" button, referred to as the mouse button.) Some mice can have three or more buttons. The buttons' uses are determined by the computer's operating system, application software, and mouse-control software.

A fairly recent enhancement is the wheel mouse. A wheel mouse has a small wheel nestled among its buttons. You can use the wheel for various purposes, one of which is scrolling through long documents.

Figure 3.8

The mouse controls the pointer, which is used to interact with items on the screen.

"click"

Click

"click click"

Double-click

Figure 3.9

Three mouse techniques.

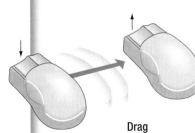

Drag

49

Figure 3.10
The Microsoft mouse features two buttons. The Macintosh mouse features one button.

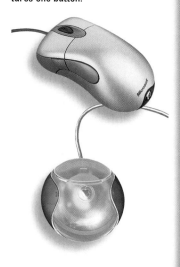

The mouse usually sits to the right of the keyboard (for right-handed people), and the user maneuvers the mouse with the right hand, pressing the left button with the right forefinger. For this reason, the left mouse button is sometimes called the primary mouse button.

Mouse Button Configurations

If you are left-handed, you can configure the right mouse button as the primary button (done by an operating system command). This configuration lets you place the mouse to the left of the keyboard, control the mouse with your left hand, and use your left forefinger for most mouse actions.

Although the primary mouse button is used for most mouse actions, an increasing number of programs also use the right mouse button. Windows 95, 98, 2000, and NT (and applications that run under these operating systems) use the right mouse button extensively to open shortcut menus. Using the right mouse button is known as **right-clicking.**

VARIANTS OF THE MOUSE

As handy as it is, some people do not like using a mouse or have difficulty maneuvering one. For some, a mouse requires too much desktop space—a real problem when you do not always work at a desk!

For these reasons and others, hardware makers have developed various input devices that duplicate the mouse's functionality but interact with the user in different ways. The primary goals of these "mouse variants" are to provide ease of use while taking up less space than a mouse. They all remain stationary and can even be built into the keyboard.

The Trackball

A trackball is a pointing device that works like an upside-down mouse. You rest your thumb on the exposed ball and your fingers on the buttons. To move the pointer around the screen, you roll the ball with your thumb. Because you do

Figure 3.11
Trackballs come in many different shapes and sizes.

not move the whole device, a trackball requires less space than a mouse. When space is limited, a trackball can be an advantage. Trackballs gained popularity with the advent of laptop computers, which typically are used on laps or on small work surfaces without room for a mouse.

Like mice, trackballs come in different models, as shown in Figure 3.11. Some trackballs are large and heavy, with a ball about the same size as a cue ball. Others are much smaller. On portable computers, trackballs may be built directly into the keyboard, slide out of the system unit in a small drawer, or clamp to the side of the keyboard. Most trackballs feature two buttons, although three-button models are also available. Trackball units also are available in right- and left-handed models.

Some trackballs are not even attached to the computer and act like a remote control for the pointer, as shown in Figure 3.12. They are especially useful when giving presentations because the presenter often walks around the room instead of sitting at a computer.

The Trackpad

The **trackpad** (also called a touchpad) is a stationary pointing device that many people find less tiring to use than a mouse or trackball. The movement of a finger across a small touch surface is translated into pointer movement on the computer screen. The touch-sensitive surface may be only 1.5 or 2 inches square, so the finger never has to move far. The trackpad's size also makes it suitable for a notebook computer. Some notebook models feature a built-in trackpad rather than a mouse or trackball (see Figure 3.13).

Like mice, trackpads usually are separate from the keyboard in desktop computers and attach to the computer through a cord. Some special keyboards feature built-in trackpads. This feature keeps the pad handy and frees a port that would otherwise be used by the trackpad.

Trackpads include two or three buttons that perform the same functions as mouse buttons. Some trackpads are also "strike sensitive," meaning you can tap the pad with your fingertip instead of using the buttons.

One drawback of trackpads is that they must be kept clean and static-free. Buildup of dust and oils from the user's fingers can affect a trackpad's performance, making it less sensitive to the touch. An unwanted static charge can make a trackpad behave erratically.

Pointers in the Keyboard

Several computer manufacturers now offer another space-saving pointing device, consisting of a small joystick positioned near the middle of the keyboard, typically between the *G* and *H* keys. The joystick is controlled with either forefinger. Because users do not have to take their hands off the keyboard to use this device, it can save a great deal of time and effort. Two buttons that perform the same function as mouse buttons are just beneath the spacebar and are pressed with the thumb. Because it occupies so little space, the device is built into many different laptop models. This type of pointing device is also available on some models of desktop computer keyboards.

Several generic terms have emerged for this device; many manufacturers refer to it as an **integrated pointing device,** while others call it a 3-D point stick. On the IBM ThinkPad line of notebook computers, the pointing device is called the **TrackPoint** (see Figure 3.14).

TrackPoint

Figure 3.12
The Trackman Live, from Logitech, is a remote-control trackball. It is especially handy for giving stand-up presentations.

Figure 3.13
Some notebook computers and desktop keyboards feature a built-in trackpad.

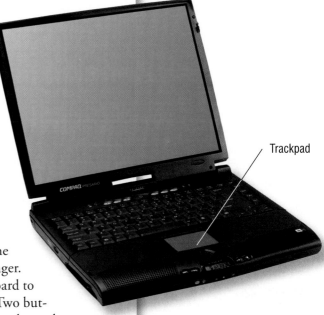

Trackpad

Figure 3.14
IBM's ThinkPad comes with the TrackPoint pointing device. Several models of desktop keyboards are equipped with similar devices. The pointer is controlled by pushing the red TrackPoint device forward, backward, left, or right. Commands are executed by clicking the TrackPoint buttons, just below the spacebar.

Norton Notebook

EQUAL-OPPORTUNITY COMPUTING

Innovations in operating systems, software applications, and hardware are making computers increasingly accessible to persons with disabilities. These technological improvements span a broad range—from general system settings that can make a PC more useful to nearly anyone, to disability-specific hardware that can help a user overcome a physical challenge as it applies to the computer.

Resetting the System

Newer operating systems provide several accessibility settings that are easy to configure. While these settings cannot make a keyboard or mouse accessible to someone with a significant mobility impairment, they can make the computer a little easier to use for persons who can use a keyboard and/or a mouse. These settings include:

◆ **Sticky Keys.** For users who have trouble pressing two keys at one time, a "sticky keys" option allows the user to activate any modifier key by pressing it once and releasing it. The key stays active until it is pressed again.

◆ **Filter Keys.** If a person cannot release a key quickly after pressing it, this option tells the computer to ignore repeated key strokes.

◆ **Mouse Keys.** In newer versions of Windows, the user can set the keyboard's cursor-movement keys to control the mouse pointer.

◆ **SerialKey Device Support.** Input devices that support the SerialKey standard can provide alternative access to the features of a keyboard or mouse.

Modern operating systems also provide various alarm methods. Hearing-impaired users can set their PCs to display visual alerts instead of sounding audible alerts.

Special Hardware and Software

Many kinds of help are available through specialized input devices, output devices, and software. Some of the major accessibility products can be categorized as follows:

◆ **Keyboard Alternatives.** This category includes software programs that enable users to input data with fewer keystrokes, or devices that replace traditional keyboards entirely.

◆ **Breath-Enabled Devices.** A breath-enabled device can perform many types of input, such as opening menus and choosing commands. By inhaling

The Accessibility Properties dialog box lets Windows users set various accessibility options.

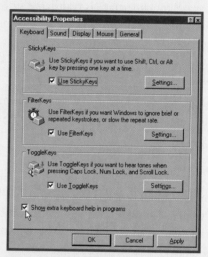

(sipping) and blowing (puffing) through a tube, the user can control different system functions.

◆ **Speech Recognition.** A speech-recognition system includes a microphone and special software that can recognize certain words and phrases. With this type of system, a user can issue commands and navigate menu systems by "talking" to the computer and can dictate text for the PC to type.

◆ **Braille Input and Output Devices.** Braille notetakers, keyboards, displays, and printers (also called embossers) are all available. Specialized software can convert standard PC keyboards to Braille input devices.

◆ **Screen Readers.** Using speech-synthesis technology, a screen reader can "read" the computer screen's contents to the user. These systems convert text to audio output for blind or visually impaired users.

◆ **Display-Enlargement Systems.** These systems "zoom" the contents of the screen so it appears large enough for the visually impaired user to read. Output-enlargement software enlarges the characters on printed output.

Accessibility has also become a concern of Web designers. By using style sheets, large fonts, text-only versions of pages, audio clips, plug-ins, and other techniques, designers are making the Web a much more user-friendly environment for persons with disabilities.

LESSON QUIZ

True/False

Answer the following questions by circling True or False.

True   False   **1.** The QWERTY keyboard layout is named after its inventor.

True   False   **2.** The keyboard keys labeled F1, F2, and so on, are called function keys.

True   False   **3.** The Delete key erases characters to the right of the cursor.

True   False   **4.** The Start and Shortcut keys are standard on all Macintosh keyboards.

True   False   **5.** On a two-button mouse, you usually click, double-click, and drag by using the left mouse button.

Multiple Choice

Circle the word or phrase that best completes each sentence.

1. On standard keyboards, keys are usually arranged in _____ groups.
   A. three   **B.** five   **C.** eight

2. On a PC keyboard, the modifier keys include _____ .
   A. Alt, Delete, and Insert   **B.** Shift, Ctrl, and Alt   **C.** Backspace, Esc, and Command

3. As you type, the system stores _____ in the keyboard buffer.
   A. interrupt requests   **B.** scan codes   **C.** neither A nor B

4. A _____ works like an upside-down mouse.
   A. trackball   **B.** trackpad   **C.** joystick

5. The term _____ is another term for integrated pointing device.
   A. trackpad   **B.** mouse   **C.** TrackPoint

LESSON LABS

Complete the following exercises as directed by your instructor.

1. Launch the Notepad text editing program and test your typing skills by clicking the Start button, pointing to Programs, clicking Accessories, then clicking Notepad. The Notepad program will open in a window. Have a classmate time you as you type the first paragraph of the Norton Notebook article on the opposite page. Do not stop to correct mistakes; keep typing until you are finished.

2. Inspect the mouse settings of your system. (Do not change any settings without your instructor's permission.)

A. Click the Start button to open the Start menu, then click Settings, Control Panel. The Control Panel dialog box opens.

B. Double-click the Mouse icon to open the Mouse Properties dialog box. Click the tabs in this dialog box and inspect your settings.

C. Experiment with the Pointer Speed and Show Pointer Trails tools and see how they affect your mouse's performance. When you are finished, click Cancel.

Alternative Methods of Input

OBJECTIVES

- List two reasons why some computer users prefer alternative methods of input over a standard keyboard or mouse.
- List three categories of alternative input devices.
- List two types of optical input devices and describe their uses.
- Describe the uses for speech-recognition systems.
- Identify two types of video input devices and their uses.

OVERVIEW:
Options for Every Need and Preference

Although the keyboard and mouse are the input devices that people use most often, several additional ways of getting data into a computer are available. Sometimes the tool is simply a matter of choice. Some users just prefer the feel of a trackball over a mouse. In many cases, however, an ordinary input device may not be appropriate. For example, in a dusty factory or warehouse, a keyboard or mouse can become clogged with dirt quickly. It takes time for grocery cashiers to input product codes and prices manually, so optical scanning devices are often used to speed the process and reduce the risk of input errors.

Alternative input devices are important parts of some special-purpose computers. Tapping an H/PC's screen with an electronic pen is a much faster way to input commands than typing on a miniature keyboard. On the other hand, a specialized device can give new purpose to a standard system. If you want to play action-packed games on your home PC, for example, you will have more fun if you use a joystick or game controller than a standard keyboard or mouse.

This lesson examines several categories of alternative input devices and discusses the special uses of each. You may be surprised at how often you see these devices, and you may decide that an alternative device will be your primary means of interacting with your computer.

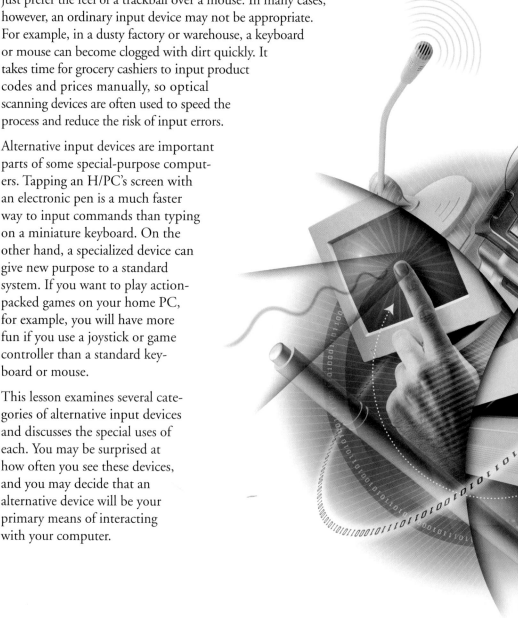

DEVICES FOR THE HAND

Most input devices are designed to be used by hand. Even specialized devices like touch screens enable the user to interact with the system by using his or her fingertips. Unlike keyboards and mice, many of these input devices are highly intuitive and easy to use without special skills or training.

Pens

Pen-based systems—including many personal digital assistants and other types of handheld computers—use a "pen" for data input. This pen-like device is sometimes called a stylus. You hold the pen in your hand and write on a special pad or directly on the screen. You can also use the pen as a pointing device, like a mouse, to select commands.

One might think that pen-based systems would be a handy way to enter text into the computer for word processing. In reality, developers have had a great deal of trouble perfecting the technology so that it deciphers people's handwriting with 100 percent reliability. Because handwriting recognition is so complex, pen-based computers are not generally used to enter large amounts of text, although they are frequently used for note-taking and creating short messages.

Pen-based computers are more commonly used for data collection, where the touch of a pen might select a yes or no box or mark a box next to a part that must be ordered or a service that has been requested (see Figure 4.1). Another common use is inputting signatures or messages that are stored and transmitted as a graphic image, such as a fax. When delivery-service drivers make deliveries, they often have recipients sign their names on such a computer-based pad (see Figure 4.2). As handwriting-recognition technology becomes more reliable, pen-based systems will undoubtedly become more common.

Touch Screens

Touch screens accept input by allowing the user to place a fingertip directly on the computer screen, usually to make a selection from a menu of choices. Most touch-screen computers use sensors in or near the computer's screen to detect the touch of a finger.

Figure 4.1
To interact with a pen-based computer, the user can point, tap, draw, and write on the computer's screen with a pen.

Figure 4.2
When you receive a package via UPS, you sign your name on a pen-based computer that stores a digital image of your signature.

Figure 4.3

A student obtains information at a public information kiosk.

Touch screens are appropriate in environments where dirt or weather would render keyboards and pointing devices useless, and where a simple, intuitive interface is important. They are well suited for simple applications such as automated teller machines or public information kiosks (see Figure 4.3). Touch screens have become common in fast-food restaurants, department stores, drugstores, and supermarkets, where they are used for all kinds of purposes, from creating personalized greeting cards to selling lottery tickets. Car-rental agencies (such as Hertz, Avis, and others) frequently provide touch-screen systems at their counters so that customers can quickly access and print out driving directions. Computerized touch screens also appear on slot machines in gambling casinos.

Some computer makers refer to pen-based systems as touch-screen systems because the user touches the screen with a pen. However, the term *touch screen* implies a system that accepts input by allowing the user to touch the screen with a fingertip.

Game Controllers

You may not think of a **game controller** as an input device, but it is. Personal computers are widely used as gaming platforms, challenging long-time video game units like the Sony PlayStation and others. Because PCs offer higher graphics resolution than standard televisions, many gamers believe a well-equipped PC provides a better game-playing experience. If your computer is connected to the Internet, you can also play games with people around the world.

A game controller can be considered an input device because a computer game is a program, much like a word processor. It accepts input from the user, processes data, and produces output in the form of graphics and sound. As computer games become more detailed and elaborate, more specialized game controllers are being developed to take advantage of their features (see Figure 4.4).

NORTON ONLINE

Visit **www.glencoe.com/norton/online/** for more information on **touch screens.**

Figure 4.4

Several game control devices are available, some of which are quite elaborate and expensive. Some controllers even provide tactile feedback, such as vibrations or pulses, to help players "feel" the action in the game.

Game controllers generally fall into two broad categories: game pads and joysticks. Joysticks have been around for a long time and can be used with applications other than games. (Some joystick users actually prefer using a joystick rather than a mouse with some business applications.) Joysticks enable the user to "fly" or "drive" through a game, directing a vehicle or character. They are popular in racing and flying games. A variant of the joystick is the racing game controller, which includes an actual steering wheel.

COMPUTERS in your career

Using Input Devices on the Job

The input devices you choose can have a large impact on your productivity, which is one reason why so many input device options are available. Different devices are designed to accommodate different needs and to make computing easier and more productive.

Your profession (or your special interests) can determine how you interact with the computer. In fact, some professions rely a great deal on specific types of input devices. Depending on your career, you may need to learn special skills to master an input device. Of course, it always helps if you know how to type.

Here are a few examples of professions that rely on specific input devices:

◆ **Programmers, Accountants, Bookkeepers.** What do these professions have in common? They require a great deal of accuracy. If you write programming code, prepare a client's taxes, or make hundreds of entries each day in balance sheets, accuracy is critical to your success. In such professions, a good keyboard and accurate typing skills are musts. Some users prefer a standard 101-key keyboard, while others prefer ergonomically correct keyboards that fit the position of the hand, wrist, and forearm more naturally while typing. A worn-out or poorly designed keyboard not only slows you down and causes typing errors, it can also result in injuries. Many professionals who must enter numerical data prefer to add a separate ten-key keypad to their system. This type of device is a handy add-on for notebook computers, whose numeric keys can be difficult to use.

◆ **Graphic Artists, Illustrators.** Keyboarding is secondary for some professionals. If your job requires you to draw on the computer—or even to drag blocks around the screen—then you may rely more on a pointing device than on a keyboard. Many graphic artists use large trackballs because they are more comfortable than mice and they require less hand movement.

◆ **Architects, Engineers.** Precise, flexible input devices are essential to professionals who create intricate designs such as buildings, bridges, and satellites. Users of computer-aided design or drafting tools (CAD programs) typically use very specialized input devices, which are not covered in this unit. Such devices include pucks, which are special mice that feature multiple buttons and a crosshair sight that helps the user position the crosshair accurately on a digitizing tablet. A digitizing tablet provides an electronic drawing surface that tracks the puck's movements and translates them into lines on the screen.

Many digitizing tablets also provide lists of commands that the user can select with the puck instead of using a menu on the computer's screen. Digitizing tablets vary in size; the smallest are about the size of a pad of paper and the largest are as big as a tabletop. Some tablets work with an electronic light pen rather than a puck.

◆ **Secretaries, Transcriptionists, Writers.** Some professions require the computer user to enter endless streams of text. For these users, a keyboard may not be enough to handle the task. Scanners are handy for entering text from a printed source, as is required when old documents must be transcribed to disk. Speech-recognition systems are becoming increasingly popular among professionals who type a great deal.

Many types of input devices are available to meet special needs.

◆ **Game Designers, Testers.** Believe it or not, some people play games for a living. Professional computer game testers spend a lot of time with a joystick or game pad in hand, making sure the latest games perform as expected. For some types of games, testers use ordinary keyboards and mice. More sophisticated games require multibutton game pads, sensitive joystick devices, steering wheels, and even foot-pedal systems.

If you have ever used a video gaming system, you are familiar with game pads. A **game pad** is a small, flat device that usually provides two sets of controls—one for each hand. These devices are extremely flexible and are used to control many game systems. If you do not have a joystick, you can use a game pad to control most racing and flying games. (Many computer games still provide support for a mouse or keyboard, so you do not have to buy a dedicated game controller.)

OPTICAL INPUT DEVICES

For a long time, futurists and computer scientists have had the goal of enabling computers to "see." Computers may never see in the same way that humans do, but new technologies allow computers to use light as a source of input. These tools fall into the category of optical input devices.

Bar Code Readers

The most widely used input device after the keyboard and mouse is a **bar code reader.** The most common type of bar code reader is the flatbed model, which is commonly found in supermarkets and department stores (see Figure 4.5). Workers for delivery services, such as Federal Express, also use handheld bar code readers to identify packages in the field (see Figure 4.6).

Figure 4.5
To enter prices and product information into a cash register, a cashier passes groceries over a bar code reader. The bar code reader projects a web of laser beams onto the bar code and measures the pattern of the reflected light.

Figure 4.6
Handheld bar code readers are used to track FedEx packages.

These devices convert a **bar code,** which is a pattern of printed bars on products, into a code the computer can understand. The bar code reader emits a beam of light—frequently a laser beam—that is reflected by the bar code image. A light-sensitive detector identifies the bar code image by recognizing special bars at both ends of the image. These special bars are different, so the reader can tell whether the bar code has been read right-side up or upside down.

After the detector has identified the bar code, it converts the individual bar patterns into numeric digits. The bar code reader then feeds that number to the computer, as though the number had been typed on a keyboard.

Image Scanners and Optical Character Recognition (OCR)

The bar code reader is a special type of image scanner. **Image scanners** (also called scanners) convert any printed image into electronic form by shining light onto the image and sensing the intensity of the light's reflection at every point. Figure 4.7 illustrates the process.

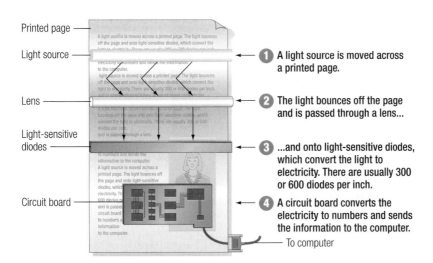

Figure 4.7
How an image is scanned.

Color scanners use filters to separate the components of color into the primary additive colors (red, green, and blue) at each point. Red, green, and blue are known as primary additive colors because they can be combined to create any other color. Processes that describe color in this manner are said to use RGB color.

The image scanner is useful because it translates printed images into an electronic format that can be stored in a computer's memory. You can then use software to organize or manipulate the electronic image. For example, if you scan a photo, you can use Adobe Photoshop—a graphics program—to increase the contrast or adjust the colors. If you have scanned a text document, you might want to use **optical character recognition (OCR)** software to translate the image into text that you can edit. When a scanner first creates an image from a page, the image is stored in the computer's memory as a bitmap. A bitmap is a grid of dots, each dot represented by one or more bits. The job of OCR software is to translate that array of dots into text that the computer can interpret as letters and numbers.

To translate bitmaps into text, the OCR software looks at each character and tries to match the character with its own assumptions about how the letters should look. Because it is difficult to make a computer recognize an unlimited number of typefaces and fonts, OCR software is extremely complex. Figure 4.8 shows a few of the many ways the letter *g* can appear on a printed page.

Despite the complexity of the task, OCR software has become quite advanced.

Figure 4.8
A few of the ways that a lowercase *g* can appear in print.

NORTON ONLINE

Visit **www.glencoe.com/norton/online/** for more detailed information on **scanning** and **OCR**.

Today, many programs can decipher a page of text received by a fax machine. In fact, computers with fax modems can use OCR software to convert faxes directly into text that can be edited with a word processor.

Scanners come in a range of sizes, from handheld models to flatbed scanners that sit on a desktop (see Figures 4.9 and 4.10). Handheld scanners are more portable but typically require multiple passes over a single page because they are not as wide as letter-size paper. Flatbed scanners offer higher-quality reproduction than do handheld scanners and can scan a page in a single pass. (Multiple scans are sometimes required for color, however.) To use a flatbed scanner, you place the printed image on a piece of glass similar to the way a page is placed on a photocopier. There are also medium-sized scanners that are sheet-fed; that is, you feed the sheet through the scanner, similar to the way a page is fed through a fax machine.

Figure 4.9
To use a handheld scanner, you roll the end of the scanner across the image. If the image is wider than the scanner, you can make multiple passes.

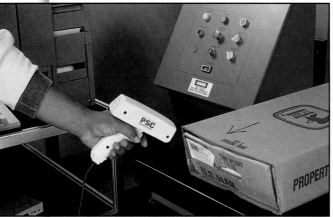

Self Check

Answer the following questions by filling in the blank(s).

1. _____ are often used for note-taking or creating short messages.

2. Game controllers generally fall into the categories of _____ and _____ .

3. _____ can translate a scanned image of a text document into text that can be edited.

Figure 4.10
Large-format, flatbed scanners produce high-resolution, digitized versions of documents. Graphic artists prefer this type of scanner because it yields the highest quality scans of photographs and other images.

AUDIOVISUAL INPUT DEVICES

Today, it is nearly impossible to buy a new PC that does not have complete multimedia capabilities. New computers have features that enable them to record audio and video input and play it back.

Microphones and Speech Recognition

Now that sound capabilities are standard in computers, microphones are becoming increasingly important as input devices to record speech.

Spoken input is used most often in multimedia, where the presentation can benefit from narration. Most PCs now have phone-dialing capabilities, so if you have a microphone and speakers (or a headset microphone with an earphone), you can use your PC to make telephone calls.

Microphones also make the PC useful for audio conferencing over the Internet. For this type of sound input, you need a microphone and a sound card that translates the analog signal (that is, sound waves) from the microphone into digital codes the computer can store and process. This process is called **digitizing.** Sound cards can also translate digital sounds back into analog signals that can then be sent to the speakers. (You will learn more about sound cards and their function in Lesson 5, "Monitors and Sound Systems".)

Using simple audio recording software built into your Windows or Macintosh operating system, you can use a microphone to record your voice, thus creating files on disk (see Figure 4.11). You can embed these files in documents, use them in Web pages, or e-mail them to other people.

There is also a demand for translating spoken words into text, much as there is a demand for translating handwriting into text. Translating voice to text is a capability known as **speech recognition** (or **voice recognition**). With it, you can dictate to the computer instead of typing, and you can control the computer with simple commands, such as "Open" or "Cancel."

Speech-recognition software takes the smallest individual sounds in a language, called phonemes, and translates them into text or commands. Even though English uses only about forty phonemes, a sound can have several different meanings (*two* versus *too*, for example), making reliable translation difficult. The challenge for speech-recognition software is to deduce a sound's meaning correctly from its context and to distinguish meaningful sounds from background noise.

Speech-recognition software has been used in commercial applications for years but traditionally has been extremely costly, as well as difficult to develop and use. Low-cost commercial versions of speech-recognition software are now available and promise to be a real benefit to users who cannot type or have difficulty using a keyboard. Commercial speech-recognition software packages have large stored vocabularies, or words they can recognize.

Newer generation speech-recognition programs are much more reliable than they were a few years ago. Some packages can accurately recognize 80 percent of spoken words. The user may need to "train" the software to recognize speech patterns or the pronunciation of some words, but this is relatively simple. Another enhancement to speech-recognition programs is their ability to recognize continuous speech. Older systems required the user to pause between words. This improved accuracy but greatly slowed the data-entry process.

Speech-recognition programs usually require the use of a noise-canceling microphone (a microphone that filters out background noise). Most commercial packages come with a microphone (see Figure 4.12).

Figure 4.11
Your PC may enable you to record spoken messages with a microphone and sound card.

Figure 4.12
Microphones are becoming increasingly popular as input devices. A multimedia PC usually comes with a microphone—sometimes the "mic" will be on a stand, or it may be built into the computer's monitor.

Video Input

With the growth of multimedia and the Internet, computer users are adding video input capabilities to their systems in great numbers. Applications such as videoconferencing enable people to use full-motion video images, captured by a **PC video camera,** and transmit them to a limited number of recipients on a network or to the world on the Internet. Videos are commonly used in presentations and on Web pages where the viewer can start, stop, and control various aspects of the playback.

The video cameras used with computers are similar to those used in production studios. PC video cameras, however, digitize images by breaking them into individual pixels. (A pixel is one or more dots that express a portion of an image. Pixels are discussed in more detail in Unit 3, "Output Devices.") Each pixel's color and other characteristics are stored as digital code. This code is then compressed (video images can be very large) so that it can be stored on disk or transmitted over a network.

Many PC video cameras attach to the top of the PC screen, enabling the user to "capture" images of himself or herself while working at the computer (see Figure 4.13). This arrangement is handy for videoconferencing, where multiple users see and talk to one another in real time over a network or Internet connection (see Figure 4.14).

Figure 4.13
Using a PC video camera system, you can conduct online videoconferences and include full-motion video in your documents or e-mail.

Figure 4.14
PC video cameras enable you to conduct video phone calls. Many newer model PCs feature built-in software that transforms a conventional telephone call into a two-way video phone call.

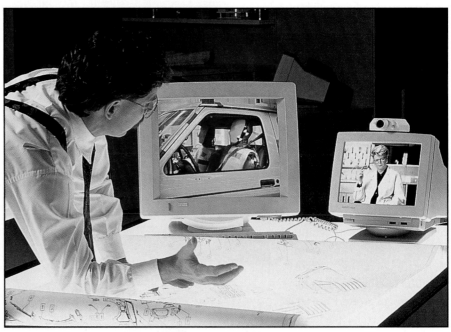

Using a **video capture card,** the user can also connect other video devices, such as VCRs and camcorders, to the PC. This enables the user to transfer images from the video equipment to the PC, and vice versa. Affordable video capture cards are enabling home users to edit their videotapes like professionals. Newer versions of the Windows operating system (specifically Windows 98 and 2000) offer support for cable-television hookups so you can connect your PC to your building's television cable system.

Digital Cameras

Digital cameras work much like PC video cameras, except that digital cameras are portable, handheld devices that capture still images (see Figure 4.15). Whereas normal film cameras capture images on a specially coated film, digital cameras capture images electronically. The digital camera digitizes the image, compresses it, and stores it on a special disk or memory card. The user can then copy the information to a PC, where the image can be edited, copied, printed, embedded in a document, or transmitted to another user.

Most digital cameras can store dozens of high-resolution images at a time, and most cameras accept additional memory that increases their capacity even further. Moving digital images from a digital camera to a computer is a simple process, using standard cables, disks, or even infrared networking capabilities. A wide range of digital cameras is available, from inexpensive home-use models (with prices starting at just over $100) to professional versions costing several thousand dollars.

Visit **www.glencoe.com/norton/online/** for information on **PC video cameras** and **digital cameras**.

Figure 4.15
Although most digital cameras look like traditional film cameras, they work very differently.

Digital cameras have become standard equipment for designers of all kinds. In the field of Web page design, for example, digital cameras enable designers to shoot a subject and quickly load the images onto their computer. This saves the step of acquiring existing photographs or developing and printing film-based photos—which must be scanned into the computer. Using digital cameras, a designer can update a Web site's illustrations quickly and regularly.

Using photo-manipulation software, graphic designers can edit and enhance digital photographs in innumerable ways. A landscape designer can use a digital camera to take a picture of a house, for example, then use landscape design software to modify the image to show how the house might appear with different landscaping.

Professional photographers use photo-manipulation software to edit blemishes out of their images, to correct color imbalances, to correct "red eye," and even to move or erase unwanted parts of an image.

Techview

A BRIEF HISTORY OF THE MOUSE

As recently as fifteen years ago, most people saw no future for the mouse. Many computer experts regarded it as a toy, a gimmick with no real value. Only a few people regarded the mouse as being ahead of its time. Today, we can hardly imagine using a computer without one. The device literally changed the face of computing—indeed, the entire computing industry—by changing the way people interacted with their computers.

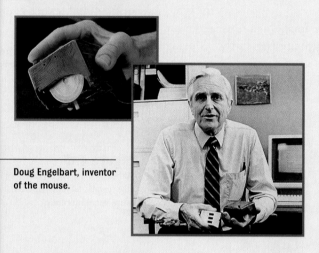

Doug Engelbart, inventor of the mouse.

The Stuff of Legends?

As simple and unassuming as it looks, the mouse is actually surrounded by myth. Many experienced computer users believe that Apple Computer, Inc. created the mouse. Even though Apple was the first company to distribute the mouse as a standard component with personal computers, Apple did not conceive the tailed input device.

Some people believe Apple's management team "stole" the mouse—or at least bought it for a song—from its creators at the Xerox Corporation's Palo Alto Research Center (PARC) in the early 1980s. (This story was embraced by the producers of a 1999 made-for-television movie, titled *Pirates of Silicon Valley*.) In fact, the mouse was not invented at PARC, although PARC's brilliant researchers can take credit for many other inventions. Xerox did, however, own the rights to mouse technology, which it licensed to Apple for a fee. Whether the fee was adequate is the subject of some dispute.

Augmenting Human Intellect

The mouse's history actually goes back to the early 1960s and a group of scientists and engineers at the Stanford Research Institute (SRI) in California. One of those scientists—Doug Engelbart—was part of a team charged with developing ways to "augment human intellect." Specifically, Engelbart's group was looking for ways to use computer systems to help people solve complex problems.

In his vision of this problem-solving system, Engelbart saw the need for a device that would enable the computer user to input data more efficiently than could be done using other standard input devices of the time, such as keyboards, light pens, and joysticks. With funding from NASA, Engelbart's team developed a series of simple tests to determine which input device enabled users to move a cursor around the screen in the least amount of time and with the least effort. In those tests, all the other devices were outdone by a simple wooden gadget—the mouse—that Engelbart had created with fellow scientist Bill English.

The first mouse was a small wooden box. Rather than the hard rubber ball used in modern mice, Engelbart's mouse actually used two small wheels, placed perpendicular to one another on the mouse's underside. The user could move the mouse only up and down or side to side (moving diagonally was a problem), but the device worked well nonetheless and served as a prototype for the mouse we know today.

On to Fame, With a Side-Trip to Obscurity

The mouse was not noticed immediately by industry titans. In fact, few people, including leaders at SRI and PARC, saw the mouse's value. Many did not see much of a future for computers in general, except for use by the military and some large businesses.

This lack of vision, however, did not stop (or even slow) the visionary Engelbart. Throughout his career, he has described or developed technology that was considered to be ahead of its time. His discoveries and inventions in the fields of networking, hypertext, user interface technologies, and other computing disciplines continue to affect everyday computer users. Although the mouse did not make him rich, it helped launch one of the most brilliant and innovative careers in the history of computing science. Today, Engelbart devotes his energies to heading The Bootstrap Institute, a private organization devoted to promoting technology and forward-thinking strategies as ways to build more efficient organizations.

LESSON QUIZ

True/False

Answer the following questions by circling True or False.

True False **1.** Because handwriting-recognition technology is 100 percent reliable, pen-based input devices are ideal for inputting large amounts of text.

True False **2.** A game controller is not really an input device.

True False **3.** Bar code readers use laser beams to convert patterns of printed bars into codes the computer can understand.

True False **4.** If you scan a text document into your computer, you can use optical character recognition software to convert the scanned image into text that can be edited.

True False **5.** All speech-recognition programs require you to pause between words as you talk.

Multiple Choice

Circle the word or phrase that best completes each sentence.

1. For a bar code reader to read a bar code correctly, the code must be positioned _____ .
  A. right-side up   **B.** upside down   **C.** neither A nor B

2. When a sound card translates signals from a microphone into codes the computer can use, it uses a process called _____ .
  A. scanning   **B.** digitizing   **C.** inputting

3. Translating voice to text is a capability known as _____ .
  A. speech recognition   **B.** voice recognition   **C.** both A and B

4. PC video cameras digitize images by breaking them into individual _____ .
  A. pixels   **B.** bar codes   **C.** waves

5. Using a _____ , you can connect devices such as a VCR or camcorder to your PC.
  A. WebTV   **B.** sound card   **C.** video capture card

LESSON LABS

Complete the following exercise as directed by your instructor.

If your computer has a microphone and sound card, record a message and play it back:

A. Click the Start button to open the Start menu; then click Programs, Accessories, Entertainment, and Sound Recorder.

B. When the Sound Recorder program opens, click the record button and speak into your computer's microphone; then click the Stop button.

C. Click Play to hear your message.

D. Close the program by clicking the Close button (with an **X** on it) in the upper right corner of the window. If Windows prompts you to save the file, click No.

LESSON 3: Standard Methods of Input

The Keyboard

- A standard computer keyboard has about 100 keys; each key sends a different signal to the CPU.

- Most keyboards follow a similar layout, with their keys arranged in five groups. Those groups include the alphanumeric keys, numeric keypad, function keys, modifier keys, and cursor-movement keys.

- Most keyboards use the QWERTY layout, which gets its name from the first six keys in the top row of letters.

- Several ergonomically correct keyboards are available to help users prevent hand and wrist injuries.

- When you press a key, the keyboard controller notes that a key was pressed and places a code in the keyboard buffer to indicate which key was pressed. The keyboard sends the computer an interrupt request, which tells the CPU to accept the keystroke.

The Mouse

- The mouse is a pointing device that lets you control the position of a graphical pointer on the screen without using the keyboard.

- Using the mouse involves five techniques: pointing, clicking, double-clicking, dragging, and right-clicking.

Variants of the Mouse

- A trackball is like a mouse turned upside-down. It provides the functionality of a mouse—but takes less space on the desktop.

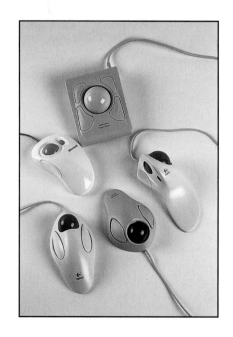

- A trackpad is a touch-sensitive pad that may be built into the keyboard or added to the PC as a separate unit. It provides the same functionality as a mouse. To use a trackpad, you glide your finger across its surface.

- Many notebook computers provide a joystick-like pointing device built into the keyboard. You control the pointer by moving the joystick. On IBM systems, this device is called a TrackPoint. Generically, it is called an integrated pointing device.

VISUAL SUMMARY

LESSON 4: Alternative Methods of Input

Devices for the Hand

- With a pen-based system, you use a "pen" (also called a stylus) to write on a special pad or directly on the screen.

- Pen-based computers are handy for writing notes or selecting options from menus, but they are not well suited for inputting long text documents because handwriting-recognition technology has not yet achieved 100 percent reliability.

- Touch-screen systems accept input directly through the monitor. Touch-screen systems are useful for selecting options from menus, but they are not useful for inputting text or other types of data in large quantities.

- A game controller is a special input device that accepts the user's input for playing a game. The two primary types of game controllers are joysticks and game pads.

Optical Input Devices

- Bar code readers, such as those used in grocery stores, can read bar codes, translate them into numbers, and input the numbers into a computer system.

- Image scanners convert printed images into digitized formats that can be stored and manipulated in computers.

- An image scanner equipped with OCR software can translate a page of text into a string of character codes in the computer's memory.

Audiovisual Input Devices

- Microphones can accept auditory input. Using speech-recognition software, you can use your microphone as an input device for dictating text, navigating programs, and choosing commands.

- To use a microphone or other audio devices for input, your computer must have a sound card installed.

- A sound card takes analog sound signals and digitizes them. A sound card can also convert digital sound signals to analog form.

- PC video cameras and digital cameras can digitize full-motion and still images, which can be stored and edited on the PC or transmitted over a LAN or the Internet.

KEY TERMS

After completing this unit, you should be able to define the following terms.

alphanumeric keys, *42*
bar code, *58*
bar code reader, *58*
clicking, *49*
cursor, *44*
cursor-movement keys, *44*
digitizing, *61*
double-clicking, *49*
dragging, *49*
drag-and-drop editing, *49*
function keys, *44*
game controller, *56*
game pad, *58*
image scanner, *59*
insertion point, *44*
integrated pointing device, *51*
interrupt request, *46*
keyboard buffer, *46*

keyboard controller, *46*
keyboarding, *42*
modifier keys, *43*
numeric keypad, *44*
optical character recognition
  (OCR), *59*
PC video camera, *62*
pointer, *48*
pointing device, *48*
QWERTY, *42*
repeat rate, *48*
right-clicking, *50*
scan code, *46*
speech recognition, *61*
trackpad, *51*
TrackPoint, *51*
video capture card, *63*
voice recognition, *61*

KEY TERMS QUIZ

Fill in each blank with one of the terms listed under Key Terms.

1. IBM-compatible PCs have ten or twelve _____ , but Macintosh computers often have fifteen.

2. _____ is the process that PC video cameras use to break images into individual pixels.

3. In addition to pointing, the four primary mouse techniques are _____ , _____ , _____ , and _____ .

4. In many programs, an on-screen symbol called a(n) _____ or a(n) _____ shows you where you are in a document.

5. A keyboard communicates with programs by sending _____ to the CPU.

6. You use the mouse (or one of its variants) to position a(n) _____ on the screen.

7. After you press a key on the keyboard, a(n) _____ tells the computer which key has been pressed.

8. Using _____ software, you can issue simple commands and dictate text to the computer instead of typing.

9. A(n) _____ lets you control the pointer by sliding your finger across a touch-sensitive pad.

10. The keyboard's _____ determines how long you must hold down a key before a character is typed again.

REVIEW QUESTIONS

In your own words, briefly answer the following questions.

1. Most standard keyboards include five major groups of keys. List them.

2. Some typing experts support the DVORAK keyboard layout. What is special about it?

3. What does the Ctrl key do?

4. You can perform five primary actions with a two-button mouse. List them.

5. How do you double-click an item with a mouse?

6. Some trackpads are "strike sensitive," which means what?

7. Why is a game controller considered an input device?

8. What is a bar code, and how does a bar code reader recognize one?

9. What does optical character recognition (OCR) software do?

10. A sound card performs two basic functions. What are they?

DISCUSSION QUESTIONS

As directed by your instructor, discuss the following questions in class or in groups.

1. Despite the rapid advancements being made with handwriting-recognition software, do you think that the keyboard will continue to be the preferred input device for generating text? Which alternative—speech recognition or handwriting recognition—do you think has a better chance of ultimately replacing the keyboard as the primary device for inputting text?

2. Suppose that you are responsible for computerizing a gourmet restaurant's order-entering system. What type of input device do you think would work best for waiters to input orders to the kitchen?

ETHICAL ISSUES

A computer's input devices make it useful to people. With this thought in mind, discuss the following questions in class.

1. Currently, commercially available PCs are configured for use by persons who do not suffer from physical impairments or disabilities. If a person with a physical impairment wants to use a computer, he or she may need to purchase special equipment or software. Do you think this is fair? Should every PC be accessible to everyone, whether they have physical impairments or not?

2. You have applied for a job as a reporter for a newspaper. Your journalistic skills are excellent. You are not a touch typist, however, and your typing is very slow. For this reason, the managing editor is reluctant to hire you at the position's advertised salary. How would you feel in this situation? Is the editor right? Would you be willing to learn to type or accept the job at a lower salary?

UNIT LABS

You and the Computer

Complete the following exercises using a computer in your classroom, lab, or home. No other materials are needed.

1. **Check Your Keyboard's Repeat Rate.** You can control the length of time your keyboard "waits" as you hold down an alphanumeric key before it starts repeating the character. You can also set the repeat speed. In this exercise, check the repeat settings but do not change any settings without your instructor's permission.

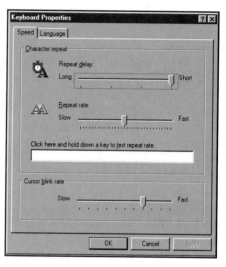

   A. Click the Start button on the Windows taskbar.

   B. Click Settings, then click Control Panel. Double-click the Keyboard icon in the Control Panel dialog box.

   C. Click the tabs at the top of the Keyboard Properties dialog box and inspect the current settings.

   D. Click the Speed tab. Drag the Repeat delay and Repeat rate indicators all the way to the right, then to the left, and in different combinations. Test the repeat rate at each setting by clicking in the test box and then holding down an alphanumeric key.

   E. Drag the Cursor blink rate indicator to the right and left. How fast do you want your cursor to blink?

   F. Click Cancel to close the dialog box without making changes.

2. **Mouse Practice.** Take the following steps:

   A. Click the Start button on the Windows taskbar to open the Start menu.

   B. Click Programs, then Accessories, then WordPad. The WordPad program will open in its own window. (WordPad is a "lightweight" word processing application.) Notice the blinking insertion point in the window.

   C. Type: **Now is the time for all good men to come to the aid of their country.**

   D. Using your mouse, click in different parts of the sentence. The insertion point moves wherever you click.

   E. Double-click the word *good*. It becomes selected: the letters change from black to white, and the background behind the word changes color.

   F. Right-click the selected word. A shortcut menu appears.

   G. Choose the Cut option. The highlighted word disappears from your screen.

   H. Click in front of the word *country* to place the insertion point; right-click again. When the shortcut menu appears, choose Paste. The word *good* reappears.

   I. Double-click the word *good* again to select it. Now click on the selected word and drag it to the left while holding down the mouse button. (A little mark appears on the mouse pointer, indicating that you are dragging something.) When the mouse pointer arrives in front of the word *men*, release the mouse button. The word *good* is returned to its original place.

   J. Continue practicing your mouse techniques. When you are finished, close the WordPad program by clicking the Close button (the button marked with an **X**) in the upper right corner of the window. The program will ask if you want to save the changes to your document; choose No.

Internet Labs

To complete the following exercises, you need a computer with an Internet connection and a Web browser. (For more information on using these tools, see "Prerequisites" at the front of this textbook.)

1. **Was Dvorak Right?** There are several Web sites that provide data about the Dvorak keyboard layout. Visit these sites. Follow the links and study their information.

   - Dvorak International—**http://www.dvorakint.org/**
   - The Dvorak International List of Frequently Asked Questions (FAQ) **http://www.cse.ogi.edu/~dylan/dvorak/DvorakIntl.html**
   - The Dvorak Keyboard—**http://www.mit.edu/people/jcb/Dvorak/**

   Next, launch WordPad (as you did in the second lab exercise on page 70) and write a three-paragraph report entitled "Advantages of the Dvorak Keyboard." Be sure to include your name on the report. When you are finished, click the Print button (the button with a picture of a printer) to print your report.

2. **Pick Your Favorite Pointing Device.** Visit these commercial Web sites for information on various types of pointing devices.

   - Altra—**http://www.altra.com/**
   - AVB Products—**http://www.avbtech.com/**
   - Cirque—**http://www.cirque.com/**
   - Hunter Digital— **http://www.footmouse.com/**
   - Logitech—**http://www.logitech.com/**
   - Mouse Systems— **http://www.mousesystems.com/**
   - Pegasus Technologies— **http://www.pegatech.com/**

   When you are finished, decide which device would work best for you. Be prepared to tell your classmates about the device and explain why you selected it.

IBE Labs

If you have the Interactive Browser Edition (IBE) CD-ROM for this textbook, you may complete the following interactive exercises using the instructions provided in the IBE.

1. **Matching.** Play this game of matching key terms with their definitions.

2. **Labeling.** Create a chart to "show the flow" of input and output in a computer system.

3. **What's Your Recommendation?** Based on the scenarios provided, make input device recommendations for users.

4. **Typing Test.** Use this exercise to test your typing skills.

UNIT 3

Output Devices

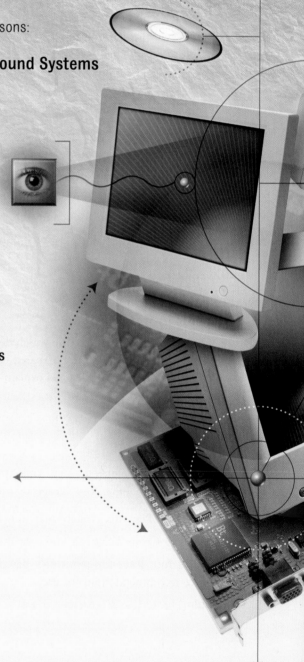

UNIT OBJECTIVES

Explain the role of output devices in computer use.

Describe the basic function of a standard computer monitor.

Explain how digital sound systems function in a PC.

List three popular printing devices and describe their function.

UNIT CONTENTS

This unit contains the following lessons:

Lesson 5: Monitors and Sound Systems

- ► Monitors
- ► PC Projectors
- ► Sound Systems

Lesson 6: Devices That Output Hard Copy

- ► Overview of Printers
- ► Dot Matrix Printers
- ► Ink Jet Printers
- ► Laser Printers
- ► Snapshot Printers
- ► Other High-Quality Printers

Monitors and Sound Systems

OVERVIEW:
Reaching Our Senses
With Sight and Sound

In its infancy, computing was anything but a sensory experience. The earliest computers were little more than gigantic calculators controlled by large panels of switches, dials, and buttons. Visual displays—which today are universally associated with computers—were uncommon until the 1960s.

Now, computers can communicate information to you in several ways, but the most exciting types of output are those that appeal to the senses. It is one thing to read text on a printed page, but quite another to see a document take shape before your eyes—and still another to watch moving, seemingly three-dimensional images on a large, colorful screen while surrounded by stereophonic sounds.

Modern display and sound systems make the computing experience a more inviting one. Because of these sophisticated output technologies, computers are easier to use, data is easier to manage, and information is easier to access. These technologies enable us to play games and watch movies, experience multimedia events, and use the PC as a telecommunications tool.

This lesson introduces you to monitors and sound systems. You will learn about the different types of monitors commonly used with computers and how they work. You will also learn some important criteria for judging a monitor's performance. This lesson also shows you how computers can output sounds by merging new (digital) and old (analog) technologies.

OBJECTIVES

- List the two most commonly used types of computer monitors.
- Explain how a CRT monitor displays images.
- Identify two types of flat-panel monitors and explain their differences.
- List four characteristics you should consider when comparing monitors.
- Explain how a computer outputs sound.

MONITORS

The keyboard is the most commonly used input device, and the monitor is the most commonly used output device on most personal computer systems. As you use your computer—whether you are typing, issuing commands, surfing the Internet, or even listening to music on the system's CD-ROM drive—hardly a moment goes by when you are not looking at your monitor.

Flat-panel displays   CRT monitor

Figure 5.1
The most common types of monitors used with PCs.

People often form an opinion about a computer just by looking at the monitor. They want to see whether the image is crisp and clear, and whether the monitor can display colorful graphics well. Two important hardware devices determine the quality of the image you see on any monitor: the monitor itself and the video controller. In this lesson, you will learn about both of these devices in detail and find out how they work together to display text and graphics.

Two basic types of monitors are used with PCs (see Figure 5.1). The first is the typical monitor that you see on a desktop computer, which looks a lot like a television screen and works the same way. This type of monitor uses a large vacuum tube, called a **cathode ray tube (CRT).** The second type, known as a **flat-panel display,** is used primarily with portable computers but is becoming an increasingly popular feature with desktop computers.

Figure 5.2
Monochrome monitors are often used for text-only displays.

Figure 5.3
Color monitors are almost always included with new computers. This screen is set to display more than 16 million colors, making it a good choice for viewing multimedia content and browsing the World Wide Web.

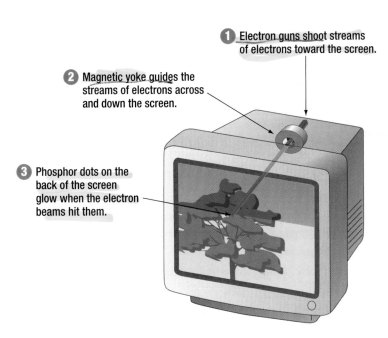

1 Electron guns shoot streams of electrons toward the screen.

2 Magnetic yoke guides the streams of electrons across and down the screen.

3 Phosphor dots on the back of the screen glow when the electron beams hit them.

Figure 5.4
How a CRT monitor creates an image.

All monitors can be categorized by the way they display colors:

◆ **Monochrome Monitors.** **Monochrome monitors** display only one color (such as green, amber, or white) against a contrasting background, which is usually black. These monitors are used for text-only displays where the user does not need to see color graphics (see Figure 5.2).

◆ **Grayscale Monitors.** **Grayscale monitors** display varying intensities of gray (from a very light gray to black) against a white or off-white background, and are essentially a type of monochrome monitor. They are used in low-end portable systems (especially handheld computers) to keep costs down.

◆ **Color Monitors.** **Color monitors** can display anywhere from 16 colors to 16 million colors (see Figure 5.3). Today, most new monitors display in color. Many color monitors can be set to work in monochrome or grayscale mode.

CRT Monitors

Figure 5.4 shows how a typical CRT monitor works. Near the back of a monochrome or grayscale monitor housing is an electron gun. The gun shoots a beam of electrons through a magnetic coil, which aims the beam at the front of the monitor. The back of the monitor's screen is coated with phosphors, chemicals that glow when they are struck by the electron beam. The screen's phosphor coating is organized into a grid of dots. The smallest number of phosphor dots that the gun can focus on is called a **pixel,** a contraction of the term *pic*ture *ele*ment. Modern monochrome and grayscale monitors can focus on pixels as small as a single phosphor dot.

Actually, the electron gun does not just focus on a spot and shoot electrons at it. It systematically aims at every pixel on the screen, starting at the top left corner and scanning to the right edge. Then it drops down a tiny distance and scans another line, as shown in Figure 5.5.

Like human eyes reading the letters on a page, the electron beam follows each line of pixels across the screen until it reaches the bottom of the screen. Then it starts over. As the electron gun scans, the circuitry driving the monitor adjusts the intensity of

Figure 5.5
The scanning pattern of the CRT's electron gun.

1 The electron gun scans from left to right,

2 and from top to bottom,

3 refreshing every phosphor dot in a zig-zag pattern.

each beam to determine whether a pixel is on or off or, in the case of grayscale, how brightly each pixel glows.

A color monitor works like a monochrome one, except that there are three electron beams instead of one. The three guns represent the primary additive colors (red, green, and blue), although the beams they emit are colorless. In a color monitor, each pixel includes three phosphors—red, green, and blue—arranged in a triangle. When the beams of each of these guns are combined and focused on a pixel, the phosphors light up. The monitor can display different colors by combining various intensities of the three beams.

A CRT monitor contains a **shadow mask,** which is a fine mesh made of metal, fitted to the shape and size of the screen. The holes in the shadow mask's mesh are used to align the electron beams, to ensure that they strike precisely the correct phosphor dot. In most shadow masks, these holes are arranged in triangles.

Flat-Panel Monitors

CRT monitors have long been the standard for use with desktop computers because they provide the brightest and clearest picture for relatively low cost. There are two major disadvantages, however, associated with CRT monitors:

A. Because they are big, they take up desktop space and can be difficult to move. Flat-panel monitors are gaining popularity because of their comparatively light weight.

B. CRT monitors require a lot of power. They are not practical for notebook computers, which must be small and need a battery built into the computer to run. Instead, notebooks use flat-panel monitors that are less than 1 inch thick.

There are several types of flat-panel monitors, but the most common is the **liquid crystal display (LCD)** monitor. The LCD monitor creates images with a special kind of liquid crystal that is normally transparent but becomes opaque when charged with electricity. If you have a handheld calculator or a digital watch, it probably uses a liquid crystal display.

One disadvantage of LCD monitors is that, unlike phosphor, the liquid crystal does not emit light, so there is not enough contrast between the images and the background to make them legible under all conditions. The problem is solved by backlighting the screen. Although this makes the screen easier to read, it requires additional power.

Another disadvantage of LCD monitors is their limited **viewing angle**—that is, the angle from which the display's image can be viewed clearly (see Figure 5.6).

Visit **www.glencoe.com/norton/online/** for more information on **flat-panel monitors.**

Figure 5.6
Flat-panel displays typically have a smaller viewing angle than CRT monitors.

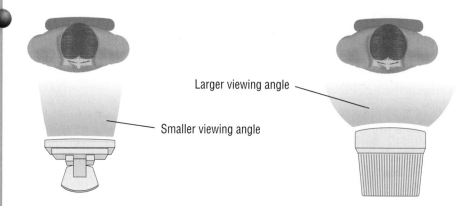

Larger viewing angle

Smaller viewing angle

With most CRT monitors, you can see the image clearly even when standing at an angle to the screen. In LCD monitors, however, the viewing angle shrinks; as you increase your angle to the screen, the image becomes fuzzy quickly. In many older flat-panel systems, the user must face the screen nearly straight on to see the image clearly. Technological improvements have extended the viewing angles of flat-panel monitors but have also caused their prices to increase.

There are two main categories of liquid crystal displays: active matrix and passive matrix. **Passive matrix LCD** relies on transistors for each row and each column of pixels, thus creating a grid that defines the location of each pixel. The color displayed by a pixel is determined by the electricity coming from the transistors at the end of the row and the top of the column. The advantage of passive matrix monitors is that they are less expensive than active matrix, a major consideration in laptops where the monitor can account for one-third the cost of the entire computer. One disadvantage is that passive matrix LCD displays have a narrow viewing angle. Another disadvantage is that passive matrix displays do not "refresh" the pixels very often. If you move the pointer too quickly, it seems to disappear, an effect known as submarining. Also, animated graphics can appear blurry.

Most notebooks that use passive matrix technology now refer to their screens as **dual-scan LCD.** In dual-scan LCD, the problem of the refresh rate is lessened by scanning through the pixels twice as often. Thus, submarining and blurry graphics are less troublesome than they were before the dual-scan technique was developed. (Refresh rate is described in more detail later in this lesson.)

Active matrix LCD technology assigns a transistor to each pixel, and each pixel is turned on and off individually. This enhancement allows the pixels to be refreshed much more rapidly, so submarining is not a problem with these monitors. In addition, active matrix screens have a wider viewing angle than dual-scan screens. Active matrix displays are often called **thin-film transistor (TFT)** displays because many active matrix monitors are based on TFT technology, which employs as many as four transistors per pixel. Active matrix displays are considerably more complex than passive matrix screens and are therefore considerably more expensive. The performance gains, however, are worth the cost for many users.

Although flat-panel monitors have so far been used primarily on portable computers, a new generation of large, high-resolution, flat-panel displays is gaining popularity among users of desktop systems (see Figure 5.7). These new monitors provide an equal or larger diagonal display area, but they take up less desk space and run cooler than traditional CRT monitors. Flat-panel displays for desktops, however, are expensive and produced only by a limited number of vendors. Prices of flat-panel monitors have fluctuated instead of dropping over time because manufacturers have found it difficult to produce flat-panel displays in large numbers. So, supply seldom meets consumer demands.

Figure 5.7
Flat-panel monitors for desktops are becoming increasingly popular.

Other Types of Monitors

While CRT and flat-panel monitors are the most frequently used types of displays in PC systems, there are other kinds of monitors. These displays use specialized technologies and have specific uses:

◆ **Paper-White Displays.** This type of monitor is sometimes used by document designers, such as desktop publishing specialists, newspaper or magazine compositors, and other persons who create high-quality printed documents. A paper-white display produces a very high contrast between the monitor's white background and displayed text or graphics, which usually appear in black. An LCD version of the paper-white display is called the page-white display. Page-white displays utilize a special technology, called supertwist, to create higher contrasts.

◆ **Electroluminescent (ELD) Displays.** ELD displays are similar to LCD monitors but use a phosphorescent film held between two sheets of glass. A grid of wires sends current through the film to create an image.

◆ **Plasma/Gas Plasma Displays.** These thin displays are created by sandwiching a special gas (such as neon or xenon) between two sheets of glass. When the gas is electrified via a grid of small electrodes, it glows. By controlling the amount of voltage applied at various points on the grid, each point acts as a pixel to display an image. Plasma and gas plasma displays are expensive, but they provide high-quality images and can be much larger than typical LCDs. Some plasma displays are big enough to be hung on a wall and used like a large-screen television.

Visit **www.glencoe.com/norton/online/** for more information on **monitor manufacturers.**

Comparing Monitors

When buying a monitor, it is important to do some comparison shopping first. In addition to being aesthetically pleasing, a good monitor is easier on your eyes, allowing you to work longer and more comfortably. A poor monitor will cause eyestrain and headaches and can even cause long-term vision problems.

When shopping for a monitor, first look closely at the display. Look at a screen full of text and examine how crisp the letters are, especially near the corners of the screen. Also, if you are going to work with graphics, display a picture with which you are familiar and see whether the colors look accurate. If possible, spend some time surfing the World Wide Web to display different pages and see how they look.

Even if the monitor looks good (or if you are buying it through the mail), you need to check several specifications. These are the most important:

◆ Size ◆ Refresh rate
◆ Resolution ◆ Dot pitch

Monitor Size

The physical size of a monitor's display area has an obvious bearing on how well you can see images. With a larger monitor, like the 17-inch model shown in Figure 5.8,

Figure 5.8

Comparison of a 17-inch monitor to a 15-inch monitor.

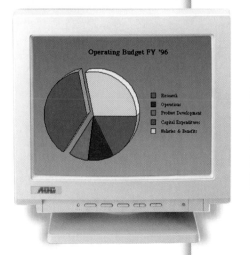
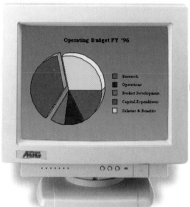

you can make the objects on the screen appear bigger, or you can fit more of them on the screen. In other words, bigger is better, although bigger costs more.

Like televisions, monitors are measured diagonally, in inches, across the front of the screen. For example, a 15-inch monitor measures 15 inches from the lower left to the upper right corner. Actually, the picture that appears on a monitor is smaller than is indicated by the monitor size because the image cannot extend too far into the corners of the CRT without becoming distorted. The picture on a 15-inch monitor, for example, usually measures about 13 inches diagonally. On a 17-inch monitor, the viewing area is a little over 15 inches.

For the past few years, the 15-inch monitor was the standard size with most desktop computer systems. Today, most new desktop systems are sold with 17-inch monitors. The norm may soon creep up to 19 inches or even 21 inches.

Flat-panel monitors are rapidly gaining in size, too. Today, flat-panel displays rival CRT monitors in terms of viewing area, but they do not consume as much desktop space. When viewed side by side, for example, a 17-inch flat-panel monitor provides nearly the same viewing area as a 17-inch CRT monitor. LCD monitors are constantly getting bigger in portable systems, as well. In many higher-end notebook computers, the display has a viewable area of just over 14 inches (measured diagonally).

Visit www.glencoe.com/norton/online/ for more information on **monitor resolution.**

Resolution

The **resolution** of a computer monitor is classified by the number of pixels on the screen, expressed as a matrix. For example, a resolution of 640 × 480 means that there are 640 pixels horizontally across the screen and 480 pixels vertically down the screen. Because the actual resolution is determined by the video controller, not by the monitor itself, most monitor specifications list a range of resolutions. (Video controllers are discussed later in this lesson.) For example, most 17-inch monitors have pixel grids that allow for five settings: 640 × 480, 800 × 600, 1024 × 768, 1152 × 864, and 1280 × 1024, as shown in Figure 5.9.

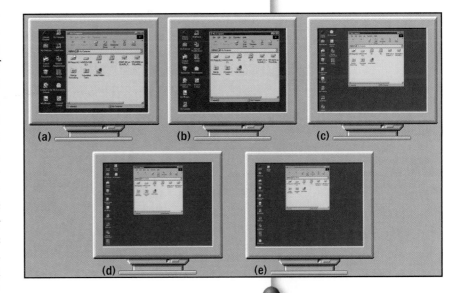

(a) (b) (c) (d) (e)

Figure 5.9
Microsoft Windows 95 and 98 use this kind of monitor to show how screen items appear at different resolutions: (a) the monitor at a resolution of 640 × 480, (b) at 800 × 600, (c) at 1024 × 768, (d) at 1152 × 864, (e) at 1280 × 1024. Notice that more items can fit on the screen at higher resolutions, but the items appear smaller. These resolutions are typical for a 17-inch monitor.

In the mid-1980s, IBM established the **Video Graphics Array (VGA)** standard of 640 × 480 pixels. The **Super VGA (SVGA)** standard expanded the resolutions to 800 × 600 and 1024 × 768. A few 15-inch monitors, and any good monitor bigger than 15 inches, will include even higher settings. Higher settings are not always better, however, because they can cause objects on the screen to appear too small, which can result in squinting and eyestrain. Most users with 15-inch monitors set them to display at either 640 × 480 or 800 × 600. Users with 17-inch monitors typically set their monitors at a resolution of 800 × 600 or 1024 × 768. The largest desktop monitors measure 21 inches or 24 inches and can display more than 16 million colors at resolutions of 1600 × 1200 and even 1920 × 1200.

Refresh Rate

When shopping for a monitor, the size and resolution are simple choices. The size is likely to be determined by your budget (although you may want to spend more on a big monitor if you are working with graphics). The resolutions tend to be standard. The **refresh rate** of the monitor, however, is neither obvious nor standard. The refresh rate is the number of times per second that the electron guns scan every pixel on the screen and is measured in Hertz (Hz), or in cycles per second. The monitor refreshes itself at least several dozen times each second.

The refresh rate is an important concern because phosphor dots fade quickly after the electron gun passes over them. Therefore, if the screen is not refreshed often enough, it appears to flicker, and flicker is one of the main causes of eyestrain. The problem is compounded because you may not even detect the flicker; in the long run, it can still cause eyestrain.

Opinions vary as to what is an acceptable refresh rate. In general, a refresh rate of 72 Hz or higher should not cause eyestrain. Note that some monitors have different refresh rates for different resolutions. Make sure the refresh rate is adequate for the resolution you will be using.

Dot Pitch

The last critical specification of a color monitor is the **dot pitch,** the distance between the phosphor dots that make up a single pixel (see Figure 5.10). Recall that in a color monitor there are three dots—one red, one green, and one blue—in every pixel. If these dots are not close enough together, the images on the screen will not be crisp. Once again, it is difficult to detect slight differences in dot pitch, but blurry pixels will cause eyestrain anyway. In general, when you are looking for a color monitor, look for a dot pitch no greater than 0.28 millimeter.

Figure 5.10
Dot pitch is the distance between the phosphor dots that make up a single pixel. The smaller the dot pitch, the crisper the display image.

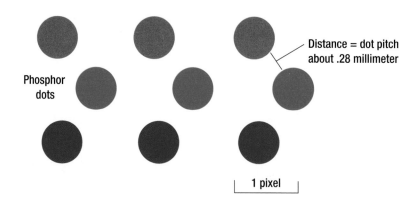

Self Check

Answer the following questions by filling in the blank(s).

1. _____ monitors are used for text-only displays where the user does not need to view color graphics.

2. In a monitor, a(n) _____ aims a beam of electrons at the front of the monitor.

3. A disadvantage of LCD monitors is their limited _____ .

PRODUCTIVITY Tip

Flat-Panel Versus CRT Monitors

Whether you are shopping to equip a future office or to buy a home computer, you have quite a few monitor options to choose from. Basically, you can pick from two categories of desktop monitors: CRTs and flat-panel displays. Of course, you will get an LCD monitor if you buy a laptop system, but do not forget that most laptops have a port for connecting a desktop monitor. Both types of desktop monitor offer advantages and disadvantages.

In Some Ways, They Are All the Same

Flat-panel technology has made some big leaps in the last few years. Whereas flat-panel monitors used to be small, low-resolution devices found mostly on portable systems, they now rival CRT monitors feature for feature. When it comes to resolution, colors, refresh rate, and viewable area, flat-panel and CRT monitors compete head to head. Whatever monitor you buy, make sure it meets your requirements in each of these areas.

But in Other Ways, They Are Not

While all monitors may be created equal (or fairly equal) in terms of the resolutions and colors they can display, there are significant differences you need to consider:

◆ **Desktop Space Requirements.** Obviously, this is the criterion where CRT monitors cannot match flat-panels. A typical CRT monitor with a 15.8-inch viewable area stands about 19 inches high (including the base) and is about 16 inches wide and about 19 inches deep. A typical flat-panel monitor with a 15-inch viewable area stands about 18 inches high (including the base) and is about 16 inches wide, but it is only about 10 inches deep—4 inches without the base. Many flat-panel monitors can be hung on a wall or mounted on a swing-arm stand, further reducing their desktop space requirements.

◆ **Viewable Area.** CRT monitors offer viewable areas ranging from just over 13 inches to more than 22 inches. Flat-panels for the desktop range from about 14 inches to more than 18 inches, but larger viewing areas are being developed all the time.

◆ **Viewing Angle.** CRT monitors are usually handsdown winners in this category, but flat-panel systems are catching up. If you do not usually need to

Flat-panel

Flat-panel monitors are becoming increasingly popular, but their cost is too high for many users.

CRT

look at the monitor from an angle and if you do not typically have several people looking at the monitor at one time, the flat-panel's restricted viewing angle should not be a problem.

◆ **Screen Curvature.** CRT screens are flatter than they once were, and some higher-end models are almost completely flat. With most moderately priced CRTs, however, some curvature of the screen is normal and can easily be seen. If you use a computer for long periods, this curvature can cause minor distortions in the picture that lead to eyestrain. Because LCD monitors are flat, they do not pose this problem.

◆ **Power Consumption.** Flat-panel systems win in this category. CRT monitors consume a great deal of electricity to keep the screen refreshed. Conversely, LCD systems are energy efficient because of their tiny transistors. As an added benefit, flat-panel displays run cooler than CRTs.

◆ **Radiation Emissions.** CRT monitors emit low-level radiation. This radiation is not thought to be harmful, but it is there just the same. LCD monitors do not emit radiation.

◆ **Cost.** This category is usually the tie-breaker for shoppers who cannot decide between a flat-panel and CRT monitor. Despite their many advantages, flat-panel displays are much more expensive than CRT monitors. In fact, if you compare a flat-panel and CRT monitor with similar viewing areas, resolutions, and other features, the flat-panel system can cost three or four times as much as the CRT display.

The Video Controller

The quality of the images that a monitor can display is defined as much by the **video controller** as by the monitor itself. As shown in Figure 5.11, the video controller is an intermediary device between the CPU and the monitor. It contains the video-dedicated memory and other circuitry necessary to send information to the monitor for display on the screen. It consists of a circuit board, usually referred to simply as a card (the terms *video card* and *video controller* have the same meaning), which is attached to the computer's motherboard. Within the monitor's constraints, the controller's processing power determines the refresh rate, resolution, and number of colors that can be displayed.

Figure 5.11
The video controller connects the CPU, via the data bus on the motherboard, to the monitor.

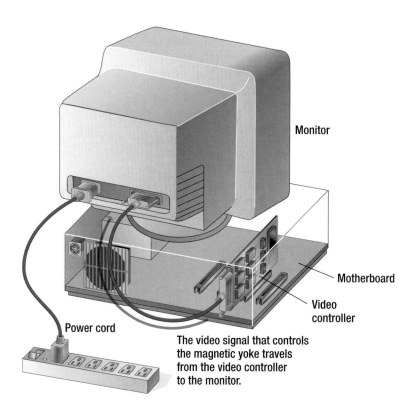

Monitor

Motherboard

Video controller

Power cord

The video signal that controls the magnetic yoke travels from the video controller to the monitor.

During the 1980s, when most PCs were running DOS and not Windows, the screen displayed text characters. Doing so took little processing power because there were only 256 possible characters and 2000 text positions on the screen. Rendering each screen required only 4000 bytes of data. With the advent of the Macintosh computer and the Windows operating environment, computers were required to display colors and graphics at high resolutions. This requires the CPU to send information to the video controller about every pixel on the screen. At the minimum resolution of 640 × 480, there are 307,200 pixels to control. Most users run their monitors at 256 colors, so each pixel requires one byte of information. Thus, the computer must send 307,200 bytes to the monitor for each screen. And remember that the screen changes constantly as you work.

If the user wants more colors or a higher resolution, the amount of data can be much higher. For example, for the maximum amount of color (24 bits, or 3 bytes, per pixel will render millions of colors) at 1024 × 768, the computer must send 2,359,296 bytes to the monitor for each screen.

The result of these processing demands is that video controllers have increased dramatically in power and importance. There is a microprocessor on the video controller, which frees the CPU from the burden of making the millions of calculations required for displaying graphics. The speed of this chip determines the speed at which the monitor can be refreshed.

Most video controllers today also include at least 4 MB of **video RAM, or VRAM** (in addition to the RAM that is connected to the CPU). VRAM is dual-ported, meaning that it can send a screen full of data to the monitor and at the same time receive the next screen full of data from the CPU. It is faster and more expensive than DRAM (dynamic RAM), the type of memory chip used as RAM for the CPU. Users with large monitors or with heavy graphics needs will usually require more than 4 MB of video RAM. Special video controllers—designed for use with large monitors or for fast, full-motion video—may have as much 32 MB of onboard RAM and support resolutions up to 1900 × 1200.

PC PROJECTORS

Portable computers are rapidly replacing old-fashioned slide projectors and overhead projectors as the source of presentations. Instead of creating, printing, and sorting through dozens of 35-millimeter photographic slides, more and more people are using software to create colorful slide shows and animated presentations. These images can be presented directly from the computer and displayed on the PC's screen or projected on a wall or large screen.

To get these presentations onto the "big screen," **PC projectors** are becoming increasingly common. A PC projector plugs into one of the computer's ports, then projects the video output onto an external surface (see Figure 5.12). These small devices typically weigh less than 10 pounds and can display over 16 million colors at resolutions up to 1024 × 768. Some PC projectors can be converted from still-video (slide) mode to full-video (animation) mode, to display output from a VCR or DVD drive.

Most PC projectors use LCD technology to create images. Like most types of light projectors, LCD projectors require the room to be darkened. They display blurry images in less-than-optimal lighting conditions.

Newer models use **digital light processing (DLP)** technology to project brighter, crisper images. DLP devices use a special microchip, called a digital micromirror device, which actually uses mirrors to control the image display. Unlike LCD-based projectors, DLP units can display clear images in normal lighting conditions.

Visit **www.glencoe.com/norton/online/** for more information on **PC projectors**.

Figure 5.12
PC projectors are rapidly gaining in popularity. The vast majority of projectors sold today are PC projectors rather than traditional slide projectors.

Figure 5.13

Speakers are common features on today's multimedia PCs. Top-of-the-line PC audio systems include premium sound cards and premium speakers with tweeters, midrange speakers, and subwoofers for sound quality that rivals home stereo systems.

SOUND SYSTEMS

Microphones are now important input devices, and speakers and their associated technology are key output systems (see Figure 5.13). Today, when you buy a **multimedia PC,** you receive a machine that includes a CD-ROM (or DVD) drive, a high-quality video controller with plenty of video RAM, speakers, and a sound card.

The speakers attached to these systems are similar to those you connect to a stereo. The only difference is that they are usually smaller, and they contain their own small amplifiers. Otherwise, they do the same thing any speaker does: they transfer a constantly changing electric current to a magnet, which pushes the speaker cone back and forth. The moving speaker cone creates pressure vibrations in the air—in other words, sound (see Figure 5.14).

The more complicated part of the sound output system is in the sound card. The **sound card** translates digital sounds into the electric current that is sent to the speakers. Sound is defined as air pressure varying over time. To digitize sound, the waves are converted to an electric current measured thousands of times per second and recorded as a number. When the sound is played back, the sound card reverses this process, translating the series of numbers into electric current that is sent to the speakers. The magnet moves back and forth with the changing current, creating vibrations.

With the right software, you can do much more than simply record and play back digitized sound. Sound editing programs provide a miniature sound studio, allowing you to view the sound wave and edit it. In the editing, you can cut bits of sound, copy them, and amplify the parts you want to hear more loudly; cut out static; and create many exotic audio effects.

Figure 5.14

How a speaker creates sound.

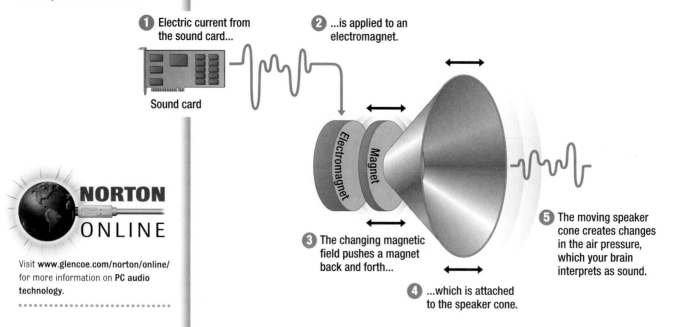

1. Electric current from the sound card...

Sound card

2. ...is applied to an electromagnet.

3. The changing magnetic field pushes a magnet back and forth...

4. ...which is attached to the speaker cone.

5. The moving speaker cone creates changes in the air pressure, which your brain interprets as sound.

Techview

THE PC AS AN ENTERTAINMENT CENTER

Except for the occasional beep, computers were once silent machines. And they were not much to look at, with their black-and-white screens displaying nothing but rows of text. But the increasing demand for multimedia has made color, graphics, animation, full-motion video, and stereo sound important capabilities for nearly every new computer and many software applications.

With the introduction of sound cards in the late 1980s, computers could play recorded sounds and music (from an application or a compact disk) and even synthesize sounds. Thanks to recent innovations in computer audio, sound has become an integral part of everyday computing, and computers have become an integral part of the audio industry.

The same is true with graphics and video. The PCs of a decade ago could barely display menus, let alone graphics with millions of colors, animation, and video. As video technologies have improved, however, users expect their computers to function like a television. The advent of graphically rich programs, multimedia events, the Internet, and—most recently—DVD has made the PC a video-on-demand resource. For a growing number of users, the PC is part of the home entertainment system or is replacing some home entertainment components entirely. Here are just a few examples of entertainment options that you can access with a typical multimedia PC:

◆ **Music on CD.** If your PC includes a CD-ROM drive, a sound card, and speakers, you can play music from any audio compact disk. Most multimedia PCs include simple audio-playback software that lets you start, stop, pause, and random-play songs from a CD. Many audio-playback programs let you create favorites lists and log your CDs to identify artists and tracks.

◆ **Movies on DVD.** Many newer model multimedia PCs include DVD drives rather than CD-ROM drives. DVD drives can play audio compact disks just like CD-ROM drives but can also play digital video disks. You can watch full-length movies with stereophonic sound at your PC.

◆ **Watch Television.** If your PC has a television tuner card (a special video card that can accept a broadcast signal through television antennae or cable), you can use your PC as a television. Special services like WebTV enable users to access program listings, set reminders to tune in, and more.

Using software such as RealPlayer, you can listen to streaming audio and view streaming video on your PC. Of course, performance is best if you have a broadband Internet connection, such as a cable modem.

◆ **Listen to Radio.** Around the world, hundreds of radio stations are now Webcasting their programs over the Internet. Multimedia players, such as Windows Media Player, RealPlayer G2, and others, enable you to tune into traditional broadcast stations and dozens of net radio outlets, which distribute their audio exclusively over the World Wide Web. Most of these stations broadcast live, in real time, on the Internet. Some also provide prerecorded programming. Formats include music of all kinds, news and sports, talk, call-in, and more.

◆ **Watch Streaming Video and Audio.** With an Internet connection and a player like RealPlayer G2, you can tune into The Weather Channel, CNN, and other cable television channels without connecting cable TV or an antenna to your PC. These services use streaming audio and video technology to transmit programming to your PC so it plays smoothly. For best results, you need a fast PC and a broadband Internet connection, such as a cable modem or an ISDN line.

◆ **Enjoy Recorded Music Over the Internet.** Using technologies like RealPlayer, LiquidAudio, and others, you can listen to prerecorded music over your Internet connection. Using newer multimedia file-compression technologies like MP3 or a2b, you can download songs to your computer and listen to them any time. If you have a CD-ROM drive that records compact disks or a portable MP3 player (such as Diamond Multimedia's Rio player), you can take your recordings with you anywhere.

LESSON QUIZ

True/False

Answer the following questions by circling True or False.

True False **1.** A cathode ray tube monitor looks and works much like a television screen.

True False **2.** A CRT monitor uses a gun to shoot pixels at the front of the screen.

True False **3.** LCD monitors typically offer a wider viewing angle than do CRT monitors.

True False **4.** Flat-panel displays are used only with notebook computers.

True False **5.** Some PC projectors can display 16 million colors at resolutions up to 1024 × 768.

Multiple Choice

Circle the word or phrase that best completes each sentence.

1. _____ monitors are most commonly used with desktop computers.
   A. Flat-panel display   **B.** Cathode ray tube (CRT)   **C.** Neither A nor B

2. A(n) _____ LCD relies on transistors for each row and each column of pixels.
   A. active matrix   **B.** passive matrix   **C.** flat-panel

3. The _____ of a computer monitor is classified by the number of pixels on the screen, expressed as a matrix.
   A. resolution   **B.** viewing angle   **C.** dot pitch

4. A video controller contains a _____ , which frees the CPU from making the calculations required for the display of graphics.
   A. cable   **B.** video RAM   **C.** microprocessor

5. Sound can be defined as _____ .
   A. multimedia   **B.** electric current   **C.** air pressure varying over time

LESSON LABS

Complete the following exercises as directed by your instructor.

1. Examine your computer's video setup. First, look at the monitor attached to your computer. What brand is it? What model? What other information can you get from the monitor by examining its exterior? (Remember to look at the back.) Next, measure your monitor. What is the diagonal measurement of the monitor's case? What is the viewing area, measured diagonally? If you are connected to the Internet, go to the manufacturer's Web site and find your monitor. Write down the resolution and refresh rate.

2. If your PC has speakers attached to it, you can easily check or change the speaker volume. Move the mouse pointer to the Windows taskbar. Look for a speaker icon and click it. A small volume control will appear on the screen. You can use the mouse to drag the volume control up or down to change the volume setting, or select the Mute checkbox to silence the sound system entirely. Click anywhere outside the volume control to close it.

Devices That Output Hard Copy

OVERVIEW:
Making the Digital Tangible

For most computer users, whether at home or work, the printer is indispensable. While monitors and sound systems allow us to see and hear our work, printers give us something we can touch, carry, and share with others. Printed documents are essential in many working environments, where people must share reports, budgets, memos, and other types of information.

Over the past decade, the variety of available printing devices has exploded, even though three types of printers have become the most popular: dot matrix, ink jet, and laser. Within those three groups, consumers have hundreds of options, ranging widely in price and features. Several other types of special printing devices are available for users with special needs, such as large-format printouts or images with extremely accurate color and high resolution.

This lesson introduces you to the basics of hard-copy output devices. You will learn about the most common types of printers and see how each creates an image on paper. You will learn the criteria for evaluating different printers and examine some of the specialized printing devices designed for professional use.

OBJECTIVES

- List the three most commonly used types of printers.
- List the four criteria you should consider when evaluating printers.
- Describe how a dot matrix printer creates an image on a page.
- Explain the process by which a laser printer operates.
- List five types of high-quality printing devices commonly used in business.

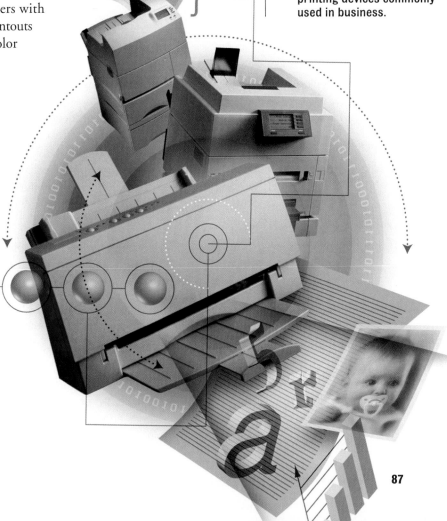

OVERVIEW OF PRINTERS

Besides the monitor, the other important output device is the printer. Generally, printers fall into two categories: impact and nonimpact. An **impact printer** creates an image by pressing an inked ribbon against the paper, using pins or hammers to shape the image. A simple example of an impact printer is a typewriter, which uses small hammers to strike the ribbon. Each hammer is embossed with the shape of an alphanumeric character; that shape is transferred through the inked ribbon onto the paper, resulting in a printed character.

Many modern electric typewriters can be connected to a PC and used as a letter-quality printer. As a printer, however, even a good typewriter is slow and limited in the kinds of images it can produce. The most common type of impact printer is the dot matrix printer. Other types of impact printers are line printers and band printers.

Nonimpact printers use other means to create an image. Ink jet printers, for example, use tiny nozzles to spray droplets of ink onto the page. Laser printers work like photocopiers, using heat to bond microscopic particles of dry toner to specific parts of the page (see Figure 6.1).

Figure 6.1
A dot matrix printer (left) is an example of an impact printer. A laser printer (right) is a nonimpact printer.

In the early years of computing, dot matrix printers were the most commonly used printing devices. They are not as prevalent now, although dot matrix printers are still popular in business and academic settings because they are relatively fast and inexpensive to operate, and they do a good job of printing text and simple graphics. Because ink jet printers now offer much higher quality for about the same price, they have become more popular than dot matrix printers in homes and small businesses. Laser printers are also popular in homes and businesses, even though they are more expensive to buy and operate than either ink jet or dot matrix devices.

When you are ready to buy a printer, one consideration is most important; that is, how do you plan to use the printer? Do you need to print only text, or are graphics capabilities also important? Do you need to print in color? Will you need to print a wide variety of fonts in many sizes? How quickly do you want your documents to be printed?

When evaluating printers, four additional criteria are important:

◆ **Image Quality.** Image quality, also known as print resolution, is usually measured in **dots per inch (dpi)**. The more dots per inch a printer can produce, the higher its image quality. For example, most medium-quality ink jet and laser printers can print 300 or 600 dots per inch, which is fine for most daily business applications. A 600 dpi printer actually provides four times the resolution of a 300 dpi printer. Professional-quality printers, used

NORTON
ONLINE

Visit **www.glencoe.com/norton/online/** for more information on **evaluating printers.**

for creating colorful presentations, posters, or renderings, offer resolutions of 1800 dpi or more.

◆ **Speed.** Printer speed is measured in the number of **pages per minute (ppm)** the device can print. Most printers have different ppm ratings for text and graphics because graphics generally take longer to print. As print speed goes up, so does cost. Most consumer-level laser printers offer print speeds of 6 or 8 ppm, but high-volume professional laser printers can exceed 20 ppm.

◆ **Initial Cost.** The cost of new printers has fallen dramatically in recent years, while their capabilities and speed have improved just as dramatically. It is possible to buy a good-quality ink jet printer for personal use for $100 or even less; low-end laser printers can be found for $250 or less. Professional-quality, high-output systems can range in price from $1000 to tens of thousands of dollars. Color printers always cost more than black-and-white printers.

◆ **Cost of Operation.** The cost of ink or toner and maintenance varies with the type of printer. Many different types of printer paper are available, too, and the choice can affect the cost of operation. Low-quality recycled paper, for example, is fine for printing draft-quality documents and costs less than a penny per sheet. Glossy, thick photo-quality stock, used for printing photographs, can cost several dollars per sheet depending on size.

DOT MATRIX PRINTERS

Dot matrix printers are commonly used in workplaces where physical impact with the paper is important, such as when the user is printing to carbon-copy/pressure-sensitive forms. These printers can produce sheets of plain text very quickly. They are also used to print very wide sheets, as data processing departments often use when generating large reports with wide columns of information.

A dot matrix printer creates an image by using a mechanism called a **print head,** which contains a cluster (or matrix) of short pins arranged in one or more columns. On receiving instructions from the PC, the printer can push any of the pins out, in any combination. By pushing out pins in various combinations, the print head can create alphanumeric characters (see Figures 6.2 and 6.3).

Figure 6.2
A dot matrix printer forms a character by creating a series of dots.

Figure 6.3
How a dot matrix printer creates an image.

When pushed out from the cluster, the protruding pins' ends strike a ribbon, which is held in place between the print head and the paper. When the pins strike the ribbon, they press ink from the ribbon onto a piece of paper. Where a single pin strikes the ribbon, a single dot of ink is printed on the page, hence the printer name, *dot matrix*. The more pins that a print head contains, the higher the printer's resolution. The lowest resolution dot matrix printers have only nine pins; the highest resolution printers have twenty-four pins.

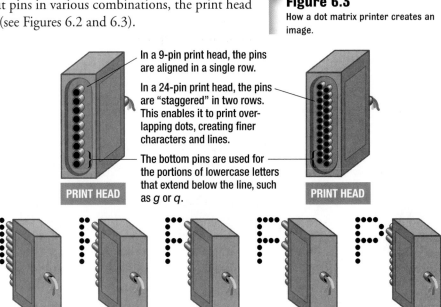

In a 9-pin print head, the pins are aligned in a single row.

In a 24-pin print head, the pins are "staggered" in two rows. This enables it to print overlapping dots, creating finer characters and lines.

The bottom pins are used for the portions of lowercase letters that extend below the line, such as *g* or *q*.

PRINT HEAD

PRINT HEAD

Direction of print head

Whereas other types of printers have their speed measured in pages per minute, dot matrix printers are measured in **characters per second (cps).** The slowest dot matrix printers create fifty to seventy characters per second; the fastest print more than 500 cps.

Like most types of impact printers, dot matrix printers can use **tractor-feed paper** (also called **continuous-feed paper**). Sheets of paper are joined, end to end, with perforations between sheets. A row of holes runs down both long edges of each page. The printer uses a tractor feeder mechanism to pull the paper through. Many impact printers can also be sheet fed; that is, they can accept single sheets of paper that lie stacked in a paper tray. Most nonimpact printers are sheet fed.

Although dot matrix printers are not commonly used in homes, they are still widely used in business, as are other types of impact printers:

◆ **Line Printers.** This special type of impact printer works like a dot matrix printer but uses a special wide print head that can print an entire line of text at one time (see Figure 6.4). Line printers do not offer high resolutions but are incredibly fast; the fastest can print 3000 lines of text per minute.

◆ **Band Printers.** A band printer features a rotating band that is embossed with alphanumeric characters. To print a character, the machine rotates the band to the desired character, then a small hammer taps the band, pressing the character against a ribbon. Although this sounds like a slow process, band printers are very fast and very robust. Depending on the character set used, a good-quality band printer can generate 2000 lines of text per minute.

◆ **Daisy Wheel Printers.** This type of printer is nearly obsolete but can still be found where older systems are used. These printers use a spinning wheel with characters embossed around its edge. A hammer strikes the wheel from behind, pressing a character against a ribbon. Daisy wheel printers can create clean text but cannot print graphics. They are also very slow in comparison to other printers.

Figure 6.4
Line printers are incredibly fast and can generate several pages of plain text in a minute.

INK JET PRINTERS

Ink jet printers create an image directly on the paper by spraying ink through tiny nozzles (see Figure 6.5). The popularity of ink jet printers jumped around 1990 when the speed and quality improved, and the price plummeted. Today, good ink jet printers are available for as little as $100. These models typically attain print resolutions of at least 360 dots per inch, comparable to that of most laser printers sold before 1992. These same models can print from two to four pages per minute (only slightly slower than the slowest laser printers).

Compared to laser printers, the operating cost of an ink jet printer is relatively low. Expensive maintenance is rare, and the only part that needs routine replacement is the ink cartridge, which ranges in price from $20 to $35. Many ink jet printers use one cartridge for color printing and a separate

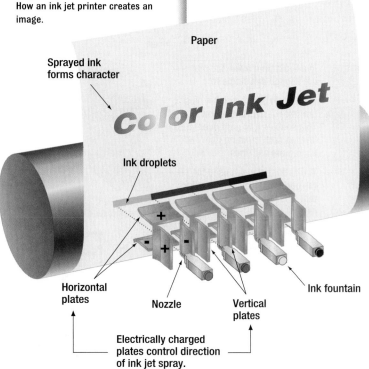

Figure 6.5
How an ink jet printer creates an image.

Paper

Sprayed ink forms character

Ink droplets

Horizontal plates

Nozzle

Vertical plates

Ink fountain

Electrically charged plates control direction of ink jet spray.

black-only cartridge for black-and-white printing. This feature saves money by reserving colored ink only for color printing.

Another improvement in ink jet printers has been in the paper they require. For many years, they needed a special paper, and each sheet had to dry before you could touch it. Today, you can run normal photocopy paper through most ink jet printers (although glossy paper looks slightly better), and the ink is dry within a few seconds.

Finally, ink jet printers offer a cost-effective way to print in color. Color ink jet printers have four ink nozzles: cyan (blue), magenta (red), yellow, and black. These four colors are used in almost all color printing because it is possible to combine them to create any color in the visible spectrum. Notice that the colors are different from the primary additive colors (red, green, and blue) used in monitors. Printed color is the result of light bouncing off the paper, not color transmitted directly from a light source. Consequently, cyan, magenta, yellow, and black are sometimes called subtractive colors and color printing is sometimes called four-color printing.

Ink jet printers are now being combined with other technologies to create complete, all-in-one office machines (see Figure 6.6). Manufacturers such as Hewlett-Packard, Canon, and others are now offering combination printers, copiers, fax machines, and scanners based on ink jet technology. A basic all-in-one unit with black-and-white printing can be purchased for less than $800. High-resolution color systems are considerably more expensive.

LASER PRINTERS

Laser printers are more expensive than ink jet printers, their print quality is higher, and most are faster. As their name implies, a laser is at the heart of these printers. A separate CPU and memory are built into the printer to interpret the data that it receives from the computer and to control the laser. The result is a complicated piece of equipment that uses technology similar to that in photocopiers. Figure 6.7 shows how a laser printer works. The quality and speed of laser printers make

Figure 6.6
Ink jet technology is the basis for many new "all-in-one" office systems.

NORTON
ONLINE

Visit **www.glencoe.com/norton/online/** for more information on **ink jet printers** and **laser printers**.

Figure 6.7
How a laser printer creates a printed page.

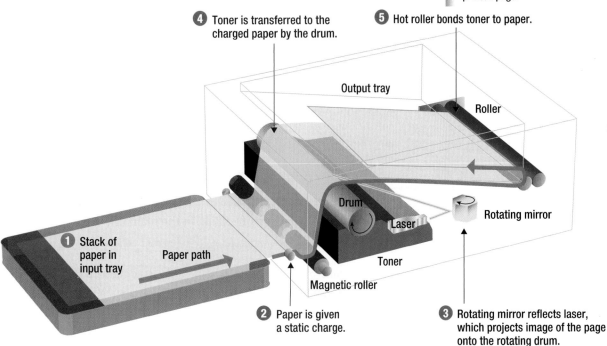

4 Toner is transferred to the charged paper by the drum.

5 Hot roller bonds toner to paper.

Output tray

Roller

Drum

Laser

Rotating mirror

1 Stack of paper in input tray

Paper path

Toner

Magnetic roller

2 Paper is given a static charge.

3 Rotating mirror reflects laser, which projects image of the page onto the rotating drum.

them ideal for office environments, where several users can easily share the same printer via a LAN.

Just as the electron gun in a monitor can target any pixel, the laser in a laser printer can aim at any point on a drum, creating an electrical charge. **Toner,** which is composed of tiny particles of oppositely charged ink, sticks to the drum in the places the laser has charged. Then, with pressure and heat, the toner is transferred off the drum onto the paper. Also like a monitor and its video controller, the amount of special memory that laser printers contain determines the speed at which documents are printed. A color laser printer (see Figure 6.8) works like a single-color model, except that the process is repeated four times and a different toner color is used for each pass. The four colors used are the same as in the color ink jet printers: cyan, magenta, yellow, and black.

Single-color (black) laser printers typically can produce between four and sixteen pages of text a minute. If you are printing graphics, the output can be a great deal slower. The most common laser printers have resolutions of 300 or 600 dpi, both horizontally and vertically, but some high-end models have resolutions of 1200 or 1800 dpi. The printing industry stipulates a resolution of at least 1200 dpi for top-quality professional printing. It is difficult to detect the difference between text printed at 600 dpi and at 1200 dpi; the higher resolution is most noticeable in graphics reproduction such as photographs and artwork.

Convenience is another advantage of laser printers. Most can use standard, inexpensive copy paper that is loaded into a paper tray. The disadvantages of laser printers are the price and the cost of operation. Laser printers start at about $300, and the price increases dramatically if you want speed, high resolution, or color. In addition, laser printers require new toner cartridges after a few thousand pages, and toner cartridges cost from $40 to $80 for black toner. Toner cartridges are typically rated on double-spaced text pages rather than graphics, which can greatly reduce the life of the cartridge.

On the other hand, the cost of laser printers has come way down. In 1990, a 300 dpi laser printer that printed four pages per minute cost about $1000. Today, you can get 600 dpi and about the same speed for less than $500. At the same time, color laser printers have also become more affordable, although most still cost more than $1000.

Figure 6.8
Laser printers produce high-resolution output quickly and quietly; however, they tend to cost more than ink jet printers. Color laser printers can cost several thousand dollars.

Self Check

Answer the following questions by filling in the blank(s).

1. Image quality is also known as _____ when discussing printers.

2. In a dot matrix printer, a(n) _____ contains a cluster (or matrix) of pins.

3. _____ printers are nearly obsolete.

Norton Notebook

A PAPERLESS SOCIETY?

In the mid-1980s, as businesses and schools began connecting their computers in greater numbers, people began to see the advantages of sharing information over networks. By accessing data on a centralized server or sharing files by electronic mail, users found they could greatly reduce their reliance on printed documents.

Experts envisioned a paperless society: a world where documents are created, distributed, and read on computer systems. They imagined a world where people gathered all their information online and shared written communications across networks. At least, experts thought, we can achieve a paperless office: work environments where printed documents were no longer used.

The Problems of Too Much Printing

In 1985, when the notion of the paperless office entered public debate, Xerox Corporation estimated that American businesses produced nearly 1.5 trillion paper documents. Even though it only cost a few cents per page to create printed documents, the accumulated cost of billions of pages was astronomical.

According to the American Forest and Paper Association, shipments of office paper increased 33 percent between 1986 and 1997. Businesses now use nearly 6.5 million tons of paper every year. Americans use about 200 pounds of paper per person, every year, according to a May 1999 report in *USA Today*.

Despite the promise of improved computer systems and networking technologies, the paperless society has yet to materialize, and most experts now believe it never will. Here is why:

◆ **Printers and Paper Are Cheap and Plentiful.** Ink jet printers cost as little as $100. Many new computer systems include a printer, making it an irresistible option. A box of printer paper can be purchased for about $20.

◆ **People Simply Prefer Paper Documents.** Although portable computers are increasingly affordable, they do not necessarily

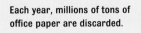
Each year, millions of tons of office paper are discarded.

make reading and writing easier. Most people find paper documents more comfortable to use, lighter, and easier on the eyes.

◆ **Not Everyone Has a Computer.** About 50 percent of Americans still do not have computers in their homes. Many have no intention of ever buying one. For these people, the demand for printed documents will not decrease.

◆ **Paper Provides Security.** Even in businesses where documents are generated and distributed electronically, many people still print them out and file them. This practice is rooted in an ongoing distrust of computers. A paper copy makes the distrustful computer user feel more secure.

Despite the reasons for printing documents, computer users should consider the negative effects of producing so many hard copies. First, deforestation is a global problem because we cut down trees to make paper. Second, if printed documents are not archived, they are discarded, adding to the world's solid waste problems. Third, printing requires a lot of energy—from producing the paper to running it through a printer.

What Can You Do?

Computer users should be responsible about using paper and energy. This practice requires thought and discipline but can actually make your work life easier and less expensive, saving you time, storage space, and money. Here are three simple steps you can take:

1. **Think Before You Print.** Do you really need a hard copy? Are people asking for a hard copy when an e-mail attachment would work just as well? If you plan to stick the printout in a file cabinet, add it to a stack of papers, or throw it out, you may not need to print it.

2. **Archive on Disk.** If you are concerned that your electronic documents will be lost or altered, back them up and store them on removable media such as a floppy disk. Kept in a safe place, the electronic copy will not change and will always be accessible.

3. **Encourage Others to Print Wisely.** When someone brings you a printed document, ask him or her to send it by e-mail or to give it to you on disk next time. These practices can actually be faster than waiting for a printout.

SNAPSHOT PRINTERS

With digital cameras and scanners becoming increasingly popular, users want to be able to print the images they create or scan. While the average color ink jet or laser printer can handle this job satisfactorily, many people are investing in special **snapshot printers** (see Figure 6.9). These small-format printers use special glossy paper to create medium-resolution prints of 150 to 200 dpi. The best snapshot printers can create images that look nearly as good as a photograph printed using traditional methods.

Snapshot printers work slowly (a printout can take between two and four minutes, on average) and generally create prints no larger than a standard 4-by-6-inch snapshot. Also, because they spray so much ink on the paper, it can take several

minutes for a printout to dry, so smearing can be a problem. Still, they give digital photography enthusiasts a way to print and display their photos in hard-copy form. Snapshot printers can be found for $400 to $500, and the cost per print ranges from fifty cents to a dollar (several times more expensive than traditional film processing).

Figure 6.9
Snapshot printers are popular for printing digital photographs.

OTHER HIGH-QUALITY PRINTERS

Although most offices and homes use ink jet or laser printers, other types of printers are used for special purposes. These printers are often used by publishers and small print shops to create high-quality output, especially color output. The last type discussed in this section, the plotter, is designed specifically for printing large-format construction and engineering documents.

Thermal-Wax Printers

Thermal-wax printers are used primarily for presentation graphics and handouts. They create bold colors and have a low per-page cost for pages with heavy color requirements. The process provides vivid colors because the inks do not bleed into each other or soak the specially coated paper. Thermal-wax printers operate with a ribbon coated with panels of colored wax that melts and adheres to plain paper as colored dots when passed over a focused heat source.

Dye-Sub Printers

Desktop publishers and graphic artists get realistic quality and color for photo images using **dye-sub** (for **dye-sublimation**) **printers.** In dye-sublimation technology, a ribbon containing panels of color is moved across a focused heat source capable of subtle temperature variations. The heated dyes evaporate from the ribbon and diffuse on specially coated paper, where they form areas of different colors. The variations in color are related to the intensity of the heat applied. (Many snapshot printers use dye-sublimation technology.) Dye-sub printers create extremely sharp images, but they are slow and costly. The special paper they require can make the per-page cost as high as $3 to $4.

Fiery Printers

One high-quality form of printing takes advantage of digital color copiers. The **fiery print server** is a special-purpose computer that transmits documents to a digital color copier, where they are printed. Fiery printers are used in print shops as an alternative to press printing.

IRIS Printers

IRIS printers are used by print shops to produce high-resolution presentation graphics and color proofs that resemble full-color offset printed images. The IRIS is a high-tech form of ink jet printing in which individual sheets of paper are mounted onto a drum. The nozzles on the ink jet printing head pass from one end of the spinning drum to the other, spraying minute drops of colored ink to form the image. This type of printer can produce an image with a resolution of 1800 dpi.

Plotters

A **plotter** is a special kind of output device. It is like a printer because it produces images on paper, but the plotter is typically used to print large-format images, such as construction or engineering drawings created in a CAD system.

Early plotters were bulky, mechanical devices that used robotic arms, which literally drew the image on a piece of paper. Table plotters (or flatbed plotters) use two robotic arms, each of which holds a set of colored ink pens, felt pens, or pencils. The two arms work in concert, operating at right angles as they draw on a stationary piece of paper. In addition to being complex and large (some are almost as big as a billiard table), table plotters are notoriously slow; a large, complicated drawing can take several hours to print.

A variation on the table plotter is the roller plotter (also known as the drum plotter) which uses only one drawing arm but moves the paper instead of holding it flat and stationary (see Figure 6.10). The drawing arm moves side to side as the paper is rolled back and forth through the roller. Working together, the arm and roller can draw perfect circles and other geometric shapes, as well as lines of different weights and colors.

In recent years, mechanical plotters have been displaced by thermal, electrostatic, and ink jet plotters, as well as large-format dye-sub printers. These systems, which also produce large-size drawings, are faster and cheaper to use than their mechanical counterparts. They can also produce full-color renderings as well as geometric line drawings, making them more useful than standard mechanical plotters (see Figure 6.11).

Figure 6.10
A roller plotter uses a robotic arm to draw with colored pens on oversized paper. Here, an architectural elevation is being printed.

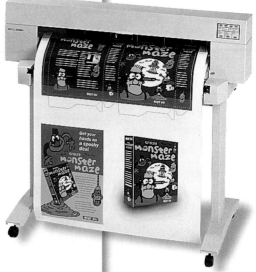

Figure 6.11
Like desktop ink jet printers, an ink jet plotter uses a spray system to create either simple line drawings or detailed artistic renderings.

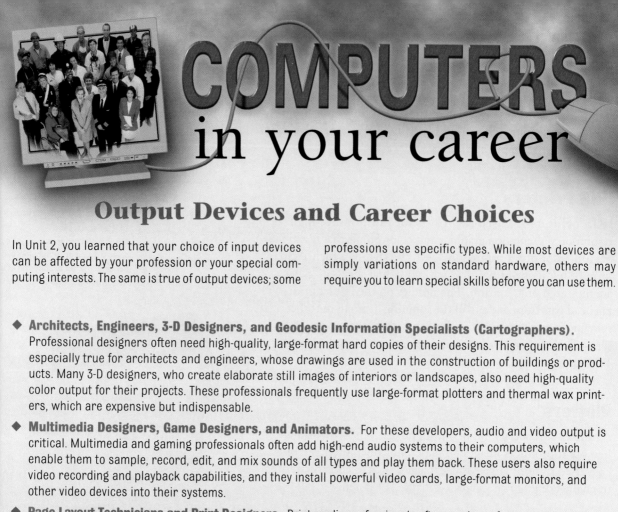

COMPUTERS
in your career

Output Devices and Career Choices

In Unit 2, you learned that your choice of input devices can be affected by your profession or your special computing interests. The same is true of output devices; some professions use specific types. While most devices are simply variations on standard hardware, others may require you to learn special skills before you can use them.

◆ **Architects, Engineers, 3-D Designers, and Geodesic Information Specialists (Cartographers).** Professional designers often need high-quality, large-format hard copies of their designs. This requirement is especially true for architects and engineers, whose drawings are used in the construction of buildings or products. Many 3-D designers, who create elaborate still images of interiors or landscapes, also need high-quality color output for their projects. These professionals frequently use large-format plotters and thermal wax printers, which are expensive but indispensable.

◆ **Multimedia Designers, Game Designers, and Animators.** For these developers, audio and video output is critical. Multimedia and gaming professionals often add high-end audio systems to their computers, which enable them to sample, record, edit, and mix sounds of all types and play them back. These users also require video recording and playback capabilities, and they install powerful video cards, large-format monitors, and other video devices into their systems.

◆ **Page Layout Technicians and Print Designers.** Print media professionals often use large-format paper-white or page-white monitors in their systems. These monitors typically are vertically oriented rather than horizontally oriented, thus displaying a full printed page on the screen. With their high-contrast displays and vivid white backgrounds, these monitors enable the designer to view fine details of the page's appearance and to make more accurate choices about fonts, borders, placement of graphics, and more.

◆ **Sales and Marketing Professionals, Instructors, and Seminar Leaders.** The presentation is the center of the workday for many people. Sales representatives and instructors, for example, frequently present slide shows to provide information for customers, students, or coworkers. A good PC projection system enables these professionals to create and modify presentations on disk and to show them without printing hard copies of slides.

LESSON QUIZ

True/False

Answer the following questions by circling True or False.

True   False   **1.** The two categories of printers are impact and nonimpact.

True   False   **2.** Printer speed is measured in dots per inch (dpi).

True   False   **3.** A dot matrix printer works by pushing pins against an inked ribbon, thus creating a series of dots on the paper.

True   False   **4.** All ink jet printers require special glossy paper.

True   False   **5.** Dye-sublimation is another term for laser printing.

Multiple Choice

Circle the word or phrase that best completes each sentence.

1. The speed of dot matrix printers is measured in _____ .
  A. dots per inch (dpi)   **B.** characters per second (cps)   **C.** pages per minute (ppm)

2. A laser printer creates an image by placing _____ at specific points on the page.
  A. toner   **B.** electric charges   **C.** neither A nor B

3. Special _____ printers are gaining popularity for printing photographic quality images.
  A. ink jet   **B.** snapshot   **C.** fiery

4. A(n) _____ printer is a high-tech version of an ink jet printer, capable of printing at resolutions of 1800 dpi.
  A. dot matrix   **B.** fiery   **C.** IRIS

5. _____ are ideal for creating large-format drawings, like those required by architects and engineers.
  A. Dot matrix printers   **B.** Plotters   **C.** Snapshot printers

LESSON LABS

Complete the following exercises as directed by your instructor.

1. Find out what type of printer is connected to your computer. Click the Start button; then click Settings, Printers. If a printer is connected to your system, it will appear in the Printers window. Right-click the printer's icon to open a shortcut menu. Then choose Properties to open the Properties dialog box for the printer. Write down the data in the dialog box. Do not make any changes in the dialog box, but leave it open for the next exercise.

2. With your printer's Properties dialog box open, click the General tab. Near the bottom of the tab, click the button labeled Print Test Page. A new dialog box appears, asking you to confirm that your printer produced a test page. If your printer produces a test page, click Yes. If not, click No and ask your instructor for assistance. When you are finished, Click Cancel to close the dialog box.

LESSON 5: Monitors and Sound Systems

Monitors

- Computer monitors are roughly divided into two categories: CRT and flat-panel displays.

- Monitors can also be categorized by the number of colors they display. Monitors are usually monochrome, grayscale, or color.

- A CRT monitor works with one or more electron guns that systematically aim a beam of electrons at every pixel on the screen.

- Most LCD displays are either active matrix or passive matrix.

- When purchasing a monitor, you should consider its size, resolution, refresh rate, and dot pitch.

- The video controller is an interface between the monitor and the CPU. The video controller determines many aspects of a monitor's performance; for example, the video controller lets you select a resolution or set the number of colors to display.

- The video controller contains its own on-board processor and memory, called video RAM.

PC Projectors

- A PC projector is a portable light projector that connects to a PC. This type of projector is rapidly replacing traditional slide projectors and overhead projectors as a means for displaying presentations.

- Many PC projectors provide the same resolutions and color levels as high-quality monitors, but they project the image on a large screen.

- The newest PC projectors use digital light processing to project bright, crisp images. A DLP projector uses a special microchip that contains tiny mirrors to produce images.

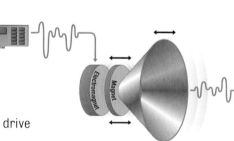

Sound Systems

- Multimedia PCs generally come with sound systems, which include a sound card, speakers, a CD-ROM or DVD drive, and a video controller.

- The sound card translates digital signals into analog signals that drive the speakers.

LESSON 6: Devices That Output Hard Copy

Overview of Printers

- Printers fall into two general categories: impact and nonimpact.

- Impact printers create an image on paper by using a device to strike an inked ribbon, pressing ink from the ribbon onto the paper. Nonimpact printers use various methods to place ink (or another colored substance) on the page.

- When evaluating printers for purchase, you should consider four criteria: image quality, speed, initial cost, and cost of operation.

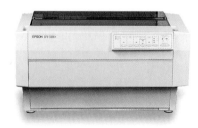

Dot Matrix Printers *like typewriter*

■ A dot matrix printer is a common type of impact printer.

■ A dot matrix printer uses a print head, which contains a cluster of pins. The printer can push the pins out to form patterns, in rapid sequence. The pins are used to press an inked ribbon against paper, thus creating an image.

■ The lowest resolution dot matrix printers have an array of nine pins; the highest resolution dot matrix printers have twenty-four pins.

■ The speed of dot matrix printers is measured in characters per second. The fastest ones can print 500 characters each second.

Ink Jet Printers *Sprays ink cheap*

■ An ink jet printer is an example of a nonimpact printer. It creates an image by spraying tiny droplets of ink onto the paper.

■ Ink jet printers are inexpensive for both color and black printing, have low operating costs, and offer quality and speed comparable to low-end laser printers.

Laser Printers *high quality fast*

■ Laser printers produce higher-quality print and are fast and convenient to use, but they are also more expensive than ink jet printers.

■ Laser printers are nonimpact printers. They use heat and pressure to bond tiny particles of toner (a dry ink) to paper.

■ Laser printers are available in both color and black and white, and the highest end laser printers provide resolutions of 1200 dpi and greater.

Snapshot Printers *for digital photos*

■ Snapshot printers are specialized, small-format printers used to print small color photographs.

■ Snapshot printers are popular among users who own digital cameras.

■ Snapshot printers are fairly slow, and they can be more expensive to operate than standard ink jet or laser printers.

Other High-Quality Printers

■ Thermal-wax, dye-sublimation, fiery, and IRIS printers are used primarily by print shops and publishers to create high-quality color images. *print shops*

■ Plotters create large-format images, usually for architectural or engineering purposes, using mechanical drawing arms, ink jet technology, or thermal printing technology. *architects, engineers*

UNIT REVIEW

KEY TERMS

After completing this unit, you should be able to define the following terms.

active matrix LCD, *77*
cathode ray tube (CRT), *74*
characters per second (cps), *90*
color monitor, *75*
continuous-feed paper, *90*
digital light processing (DLP), *83*
dot matrix printer, *89*
dot pitch, *80*
dots per inch (dpi), *88*
dual-scan LCD, *77*
dye-sublimation (dye-sub) printer, *94*
fiery print server, *95*
flat-panel display, *74*
grayscale monitor, *75*
impact printer, *88*
ink jet printer, *90*
IRIS printer, *95*
laser printer, *91*
liquid crystal display (LCD), *76*
monochrome monitor, *75*
multimedia PC, *84*

nonimpact printer, *88*
pages per minute (ppm), *89*
passive matrix LCD, *77*
PC projector, *83*
pixel, *75*
plotter, *95*
print head, *89*
refresh rate, *80*
resolution, *79*
shadow mask, *76*
snapshot printer, *94*
sound card, *84*
Super VGA (SVGA), *79*
thermal-wax printer, *94*
thin-film transistor (TFT), *77*
toner, *92*
tractor-feed paper, *90*
video controller, *82*
Video Graphics Array (VGA), *79*
video RAM (VRAM), *83*
viewing angle, *76*

KEY TERMS QUIZ

Fill in each blank with one of the terms listed under Key Terms.

1. A(n) _____ displays only one color, usually against a black background.

2. The term _____ is a contraction of the term *picture element.*

3. All CRT monitors use _____ with holes in them to align the beams from the electron gun.

4. A(n) _____ matrix LCD monitor assigns one transistor to each row and each column of pixels.

5. A monitor's _____ is classified by the numbers of pixels on the screen, expressed as a matrix.

6. A(n) _____ translates digital sounds into the electric current that is sent to the speakers.

7. _____ is composed of charged particles of ink that bond to the paper in a laser printer.

8. A(n) _____ printer is designed to print digital photographs.

9. A(n) _____ printer uses heat to diffuse special dyes from a ribbon onto the paper.

10. _____ are used to create large-format images such as construction drawings.

REVIEW QUESTIONS

In your own words, briefly answer the following questions.

1. There are two basic types of monitor used with PCs. List them.
2. How does a color CRT monitor produce images on the screen?
3. What is the most common type of flat-panel monitor?
4. How does a dual-scan LCD monitor produce a clearer image than an ordinary passive matrix monitor?
5. You should consider four specifications when comparing monitors. List them.
6. How can digital light processing (DLP) projectors project better images than standard LCD projectors?
7. You should consider four specifications when evaluating printers. List them.
8. What units of measure are used to express the speed of a dot matrix printer and a laser printer?
9. Color ink jet printers use four colors of ink. List them.
10. Why are plotters special output devices?

DISCUSSION QUESTIONS

As directed by your instructor, discuss the following questions in class or in groups.

1. When you think about the two most frequently used output devices for computers—monitors and printers—why will color technology for printers become more commonplace, more affordable, and more necessary to many users?
2. Many computer users now think that a computer system is not complete unless it is equipped with a printer, a microphone, and speakers. Do you think this is true? Would you be happy (or able) to do your work at a PC that lacked these pieces of hardware? Why?

 **ETHICAL ISSUES** We may think we cannot use a computer unless it has a full array of output devices, but is this true? With this thought in mind, discuss the following questions in class.

1. Many people overuse their PC's printer, and the number of unnecessary printouts is growing every year. This practice wastes paper, electricity, storage space, and natural resources. It also contributes to pollution and landfill use. If you could do one thing to reduce the practice of unnecessary printing, what would it be? Would you restrict printer use in offices? Would you ration paper? Would you take printers away from certain types of workers? In your view, are such radical actions necessary? If you do not agree, what types of actions would you support?

2. Because PCs provide an ever-increasing variety of multimedia options, people are spending more and more time at their computers. Much of this time is spent playing games, downloading music from the Internet, Web surfing, and so on. In fact, recent studies indicate that nearly 14 percent of computer users are addicted to the Internet or to game playing. Do these facts bother you? Why? Do you worry that you spend too much time at your computer? What would you do to help a friend or coworker if you thought he or she was devoting too much time to the computer?

UNIT LABS

You and the Computer

Complete the following exercises using a computer in your classroom, lab, or home. No other materials are needed.

1. **Change Your Color Settings.** By experimenting with your PC's color settings, you can determine the settings that work best for you. For example, if you do not plan to browse the World Wide Web or use multimedia products, you probably do not need to use the system's highest color settings; if you do, you need to make sure your monitor's settings are up to the task or you will not get the most from your computing experiences. Before you take the following steps, close any running programs and make sure there is no disk in your system's floppy disk drive.

   A. Click the Start button to open the Start menu. Next, click Settings; then click Control Panel. The Control Panel dialog box appears.

   B. Double-click the Display icon. The Display Properties dialog box opens.

   C. Click the Settings tab. Note the setting in the Colors box and write it down.

   D. Click the Colors drop-down list arrow and choose the lowest color setting. Then click Apply. A dialog box will appear, asking you to restart the computer. Click Yes.

   E. After the system restarts, open a program or two and look at the screen. How does it look? Note your impressions.

   F. Repeat steps A to E, this time choosing the highest color setting. Again, note your impressions.

   G. Repeat steps A to E, and select the system's original color setting.

2. **What Is Your Resolution?** Like the color setting, your system's screen resolution can affect the quality of your computing experience. If your resolution is set too high, text and icons may be too small to view comfortably and you may strain your eyes. If the resolution is too low, you will spend extra time navigating to parts of your applications that do not fit on the screen. Try different settings to find what works best for you.

   A. Click the Start button to open the Start menu. Next, click Settings; then click Control Panel. The Control Panel dialog box appears.

   B. Double-click the Display icon. The Display Properties dialog box opens.

   C. Click the Settings tab. Note the current setting in the Screen area box and write it down.

   D. Click the Screen area slider control and drag it to the lowest setting. Then click Apply. A dialog box will appear, asking you to restart the computer. Click Yes.

   E. After the system restarts, open a program or two and look at the screen. How does it look? Note your impressions.

   F. Repeat steps A to E, this time choosing the highest setting. Again, note your impressions.

   G. Repeat steps A to E, and select the system's original resolution setting.

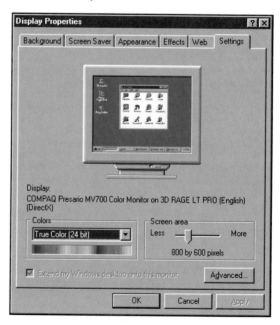

Internet Labs

To complete the following exercises, you need a computer with an Internet connection and a Web browser. (For more information on using these tools, see "Prerequisites" at the front of this textbook.)

1. **Tunes on the 'Net.** Thanks to multimedia programs like Windows Media Player, you can listen to music over the Internet. Several programs such as LiquidAudio and RealPlayer are available for this purpose, but Media Player is built into Windows.

    A. Click the Start button to open the Start menu. Next, click Programs; then click Accessories. If you use Windows 98, click Entertainment. If you use Windows 95, click Multimedia. When the submenu opens, click Windows Media Player.

    B. Click the Radio button. If you are connected to the Internet, your Web browser opens and displays the Radio page of the WindowsMedia.com Web site.

    C. Scroll through this Web page, then click a link to any radio station listed. After a moment, the station's programming should begin playing.

    D. On the Windows taskbar, click Windows Media Player. The player's window will reappear on your screen.

    E. Use the Media Player's controls to set the volume. Then pick another station.

    F. Close Windows Media Player and your browser.

2. **Pick Your Dream Printer.** Visit these Web sites for information on various types of printers:

    - Canon—**http://www.ccsi.canon.com/**
    - Epson—**http://www.epson.com/**
    - Hewlett-Packard—**http://www.hp.com/**
    - Lexmark—**http://www.lexmark.com/**
    - NEC Technologies—**http://www.nectech.com/**
    - Okidata—**http://www.okidata.com/**
    - Tektronix—**http://www.tek.com/**

    When you are finished, decide which device would work best for you. Be prepared to tell your classmates about the device and to explain why you selected it.

IBE Labs

If you have the Interactive Browser Edition (IBE) CD-ROM for this textbook, you may complete the following interactive excercises using the instructions provided in the IBE.

1. **Trivia Game.** Choose a category; then test your knowledge.

2. **Labeling.** Identify the output devices in this exercise.

3. **What's Your Recommendation?** Based on the scenarios provided, make printer recommendations for users.

4. **Experiment With Sound.** "Play with the controls" in this exercise to create different sounds.

Processing Data

UNIT OBJECTIVES

Explain the difference between data and information.

List the three primary text code systems.

Describe one way to provide a device with access to the system's processor.

Identify the four primary manufacturers of PC processors.

Differentiate between RISC and CISC processors.

Define the term *parallel processing* and describe how it makes computers faster.

UNIT CONTENTS

This unit contains the following lessons:

LESSON 7

[handwritten:] transistors = tiny electronic switches in the CPU on/off

Transforming Data Into Information

OVERVIEW: The Difference Between Data and Information

It often seems as though computers must understand us because we understand the information they produce. However, computers cannot understand anything. All computers do is recognize two distinct physical states produced by electricity, magnetic polarity, or reflected light. Essentially, all they can understand is whether a switch is on or off. In fact, the "brain" of the computer, the CPU, consists of several million tiny electronic switches, called **transistors.**

A computer appears to understand information only because it contains so many transistors and operates at such phenomenal speeds, assembling its individual on/off switches into patterns that are meaningful to us.

Data is the term used to describe the information represented by groups of on/off switches. Even though the words *data* and *information* are often used interchangeably, there is an important distinction between them. In the strictest sense, data consists of the raw numbers that computers organize to produce information.

You can think of data as facts out of context, like the individual letters on this page. Taken individually, most of them do not have meaning. Grouped together, however, they convey specific meanings. Just as a theater's marquee can combine thousands of lights to spell the name of the current show, a computer turns meaningless data into useful information, such as spreadsheets, graphs, and reports.

OBJECTIVES

- List two reasons why computers use the binary number system.
- List the two main parts of the CPU and explain how they work together.
- Explain the difference between RAM and ROM.
- Identify two RAM technologies used in PCs.
- List three hardware factors that affect processing speed.
- Identify four connections used to attach devices to a PC.

HOW COMPUTERS REPRESENT DATA

To a computer, everything is a number. Numbers are numbers; letters and punctuation marks are numbers; sounds and pictures are numbers. Even the computer's own instructions are numbers. When you see letters of the alphabet on a computer screen, you are seeing just one of the computer's ways of representing numbers. For example, consider this sentence: *Here are some words.* It may look like a string of alphabetic characters to you, but to a computer it looks like the string of ones and zeros shown in Figure 7.1.

Figure 7.1

These 1s and 0s represent a sentence. The decimal system uses ten symbols and multiple digits for numbers above 9.

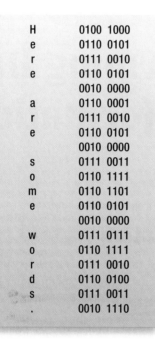

H	0100 1000
e	0110 0101
r	0111 0010
e	0110 0101
	0010 0000
a	0110 0001
r	0111 0010
e	0110 0101
	0010 0000
s	0111 0011
o	0110 1111
m	0110 1101
e	0110 0101
	0010 0000
w	0111 0111
o	0110 1111
r	0111 0010
d	0110 0100
s	0111 0011
.	0010 1110

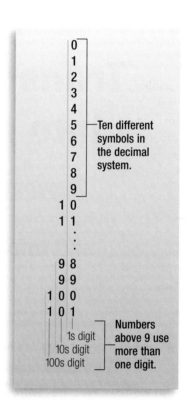

0
1
2
3
4
5 — Ten different
6   symbols in
7   the decimal
8   system.
9
1 0
1 1
· ·
· ·
9 8
9 9
1 0 0
1 0 1

1s digit
10s digit
100s digit

Numbers above 9 use more than one digit.

Computer data looks especially strange because people normally use base 10 to represent numbers. The system is called base 10, or the **decimal number system** (*deci* means "10" in Latin) because ten symbols are available: 0, 1, 2, 3, 4, 5, 6, 7, 8, and 9. When you need to represent a number greater than 9, you use two symbols together, as in 9 + 1 = 10. Each symbol in a number is called a digit, so 10 is a two-digit number.

In a computer, however, all data is represented by the state of the computer's electrical switches. A switch has only two possible states—on and off—so it can represent only two numeric values. To a computer, when a switch is off, it represents a 0; when a switch is on, it represents a 1 (see Figure 7.2). Because there are only two values, computers are said to function in base 2, which is also known as the **binary number system** (*bi* means "2" in Latin).

When a computer needs to represent a quantity greater than 1, it does the same thing you do when you need to represent a quantity greater than 9: it uses two (or more) digits. To familiarize yourself with the binary system, look at Table 7.1.

Figure 7.2

In a computer, data is represented by the state of electrical switches. An on switch represents a 1. An off switch represents a 0.

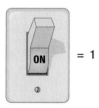

= 1

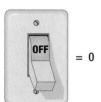

= 0

Bits and Bytes

When referring to computerized data, the value represented by each switch's state—whether the switch is turned on or off—is called a **bit.** The term *bit* is a combination of *bi*nary dig*it*. A bit is the smallest possible unit of data a computer can recognize or use. To represent anything meaningful (in other words, to convey information), the computer uses bits in groups.

A group of 8 bits is called a byte (see Figure 7.3). With 1 byte, the computer can represent one of 256 different symbols or characters because the eight 1s and 0s in a byte can be combined in 256 different ways.

Table 7.1	Counting in Base 10 and Base 2	
Base 10	**Base 2**	
0	0	
1	1	
2	10	
3	11	
4	100	
5	101	
6	110	
7	111	
8	1000	
9	1001	
10	1010	

NORTON
ONLINE

Visit **www.glencoe.com/norton/online/** for more information on **number systems.**

The byte is an extremely important unit because there are enough different 8-bit combinations to represent all the characters on the keyboard, including all the letters (uppercase and lowercase), numbers, punctuation marks, and other symbols. In Figure 7.1, you will notice that each of the characters (or letters) in the sentence *Here are some words.* is represented by 1 byte (8 bits) of data.

Figure 7.3
One byte is composed of eight bits.

1 bit

8 bits = 1 byte

Text Codes

Early programmers realized that they needed a standard **text code**—a system they could all agree on—in which numbers represented the letters of the alphabet, punctuation marks, and other symbols. This standard code system would enable any programmer or program to use the same combinations of numbers to represent the same individual pieces of data. EBCDIC, ASCII, and Unicode are three of the most popular text code systems invented.

Processing Data   **107**

EBCDIC

The BCD (binary coded decimal) system, defined by IBM for one of its early computers, was one of the first complete systems to represent symbols with bits. BCD codes consisted of 6-bit codes, which allowed a maximum of sixty-four possible symbols. BCD computers could work only with uppercase letters and with very few other symbols; thus, this system was short-lived.

The need to represent more characters led to IBM's development of the EBCDIC system. **EBCDIC** (pronounced EB-si-dic) stands for Extended Binary Coded Decimal Interchange Code. EBCDIC is an 8-bit code that defines 256 symbols. EBCDIC is still used in IBM mainframe and midrange systems, but it is rarely encountered in personal computers. By the time small computers were being developed, the American National Standards Institute (ANSI) had begun to define new text code standards for computers.

ASCII

ANSI's solution to representing symbols with bits of data was the ASCII character set. **ASCII** (pronounced AS-key) stands for the American Standard Code for Information Interchange. Today, the ASCII character set is by far the most commonly used in computers of all types. Table 7.2 shows the first 128 ASCII codes.

The characters from 0 to 31 and 127 are control characters; from 32 to 64, special characters and numbers; from 65 to 96, uppercase letters and a few symbols; from 97 to 126, lowercase letters plus a handful of common symbols. Because ASCII, an 8-bit code, specifies characters up to only 127, there are many variations that specify different character sets for codes 128 through 255. The International Standards Organization (ISO) standard expanded on the ASCII character set, to offer different sets of characters for different language groups. This organization works to establish international standards and publishes documents describing each technology. For example, ISO 8859-1 covers Western European languages. There are many other character sets for languages that use a different alphabet.

Unicode

An evolving standard for data representation, called the **Unicode** Worldwide Character Standard, provides 2 bytes—16 bits—to represent each letter, number, or symbol. With 2 bytes, enough Unicode codes can be created to represent more than 65,536 different characters or symbols. This total is enough for every unique character and symbol in the world, including the vast Chinese, Korean, and Japanese character sets and those found in known classical and historical texts.

One major advantage that Unicode has over other text code systems is its compatibility with ASCII codes. The first 256 codes in Unicode are identical to the 256 codes used by ASCII systems. Unicode then extends far beyond the standard ASCII character set.

The Unicode standard was developed in 1991 by a joint engineering team from Apple Computer Corporation and Xerox Corporation. It has been updated continually since its inception. In fall 1999, version three of the worldwide Unicode standard was released by the Unicode Consortium, a group of developers, corporations, researchers, and other groups working in conjunction with the ISO. In version three, the Unicode standard includes a total of 57,709 16-bit code values.

Visit **www.glencoe.com/norton/online/** for more information on the **ASCII text code system.**

Table 7.2 ASCII Codes

ASCII Code	Decimal Equivalent	Character	ASCII Code	Decimal Equivalent	Character	ASCII Code	Decimal Equivalent	Character
0000 0000	0	Null prompt	0010 1011	43	+	0101 0110	86	V
0000 0001	1	Start of heading	0010 1100	44	,	0101 0111	87	W
0000 0010	2	Start of text	0010 1101	45	-	0101 1000	88	X
0000 0011	3	End of text	0010 1110	46	.	0101 1001	89	Y
0000 0100	4	End of transmit	0010 1111	47	/	0101 1010	90	Z
0000 0101	5	Enquiry	0011 0000	48	0	0101 1011	91	[
0000 0110	6	Acknowledge	0011 0001	49	1	0101 1100	92	\
0000 0111	7	Audible bell	0011 0010	50	2	0101 1101	93	]
0000 1000	8	Backspace	0011 0011	51	3	0101 1110	94	^
0000 1001	9	Horizontal tab	0011 0100	52	4	0101 1111	95	_
0000 1010	10	Line feed	0011 0101	53	5	0110 0000	96	`
0000 1011	11	Vertical tab	0011 0110	54	6	0110 0001	97	a
0000 1100	12	Form feed	0011 0111	55	7	0110 0010	98	b
0000 1101	13	Carriage return	0011 1000	56	8	0110 0011	99	c
0000 1110	14	Shift out	0011 1001	57	9	0110 0100	100	d
0000 1111	15	Shift in	0011 1010	58	:	0110 0101	101	e
0001 0000	16	Data link escape	0011 1011	59	;	0110 0110	102	f
0001 0001	17	Device control 1	0011 1100	60	<	0110 0111	103	g
0001 0010	18	Device control 2	0011 1101	61	=	0110 1000	104	h
0001 0011	19	Device control 3	0011 1110	62	>	0110 1001	105	i
0001 0100	20	Device control 4	0011 1111	63	?	0110 1010	106	j
0001 0101	21	Neg. acknowledge	0100 0000	64	@	0110 1011	107	k
0001 0110	22	Synchronous idle	0100 0001	65	A	0110 1100	108	l
0001 0111	23	End trans. block	0100 0010	66	B	0110 1101	109	m
0001 1000	24	Cancel	0100 0011	67	C	0110 1110	110	n
0001 1001	25	End of medium	0100 0100	68	D	0110 1111	111	o
0001 1010	26	Substitution	0100 0101	69	E	0111 0000	112	p
0001 1011	27	Escape	0100 0110	70	F	0111 0001	113	q
0001 1100	28	File separator	0100 0111	71	G	0111 0010	114	r
0001 1101	29	Group separator	0100 1000	72	H	0111 0011	115	s
0001 1110	30	Record separator	0100 1001	73	I	0111 0100	116	t
0001 1111	31	Unit separator	0100 1010	74	J	0111 0101	117	u
0010 0000	32	Blank space	0100 1011	75	K	0111 0110	118	v
0010 0001	33	!	0100 1100	76	L	0111 0111	119	w
0010 0010	34	"	0100 1101	77	M	0111 1000	120	x
0010 0011	35	#	0100 1110	78	N	0111 1001	121	y
0010 0100	36	$	0100 1111	79	O	0111 1010	122	z
0010 0101	37	%	0101 0000	80	P	0111 1011	123	{
0010 0110	38	&	0101 0001	81	Q	0111 1100	124		
0010 0111	39	'	0101 0010	82	R	0111 1101	125	}
0010 1000	40	(	0101 0011	83	S	0111 1110	126	~
0010 1001	41	)	0101 0100	84	T	0111 1111	127	Delete or rubout
0010 1010	42	*	0101 0101	85	U			

Many software publishers, including IBM, Microsoft, Netscape, and others, encourage their developers to use Unicode in their programs. Unicode is supported by some operating systems (such as Windows 2000 and OS/2) and applications. Even so, it has not yet been universally adopted by software developers. Still, the goal is a worthwhile one. If a single character set were available to cover all languages, computer programs and data would be interchangeable.

HOW COMPUTERS PROCESS DATA

Two components handle processing in a computer: the central processing unit, or CPU, and the memory. Both are located on the computer's motherboard (see Figure 7.4), the circuit board that connects the CPU to the other hardware devices.

The CPU

The CPU is the "brain" of the computer, the place where data is manipulated. In large computer systems, such as supercomputers and mainframes, processing tasks may be handled by multiple processing chips. (Some powerful computer systems use hundreds or even thousands of separate processing units.) In the average microcomputer, the entire CPU is a single unit, called a microprocessor.

Most microprocessors are single chips mounted on a piece of plastic with metal wires attached to it. Some newer microprocessors include multiple chips and are encased in their own cover, which fits into a special socket on the motherboard. Regardless of its construction, every CPU has at least two basic parts: the control unit and the arithmetic logic unit.

The Control Unit

All the computer's resources are managed from the **control unit.** Think of the control unit as a traffic cop directing the flow of data through the CPU, and to and from other devices. The control unit is the logical hub of the computer (see Figure 7.5).

The CPU's instructions for carrying out commands are built into the control unit. The instructions, or **instruction set,** list all the operations that the CPU can perform. Each instruction in the instruction set is expressed in **microcode**—a series of basic directions that tells the CPU how to execute more complex operations.

Figure 7.4
Processing devices.

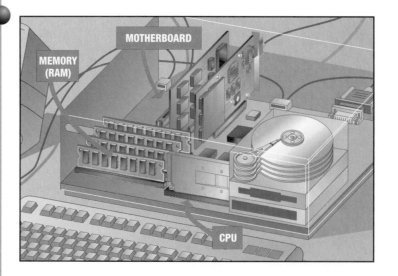

The Arithmetic Logic Unit

Because all computer data is stored as numbers, much of the processing that takes place involves comparing numbers or carrying out mathematical operations. In addition to establishing ordered sequences and changing those sequences, the computer can perform two types of operations: **arithmetic operations** and **logical operations.** Arithmetic operations include addition, subtraction, multiplication, and division. Logical operations include comparisons, such as determining whether one number is equal to, greater than, or less than another number. Also, every logical operation has an opposite. For example, in addition to "equal to" there is "not equal to." Table 7.3 shows the symbols for all the arithmetic and logical operations.

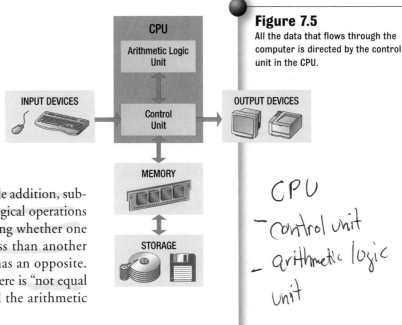

Figure 7.5
All the data that flows through the computer is directed by the control unit in the CPU.

CPU
- control unit
- arithmetic logic unit

Table 7.3	Operations Performed by the Arithmetic Logic Unit	

Arithmetic Operations		Logical Operations	
+	add	=, ≠	equal to, not equal to
−	subtract	>, ≯	greater than, not greater than
×	multiply	<, ≮	less than, not less than
÷	divide	≧, ≩	greater than or equal to, not greater than or equal to
∧	raise by a power	≦, ≨	less than or equal to, not less than or equal to

Remember that some of the logical operations can be done on text data. For example, when you want to search for a word in a document, the CPU carries out a rapid succession of "equals" operations to find a match for the sequence of ASCII codes that make up the word for which you are searching.

Many instructions carried out by the control unit involve simply moving data from one place to another—from memory to storage, from memory to the printer, and so forth. When the control unit encounters an instruction that involves arithmetic or logic, however, it passes that instruction to the second component of the CPU, the **arithmetic logic unit,** or **ALU.** The ALU actually performs the arithmetic and logical operations described earlier.

The ALU includes a group of **registers**—high-speed memory locations built directly into the CPU that are used to hold the data currently being processed. For example, the control unit might load two numbers from memory into the registers in the ALU. Then it might tell the ALU to divide the two numbers (an arithmetic operation) or to see whether the numbers are equal (a logical operation).

Machine Cycles

Each time the CPU executes an instruction, it takes a series of steps. The completed series of steps is called a **machine cycle.** A machine cycle itself can be broken down into two smaller cycles: the **instruction cycle** and the **execution cycle.** At the beginning of the machine cycle (that is, during the instruction cycle), the CPU takes two steps:

1. **Fetching.** Before the CPU can execute an instruction, the control unit must retrieve (or "fetch") a command or data from the computer's memory.

2. **Decoding.** Before a command can be executed, the control unit must break down (or **decode**) the command into instructions that correspond to those in the CPU's instruction set.

At this point, the CPU is ready to begin the execution cycle:

1. **Executing.** When the command is executed, the CPU carries out the instructions in order by converting them into microcode.

2. **Storing.** The CPU may be required to **store** the results of an instruction in memory (but this condition is not always required).

Depending on the type of processor in use, a machine cycle may include other steps. For example, some processors employ multiple decoders when translating instructions to microcode; other processors skip this step. Some processors retire the instructions after they have been executed and collect the results in the proper order. This step may be needed if the processor can execute instructions out of order.

Although the process is complex, the computer can accomplish it at an incredible speed, translating millions of instructions every second. In fact, CPU performance is often measured in millions of instructions per second (MIPS).

Even though most microprocessors execute instructions rapidly, newer ones can perform even faster by using a process called **pipelining** (or pipeline processing). In pipelining, the control unit begins a new machine cycle—that is, it begins executing a new instruction—before the current cycle is completed. Executions are performed in stages: when the first instruction completes the "fetching" stage, it moves to the "decode" stage and a new instruction is fetched. Using this technique, some microprocessors can execute up to six instructions simultaneously.

Memory

The CPU contains the basic instructions needed to operate the computer, but it cannot store entire programs or large sets of data permanently. The CPU does contain registers, but these are small areas that can hold only a few bytes at a time. In addition to registers, the CPU needs to have millions of bytes of randomly accessed space where it can quickly read or write programs and data while they are being used. This area is called memory.

Physically, memory consists of chips either on the motherboard or on a small circuit board attached to the motherboard. This electronic memory allows the CPU to store and retrieve data quickly.

There are two types of built-in memory: permanent and nonpermanent (see Figure 7.6). Some memory chips always retain the data they hold, even when the computer is turned off. This type of memory is called **nonvolatile.** Other chips— in fact, most of the memory in a microcomputer—lose their contents when the computer's power is shut off. These chips have **volatile** memory.

NORTON
ONLINE

Visit **www.glencoe.com/norton/online/** for more information on **computer memory.**

ROM

Nonvolatile chips always hold the same data; the data in them cannot be changed except through a special process that overwrites the data. In fact, putting data permanently into this kind of memory is called "burning in the data," and it is usually done at the factory. During normal use, the data in these chips is only read and used—not changed—so the memory is called read-only memory (ROM).

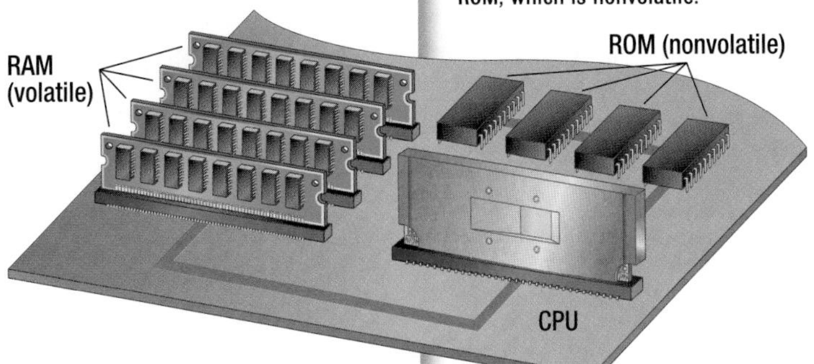

One important reason a computer needs ROM is that it must know what to do when the power is first turned on. Among other things, ROM contains a set of start-up instructions, which ensures that the rest of memory is functioning properly, checks for hardware devices, and checks for an operating system on the computer's disk drives.

RAM

Memory that can be instantly changed is called read-write memory or random-access memory (RAM). When people talk about computer memory in connection with microcomputers, they usually mean the volatile RAM. The purpose of RAM is to hold programs and data while they are in use. Physically, RAM consists of some chips on a small circuit board (see Figure 7.7).

A computer does not have to search its entire memory each time it needs to find data because the CPU uses a **memory address** to store and retrieve each piece of data (see Figure 7.8 on page 114). A memory address is a number that indicates a location on the memory chips, just as a post office box number indicates a slot into which mail is placed. Memory addresses start at zero and go up to one less than the number of bytes of memory in the computer.

This type of memory is referred to as random-access memory because of its ability to access each byte of data directly. Actually, read-only memory (ROM) is "random access" as well, so the names for the two types of memory can be misleading. It is best simply to remember that the data in ROM does not change while the data in RAM changes constantly.

RAM is not just used in conjunction with the computer's CPU. RAM can be found in various places in a computer system. For example, most newer video and sound cards have their own built-in RAM, as do many types of printers.

There are two types of RAM: dynamic and static. **Dynamic RAM (DRAM)** gets its name from the fact that it must be refreshed frequently. (The term *refreshing* means recharging the RAM chips with electricity.) DRAM chips must be recharged many times each second, or they will lose their contents. **Static RAM (SRAM),** on the other hand, does not need to be refreshed as often and can hold its contents longer than dynamic RAM. SRAM is also considerably faster than DRAM. Most DRAM technologies support access times of around 60 nanoseconds. (A nanosecond is one-billionth of a second!) The term *nanosecond* is often abbreviated as *ns*. Faster SRAM chips support access times of around 10 nanoseconds. Consequently, SRAM is more expensive than DRAM and is not used as frequently in PCs.

Figure 7.6
The CPU is attached to two kinds of memory: RAM, which is volatile, and ROM, which is nonvolatile.

Figure 7.7
In personal computers, RAM chips are normally mounted on a small circuit board, which is plugged into the motherboard.

NORTON ONLINE

Visit **www.glencoe.com/norton/online/** for information on **RAM technologies.**

Figure 7.8
To request a byte of data, the CPU sends a memory address to RAM.

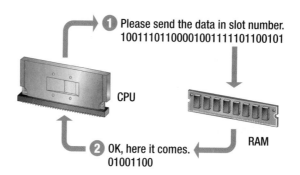

① Please send the data in slot number.
100111011000010011111101100101

CPU

RAM

② OK, here it comes.
01001100

Flash Memory

Standard RAM is volatile; when power to the PC is lost, all data currently stored in RAM is lost. This fact explains why you must save your work when using an application. One type of memory, called **flash memory,** stores data even when the power is turned off. ROM is a form of flash memory used in PCs. Other machines that use flash memory are digital cameras. When you take pictures with some digital cameras, the pictures are stored in a flash memory chip rather than on photographic film. Because you do not want to lose the pictures you have taken, the memory must store the pictures until you can transfer them to your PC, even when the camera is turned off.

Self Check

Answer the following questions by filling in the blank(s).

1. A computer's CPU consists of millions of tiny switches called _____ .

2. Base 2 is another name for the _____ .

3. _____ can represent more than 65,536 different characters or symbols.

FACTORS AFFECTING PROCESSING SPEED

The circuitry design of a CPU determines its basic speed, but several additional factors can make chips already designed for speed work even faster. You have already been introduced to some of these, such as the CPU's registers and the memory. In this section, you will see how these two components, as well as a few others—such as the cache memory, clock speed, and data bus—affect a computer's speed. Figure 7.9 shows how these components might be arranged on the computer's motherboard.

How Registers Affect Speed

The registers in the first PCs could hold two bytes—16 bits—each. Most CPUs sold today, for both PCs and Macintosh computers, have 32-bit registers. Many newer PCs, as well as minicomputers and high-end workstations, have 64-bit registers.

The size of the registers, which is sometimes called the **word size,** indicates the amount of data with which the computer can work at any given time. The bigger the word size, the more quickly the computer can process a set of data. Occasionally, you will hear people refer to "32-bit processors," or "64-bit processors," or even "64-bit computers." This terminology refers to the size of the registers in the processor. If all other factors are kept equal, a CPU with 32-bit registers can process data twice as fast as one with 16-bit registers.

Memory and Computing Power

The amount of RAM in a computer can have a profound effect on the computer's power. More RAM means the computer can use bigger, more powerful programs, and those programs can access bigger data files.

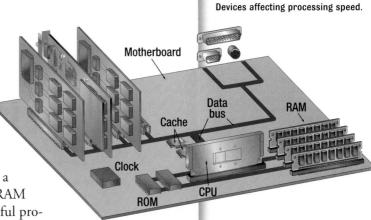

Figure 7.9
Devices affecting processing speed.

More RAM also can make the computer run faster. The computer does not necessarily have to load an entire program into memory to run it. However, the greater the amount of the program that fits into memory, the faster the program runs. For example, a PC with 16 MB of RAM is able to run Microsoft Windows 98, even though the program actually occupies about 195 MB of disk storage space. When you run Windows, the program does not need to load all its files into memory to run properly. It loads only the most essential parts into memory. When the computer needs access to other parts of the program on the disk, it can unload, or **swap out,** nonessential parts from RAM to the hard disk. Then the computer can load,

With more RAM available, more of the operating system can be loaded from the hard disk at startup.

7 MB copied from the hard disk to RAM at startup.

16 MB RAM

16 MB copied from the hard disk to RAM at startup.

64 MB RAM

Figure 7.10
How RAM affects speed.

If more of the operating system can be loaded into RAM, then less needs to be swapped while the computer is running.

Lots of swapping needed.

The hard disk is much slower than RAM, so less swapping makes for a faster computer.

16 MB RAM

SLOW

Little swapping needed.

64 MB RAM

FAST

Figure 7.11
On the top is a SIMM; on the bottom
is an example of a DIMM.

or **swap in,** the program code or data it needs. While this is an effective method for managing a limited amount of memory, it can result in slow system performance because the CPU, memory, and disk are continuously occupied with the swapping process. As shown in Figure 7.10 on page 115, if your PC has 64 MB of RAM (or more), you will notice a dramatic difference in how fast Microsoft Windows 98 runs because the CPU will need to swap program instructions between RAM and the hard disk much less often.

If you purchase a new computer system, it will probably come with at least 64 MB of RAM, although 128 MB is rapidly becoming the standard minimum for PCs. If you are willing to pay a little more, you can get a new PC with 128 MB or even 256 MB of RAM. Many new computers can hold as much as 1 GB of RAM.

Fortunately, if you already own a PC and decide that it needs more RAM, you should be able to buy more, open up your computer, and plug it in. (Some newer PCs come "stuffed" with all the RAM they can hold, making it difficult to upgrade.) In today's computers, chips are usually grouped together on small circuit boards called **single in-line memory modules (SIMMs)** or **dual in-line memory modules (DIMMs),** both of which are shown in Figure 7.11. Each SIMM or DIMM can hold between 1 MB and 64 MB of RAM and connects to the motherboard with 30-pin, 72-pin, or 168-pin connections. The cost of upgrading the memory of a computer has actually gone down, so upgrading RAM is often the most cost-effective way to get more speed from your computer.

The Computer's Internal Clock

Every microcomputer has a **system clock,** but the clock's primary purpose is not to keep the time of day. Like most modern wristwatches, the clock is driven by a quartz crystal. When electricity is applied, the molecules in the crystal vibrate millions of times per second, a rate that never changes. The speed of the vibrations is determined by the thickness of the crystal. The computer uses the vibrations of the quartz in the system clock to time its processing operations.

Over the years, system clocks have become steadily faster. For example, the first PC operated at 4.77 megahertz. **Hertz (Hz)** is a measure of cycles per second. **Megahertz (MHz)** means "millions of cycles per second."

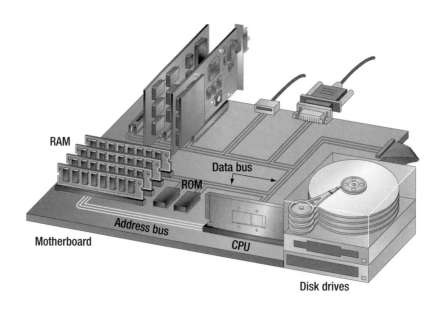

The computer's operating speed is tied to the speed of the system clock. For example, if a computer's **clock speed** is 300 MHz, it "ticks" 300 million times per second. A **clock cycle** is a single tick, or the time it takes to turn a transistor off and back on again. A processor can execute an instruction in a given number of clock cycles. As the system's clock speed increases, so does the number of instructions it can carry out each second.

Clock speed has a tremendous impact on CPU performance. A CPU operating at 300 MHz can process data nearly twice as fast as the same one operating at 166 MHz.

Clock speeds of 500 MHz and higher are common, and processor speeds are increasing rapidly. By the time you read this sentence, clock speeds exceeding 800 MHz will probably be common. Clock speeds of 1 GHz (gigahertz) have already been achieved (early 2000).

The Bus

In microcomputers, the term **bus** refers to the path between the components of a computer. There are two main buses in a computer: the internal (or system) bus and the external (or expansion) bus. The system bus resides on the motherboard and connects the CPU to other devices that reside on the motherboard. An expansion bus connects external devices, such as the keyboard, mouse, modem, printer, etc., to the CPU. Cables from disk drives and some other internal devices may also be plugged into the bus. The system bus has two parts: the data bus and the address bus (see Figure 7.12).

The Data Bus

The **data bus** is an electrical path that connects the CPU, memory, and the other hardware devices on the motherboard. Actually, the bus is a group of parallel wires. The number of wires in the bus affects the speed at which data can travel between hardware components, just as the number of lanes on a highway affects how long it takes people to reach their destinations. Because each wire can transfer 1 bit of data at a time, an 8-wire bus can move 8 bits at a time, which is a full byte (see Figure 7.13). A 16-bit bus can transfer 2 bytes, and a 32-bit bus can transfer 4 bytes at a time. Newer model computers have a 64-bit data bus, which transfers 8 bytes at a time.

The Address Bus

The **address bus** is a set of wires similar to the data bus (see Figure 7.14). The address bus connects only the CPU and RAM and carries only memory addresses. (Remember, each byte in RAM is associated with a number, which is its memory address.) In theory, today's CPUs have address buses that are wide enough to address 64 GB of RAM.

NORTON
ONLINE

Visit **www.glencoe.com/norton/online/** for more information on **processor speeds**.

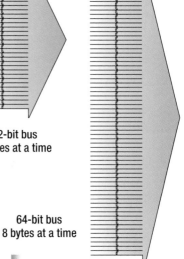

Figure 7.13
With a wider bus, the computer can move more data in the same amount of time (or the same amount of data in less time).

16-bit bus
2 bytes at a time

32-bit bus
4 bytes at a time

64-bit bus
8 bytes at a time

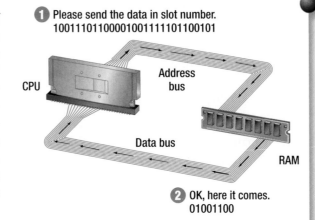

① Please send the data in slot number.
100111011000010011111101100101

CPU

Address bus

Data bus

RAM

② OK, here it comes.
01001100

Figure 7.14
Requests for data are sent from the CPU to RAM along the address bus. The request consists of a memory address. The data comes back to the CPU via the data bus.

Bus Types

PC buses are designed to match the capabilities of the devices attached to them. When CPUs could send and receive only 1 byte of data at a time, there was no point in connecting them to a bus that could move more data. As microprocessor technology improved, however, chips were built that could send and receive more data at once, and improved bus designs created wider paths through which the data could flow. Common bus technologies include:

Visit **www.glencoe.com/norton/online/** for more information on **bus technologies**.

- ◆ The **Industry Standard Architecture (ISA)** bus is a 16-bit data bus. ISA became the de facto industry standard on its release in the mid-1980s and is still used in many computers to attach slower devices (such as modems and input devices) to the CPU.

- ◆ **Local bus** technology was developed to attach faster devices to the CPU. A local bus is an internal system bus that runs between components on the motherboard. Most system buses use some type of local bus technology today and are coupled with one or more kinds of expansion bus.

- ◆ The **Peripheral Component Interconnect (PCI)** bus is a type of local bus designed by Intel to make it easier to integrate new data types, such as audio, video, and graphics.

- ◆ The **Accelerated Graphics Port (AGP)** bus incorporates a special architecture that allows the video card to access the system's RAM directly, greatly increasing the speed of graphics performance. The AGP standard has led to the development of many types of accelerated video cards that support 3-D and full-motion video. While AGP improves graphics performance, it cannot be used with all PCs. The system must use a chip set that supports the AGP standard. Most new computers feature AGP graphics capabilities in addition to a PCI system bus and an expansion bus.

- ◆ Two new expansion bus technologies promise to replace most existing buses in the future. These bus types—**Universal Serial Bus (USB)** and **IEEE 1394** (called **FireWire** on Macintosh computers)—not only provide fast data transfer speeds, they also eliminate the need for expansion slots and boards. Most new PCs and Macintosh computers feature at least one USB port, and each USB port can support 127 different devices. If you have USB-compliant devices such as keyboards, mice, printers, and modems, you can plug them all into a single USB port.

Traditionally, the performance of computer buses was measured by the number of bits they could transfer at one time. Hence, the newest 64-bit buses are typically considered the fastest available. However, buses are now also being measured according to their **data transfer rates**—the amount of data they can transfer in a second. This type of performance is usually measured in **megabits per second (Mbps)** or **megabytes per second (MBps).**

For example, a USB bus has a data transfer rate of 12 Mbps. An IEEE 1394 bus has a data transfer rate of 400 Mbps. AGP buses are typically rated at 266 MBps but can support data transfer rates of more than 1 GBps. PCI buses offer data transfer rates of 133 MBps.

Some manufacturers also rate the speed of their system buses in megahertz. For years, system buses ran at a speed of 66 MHz; contemporary systems offer bus speeds of 100 MHz and 200 MHz. When coupled with a fast processor, a high-speed bus can result in an exceptionally high-performance system.

Cache Memory

Moving data between RAM and the CPU's registers is one of the most time-consuming operations a CPU must perform, simply because RAM is much slower than the CPU. A partial solution to this problem is to include a cache memory in the CPU. **Cache** (pronounced *cash*) **memory** is similar to RAM, except that it is extremely fast compared to normal memory and it is used in a different way.

Figure 7.15 shows how cache memory works with the CPU and RAM. When a program is running and the CPU needs to read data or program instructions from RAM, the CPU checks first to see whether the data is in cache memory. If the data is not there, the CPU reads the data from RAM into its registers, but it also loads a copy of the data into cache memory. The next time the CPU needs that same data, it finds it in the cache memory and saves the time needed to load the data from RAM.

Since the late 1980s, cache memory has been built into most PC CPUs. This CPU-resident cache is often called **Level-1 (L1) cache.** The first CPU caches came with 0.5 KB, then 8 KB, then 16 KB, then 32 KB. Today, many CPUs have as much as 256 KB built in.

In addition to the cache memory built into the CPU, cache is also added to the motherboard. This motherboard-resident cache is often called **Level-2 (L2) cache.** Many PCs sold today have 512 KB or 1024 KB of motherboard cache memory; higher-end systems can have as much as 2 MB of L2 cache.

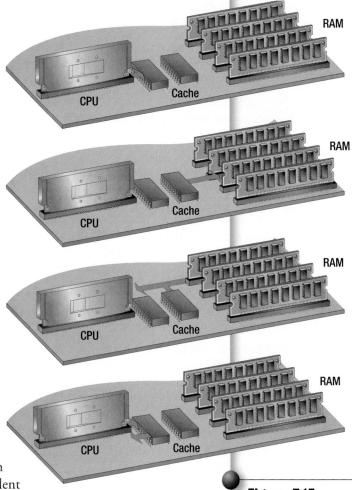

Figure 7.15
The cache speeds processing by storing frequently used data or instructions in its high-speed memory. External (Level-2) cache is shown here, but most computers also have internal (Level-1) cache memory circuitry built into the CPU.

EXTENDING THE PROCESSOR'S POWER TO OTHER DEVICES

You have already learned that all the components of a computer tie into the computer's CPU by way of the bus. When you need to add a new piece of hardware to your computer, you need to know how to connect it to the bus. In some cases, you can plug the device into an existing socket, or port, on the back of the computer. Most computers have several types of ports, each with different capabilities and uses. Older computers feature only three or four distinct types of ports, but new systems provide a wide array of specialized ports. When a port is not available, you need to install a circuit board that includes the port you need.

NORTON
ONLINE

Visit **www.glencoe.com/norton/online/** for more information on **cache memory.**

Techview

UNIVERSAL SERIAL BUS

The Advantages of USB

The USB standard may someday eliminate the need for multiple types of buses in a single computer. Currently, a USB port can accept as many as 127 devices, extending the system's bus to many peripherals. The USB standard also provides for a data transfer rate of 12 Mb per second, which compares favorably to standard parallel and serial port throughput and is more than adequate for many peripheral devices.

Specifically, the USB standard provides the following advantages over traditional expansion bus designs:

◆ **No Expansion Cards.** You simply plug a USB-compliant device into the computer's existing USB port. Because the computer's USB port is already built in, you do not need to add a new port to the computer by installing an expansion card.

◆ **You Can Leave Your System in One Piece.** Installing an expansion board means opening your computer—a daunting task for most users. Because the USB port is already built into newer systems, you may never need to remove the system's cover again.

◆ **True "Plug and Play."** Whenever you add an expansion card to a computer, you may need to make other changes to enable the card to work. USB devices require no special settings, which means that the dream of true "Plug and Play" is nearly a reality. Because USB devices all adhere to the same standards, you plug the new device into the USB port, turn it on (an optional step for some devices), and start using it. The system will recognize the new device right away, which means that you will not need to reboot the computer.

◆ **Never Run Out of Ports.** With traditional expansion bus technologies, you are limited to the number of available expansion slots. Once they are filled, you cannot add any other devices, unless you want to invest in a SCSI adapter and SCSI-compliant devices. (SCSI devices are considerably more expensive than non-SCSI devices.) Most USB-compliant computers have two built-in ports, each capable of supporting 127 devices at one time. To connect multiple peripherals, you can use an inexpensive USB "hub," which provides additional ports for chaining multiple devices together.

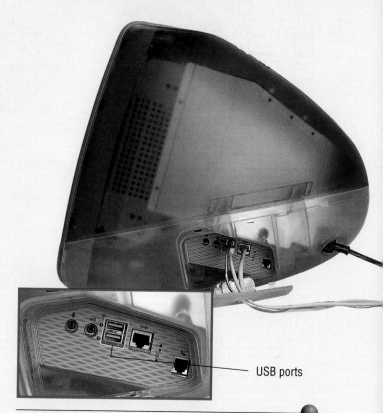

USB ports

The iMac computer features multiple USB ports, which greatly simplifies the process of adding peripheral devices.

◆ **More Power and Control.** The USB port supplies power to the connected devices, which means that you do not have to plug them into a power supply. Most USB devices can be controlled from the PC, so you do not have to adjust settings manually.

USB Devices

The USB standard is being developed through a joint effort of leaders in the computer and telecommunications industries, including Intel, Microsoft, and several others. If the standard is universally adopted (hence its name), its proponents believe that it will apply to almost any device that can be plugged into a computer, including keyboards, pointing devices, monitors, scanners, digital cameras, game controllers, printers, modems, and more.

120

Serial and Parallel Ports

A PC's internal components communicate through the data bus, which consists of parallel wires. Similarly, a **parallel interface** is a connection of eight or more wires through which data bits can flow simultaneously. Most computer buses transfer 32 bits simultaneously. However, the standard parallel interface for external devices like printers usually transfers 8 bits (1 byte) at a time over eight separate wires.

With a **serial interface,** data bits are transmitted one at a time through a single wire (however, the interface includes additional wires for the bits that control the flow of data). Inside the computer, a chip called a **universal asynchronous receiver-transmitter (UART)** converts parallel data from the bus into serial data that flows through a serial cable. Figure 7.16 shows how data flows through a 9-pin serial interface.

As you would expect, a parallel interface can handle a higher volume of data than a serial interface because more than 1 bit can be transmitted through a parallel interface simultaneously. Figure 7.17 shows how data moves through a parallel interface.

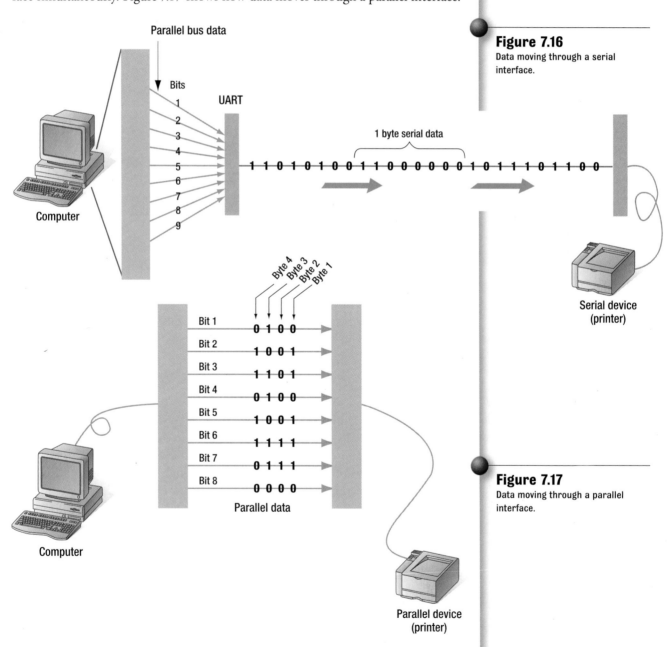

Figure 7.16
Data moving through a serial interface.

Figure 7.17
Data moving through a parallel interface.

SCSI, MIDI, and Other Specialized Expansion Ports

In addition to the standard collection of expansion ports, many PCs include specialized ports. These ports allow the connection of special devices, which extends the computer's bus in unique ways.

SCSI

The **Small Computer System Interface** (**SCSI,** pronounced *scuzzy*) takes a different approach from ports discussed so far and overcomes the constraints of a limited number of expansion slots on the motherboard. Instead of forcing the user to plug multiple cards into the computer's expansion slots, a single SCSI adapter extends the bus outside the computer by way of a cable. Thus, SCSI is like an extension cord for the data bus. Like plugging one extension cord into another to lengthen a circuit, you can plug one SCSI device into another to form a chain.

The emerging standard is SCSI-3, which can link as many as 127 devices. The newest SCSI standard, Ultra3 SCSI, supports a 32-bit bus and can transfer data at a rate of 160 Mbps, more than thirty times faster than the earliest SCSI.

Figure 7.18
SCSI peripherals daisy-chained together.

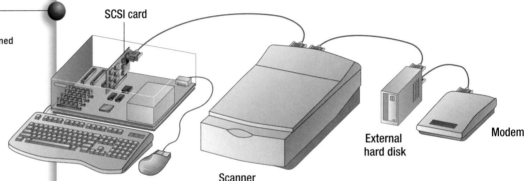

SCSI card

External hard disk

Modem

Scanner

To provide a PC with a SCSI port, insert a SCSI adapter board into one of the PC's available expansion slots. Many devices use the SCSI interface. Fast, high-end hard disk drives often have SCSI interfaces, as do scanners, tape drives, and optical storage devices such as CD-ROM drives. Like the USB and IEEE 1394 standards, SCSI enables you to plug multiple devices into a single port. This process is called daisy-chaining (see Figure 7.18).

USB

As mentioned previously, the Universal Serial Bus (USB) standard is rapidly gaining popularity for PCs—both IBM-compatible and Macintosh systems. Because the USB standard allows 127 devices to be connected to the bus via a single port, many experts believe that USB will emerge as the single bus standard of the future. Today, most new computers feature at least one or two USB ports.

IEEE 1394 (FireWire)

Like the USB standard, the IEEE 1394 (or FireWire) standard extends the computer's bus to many peripheral devices through a single port. Because IEEE 1394-compliant technology is so expensive, however, it is not expected to become the dominant bus technology, although it may gain wide acceptance as a standard for plugging video and other high-data-throughput devices to the system bus.

Musical Instrument Digital Interface (MIDI)

The **Musical Instrument Digital Interface (MIDI)** has been in use since the early 1980s, when a group of musical instrument manufacturers developed the technology to enable electronic instruments to communicate. Since then, MIDI has been adapted to the personal computer. Many sound cards are MIDI-compliant and feature a special MIDI port. Using a MIDI port, you can plug a wide variety of musical instruments and other MIDI-controlled devices into the computer. MIDI systems are widely used in recording and performance to control settings for electronic synthesizers, drum machines, light systems, amplification, and more.

Expansion Slots and Boards

PCs are designed so that users can adapt, or **configure,** the machines to their own particular needs. PC motherboards have two or more **expansion slots,** which are extensions of the computer's bus that provide a way to add new components to the computer. The slots accept **expansion boards,** also called **cards, adapters,** or sometimes just **boards.** Figure 7.19 shows a PC expansion board being installed. The board is being attached to the motherboard—the main system board to which the CPU, memory, and other components are attached.

NORTON
ONLINE

Visit **www.glencoe.com/norton/online/** for information on installing **expansion boards.**

Figure 7.19
An expansion board being inserted into an expansion slot.

The expansion slots on the motherboard are used for three purposes:

◆ To give built-in devices—such as hard disks and diskette drives—access to the computer's bus via controller cards. (Note that the use of controller cards is waning as disk controllers are more commonly built into the system's motherboard or directly onto the disk drive.)

◆ To provide I/O ports on the back of the computer for external devices such as monitors, external modems, printers, and game controllers (for computers that do not have built-in ports for such devices, or where existing ports are already in use by other devices).

◆ To give special-purpose devices access to the computer. For example, a computer can be enhanced with an **accelerator card,** a self-contained device that enhances processing speed through access to the computer's CPU and memory by way of the bus.

VISUAL ESSAY: EXPANDING YOUR COMPUTER WITH PORTS, SLOTS, AND BOARDS

A A 9-pin serial port is provided for an external communication device (such as a modem) or an input device (such as a mouse). Some types of printers and other devices can also use this type of port.

B A 25-pin parallel port is typically used by a printer but can also be used by backup devices, such as tape drives, Zip drives, and others.

C These small ports are devoted specifically to the keyboard and mouse. Most newer systems use a 6-pin "mini-DIN" connector for these devices, although some systems use a larger, 5-pin DIN plug.

D Most PCs feature a special 15-pin port specifically for the monitor.

E Multimedia PCs include a built-in sound card that provides single-pin miniplugs such as an input jack for a microphone or a stereo output jack for a set of speakers or headphones. Other plugs are dedicated audio line input and output jacks for devices such as tape decks or CD players.

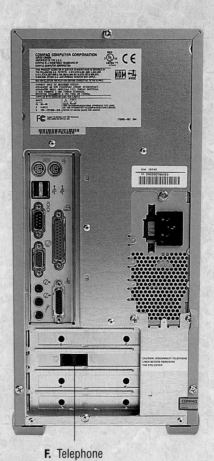

F. Telephone & modem

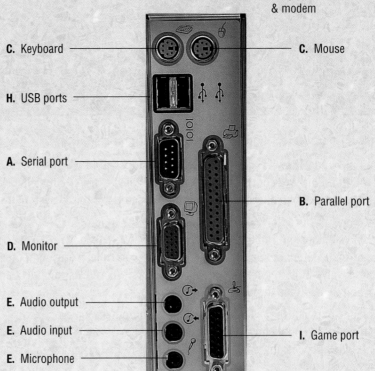

C. Keyboard

C. Mouse

H. USB ports

A. Serial port

B. Parallel port

D. Monitor

E. Audio output

E. Audio input

I. Game port

E. Microphone

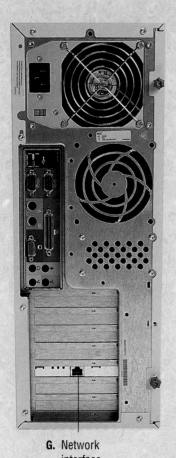

F

If the PC includes a built-in modem card, the card provides two standard phone-line (RJ-11) plugs. One plug is for the modem line; the other enables you to plug a telephone directly into the PC.

G

Most business-class computers and many home computers feature built-in network interface cards that enable the computer to be connected to a network. In home computers, this card enables the user to create a home network or to connect to a cable modem system. The type of plug used depends on the networking protocols supported by the card.

G. Network interface

H. USB ports

A. Serial ports

H

All new Macintosh computers and a growing number of IBM-compatible PCs feature one or more universal serial bus (USB) ports. As many as 127 USB-compliant devices can be connected to a single USB port. These devices include printers, keyboards, mice, video devices, and other peripherals.

C. Mouse

C. Keyboard

B. Parallel port

D. Monitor

E. Headphones

E. Microphone

I

Many newer PCs include a dedicated port for game controllers such as a joystick.

E. Audio output

E. Audio input

Adapters that serve input and output purposes provide a port to which devices can be attached and act as translators between the bus and the device itself. Some adapters also do a significant amount of data processing. For example, a video controller is a card that provides a port on the back of the PC into which you can plug the monitor. It also contains and manages the video memory and does the processing required to display images on the monitor. Other I/O devices that commonly require the installation of a card into an expansion slot include sound cards, internal modems or fax/modems, network interface cards, and scanners.

PC Cards

Another type of expansion card—the **PC Card** (initially called a Personal Computer Memory Card International Association or PCMCIA card)—is a small device about the size of a credit card (see Figure 7.20). This device was designed initially for use in notebook computers and other computers that are too small to accept a standard expansion card. A PC Card fits into a slot on the back or side of the notebook computer. PC Card adapters are also available for desktop computers, enabling them to accept PC Cards. Even some types of digital cameras accept PC Cards that store digital photographs. PC Cards are used for a wide variety of purposes and can house modems, network cards, memory, and even fully functioning hard disk drives.

Figure 7.20
Small PC Card devices provide memory, storage, communications, and other capabilities.

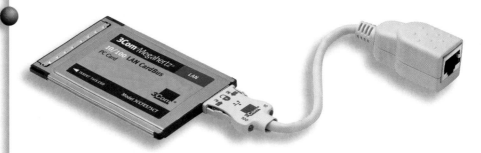

There are three categories of PC Card technologies: Type I, Type II, and Type III. The different types are typically defined by purpose. For example, Type I cards usually contain memory, Type II cards are used for network adapters, and Type III cards usually house tiny hard drives. Type I PC Cards are the thinnest available and have the fewest uses. Type III cards are the thickest and enable developers to fit disk storage devices into the card-size shell. Some PC Card adapters can hold multiple cards, greatly expanding the capabilities of the small computer.

Plug and Play

With the introduction of Windows 95, Intel-based PCs began supporting the **Plug and Play** standard, making it easier to install hardware via an existing port or expansion slot. If you use hardware that complies with Windows' Plug and Play standard, the operating system can detect a new component automatically, check for existing driver programs that will run the new device, and load necessary files. In some cases, Windows will prompt you to install the needed files from a disk. This may require restarting the system for the new hardware's settings to take effect. Still, this process is much simpler than the one required prior to Plug and Play technology, which usually forced the user to manually resolve conflicts between the new hardware and other components.

Norton Notebook

MUSICAL COMPUTERS

MIDI (Musical Instrument Digital Interface) is a digital communication protocol and hardware specification that allows electronic instruments, controllers, and computers to talk to one another. The MIDI protocol gives musicians a language to use when talking to electronic musical equipment. MIDI thus allows a musician to focus on creating and playing music rather than worrying about the ins and outs of digital communications or computer circuitry.

MIDI commands can work in real time to allow you to control several pieces of interconnected equipment from one central point. However, you can also store MIDI commands in a MIDI file. Once stored, you can re-create your sound again and again by playing the MIDI file back through a MIDI instrument or MIDI sound card with speakers.

Musicians and engineers proposed MIDI in the early 1980s as a way of standardizing the communications protocols used in the growing field of synthesized music, which at the time included keyboard synthesizers and their controllers, called sequencers. (A sequencer tells a synthesizer to play specific sounds in specific patterns). Prior to any standard, there was no guarantee that synthesizers and sequencers from different companies could talk to one another.

Since the development of the MIDI standards, MIDI has grown to include controls for many types of equipment:

◆ **MIDI Instruments.** MIDI instruments are the devices that actually make sound when they receive a MIDI signal. These devices are synthetic instruments, so they are called synthesizers. The most common MIDI instrument is a keyboard synthesizer. Other MIDI instruments include drum machines and guitar synthesizers.

◆ **MIDI Sequencers.** MIDI sequencers are devices that record, edit, and output MIDI signals. Sequencers may be hardware, similar to a traditional studio soundboard, or they may be software within a computer.

◆ **Other Devices.** With compatible MIDI hardware, a stage manager can turn on a microphone or fade out a light from the same sequencer used to control a drum machine or keyboard.

Because MIDI commands tell a device what to do rather than actually describing a sound, it is possible for MIDI instruments and their controllers to communicate back and forth. A musician can create music with these devices in several ways:

◆ **Instrument to Sequencer.** A musician can use a MIDI instrument to program a sequencer. The musician plays a song on an instrument like a keyboard. The keyboard then transmits a MIDI description back to the sequencer. Once the MIDI code is stored on the sequencer, the musician can convert the codes to written music or transmit the codes to a different instrument to get a different sound.

◆ **MIDI Codes.** A second option is for the musician to create a MIDI file manually on a sequencer. This file contains the MIDI codes that describe each MIDI event, such as playing a particular note on a keyboard.

◆ **Sheet Music.** The final option is for the musician to write the music using the sequencer's software and then let the sequencer interpret the musical notation and turn it into MIDI codes.

MIDI devices have their own built-in computers to interpret MIDI commands. However, PC sound cards may also be MIDI devices. To work with MIDI on your PC, you must have a MIDI-compatible sound card, a set of speakers or a MIDI instrument, and sequencer software.

Using MIDI-compliant sound cards and instruments, musicians can use the PC to control the creative, recording, and performing processes. A single MIDI controller can run various instruments connected together.

LESSON QUIZ

True/False

Answer the following questions by circling True or False.

True   False   **1.** The only things a computer can understand are yes and no.

True   False   **2.** Base 2 is another name for the decimal number system.

True   False   **3.** Unicode is by far the most commonly used text code system.

True   False   **4.** The CPU's control unit contains a list of all the operations that the CPU can perform.

True   False   **5.** Static RAM is considerably faster than dynamic RAM.

Multiple Choice

Circle the word or phrase that best completes each sentence.

1. The _____ standard promises to provide enough characters to cover all the world's languages.

    A. ASCII   **B.** Unicode   **C.** ISO

2. _____ are high-speed memory locations built directly into the CPU.

    A. Registers   **B.** Logic units   **C.** Neither A nor B

3. The CPU uses a _____ to store and retrieve each piece of data in memory.

    A. control unit   **B.** cache   **C.** memory address

4. The computer can move data and instructions between storage and memory, as needed, in a process called _____ .

    A. swapping   **B.** volatility   **C.** pipelining

5. A bus's _____ is measured in Mbps or MBps.

    A. clock speed   **B.** daisy chain   **C.** data transfer rate

LESSON LABS

Complete the following exercises as directed by your instructor.

1. Using the list of ASCII characters in Table 7.2, compose a sentence using ASCII text codes. Make sure the sentence includes at least six words and make it a complete sentence. Swap your ASCII sentence with a classmate, then translate his or her sentence into alphabetical characters. Time yourself. How long did it take you to translate the sentence? What does this tell you about the speed of a computer's processor?

2. Using the photographs and descriptions in this lesson's Visual Essay as a guide, determine what ports are available on your system. Then list the devices that are plugged into each port. Are any ports not in use?

3. See how much RAM your computer has. Click Start to open the Start menu; click Settings, and then click Control Panel. In the Control Panel window, double-click the System icon. In the System Properties window, click the General tab. General information about your system should appear on this tab. Note the amount of RAM, and then close all dialog boxes.

CPUs Used in Personal Computers

OVERVIEW:
The Race for the Desktop

How fast is fast enough? How powerful does a PC need to be? As software developers and users place ever-increasing demands on microcomputer systems, processor developers respond with chips of ever-increasing speed and power. Chip makers such as Intel, Motorola, Advanced Micro Devices (AMD), and others keep proving that there seems to be no end to the potential power of the personal computer.

For two decades after the birth of the personal computer, the biggest player in the PC CPU market was Intel Corporation. This dominance began to change in 1998 when several leading computer makers (most notably Compaq and Gateway, as well as others) began offering lower-priced systems using chips made by AMD and Cyrix. These microprocessors were comparable in many respects to chips made by Intel but typically offered less performance at a lower price. That situation is quickly changing, however, as Intel's competitors make rapid advances in their products' performance and chip prices become increasingly competitive.

Meantime, computer users watched the rebirth of Apple Computer, which nearly folded after losing most of its market share to competitors. Apple's savior, as it turned out, was an odd-looking PC named the iMac—a low-priced system that performed as well as higher-priced IBM-compatible PCs. Like other Macintosh systems, the iMac uses processors made by Motorola.

This lesson looks at the processors most commonly found in personal computers, and their manufacturers. You will learn how these CPUs are typically differentiated from one another, and see how their performance is measured.

OBJECTIVES

- Name the three best-known families of CPUs and list their differences.
- List all the processors in Intel's 80x86 line of processors.
- Identify the key processor families from AMD and Cyrix.
- Differentiate the processors used in Macintosh and IBM-compatible PCs.
- Define the terms *CISC* and *RISC*.
- Identify one advantage of using multiple processors in a computer.

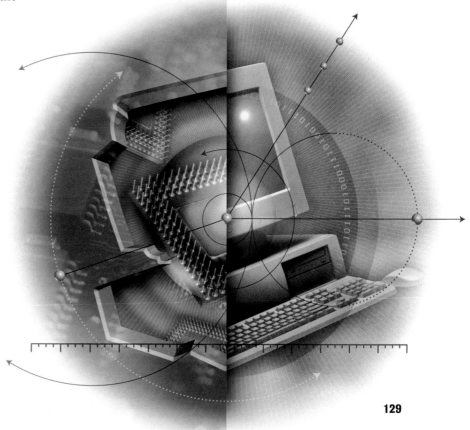

INTEL PROCESSORS

The Intel Corporation is the largest manufacturer of microchips in the world and is historically the leading provider of chips for PCs. In fact, Intel invented the microprocessor, the so-called computer on a chip, in 1971 with the 4004 model (see Figure 8.1). This led to the first microcomputers that began appearing in 1975. Even so, Intel's success in this market was not guaranteed until 1981 when IBM released the first IBM PC, which was based on the Intel 8088 microprocessor.

Since 1981, all IBM personal computers and compatibles based on IBM's design have been created around Intel's chips. A list of those chips, along with their basic specifications, is shown in Table 8.1. Although the 8088 was the first chip to be used in an IBM PC, IBM actually used an earlier chip, the 8086, in a subsequent model called the IBM PC XT. The chips that came later—80286, 80386, 80486, Pentium, Pentium Pro, Pentium II, Pentium III, Celeron, and Xeon lines—correspond to certain design standards established by the 8086. This line of chips is often referred to as the 80*x*86 line.

The basic structural design of each chip, known as **architecture,** has grown steadily in sophistication and complexity. The architecture of the 8086 contained only a few thousand transistors, but today's powerful Pentium III Xeon processors contain 9.5 million. This increasingly complex architecture is primarily responsible for the continually increasing power and speed of the Intel processor line.

Figure 8.1
Intel's first microprocessor, the 4004.

Table 8.1		Intel Chips and Their Specifications					
Model	Intro. Year	Data Bus Capacity	Register Size	Addressable Memory	Clock Speeds		Number of Transistors
8086	1978	16 bit	16 bit	1 MB	5 MHz, 8 MHz, 10 MHz		29,000
8088	1979	8 bit	16 bit	1 MB	5 MHz, 8 MHz		29,000
80286	1982	16 bit	16 bit	16 MB	6 MHz, 8 MHz, 10 MHz, 12 MHz, 25 MHz		134,000
80386	1985	32 bit	32 bit	4 GB	16 MHz, 20 MHz, 25 MHz, 33 MHz		275,000
80486	1989	32 bit	32 bit	4 GB	25 MHz, 33 MHz, 50 MHz, 66 MHz, 75 MHz, 100 MHz		1.2 million
Pentium	1993	64 bit	32 bit	4 GB	60 MHz, 66 MHz, 100 MHz, 120 MHz, 133 MHz, 150 MHz, 166 MHz		3.1 million
Pentium Pro	1995	64 bit	32 bit	64 GB	150 MHz, 166 MHz, 200 MHz		5.5 million
Pentium II	1997	64 bit	32 bit	64 GB	233 MHz, 266 MHz, 300 MHz, 333 MHz, 350 MHz, 400 MHz, 450 MHz		7.5 million
Pentium II Xeon	1998	64 bit	64 bit	64 GB	400 MHz, 450 MHz, and higher		7.5 million
Pentium II Celeron	1998	64 bit	64 bit	64 GB	266 MHz, 300 MHz, 333 MHz, 366 MHz, 400 MHz, 433 MHz, 466 MHz, 500 MHz		7.5 million*
Pentium III	1999	64 bit	64/128 bit	64 GB	450 MHz, 500 MHz, 550 MHz, 600 MHz, 750 MHz, 1 GHz, and higher		9.5 million
Pentium III Xeon.	1999	64 bit	64/128 bit	64 GB	500 MHz, 550 MHz, and higher		9.5 million

*Later versions of the Celeron processor have a total of 19 million transistors

Pre-Pentium Processors

Intel's first microprocessors were fairly simple by today's standards but provided a level of computing power never before seen in a single processing chip (see Figure 8.2). As the 8086 grew into the 80286, Intel developed methods for squeezing more transistors onto the surface of its chips and enabling processors to handle more instructions per second and access greater amounts of memory.

The growing complexity of the architecture also allowed Intel to incorporate some sophisticated techniques for processing. One major improvement that came with the 80386 is called **virtual 8086 mode.** In this mode, a single 80386 chip could achieve the processing power of sixteen separate 8086 chips, each running a separate copy of the operating system. The capability for virtual 8086 mode enabled a single 80386 chip to run different programs at the same time—a technique known as **multitasking.** All the chips following the 386 have the capacity for multitasking.

Introduced in 1989, the 80486 did not feature any radically new processor technology. Instead, it combined a 386 processor, a math coprocessor, and a cache memory controller on a single chip. Because these chips were no longer separate, they no longer had to communicate through the bus. This innovation increased the speed of the system dramatically.

Figure 8.2
Intel's first family of processors—the 8086, 8088, 80286, 80386, and 80486—formed the foundation of personal computers for more than a decade.

0-1 binary bits
byte-8bits
characters

The Pentium

The next member of the Intel family of microprocessors was the **Pentium** (see Figure 8.3), introduced in 1993. With the Pentium, Intel broke its tradition of numeric model names—partly to prevent other chip manufacturers from using similar numeric names, which implied that their products were functionally identical to Intel's chips. The Pentium, however, is still considered part of the 80x86 series.

The Pentium chip itself represented another leap forward for microprocessors. The speed and power of the Pentium dwarfed all its predecessors' performance in the Intel line. In practical terms, the Pentium runs application programs approximately five times faster than a 486 at the same clock speed. Part of the Pentium's speed comes from a **superscalar** architecture, which allows the chip to process more than one instruction in a single clock cycle.

Figure 8.3
The Intel Pentium.

Figure 8.4
The Intel Pentium Pro.

The Pentium Pro

Introduced in 1995, the **Pentium Pro** reflected still more design breakthroughs (see Figure 8.4). The Pentium Pro can process three instructions in a single clock cycle—one more than the Pentium. In addition, the Pentium Pro can achieve faster clock speeds.

Intel coined the phrase *dynamic execution* to describe the chip's capability of executing program instructions most efficiently, but not necessarily in the order in which they were written. This out-of-order execution means that instructions that cannot be executed immediately are put aside while the Pentium Pro begins processing other instructions.

Pentium With MMX Technology

The Pentium also supports a technology called **MMX.** MMX includes three primary architectural design enhancements: new instructions, SIMD process, and additional cache. MMX includes a set of fifty-seven instructions that increase the multimedia capabilities of a computer chip. These instructions process audio, video, and graphical data more efficiently than non-MMX processors. The MMX **single instruction multiple data (SIMD)** process enables one instruction to perform the same function on multiple pieces of data, reducing the number of loops required to handle video, audio, animation, and graphical data.

The Pentium II

Figure 8.5
The Intel Pentium II.

Intel released the **Pentium II** processor in the summer of 1997. The Pentium II has 7.5 million transistors and execution ratings of up to 450 MHz. Like the Pentium Pro, the Pentium II supports MMX technology and dynamic execution.

The Pentium II differs from other Pentium models because it is encased in a plastic and metal cartridge instead of the wafer format used for other chips. This cartridge is necessary because of the Pentium II's **single edge connector** connection scheme (see Figure 8.5). Instead of plugging into the regular chip slot on the motherboard, the Pentium II plugs into a special slot called Slot One, which requires a motherboard design different from that used with previous Intel processors. Enclosed within the Pentium II cartridge is the core processor and the L2 cache chip, which enables high-performance operations.

In 1998, Intel expanded the Pentium II family by announcing two new processors—**Celeron** and **Xeon**—which adapted Pentium II technology for new markets. The Celeron processor features many of the capabilities of the Pentium II but operates at slightly slower speeds and is designed for entry-level personal computers priced in the $1000 range. The Xeon Pentium II incorporates a larger Level-2 cache and features enhanced multiprocessing capabilities. The Xeon is designed for use in network server computers and workstations.

Another advantage of the Pentium II is its ability to work with a 100 MHz data bus. Prior to the release of the Pentium II, data buses typically ran at speeds of 66 MHz or less. Improved data bus speeds mean faster overall performance.

The Pentium III

In 1999, Intel introduced the **Pentium III** processor (see Figure 8.6), which features several enhancements and incremental performance gains over the Pentium II. With speeds that reached 1 GHz in March 2000, the Pentium III includes seventy new built-in instructions and improved multimedia-handling features. The Pentium III's biggest single enhancement is **streaming SIMD extensions (SSE),** an improved version of the MMX technology that results in faster video and graphics handling. Like the Pentium II, the Pentium III uses a cartridge-and-slot configuration, but the Pentium III uses a newer Slot 2 system.

Early Pentium III systems took advantage of the 100 MHz bus, like the Pentium II. Shortly after the Pentium III's release, Intel announced a 133 MHz bus, further improving the Pentium III's overall performance.

A Xeon version of the Pentium III was released later in 1999. Like the Pentium II Xeon, the newer Xeon provides even faster performance than the ordinary Pentium III by offering larger cache (up to 2 MB).

ADVANCED MICRO DEVICES (AMD) PROCESSORS

In 1998, **Advanced Micro Devices (AMD)** emerged as a primary competitor to Intel's dominance in the IBM-compatible PC market. Until that time, AMD processors were typically found in low-end, low-priced home and small business computers selling for less than $1000. With the release of the K6 and Athlon processor series (see Figure 8.7), AMD proved that it could compete feature for feature with many of Intel's best-selling products. AMD even began a new race for the fastest PC processor.

The K6 Processors

Known for years as a maker of budget processors, AMD burst into prominence with its **K6** line of chips, which quickly became popular among major computer makers for both desktop and notebook PCs. While the K6 was not entirely compatible with Intel processors and initially performed at slower speeds, AMD continued to improve the line and eventually began to overtake Intel in some markets.

AMD's K6-2 processor was released in 1998. With speeds ranging from 300 to 475 MHz and a 100 MHz data bus, the K6-2 offers Level-2 cache sizes as great as 2 MB (compared to the Pentium II's 512 KB L2 cache). The K6-2 also features 64-bit registers and can address 4 GB of memory.

In early 1999, AMD released the K6-III as a head-to-head competitor with the Pentium III. Operating at speeds of 400 and 450 MHz, the K6-III provides a smaller L2 cache but features a new Level-3 cache (up to 2 MB) not found in the Pentium III.

K6 chips feature MMX technology. Although neither K6 offers SSE instructions, both feature AMD's 3DNow! technology, which provides enhanced multimedia performance.

Figure 8.6
The Intel Pentium III.

NORTON
ONLINE

Visit **www.glencoe.com/norton/online/** for more information on **Advanced Micro Devices'** line of microprocessors.

Figure 8.7
The AMD K6-III and the AMD Athlon.

The Athlon Processor

With its release in August 1999, AMD's **Athlon** processor was the fastest microprocessor available, operating at speeds up to 650 MHz. (In March 2000, the Athlon was the first PC-class CPU to reach an operating speed of 1 GHz.) The Athlon outperformed the Pentium III in tests because it could perform more instructions at one time. Utilizing a bus speed of 100 MHz at the time of its release, the Athlon processor was actually designed to work with bus speeds of 200 MHz. The Athlon includes a 64 KB Level-1 cache and 512 KB of Level-2 cache. Capable of addressing 64 GB of memory, the Athlon also features 64-bit registers.

Self Check

Answer the following questions by filling in the blank(s).

1. The basic structural design of a processor is called its _Architecture_.

2. A processor's ability to run different programs at one time is called _Multitasking_

3. The _Athlon_ processor can operate at bus speeds of up to 200 MHz.

NORTON ONLINE

Visit **www.glencoe.com/norton/online/** for more information on **Cyrix** products.

CYRIX PROCESSORS

Cyrix began as a maker of specialized microchips, but in the mid-1990s the company began making processors that competed with Intel's products. Cyrix focuses its attention on PCs that sell for less than $1000.

In 1997, Cyrix introduced the **MediaGX** processor, a Pentium-compatible microprocessor that integrated audio and graphics functions and operated at speeds of 233 MHz and higher. In 1999, however, Cyrix was sold by National Semiconductor, Inc., who maintained ownership of the MediaGX product line. At the time of the sale, National's intention was to market the MediaGX technology for use in smart appliances, network computers, and other small computing devices.

Under the auspices of its new owner, VIA Technologies, Inc., Cyrix continued to develop its **MII** line of microprocessors (see Figure 8.8). This Pentium II–class processor operates at speeds of 433 MHz and can be found in PCs from various manufacturers.

Figure 8.8
The Cyrix MII processor.

MOTOROLA PROCESSORS

Motorola Corporation is another major manufacturer of microprocessors for small computers. As mentioned earlier, Apple's Macintosh computers use Motorola processors. Other computer manufacturers, including workstation manufacturers such as Sun Microsystems, have also relied heavily on Motorola chips. They were an early favorite among companies that built larger, UNIX-based computers, such as the NCR Tower series and the AT&T 3B series.

Motorola offers two families of processor chips. The first is known as the $680x0$ family. The second, designated MPC, has a different architecture and is known as the PowerPC family.

COMPUTERS
in your career

Processors and Your Career

If your career involves the use of a computer, it is wise to become familiar with how a computer processes data. Even if your activities are limited to using a computer and not supporting or building one, it is helpful to have an idea of which components are most important in processing data and which components affect the speed of your computer. This knowledge will enable you to make sound decisions on upgrading and replacing your hardware.

Depending on your career track, it may be necessary to learn all you can about how a computer processes data. The following list describes some of the fields in which you need to know the details of how computers process data.

♦ **Information Systems (IS) Managers and Technicians.** If you are interested in a career in information systems, an understanding of how a PC processes data is a must. In many organizations, IS managers have the responsibility of choosing the types of computers that a company uses. Further, the IS department usually must set up and administer a company's PC installation. All three of these tasks require that the IS manager and staff have an in-depth knowledge of how PCs process data, use RAM, and are affected by CPU type and speed. IS personnel must also understand the different types of data bus architecture.

♦ **Software Engineers and Programmers.** Although software is usually described as separate from hardware, software engineers and programmers must understand how a PC processes data to be able to write computer programs. Software engineers and programmers must know how to optimize their program to take advantage of the CPU architecture and the RAM that a computer uses. Also, programmers working with certain types of software must become proficient in the different text codes used by the PCs they work on, in particular the ASCII and Unicode tables.

♦ **Hardware Configuration Personnel.** If you are interested in a hardware support career, knowing how a computer represents data in binary code is a must. This knowledge will enable you to troubleshoot many problems that users encounter between the hardware and operating system. A thorough knowledge of how a computer uses the CPU to process data and keeping up-to-date on the types of CPUs available are essential to success in a hardware support position. Finally, to round out your knowledge and thus handle as many hardware problems as possible, you should become familiar with the different types of memory a PC uses and the types of data buses available.

♦ **System Designers and Engineers.** If your plans lead to a career in computer hardware design or engineering, an in-depth knowledge of processors and their function is a must. Whether you are building PCs or designing cutting-edge manufacturing systems, you will need to know how to choose or create the right processor for the job.

The 680x0 Series

Although the 68000 chip is best known as the foundation of the original Macintosh, it actually predates the Mac by several years. In fact, IBM considered using the 68000 in the first IBM PC. Although Motorola's 68000 chip (introduced in 1979) was more powerful than Intel's 8088, subsequent improvements to the Motorola chip were made in smaller increments than Intel's giant performance leaps. By the time Motorola introduced the 68060 chip in 1993, Intel was promoting the Pentium. In an attempt to regain market share, Motorola initiated the development of the new PowerPC chip.

The PowerPC Series

The **PowerPC** chip had an unusual beginning. Two industry rivals, IBM and Apple, joined forces with Motorola in 1991, ostensibly to dethrone Intel from its preeminence in the PC chip market. The hardware portion of their efforts focused on the PowerPC chip, the first of which was the 601. Following closely on its heels was the 603, a low-power processor suitable for notebook computers. Its successors, the 604 and 604e, are high-power chips designed for high-end desktop systems. With the introduction of the 620 late in 1995, PowerPC chips established a new performance record for microprocessors. A handful of small 620-based machines working together offers about the same computing power as an IBM 370 mainframe. The PowerPC 750 chip (266 MHz) was released for desktop and mobile computers that need significant computing power in a low-voltage processor. The PowerPC 750 was designed for multimedia, small business, and mobile applications.

Figure 8.9
Apple's Power Mac G4 system is based on the powerful PowerPC G4 processor.

The **G3** chip, released in 1998, provides even more power for such applications. Apple's iMac and Power Mac personal computer lines are built around the G3 chip and offer better performance and speed than Pentium II–based systems at a lower cost.

In 1999, Apple released the newest member of the PowerPC family—the **G4**—and described the processor as having "the heart of a supercomputer miniaturized onto a sliver of silicon" (see Figure 8.9). Operating at speeds of 500 MHz and higher, the G4's 128-bit processor is capable of performing 1 billion floating-point operations (one **gigaflop**) per second. The G4 processor features 1 MB of Level-2 cache and a bus speed of 100 MHz. As you will see in the next section, PowerPC, G3, and G4 chips are different from the earlier 68000 series from the ground up.

RISC PROCESSORS

Both the Motorola 680x0 and Intel 80x86 families are **complex instruction set computing (CISC)** processors. The instruction sets for these CPUs are large, typically containing 200 to 300 instructions.

A newer theory in microprocessor design holds that if the instruction set for the CPU is kept small and simple, each instruction will execute in much less time, allowing the processor to complete more instructions during a given period. CPUs designed according to this theory are called **reduced instruction set computing**

(**RISC**) processors. RISC instruction sets are considerably smaller than those used by CISC processors. The RISC design, which is used in the PowerPC but was first implemented in the mid-1980s, results in a faster and less expensive processor. Because of the way the Pentium and its spin-offs process instructions, they are called RISC-like, but their architecture is still based on complex instruction set computing.

RISC technology has been the engine of midsize computers such as the IBM RS/6000 and high-end UNIX workstations such as those built by Sun Microsystems, Hewlett-Packard, and NCR. RISC CPUs are also found in printers and other devices that have their own internal CPUs. The PowerPC and G3/G4 processors reflected a major move on the part of industry giants toward using RISC technology in desktop and notebook computers.

Motorola is not alone in producing both RISC and CISC processors. In 1989, Intel introduced the i860, which was a 64-bit RISC chip that earned the distinction of being the first chip to contain more than 1 million transistors. Other RISC processors include the Intel i960, the Motorola 88100, the NEC Electronics VR4000 series, and the Compaq (formerly Digital Equipment Corporation) Alpha (see Figure 8.10). Sun Microsystems also produces a RISC processor, known as SPARC, which it uses in its UNIX workstations.

Figure 8.10
This AlphaServer 1200 system is a RISC-based enterprise server. Some of the most powerful network servers and workstations are based on RISC technology.

Whether CISC or RISC technology will be the basis of most future microprocessors has yet to be determined, but early bets are on models of RISC chips with reduced power consumption.

PARALLEL PROCESSING

An emerging school of thought on producing faster computers is to build them with more than one processor. This type of system uses **parallel-processing** techniques; that is, the system harnesses multiple processors that share the processing workload. The result is a system that can handle a much greater flow of data, complete more tasks in a shorter time, and deal with the demands of many input and output devices. Parallel processing is also called **multiprocessing (MP)** or **symmetric multiprocessing (SMP).**

Parallel processing is not a new idea in the minicomputer, mainframe, and supercomputer arenas. Many powerful midrange systems (such as the Compaq AlphaServer 1200), mainframes (like the IBM 3090), and supercomputers (including the Cray X MP 4 and others) support multiple processors. Some companies are developing computers with 256, 512, and even thousands of microprocessors, known as **massively parallel processors (MPP).**

At the other end of the spectrum, dual-processor and quad-processor versions of PCs are available today and are commonly used as network servers, Internet host computers, and stand-alone workstations. In fact, recent generations of standard PC microprocessors incorporate a measure of parallel processing by using pipelining techniques to execute more than one instruction at a time.

Visit **www.glencoe.com/norton/online/** for more information on **RISC** processors.

FUTURE

The Future of Processing

It is safe to say that computers will be faster in the future. In fact, many computer industry experts agree that the current rate of progress should hold true for the next twenty years. Where experts disagree, however, is how computers will become faster. Existing technologies eventually will reach their limits; for example, standard silicon processors will someday hold all the microscopic transistors they possibly can.

New materials and methods will be required if PC makers want to continue building higher-performance systems. A few developments are visible on the horizon that may already be available by the time you read this text:

◆ **Coppermine.** Intel's next version of the Pentium III, code-named Coppermine, is expected to be paired with a 133 MHz bus and increased cache memory, and should provide initial clock speeds of 500 MHz. Coppermine is expected to be Intel's first processor based on 0.18-micron technology. This measurement refers to the distance between processors imprinted on the chip. The closer that transistors can be placed to one another, the more that can be fit on a chip. On the first Pentium III processor, for example, transistors are spaced 0.25 microns apart. A micron equals 1000 nanometers, or one-billionth of a meter.

◆ **Merced.** Intel's first 64-bit processor, code-named Merced, has been in the news since 1997, when it was first announced as a joint development project by Intel and Hewlett-Packard. Merced's primary innovations will be the combination of CISC and RISC processors on a single chip and the use of 0.18-micron technology. Merced is expected to execute as many as 8 billion instructions per second, with initial operating speeds of 800 MHz.

◆ **Willamette and McKinley.** These Intel next-generation processors follow Merced. Using 0.18-micron technology, these processors are expected to provide still faster performance levels.

Look for other developments in and around the processor, all of which may lead to even faster PCs in the future:

◆ **Faster Buses.** Intel and AMD have already proved that faster bus technologies lead to faster overall performance because they enable the processor to move data from point to point in less time. Someday, bus speeds may be matched to processor speed. Computers may also gain improved performance when a single data bus standard (such as the USB standard) is adopted for all devices.

◆ **Larger Caches.** AMD has added a third level of cache memory to its K6-III processor, and other vendors may do the same. While cache memory levels have remained fairly static for the past several years, they will likely increase dramatically. Look for cache speeds to increase, as well. The fastest L2 caches operate at about half the processor's speed, which makes cached data available almost instantly. Larger and faster cache systems consume more power and memory management, and increase the cost of the processor.

◆ **Copper Transistor Technology.** In 1997, IBM developed a method for using copper rather than aluminum for the transistors on microprocessor circuits. This method enables transistors to be placed closer together. Because copper is a better conductor of electricity, copper-based transistors run faster than aluminum transistors. Copper-based transistors are now available in Intel's newest chips and in the Macintosh G4 computer.

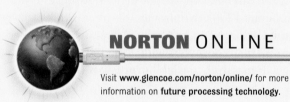

NORTON ONLINE

Visit **www.glencoe.com/norton/online/** for more information on **future processing technology.**

LESSON QUIZ

True/False

Answer the following questions by circling True or False.

True   False   **1.** Intel's line of PC processors is sometimes called the 80x86 line.

True   False   **2.** Superscalar architecture enables computers to use more than one processor at a time.

True   False   **3.** AMD's K6-III processor features a Level-3 cache, which is not found in the Pentium III.

True   False   **4.** A gigaflop is the equivalent of one-billionth of a meter.

True   False   **5.** Parallel processing uses multiple processors to share the workload.

Multiple Choice

Circle the word or phrase that best completes each sentence.

1. By running in virtual 8086 mode, the Intel 80386 processor can perform _____ .
   A. multitasking   **B.** parallel processing   **C.** neither A nor B

2. The _____ process enables one instruction to perform the same function on multiple pieces of data.
   A. superscalar   **B.** symmetric multiprocessing   **C.** single instruction multiple data

3. The Pentium III processor attaches to the motherboard via the _____ system.
   A. Slot 1   **B.** Slot 2   **C.** Slot 3

4. The _____ chip originated through a partnership of IBM and Apple.
   A. MediaGX   **B.** PowerPC   **C.** Alpha

5. The instruction set for a _____ processor usually contains 200 to 300 instructions.
   A. CISC   **B.** SMP   **C.** RISC

LESSON LABS

To view information about your computer's components, follow these steps:

A. Click the Start button, click Settings, and then click Control Panel. In the Control Panel window, double-click the System icon.

B. In the System Properties dialog box, click the Device Manager tab to view the list of categories of devices attached to your system. If a category is preceded by a plus sign (+), click this symbol to display all the devices in that category.

C. To read about a device, click its name; then click Properties. A dialog box will appear displaying information about the selected device. *Warning:* Do not make any changes.

D. Review the properties for your system's disk drives, ports, and system devices.

E. Click Cancel to close any dialog boxes. When finished, close the Control Panel window.

LESSON 7: Transforming Data Into Information

How Computers Represent Data

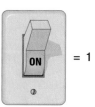

= 1

- Computer data is reduced to binary numbers because computer processing is performed by transistors that have only two possible states: on and off.

- The binary number system works the same way as the decimal system, except that it has only two available symbols (0 and 1) rather than ten (0, 1, 2, 3, 4, 5, 6, 7, 8, and 9).

= 0

- A single unit of data is called a bit; 8 bits make up 1 byte.

- In the most common text-code set, ASCII, each character consists of 1 byte of data. In the Unicode text-code set, each character consists of 2 bytes of data.

How Computers Process Data

- A microcomputer's processing takes place in the central processing unit, the two main parts of which are the control unit and the arithmetic logic unit (ALU).

- Within the CPU, program instructions are retrieved and translated with the help of an internal instruction set and the accompanying microcode.

- The CPU follows a set of steps for each instruction it carries out. This set of steps is called the machine cycle. By using a technique called pipelining, many CPUs can process more than one instruction at a time.

- The actual manipulation of data takes place in the ALU, which is connected to the registers that hold data and program instructions while they are being processed.

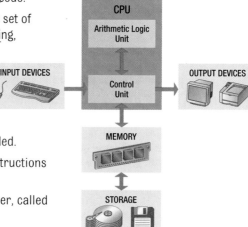

- Random-access memory (RAM) is volatile (or temporary). Programs and data can be written to and erased from RAM as needed.

- Read-only memory (ROM) is nonvolatile (or permanent). It holds instructions that run the computer when the power is first turned on.

- The CPU accesses each location in memory by using a unique number, called the memory address.

Factors Affecting Processing Speed

- The size of the registers, also called word size, determines the amount of data with which the computer can work at one time.

- The amount of RAM can affect speed because the CPU can keep more of the active program and data in memory, which is faster than storage on disk.

- The computer's system clock sets the pace for the CPU by using a vibrating quartz crystal. The faster the clock, the more instructions the CPU can process per second.

- The system bus has two parts—the data bus and the address bus—both of which are located on the motherboard.

- The width of the data bus determines how many bits can be transmitted at a time between the CPU and other devices.

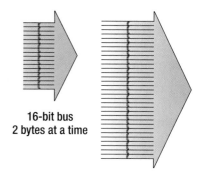

16-bit bus
2 bytes at a time

32-bit bus
4 bytes at a time

- Peripheral devices can be connected to the CPU by way of an expansion bus.

- Cache memory is a type of high-speed memory that contains the most recent data and instructions that have been loaded by the CPU. The amount of cache memory has a tremendous impact on the computer's speed.

Extending the Processor's Power to Other Devices

- External devices—such as those used for input and output—are connected to the system by ports on the back of the computer.

- Most computers come with a serial port and a parallel port. A serial port transmits 1 bit of data at a time; a parallel port transmits 1 byte (8 bits) of data at a time.

- If the computer does not have the right type of port for an external device (or if all the existing ports are in use), you can install an expansion board into one of the PC's empty expansion slots.

- Bus technologies such as Universal Serial Bus (USB) and IEEE 1394 enable the user to connect many devices through a single port.

- Small Computer System Interface (SCSI) is an older standard for extending the bus to multiple devices through a single port.

LESSON 8: CPUs Used in Personal Computers

Processors

- Since 1978, Intel's processors have evolved from the 8086 and the 8088 to the 80286, 80386, and 80486, and then to the Pentium family of processors (which includes the Pentium, Pentium Pro, Pentium with MMX, Pentium II, Pentium III, Celeron, and Xeon processors). With the Pentium III processor, Intel achieved clock speeds greater than 500 MHz.

- Advanced Micro Devices (AMD) was long known as a provider of low-performance processors for use in low-cost computers. That reputation changed in 1998, however, with the release of the K6 line of processors, which challenged Intel's processors in terms of both price and performance. With the K6-III processor, AMD broke the 600 MHz barrier, claiming the fastest processor title for the first time in IBM-compatible computers.

- Cyrix began as a specialty chip maker but eventually began producing microprocessors including the MediaGX processor and now the MII series of processors.

- Motorola makes the CPUs used in Macintosh and PowerPC computers. Macintosh processors use a different architecture than IBM-compatible PC processors.

- PowerPC processors are RISC processors. Instruction sets for RISC processors are kept smaller than those used in CISC chips. This smaller size enables the processor to run faster and process more instructions per second. RISC processors are found in Apple microcomputers, some workstations, and many minicomputers and mainframe systems. They are also the basis for many small digital devices, such as H/PCs.

Parallel Processing

- A parallel-processing system harnesses the power of multiple processors in a single system, enabling them to share processing tasks.

- In a massively parallel processor (MPP) system, many processors are used. Some MPP systems use thousands of processors simultaneously.

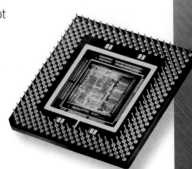

UNIT REVIEW

KEY TERMS

After completing this unit, you should be able to define the following terms.

Accelerated Graphics Port (AGP), 118
accelerator card, 123
adapter, 123
address bus, 117
Advanced Micro Devices (AMD), 133
architecture, 130
arithmetic logic unit (ALU), 111
arithmetic operation, 111
ASCII, 108
Athlon, 134
binary number system, 106
bit, 107
board, 123
bus, 117
cache memory, 119
card, 123
Celeron, 132
clock cycle, 117
clock speed, 117
complex instruction set computing (CISC), 136
configure, 123
control unit, 110
Cyrix, 134
data bus, 117
data transfer rate, 118
decimal number system, 106

decode, 112
dual in-line memory module (DIMM), 116
dynamic RAM (DRAM), 113
EBCDIC, 108
execution cycle, 112
expansion board, 123
expansion slot, 123
fetch, 112
FireWire, 118
flash memory, 114
G3, 136
G4, 136
gigaflop, 136
hertz (Hz), 116
IEEE 1394, 118
Industry Standard Architecture (ISA), 118
instruction cycle, 112
instruction set, 110
K6, 133
Level-1 (L1) cache, 119
Level-2 (L2) cache, 119
local bus, 118
logical operation, 111
MII, 134
machine cycle, 112
massively parallel processors (MPP), 137
MediaGX, 134

megabits per second (Mbps), 118
megabytes per second (MBps), 118
megahertz (MHz), 116
memory address, 113
microcode, 110
MMX, 132
Motorola, 134
multiprocessing (MP), 137
multitasking, 131
Musical Instrument Digital Interface (MIDI), 123
nonvolatile, 112
parallel interface, 121
parallel processing, 137
PC Card, 126
Pentium, 131
Pentium II, 132
Pentium III, 133
Pentium Pro, 132
Peripheral Component Interconnect (PCI), 118
pipelining, 112
Plug and Play, 126
PowerPC, 136
reduced instruction set computing (RISC), 136
register, 111
serial interface, 121

single edge connector, 132
single in-line memory module (SIMM), 116
single instruction multiple data (SIMD), 132
Small Computer System Interface (SCSI), 122
static RAM (SRAM), 113
store, 112
streaming SIMD extensions (SSE), 133
superscalar, 131
swap in, 116
swap out, 115
symmetric multiprocessing (SMP), 137
system clock, 116
text code, 107
transistor, 105
Unicode, 108
universal asynchronous receiver-transmitter (UART), 121
Universal Serial Bus (USB), 118
virtual 8086 mode, 131
volatile, 112
word size, 114
Xeon, 132

KEY TERMS QUIZ

Fill in each blank with one of the terms listed under Key Terms.

1. People use the ___decimal___ number system, but computers use the ___binary___ number system.

2. The term ___bit___ is a combination of the words *binary digit.*

3. The term ___ASCII___ stands for the American Standard Code for Information Interchange.

4. A processor's built-in instructions are stored as ___memory___ .

5. _____ are high-speed memory locations built directly into the CPU, which hold data while it is being processed.

6. In the first step of a machine cycle, the control unit must _____ a command or data from memory.

7. Two new bus types, called _____ and _____ , provide fast data transfer speeds and eliminate the need for expansion slots and boards.

8. CPU-resident cache memory is often called _____ cache. Motherboard-resident cache memory is often called _____ cache.

9. With a(n) _____ interface, data bits are transmitted one at a time through a single wire.

10. The _____ enables electronic instruments and computers to communicate with one another.

REVIEW QUESTIONS

In your own words, briefly answer the following questions.

1. What is the difference between data and information?

2. How many characters or symbols can be represented by one 8-bit byte?

3. What is the primary advantage of the Unicode Worldwide Character Standard?

4. What is the difference between arithmetic operations and logical operations, which are performed by a CPU?

5. What is the advantage of pipelining and how does it work?

6. What does someone mean when he or she refers to a "32-bit processor"?

7. What is a data bus?

8. Describe the purpose of expansion slots in a PC.

9. Intel has introduced two variations on the Pentium II processor. Name and describe them.

10. What is the primary difference between a CISC processor and a RISC processor?

DISCUSSION QUESTIONS

As directed by your instructor, discuss the following questions in class or in groups.

1. Do you think the international interchange of data provided by the Unicode character set is a worthwhile goal for computing technology? Do you see any other benefits to Unicode's widespread implementation?

2. Why is the CPU commonly referred to as the computer's "brain"? Do you think it is a good idea to use this term to describe the CPU? Why?

ETHICAL ISSUES

Computers are becoming more powerful all the time. Many people see this capability as a source of limitless benefits, but others view it as a threat. With this thought in mind, discuss the following questions in class.

1. As technology improves, processing becomes faster. It can be argued that computer technology has made Americans less patient than they were a decade ago. Do you agree? If so, do you see it as a benefit of our technological progress or a drawback? Should we restrain our urge to increase the pace of life? Be prepared to explain your position.

2. Computers are not just getting faster, they are becoming exponentially more powerful all the time. For example, many think that in the next decade artificial intelligence will be developed to the point that computers can begin reasoning—weighing facts, solving problems, perhaps even making decisions. Will people relinquish even a tiny bit of control to computers? If so, what kinds of decisions will we allow them to make for us? What risks do we run by enabling computers to become "smart" enough to solve problems or ultimately to think?

You and the Computer

Complete the following exercises using a computer in your classroom, lab, or home. No other materials are needed.

1. **Plug It In.** With your instructor observing, turn your computer and monitor off and unplug them from their power source. Then take these steps:

   A. Move to the back of the computer and inspect all the cables plugged into it. Which devices are connected to the PC and by which cables? Which port is connected to each device? Make a chart of these connections.

   B. Unplug each connection. After all students have unplugged their devices, switch places with someone and reconnect all the devices. Does the other student's system have the same connections as yours? If not, can you reconnect all its devices correctly?

   C. Return to your PC. Use your chart to see whether your system has been reconnected correctly. If not, correct the other student's mistakes. When you are sure all devices are plugged into the right ports, reconnect the PC and monitor to their power source. Turn the PC on and make sure everything is working correctly.

2. **Watch Those Files Grow.** The concept of bits and bytes may seem unimportant until you begin creating files on your computer. Then you can begin to understand how much memory and storage space your files take up (in bytes, of course). Create a file in Notepad, save it to disk, and add to the file to see how it grows by taking the following steps:

   A. On the Windows taskbar, click Start to open the Start menu. Then click Programs, Accessories, and Notepad. The Notepad text editor will open.

   B. Type two or three short paragraphs of text. When you are done, click the File menu, then click the Save As command.

   C. In the Save As dialog box, choose a drive and folder to save the new file in, and give the file a short name you can remember easily, such as SIZE-TEST.TXT.

   D. With Notepad running, click Start, then Programs, then Windows Explorer.

   E. In the Exploring window, navigate to the drive and folder where you saved your Notepad file. When you find the file, look for its size in the Size column and write it down. Close the Exploring window.

   F. Return to the Notepad window and add two or three more paragraphs of text. Then click the File menu and click the Save command to resave the file under the same name.

   G. Reopen the Exploring window. Has the file's size changed? By how much?

Internet Labs

To complete the following exercises, you need a computer with an Internet connection and a Web browser. (For more information on using these tools, see "Prerequisites" at the front of this textbook.)

1. **Learn More About Unicode.** The Unicode text code system may become universally accepted in the next few years. All operating systems, application programs, data, and

hardware architectures will start to conform to it. For this reason, learn as much as you can about Unicode and how it may affect your computing in the future. Visit the following Web sites:

- The Unicode Consortium— **http://www.unicode.org/**

- An Introduction to the Unicode Standard— **http://www.asca.com/unicode.html**

What particular aspect of Unicode do you think is most important? Why? When you are finished reviewing these Web sites, launch the Notepad application on your computer. Write and print out a three- or four-paragraph essay explaining your thoughts.

2. **Pick the Perfect Processor.** For this exercise, imagine you are planning to buy a new PC. Set a budget for yourself, then use the following links to decide which processor meets your needs best, based on your budget:

- Intel—**http://www.intel.com/**

- Apple—**http://www.apple.com/**

- Motorola—**http://www.motorola.com/**

- AMD—**http://www.amd.com/**

- Cyrix—**http://www.cyrix.com/**

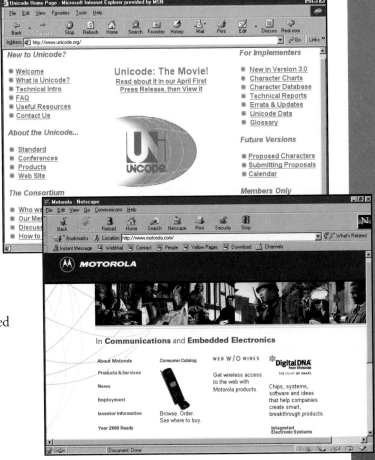

Visit the following sites and search for reviews of processors. Look for head-to-head comparisons and price/performance analysis:

- *PC Magazine*—**www.zdnet.com/pcmag/**

- Microprocessor Report—**http://www.mdronline.com/x86/microarchitecture/**

- Dr. Dobb's Microprocessor Center—**http://www.x86.org/**

When you are finished, compare your findings with your classmates. What processors did they pick? What price/performance criteria did they use as the basis for their decisions?

IBE Labs

If you have the Interactive Browser Edition (IBE) CD-ROM for this textbook, you may complete the following interactive exercises using the instructions provided in the IBE.

1. **Data or Information?** Classify the examples provided.

2. **Labeling.** Create a chart to show how computers process data.

3. **Scavenger Hunt.** Answer questions to find a clue toward solving the puzzle.

4. **Click the Switch.** Turn ASCII switches on and off to achieve results.

UNIT 5

Storing Information in a Computer

UNIT OBJECTIVES

Identify the two main categories of storage technology.

Explain how storage devices record and retrieve data.

Explain how a computer locates data stored on magnetic media.

List three criteria for measuring the performance of storage devices.

Name four types of common disk drive interfaces.

UNIT CONTENTS

This chapter contains the following lessons:

Lesson 9: Types of Storage Devices

➤ Categorizing Storage Devices
➤ Magnetic Storage Devices
➤ Optical Storage Devices

Lesson 10: Measuring Drive Performance

➤ Average Access Time
➤ File Compression
➤ Data Transfer Rate
➤ Drive-Interface Standards

Types of Storage Devices

OVERVIEW:
An Ever-Increasing Need

If you ask several people to name the most important feature in a computer, you will probably get two answers. Many people believe a fast processor and lots of RAM are essential to a satisfying PC experience. Just about as many people (especially experienced users) believe that storage is the most important feature in a PC. After all, a fast processor will not help if the computer cannot store all the data and programs you want to use.

Software developers help drive the need for larger, faster storage devices. Applications and operating systems grow larger all the time, requiring more and more storage space. WordPerfect Office 2000, for example, requires about 280 MB of disk space for a typical installation, while Microsoft Windows 98 can take up 295 MB. New versions of applications typically produce larger data files (and operating systems create bigger system files) than previous versions did, placing storage space at a higher premium.

For these reasons, computer storage systems have grown in capacity and speed at about the same rate as processors. The newest home PCs feature storage capacities once found only in the most sophisticated corporate systems. Users can choose from a dizzying and constantly changing array of storage options to complement their systems' built-in storage devices.

OBJECTIVES

- List four common types of magnetic storage devices.
- Identify three common uses for floppy disks.
- Name the four areas that are created on a magnetic disk.
- Explain how data is stored on the surface of a magnetic disk.
- Identify four common types of optical storage devices.
- Explain how data is stored on the surface of an optical disk.
- List three variations on optical disk technology.

CATEGORIZING STORAGE DEVICES

The physical components or materials on which data is stored are called **storage media.** The hardware components that write data to, and read it from, storage media are called **storage devices.** For example, a diskette (sometimes called a floppy disk or simply a "floppy") is a storage medium (medium is the singular form of media), whereas a diskette drive is a storage device.

The two main categories of storage technology used today are **magnetic storage** and **optical storage.** Although most storage devices and media employ one technology or the other, some use both.

The primary types of magnetic storage are as follows:

◆ Diskettes

◆ Hard disks (both fixed and removable)

◆ High-capacity floppy disks

◆ Disk cartridges

◆ Magnetic tape

The primary types of optical storage are as follows:

◆ Compact Disk Read-Only Memory (CD-ROM)

◆ Digital Video Disk Read-Only Memory (DVD-ROM)

◆ CD-Recordable (CD-R)

◆ CD-ReWritable (CD-RW)

◆ PhotoCD

MAGNETIC STORAGE DEVICES

The purpose of storage devices is to hold data—even when the computer is turned off—so the data can be used whenever it is needed. Storage involves the processes of writing data to the storage medium and reading data from the storage medium. Writing data means recording data on the surface of the disk, where it is stored for later use. Reading data means retrieving the data from the disk's surface and transferring it into the computer's memory for use by the operating system or an application program.

Because they all use the same medium (the material on which the data is stored), diskette drives, hard disk drives, and tape drives use similar techniques for writing and reading data. The surfaces of diskettes, hard disks, and magnetic tape are all coated with a magnetically sensitive material, such as iron oxide, which reacts to a magnetic field.

You may remember from high school science projects that one magnet can be used to make another. For example, you can make a magnet by taking an iron bar and stroking it in one direction with a magnet. The iron bar becomes a magnet itself because its iron molecules align themselves in one direction. Thus, the iron bar becomes **polarized;** that is, its ends have opposite magnetic polarity (see Figure 9.1).

Magnetic storage devices use a similar principle to store data. Just as a transistor can represent binary data as "on" or "off," the orientation of a magnetic field can be used to represent data. A magnet has one important advantage over a transistor: it can represent "on" and "off" without a continual source of electricity.

Visit **www.glencoe.com/norton/online/** for more information on **magnetic storage media.**

Another way to make a magnet is to wrap a wire coil around an iron bar and send an electric current through the coil. This produces an *electromagnet*.

If you reverse the direction of the current, the polarity of the magnet also reverses.

Figure 9.1
How an electromagnet creates a field on a magnetic surface.

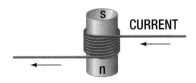

If you place the electromagnet against a magnetic surface, such as the coating of a diskette...

...the electromagnet's pole induces a magnetic field on the diskette's surface.

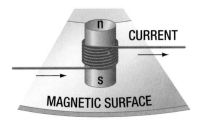

The surfaces of disks and magnetic tapes are coated with millions of tiny iron particles so that data can be stored on them. Each of these particles can act as a magnet, taking on a magnetic field when subjected to an **electromagnet.** The read/write heads of a hard disk drive, diskette drive, or tape drive contain electromagnets, which generate magnetic fields in the iron on the storage medium as the head passes over the disk or tape. As shown in Figure 9.2, the read/write heads record strings of 1s and 0s by alternating the direction of the current in the electromagnets.

To read data from a magnetic surface, the process is reversed. The read/write head passes over the disk or tape while no current is flowing through the electromagnet. Because the storage medium has a magnetic field but the head does not, the storage medium charges the magnet in the head, which causes a small current to flow through the head in one direction or the other depending on the polarity of the field. The disk or tape drive senses the direction of the flow as the storage medium passes by the head, and the data is sent from the read/write head into memory.

Magnetic Disks

As mentioned earlier, diskette drives and hard disk drives are the most commonly used storage devices in PCs. Both fall into the category of magnetic storage because they record data as magnetic fields. You will study diskettes and hard disks in detail later. This section looks at the fundamental differences and similarities between these two types of devices.

Figure 9.2
Data being recorded by a read/write head.

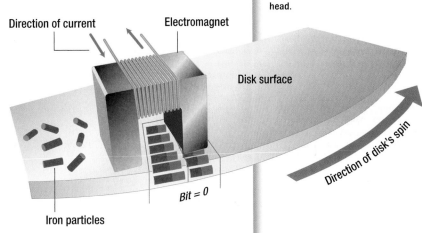

VISUAL ESSAY: POPULAR STORAGE TECHNOLOGIES

A Most new PCs come with a diskette drive, a hard disk drive, and a CD-ROM or DVD drive. Many new PCs also feature a drive for removable, high-capacity floppy disks.

B Floppy disks are common storage media, although they provide limited storage capacities. Floppies are popular because they are extremely portable and inexpensive.

C A hard disk is standard equipment on any personal computer. Because a standard hard disk is built into the system unit (and is called an internal device), you cannot see it. Most PCs feature an indicator light that blinks when the hard disk is accessed.

D Not all hard drives are internal. External hard drives, like this one made by Hewlett-Packard, can be plugged into one of the PC's ports.

E The Iomega Zip system is an example of a high-capacity floppy disk. These disks store data in quantities of 100 MB and 250 MB. All high-capacity floppy disks require a drive made especially for their use.

F This Spressa drive, made by Sony Electronics, Inc., is an example of CD-ReWritable (CD-RW) technology. Such drives enable users to create their own CD-ROM disks and to play standard audio and data compact disks.

G These two tape drives are made by Seagate Technology, Inc. Although tape drives are considered to be add-ons, many tape drives can be inserted into the system unit's drive bays, which makes them an integral part of the system. Other tape drives are external and connect to the system via an expansion slot.

CD-ROM (or DVD) drive

Diskette drive

High-capacity floppy disk drive

There are several fundamental differences between a diskette and a hard disk:

◆ A diskette contains a single, flat piece of plastic (the disk), coated with iron oxide and enclosed in a vinyl or plastic cover. A hard disk contains one or more rigid metal platters, coated with iron oxide, which are permanently encased in the hard disk drive.

◆ Diskettes are small and portable (they can be removed from diskette drives), but hard disks are usually built into the computer, so they are not portable (unless the entire computer is). Built-in hard disk drives cannot be moved easily from one computer to another. There are many different standards in use for hard drives, and the user must make sure that the computer can recognize the hard drive before the two can be used together. Exceptions are removable hard drives and external hard drives, which can simply be detached from the system.

◆ Most floppy disks store only 1.44 MB, although special floppy disks offer higher capacities. New hard disks can store several thousand times as much data as a diskette.

◆ Hard disk drives are much faster than diskette drives; their disks spin faster and they can locate data on the disk's surface in much less time.

Almost all PCs sold today come with a hard disk and one diskette drive. Many new computers also feature a third built-in magnetic storage device—a drive that uses high-capacity floppy disks.

How Data Is Organized on a Magnetic Disk

Before the computer can use a diskette to store data, the disk's surface must be magnetically mapped so that the computer can go directly to a specific point on it without searching through data. The process of mapping a diskette is called **formatting** or **initializing.** Actually, when you purchase new diskettes, they should be preformatted for either a PC or a Macintosh computer.

You may find it helpful to reformat diskettes from time to time because the process ensures that all data is deleted from the disk. During the formatting process, you can also determine whether the disk's surface has faulty spots, and you can copy important system files to the disk. You can format a floppy disk by using operating system commands, as shown in Figure 9.3.

Hard disks must also be formatted so the computer can locate data on them. When you buy a computer, its hard disk has already been formatted correctly and probably already contains some programs and data. You can format your hard disk, if necessary, but the process is a little different from formatting a floppy disk.

Modern diskettes store data on both sides of the disk (numbered as side 0 and side 1), and each side has its own read/write head. When formatting a disk, the disk drive creates a set of magnetic concentric circles, called **tracks,** on each side of the disk. The number of tracks required depends on the type of disk. Most high-density diskettes have 80 tracks on each side of the disk. A hard disk may have several hundred tracks on each side of each platter. Each track is a separate circle, like the circles on a bull's-eye target. The tracks are numbered from the outermost circle to the innermost, starting with zero, as shown in Figure 9.4 on page 152.

NORTON
ONLINE

Visit **www.glencoe.com/norton/online/** for more information on **formatting a disk.**

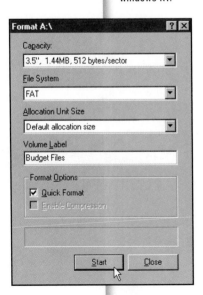

Figure 9.3
Formatting a floppy disk in Windows NT.

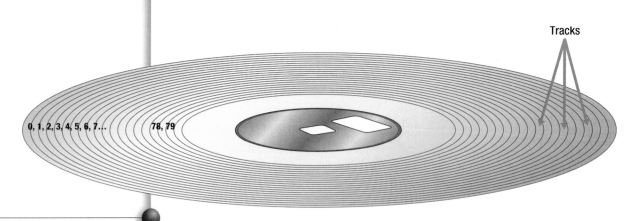

Tracks

Figure 9.4
Tracks are concentric circles
numbered from the outside in.

Each track on a disk is also split into smaller parts. Imagine slicing a disk the way you cut a pie. As shown in Figure 9.5, each slice would cut across all the disk's tracks, resulting in short segments, or **sectors.** In both diskettes and hard disks, a sector can store up to 512 bytes (0.5 KB). All the sectors on the disk are numbered in one long sequence so that the computer can access each small area on the disk with a unique number. This scheme simplifies what would be a set of two-dimensional coordinates into a single numeric address.

If a diskette has eighty tracks on each side, and each track contains eighteen sectors, then the disk has 1440 sectors (80 × 18) per side, for a total of 2880 sectors. This configuration is true regardless of the length of the track. The diskette's outermost track is longer than the innermost track, but each track is still divided into the same number of sectors. Regardless of physical size, all of a diskette's sectors hold the same number of bytes; that is, the shortest, innermost sectors hold the same amount of data as the longest, outermost sectors.

Of course, a diskette's allocation of sectors per track is somewhat wasteful because the longer outer tracks could theoretically store more data than the shorter inner tracks. For this reason, most hard disks allocate more sectors to the longer tracks on the disk's surface. As you move toward the hard disk's center, each subsequent track has fewer sectors. This arrangement takes advantage of the hard disk's potential capacity and enables a typical hard disk to store data more efficiently than a floppy disk. Because many hard disks allocate sectors in this manner, their sectors-per-track specification is often given as an average. Such hard disks are described as having "an average of *x* sectors per track."

Because files are not usually a size that is an even multiple of 512 bytes, some sectors contain unused space after the end of the file. In addition, the Windows operating system allocates a group of sectors, called a **cluster,** to each file stored on a disk. Cluster sizes vary, depending on the size and type of the disk, but they can

Figure 9.5
Sectors on a disk, each with
a unique number.

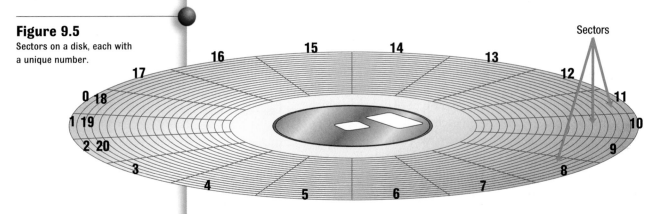

Sectors

range from four sectors for diskettes to sixty-four sectors for some hard disks. A small file that contains only 50 bytes will use only a portion of the first sector of a cluster assigned to it, leaving the remainder of the first sector, and the remainder of the cluster, allocated but unused.

The different capacities of disks are generally a function of the number of sides, tracks, and sectors per track. These differences are easy to demonstrate in floppy disks because there are only a few standard types and formats for diskettes. Hard disks, on the other hand, come in a wide variety of sizes (and may allocate sectors and clusters in different ways), so their capacities vary greatly. Diskette storage capacities are discussed in detail later in this lesson.

A sector is the smallest unit with which any disk drive (diskette drive or hard drive) can work. Each bit and byte within a sector can have different values, but the drive can read or write only whole sectors at a time. If the computer needs to change just 1 byte out of 512, it must rewrite the entire sector.

How the Operating System Finds Data on a Disk

A computer's operating system can locate data on a disk (diskette or hard drive) because each track and sector is labeled, and the location of all data is kept in a special log on the disk. The labeling of tracks and sectors is called performing a **logical format.** (This type of formatting is also called **low-level formatting** or **soft formatting.**) A commonly used logical format performed by Windows creates four disk areas: master boot record (MBR), file-allocation table (FAT), root folder or directory, and **data area** (see Figure 9.6).

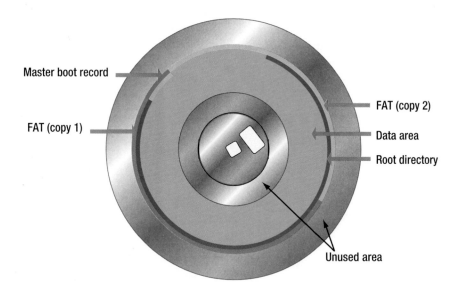

Master boot record

FAT (copy 1)

FAT (copy 2)

Data area

Root directory

Unused area

Figure 9.6
When a disk is formatted, these four areas are defined.

The **master boot record** is a program that runs when you first start the computer. This program determines whether the disk has the basic components that are necessary to run the operating system successfully. If the program determines that the required files are present and the disk has a valid format, it transfers control to one of the operating system programs that continues the process of starting up. This process is called **booting**—because the boot program makes the computer "pull itself up by its bootstraps." The boot record also describes other disk characteristics, such as the number of bytes per sector and the number of sectors per track—information that the operating system needs to access the data area of the disk.

NORTON
ONLINE

Visit **www.glencoe.com/norton/online/** for more information on **file systems**.

The **file-allocation table (FAT)** is a log that records the location of each file and the status of each sector. When you write a file to a disk, the operating system checks the FAT for an open area, stores the file, and then identifies the file and its location in the FAT. This process is shown in Figure 9.7.

The FAT solves a common filing problem: What happens when you load a file, increase its size by adding text to it, and then save it again? For example, you need to add 5000 bytes to a 10,000-byte file that has no open space around it. The disk drive could move the surrounding files to make room for the 5000 bytes, but that would be time consuming. Instead, the operating system checks the FAT for free areas and then places pointers in it that link together the nonadjacent parts of the file. In other words, it splits the file by allocating new space for the overflow; the pointers in the FAT enable the operating system to put the file's pieces back together again.

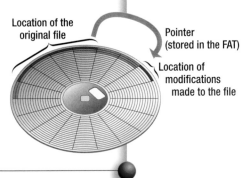

Figure 9.7
When new data must be added to a file and there is no more room next to the cluster where the original data is stored, the operating system records the new information in an unused cluster on the disk. The FAT lists both clusters, and a pointer at the end of the first cluster connects it to the second.

When the operating system saves a file in this way, the file becomes **fragmented.** Its parts are located in nonadjacent sectors. Fragmented files cause undesirable side effects, the most significant being that it takes longer to save and load them.

Users do not see the information listed in the FAT, but they often use the information. A **folder,** also called a **directory,** is a tool for organizing files on a disk. Folders can contain files or other folders, so it is possible to set up a hierarchical system of folders on your computer, just as you have folders within other folders in a file cabinet. The top folder on any disk is known as the root. (Experienced computer users may refer to this folder as the **root folder** or **root directory.**) When you use the operating system to view the contents of a folder, the operating system lists specific information about each file in the folder, such as the file's name, its size, the time and date that it was created or last modified, and so on. Figure 9.8 shows a typical folder listing on a Windows NT system.

Figure 9.8
A Windows NT folder listing.

The folder named C: is the root and contains all other folders on this disk.

Folders can contain other folders and individual files.

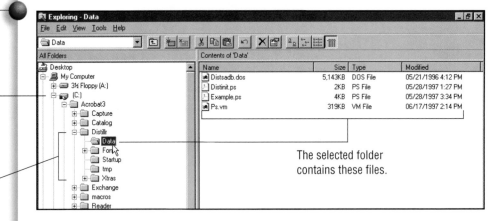
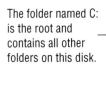

The part of the disk that remains free after the boot sector, FAT, and root folder have been created is called the **data area** because that is where the data files (or program files) are actually stored.

Diskettes (Floppy Disks)

Figure 9.9 shows a diskette and a diskette drive. The drive includes a motor that rotates the disk on a spindle and read/write heads that can move to any spot on the disk's surface as the disk spins. This capability is important because it allows the heads to access data randomly rather than sequentially. In other words, the heads can skip from one spot to another without having to scan through all of the data in between.

Diskettes spin at approximately 300 revolutions per minute. Therefore, the longest it can take to position a point on the diskette under the read/write heads is the amount of time required for one revolution—about 0.2 second. The farthest the heads have

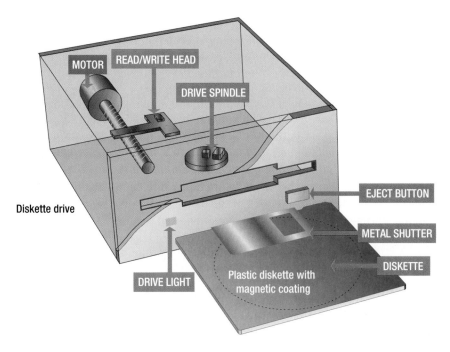

Diskette drive

MOTOR
READ/WRITE HEAD
DRIVE SPINDLE
EJECT BUTTON
METAL SHUTTER
DISKETTE
Plastic diskette with magnetic coating
DRIVE LIGHT

Figure 9.9
Parts of a diskette and diskette drive.

to move is from the center of the diskette to the outside edge (or vice versa). The heads can move from the center to the outside edge in even less time— about 0.17 second. Because both operations (rotating the diskette and moving the heads from the center to the outside edge) take place simultaneously, the maximum time to position the heads over a given location on the diskette— known as the maximum access time—remains the greater of the two times, or 0.2 second (see Figure 9.10).

The maximum access time for diskettes can be even longer, however, because diskettes do not spin when they are not being used. It can take about ½ second to rotate the disk from a dead stop.

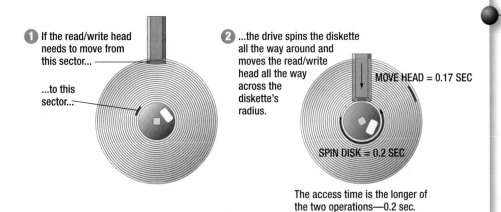

1 If the read/write head needs to move from this sector...

...to this sector...

2 ...the drive spins the diskette all the way around and moves the read/write head all the way across the diskette's radius.

MOVE HEAD = 0.17 SEC

SPIN DISK = 0.2 SEC

The access time is the longer of the two operations—0.2 sec.

Figure 9.10
How maximum access time is determined for a diskette drive.

Listed below are the three most common uses of diskettes:

◆ **Moving Files Between Computers That Are Not Connected Through Network or Communications Hardware.** One of the easiest ways to move data between computers is to copy the data to a diskette, remove the diskette from the first computer's drive, and insert it in another computer's drive.

◆ **Loading New Programs Onto a System.** Although large programs are often delivered on CD-ROM, many programs are still sold on diskettes. When you buy a program from a software retailer, you install it by copying the contents of the diskettes onto your hard disk drive or by running a small program on the diskettes that installs the files on your hard drive automatically.

◆ **Backing Up Data or Programs.** The primary copy of data or programs is stored on a hard disk drive. **Backing up** is the process of creating a duplicate set of programs and/or data files for safekeeping. Most people rely on a hard disk drive for the bulk of their storage needs, but what if the hard drive malfunctions or is damaged? To protect against data loss, it is always wise to back up a hard disk. One common way to do so is to copy files onto diskettes, tapes, or some other removable storage medium. Because diskettes provide limited storage capacity, they are most often used to back up small groups of data files rather than programs or the entire hard disk.

Types of Diskettes

During the 1980s, most PCs used 5.25-inch diskettes. Today, the 3.5-inch diskette has almost completely replaced its 5.25-inch cousin. In fact, you will encounter 5.25-inch disks only when using older computer systems. New systems use the smaller diskette almost exclusively, unless a 5.25-inch disk drive has been added. The size refers to the diameter of the disk and is not an indication of the disk's capacity. The 5.25-inch type, shown in Figure 9.11, is encased in a flexible vinyl envelope with an oval cutout that allows the read/write head to access the disk. The 3.5-inch diskette, shown in Figure 9.12, is encased in a hard plastic shell with a sliding metal shutter. When the disk is inserted into the drive, the shutter slides back to expose the disk's surface to the read/write head.

Figure 9.11
A 5.25-inch diskette.

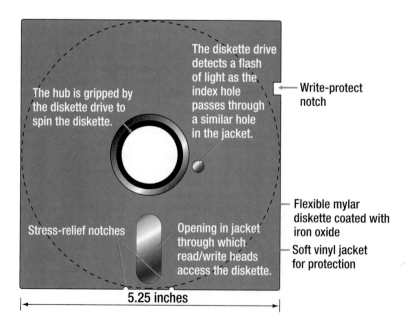

The hub is gripped by the diskette drive to spin the diskette.

The diskette drive detects a flash of light as the index hole passes through a similar hole in the jacket.

Write-protect notch

Flexible mylar diskette coated with iron oxide

Soft vinyl jacket for protection

Stress-relief notches

Opening in jacket through which read/write heads access the diskette.

5.25 inches

Diskette Capacities

Both types of diskette have evolved from lower to higher densities. The **density** of the disk is a measure of the capacity of the disk surface: the higher the density, the more closely the iron-oxide particles are packed, and the more data the disk can store. Early versions of diskettes were double density (DD). As diskette media improved, storage capacities increased; the double-density diskettes have been almost completely replaced by high-density (HD) diskettes, which provide significantly more storage.

As Table 9.1 shows, the physically smaller disks can actually hold more data than the larger ones, thanks to newer technology. Because of their hard plastic shell and the sliding metal shutter, the 3.5-inch diskettes are also more durable.

The sizes given in the table are for DOS- and Windows-based machines. Macintosh computers have never used 5.25-inch disks. A double-density diskette with a Macintosh format holds 800 KB, not 720 KB—a result of the different ways the two machines use the disks. A Macintosh high-density diskette holds 1.44 MB, the same capacity as a DOS- or Windows-based high-density diskette.

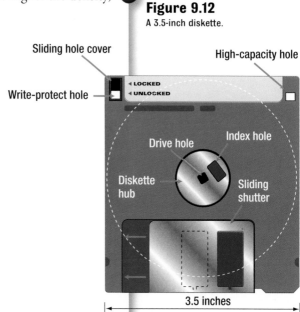

Figure 9.12
A 3.5-inch diskette.

Diameter (Inches)	Type	Tracks	Sectors/ Track	Sectors	Bytes/ Sector	Total Bytes	Bytes Expressed in KB	MB
5.25	Double density (DD)	40	9	720	512	368,640	360	.36
5.25	High density (HD)	80	15	2400	512	1,228,800	1200	1.2
3.5	Double density (DD)	80	9	1440	512	737,280	720	.7
3.5	High density (HD)	80	18	2880	512	1,474,560	1440	1.44
3.5	Extra-high density (ED)	80	36	5760	512	2,949,150	2880	2.88

Table 9.1 — Formatting Specifications for Floppy Disks

Although the "extra-density" ("ED") 2.88 MB floppy disk holds more data than the standard high-density 1.44 MB diskette, you need a special floppy disk drive to read the extra-density disk. The 2.88 MB floppy disk drive was released by Toshiba Corporation in 1987 and was adopted by IBM for the PS/2 system in 1991. Most other PCs, however, do not include 2.88 MB floppy disk drives.

Hard Disks

Although a shift toward optical technology is occurring, the hard disk is still the most common storage device for all computers. Much of what you have learned about diskettes and diskette drives applies to hard disks as well. Like diskettes, hard disks store data in tracks divided into sectors. Physically, however, hard disks look quite different from diskettes.

A hard disk includes one or more metal platters mounted on a central spindle, like a stack of rigid diskettes. Each platter is covered with a magnetic coating, and the entire unit is encased in a sealed chamber. Unlike diskettes, where the disk and drive are separate, the hard disk and drive are a single unit. It includes the hard disk, the motor that spins the platters, and a set of read/write heads (see Figure 9.13). Because you cannot remove the disk from its drive (unless it is a removable or external hard disk), the terms *hard disk* and *hard drive* are used interchangeably.

Hard disks have become the primary storage device for PCs because they are convenient and cost-efficient. In both speed and capacity, they outperform diskettes. A high-density 3.5-inch diskette can store 1.44 MB of data. Hard disks, in contrast, offer capacities from about several hundred megabytes and more. Most entry-level consumer PCs now come with hard disks of at least 6.8 GB, but minimum capacities are continually increasing. At the time this was written, home and business-class PCs could easily be found with hard disk capabilities of 13GB, 20GB, and even greater.

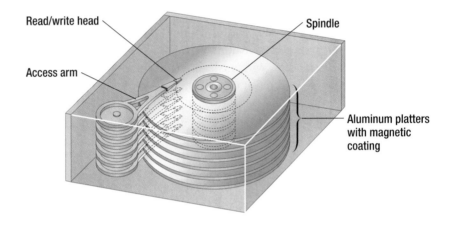

Figure 9.13
Parts of a hard disk.

Read/write head

Spindle

Access arm

Aluminum platters with magnetic coating

Two important physical differences between hard disks and diskettes account for the differences in performance. First, hard disks are sealed in a chamber, and second, the hard disk consists of a rigid metal platter (usually aluminum), rather than flexible mylar.

The hard disks found in most PCs spin between 3600 rpm and 7200 rpm. (Compare these figures to a diskette's spin rate of 300 rpm.) Some new high-performance hard disks can spin as fast as 10,000 rpm. The speed at which the disk spins is a major factor in the overall performance of the drive.

The rigidity of the hard disk and the high speed at which it rotates allow more data to be recorded on the disk's surface. As you may recall, waving a magnet past an electric coil like the one in a drive's read/write head causes a current to flow through the coil. The faster you wave the magnet and the closer the magnet is to the coil, the larger the current it generates in the coil. Therefore, a disk that spins faster can use smaller magnetic charges to make current flow in the read/write head. The drive's heads can also use a lower-intensity current to record data on the disk.

Not only do hard disks pack data more closely together, they also hold more data because they usually include multiple platters, stacked one on top of another. To the computer system, this configuration means that the disk has more than two sides; in addition to a side 0 and side 1, there are sides 2, 3, 4, and so on. Larger capacity hard disk drives may use twelve platters, but both sides of every platter are not always used.

With hard disks, the number of sides that the disk uses is specified by the number of read/write heads. For example, a particular hard disk drive might have six disk

NORTON
ONLINE

Visit **www.glencoe.com/norton/online/** for more information on **hard disks**.

platters (that is, twelve sides) but only eleven heads, indicating that one side is not used to store data. Often, the unused side is the bottom side of the bottom disk, as shown in Figure 9.14.

Because hard disks are actually a stack of platters, the term **cylinder** is used to refer to the same track across all the disk sides, as shown in Figure 9.15. For example, track 0 (the outermost track) on every disk is cylinder 0.

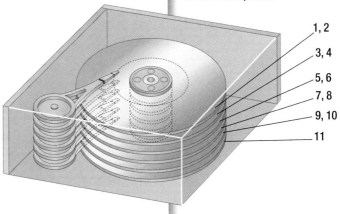

Figure 9.14
Read/write heads on each side of each platter, except the bottom side of the bottom platter.

1, 2
3, 4
5, 6
7, 8
9, 10
11

Like diskettes, hard disks generally store 512 bytes of data in a sector, but because of their higher tolerances, hard disks can have more sectors per track—fifty-four, sixty-three, or even more sectors per track are not uncommon.

The computation of a hard disk's capacity is identical to that for diskettes, but the numbers are larger—in some cases, much larger. Here is how you would break down the capacity for an extremely large (50 GB) hard disk, assuming that the disk has eleven platters, 264,528 tracks, and about 369 sectors per track:

12,024 cylinders $\times$ 22 heads (sides) $=$ 264,528 total tracks

264,528 tracks $\times$ 369 avg. sectors/track $=$ 97,610,823 sectors

97,610,823 sectors $\times$ 512 bytes/sector $=$ 49,976,745,984 bytes (approximately)

The total number of bytes is approximate because this simple calculation is based on the average number of sectors per track. (Recall that many hard drives have varying numbers of sectors per track, so an average may be used.) If the actual number of sectors per track were taken into account, the calculation would be more difficult and the resulting number of bytes would be somewhat higher.

In spite of all the capacity and speed advantages, hard disks have one major drawback. To achieve optimum performance, the read/write head must be extremely close to the surface of the disk without actually touching the disk. In fact, the read/write heads fly so close to the surface of the disk that if a human hair, a dust particle, or even a fingerprint were placed on the disk, it would bridge the gap between the head and the disk and cause the head to crash. A **head crash,** in which the head touches the disk, can destroy the data stored in the area of the crash. A severe head crash not only damages the surface of the disk, it can also destroy a read/write head. Figure 9.16 on page 160 shows the height at which a hard disk head floats compared to the sizes of dust particles, fingerprints, and the width of a hair.

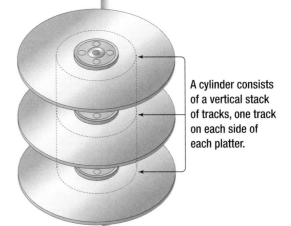

A cylinder consists of a vertical stack of tracks, one track on each side of each platter.

Figure 9.15
A cylinder on a hard disk.

Removable High-Capacity Magnetic Disks

Removable high-capacity disks and drives attempt to combine the speed and capacity of a hard disk with the portability of a diskette. This category includes many different types of devices. Choosing the best type is usually a matter of balancing your needs for speed, storage capacity, compatibility (will it work in different computers?), and price.

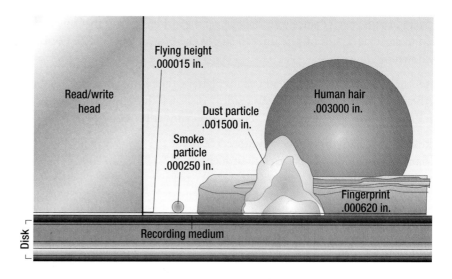

Figure 9.16

The distance between a hard disk's read/write head and the disk's surface compared to the size and/or width of possible contaminants.

Flying height
.000015 in.

Read/write head

Dust particle
.001500 in.

Human hair
.003000 in.

Smoke particle
.000250 in.

Fingerprint
.000620 in.

Recording medium

Disk

Figure 9.17

The Sony HiFD system is an example of the new high-capacity floppy disk drives.

◆ **High-Capacity Floppy Disks.** Many computer users are adding **high-capacity floppy disk** drives to their systems. These disks, which have the same dimensions as a 3.5-inch diskette or are slightly larger, have a much greater capacity than a standard diskette. In fact, many computer manufacturers now offer high-capacity floppy disk drives on their systems. The drive may be offered in addition to a standard diskette drive, but some of these specialty drives can read both standard and high-capacity floppy disks. Popular high-capacity floppy disks include the following:

- A HiFD (high-capacity floppy disk), made by Sony Electronics, Inc., looks just like a normal 3.5-inch floppy disk but can store up to 200 MB of data. A HiFD disk drive (see Figure 9.17) can read and format double-density and high-density floppy disks in addition to HiFD disks.

- The SuperDisk, made by Imation, has the same dimensions as a standard 3.5-inch diskette but is formatted to hold 120 MB of data. SuperDisk drives are compatible with high-density 3.5-inch diskettes.

- Zip disks, made by Iomega Corp., are available in 100 MB and 250 MB capacities and require a special disk drive and utility software. Unlike HiFD and SuperDisk disks, Zip disks are slightly larger than normal diskettes, and Zip disk drives are not compatible with ordinary floppy disks.

◆ **Hot-Swappable Hard Disks.** At the high end in terms of both price and performance are **hot-swappable hard disks.** These disks are sometimes used on high-end workstations or servers that require large amounts of storage. They allow the user to remove swap out a hard disk and insert (swap in) another while the computer is still on (hot). Hot-swappable hard disks are like removable versions of normal hard disks. The removable box includes the disk, drive, and read/write heads in a sealed container.

◆ **Disk Cartridges.** Most removable hard disks used with PCs are different from the hot-swappable design. Most work a bit like a diskette, with a disk in a plastic case that is inserted into or removed from the drive. The disk and case are often called a **disk cartridge.** While these devices do not offer the same storage capacities as true hard disks (or many hot-swappable hard disks), they hold

NORTON
ONLINE

Visit **www.glencoe.com/norton/online/** for more information on **removable magnetic disks.**

significantly more data than a floppy disk and are faster and just as portable. A popular disk cartridge system is the Jaz disk made by Iomega Corporation. Jaz disks are available in 1 GB and 2 GB capacities (see Figure 9.18).

Tape Drives

Tape drives read and write data to the surface of a tape the same way an audiocassette recorder does. The difference is that a computer tape drive writes digital data rather than analog data—discrete 1s and 0s rather than the finely graduated signals created by sounds in an audio recorder.

Figure 9.18
With storage capacities of 2 GB, Jaz disks and other disk cartridges are popular for backing up data from hard drives.

The best use of tape storage is for data that you do not use often, such as backup copies of your hard disk (which you will need only if your hard drive malfunctions or you accidentally delete a valuable file). Because a tape is a long strip of magnetic material, the tape drive has to write data to it serially—1 byte after another. Serial access is inherently slower than the direct access provided by media such as disks. When you want to access a specific set of data on a tape, the drive has to scan through all the data you do not need to get to the data you want. The result is a slow access time. In fact, the access time varies depending on the speed of the drive, the length of the tape, and the position on the tape to which the head wrote the data in the first place.

Despite the long access times, however, tape drives are well suited for certain purposes, especially for backing up your system's entire hard disk. Because hard disks usually have capacities much greater than diskettes, backing up or restoring a system with diskettes can be a long and tedious process requiring dozens or even hundreds of diskettes. Backing up using high-capacity floppy disks or disk cartridges is usually expensive, and even though these media store more data than standard diskettes can, you still need more than one to back up a hard drive larger than 2 GB. Many people now use recordable compact disks to back up data because of their high storage capacities. This option is more expensive than tape, however, and unless rewritable CDs are used, the data cannot be overwritten. (Optical disks are covered later in this lesson.) With capacities as high as 50 GB, 100 GB, and higher, tape offers an inexpensive way to store a lot of data on a single cassette (see Figure 9.19).

Visit **www.glencoe.com/norton/online/** for more information on **tape drives**.

A special type of tape drive uses **digital audiotape (DAT)** to achieve high storage capacities. DAT drives typically have multiple read and write heads built into a small wheel or cylinder that spins near the tape at a high speed. The tape moves past the heads at a much slower speed. The write heads on the spinning wheel each write data with opposite magnetic polarities on overlapping areas of the tape. Each read head reads only one polarity or the other. The result is a high data density per inch of tape. Although DAT tapes are relatively inexpensive, the drives can be expensive when compared to standard tape drives.

Figure 9.19
New generation tape drives, like this Sony SDX-300-C, feature data capacities up to 70 GB and data transfer rates of several megabytes per second.

PRODUCTIVITY Tip

Insurance for Your Data

Backing up your data simply means making a copy of it, separate from the original version on your computer's hard disk. You can back up the entire disk, programs and all, or you can back up your data files. If your original data is lost, you can restore the backup copy, then resume your work with no more than a minor inconvenience. Here are some tips to help you start a regular backup routine.

Choose Your Medium

The most popular backup medium is the floppy disk, but you may need dozens of them to back up all your data files. A tape drive, removable hard disk, disk cartridge, or CD-RW drive may be a perfect choice if the medium provides enough storage space to back up your entire disk. When choosing your own backup medium, the first rule is to make sure it can store everything you need. It should also enable you to restore backed-up data and programs with little effort. You can find medium-capacity tape drives and Zip or Jaz drives for as little as $100 to $300. Prices increase with speed and capacity.

Remote backup services are a growing trend. For a fee, such a service can connect to your computer remotely (via an Internet or dial-up connection) and back up your data to their servers. You can restore data remotely from such a system.

Make Sure You Have the Right Software

For backing up your entire hard disk to a high-capacity device, use the file-transfer software that came with the device. Your operating system may also have a built-in backup utility that works with several devices. The critical issue when choosing backup software is that it should enable you to organize your backups, perform partial backups, and restore selected files at will.

Set a Schedule and Stick to It

Your first backup should be a full backup—everything on your hard disk—and it should be repeated once a week. Beyond that, you can do a series of partial backups—either incremental (files that have changed since

Online backup services like @Backup can back up your system's hard drive over an Internet connection, on any schedule.

the last partial backup) or differential (files that have changed since the last full backup).

Keep Your Backups Safe

Be sure to keep your disks or tapes in a safe place. Experts suggest keeping them somewhere away from the computer. If your computer is damaged or stolen, your backups will not suffer the same fate. Some organizations routinely ship their media to a distant location, such as a home office or a commercial warehouse, or store them in weather- and fireproof vaults. Home users may want to keep their backups in a fireproof box. Companies often keep three or more full sets of backups, all at different sites. Such prudence may seem extreme, but where crucial records are at stake, backups can mean the life or death of a business.

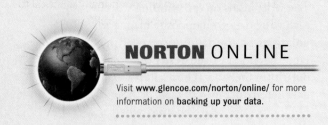

NORTON ONLINE

Visit **www.glencoe.com/norton/online/** for more information on **backing up your data**.

Answer the following questions by filling in the blank(s).

1. The physical components or materials on which data is stored are called _____ .

2. The read/write heads of a disk drive or tape drive contain _____ .

3. Some operating systems allocate a group of sectors, called _____ , to each file they store on a disk.

OPTICAL STORAGE DEVICES

Because of the continuing demand for greater storage capacity, hardware manufacturers are always searching for alternative storage media. Today, the most popular alternatives to magnetic storage systems are optical systems. The most widely used type of optical storage medium is the compact disk (CD), which is used in CD-ROM, DVD-ROM, CD-Recordable, CD-ReWritable, and PhotoCD systems.

Since the mid-1990s, nearly all new PCs have been sold with a built-in CD-ROM drive. However, consumers are buying more and more systems with DVD-ROM drives rather than standard CD-ROM units. These devices fall into the category of optical storage because they store data on a reflective surface so it can be read by a beam of laser light. A laser uses a concentrated, narrow beam of light, focused and directed with lenses, prisms, and mirrors. The tight focus of the laser beam is possible because all the light is the same wavelength.

CD-ROM

The familiar audio compact disk is a popular medium for storing music. In the computer world, however, the medium is called compact disk, read-only memory (CD-ROM). CD-ROM uses the same technology used to produce music CDs. In fact, if your computer has a CD-ROM drive, a sound card, and speakers, you can play audio CDs on your PC (see Figure 9.20).

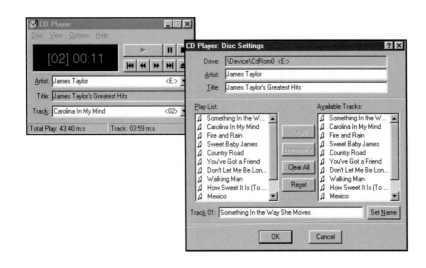

Figure 9.20
Newer operating systems include utilities for playing audio compact disks on the computer. This utility, which is part of Windows 98, lets you set up play lists for your CDs, set the order in which you want songs to play, and even skip specific tracks.

The CD-ROM drive for music or data reads 0s and 1s from a spinning disk by focusing a laser on the disk's surface. Some areas of the disk reflect the laser light into a sensor, and other areas scatter the light. A spot that reflects the laser beam into the sensor is interpreted as a 1, and the absence of a reflection is interpreted as a 0.

Data is laid out on a CD-ROM disk in a long, continuous spiral that starts at the outer edge and winds inward to the center. Data is stored in the form of **lands,** which are flat areas on the metal surface, and **pits,** which are depressions or hollows. As Figure 9.21 shows, a land reflects the laser light into the sensor (indicating a data bit of 1), and a pit scatters the light (indicating a data bit of 0). On a full CD-ROM, the spiral of data stretches almost three miles long! A standard compact disk can store 650 MB of data, or about seventy minutes of audio.

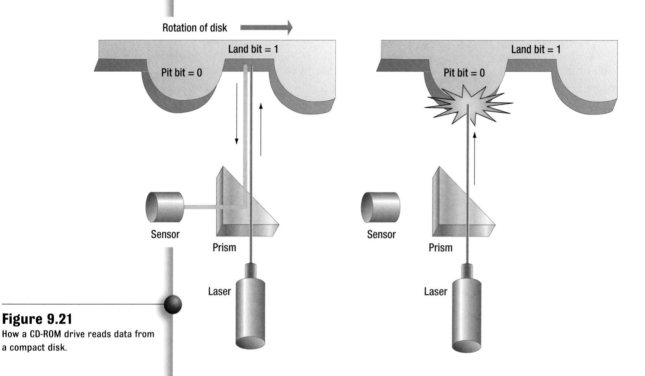

Figure 9.21
How a CD-ROM drive reads data from a compact disk.

NORTON
ONLINE

Visit **www.glencoe.com/norton/online/** for more information on **CD-ROM** drives.

CD-ROM Speeds

Compared to hard disk drives, CD-ROM drives are quite slow, in part because the laser reads pits and lands one bit at a time. Another reason has to do with the changing rotational speed of the disk. Like a track on a magnetic disk, the track of an optical disk is split into sectors. However, the sectors are laid out quite differently than they are on magnetic disks (see Figure 9.22).

The sectors near the middle of the CD wrap farther around the disk than those near the edge. For the drive to read each sector in the same amount of time, it must spin the disk faster when reading sectors near the middle and slower when reading sectors near the edge. Changing the speed of rotation takes time—enough to seriously impair the overall performance of the CD-ROM drive. The first CD-ROM drives read data at 150 KBps (kilobytes per second) and were known as single speed drives. This rate is much slower than that of a typical hard drive, which transfers data at rates of 5 to 15 MBps (megabytes per second). At the time this book was published, CD-ROM drives read data two (300 KBps) to fifty-two (7800 KBps) times faster than the first models. By the time you read this sentence, the speed will undoubtedly be higher.

SECTORS ON A MAGNETIC DISK

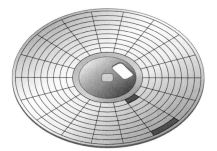

Sectors are wider at the edge
than they are near the middle.

SECTORS ON A CD-ROM

Sectors form a continuous spiral,
and each sector is the same width.

Figure 9.22
How sectors are laid out on a compact disk versus a magnetic disk.

Even with the changing speed of the disk, reading data from an optical medium is a relatively simple undertaking. Writing data, however, is another matter. The medium is a foil disk that is physically pitted to reflect or scatter the laser beam. The disk is then covered in a plastic coating, and it is difficult to alter the surface of the disk after it has been stamped. (As you will see, there are newer optical technologies that allow you to write and rewrite data onto the surface of an optical disk.)

CD-ROM Uses

The fact that you must use special technologies to write data to an optical disk does not mean that this storage medium is not useful. In fact, many applications rely on huge volumes of data that rarely change. For example, dictionaries, encyclopedias, professional reference libraries, music, and video all require tremendous amounts of data that you would not normally want to alter even if you could (see Figure 9.23). Because of the high precision and data density possible with CD-ROM, a single CD typically can hold about 650 MB of data.

In addition to these uses, software companies can distribute their products on CD-ROM. Because of their high capacity and the fact that one CD is much

Figure 9.23
A CD-ROM is a perfect medium for electronic encyclopedias. CD-ROMs are far less expensive to print than a set of books, and the CD-ROM can contain video and sound in addition to text and pictures.

cheaper to produce than a set of diskettes, many software publishers regard CDs as the distribution medium of choice. For example, Microsoft Office is available on one or two compact disks (depending on the version you buy) and includes an online version of the printed manuals, thousands of clip art images, sample files, and more. Instead of installing the programs from dozens of diskettes, the user must insert only one or two CDs.

Figure 9.24

If your PC features a DVD drive, you can watch movies in DVD format on your computer's screen.

DVD-ROM

Standard compact disks and CD-ROM drives are beginning to be replaced on computer systems by digital video disk read-only memory (DVD-ROM), also called digital video disk or digital versatile disk. DVD-ROM is a high-density medium capable of storing a full-length movie on a single disk the size of a CD. DVD-ROM achieves such high storage capacities by using both sides of the disk and special data-compression technologies, and by using extremely small tracks for storing data. The latest generation of DVD-ROM disks actually use layers of data tracks, effectively doubling their capacity. The device's laser beam can read data from the first layer, and then look through it to read data from the second layer.

In fact, DVDs look like CDs (see Figure 9.24), and DVD-ROM drives can play ordinary CD-ROM disks. A slightly different player, the DVD movie player, connects to your television and plays movies like a VCR (see Figure 9.25). The DVD movie player will also play audio CDs.

Each side of a standard DVD-ROM disk can hold up to 4.7 GB. Therefore, these two-sided disks can contain as much as 9.4 GB of data. Dual-layer DVD-ROM disks can hold 17 GB of data.

Figure 9.25

DVD-ROM movie players can read video, audio, and data from DVD-ROM and CD-ROM disks and are becoming popular additions to home entertainment centers. In PC systems, built-in DVD-ROM drives look just like standard CD-ROM drives.

DVD-ROM drive

CD-Recordable, CD-ReWritable, and PhotoCD

For large quantities, CD-ROM disks can be produced by manufacturers with expensive duplication equipment. For fewer copies or even single copies, a CD-Recordable (CD-R) drive can be attached to a computer as a regular peripheral device. CD-R drives allow you to create your own CD-ROM disks that can be read by any CD-ROM drive. After information has been written to part of the CD, that information cannot be changed. With most CD-R drives, however, you can continue to record information to other parts of the disk until it is full.

Using newer generation CD-ReWritable (CD-RW) drives, however, users can write and overwrite data onto compact disks (see Figure 9.26). With a CD-ReWritable drive, users can leverage the high storage capacity of compact disks but revise the data on them in the same manner as a floppy disk.

A new type of CD-R device does not need to be attached to a PC but can be, if needed. These devices feature a large built-in hard disk, which can record data or music from the user's PC or from an audio or data CD. The

Figure 9.26
With a CD-RW drive, you can record and re-record audio or data on compact disks.

device stores the data on its disk and then can copy the data onto a fresh CD-R or CD-RW disk. This type of drive is handy because it can create CDs without tying up resources on the user's PC.

One popular form of recordable CD is PhotoCD, a standard developed by Kodak for storing digitized photographic images on a CD. Many film developing stores now have PhotoCD drives that can store your photos and put them on a CD. You can then put the PhotoCD in your computer's CD-ROM drive (assuming that it supports PhotoCD, and most do) and view the images on your computer. You can also paste them into other documents (see Figure 9.27). With a PhotoCD, you can continue to add images until the disk is full. After an image has been written to the disk using a field of lasers, however, it cannot be erased or changed.

Figure 9.27
After your pictures have been processed and stored on a PhotoCD, you can see them on your computer screen and copy them into documents.

NORTON ONLINE

Visit **www.glencoe.com/norton/online/** for more information on **DVD-ROM**, **CD-R**, and **CD-RW** devices.

COMPUTERS
in your career

Storage Devices in Your Career

If computers will play a large part in your career, you need to be familiar (if not intimate) with the way computers store data. If you plan to support, maintain, or build computers, for example, you will rely heavily on your knowledge of storage device specifications. The following professionals, for example, must have a thorough understanding of storage technologies:

◆ **Network Administrators.** One of the network administrator's primary responsibilities is making backups of data stored on the network server(s) and on users' desktop PCs. This task involves knowing when to make the backups and what backup media and devices are the best for the job. Any company uses various storage devices, and the administrators must understand how each one stores data to allocate storage resources on the network depending on the data that users create.

◆ **Help Desk Operators.** When a user calls the help desk for technical support on a hard disk problem, such as the inability to store or retrieve data, the operator must be able to understand the problem quickly and offer solutions. Help desk operators should become familiar with the different file systems that operating systems use and how these operating systems work with different storage devices. Many help desk operators must walk users through the process of installing or configuring storage devices.

◆ **Database Designers.** As database designers create databases, they need to know the type of storage media being used. Databases created for CD-ROMs, for instance, will allow users only the ability to access, not change, data. For databases created for hard disks, the designer must know the maximum size that the database can grow to (which includes the data already in the database as well as the data that will be added in the future) based on the size of the storage media. If a larger storage device is needed after the database designer assesses the existing storage requirements, he or she must consider downgrading the database storage requirements or upgrading the existing storage hardware.

Even if you do not plan to work with computer systems, you need to understand the basics of data storage. In fact, every user should understand how a computer stores data. You may not need to know how often a hard drive is backed up (unless that task becomes your responsibility) or even where a particular file is stored. However, you do need to understand the differences among floppy disks, hard drives, CD-ROM drives, and removable storage.

LESSON QUIZ

True/False

Answer the following questions by circling True or False.

True   False   **1.** The hardware components that write data to storage media are called storage devices.

True   False   **2.** Writing data means recording data on the surface of a disk.

True   False   **3.** The process of mapping a disk's surface is called organizing data.

True   False   **4.** A cluster is a group of sectors.

True   False   **5.** The top folder on any disk is known as the master boot sector.

Multiple Choice

Circle the word or phrase that best completes each sentence.

1. A _____ is an example of a magnetic storage device.
   A. hard disk drive   **B.** PhotoCD drive   **C.** neither A nor B

2. A floppy disk's read/write head uses a(n) _____ to read and write data on a disk.
   A. tape drive   **B.** pit   **C.** electromagnet

3. The _____ is a small program that runs when you start the computer.
   A. file allocation table   **B.** master boot record   **C.** sector

4. _____ is the process of creating a duplicate set of programs or data files for safekeeping.
   A. Backing up   **B.** Initializing   **C.** Neither A nor B

5. A(n) _____ hard disk can be inserted and removed while the computer is running.
   A. cartridge   **B.** optical   **C.** hot-swappable

LESSON LABS

Complete the following exercises as directed by your instructor.

1. Format a blank floppy disk:
   A. Make sure the disk's write-protect tab is closed. Place the disk in the diskette drive.
   B. Click the Start button, click Programs, and then click Windows Explorer.
   C. Right-click the floppy disk icon in the left pane. Click Format on the shortcut menu.
   D. In the Format dialog box, choose a capacity for the disk. Click the "Quick (erase)" option. Make sure the "Display summary when finished" option is checked. Click Start.
   E. Click Close twice. Remove the disk from the drive. Leave the Exploring window open.

2. Explore the contents of your hard disk. In the Exploring window's left pane, click the system's hard disk icon labeled (C:). Look at the status bar at the bottom of the window. How many "objects" (folders) are stored on the hard disk? How much free space is available? Click several folders and review their contents in the right pane. When finished, close the Exploring window.

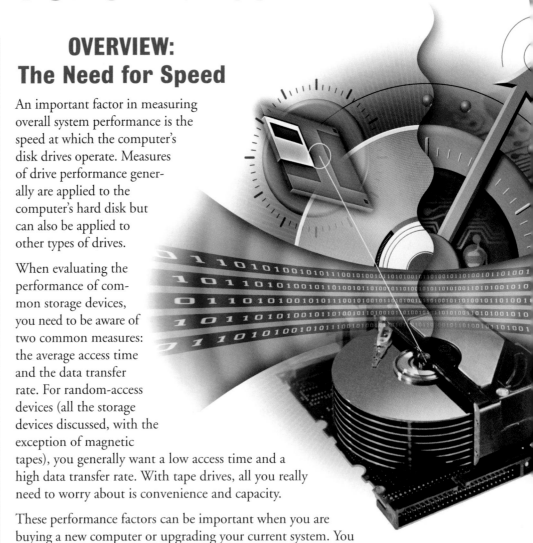

Measuring Drive Performance

OBJECTIVES

- Explain the importance of understanding drive performance.
- Define the term *average access time* and describe how it is measured.
- Explain why file compression is a factor in drive performance.
- Define the term *data transfer rate* and describe how it is measured.
- Identify four drive interface standards commonly used in PCs.

OVERVIEW: The Need for Speed

An important factor in measuring overall system performance is the speed at which the computer's disk drives operate. Measures of drive performance generally are applied to the computer's hard disk but can also be applied to other types of drives.

When evaluating the performance of common storage devices, you need to be aware of two common measures: the average access time and the data transfer rate. For random-access devices (all the storage devices discussed, with the exception of magnetic tapes), you generally want a low access time and a high data transfer rate. With tape drives, all you really need to worry about is convenience and capacity.

These performance factors can be important when you are buying a new computer or upgrading your current system. You want to make sure that your drives operate at a speed that complements your processor's capabilities. You also want to make sure that the drive uses an interface that is compatible with any other devices you may add to the computer.

AVERAGE ACCESS TIME

For a storage device, **average access time** (or **seek time**) is the amount of time the device takes to position its read or read/write heads over any spot on the medium. It is important that the measurement be an average because access times can vary greatly depending on the distance between the heads' original location and their destination. To measure the access time of a drive effectively, you must test many reads of randomly chosen sectors—a method that approximates the actual read instructions a disk drive would receive under normal circumstances.

For storage devices, access times are measured in **milliseconds (ms),** or one-thousandths of a second. For memory devices, access times are measured in **nanoseconds (ns),** or one-billionths of a second.

In a disk drive, access time depends on a combination of two factors: the speed at which a disk spins (revolutions per minute, or rpm), and the time it takes to move the heads from one track to another. In Lesson 9, you saw that the longest it takes a diskette drive's read/write head to access any point is about 0.2 second: the amount of time it takes the disk to complete one revolution at 300 rpm. The maximum access time for diskettes, therefore, is 0.2 second, or 200 milliseconds. The average access time is about one half the maximum, or 100 milliseconds.

Average access times for hard drives can vary, but most good drives work at rates of 6 to 12 milliseconds, many times faster than diskette drives. Access time is used as a measure for many different computer components, including RAM and ROM (see Table 10.1).

As you can see, access times for CD-ROM drives tend to be quite slow by hard disk drive standards, but tape drives offer the longest average access times of any storage device. Depending on the type of drive and format used, tape drives can take from a few seconds to a few minutes to find a specific piece of data on the tape's surface.

The easiest way to determine the average access time for a device is to check the manufacturer's specifications. You should be able to find the specifications for a device in its packaging or documentation, or you may be able to get them from the manufacturer's Web site (see Figure 10.1). Popular computer-related magazines—such as *PC Magazine*, *PC World*, and others—regularly test new drives to measure various performance factors.

FILE COMPRESSION

Even with the large storage devices available, many users still find themselves pushing the limits of what they can store on their PCs. One solution to this storage problem, besides upgrading to larger devices, is to compress data. **File compression,** or **data compression,** is the technology for shrinking the size of a file, thereby freeing up space for more data and programs to reside on the disk.

Table 10.1	Typical Access Times
Device	**Typical Access Time**
Static RAM (SRAM)	5–15 ns
Dynamic RAM (DRAM)	50–70 ns
Read-only memory (ROM)	55–250 ns
Hard disk drives	6–12 ms
CD-ROM drives	80–800 ms
Tape drives	20–500 seconds

Source: *Copyright 1999 internet.com Corporation. All Rights Reserved. Reprinted with permission from* **http://www.pcwebopedia.com.**

Figure 10.1
Like many storage device manufacturers, Seagate Technology, Inc., provides product specifications on its
Web site. This page shows the specifications for one of Seagate's hard
disks.

ST31270A
Medalist 1270 Family

Spec Sheet
Install Guide-pdf
Manual-pdf

Cylinders: 621
Heads: 64
Sectors: 63

Capacity: 1.28 GB
Speed: 4500 rpm
Seek time: 12 ms avg
SeaFAX#: 312702

J8 Options
jumper block

J8 pin 1

J1 Interface
connector

pin 1

J3 Standard
power connector

The average access
time for this drive
is 12 ms.

Figure 10.2
This illustration shows the WinZip
file compression utility at work.

Compressing files will not necessarily improve a disk's performance; that is, compressing files will not reduce a disk's access time. However, file compression can
enable you to store more data on a disk, effectively increasing the disk's capacity.

Entire hard disks, floppy disks, or individual files can be compressed by as much as
a 3:1 ratio (so that 300 MB of data fills only 100 MB of space, for instance). File
compression is performed by software that uses mathemati-
cal algorithms to squeeze data into smaller chunks by removing information that is not vital to the file or data. When
the file is returned to its original state, this data is reinserted
so that the original data is reproduced exactly as it was before
compression.

Some favorite compression programs for PCs include PKZIP,
WinZip, and DriveSpace 3 (DriveSpace 3 is part of the
Windows 98 operating system). StuffIT is a favorite compres-
sion utility among Macintosh enthusiasts.

Most file-compression utilities are useful for compressing
one or more files to reduce their storage requirements. When
you use a utility like WinZip, the program actually shrinks
the selected files and then saves them together inside a new
file, with its own name. The resulting file is called an **archive file** because it stores
the compressed files inside it. Archive files are commonly used for exactly that purpose—archiving unneeded data files.

Figure 10.2 shows an example of a file compression utility at work. Depending on
the circumstances (the compression software used, the data file's native program,
and other factors), the user may need to **extract** the compressed files manually
(that is, return them to their uncompressed state) before using them. Most file
compression utilities enable the user to create self-extracting archive files—files
that can extract themselves automatically.

Utilities like WinZip, PKZIP, or StuffIT generally are not used to compress the
contents of an entire hard disk. Because such files must be expanded manually, a

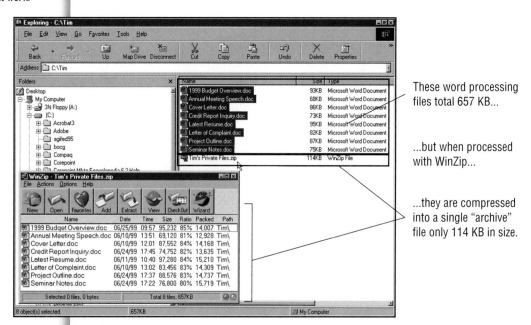

These word processing
files total 657 KB...

...but when processed
with WinZip...

...they are compressed
into a single "archive"
file only 114 KB in size.

lot of effort would be required to compress a disk's contents, select and expand files when you want to use them, and then recompress them. For this reason, programs such as DriveSpace 3 are helpful.

DriveSpace 3 effectively doubles the storage capacity of a hard disk by compressing all its contents. You can use your programs and data in compressed form without expanding them manually; DriveSpace 3 handles those tasks for you. Full-disk compression schemes are not without risks, however. For example, a disk may perform more slowly because of all the compressing and expanding that occurs in the background, and the likelihood of data errors increases.

DATA TRANSFER RATE

The other important statistic for measuring drive performance is the speed at which it can transfer data— that is, how long it takes for one device to transfer data to another device. Speeds are expressed as a rate, or as some amount of data per unit of time. When measuring any device's data transfer rate (also called **throughput**), time is measured in seconds, but units of data may be measured in bytes, KB, MB, or GB. Figure 10.3 illustrates data transfer rate.

5 Megabytes = 0.25 sec.

Transfer rate = 20 MB/sec.

Figure 10.3
The data transfer rate is the time required to move a specific amount of data (for example, 20 MB) from one device to another, such as from the hard disk to memory.

As is the case with access times, data transfer rates can vary greatly from one device to another. Speeds for hard disks are generally high, from about 15 MBps for low end home systems to 80 MBps and higher for the faster drives designed for high-performance workstations and servers. When buying a hard disk, the data transfer rate is at least as important a factor as the access time.

CD-ROMs and diskettes are the slowest storage devices. CD-ROMs range from 300 KBps for a double-speed player, to 900 KBps for a 6X drive, to even higher speeds, with the data transfer rate corresponding to the drive's speed. Diskette drives average about 45 KBps. Removable hard disks range from about 1.25 MBps up into the hard disk range.

Some drive manufacturers and dealers advertise their drives' data transfer rates in units of megabytes per second (MBps); others express them in megabits per second (Mbps). When shopping, note if the rate specified is "MBps" or "Mbps."

Self Check

Answer the following questions by filling in the blank(s).

1. For storage devices, access times are measured in _____ .

2. _____ is the technology for shrinking the size of a file.

3. *Throughput* is another term for _____ .

DRIVE-INTERFACE STANDARDS

Another important factor in determining how quickly a drive can read and write data is the type of controller that the drive uses. Just as a video monitor requires a controller to act as an interface between the CPU and the display screen, storage

NORTON
ONLINE

Visit **www.glencoe.com/norton/online/** for more information on **data compression.**

Norton Notebook

DATA WAREHOUSES, PART I

For years, companies have gathered and managed vast amounts of data of every imaginable kind. Since data truly is the lifeblood of a corporation, then you can think of the corporation's data storage system as its heart. The bigger and stronger that system is, the more information it can handle and the more effectively it will operate.

Large and medium-size companies are taking new approaches to storing and managing their huge collections of data. On the storage side of the equation is the data warehouse—a massive collection of corporate information, often stored in gigabytes or terabytes of data. Setting up a data warehouse is much more complicated than simply dumping all kinds of data into one storage place. Companies must consider several factors before investing in a data warehousing structure:

◆ **Storage Space.** One of the most popular mass-storage schemes is based on a redundant array of independent disks (RAID). RAID is a storage system that links any number of disk drives so that they act as a single disk. In this system, information is written to two or more disks simultaneously to improve speed and reliability, and to ensure that data is available to users at all times. Current RAID systems offer up to 10 TB of storage and incredibly fast access and data transfer times.

◆ **Processing Scheme.** Generally, two technologies are used to control data warehouses: symmetrical multiprocessing (SMP) or massively parallel processing (MPP). Using special RAID controllers, such systems can rapidly collect data, check it for errors, and retrieve a backup copy of the data if necessary.

◆ **Backup Strategy.** RAID's capabilities are based on three basic techniques: (1) mirroring, (2) striping, and (3) striping-with-parity. In a mirrored system, data is written to two or more disks simultaneously, providing a complete copy of all the information on a drive should one drive fail. Striping provides the user with a speedy response by spreading data across several disks. Striping alone, however, does not provide backup if one of the disks in an array fails. Striping-with-parity provides the speed of striping with the reliability of mirroring. In this scenario, the system stores parity information, which can be used to reconstruct data if a disk drive fails.

◆ **Speed.** Newer data-warehousing systems not only incorporate huge disk drives, but some interconnect the drives with fiber-optic lines rather than standard wire-based buses. Fiber-optic lines use beams of pulsing light to transmit data and operate many times faster than standard data-bus technologies.

Huge data warehouses can supply the data requirements for tens of thousands of users in a large organization. They are also used to store and support thousands or millions of transactions per day on active Web sites, such as the popular electronic auction and retail Web sites.

Having a place to store all that data, however, leads to another question: how do you find what you need in all that data? The answer is a process called data mining, and it is explained in Part II of this discussion, in Lesson 16.

In a simple RAID array like this, data is written to two or more disks at once, resulting in multiple copies. This protects the data in case one disk fails. In more sophisticated RAID configurations, data from a single file is spread over multiple disks, and duplicates are also made. Error-checking is also provided in such arrays.

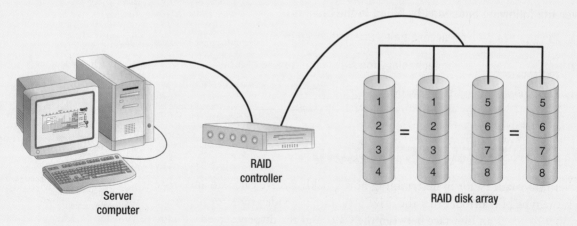

Server computer

RAID controller

RAID disk array

devices also need a controller to act as an intermediary between the drive and the CPU. A **disk controller** connects the disk drive to the computer's bus, enabling the drive to exchange data with other devices.

Currently, most personal computers use one of two drive-interface standards: EIDE or SCSI. A lot of confusion has surrounded drive-interface standards because competing developers have introduced many variations of and names for these technologies. If you buy a PC today, it will almost certainly feature one of these two drive interfaces. If you plan to purchase a drive for an existing PC, be sure that the new drive is compatible with the computer's drive interface.

Visit **www.glencoe.com/norton/online/** for more information on **drive-interface standards.**

Enhanced Integrated Drive Electronics (EIDE)

Enhanced integrated drive electronics (EIDE) is an enhanced version of an older drive-interface standard simply called integrated drive electronics (IDE). While the IDE standard still exists and is the basis for several drive interfaces, the standard now goes by about a half-dozen different names, and EIDE is widely regarded as the catch-all term for drive interfaces based on this standard.

As a result, most new computer systems use the EIDE drive-interface standard (or one like it). The latest version of EIDE supports data transfer rates of 33 MBps. The EIDE standard's variants go by many different names (including Fast IDE, ATA, Fast ATA, ATA-2, ATA-3, ATA-4, and Ultra ATA) and offer somewhat different features and performance.

Small Computer System Interface (SCSI)

The history of the small computer system interface (SCSI) goes back to the 1970s. SCSI was originally developed as a way to connect third-party peripheral devices to mainframe computers—specifically, IBM mainframe computers. SCSI went through many transformations before the American National Standards Institute (ANSI) established a definition for the interface in 1986. Since then, the definition of SCSI continued to evolve into SCSI-2, Wide SCSI, Fast SCSI, Fast Wide SCSI, Ultra SCSI, SCSI-3 (also known as Ultra-Wide SCSI), Ultra 2 SCSI, and Wide Ultra 2 SCSI.

Because the original concept of SCSI was to provide peripherals (not just hard disk drives) access to the computer system's bus, one way to think of SCSI is as an extension of the computer's bus. As such, all interface circuitry needed by the device has to be on the device itself.

One benefit of SCSI is that bringing the computer's bus directly into the drive improves efficiency. It allows even higher data transfer rates than are possible with EIDE. SCSI-2 began by supporting transfer rates up to 5 MBps. SCSI-3 raised the ante again to 40 MBps. Wide Ultra 2 SCSI supports a 16-bit data bus and data transfer rates of 80 MBps. Because of its speed, flexibility, and high throughput rates, the SCSI drive interface standard is usually found in higher-end business systems, servers, and workstations (see Figure 10.4).

Figure 10.4
SCSI drive interfaces are often found in high-performance desktop computers, workstations, and network servers.

FUTURE

The Future of Data Storage

Some of the most exciting changes in computer hardware over the next few years are likely to occur in the area of storage technology. Important developments are taking place right now that will affect the storage options you can choose from, the basic technologies on which future storage devices will be based, and the need for storage as it relates to networks and the Internet.

◆ Similar holographic techniques and crystals will be used to store terabytes of data in devices the size of sugar cubes.

◆ Data compression technologies, such as MP3 and others, will find wider applications, enabling developers to squeeze huge amounts of data down to miniscule sizes.

Options

◆ Home and business users will continue to enjoy an increasing variety of storage options, and those options will offer ever-increasing capacities and speed.

◆ Many experts predict that the lowly floppy disk will disappear in the next two or three years as high-capacity floppy disks become the standard for portable storage.

◆ By 2001, DVD-ROM drives will probably replace CD-ROM drives as the standard optical drive on desktop computers, offering capacities of at least 17 GB. By 2002 or 2003, 1 TB (that's terabyte, or 1 trillion bytes) hard disks will become standard equipment on desktop computers.

Methodologies

Corporate and e-commerce network administrators say that the need for data storage doubles every year. As a result, new mass data storage methods are being developed, including some that use fiber-optic connections for the fastest possible data transfer rates. New storage subsystems are being invented for companies that handle thousands of transactions a day, and these systems will use vast disk arrays capable of storing dozens of terabytes. By leveraging such technologies, new online services will offer mass data storage services (primary storage, not backup) for home and small business users.

Technologies

Other changes will arrive soon in the form of new standards and new technologies.

◆ Look for optical disks that have tremendous storage capacities because of crystal technology and holographic imaging that store multiple layers of information.

NORTON ONLINE

Visit **www.glencoe.com/norton/online/** for more information on **storage devices**.

LESSON QUIZ

True/False

Answer the following questions by circling True or False.

True   False   **1.** To measure the access time of a drive, you must test the way the drive reads data from a single sector.

True   False   **2.** One purpose of file compression technology is to create free space on a disk.

True   False   **3.** Data transfer rates should not vary from one device to another.

True   False   **4.** EIDE and SCSI are the two most common drive-interface standards used in PCs.

True   False   **5.** SCSI allows higher data transfer rates than are possible with EIDE.

Multiple Choice

Circle the word or phrase that best completes each sentence.

1. The amount of time a storage device takes to position its head over any spot on the medium is called _____ .

  A. average access time   **B.** seek time   **C.** both A and B

2. For storage devices, access times are measured in _____ .

  A. nanoseconds   **B.** milliseconds   **C.** seconds

3. File compression utilities shrink selected files and save them together in a new file, called a(n) _____ .

  A. data file   **B.** extraction file   **C.** archive file

4. A device's data transfer rate may also be called _____ .

  A. throughput   **B.** bandwidth   **C.** seek time

5. The term MBps stands for _____ .

  A. megabits per second   **B.** megabytes per second   **C.** neither A nor B

LESSON LABS

Complete the following exercise as directed by your instructor.

Learn what kind of hard disk controllers are installed in your computer.

  A. Click the Start button, point to Settings, then click Control Panel.

  B. Double-click the System icon to open the System Properties dialog box.

  C. Click the Device Manager tab. Click the plus sign (+) in front of Hard Disk Controllers.

  D. Click to highlight an item listed under Hard Disk Controllers, then click the Properties button. Write down the data for the selected controller, then click Cancel.

  E. Repeat step D for each item listed under Hard Disk Controllers. When finished, click Cancel to close the System Properties dialog box. Then close the Control Panel dialog box.

VISUAL SUMMARY

Lesson 9: Types of Storage Devices

Categorizing Storage Devices

- Storage devices can be categorized as magnetic or optical.

- The most common magnetic storage devices are diskettes, hard disks, high-capacity floppy disks, disk cartridges, and magnetic tape.

- The primary types of optical storage are compact disk read-only memory (CD-ROM), digital video disk read-only memory (DVD-ROM), CD-Recordable (CD-R), CD-ReWritable (CD-RW), and PhotoCD.

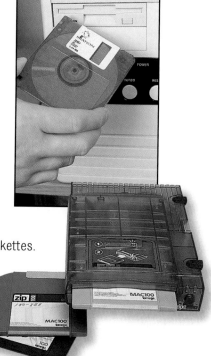

Magnetic Storage Devices

- Magnetic storage devices work by polarizing tiny pieces of iron on the magnetic medium.

- Read/write heads contain electromagnets that create magnetic charges on the medium.

- Diskette drives, also known as floppy disk drives, read and write to diskettes.

- Diskettes are used most often to transfer files between computers, as a means for distributing software, and as a backup medium.

- Diskettes are available in two sizes: 5.25 inch and 3.5 inch. The 5.25-inch diskette is rarely used today.

- Before a magnetic disk can be used, it must be formatted—a process that maps the disk's surface and creates tracks and sectors where data can be stored.

- When a disk is formatted, the operating system creates four distinct areas on its surface: the boot sector, FAT, root folder, and data area.

- Hard disks can store more data than diskettes because of their higher-quality media, faster rotational speed, and the tiny distance between the read/write head and the disk's surface.

- Removable hard disks combine high capacity with the convenience of diskettes.

- High-capacity floppy disks are becoming a popular add-on for many computers. They offer capacities up to 250 MB and the same portability as standard floppy disks.

- Data cartridges are like small removable hard disks and can store up to 2 GB.

- Magnetic tape systems offer slow data access, but because of their large capacities and low cost, they are a popular backup medium.

Optical Storage Devices

- CD-ROM uses the same technology as a music CD does; a laser reads lands and pits on the surface of the disk.

- Standard CD-ROM disks can store up to 650 MB. Once data is written to the disk, it cannot be changed.

- DVD-ROM technology is a variation on standard CD-ROM. DVDs offer capacities up to 17 GB.

- Other popular variations on CD-ROM are CD-Recordable, CD-ReWritable, and PhotoCD.

Lesson 10: Measuring Drive Performance

Average Access Time

- In storage devices, the average access time is the time it takes a read/write head to move to a spot on the storage medium.

- Diskette drives offer an average access time of 100 milliseconds. Hard drives are many times faster.

- Tape drives provide the slowest average access times of all magnetic storage devices; optical devices are also much slower than hard disks.

File Compression

- File compression technology is used to shrink the size of files so that they take up less disk space.

- By using compression utilities, you can shrink multiple files into a single archive file.

- Utilities such as Windows' DriveSpace enable you to compress the entire contents of your hard disk.

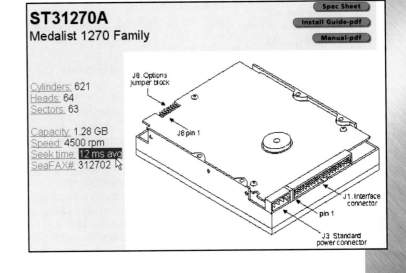

ST31270A
Medalist 1270 Family

Spec Sheet
Install Guide-pdf
Manual-pdf

Cylinders: 621
Heads: 64
Sectors: 63

Capacity: 1.28 GB
Speed: 4500 rpm
Seek time: 12 ms avg
SeaFAX# 312702

J8. Options jumper block
J8 pin 1
J1. Interface connector
pin 1
J3. Standard power connector

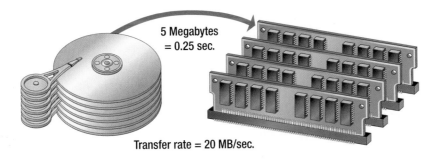

5 Megabytes = 0.25 sec.

Transfer rate = 20 MB/sec.

Data Transfer Rate

- The data transfer rate is a measure of how long it takes a given amount of data to travel from one device to another.

- Hard disks offer the fastest data transfer rates of any storage device.

Drive-Interface Standards

- All PCs use a disk controller as an interface between a disk drive and the CPU.

- Two drive-interface standards are commonly used today: EIDE and SCSI.

- EIDE has evolved over the years and has several variants, all of which go by different names.

- SCSI is a faster, more flexible drive-interface standard found in high-performance computers.

UNIT REVIEW

KEY TERMS

After completing this unit, you should be able to define the following terms.

archive file, *172*
average access time, *171*
backing up, *156*
booting, *153*
cluster, *152*
cylinder, *159*
data area, *153*
data compression, *171*
density, *157*
digital audiotape (DAT), *161*
directory, *154*
disk cartridge, *160*
disk controller, *175*
electromagnet, *149*
enhanced integrated drive
    electronics (EIDE), *175*
extract, *172*
file compression, *171*
file-allocation table (FAT), *154*
folder, *154*
formatting, *151*
fragmented, *154*
head crash, *159*

high-capacity floppy disk, *160*
hot-swappable hard disk, *160*
initializing, *151*
land, *164*
logical format, *153*
low-level formatting, *153*
magnetic storage, *148*
master boot record, *153*
millisecond (ms), *171*
nanosecond (ns), *171*
optical storage, *148*
pit, *164*
polarized, *148*
root directory, *154*
root folder, *154*
sector, *152*
seek time, *171*
soft formatting, *153*
storage device, *148*
storage media, *148*
throughput, *173*
track, *151*

KEY TERMS QUIZ

Fill in each blank with one of the terms listed under Key Terms.

1. When an iron bar is _____ , its ends have opposite magnetic polarity.

2. When formatting a disk, the disk drive starts by creating a set of _____ on its surface.

3. The process of logical formatting is also called _____ or _____ .

4. A disk's _____ records the location of each file and the status of each sector.

5. _____ is the process of creating a duplicate set of programs and/or data files for safekeeping.

6. A disk's _____ is a measure of its capacity.

7. On the surface of a magnetic disk, each track is divided into a series of _____ .

8. You can organize the files on a disk by setting up _____ .

9. If you use a data compression utility to compress some files, you may need to _____ the files before using them.

10. The _____ standard has several variants, which are known by names like Fast IDE, ATA, and others.

REVIEW QUESTIONS

In your own words, briefly answer the following questions.

1. List the primary types of magnetic storage.

2. List the primary types of optical storage.

3. In terms of storing data, what important advantage does a magnetic disk have over memory?

4. Describe how a read/write head can pass data to and from the surface of a magnetic disk.

5. Describe how a computer's operating system can locate data on a disk's surface.

6. Why is the process of starting a computer called "booting"?

7. Describe the function of lands and pits on the surface of an optical disk.

8. What is the primary use of data compression utilities such as WinZip and StuffIT?

9. What are some of the benefits of using compact disks rather than diskettes?

10. What primary benefit does SCSI provide for disk drives?

DISCUSSION QUESTIONS

As directed by your instructor, discuss these questions in class or in groups.

1. Why do you think a basic truth in computing is that one never has enough storage space? What factors contribute to this situation? As hard disks get larger and larger, do you think we will reach a point where the standard desktop computer has more than enough storage space for the average user's needs? Have we reached that point already?

2. Suppose that your class is actually one department within a medium-size company. You need to adopt a backup system for the department's data. As a group, what factors should you consider in making this decision? What backup technologies should you consider? What type of backup schedule should you follow?

 ETHICAL ISSUES Many storage device options are available. These choices are beneficial for many users, but they can also be drawbacks for software companies, music publishers, and others. With this thought in mind, discuss the following questions in class:

1. CD-ReWritable (CD-RW) devices are getting cheaper and more popular. They let you create backups and store data in a safe format. However, people also use them to make illegal duplicates of software and audio CDs. If you had a CD-RW system, would you consider making illegal duplicates? Do you think such copying should be illegal? Defend your answer.

2. You have seen that large companies store gigabytes of data about their customers. Do you know that many companies sell this information to other companies? As more organizations build databases about individuals, do you believe they should be free to exchange or sell this information? Why?

You and the Computer

Complete the following exercises using a computer in your classroom, lab, or home. No other materials are needed.

1. **Defragment a Disk.** As you learned in this unit, a file becomes fragmented when the entire file cannot be stored in consecutive sectors. If you are using a Windows 95, 98, or 2000 computer, you can defragment a disk by using Windows' Disk Defragmenter utility. Defragment a floppy disk by taking the following steps:

   A. Insert a diskette into your computer's floppy disk drive.

   B. Click the Start button, point to Programs, point to Accessories, point to System Tools, and then click Disk Defragmenter. The Select Drive window opens.

   C. Click the drop-down arrow next to the *Which drive do you want to defragment?* box. Choose your computer's floppy disk drive, which should be Drive A.

   D. Click OK. The Defragmenting Drive A dialog box appears, and Windows begins defragmenting the disk. Quickly click the Show Details button. The dialog box expands and provides details about the disk's surface.

   E. Click the Legend button. Windows displays a second dialog box, which explains the details in the defragmentation window. Now watch as Windows finishes defragmenting the disk. (This process could last a few minutes or it could last a few hours if the disk is severely fragmented.)

   F. A new dialog box appears, asking if you want to quit Disk Defragmenter. Choose Yes, then remove the diskette from the drive.

2. **Check a Disk for Errors.** Several disk errors can occur and harm the disk's performance and cause data loss. Your operating system should provide a utility that lets you check a magnetic disk for different types of errors. In Windows 95 and 98, this utility is called ScanDisk. It looks for unclaimed files (files or pieces of files that do not belong to a specific program), problems on the surface of a disk, and more. In this exercise, you will run your disk-checking utility on a floppy disk, using settings your instructor provides. Take the following steps:

   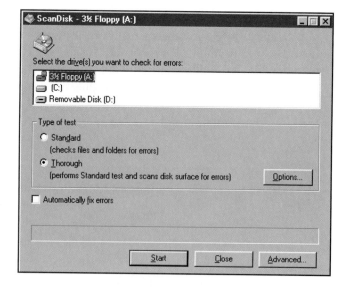

   A. Insert a diskette into your diskette drive.

   B. Click the Start button, point to Programs, point to Accessories, point to System Tools, and then click ScanDisk. The ScanDisk window opens.

   C. In the "Select the drive(s) you want to check for errors" list, click 3½ Floppy.

   D. Choose other settings as directed by your instructor, then click Start.

   E. Watch as ScanDisk checks the disk for data and surface errors. If it reports finding an error, ask your instructor for assistance in dealing with the problem.

   F. When ScanDisk is done, click Close and remove the diskette from its drive.

Internet Labs

To complete the following exercises, you need a computer with an Internet connection and a Web browser. (For more information on using these tools, see "Prerequisites" at the front of this textbook.)

1. **Go Shopping.** Suppose you are in the market for a CD-ReWritable drive, which you want to add to your computer system. Visit the following Web sites and gather information about the CD-RW products offered by these vendors:

   - Hewlett-Packard—**http://www.hewlett-packard.com/**
   - Iomega Corp.—**http://www.iomega.com/**
   - Memorex—**http://www.memorex.com/**
   - Philips Consumer Electronics—**http://www.philips.com/**
   - Ricoh Consumer Products Group—**http://www.ricohcpg.com/**
   - Yamaha—**http://www.yamaha.com/**

   When you are done, launch Notepad and write a one-page paper summarizing your findings and explaining which CD-RW unit you would purchase. Give your reasons for choosing that unit. Print the paper and give a copy to your instructor.

2. **Backup Online.** Suppose you want to back up the hard disk on your home computer, but you do not want to research, purchase, and set up a backup system. Instead, you decide to check out some of the online backup services that can back up your data over the Internet. Visit the Web sites for the following online backup services:

   - @Backup—**http://www.backup.com/**
   - BackJack Online Backup Service—**http://www.backjack.com/**
   - Data Protection Services, LLC—**http://www.dataprotection.net/**
   - NetMass, Inc.—**http://www.systemrecovery.com/**

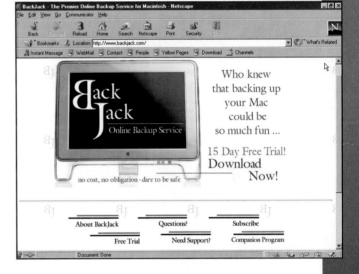

IBE Labs

If you have the Interactive Browser Edition (IBE) CD-ROM for this textbook, you may complete the following interactive exercises using the instructions provided in the IBE.

1. **Trivia Game.** Test your knowledge of storage devices.

2. **Labeling.** The focus of this exercise is on disk drive interfaces.

3. **Association Game.** Challenge your understanding of storage technology by arranging information correctly in a table.

4. **How Good Is Your Drive Performance?** Depending on your choices, the "system's" drive performance may increase or decrease.

UNIT 6

The Operating System and User Interface

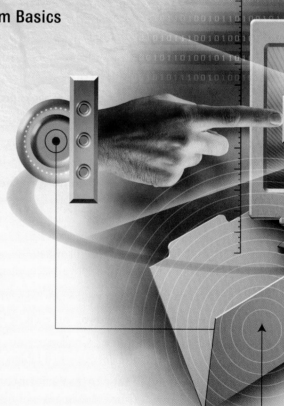

Operating System Basics

OVERVIEW:
The Role of the Operating System

An operating system (OS) is a software program, but it is different from word processing programs, spreadsheets, and all the other software programs on your computer. The OS is the computer's master control program. The OS provides you with the tools (commands) that enable you to interact with the PC. When you issue a command, the OS translates it into code that the machine can use. The OS also ensures that the results of your actions are displayed on screen, printed, and so on.

The operating system performs the following functions:

> ► Provides the instructions to display the on-screen elements with which you interact. Collectively, these elements are known as the user interface.

> ► Loads programs (such as word processing and spreadsheet programs) into the computer's memory so that you can use them.

> ► Coordinates how programs work with the CPU, RAM, keyboard, mouse, printer, and other hardware as well as with other software.

> ► Manages the way information is stored on and retrieved from disks.

The functioning of the OS can be extended by adding utility software.

OBJECTIVES

- Identify four components found in most graphical user interfaces.
- Describe the operating system's role in running software programs.
- Explain how the operating system enables users to manage files.
- List three ways the operating system manages the computer's hardware.
- Name five types of utilities that enhance an operating system's functioning.

OPEN

SAVE

PRINT

COPY

PASTE

THE USER INTERFACE

With an operating system, you see and interact with a set of items on the screen: the **user interface.** In the case of most current operating systems, the user interface looks like a collection of objects on a colored background (see Figure 11.1).

Figure 11.1
The screen of a typical Windows 98 computer. The items that appear on the screen depend on the contents of the computer's disk and the resources to which the computer has access. For this reason and others, any two Windows 98 systems can look different.

Graphical User Interfaces

Most current operating systems, including all versions of Windows, the Macintosh operating system, OS/2, and some versions of UNIX, provide a **graphical user interface (GUI,** pronounced GOO-ee). Apple Computer introduced the first successful GUI with its Macintosh computer in 1984. Graphical user interfaces are so called because you use a mouse (or some other pointing device) to point at graphical objects on the screen. Figure 11.2 shows the Windows 98 interface with the Start menu open, a program running, and a dialog box open.

Figure 11.2
Many graphical operating systems provide the features shown here. *Note:* The taskbar, Start button, and Start menu are unique to Windows 95, 98, and 2000 and Windows NT version 4.0 and later.

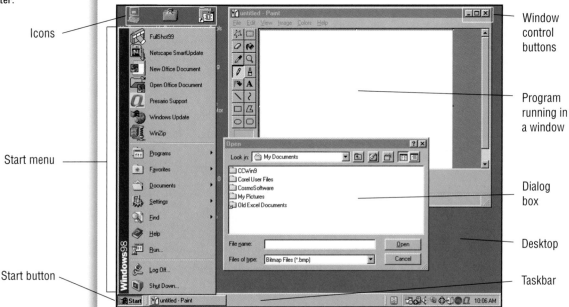

Icons

Start menu

Start button

Window control buttons

Program running in a window

Dialog box

Desktop

Taskbar

The Desktop

Software makers call the colored area you see on screen the **desktop** because they want you to think of it as just like the surface of a desk. The pictures, too, stand for items you might have in your office—in the case of Windows, these items include My Computer, a Recycle Bin, an Inbox, and a Briefcase.

Icons

Icons are pictures that represent the parts of the computer you work with—printers, fonts, document files, folders (a way to organize files into logical groups), disk drives, programs, and so on. Software designers try to design the icons so that they look like what they represent, thus making it easy to identify the icon you need. In Figure 11.3, for example, the PaintShop Pro icon represents the PaintShop Pro program, which resides on the computer's disk.

You interact with your computer's resources by activating the icons that represent the resources, which is done most easily by using a pointing device, such as a mouse. You learned about basic mouse usage in Lesson 3, "Standard Methods of Input." With most GUI-based operating systems, rules for using the mouse to interact with icons are fairly consistent:

◆ You click an icon to **select** it. This indicates that you plan to work with it.

◆ You double-click on an icon to **choose,** or **activate** it. For instance, you double-click the icon of a word processing program to load that program into memory and start using it. This action is also called launching the program.

◆ If you click an icon and hold down the mouse button, you can drag the mouse to move the icon to another location on the desktop. Sometimes you drag an icon to another icon to perform an action. For instance, you can drag an icon for a file from one folder to another and thus move the file.

◆ If you right-click many parts of the desktop for Windows 9*x*, NT, and 2000 operating systems, you will see a small menu containing the most common commands associated with that part. Depending on the version of Windows you are using and whether you are using a specific application, this type of menu may be called a **shortcut menu** or a **context menu.** Either way, its function is the same—to provide quick access to commonly used commands related to the item you have right-clicked.

Although icons generally look like the object they represent, another class of symbols, called buttons, generally look the same from program to program. **Buttons** are areas of the screen you can click to start an action or task. Most buttons feature a name and/or a picture surrounded by a black border. You may find many kinds of buttons in your program windows and dialog boxes; each one enables you to perform a specific task. For example, the Open button and the Cancel button are found in many dialog boxes, as shown in Figure 11.2.

The Taskbar and the Start Button (Windows Only)

Whenever you start a program in certain versions of Windows (including Windows 95, 98, 2000, or NT version 4.0 or later), a button for it appears on the **taskbar**— an area at the bottom of the screen whose purpose is to display the buttons for the programs you are running. The **Start button** (see Figure 11.4) is a permanent feature of the taskbar. You click it to open the **Start menu** (see Figure 11.2). From the Start menu, you can click a program icon to start a program, choose Help to

Figure 11.3
If icons like these appear on your operating system's desktop, you can use them to launch programs or to access different devices on your computer.

Figure 11.4
The Start button is a standard feature of the Windows 95, 98, 2000, and NT operating systems. You use it to open the Start menu, which provides access to the programs and devices on your disk.

Visit **www.glencoe.com/norton/online/** for more information on **graphical user interfaces.**

find information to assist you as you work, or choose Shut Down when you are ready to turn off your computer.

Programs Running in Windows

In a graphical operating system, you can launch a program by choosing its program icon on the desktop. (In Windows 95, 98, and 2000, you can also launch a program by choosing its name from the Start menu.) The program is then loaded into memory and begins to run. A running program may take up the whole screen or it may appear in a rectangular frame, called a **window.** Windows give you access to all the resources on your computer. For example, you can view the contents of a disk in a window, run a program and edit a document inside a window, view a Web page in a window, or change system settings in a window. A different window appears for each resource you want to use.

Most windows share many of the characteristics shown in Figure 11.5. For example, all windows include a **title bar** across the top that identifies the window's contents. In addition to providing useful information, the title bar has another purpose: you can move the entire window by clicking the title bar and dragging the window to a new location on the desktop. Below the title bar, most programs contain a menu bar and toolbars that give you quick access to options and commands.

In all versions of Microsoft Windows, OS/2, and the Macintosh operating system, windows also have adjustable borders and corners. If you drag the corners or sides of the windows, you can make the windows larger or smaller so that you see more or less of their contents. Many windows also provide **scroll bars** with scroll arrows and scroll boxes, which enable you to view the different parts of the program or file that do not fit in the window.

Graphical operating systems enable you to have multiple programs and resources running at the same time, but you can work in only one window at a time. The window that is currently in use is called the **active window;** it is the window where your next action will take effect. If you have more than one window open, as shown in Figures 11.6 and 11.7, you can identify the active window in several ways:

Figure 11.5
Typical components of a program window in a graphical user interface.

Title bar
Menu bar
Toolbar

Click the Minimize button to reduce the program to a button on the taskbar.

Click the Maximize button to restore the window to its previous size.

Click the Close button to close the window altogether.

Scroll arrow
Scroll box
Scroll bar
Scroll arrow

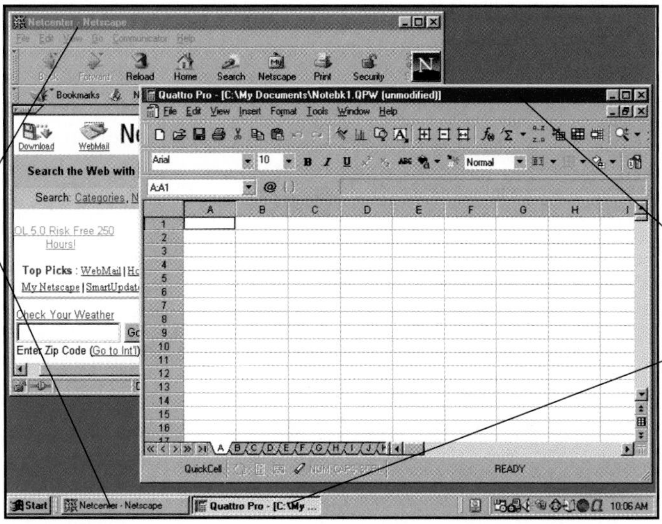

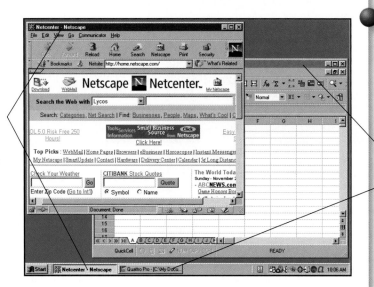

Figure 11.6
Two programs running under Windows 98. Quattro Pro is the active program.

Netscape Navigator is in the background. Its title bar is grayed out and its taskbar button is not highlighted.

Quattro Pro is on top, ready to be used. Its title bar and taskbar button are highlighted.

Figure 11.7
The same two programs running under Windows 98. Now, Netscape Navigator is active.

Netscape Navigator is now the active program. Its title bar and taskbar button are highlighted.

Quattro Pro is now in the background. Its title bar is grayed out and its taskbar button is no longer highlighted.

◆ Unless all open windows are arranged side by side, the active window will appear on top of the other windows. Inactive windows appear to be in the background.

◆ The active window's title bar is highlighted—that is, it is displayed in color. The title bar of an inactive window is "grayed out," meaning that it appears in gray rather than in color.

◆ If you are using a Windows system with a taskbar, the active window's taskbar button is highlighted—that is, it appears to be "pushed in." An inactive program's taskbar button appears to be "popped out."

If you have more than one window open, you must select the window you want to use before you can access its contents. The process of moving from one open window to another is called **task switching,** and different operating systems let you task switch in different ways. In any graphical operating system, you can simply click in any open window to make it active. Your OS may also provide a special dialog box or a keyboard shortcut for performing task switching. In Windows 95, 98, and 2000, you can also click an open program's taskbar button to activate its window.

Menus

Although you initiate many tasks by clicking icons and buttons, you can also start tasks by choosing commands from lists called **menus.** You have already seen the Start menu, which appears when you click the Start button in some versions of Windows. The more standard type of menu, however, appears at the top of many windows in a horizontal list called the **menu bar.**

Figure 11.8

The File menu in WordPerfect. Notice that if any keyboard shortcuts are available, you can see them on the menu.

The underlined F indicates that you can press Alt+F to open the File menu.

With the File menu open, you can press P to execute the Print command.

As a one-step shortcut, you can press Ctrl+P to execute the Print command without opening the File menu.

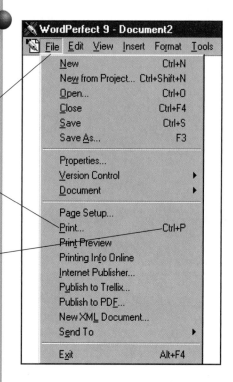

Figure 11.8

The File menu in WordPerfect. Notice that if any keyboard shortcuts are available, you can see them on the menu.

The underlined F indicates that you can press Alt+F to open the File menu.

With the File menu open, you can press P to execute the Print command.

As a one-step shortcut, you can press Ctrl+P to execute the Print command without opening the File menu.

When you click a menu's name, a menu "drops down" and displays a list of commands. (These menus are sometimes called pull-down menus or drop-down menus.) For example, many programs feature a File menu, which typically contains commands for opening, closing, saving, and printing files. Figure 11.8 shows the File menu in WordPerfect. To execute or run one of the menu commands, you click it.

As a shortcut, you can also execute many commands from the keyboard. For example, in Windows programs, one letter is underlined in the name of each menu and in many menu commands. To open a menu, hold down the Alt key and type the underlined letter in the menu's name at the same time. After the menu is opened, just type the underlined letter in the name of the command you want to issue. If you want to open a new file in Microsoft Word, for example, you can press Alt+F to open the File menu, then press O to access the Open dialog box.

Some commands are used so frequently they have keyboard shortcuts that bypass the menu system altogether. Many programs use the keyboard's function keys (F1, F2, and others) as shortcut keys. For example, in most programs you can press F1 to access the online help system. You issue many keyboard shortcuts by pressing multiple keys at the same time, such as a modifier key and an alphanumeric key. The Save command is a good example. In many programs, for instance, you can press a key combination such as Ctrl+S to save the currently open file to disk. Different operating systems and programs provide different sets of keyboard shortcuts. When you learn these shortcuts, you may find them much more efficient than opening menus to issue commands.

Dialog Boxes

Dialog boxes are special-purpose windows that appear when you need to tell a program (or the operating system) what to do next. For example, if you choose Find and then choose Files or Folders from the Windows Start menu, a dialog box appears, asking you to describe the file or folder you want to find. A dialog box is so named because it conducts a "dialog" with you as it seeks the information it needs to perform a task. Figure 11.9 shows a typical dialog box and describes some of the most common dialog box features.

Figure 11.9
A dialog box can provide a wide variety of tools, thus allowing you to perform specialized tasks in an application or operating system.

Click a tab to display different "pages" of the dialog box. The Index section is currently visible.

Option buttons let you select one option from a set of choices.

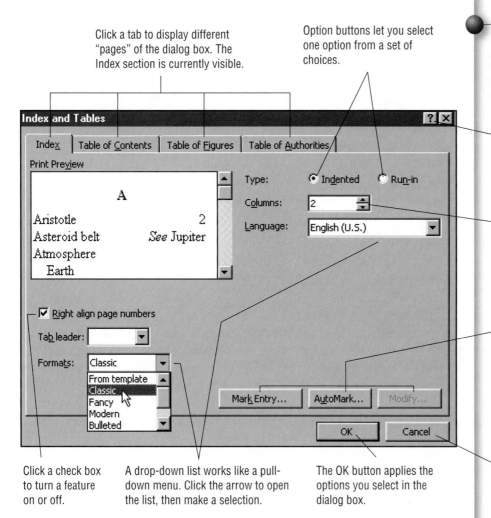

The Help button provides information about the tools of the dialog box.

Spinner (or counter) buttons usually contain numbers. Use the controls to increase or decrease the value.

These three buttons are called command buttons. Click one to initiate an action right away. If a button's name is followed by an ellipsis (...), then a second dialog box appears.

The Cancel button closes the dialog box without making any changes.

Click a check box to turn a feature on or off.

A drop-down list works like a pull-down menu. Click the arrow to open the list, then make a selection.

The OK button applies the options you select in the dialog box.

Command-Line Interfaces

The graphical user interface has become the standard because the Macintosh and Windows operating systems use it. For years, however, computer operating systems used command-line interfaces, which are environments that use typewritten commands rather than graphical objects to execute tasks and process data.

During the 1980s, the most popular command-line interfaces were Microsoft's MS-DOS, its near twin PC-DOS from IBM, and UNIX. Users interact with a **command-line interface** by typing strings of characters at a **prompt** on the screen. In DOS, the prompt usually includes the identification for the active disk drive (a letter followed by a colon), a backslash (\), and a greater-than symbol, as in C:\>. Figure 11.10 shows the DOS prompt, which is still available in Windows 95 and 98 for those who want to run DOS programs or to work with DOS keyboard commands.

Some experienced users of command-line interfaces argue that they are simpler and faster, and provide better information than GUI operating systems. However, GUIs became the standard because most users preferred them, in part because they are easier to learn. Finding and starting programs from a command-line prompt can be compared to traveling at night with a road map in your head. Instead of clicking icons, you type a series of memorized commands. For instance, in DOS, you type DIR at the prompt to see a list of files in a particular "directory" (the equivalent of a folder).

NORTON ONLINE

Visit www.glencoe.com/norton/online/ for more information on command-line interfaces.

Figure 11.10
The DOS prompt.

C:\>_

COMPUTERS
in your career

Operating Systems and You

Although you will spend most of your computing time using an application rather than working directly with an operating system, it is still useful to learn as much as you can about your operating system. Not only can you get more power from your computer and its resources, you will get more from your applications also.

If you find yourself in a career that involves the use of computers—specifically, as a tool to get your job done—you will probably be working with only one operating system. In most general businesses, that operating system will probably be a variation of Windows or Windows NT. Many careers in the publishing and design industries, however, involve Apple computers and the Macintosh operating system. As shown below, the medical and engineering fields commonly make use of high-powered systems that include a variation of UNIX.

In all these cases, however, your experience will probably be limited to a single operating system, which means you need to learn about only one. This rule does not apply to other careers, some of which demand a mastery of different hardware platforms, operating systems, and network systems:

◆ **Network Administrators and Hardware Technicians.** Careers in data services may require you to work with several different hardware platforms and operating systems. Network managers, for example, typically have to deal with different versions of Windows and a separate network operating system (such as NetWare). You can easily find "mixed" networks, where Macintosh PCs, mainframe systems, and other platforms have been combined. These environments require network administrators to have a broad understanding of different operating systems, their capabilities, and their command sets.

◆ **Programmers.** Some specialized careers may require you to master—or at least understand—several operating systems. For example, many programmers must write different versions of programs to run on different operating systems. Programmers must know the many differences between operating systems and the way they interact with the architecture of the computer itself. Many programmers use various development tools and languages to assist in these efforts.

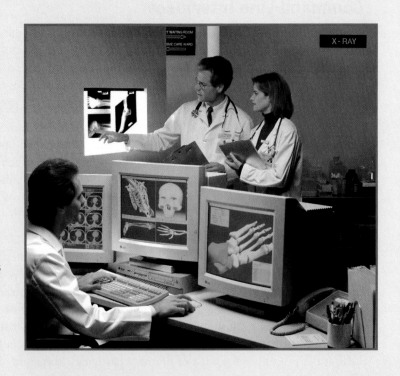

◆ **Graphic Artists and Desktop Publishers.** In the world of computer graphics, artists and designers use many different hardware and software tools. Different platforms offer unique strengths and features. In digital studios, therefore, you can commonly find Windows, Macintosh, and UNIX systems all on the same network, with users switching from one system to another as needed.

Answer the following questions by filling in the blank(s).

1. In most current operating systems, the _____ looks like a collection of objects on a colored background.

2. The taskbar and Start button are found exclusively in certain versions of the _____ operating system.

3. The process of moving from one open window to another is called _____ .

RUNNING PROGRAMS

The operating system provides a consistent interface between the program and the user; it is also the interface between those programs and other computer resources (such as memory, a printer, or another program such as a spreadsheet application). Programmers write computer programs with built-in instructions—called **system calls**—that request services from the operating system. (They are "calls" because the program has to call on the operating system to provide some information or service.)

Figure 11.11
The Open dialog box in FullShot 99, an image-management program.

For example, when you want your word processing program to retrieve a file, you use the Open dialog box to list the files in the folder that you specify (see Figure 11.11). To provide the list, the program calls on the operating system. The OS goes through the same process to build a list of files whether it receives its instructions from you (via the desktop) or from an application. The difference is that when the request comes from an application, the operating system sends the results of its work to the application rather than to the desktop.

Some other services that an operating system provides to programs, in addition to listing files, are as follows:

◆ Saving the contents of files to a disk for permanent storage.

◆ Reading the contents of a file from disk into memory.

◆ Sending a document to the printer and activating the printer.

◆ Providing resources that let you copy or move data from one document to another, or from one program to another.

◆ Allocating RAM among various programs that you may have open.

◆ Recognizing keystrokes or mouse clicks and displaying characters or graphics on the screen.

Visit **www.glencoe.com/norton/online/**
for more information on **data sharing.**

Sharing Information

In many types of applications you may want to move chunks of data from one place to another. For example, you may want to copy a chart from a spreadsheet program and place the copy in a document in a word processor (see Figure 11.12).

Most newer operating systems accomplish this feat with a feature known as the **Clipboard.** The Clipboard is a temporary holding space (in the computer's memory) for data that is being copied or moved. For example, to move a paragraph in a word-processed document, select the paragraph, then choose the **Cut** command, which removes the data and places it on the Clipboard. (If you want to leave the original data in place, you can use the **Copy** command, which makes a copy of the data and stores it on the Clipboard but does not remove the original.) After placing the insertion point where you want to place the paragraph, you choose the **Paste** command, which copies the Clipboard's contents back into the document.

The Clipboard can also be used to move data from one document to another. For example, you can copy an address from one letter to another and thereby avoid rekeying it. The real versatility of the Clipboard, however, stems from the fact that it is actually part of the operating system, not a particular application. As a result, you can use the Clipboard to move data from one program to another.

The versatility of the Clipboard has been extended further with a feature known in Windows as **OLE,** which stands for **Object Linking and Embedding.** A simple cut and paste between applications results in object embedding. The data, which is known as an object in programming terms, is embedded in a new type of document. It retains the formatting that was applied to it in the original application, but its relationship with the original file is destroyed; that is, it is simply part of the new file.

Figure 11.12
Using the Clipboard to copy a chart from an Excel document to a WordPro document.

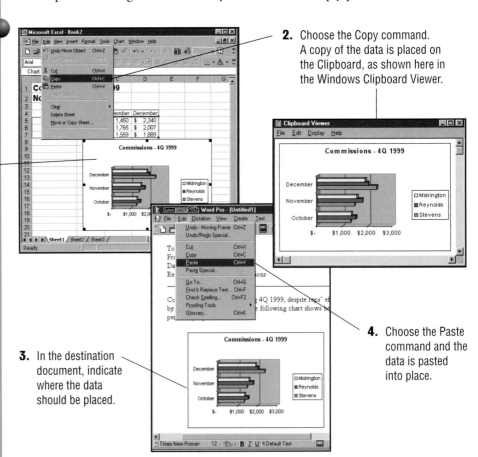

1. Select the desired data—in this case, a chart in Excel.

2. Choose the Copy command. A copy of the data is placed on the Clipboard, as shown here in the Windows Clipboard Viewer.

3. In the destination document, indicate where the data should be placed.

4. Choose the Paste command and the data is pasted into place.

Object linking adds another layer to the relationship: the data that is copied to and from the Clipboard retains a link to the original document so that a change in the original document also appears in the linked data. For example, suppose that the spreadsheet and memo shown in Figure 11.12 are generated quarterly. They always contain the same chart updated with the most recent numbers. With object linking, when the numbers in the spreadsheet are changed, the chart in the report will automatically reflect the new figures.

Multitasking

Since the mid-1990s, all PC operating systems have been able to multitask, which is a computer's version of being able to "walk and chew gum at the same time." Multitasking means much more than the capability to load multiple programs into memory. Multitasking means being able to perform two or more procedures—such as printing a multiple-paged document, sending e-mail over the Internet, and typing a letter—simultaneously (see Figure 11.13).

Software engineers use two methods to develop multitasking operating systems. The first requires cooperation between the operating system and application programs. Programs that are currently running will periodically check the operating system to see whether any other programs need the CPU. If any do, the running program will relinquish control of the CPU to the next program. This method is called **cooperative multitasking** and is used to allow activities such as printing while the user continues to type or use the mouse to input more data.

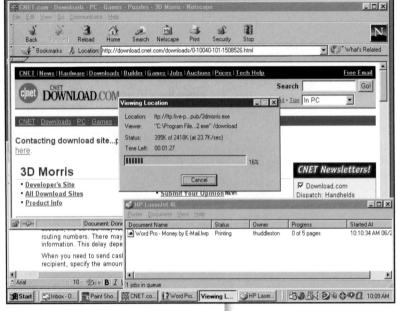

Figure 11.13
Multitasking lets you do more than one task at a time. Here the computer is printing a document from Lotus Word Pro while the user downloads a file from the Internet.

The second method is called **preemptive multitasking.** With this method, the operating system maintains a list of programs that are running and assigns a priority to each program in the list. The operating system can intervene and modify a program's priority status by rearranging the priority list. With preemptive multitasking, the operating system can preempt the program that is running and reassign the time to a higher priority task at any time. Preemptive multitasking thus has the advantage of being able to carry out higher-priority programs faster than lower-priority programs.

MANAGING FILES

The files that the operating system works with may be program or data files. Most programs come with any number—possibly thousands—of files. When you use programs, you often create your own data files, such as word processing documents, and store them on a disk under names that you assign to them. It is the responsibility of the operating system to keep track of all these files so that it can copy any one of them into RAM at a moment's notice.

NORTON
ONLINE

Visit **www.glencoe.com/norton/online/** for more information on **multitasking.**

NORTON

ONLINE

Visit **www.glencoe.com/norton/online/** for more information on **file management.**

To accomplish this feat, the operating system maintains a list of the contents of a disk on the disk itself. As you learned in Lesson 9, "Types of Storage Devices," there is an area called the file allocation table, or FAT, that the operating system creates when you format a disk. The operating system updates the information in the FAT any time a file is created, moved, renamed, or deleted. In addition, the operating system keeps track of different disks or disk drives by assigning names to them. On IBM and compatible computers, diskette drives are assigned the letters A and B, and hard disk drives are designated as the C drive and up. CD-ROM drives have the first available letter following the hard drives—often the letter D. Non-Microsoft operating systems use slightly different schemes for keeping track of disks and their contents, but each scheme accomplishes the same task.

When there are hundreds of files on a disk, finding the one you want can be time-consuming. To find files quickly, you can organize them using folders. Figure 11.14 shows a list of the main folder of a hard disk, as shown in the Windows Explorer utility. Notice how file names are accompanied by the file sizes in bytes and the date and time when the files were last modified.

Also notice that there are several folders in the list. Folders can contain other folders, so you can create a structured system known as a **hierarchical file system.** A diagram for a hierarchical file system is shown in Figure 11.15.

Figure 11.14
The Exploring window, showing the contents of the hard disk.

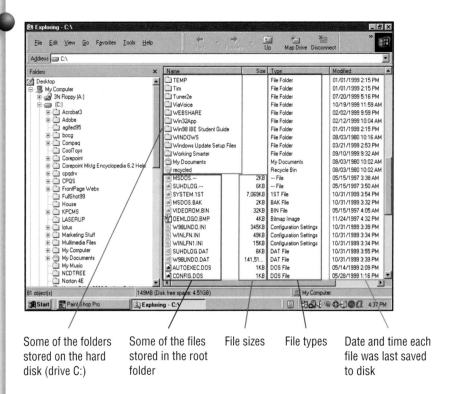

Some of the folders stored on the hard disk (drive C:)

Some of the files stored in the root folder

File sizes

File types

Date and time each file was last saved to disk

MANAGING HARDWARE

When programs run, they need to use the computer's memory, monitor, disk drives, and other devices, such as a printer. The operating system is the intermediary between programs and hardware. In a computer network, the operating system also mediates between your computer and other devices on the network. In the next sections, you will see three ways in which the operating system serves as the go-between to keep hardware running smoothly.

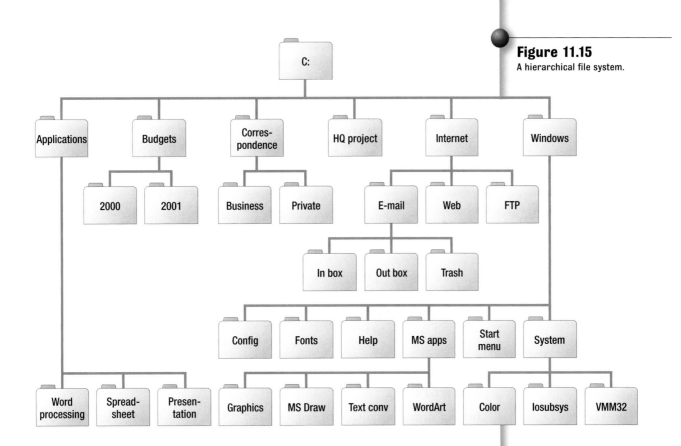

Figure 11.15
A hierarchical file system.

Processing Interrupts

The operating system responds to requests to use memory and other devices, keeps track of which programs have access to which devices, and coordinates everything the hardware does so that various activities do not overlap and cause the computer to become confused and stop working. The operating system uses interrupt requests (IRQs) to help the CPU coordinate processes. For example, if you tell the operating system to list the files in a folder, it sends an interrupt request to the computer's CPU (see Figure 11.16 on page 198).

The interrupt request procedure is a little like using parliamentary procedures in a large meeting. At first, it may seem like an extra layer of unnecessary formality. In fact, this formality is needed to keep everyone from talking at once—or in the case of interrupt requests, to keep the CPU from becoming overwhelmed with a barrage of possibly conflicting processing instructions.

Drivers

In addition to using interrupts, the operating system often provides complete programs for working with special devices, such as printers. These programs are called **drivers** because they allow the operating system and other programs to activate and use—that is, "drive"—the hardware device. When DOS reigned, drivers had to be installed separately for each program used. With modern operating systems such as Windows 9x, Windows NT, and the Macintosh OS, drivers are an integral part of the operating system. Most of the software you buy will work with your printer, monitor, and other equipment without requiring any special installation. For example, many modems use the same unified driver in Windows 9x. All that is different is the setup information the operating system uses to configure the modem to accommodate the specific capabilities of each modem.

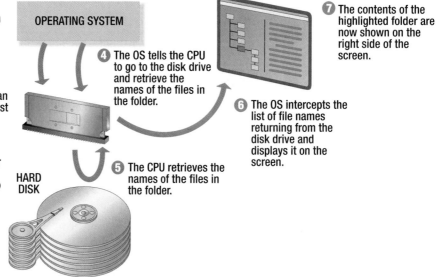

① When you click on a folder, the OS interprets the action as a command to list the files in that folder.

OPERATING SYSTEM

② The OS sends an interrupt request to the CPU.

③ When possible, the CPU pauses any other processing and checks with the OS to see what new processing job is being requested.

④ The OS tells the CPU to go to the disk drive and retrieve the names of the files in the folder.

HARD DISK

⑤ The CPU retrieves the names of the files in the folder.

⑥ The OS intercepts the list of file names returning from the disk drive and displays it on the screen.

⑦ The contents of the highlighted folder are now shown on the right side of the screen.

Figure 11.16
How the operating system communicates with the CPU.

Networking

Besides providing interrupt requests and drivers for working with individual devices, the operating system can also allow you to work with multiple computers on a network. On a network, usually each person has a separate PC with its own operating system. The network server also has its own operating system, which manages the flow of data on the file server and around the network. As operating systems continue to evolve, networking will become a more integral part of all operating systems.

UTILITY SOFTWARE

Operating systems are designed to let you do most of the tasks you normally would want to do with a computer—manage files, load programs, print files, multitask, and so on. These programs (actually, sets of programs) are sold by the behemoths of the software industry: Microsoft, Apple, IBM, Santa Cruz Operation (SCO), and Novell. However, many other talented software firms are constantly finding ways to improve operating systems. The programs they create are called **utilities.**

In the 1980s, when utilities for PCs first appeared, some of the most popular were those that helped the user back up files, detect computer viruses, and retrieve files that had been deleted. A few utility programs actually replace parts of the operating system, but the vast majority simply add helpful functioning. Because they aid the inner workings of the computer system, utilities are grouped with the operating system under the category of system software.

Popular utilities range from programs that can organize or compress the files on a disk to programs that help you remove programs you no longer use from your hard disk. Some of the major categories of utilities include **file defragmentation utilities, data compression programs, backup utilities, antivirus programs,** and **screen savers.** Each of these types of utilities is illustrated in the Visual Essay on pages 200 and 201.

NORTON ONLINE

Visit **www.glencoe.com/norton/online/** for more information on **utilities.**

PRODUCTIVITY Tip

Do-It-Yourself Tech Support

If you want to learn a new feature or need help solving a problem, the answers may be on your hard disk or the Internet.

Using Local Online Help

Most commercial operating systems and applications include an online help system that is installed on your computer with the software. New-generation help systems include descriptions, tips, audio/video demonstrations, hyperlinks, and links to Internet-based resources.

To find help on your hard drive, open the help system and look for answers. To get help with the Windows OS, for example, click the Start button and choose Help from the Start menu. In any Windows application, click the Help menu and choose Contents or Help Topics. A Help window appears, providing tools that let you search for help in different ways. Remember the following tips:

◆ **Be Patient.** You may not find your answer immediately. Be prepared to try again.

◆ **Learn Different Search Options.** Most Windows-based help systems are divided into three sections, each providing different options for finding help. The Contents section displays help topics in a hierarchical list. The Search section lets you search all topics to find those topics whose title contains a specific term. The Index tab displays all the key terms in the help system; select one or more terms and then get a list of help topics that contain those terms.

◆ **Think of the Problem in Different Ways.** For example, if you want help with making characters bold in your document, the terms *bold*, *format*, *font*, and *style* may bring up the right answers.

◆ **Use Bookmarks and Annotations.** Most help systems let you bookmark specific help topics so you can find them again quickly. You can also add your own notes to specific topics.

Using Remote Online Help

Many software makers provide several remote online help resources that you can access over the Internet.

◆ **Web-Based Technical Support.** Many software companies have a "Support" or "Help" link on their Web home page.

◆ **FAQs.** Most software companies have Web sites with lists of frequently asked questions (FAQs).

◆ **E-Mail Help.** At the company's Web site, you may find an option that lets you describe a problem and submit a request for help. A support technician will investigate the problem, or an automated system will send you a list of possible solutions.

◆ **Knowledgebases.** A knowledgebase is a sophisticated database containing detailed information about a specific topic. To use a knowledgebase, you type a term or phrase or describe a problem. After your text is matched against a database, you are presented with a list of possible solutions.

◆ **Newsgroups.** Large software companies sponsor newsgroups on the Internet. Using your newsreader, you can access these newsgroups, post questions for other users to answer, or participate in discussions about specific products and technical issues.

Before you use any remote online help resource, read all the information the company provides about it. Look for notices about fees, registration, and proof of product ownership.

The online help system is often the last place users turn for help; in fact, it should be the first place you look.

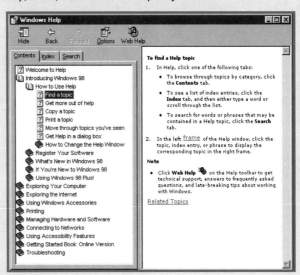

VISUAL ESSAY: UTILITY SOFTWARE

If a file is too large to be saved in a single sector on a disk, it must be broken into pieces. Each piece is saved in a separate sector. Ideally, the pieces will be stored in contiguous sectors. This setup is not always possible because enough contiguous sectors may not be available. In this case, the pieces are stored in noncontiguous sectors. When this happens to a large number of files, the disk is said to be fragmented. Fragmentation slows disk performance because the OS must spend time looking for pieces of files stored in various places.

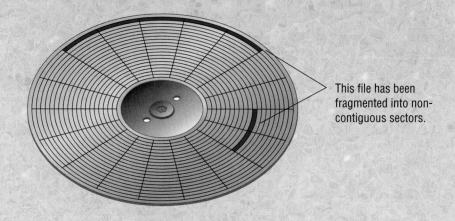

This file has been fragmented into non-contiguous sectors.

Using a utility like the Disk Defragmenter (built into Windows 95, 98, and 2000), you can rearrange the fragmented pieces of data so your files are stored in contiguous sectors. This dialog box shows the process of the utility as it defragments the files on the hard disk.

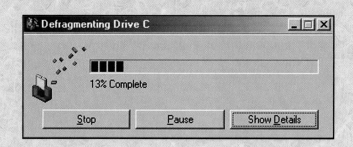

As you learned in Unit 5, you can use a data compression utility to reduce the size of files so they consume less disk space. Utilities such as WinZip, StuffIT, and others use special algorithms to search files for unnecessary bits, which are stripped out. The process can significantly shrink some types of files. In this collection of compressed files, some files have shrunk by more than 80 percent.

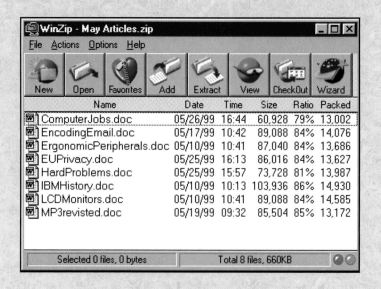

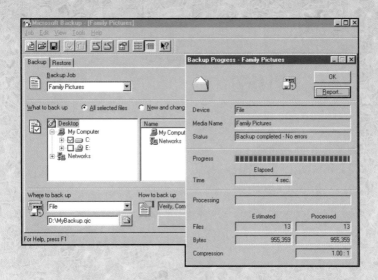

Backup software can help you copy large groups of files from your hard disk to another storage medium, such as tape or a CD-R disk. Many newer operating systems feature built-in backup utilities, but feature-rich backup software is available from other sources. These utilities not only help you transfer files to a backup medium, they also help organize the files, update backups, and restore backups to disk in case of data loss.

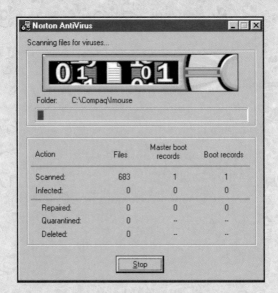

A virus is a parasitic program that can delete or scramble files or replicate itself until the host disk is full. As you will learn in Unit 15, computer viruses can be transmitted in numerous ways, and users should be especially vigilant when downloading files over the Internet or reusing old diskettes that may be infected. Antivirus utilities examine specific parts of a disk for hidden viruses and files that may act as hosts for virus code. Effective antivirus products not only detect and remove viruses, they also help you recover data that has been lost because of a virus.

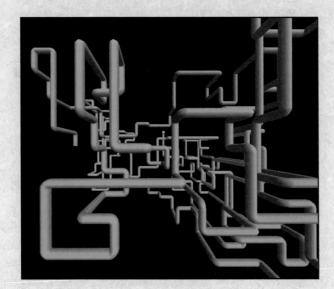

Screen savers are popular utilities, although they serve little purpose other than to hide what would otherwise be displayed on the screen. A screen saver automatically displays when the system has been unused for a specified period of time. Screen savers display a constantly moving image on the screen and were originally created to prevent constantly displayed images from "burning" into the monitor. Today's monitors do not suffer from this problem, but screen savers remain a popular utility because they add personality to the user's system.

LESSON QUIZ

True/False

Answer the following questions by circling True or False.

True   False   **1.** Graphical user interfaces are so called because you point at graphical objects on the screen.

True   False   **2.** You interact with icons by using the keyboard.

True   False   **3.** All windows are unique because none share the same features.

True   False   **4.** You can choose menu commands by using the mouse or keyboard shortcuts.

True   False   **5.** In OLE, a copied object retains a link to its original application.

Multiple Choice

Circle the word or phrase that best completes each sentence.

1. In a GUI, you work in the _____ window.
   A. active   **B.** biggest   **C.** highlighted

2. Graphical operating systems often let you choose commands from lists, called _____ .
   A. command lines   **B.** menus   **C.** neither A nor B

3. In a command-line interface (such as DOS), you enter commands at a _____ .
   A. dialog box   **B.** window   **C.** prompt

4. To remove data from one document and place it in another, you can use the _____ and _____ commands.
   A. Cut, Paste   **B.** Copy, Paste   **C.** File, Open

5. When _____ , a computer performs two or more procedures at the same time.
   A. multitasking   **B.** cooperating   **C.** preempting

LESSON LABS

Complete the following exercises as directed by your instructor.

1. Use your online help system to learn more about Windows. Click the Start button, then choose Help from the Start menu. In the Windows Help window, click the Index tab, then click in the *Type in the keyword to find* text box. Type **what's new** and then click the Display button. A list of topics appears, each describing a new feature of Windows. View each of the topics. To research further, search using terms like **operating system**, **command**, **dialog box**, **menu**, and **multitasking**. When finished, close the help windows.

2. Practice using the DOS prompt:
   A. Click the Start button.
   B. Point to Programs, then double-click the MS-DOS Prompt from the Programs menu. Write down what the DOS prompt says.
   C. At the prompt, type **DIR** and press Enter. Write down the results. Do the same with the **VER** and **EXIT** commands.

PC Operating Systems in Review

OVERVIEW:
Operating Systems Then, Now, and Beyond

The personal computer has come a long way in a relatively short time, and much of the progress is due to the continuing advancements in operating system technologies. Over the past twenty years, the evolution in operating systems has made PCs easier to use and understand, more flexible, and more reliable.

In the 1980s, nearly all PCs ran the DOS operating system, and Macintosh computers used the Mac OS. Today, users have more choices in operating systems, but the choice is not always easy. Although the vast majority of new PCs feature a consumer version of Windows, the number of exceptions is increasing.

This lesson introduces you to the primary operating systems used on personal computers and describes the basic features of each. The operating systems are discussed chronologically, in order of their appearance on the desktop. You will learn how operating systems have evolved over the past two decades.

OBJECTIVES

- List all the major PC operating systems.
- Explain why DOS is no longer the dominant OS for personal computers.
- List two advances that made the Macintosh OS popular.
- Differentiate between the terms *operating environments* and *operating systems*.
- List and differentiate the various versions of Windows.

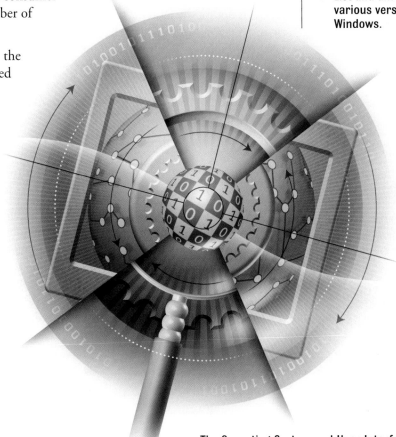

internet

UNIX — oldest operating system used on PC's

UNIX (pronounced YOO-niks) is older than all the other PC operating systems, and in many ways it served as a model for them. Initially developed by Bell Labs in the 1970s, UNIX was geared toward uses in telecommunications systems.

Instead of marketing UNIX as a commercial product, Bell Labs distributed the source code and allowed users to modify it. As a result, dozens (if not hundreds) of different versions of UNIX began springing up, especially in universities, where UNIX was widely used as a teaching and research tool by programmers and computer scientists. Today, there are two major "families" of UNIX—one developed and promoted by AT&T (called System V), and the other from Berkeley University (known as BSD UNIX). Many specific versions of UNIX exist, including A/UX for the Mac, AIX for IBM high-end workstations, Solaris for Sun Microsystems workstations, OpenVMS for Alpha workstations, SCO UNIX, XENIX, and others.

From nearly the beginning, UNIX was an incredibly powerful and flexible operating system that could run on a single computer or on a network. It provides pre-emptive multitasking, which makes efficient use of the computer's resources, especially when meeting the demands of many users or applications. UNIX allows multiple users to work from more than one keyboard and monitor attached to a single CPU, like a mainframe with dumb terminals. UNIX also supports multiprocessor systems—a PC with more than one CPU working at a time.

UNIX runs on many types of computers, including supercomputers, notebook PCs, and everything between, including mainframes and minicomputers. Because of its ability to work with so many kinds of hardware, UNIX became the backbone of the Internet. Thanks to its power and its appeal to engineers and other users of CAD and CAM software, UNIX has been popular for RISC workstations such as those from Sun Microsystems, Hewlett-Packard, and Silicon Graphics.

UNIX is not for the faint of heart because of its command-line interface and cryptic instructions, and the fact that it requires many commands to do even simple tasks (see Figure 12.1). In an attempt to make UNIX more user-friendly, developers have created windows-based GUIs for UNIX, such as MOTIF and OpenLook, which are based on a windowing standard called X-Windows (see Figure 12.2). Nonetheless, UNIX never really caught on as a consumer operating system, giving way to DOS, Windows, and the Mac OS, which generally have been perceived as easier to learn and use.

In the business world UNIX remains a popular operating system, especially among organizations that manage large databases shared by hundreds or thousands of users. Many types of specialized database-specific software have been developed for the UNIX platform and are deeply entrenched in industries such as insurance, medicine, banking, and manufacturing.

Figure 12.1

The UNIX command-line interface. Most versions of UNIX are case-sensitive: they can differentiate between upper- and lowercase letters typed at the command prompt.

```
linex2> ls
Mail/        News/        brian/      mail/
Mailboxes/   ShopCart.dat james.pl    public_html/
linex2> cd mail
linex2> ls
saved-messages      sent-mail          sent-mail-feb-1996
linex2> cd ..
linex2> ls
Mail/        News/        brian/      mail/
Mailboxes/   ShopCart.dat james.pl    public_html/
linex2> ps
  PID TT STAT  TIME COMMAND
 3023 p8 S     0:00 -csh (csh)
linex2> ftp
ftp> open ftp.netscape.com
Connected to ftp20.netscape.com.
220 ftp20 FTP server (Version wu-2.4(17) Tue Feb 20 09:08:35 PST 1996) ready.
Name (ftp.netscape.com:swankman): anonymous
331 Guest login ok, send your complete e-mail address as password.
Password:
230-Welcome to the Netscape Communications Corporation FTP server.
230-
230-If you have any odd problems, try logging in with a minus sign (-)
230-as the first character of your password.  This will turn off a feature
230-that may be confusing your ftp client program.
230-
230-Please send any questions, comments, or problem reports about
230-this server to ftp@netscape.com.
230-
230-***********  October 13, 1995  **********
230-Private ftp is now only on ftp1.netscape.com.  Anonymous is supported on
230-ftp 2 through 8.  If you are accessing a named account please use ftp1.
230-
230 Guest login ok, access restrictions apply.
ftp> bye
221 Goodbye.
linex2>
```

DOS

Microsoft's **MS-DOS** (which stands for Microsoft Disk Operating System), along with IBM's PC-DOS (Personal Computer Disk Operating System), was once the most common of all the PC operating systems. An overwhelming volume of software that ran under DOS was available, and a large installed base of Intel-based PCs ran DOS.

DOS was developed in the 1970s and distributed on some of the earliest commercial PCs. Although it ruled throughout the 1980s, DOS did not gain the upper hand without a fight. Its toughest early competitor was an operating system called CP/M (Control Program for Microprocessors). However, DOS won the early operating system marketing wars because IBM chose to license it instead of CP/M as the standard operating system for the IBM PC. It became the operating system for the huge market of IBM-compatibles.

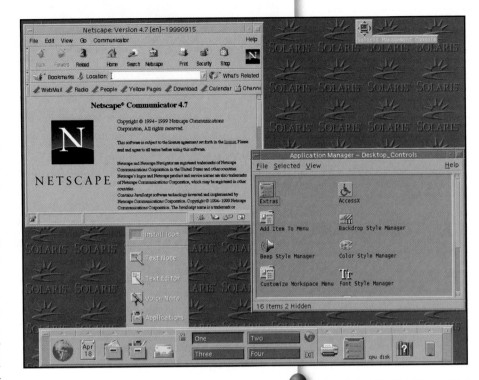

Figure 12.2
Window-based GUIs, like this one, make UNIX systems more user-friendly.

Among the strengths of DOS were its reliability and stability. On a properly configured system, DOS and DOS programs ran well; crashes and lockups were rare. Most users needed to learn only a small set of commands. Although the DOS prompt is not an elegant interface, it was not terribly hard to use once you mastered the commands you used most frequently.

DOS was adequate for the IBM-compatible PCs of the early 1980s, but its limitations became more noticeable as PCs became more powerful:

◆ Under DOS, you can load only a single application into memory at a time. To work with a second program, you have to close the first—a process that often hinders productivity.

◆ DOS supports only one user and a single processor.

◆ Because DOS did not dictate how an application's interface must look or function, developers created a wide variety of program-specific interfaces (see Figure 12.3 on page 206). Some applications appeared as nearly blank, text-only screens; to issue commands, you had to memorize keystrokes or use function keys. Others attempted to use primitive menu systems, which proved difficult for DOS users who did not have a mouse.

◆ DOS was designed to recognize only 640 KB of RAM and therefore cannot handle the large amounts of RAM commonly found in today's PCs. As a result, you must use utilities to access memory beyond the 640 KB limit.

NORTON
ONLINE

Visit www.glencoe.com/norton/online/ for more information on **DOS**.

Figure 12.3

An application running under DOS. DOS-based programs were often as difficult to use as the operating system itself, requiring users to memorize dozens of cryptic key combinations to issue commands.

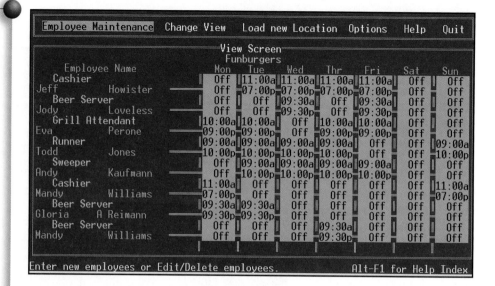

◆ DOS was designed for 8-bit and 16-bit CPUs; it cannot take advantage of the 32-bit architecture of the 486, Pentium, and later chips. DOS forces higher performance computers to work at speeds below their capacity.

◆ Hardware is difficult to install and configure under DOS because each device requires a unique driver. Often, different DOS applications use different drivers for the same device.

◆ DOS file names are limited to eight characters, plus a three-character "extension" following a period, as in the name "wordproc.doc." Windows 95 and 98 have remedied this situation by allowing file names up to 256 characters long. The UNIX and Macintosh operating systems, however, have long supported file names of up to 256 characters.

◆ Finally, as you learned in Lesson 11, many people found the DOS command-line interface more difficult to learn and use than a well-designed GUI. When Windows came along, most users were all too happy to stop typing commands and start clicking icons.

THE MACINTOSH OPERATING SYSTEM

The Macintosh is a purely graphical machine and brought the first truly graphical user interface to consumers. In its early days (mid-1980s), the Macintosh's integration of hardware and operating system, along with its GUI, made it popular among users who did not want to deal with the DOS command-line interface. Another advantage of the Macintosh was that all its applications looked alike and functioned similarly, making them easier to learn than DOS applications, most of which had their own unique "look and feel." Now that GUIs have become the standard, it is difficult to appreciate how big a breakthrough this standardization was.

The **Macintosh operating system** (or the **Mac OS**) was also ahead of Windows with many other features, such as built-in network support and Plug and Play hardware support. The Mac OS also provides multitasking and allows data sharing across different applications (see Figure 12.4). Such features quickly made even die-hard DOS enthusiasts envious and led Microsoft to develop the Windows operating environment for the IBM-compatible market.

NORTON
ONLINE

Visit **www.glencoe.com/norton/online/** for more information on the Macintosh operating system.

The fact that the Mac OS works only on Macintosh computers and compatible hardware has long been considered one of the operating system's biggest drawbacks. Similarly, DOS and all the varieties of Windows work only on IBM-compatible computers (although they can be run on PowerPC computers with a special dedicated section of the hard drive). Still, the Mac remains the first choice of many publishers, multimedia developers, graphic artists, and schools.

WINDOWS 3.x

In the mid-1980s, Microsoft accepted the popularity of the Macintosh computer and users' desire for a GUI. Microsoft's solution was **Windows,** a GUI that ran on top of DOS, replacing the command-line interface with a point-and-click system. Windows was not originally an operating system but an **operating environment,** another term for an interface that disguises the underlying operating system.

The first version of Windows did not work or sell very well, and the second version also was not a success. Not until Microsoft released Windows 3.0 in 1990 did the operating environment really take off.

Windows 3.0 was reasonably stable and succeeded in providing a GUI, (see Figure 12.5), and the capability to load more than one program into memory at a time. Users could also run their old DOS programs under Windows, either in full-screen mode (so the screen looked like a plain DOS system) or within a window.

During the early 1990s, Windows 3.0, Windows 3.1, and Windows 3.11 (called Windows for Workgroups) became the market leaders and eventually were installed on most new PCs, running on top of DOS. Meantime, thousands of users installed Windows on their existing DOS machines, instantly creating a multitasking, GUI-based system. However, DOS actually remained the most popular operating system for IBM-compatible PCs because it was required to run the Windows operating environments.

Despite its success and the capabilities it added to DOS computers, early versions of Windows did little else to overcome the built-in limitations of DOS. For example, users still had to deal with DOS memory-use limitations, although Windows made it easier to access 1 MB of memory. Plug and Play capabilities were not introduced in subsequent versions of Windows, so users still had to install drivers and configure each piece of hardware manually. Because it attempted to force DOS to support multitasking, Windows was fairly unstable and became known for crashing and locking up when the system's resources reached their limits. Although Windows featured a memory-protection scheme that reserved blocks of memory space and CPU time for individual processes, the system was not reliable and Windows users frequently lost data to crashes.

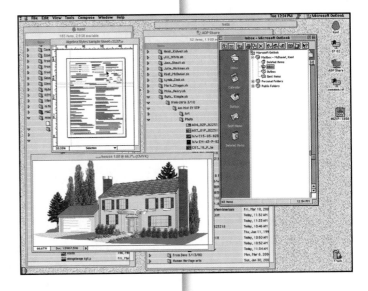

Figure 12.4
Before the advent of Windows, the Mac OS enabled users to run multiple applications in a graphical user interface.

Visit **www.glencoe.com/norton/online/** for more information on **Windows 3.x.**

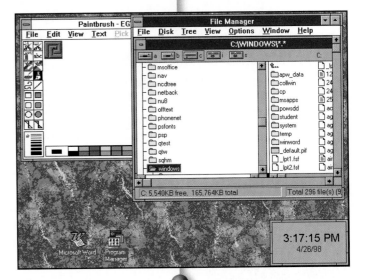

Figure 12.5
The interface for Windows 3.x has a lot in common with the Macintosh OS. Users can work with files and programs by clicking desktop icons to open windows.

Windows for Workgroups was an important step for the Windows line of operating systems because it was network-enabled. In other words, two computers running Windows for Workgroups could be networked together without the need to purchase a separate network operating system like Novell NetWare.

From time to time, you may see the term **Windows 3.x.** This term is used when referring to more than one member of the Windows 3 family.

OS/2 WARP

Although they are now rivals, IBM and Microsoft were once allies. After the introduction of the Intel 80286 processor in 1982, both companies recognized the need to take advantage of the new capabilities of this CPU. They joined forces to develop **OS/2 Warp** (originally called just OS/2), a multitasking, GUI-based operating system for Intel microprocessors (see Figure 12.6). The IBM/Microsoft partnership did not last long. The initial version suffered from many technical problems. Microsoft also decided to pursue the development of Windows as its own operating system, freeing it from ties to any specific hardware manufacturer.

Unlike Windows 3.x, OS/2 was a true operating system, not an operating environment that ran on top of DOS. OS/2 provided networking support, true multitasking and multiuser support, and other features that made it superior to DOS as an operating system for Intel-based PCs. OS/2 enabled users to run OS/2-specific applications as well as programs written for DOS and Windows 3.x. OS/2 became the first operating system to provide built-in speech recognition technology, and it could run on a wide range of hardware platforms, from PCs to multiprocessor systems with up to sixty-four processors.

In spite of its power and features, OS/2 never fully recovered from its rocky start. IBM continues to develop and market OS/2, but the product has fallen to an "also-ran" status. OS/2 systems can be found in large businesses and schools, many of which adopted the system early and never switched to a different OS.

Figure 12.6
The OS/2 Warp interface.

WINDOWS NT

Microsoft released **Windows NT,** a 32-bit operating system for PCs, in 1993. Windows NT (New Technology) was originally designed as the successor to DOS, but by the time it was ready for release, it had become too large to run on most of the PCs in use at the time. As a result, Microsoft repositioned Windows NT to be a high-end operating system designed primarily for powerful workstations and network servers. (With Windows NT released, Microsoft went back to the drawing board to create a more consumer-oriented version of Windows to replace DOS on home and office PCs. The result would be Windows 95, which is discussed later.)

At the time of its release, Windows NT addressed the market for the 32-bit, networked workstations that used some of the most powerful CPUs on the market.

Visit www.glencoe.com/norton/online/
for more information on **OS/2 Warp.**

Norton Notebook

CHANGING YOUR PC'S OPERATING SYSTEM

The operating system market has expanded over the past few years, freeing PC users to choose different operating systems. Users no longer feel locked into the OS provided by the PC's manufacturer.

Any newer model PC (if it has sufficient resources) can run nearly any current operating system. For example, if you have a Pentium II-class computer with 64 MB of RAM and a large hard disk, you do not necessarily need to run Windows 9x. Instead, you can use Windows NT, OS/2, Linux, and some versions of UNIX (but not the Mac OS). If you have a Macintosh, you may also be able to run some versions of UNIX or Linux (but not Windows).

Consider Your Needs First

Consider your need for a new operating system. Do you need a different OS to use a specific application? Is the OS used in your workplace or school, or do you need to be OS-compliant with a workgroup? Do you plan to develop or test applications that run on a specific operating system? Or will an updated operating system get better performance from your computer? If you answer yes to any of these questions, a new OS may be a good idea.

Compatibility Is a Must

Before installing an OS, make sure that your hardware is completely compatible with it. If you have any doubts, check with the manufacturers of your computer and any devices attached to it. Check with the operating system's developer to see if a "hardware compatibility list" is available. This document may answer all your hardware-related questions and may be found on the developer's Web site. If you suspect a problem, weigh the costs of replacing the hardware against installing a new OS.

If your hardware is compatible, make sure you have adequate resources for the new OS. This can be a problem for operating systems, such as Windows 2000 and Windows NT Workstation, that consume a great deal of system resources. Make sure your PC has enough power, memory, and storage, not just for the OS, but for your applications and data.

NORTON ONLINE

Visit **www.glencoe.com/norton/online/** for more information on **changing your OS.**

The Web is a convenient place to obtain updated information about your new operating system. Look for information on hardware requirements, compatibility, and installation procedures.

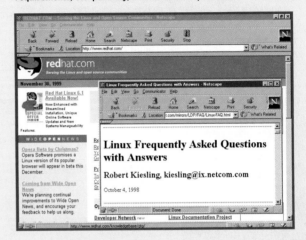

Next, make a list of all the applications you use or plan to use, and make sure they will run under the new OS. Be sure to include your utilities, Internet tools, and others. You may need to upgrade or replace some or all of your software to accommodate the new OS. Again, weigh this cost against the need for a new OS.

Taking the Big Step

Before you install anything, take these precautions:

◆ **Back Up Your Hard Disk.** If you plan to install the OS on your existing hard disk, make a complete backup beforehand. If the installation goes wrong, you can restore the disk to its previous state. Before you back up, test the disk for errors (by using ScanDisk or a similar utility), defragment the drive, and run a full virus scan.

◆ **Decide Whether to Reformat.** You may want to reformat the disk completely before installing a new OS. Reformatting erases everything related to the previous operating system and may make installation easier. If you do not know how to format a hard disk, look in your current operating system's help system and follow the directions closely.

◆ **Call for Help if You Need It.** If you have never installed a new OS, you may not be prepared for all the pitfalls involved. If the upgrade is essential, then it is worth doing right, so get help from an experienced user or a computer technician before you start.

Because these computers fell into two primary categories, Microsoft separated Windows NT into two products: Windows NT Workstation and Windows NT Server.

Windows NT Workstation

Although **Windows NT Workstation** looks almost identical to consumer versions of Windows (see Figure 12.7), its underlying operating system is almost completely different. Windows NT Workstation is designed to take better advantage of today's computers and also runs on a broader range of CPUs than do other versions of Windows, which run only on Intel, AMD, or Cyrix processor-based systems. Windows NT runs on systems that use Intel, AMD, Cyrix, Alpha, PowerPC, and other RISC-based processors. As its name implies, Windows NT Workstation is typically used on individual, stand-alone PCs that may or may not be part of a network. While Windows NT Workstation supports networking and can be used to run peer-to-peer networks, it generally is not used on network servers.

Windows NT incorporates much greater security than Microsoft's other operating systems. Windows NT requires users to have an account either on the computer they are using or on a server on the network. Resources on the local computer, as well as resources on remote servers, can be configured to limit access to specific users and groups of users. For example, files can be protected on a file-by-file basis, granting access to a file to one person or group but not to another. This exclusivity is achieved by using the NT File System (NTFS), a high-performance file system that replaces the older FAT file system introduced by MS-DOS. Users and administrators have the option of using NTFS or FAT on their Windows NT computer.

Figure 12.7
The interface for Windows NT Workstation 4.0.

Windows NT is more fault-tolerant than other Microsoft operating systems. Because of the way the OS isolates programs from one another, it is much less likely for one program to affect another adversely. Windows NT also integrates features that provide for disk mirroring, which is the capability to have online a backup hard disk that is a mirror image of another. If the primary hard disk fails, the mirrored drive takes over automatically. Lastly, Windows NT turns in better performance figures than Windows 3.*x*. Although performance varies according to your hardware and application, you can expect about a 50 percent improvement.

Windows NT Server

Windows NT Server incorporates all the features of Windows NT Workstation but also has other capabilities. Microsoft fine-tuned Windows NT Server to function as an operating system for file and print servers and on other systems that provide services for other computers on the LAN or Internet. Windows NT Server offers expanded security features for grouping and authenticating users and controlling their access to network resources.

Windows NT Server also incorporates several features not found in Windows NT Workstation. For example, Windows NT Server supports several additional levels

Visit **www.glencoe.com/norton/online/** for more information on **Windows NT**.

of Redundant Array of Independent Disks (RAID) for disk duplexing, disk striping, and disk mirroring. All these features make it possible for Windows NT Server to ensure disk and data security even in the event of a catastrophic failure of a hard disk. Features such as support for volume sets enable you to combine storage space on several different disks to look and function as a single drive.

Self Check

Answer the following questions by filling in the blank(s).

1. MOTIF and OpenLook are examples of _____ for UNIX.

2. The _____ brought the first truly graphical user interface to consumers.

3. Windows 3.x is called a(n) _____ because it is not a true operating system.

WINDOWS 95 AND 98

In 1995, Microsoft released **Windows 95,** a complete operating system and a successor to DOS for desktop computers. Windows 95 is a 32-bit, preemptive multitasking operating system with a revised GUI. All the strengths of Windows 95, which followed the Windows 3.x series, had already existed in other operating systems—most notably the Macintosh and Windows NT. In fact, purists considered it a compromise because, unlike those 32-bit operating systems, Windows 95 contains a good deal of 16-bit code needed to run older DOS and Windows programs.

Although the 16-bit code may have represented a backward glance, it was probably the greatest marketing strength of Windows 95. As a result of the 16-bit code, Windows 95 can run almost any DOS or Windows 3.x program (see Figure 12.8). Thus, if a company has already invested in many such programs, it can continue to use its familiar programs while migrating to the new operating system.

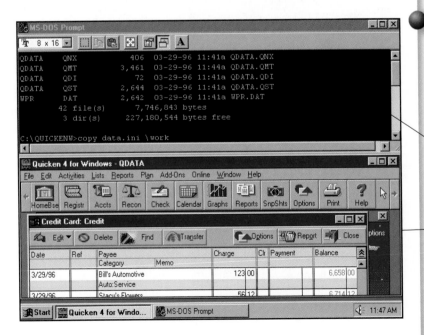

Figure 12.8
Windows 95 is designed primarily to run 32-bit applications but can run older 16-bit applications designed for Windows 3.x and DOS.

DOS, running in a window

A 16-bit application written for Windows 3.x

For users of Windows 3.*x*, Windows 95 has several attractions. First, for programs designed with 32-bit processing, the operating system can exchange information with printers, networks, and files in 32-bit pieces instead of 16-bit pieces as in Windows 3.*x* and DOS. For information moving around in the computer, the effect is like doubling the number of lanes on an expressway.

Second, Windows 95, like Windows NT, offers preemptive multitasking and not the less efficient cooperative multitasking of Windows 3.1 and the Macintosh. The self-contained 32-bit preemptive multitasking means that, if one program fails, you still have access to all the other programs loaded into memory. In most cases, you do not have to restart the computer to work with those programs, as you did with earlier versions of Windows.

Third, Windows 95 has an improved graphical interface. The Windows Explorer, for example, improves on earlier Microsoft operating systems for working with files. Windows 95 also allows users to type file names of up to 256 characters and to have spaces in those names—freedoms that had not been available on DOS-based PCs.

In addition, Windows 95 offers a Plug and Play standard for connecting new hardware. Another Windows 95 asset is compatibility with networking software such as NetWare and Microsoft Windows NT Server. With networks, you can simply identify the network operating system when you install Windows 95, and Windows 95 will be compatible with it.

Many experts considered **Windows 98** to be an update to Windows 95 rather than a major Windows operating system upgrade. In other words, the differences from Windows 95 to Windows 98 are not as significant as the differences from Windows 3.*x* to Windows 95. However, one key change in Windows 98 is the inclusion of the Internet Explorer Web browser. A new feature, called the Active Desktop, lets you browse the Internet and local computer in a similar manner (see Figure 12.9). Active Desktop enables you to integrate Internet resources such as stock tickers and news information services directly on your Windows desktop. If you have an active Internet connection, the information will update automatically.

Windows 98 also adds support for new and emerging technologies and expands other hardware support, including USB devices, DVD, and OnNow (which enables computers to be booted and ready to use almost instantly). Windows 98's capability to support up to eight monitors at one time is ideal for applications such as computer-aided design, providing large desktops and the capability to separate application and document windows. It is also a great feature for many online and interactive games.

In addition to fine-tuning in the core operating system, Windows 98 includes a new feature called Windows Update (see Figure 12.10). This Web-based resource enables Windows to

Visit www.glencoe.com/norton/online/ for more information on **Windows 95** and **Windows 98**.

Figure 12.9
The Windows 98 Active Desktop lets the operating system function like a Web browser.

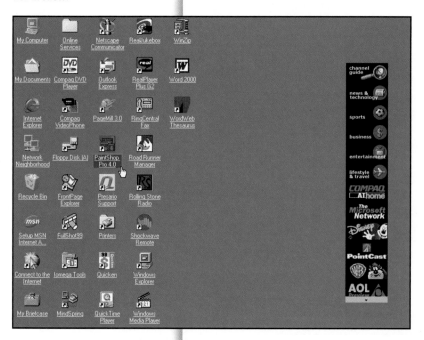

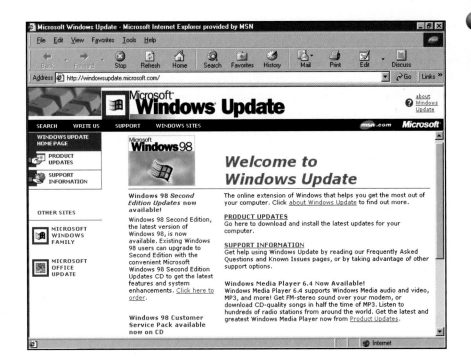

Figure 12.10
Using the Windows 98 Update feature, you can log onto the Microsoft Web site and download various upgrades to the operating system. Updates include feature enhancements, utilities, bug fixes, tools, and more.

connect to Microsoft periodically via the Internet to update your operating system, eliminating the need to buy CD-ROM or floppy disk–based upgrades. Scheduling has been expanded to enable Windows 98 to automatically perform routine maintenance such as disk scanning and repair and to optimize the system in the background.

Another feature is FAT32—a 32-bit implementation of the FAT file system that can improve file system performance. FAT32 also saves large amounts of wasted disk space by making the clusters much smaller. FAT32 is not compatible with DOS or Windows NT systems, however. If you use either of these operating systems on your computer in addition to Windows 98, you will not be able to access any FAT32 partitions from these other operating systems.

The broadcast features in Windows 98 provide built-in software to support television reception devices (such as TV/video card combinations) that enable you to watch television on your PC. These broadcast features extend beyond television reception to other technologies that enable data to be pushed from the Internet to your computer. Multimedia streams, news, and stock quotes are just a few examples of these types of data.

LINUX

Between the release of Windows 95 and Windows 98, the computer world's attention focused on another new operating system, called **Linux.** In fact, Linux (LIH-nuhks) is a new version of UNIX developed by a worldwide cooperative of programmers and is freely distributed by various sources.

Even though Linux is considered a "freeware" operating system, industry experts have been impressed by its power, capabilities, and rich feature set. Like UNIX, Linux is a full 32-bit, multitasking operating system that supports multiple users and multiple processors. Also like UNIX, Linux can run on nearly any computer and can support almost any type of application. Native Linux is driven by a command-line interface, but a windows-based GUI is also available.

Visit **www.glencoe.com/norton/online/** for more information on **Linux.**

The big difference with Linux is its price. Anyone can get a free copy of Linux on the Internet, and disk-based copies are often inserted in popular computer books and magazines. Commercial versions of Linux, which are very inexpensive when compared to the cost of other powerful operating systems, are also available from Red Hat Software, Corel Corp., and Caldera Systems, Inc. For all these reasons, Linux has quickly become a popular OS in certain circles. Students and teachers have flocked to Linux not just for its technical advances but to participate in the global community that has built up around the operating system. This community invites Linux users and developers to contribute modifications and enhancements, and it freely shares information about Linux and Linux-related issues.

Linux has also attracted a large user base among Internet service providers, who are increasingly using it as a low-cost server platform. In mid-1999, an estimated 30 percent of all new Internet servers were running on Linux, and the number was rapidly increasing. This phenomenon has prompted computer makers to announce their support for Linux, and many are offering Linux as the preinstalled OS on certain PCs and servers.

Commercial software developers have also made a commitment to Linux, and users can expect to see popular software applications to be modified to run under Linux. Among the first to commit to Linux were Corel Corp. (maker of CorelDRAW and WordPerfect) and Netscape, which released Linux versions of several products in 1999 (see Figure 12.11).

Figure 12.11
Although Linux is typically considered to be a server platform, an increasing number of software companies are porting their applications to Linux.

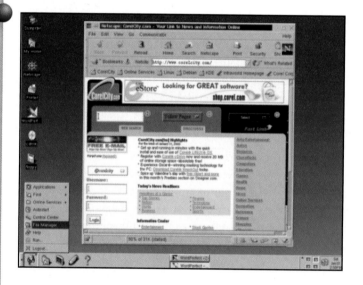

WINDOWS 2000

Windows 2000 combines the user-friendly interface and features of Windows 98 with the file system, networking, power, and stability of Windows NT and some new and improved features. This combination of features makes Windows 2000 the most powerful and easy-to-use Windows ever made and should bring a unified look and feel to all Windows-based computers (see Figure 12.12).

At the time of the writing of this textbook, Microsoft had developed the following versions of Windows 2000:

◆ **Professional.** This version is found primarily on office PCs. It includes support for symmetric multiprocessing (SMP) with up to two processors. SMP

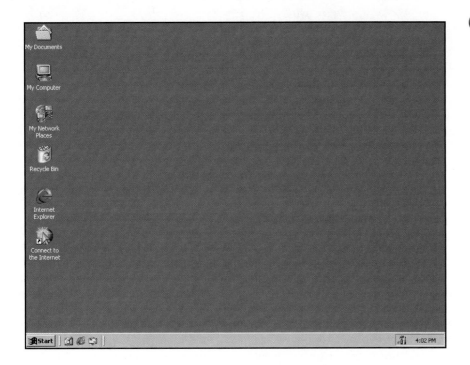

Figure 12.12
The Windows 2000 desktop.

is a protocol that allows the operating system and applications to run on multiple processors at the same time, improving performance on huge jobs.

◆ **Server Standard Edition.** This version is fine-tuned for use as a network server for the average business, with SMP support for up to two processors.

◆ **Advanced Server.** This version is a more powerful version of the server edition. It includes support for SMP with up to four processors, enhanced balancing of network and component loads, and support for more RAM. Another important feature is print server clustering. With clustering, Windows 2000 can group print servers to provide alternate printers if one print server fails.

◆ **Data Center Server.** This version is the most powerful of the server edition. It is optimized for use as a large-application server, such as a database server. It includes the Advanced Server features, plus support for SMP with up to thirty-two processors.

Some features of Windows 2000 include the following:

◆ **Improved Setup and Installation.** Although Plug and Play has existed for a few years, the protocol has improved. Windows 2000 also includes the new Windows Installer to make software installation easier.

◆ **Improved Internet Features.** New features make it easier to blend workstations, servers, intranets, and the Internet into one seamless unit.

◆ **Improved Networking.** The networking features of Windows 2000 make it easier for administrators to set up and run a network, allowing less experienced users to run office networks.

◆ **Improved Disk Management.** Windows 2000 includes a more flexible method of dividing and accessing hard drive space, as well as adding drive-maintenance programs like Disk Defragmenter that were missing in Windows NT.

If you want to use Windows 2000, you must have hardware that is Windows 2000–compatible. For example, your sound card must recognize the protocols of Windows 2000, and Windows 2000 must have a device driver that works with your sound card.

NORTON
ONLINE

Visit **www.glencoe.com/norton/online/** for more information on **Windows 2000.**

The Operating System and User Interface

Techview

LINUX: THE LITTLE OS THAT COULD

Linus Torvalds was a student at the University of Helsinki in 1991 when he decided to create a new and different "UNIX clone." Torvalds decided the new OS would be named "Linux," a combination of his name and "UNIX."

Torvalds had two goals. First, he wanted to create a powerful, feature-rich OS that provided the same functioning of UNIX. His OS would run on almost any computer,

It is easy to find information about Linux. Dozens of Usenet newsgroups and many Web sites are devoted to Linux.

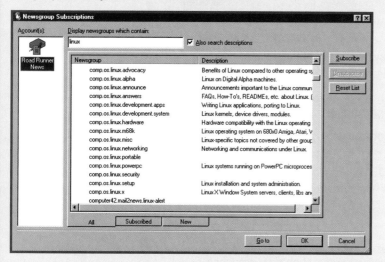

regardless of its architecture or the type of applications it hosted. Second, the OS would be completely open; anyone could contribute to its development and adapt or change its code, as long as they made their innovations public and did not take credit for anyone else's work. As part of its openness, Linux would be available for free to anyone who wanted it, although no one would be prohibited from selling their version of Linux as long as they made their innovations public and kept the OS completely open.

To achieve these goals, Torvalds decided that Linux would be built from the ground up, without using any code from any commercial version of UNIX. To keep Linux open, Torvalds posted a message on the Internet in 1991 inviting programmers around the world to help him develop the new operating system.

The call was taken up by dozens of programmers, who immediately wanted to share Torvalds' dream. Piecing the work out among themselves, different programmers tackled different aspects of the program, sharing code

and ideas over the Internet. By 1994, enough pieces had been stitched together and the first version of Linux was released to anyone who wanted to download it.

Although commercial versions of the OS now exist, Linux remains open and still attracts a community of developers interested in contributing to it. By some estimates, Linux runs on more than 10 million computers, a number that is growing rapidly. An ever-increasing number of corporate IT and database managers, Web site operators, and ISPs are using Linux as the core operating system on mission-critical computer networks.

There is probably no greater mark of Linux's acceptance, however, than the acknowledgment it has received from Microsoft. Although few people believe that Linux will ever replace Windows as the desktop operating system of choice (or replace Windows NT as the primary network OS), Microsoft executives have said that they view Linux as a legitimate competitor.

Leading hardware vendors—including Intel, IBM, Compaq, and others—have announced their support of Linux. In fact, some server-class computers are now being shipped with Linux, rather than UNIX or Windows NT, installed. In the software world, leading database companies such as Informix and Oracle have announced that their corporate database products will be tailored to run under Linux.

For computer users in the home and in most average business settings, Linux is not an issue. With its cryptic command-driven interface, Linux is not likely to become the operating system of the masses, even though developers have created a Windows-like GUI for it.

Having said all this, should you learn about Linux? In general, the more you know about operating systems, the better. But if you plan a career in programming, database management, network management, or Internet hosting, you would be well advised to get a copy of Linux and start mastering it. After all, it is free and will run on nearly any old computer. And there is a wealth of information about Linux on the Internet, along with thousands of devoted users.

LESSON QUIZ

True/False

Answer the following questions by circling True or False.

True   False   **1.** UNIX is an 8-bit, single-user OS for older mainframe computers.

True   False   **2.** DOS was designed to recognize only 640 KB of RAM.

True   False   **3.** Windows 3.*x* replaced DOS as the operating system of computers on which it was installed.

True   False   **4.** Windows NT was developed as a replacement for DOS but was too big to run on most PCs.

True   False   **5.** Windows 98 supports OnNow, which enables a computer to be booted and ready to use almost instantly.

Multiple Choice

Circle the word or phrase that best completes each sentence.

1. Windows 3.*x* is an example of an _____ .
  A. operating system   **B.** operating environment   **C.** Active Desktop

2. _____ is an operating system marketed by IBM for use on Intel-based computers.
  A. UNIX   **B.** OS/2 Warp   **C.** Neither A nor B

3. The _____ operating system runs on systems that use Intel, Alpha, PowerPC, and other RISC-based processors.
  A. Windows NT Workstation   **B.** Windows 9*x*   **C.** Mac OS

4. In Windows 98, the _____ feature lets you browse the Internet and local resources in a similar manner.
  A. Universal Serial Bus   **B.** Active Desktop   **C.** GUI

5. The primary attraction(s) of Linux is _____ .
  A. it can be acquired at no cost   **B.** it can run on virtually any computer   **C.** both A and B

LESSON LABS

Complete the following exercise as directed by your instructor.

Use your operating system's tools to find files:

A. Click the Start button, point to Programs, and click Windows Explorer.

B. Click Tools, click Find, and then click Files or Folders.

C. In the Named text box, type *.txt. This tells Windows to search for all files with the file-name extension *txt*.

D. From the Look in drop-down list, choose your computer's hard disk (typically C:).

E. If the Include subfolders check box is not selected (with a check mark), click it once.

F. Click Find Now. Windows conducts the search and displays the results at the bottom of the Find: All Files dialog box.

G. Repeat the search, specifying *.**wri**, *.**doc**, and *.**gif** as your search criteria. When you are finished, close the Find: All Files dialog box and the Exploring window.

LESSON 11: Operating System Basics

The User Interface

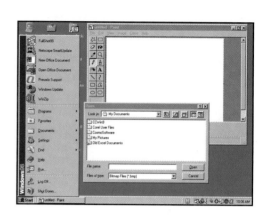

- Most modern operating systems employ a graphical user interface (GUI) with which users control the system by pointing and clicking graphical objects on the screen.

- A GUI is based on the desktop metaphor. Icons, windows, menus, dialog boxes, and other graphical objects appear on the desktop for the user to manipulate.

- Applications designed to run under a specific operating system use the same interface elements, so users can see a familiar interface no matter what programs they are using.

- Some older operating systems, such as DOS and UNIX, use command-line interfaces, which the user controls by typing commands at a prompt.

Running Programs

- The operating system manages all the other programs that run on the PC.

- The operating system also provides system-level services, including file management, memory management, printing, and others, to those programs.

- Some operating systems, such as Windows, enable programs to share information. This capability enables you to create data in one program and use it again in other programs without re-creating it.

- Modern operating systems support multitasking, which is the capability of running multiple processes simultaneously.

Managing Files

- The operating system keeps track of all the files on each disk. To track the location of each file, the operating system maintains a running list of information on each file, in a table that is typically called the file allocation table (FAT).

- Users can make their own file management easier by creating a hierarchical file system that includes folders and subfolders arranged in a logical order.

Managing Hardware

- The operating system uses interrupt requests (IRQs) to maintain organized communication with the CPU and other pieces of hardware.

- Each of the hardware devices is controlled by another piece of software, called a driver, which allows the operating system to activate and use the device.

- The operating system also provides the software necessary to link computers and form a network.

Utility Software

- A utility is a program that performs a task not typically handled by the operating system or that enhances the operating system's functioning.

- Some of the major categories of utilities include file defragmentation utilities, data compression programs, backup utilities, antivirus programs, and screen savers.

LESSON 12: PC Operating Systems in Review

UNIX

- UNIX was the first multi-user, multiprocessor, multitasking operating system available for use on PCs. UNIX served as a model for other PC operating systems.

DOS

- DOS is a single-user OS that supports only 640 KB of memory. It features a command-line interface.

The Macintosh Operating System

- The Macintosh operating system supports the graphical nature of the Macintosh computer. The Mac OS brought the first truly graphical user interface to consumers.

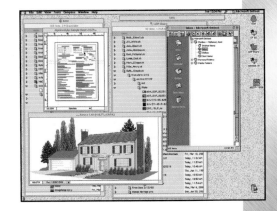

Windows 3.x

- Windows 3.0, 3.1, and 3.11 brought a graphical user interface and multitasking capabilities to PCs that ran DOS. Windows 3.x is an operating environment.

OS/2 Warp

- IBM's OS/2 Warp was the first true GUI-based operating system for Intel-based PCs. OS/2 is a multitasking operating system that provides support for networking and multiple users.

Windows NT

- Microsoft's Windows NT was originally meant as a replacement for DOS but was too resource-intensive to work on most PCs at the time of its release. Microsoft issued two versions—Windows NT Workstation and Windows NT Server.

Windows 95 and 98

- Windows 95 was Microsoft's first true GUI-based, 32-bit operating system for Intel PCs. It supports multitasking and can run older DOS and Windows 3.x programs.

- The features of Windows 98 include advanced Internet capabilities, an improved user interface, and enhanced file system performance.

Linux

- Linux is a version of UNIX and is available free or at a low cost from various sources. It is a powerful 32-bit OS that supports multitasking, multiple users, networking, and almost any application.

Windows 2000

- Windows 2000 includes the same interface and features of Windows 98, with the file system, networking, power, and stability of Windows NT. Several versions of Windows 2000 are available, each targeting a specific user or computing environment.

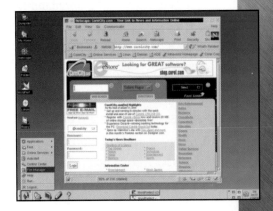

UNIT REVIEW

KEY TERMS

After completing this unit, you should be able to define the following terms.

activate, *187*
active window, *188*
antivirus program, *198*
backup utility, *198*
button, *187*
choose, *187*
Clipboard, *194*
command-line interface, *191*
context menu, *187*
cooperative multitasking, *195*
Copy, *194*
Cut, *194*
data compression program, *198*
desktop, *187*
dialog box, *190*
driver, *197*
file defragmentation utility, *198*
graphical user interface (GUI), *186*
hierarchical file system, *196*
icon, *187*
Linux, *213*
Macintosh Operating System (Mac OS), *206*
menu, *190*
menu bar, *190*
MS-DOS, *205*
Object Linking and Embedding (OLE), *194*
operating environment, *207*

OS/2 Warp, *208*
Paste, *194*
preemptive multitasking, *195*
prompt, *191*
screen saver, *198*
scroll bar, *188*
select, *187*
shortcut menu, *187*
Start button, *187*
Start menu, *187*
system call, *193*
taskbar, *187*
task switching, *189*
title bar, *188*
UNIX, *204*
user interface, *186*
utilities, *198*
window, *188*
Windows, *207*
Windows 2000, *214*
Windows 3.*x*, *208*
Windows 95, *211*
Windows 98, *212*
Windows NT, *208*
Windows NT Server, *210*
Windows NT Workstation, *210*

KEY TERMS QUIZ

Fill in each blank with one of the terms listed under Key Terms.

1. In a graphical user interface, _____ represent the parts of the computer you work with, such as files or printers.

2. All windows include a(n) _____ across the top, which identifies the window's contents.

3. The process of moving from one open window to another is called _____ .

4. You interact with a command-line interface by typing strings of characters at a(n) _____ .

5. The _____ is a temporary storage space for data that is being copied or moved.

6. With _____ , the operating system can reassign the priority of tasks at any time.

7. _____ is older than all the other PC operating systems.

8. Data compression programs, antivirus programs, and screen savers are examples of _____ .

9. _____ is the term that refers to Windows versions 3.0, 3.1, and 3.11.

10. A new version of UNIX, _____ , can be acquired easily at no cost.

REVIEW QUESTIONS

In your own words, briefly answer the following questions.

1. What are the four primary functions that an operating system performs?
2. Where do graphical user interfaces get their name?
3. In later Windows operating systems, what happens when you right-click many parts of the desktop?
4. What is the function of windows in a graphical user interface?
5. Why is task switching necessary in a multitasking operating system?
6. Describe the difference between the Cut and Copy commands.
7. What is the difference between cooperative multitasking and preemptive multitasking?
8. What does "MS-DOS" stand for?
9. Why did the Macintosh operating system become popular immediately upon its release?
10. What are the two versions of Windows NT?

DISCUSSION QUESTIONS

As directed by your instructor, discuss the following questions in class or in groups.

1. Discuss the benefits of using the object linking and embedding (OLE) capabilities of newer operating systems. Can you envision a task where this capability would be helpful? What types of documents might you create that would benefit from OLE?
2. What does multitasking mean to a user? How does the user benefit from the multitasking capabilities of an operating system?

 ETHICAL ISSUES

Many people believe that operating systems are simply becoming too powerful. With this thought in mind, discuss the following questions in class.

1. The Windows Update feature enables the Windows 98 operating system to notify the user when updated features are available for downloading on the Internet. Some observers think that future operating systems will be able to update themselves automatically, without first notifying the user. How do you feel about this possibility? What dangers could it pose to users?

2. Many observers believe that by including so many features (such as disk defragmenters, file management tools, and Internet applications) in its operating systems, Microsoft has taken market share away from other companies that might develop and sell such tools to Windows users. Do you agree with this criticism, or do you feel that an operating system should include such "extras"?

UNIT LABS

You and the Computer

Complete the following exercises using a computer in your classroom, lab, or home. No other materials are needed.

1. **Create a File System.** Suppose that your employer has asked you to create a business proposal for a new department. The proposal must be at least fifty pages in length and must include several supporting documents, such as reports, memos, budgets, customer lists, and so on. Your first task is to create a file system on your computer's hard disk where you can store and manage all these files. Using a piece of paper, design a set of folders (and subfolders, if needed) to store these files. Be prepared to share your file system with the rest of the class and to discuss the logic behind it.

2. **Take a Tour of Windows.** If you use Windows 98, you can take a multimedia tour of the operating system to learn about its features. Take the following steps:

   A. Click the Start button to open the Start menu. Point to Programs, then to Accessories, and then to System Tools. Click Welcome to Windows. The Welcome to Windows 98 window appears.

   B. Click Discover Windows 98, and the tour begins. Follow the instructions on the screen to complete the tour. (You can close the tour at any time by clicking the Close button.)

   C. When you finish the tour, close the Welcome to Windows 98 window.

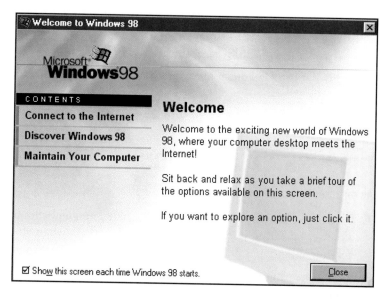

Internet Labs

To complete the following exercises, you will need a computer with an Internet connection and a Web browser. (For more information on using these tools, see "Prerequisites" at the front of this textbook.)

1. **Get the Latest on Windows 2000.** If you do not have Windows 2000 yet, chances are good that you will be using it eventually. Get a jump on the OS by finding the latest information about it on the Web.

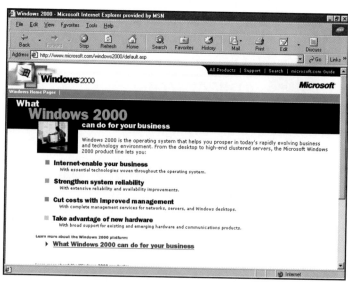

Visit the following Web sites for more information:

- **Microsoft Corp.** Visit Microsoft's main Windows 2000 page at **http://www.microsoft.com/windows2000/default.asp**

- **Windows Magazine.** For a series of articles about and links to Windows 2000, visit **http://www.winmag.com/win2000/**

- **Planet IT Windows 2000 Technology Center.** For articles, reviews, and technical information relating to Windows 2000 in enterprise settings, visit **http://www.planetit.com/techcenters/windows_2000**

2. **Learn More About Linux.** If you are curious about Linux (or UNIX in general) or want to install Linux on your system, you can find everything you need on the Internet. Visit the following Web sites for more information on Linux and to learn where you can get a free copy. (*Note:* Do not download any files from the Internet without asking your instructor for permission.)

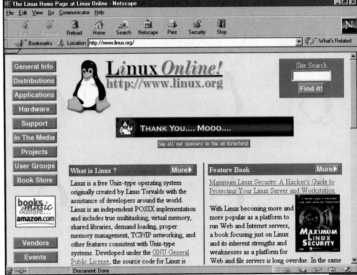

- **Linux Online.** Hosted by Linux.Org, this site provides a comprehensive array of resources. Visit **http://www.linux.org**

- **The Linux Gazette.** An online newsletter for Linux users of all levels can be found at **http://www.linuxgazette.com/**

- **Linux Planet.** For articles, reviews, technical information, and links to Linux resources, visit **http://www.linuxplanet.com/linuxplanet/**

IBE Labs

If you have the Interactive Browser Edition (IBE) CD-ROM for this textbook, you may complete the following interactive exercises using the instructions provided in the IBE.

1. **Matching.** Play this game of matching key terms with their definitions.

2. **Labeling.** Create a flowchart showing the functions of an operating system.

3. **Ask an Expert.** Compare how your recommendations match up with the expert's.

4. **Explore the World of Utility Software.** Take a closer "look" at different types of utility software.

UNIT 7

Productivity Software, Part I

224

Word Processing and Desktop Publishing Software

OVERVIEW:
The Importance of Documents in Our World

Every day, millions of people use word processing software to create and edit memos, letters, reports, and many other kinds of documents. In fact, it has been estimated that 80 to 90 percent of all personal computers have a word processor installed.

If this fact comes as a surprise, consider the number of documents that surround you. Newspapers, magazines, letters, and advertisements crowd your mailbox each day. You read books for school and for pleasure. Businesses, government agencies, schools, and individuals create an untold number of documents for myriad purposes. On desktops around the world, printers spit out tons of documents every week. Probably, just as many documents are created but never printed.

If you have not had any experience yet with productivity software, a word processor is an ideal place to start. Modern word processors are easy to use and require no special skills to master. A word processor will familiarize you with many tools and interface elements common to other applications designed for your operating system. You may find little use for other types of applications, but you may find your word processor to be a program you cannot live without.

OBJECTIVES

- Identify three basic word processing tools that simplify document editing.
- Explain what is meant by "selecting" parts of a document.
- Identify five special features commonly found in modern word processors.
- Distinguish desktop publishing software from word processing software.
- Describe how word processors can convert normal documents into World Wide Web pages.

WORD PROCESSING PROGRAMS AND THEIR USES

Figure 13.1
This simple birthday card was created in a word processing application. It features colors, rotated text, and clip art graphics.

Figure 13.2
Word processors are used frequently to create business letters and résumés. The formatting can be simple (as demonstrated by the cover letter on the left) or more elaborate (as in the résumé).

Visit **www.glencoe.com/norton/online/** for more information on **word processing software.**

Word processing software (also called a **word processor**) is an application that provides extensive tools for creating all kinds of text-based documents, as shown in Figures 13.1 through 13.3. Word processors are not limited to working with text. Word processors enable you to add images to documents and design documents that look like products of a professional print shop.

A word processor can enhance documents in other ways; you can embed sounds, video clips, and animations into them. You can link different documents together—for example, link a chart from a spreadsheet into a word processing report—to create complex documents that update themselves automatically. Word processors can even create documents for publishing on the World Wide Web, complete with hyperlinked text and graphics.

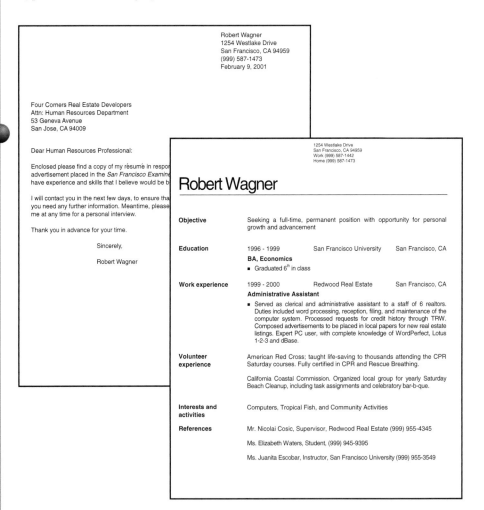

THE WORD PROCESSOR'S INTERFACE

The word processor's main editing window displays a document and several tools, as illustrated in Figure 13.4. In addition to a **document area** (or **document window**), which is where you view the document, a word processor provides several sets of tools. These tools include a menu bar displaying titles of command categories from which you can select hundreds of commands and options. One or more **toolbars** provide tools that resemble buttons; these buttons represent frequently used commands, such as those for printing and for selecting text styles. A **ruler** shows you the positioning of text, tabs, margins, indents, and other elements on the page. Horizontal and vertical scroll bars with scroll boxes let you scroll through a document that is too large to fit inside the document area. Most word processors also offer a **status bar** across the bottom of the window, which includes information related to your position in the document, the page count, and the status of keyboard keys.

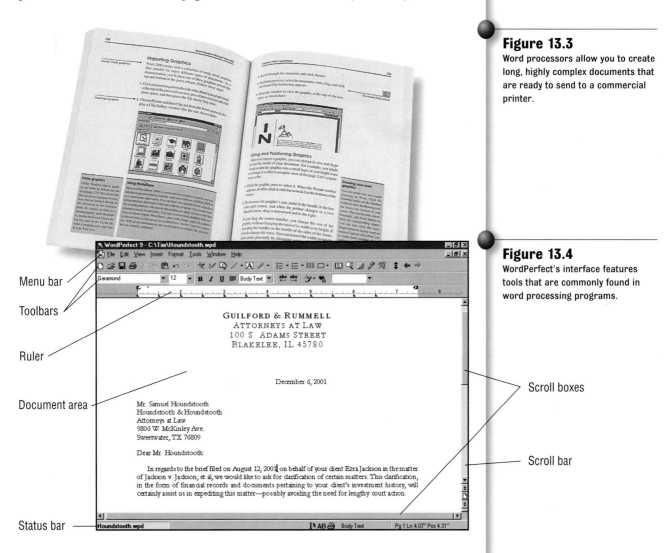

Figure 13.3
Word processors allow you to create long, highly complex documents that are ready to send to a commercial printer.

Figure 13.4
WordPerfect's interface features tools that are commonly found in word processing programs.

Menu bar

Toolbars

Ruler

Document area

Scroll boxes

Scroll bar

Status bar

ENTERING AND EDITING TEXT

You create a document by typing on the keyboard—a process known as entering text. In a new document, the program places a blinking insertion point (also called a cursor) in the upper left corner of the document window. As you type, the insertion point advances across the screen, showing you where the next character will be placed.

When your text reaches the right edge of the screen, the word processor automatically moves the insertion point to the next line, as shown in Figure 13.5 on page 228. This feature is called **word wrap.** The only time you need to press Enter is at the end of a paragraph. (In a word processor, you press Enter to start a new paragraph.)

Figure 13.5
Word wrap.

When the insertion point reaches the end of a line...

...it automatically moves down to the next line.

Unlike the typewriter, word processing software lets you change text without retyping the entire page; you retype only the text that needs to be changed. Changing an existing document is called **editing** the document. Word processing software provides several simple methods for erasing and retyping text quickly:

◆ **The Backspace and Delete Keys.** The Backspace key moves the insertion point one character to the left, erasing each character as it goes. The Delete key works like the Backspace key but deletes each character to the right of the insertion point.

◆ **Overtyping.** All word processors let you work in **overtype mode,** in which the new text you type writes over existing text. Otherwise, you work in **insertion mode,** and the word processor inserts text wherever the insertion point is located without overtyping existing text.

◆ **AutoCorrect.** Many word processors can automatically correct common misspellings, a feature called **AutoCorrect.** This feature can catch many common mistakes, such as failing to capitalize the first word of a sentence.

◆ **Undo and Redo.** If you make a change to a document and then change your mind, use the **Undo** command to return the document to its previous state. If you undo a change and then decide you like the change better than the original version, use the **Redo** command to reverse the previous Undo.

The word processor's real beauty is its ability to work with blocks of text. A **block** is a contiguous group of characters, words, lines, sentences, or paragraphs in your document that you mark for editing. To mark text for editing, you select the text to be edited. You can select text by using the mouse (dragging to select several words or lines), the keyboard (using Shift and the arrow keys to select characters, words, or lines), or both (using Ctrl while clicking to select entire sentences). When you select text, it changes color—becoming **highlighted,** as shown in Figure 13.6—to indicate that it is selected. You can erase an entire selected block by pressing the Delete key or by typing other text over the selected block. You can change the formatting of the selection by making it bold or underlined, for example, or by changing the font or font size. To **deselect** a selected block of text, click the mouse anywhere on the screen or press any arrow key. The text is displayed again as it normally would be.

flow, or a burst of waves, the reservoir cushions the banks from changing forces. A UPS is like a reservoir for electricity. As your electricity fluctuates, the UPS absorbs and supplements the flow.

To fully appreciate how helpful a UPS is, take the water analogy one step further and think of the plumbing in your home. If someone is drawing water when you start a shower, the other person notices a drop in the water pressure and you notice that the water pressure isn't as high as it should be. Then, if someone else flushes a toilet, you can expect the flow of cold water to momentarily drop even more. When the toilet finishes filling up, you can expect a sudden return of the cold water. And, when the original person drawing water stops, you notice a sudden increase in water pressure. Once you're through fiddling with the faucets, you appreciate how nice a personal reservoir could be. The electricity in your home works much the same way, so a UPS goes a long way to even out the flow as various appliances are turned on an off.

What Are the Most Common Electrical Problems?

Electrical problems come in all types, from the nearly harmless minor fluctuation in the voltage level, to

You can also copy or move a block of selected text from one part of the document to another, or even from one document to another. In a word processor, moving text is as easy as dragging the block to a new location, a technique called drag-and-drop editing. The same effect can be accomplished by cutting or copying the block to the Clipboard and then pasting it to a new location.

FORMATTING TEXT

Most word processing features are used to **format** the document. The process of formatting a document includes controlling the appearance of text, the layout of text on the page, and the use of pictures and other graphic elements. As explained in the following sections, most formatting features fall into one of three categories: character formats, paragraph formats, and document formats.

Character Formats

Character formatting includes settings that control the attributes of individual text characters, such as font, type size, type style, and color.

Fonts

The term **font** refers to the characteristics of the letters, symbols, and punctuation marks in your document. Fonts have names like Times Roman, Helvetica, and Palatino. In addition to those that come with the operating system, most word processors provide at least a handful of built-in fonts.

There are two general categories of fonts: monospace and proportional. Every character of a **monospace font,** such as Courier, takes up exactly the same amount of horizontal space (see Figure 13.7). This characteristic is useful if you need to line up columns of type. Most fonts are proportional. With a **proportional font,** such as Times, each character is as wide as it needs to be. So, for example, the letter *M* uses more horizontal space than *I* does.

Fonts also fall into two additional broad categories: serif and sans serif. As shown in Figure 13.8, **serif** fonts have curls or extra decorative lines at the ends of the strokes that make up each character; **sans serif** fonts do not (*sans* means "without" in French).

Visit **www.glencoe.com/norton/online/** for more information on **formatting documents** and **fonts.**

```
This is the Courier font, which is monospaced.
```

This is the Times font, which is proportional.

Figure 13.7

In a monospaced font, each character occupies the same amount of horizontal space. In a proportional font, characters take up only as much space as they need to be legible.

Berkeley is a serif font.

Helvetica is a sans serif font.

Figure 13.8

Serif fonts have decorative lines and curls at the ends of strokes. Sans serif fonts do not.

Type Size

A font is measured in **points,** as shown in Figure 13.9 on page 230. One point equals $1/72$ of an inch, so 72 points equal 1 inch, 36 points equal $1/2$ inch, and so forth. A common font size used in business documents is 12-point type. Characters are measured from the top of the tallest letters (such as *T* and *P*) to the bottom of letters that descend below the baseline (such as *g* and *p*). Word processors let you work with type sizes from as little as one point to as large as several hundred points.

This is 10 point Times type.

This is 12 point Times type.

This is 14 point Times type.

This is 16 point Times type.

This is 18 point Times type.

Figure 13.9
Type sizes.

Remember, however, that all programs do not treat font sizes the same. A 14-point character in one program may be considerably larger than a 14-point character in a different program. The heights of similar characters may vary greatly among different fonts, even at the same size. Sometimes the best way to determine a font's true size (and relation to other fonts on a page) is to print a document.

You can make your text **bold.**

You can use *italics,* too.

Underlining is an old standby.

Sometimes you can use ~~strike through.~~

You can also use SMALL CAPS VS. LARGE CAPS.

Figure 13.10
Type styles.

In addition to the font and type size, the appearance of characters can be controlled with **type styles** (which are often referred to as attributes or effects). The most common styles used in documents are bold, italic, and underlining, as shown in Figure 13.10. Less commonly used style attributes include strikethrough, superscript, subscript, small caps, and others.

Paragraph Formats

In word processing, the word *paragraph* has a slightly different meaning than it does traditionally. Word processing software creates a **paragraph** each time you press the Enter key. A group of sentences is a paragraph, but a two-word heading (like the one above this paragraph) is defined as a paragraph, as well.

Paragraph formatting includes settings applied only to one or more entire paragraphs. These settings include line spacing, paragraph spacing, indents, alignment, tab stops, borders, and shading. Another common type of paragraph formatting is the use of lists, either numbered lists or bulleted lists.

Line and Paragraph Spacing

Word processing software provides precise control over the amount of space between each line of text in a paragraph, a setting known as **line spacing.** Lines can be single-spaced or double-spaced or set to any spacing you want.

Paragraph spacing refers to the amount of space between each paragraph. By default, the paragraph spacing is the same as the line spacing. However, you can set the software so that extra space is included automatically before or after each paragraph. In many documents, paragraph spacing is roughly equivalent to one blank line between paragraphs.

Indents and Alignment

Margins are the white borders around the edge of the page where the text is not typed. Every document has top, bottom, left, and right margins, and in any document all four margins can be the same or different. Many documents, such as business letters, require margins of a standard width. A word processor lets you set each margin as precisely as you want, usually to an accuracy of $1/100$ inch.

Indents determine how close each line of a paragraph comes to the margins. In a report, for example, the body text lines may reach all the way to the left and right margins, but quoted material may be indented 1 inch from each margin.

Alignment refers to the orientation of the lines of a paragraph with respect to the margins. There are four alignment options—left, right, center, and justified (or full justification)—as shown in Figure 13.11. Alignment and indents are paragraph formats; the margins are part of the overall document format.

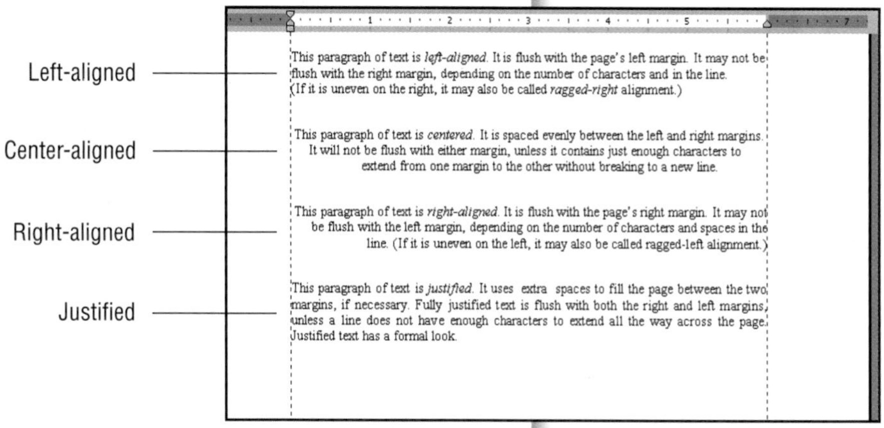

Left-aligned
Center-aligned
Right-aligned
Justified

This paragraph of text is *left-aligned*. It is flush with the page's left margin. It may not be flush with the right margin, depending on the number of characters and in the line. (If it is uneven on the right, it may also be called *ragged-right* alignment.)

This paragraph of text is *centered*. It is spaced evenly between the left and right margins. It will not be flush with either margin, unless it contains just enough characters to extend from one margin to the other without breaking to a new line.

This paragraph of text is *right-aligned*. It is flush with the page's right margin. It may not be flush with the left margin, depending on the number of characters and spaces in the line. (If it is uneven on the left, it may also be called ragged-left alignment.)

This paragraph of text is *justified*. It uses extra spaces to fill the page between the two margins, if necessary. Fully justified text is flush with both the right and left margins, unless a line does not have enough characters to extend all the way across the page. Justified text has a formal look.

Figure 13.11
The vertical dotted lines represent the left and right margins on the page. Notice how the different paragraph alignments adjust the text in relation to the margins.

Tabs and Tab Stops

The keyboard's Tab key moves the insertion point forward (to the right) until it encounters a **tab stop** (or just **tab**), inserting a fixed amount of space in the line. A tab stop is a position, both on screen and in the document, usually measured from the left margin of the document. When you create a new document, tab stops typically are defined at every fourth or fifth character, or at every 0.5-inch position. Most word processors allow you to change or remove the tab stops by displaying a ruler across the top or bottom of the screen that shows where tab stop positions are set.

Tabs are most often used to align columns of text accurately or to create tables; word processors provide at least four different types of tab stops so that you can align columns in different ways. For example, in Figure 13.12, the columns are separated by tab spacing (rather than by spaces inserted with the space bar). The first column is aligned along the left margin of the page, the second column is aligned by a left-aligned tab stop, the third by a centered tab stop, the fourth by a right-aligned tab stop, and the fifth by a decimal tab stop.

Figure 13.12
Four kinds of tab stops.

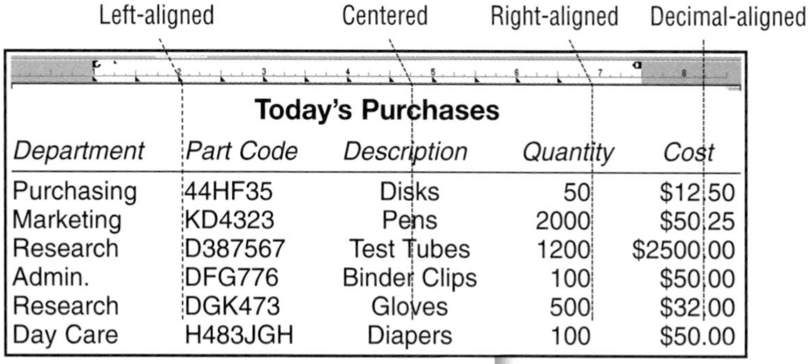

Left-aligned   Centered   Right-aligned   Decimal-aligned

Today's Purchases

Department	Part Code	Description	Quantity	Cost
Purchasing	44HF35	Disks	50	$12.50
Marketing	KD4323	Pens	2000	$50.25
Research	D387567	Test Tubes	1200	$2500.00
Admin.	DFG776	Binder Clips	100	$50.00
Research	DGK473	Gloves	500	$32.00
Day Care	H483JGH	Diapers	100	$50.00

Borders, Shading, and Shadows

Paragraphs can be formatted with borders or shading (see Figure 13.13 on page 232). A **border,** or **rule,** is a line that is drawn on one or more sides of a paragraph. **Shading** consists of a pattern or color that is displayed as a background to the text in a paragraph. A drop shadow is a partial shadow around a bordered paragraph, which creates the illusion that the paragraph is "floating" above the page.

Figure 13.13

A paragraph formatted with a border, shading, and a drop shadow.

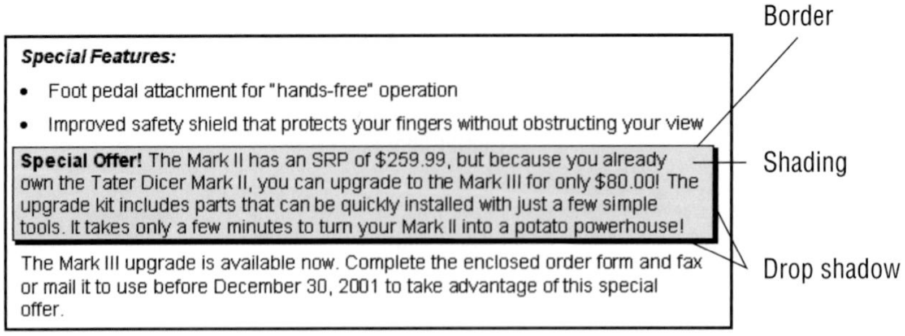

Border

Special Features:
- Foot pedal attachment for "hands-free" operation
- Improved safety shield that protects your fingers without obstructing your view

Special Offer! The Mark II has an SRP of $259.99, but because you already own the Tater Dicer Mark II, you can upgrade to the Mark III for only $80.00! The upgrade kit includes parts that can be quickly installed with just a few simple tools. It takes only a few minutes to turn your Mark II into a potato powerhouse!

The Mark III upgrade is available now. Complete the enclosed order form and fax or mail it to use before December 30, 2001 to take advantage of this special offer.

Shading

Drop shadow

Document Formats

In addition to margins, **document formats** include the size of the page, its orientation, and headers or footers. Word processing software also lets you apply special formats, such as columns, to documents. You can also divide a document into sections and give each section its own unique format.

Page Size and Orientation

Normally, documents are set up to fit on 8½- by 11-inch paper, a standard known as letter-size paper. You can set up a word processor document for other standard sizes, such as legal size (8½ by 14 inches). You can also set up a document for custom paper sizes.

Figure 13.14

Landscape printing.

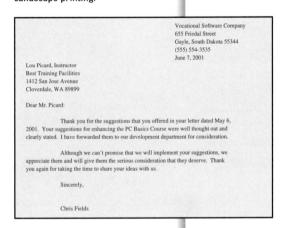

Document dimensions are also determined by the orientation of the paper. By default, documents are set up with **portrait orientation** (or tall orientation), where the document is taller than it is wide, like the pages of this textbook. You can also switch to **landscape orientation** (or wide orientation), in which the paper is turned on its side, as shown in Figure 13.14.

Headers and Footers

Long documents generally include headers, footers, or both. **Headers** and **footers** are lines of text that run along the top and bottom of every page. For example, the footers in this book include the unit number or the unit title (depending on whether they are located on a left page or a right page, respectively) and the page number. There are no headers.

Columns and Sections

Columns are effective formats for certain types of documents. Newsletters, for example, are often laid out in a two- or three-column format to make them easy to read.

Figure 13.15

A two-section document, with different document formats in each section.

Word processors also allow you to divide a document into **sections** and apply a different format to each section. In Figure 13.15, the document's top section is a heading followed by pagewide text. The second section is a three-column format.

COMPUTERS
in your career

Productivity Software and Your Career

If your work involves the use of personal computers, then you will probably find yourself using a word processor and/or spreadsheet program like those introduced in this unit. These productivity programs are the primary working tools in many organizations. Even in businesses that use other "mission-critical" applications, word processors and spreadsheets play an important role.

To improve your employability—even if you plan to use no other kind of software in your work—basic word processing and spreadsheet skills are essential. These programs are widely used, and they provide an excellent springboard to mastering other types of software. Here are a few examples of professionals who use word processors or spreadsheet programs in their daily work:

◆ **Secretaries, Writers, Journalists, Teachers, and Sales Professionals.** This list is short indeed. Many, many jobs require workers to create documents. To put it plainly, if your job requires you to write anything, no matter how brief or informal, you will most likely use a word processing program to do it. In fact, many businesses now demand that all documents be created and stored electronically, for various reasons. In the professional setting, hand- or typewritten documents are a thing of the past.

The word processor is the main (or only) tool for some professionals, like journalists and secretaries. However, word processors are important to professionals who primarily use other programs, like architects, engineers, accountants, and others who rely on design, analysis, or spreadsheet programs. They also use word processors to create other documents, such as proposals, reports, letters, and so on.

◆ **Accountants, Bookkeepers, Business Owners and Managers, and Financial Planners.** Again, this list is brief, but if your career involves managing money, then a spreadsheet will probably be an essential tool for you. Of course, many business and financial professionals use dedicated accounting programs to "keep their books," but these people also rely on spreadsheets when sharing information with clients, creating reports, or performing various types of analysis.

If your career path leads in the direction of financial planning or management, be sure to master specific skills with spreadsheet analytical tools such as what-if analysis and goal seeking. Professional spreadsheet users also suggest mastering the software's page layout features and charting capabilities to make your work look polished.

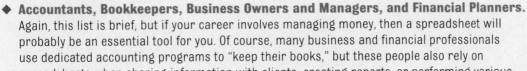

233

SPECIAL FEATURES OF WORD PROCESSING SOFTWARE

All modern word processing programs are rich in features, many of which have nothing to do with text editing or formatting. Such utilities add functions that are almost like adding new software programs to your word processor.

Language Tools

Although a word processing program cannot make you a good writer, it can help. Among the many features of word processors are language tools that assist you in finding errors in your spelling and grammar, and help you find just the right word or avoid overusing certain words. These tools include the following:

◆ **Spell Checkers.** If your word processor has a **spell checker,** you can enable it to catch spelling mistakes as you type or use it to review an entire document for spelling errors. A spell checker matches each word in a document against a built-in dictionary containing standard spellings. If the utility encounters a word that has no match in the dictionary, it lets you know. A good spell checker will provide options for replacing or ignoring the word, or adding the word to the spelling dictionary (see Figure 13.16).

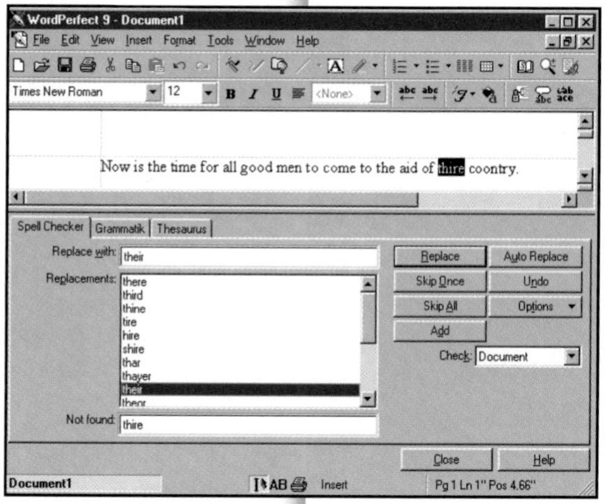

◆ **Grammar Checkers.** **Grammar checkers** work like spell checkers, but they inspect your document for grammatical problems. A grammar checker compares each sentence to a set of standard grammatical rules, notifies you if it finds a potential problem, and provides grammatically correct options.

◆ **Thesaurus.** An electronic **thesaurus** is just like a printed one—a source of alternative words. Suppose you think you are using a word incorrectly or want to find a different word with a similar meaning. You can select a word, then launch the thesaurus. A good thesaurus will display a definition of the selected word and a list of possible replacements.

Figure 13.16
Checking the spelling in a document in WordPerfect.

Tables

Although tabs can be used to set up rows and columns of information in a document, word processors provide features that let you create **tables** in just a few steps. The size of a table is limited only by the amount of page space that can be devoted to it, and tables can be formatted in dozens of ways. Tables are typically set up with a header row across the top to describe the contents of each column. Many tables also include a special first column that describes the contents of each row.

Mail Merge

A **mail merge** is the process of combining a form letter with the contents of a database, usually a name and address list, so that each copy of the letter has one entry from the database printed on it. The mail merge feature makes it easy to send the same letter to a list of different people with the correct name and address printed on each letter.

Adding Graphics and Sounds

With a word processor, you can easily add graphic images—photos, drawings, or clip art—to your documents. You set the cursor where you want the graphic to appear, tell the word processing program that you want to insert a graphic, and then locate the graphic file. After the graphic has been imported, you can move, size, crop, and add borders to it. You can even adjust the alignment so that your text flows around the picture.

You can embed sound files in your documents in much the same way that you embed a graphic file. The only difference is that an icon appears in the document (see Figure 13.7). Clicking the icon plays the sound file if the PC has a sound card and speakers. Although sound files are of no value in printed documents, they can be useful in documents that are distributed electronically—on disk, online, or across a network.

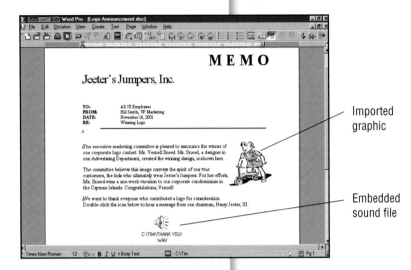

Figure 13.17
Documents can contain both graphics and sounds.

Imported graphic

Embedded sound file

Templates

Templates are predesigned documents that are blank except for preset margins, fonts, paragraph formats, headings, rules, graphics, headers, or footers (see Figure 13.18). You can open a document template, type your text into it, save it, and you're done. Templates free users from manually formatting complex documents.

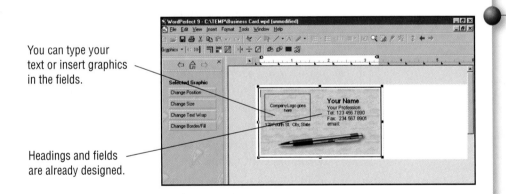

You can type your text or insert graphics in the fields.

Headings and fields are already designed.

Figure 13.18
Predesigned templates make it easy to create professional documents, from business cards to newsletters.

Self Check ✓

Answer the following questions by filling in the blank(s).

1. A(n) _____ is an application that provides tools for creating text-based documents.

2. Changing an existing document is called _____ the document.

3. _____ determine how close each line of a paragraph comes to the margins.

NORTON ONLINE

Visit **www.glencoe.com/norton/online/** for more information on **adding graphics to your documents.**

DESKTOP PUBLISHING SOFTWARE

The introduction of **desktop publishing (DTP) software** revolutionized the publishing and design industries, giving ordinary users the power to produce professional-quality documents and publications. Popular DTP software packages include Adobe PageMaker, QuarkXPress, and Adobe FrameMaker, among others.

Before DTP software, producing publications of any kind was a complex process involving multiple people with different skills. DTP software enabled one person to perform all the required tasks—design, layout, typesetting, placement of graphics, and more—and create a document that was ready to be printed.

Word processors now feature many capabilities once found only in DTP software (graphics importing, font controls, and many others), and most users find that their word processor more than satisfies their daily desktop publishing and page layout requirements. However, because DTP software is designed specifically to produce complex, multicolor, printer-ready documents, it is the better choice for professional document design. Here is a sampling of the advanced document-design features found in DTP software:

◆ **Type Controls.** Because spacing is often a concern in page layout, DTP software enables the user to control **kerning** (the spacing between individual letters, as shown in Figure 13.19) and **tracking** (a general setting for character spacing for entire blocks of text). DTP software also provides nearly infinite control of **leading** (pronounced LED-ding), which is a typesetting term for line spacing.

◆ **Graphics Controls.** DTP software gives the user direct control over the exact placement of graphics on the page, the wrapping of text around the graphic, and the use of borders or shading with graphics. This book provides many excellent examples of the graphics capabilities of DTP software.

◆ **Page Layout and Document Controls.** Because DTP software was designed for the publisher, it offers sophisticated controls for formatting documents and coordinating multiple documents in a publication. Magazines, for example, contain many different documents, with some laid out in different styles. A common page layout control in DTP software is called **master pages**—special pages that are set aside for defining elements that are common to all pages in the document, such as page numbers, headers, headings, rules, and more.

◆ **Prepress Controls.** Perhaps the most unique characteristics of DTP software are **prepress controls**—that is, its capability to prepare documents for the printing press. DTP enables the user to specify colors according to printing industry standards, such as Pantone and TruMatch, so that the printer can understand precisely what colors to use. DTP software also prepares color separations for documents printed in color. **Color separations** are separate pages created for each of the four colors that are combined to give the illusion of full color on the printed page.

Figure 13.19
Kerning can be especially important in headlines.

SUSPECT VANISHES
West-Side Police Lose James in Corn Field

SUSPECT VANISHES
West-Side Police Lose James in Corn Field

With kerning, these letters were moved closer together.

CONVERTING DOCUMENTS INTO WORLD WIDE WEB PAGES

Since 1994, thousands of companies and individuals have created electronic documents that can be accessed on the part of the Internet known as the World Wide Web. These documents are known as Web pages. To create a page for the Web, you need to format the page with special codes that explain how the page will appear and behave in a Web browser (a program like Netscape Navigator, for example). These special codes are part of a page-description language called Hypertext Markup Language, or HTML.

Newer versions of word processors—including Microsoft Word, WordPerfect, WordPro, and others—can convert standard text documents into the HTML format for you. The resulting Web page contains the original text and is formatted with HTML tags so that headings, body text, lists, and other elements will appear in a standard Web format. An example of a document coded with HTML is shown in Figure 13.20. The resulting page, as it appears on the Web, is shown in Figure 13.21.

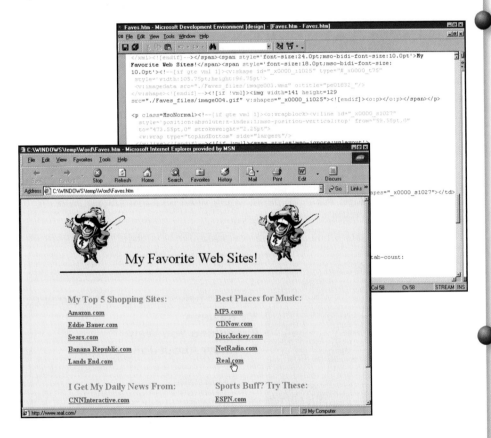

Figure 13.20
A document coded with HTML tags. This document was created in Microsoft Word's editing window like any normal document. But in HTML mode, Word provides tools for Web design and creating hyperlinks. Here is how the document appears in Word's HTML Design View window. Although the HTML codes look complicated, the user did not create any of them; they were inserted by the word processor.

Figure 13.21
The HTML document viewed in a browser.

Word processors are not the only programs that can convert documents into Web pages. Almost any new version of a spreadsheet, presentation, or database program can convert a user's files into HTML format.

Many new programs also provide HTML templates. These templates function just like normal word processing templates, which you learned about earlier in this lesson. HTML document templates provide predesigned navigation tools: places where the user can insert hyperlinks, frames, and many other features found in well-designed Web pages.

Visit **www.glencoe.com/norton/online/** for more information on the **HTML** capabilities of popular word processors.

Norton Notebook

GETTING PUBLISHED ON THE INTERNET

One of the most exciting aspects of the Internet is its openness. With the right software and an Internet account, you can go online and view materials that others have published—that is, posted on an Internet server. Add a little creativity to the mix, and you can publish your own materials for viewing by a worldwide audience. One of the easiest and fastest ways to publish your work online is to create your own page on the World Wide Web.

The Internet is not limited to big businesses. Individuals, private organizations, and small companies actually publish the vast majority of materials on the Internet. The variety of online publishing opportunities is almost limitless, and people are using them to enhance their businesses, share information, and entertain and educate others.

Before it can be viewed in a Web browser, a document must be formatted with special tags called Hypertext Markup Language (HTML) tags. These tags, which surround the text they affect, tell the browser how to display the text, whether as a heading, a table, a link, normal text, and so on.

Fortunately, you do not have to be a computer whiz to create HTML documents. In fact, you do not even need to know anything about HTML. With the right tools, you can quickly create attractive, interesting pages that are ready to be published on the Web.

Almost any new word processor, spreadsheet, database, or presentation application can convert ordinary documents into HTML files. As you saw earlier in this lesson, these features let you create any type of document, save it in HTML format, and then immediately open it in a Web browser (such as Netscape Navigator or Microsoft Internet Explorer). Many desktop applications provide tools that embed graphics, create hotlinks, and add other special features to your HTML documents.

Popular Web browsers also provide editors that enable you to create feature-rich Web pages. Using a browser's editing tools, you can create new pages from scratch or use pre-designed templates. A popular page-design method is to find a Web page you like, copy it to disk, and then open it in Edit mode in the browser. You then can use that page's HTML formatting as the basis for your page. Using a browser-based editor, you work directly with HTML tags only if you want to. If you prefer, the browser can do all the HTML formatting for you.

After you have created your pages, simply contact your Internet service provider (ISP). Your ISP can provide you with space on a Web server and an address where others can find your pages. Using your chosen HTML editing tools, you can update, expand, and refresh your Web site whenever you want.

If you want complete control over the appearance of your Web pages and like the challenge of learning a completely new software program, then you can use one of the many Web design programs now available. The programs, such as Microsoft's FrontPage or Adobe's PageMill, are a combination word processor, HTML editor, and graphics program. These applications give you all the tools you need to create complex, feature-rich Web sites with as many pages as you like.

By the thousands, people are using basic application software to create Web pages. This is a simple résumé page, viewed in Netscape Navigator, which was created in a word processor.

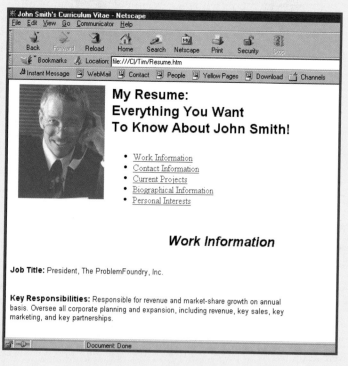

LESSON QUIZ

True/False

Answer the following questions by circling True or False.

True   False   **1.** Word processing programs are designed to work with text only.

True   False   **2.** As you enter text in a word processor, you do not need to press Enter at the end of a line unless you want to start a new paragraph.

True   False   **3.** To mark text for editing, you select it.

True   False   **4.** All characters in a serif font use the same amount of horizontal space.

True   False   **5.** In a document, the left and right margins must always be the same.

Multiple Choice

Circle the word or phrase that best completes each sentence.

1. Most word processors feature one or more _____ , which provide tools that resemble buttons.
   A. menu bars   **B.** toolbars   **C.** status bars

2. The _____ key moves the insertion point one character to the left, erasing each character as it goes.
   A. Tab   **B.** Delete   **C.** Backspace

3. On the screen, selected text is _____ .
   A. highlighted   **B.** deleted   **C.** neither A nor B

4. A(n) _____ is a position, on screen and in a document, measured from the left margin.
   A. tab stop   **B.** Backspace   **C.** insertion point

5. Newsletters are commonly laid out in a _____ format.
   A. sans serif   **B.** tabbed   **C.** column

LESSON LABS

If a word processor is installed on your computer, complete the following exercise as directed by your instructor.

Practice some basic formatting:

A. In your word processor's document area, type a few lines of text, allowing the lines to wrap when they reach the right edge of the screen. Press Enter and type a new paragraph. Create several more paragraphs.

B. Using the mouse, select a word. (Double-click the word or drag the mouse pointer across it.) Click the Bold tool. Then deselect the word by pressing an arrow key on the keyboard. Select the word again and click the Bold tool to turn off the effect.

C. Select different words, lines, and paragraphs and practice using other tools such as a Font tool, a Font size tool, Italic, and Underline.

D. Select an entire paragraph and use the alignment tools to change its alignment. Deselect the paragraph when you are done.

E. Select two or more paragraphs and use the Bullet and Numbering tools.

F. Close the program by clicking the Close button (the button marked with an **X** on the title bar). If the program prompts you to save the file, choose No.

Spreadsheet Software

OBJECTIVES

- Define and differentiate the terms *worksheet* and *spreadsheet*.
- Identify four types of data that can be entered in a worksheet.
- Explain how cell addresses are used in spreadsheet programs.
- Explain what a formula is and how formulas can be used in spreadsheet programs.
- List three types of data-analysis tools commonly found in spreadsheets and describe their use.

OVERVIEW:
Crunching Data and Presenting the Results

We live in a world that is run "by the numbers." It seems that we must work with more numerical data and financial information each day. Corporations track profits and losses, accountants manage huge balance sheets, and people balance their checkbook registers or try to maintain a household budget.

Whether their task is big or small, people use spreadsheet programs to juggle all those numbers. If you have ever heard of someone "crunching the numbers," that person was probably using a spreadsheet.

As you will learn in this lesson, spreadsheets are amazing applications that can hold large amounts of numerical data arranged in rows and columns. A typical spreadsheet program provides all sorts of tools for arranging data, performing calculations, generating charts, and creating reports.

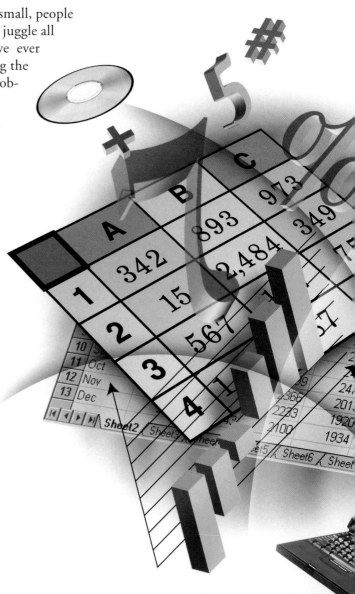

SPREADSHEET PROGRAMS AND THEIR USES

A **spreadsheet** program is a software tool for entering, calculating, manipulating, and analyzing sets of numbers. Spreadsheets have a wide range of uses—from family budgets to corporate earnings statements. As shown in Figure 14.1, you can set up a spreadsheet to show information in numerous ways, such as the traditional ledger row-and-column format or a slick report format with headings and charts.

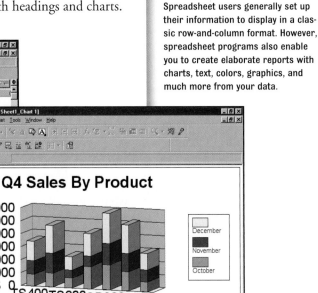

Figure 14.1
Spreadsheet users generally set up their information to display in a classic row-and-column format. However, spreadsheet programs also enable you to create elaborate reports with charts, text, colors, graphics, and much more from your data.

THE SPREADSHEET'S INTERFACE

Like a word processing program, a spreadsheet lets you work in a main document area (also called a document window), which displays your data and various tools.

Like a word processor, modern spreadsheets provide a document area, which is where you view the document. In a spreadsheet program, you actually work in a document called a **worksheet** (or sheet, as it is also called), and you can collect related worksheets in a **workbook.** Worksheets can be named, and a workbook can contain as many individual worksheets as your system's resources will allow.

A typical spreadsheet interface also provides a menu bar, toolbars, and a special **formula bar,** where you can create or edit data and formulas in the worksheet. Scroll bars help you navigate a large worksheet, and at the bottom of the window, a status bar tells you specific information about the worksheet.

An empty worksheet (one without any data) looks like a grid of rows and columns. The intersection of any column and row is called a **cell,** as shown in Figure 14.2 on page 242. You interact with a spreadsheet primarily by entering data into individual cells. A typical worksheet contains thousands of individual cells.

NORTON
ONLINE

Visit **www.glencoe.com/norton/online/** for a wide variety of information on **spreadsheets.**

Figure 14.2

Microsoft Excel's interface features tools common to nearly all Windows and Macintosh spreadsheets.

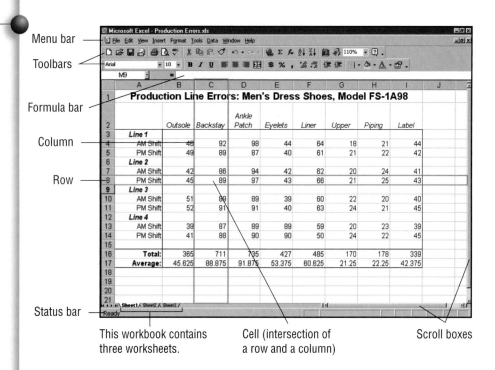

Menu bar
Toolbars
Formula bar
Column
Row
Status bar

This workbook contains three worksheets.

Cell (intersection of a row and a column)

Scroll boxes

Early spreadsheet programs provided only one worksheet at a time. Unlike current workbooks, which provide multiple sheets, earlier programs could support only one worksheet per file. Now programs provide **3-D worksheets,** which are like a pad of worksheets (see Figure 14.3). This feature lets you perform calculations in one worksheet, but your calculations can also use data from a different worksheet in the same workbook, or from worksheets in other workbooks.

ENTERING DATA IN A WORKSHEET

A worksheet's cells can hold several types of data, including labels (ordinary text), values (numbers), dates, and formulas (statements that perform calculations). Cells can also hold graphics, audio files, and video or animation files. To the spreadsheet program, each type of data has a particular use and is handled in a unique manner.

Entering data in a worksheet is simple. Using the mouse or arrow keys, you select a cell to make it active. The active cell is indicated by a **cell pointer,** a rectangle that makes the active cell's borders look bold (see Figure 14.4).

To navigate the worksheet, you need to understand its system of **cell addresses.** All spreadsheets use row and column identifiers as the basis for their cell addresses. If you are working in the cell where column B intersects with row 3, for example, then cell B3 is the active cell.

When you have selected a cell, you simply type the data into it. When a cell is active, you can also type its data into the formula bar. The formula bar is handy because it displays much more data than the cell can. If a cell already contains data, you can edit it in the formula bar.

Figure 14.3

3-D worksheets let you calculate in three directions. For example, you can create three worksheets, each containing sales data for a different month. A fourth worksheet is used to create totals for the quarter.

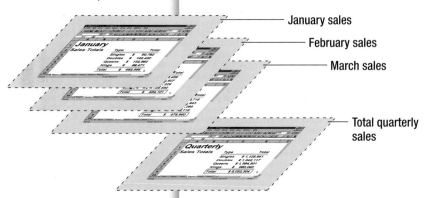

January sales
February sales
March sales
Total quarterly sales

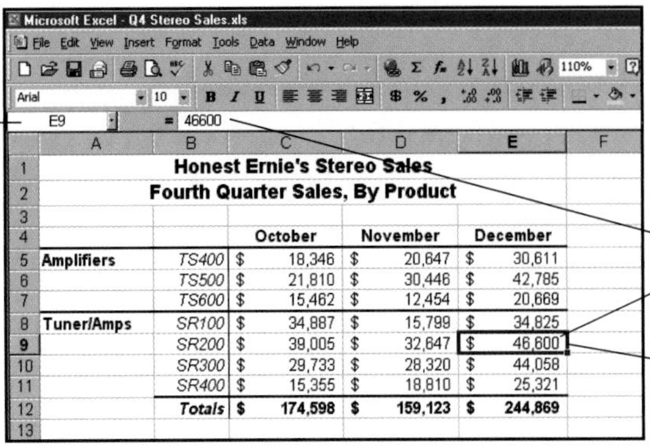

The address of the active cell is displayed here.

You can enter data in the cell or in the formula bar.

The cell pointer indicates the active cell.

You can also use the spreadsheet's cut, copy, and paste features to duplicate and move data to various parts of the worksheet. These features work among the different sheets in a workbook, from one workbook to another, and between the spreadsheet and other applications.

Labels

Worksheets can contain text—called **labels** (names for data values)—as well as values and formulas. In spreadsheets, text is referred to as a label because it is usually used to identify a value or series of values (as in a row or column heading) or to describe the contents of a specific cell (such as a total). Labels help you make sense of a worksheet's contents (see Figure 14.5).

You can place labels in any cell in a worksheet and can easily move or delete labels. In fact, you can use spreadsheets to create and manage large lists that contain nothing but text. The spreadsheet program recognizes labels as such and differentiates between labels and values or formulas. (Remember that values and formulas can be used in calculations but labels cannot.)

Spreadsheet programs provide many of the same text-formatting features found in word processors. You can format text in a spreadsheet by applying different fonts, font sizes, styles, alignments, and special effects to your labels. These formatting capabilities let you create professional, easily understood worksheets and reports.

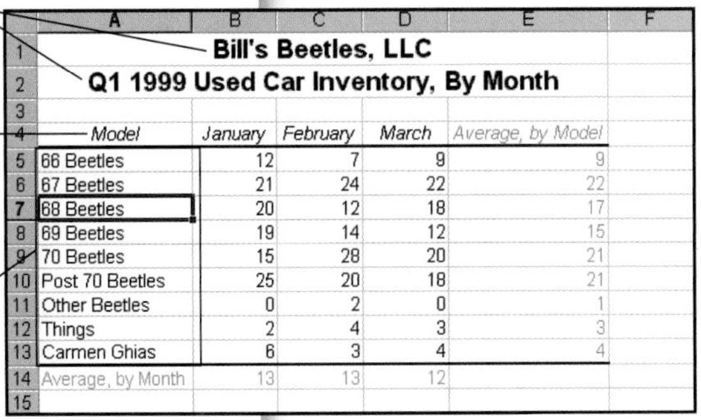

These labels are used as titles for the worksheet.

These labels are column headings that describe the contents of the cells below them.

These labels identify the data in the cells to their right.

Figure 14.5
Labels help organize the information in a worksheet.

Values

In a spreadsheet, a **value** is any number you enter or that results from a computation. You might enter a series of values in a column so that you can total them. Or you might enter several different numbers that are part of an elaborate calculation.

Spreadsheets can work with whole numbers, decimals, negative numbers, currency, and other types of values, including scientific notation. In fact, some spreadsheet programs are intelligent enough to understand the types of values you enter. Most spreadsheets recognize currency entries easily, depending on the context of the values being entered.

Dates

Dates are a necessary part of most worksheets, and spreadsheet programs can work with date information in many ways. A date may be added to a worksheet simply to indicate when it was created, or a date function may be updated whenever the worksheet is opened.

Spreadsheets can also use dates in performing calculations. An example might be the calculation of late payments on a loan. If the spreadsheet knows the payment's due date, it can calculate late fees based on that date.

Formulas

The power of the spreadsheet lies in **formulas**, which calculate numbers based on values or formulas in other cells. You can create many kinds of formulas manually to do basic arithmetic operations, calculus or trigonometric operations, and so on.

Spreadsheets make it simple to perform calculations on a set of numbers. Suppose, for example, that the manager of a real estate office wants to calculate the commissions paid to agents over a specific time period. Figures 14.6 and 14.7 show a simple formula that takes the total sales amount for each agent and calculates the commission for that total. If any part of the formula (either the sales total or the commission percentage) changes, the formula can automatically recalculate the resulting commission.

Figure 14.6

An example of a formula used to calculate simple percentages.

Figure 14.7

Spreadsheet formulas recalculate automatically if any of their base data changes.

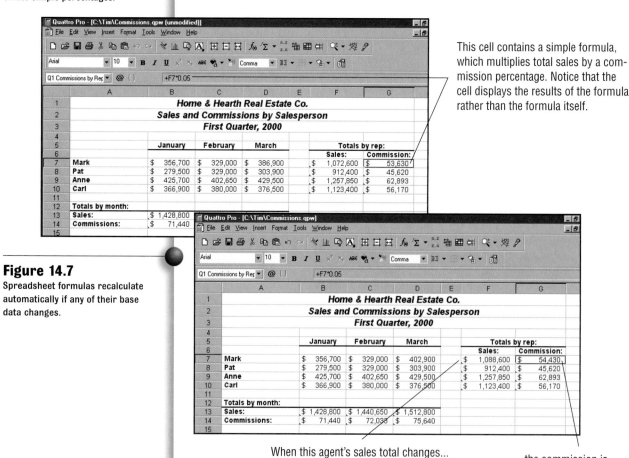

This cell contains a simple formula, which multiplies total sales by a commission percentage. Notice that the cell displays the results of the formula rather than the formula itself.

When this agent's sales total changes...

...the commission is recalculated automatically.

Cell References and Ranges

Formulas typically refer to the values in other cells throughout the worksheet. To reduce time and errors, you can use a cell reference in formulas. A **cell reference** tells the formula to look up the contents of the referenced cell; this feature saves you the trouble of typing the referenced cell's contents into the formula. If the referenced cell's contents change, the change is reflected automatically in the formula that refers to the cell.

The most common method is to refer to the cell by its address, such as A1, B10, or Y254. Therefore, if you want to add the values in cells B13 and C16, your formula might look like this: =B13+C16. A cell reference can refer to one or more cells in the same worksheet, in a different worksheet from the same workbook, or in a different workbook. Sophisticated worksheets that draw data from many different sources may use dozens or even hundreds of formulas containing cell references.

If your formula uses cells that are contiguous, you can refer to all the cells at once as a **range** (also called a block). For example, in Excel, the formula =SUM(B4,C4,D4) can be written =SUM(B4:D4). (The SUM function calculates the total of the values in a specified range of cells.) Ranges can consist of a group of cells in a column, a row, or even a group that includes several rows and columns. For example, a range of B3:D14 includes the whole block that has B3 as the upper left corner and D14 as the lower right corner.

You can even give names to cells or cell ranges instead of using their row and column address. After you assign a name to a cell, you can include the name rather than the cell address in formulas. The formula =SUM(B4,C4,D4) could appear as =SUM (April_Income, May_Income, June_Income). This makes the formula much more comprehensible because words convey more meaning than cell addresses.

NORTON ONLINE

Visit **www.glencoe.com/norton/online/** for more information on **spreadsheet functions and arguments.**

Functions

Spreadsheets come with many built-in formulas, called **functions,** that perform specialized calculations automatically. You can include these functions in your own formulas. Some functions are simple, such as the COUNT function, which counts how many values are in a range of cells. Many functions are complex. You may not know the mathematical equations for a loan payment or the depreciation of an asset using the double declining balance method. By using spreadsheet functions, however, you can arrive at the answer.

You add **arguments** within the parentheses of the function. Arguments are the values (often cell references) that the function uses in its operation. The number and type of arguments used depend on the function.

The most commonly used function is the SUM function (see Figure 14.8), which adds a list of numbers to get a total. In the following formula, the SUM function's argument is a range: @SUM(D9..D5). This formula adds the values in the five cells that comprise the range D5 through D9.

Figure 14.8
An example of the SUM function in a Lotus 1-2-3 worksheet.

A	B	C	D	E	F
Hammaker's Hammocks					
Third Quarter 1999 Sales					
	July	*August*	*September*		
Complete Systems	$12,985	$13,996	$11,804		
Beds	$2,349	$3,002	$2,123		
Stands	$5,786	$4,879	$3,989		
Repairs	$8,665	$7,501	$6,989		
Special Orders	$4,023	$3,209	$3,599		
Total Monthly Sales	**$33,808**	**$32,587**	**$28,504**		

This cell contains a SUM function, which adds the values in the cells above it.

Answer the following questions by filling in the blank(s).

1. A(n) _____ is a software tool for entering, calculating, manipulating, and analyzing numbers.

2. In a worksheet, the active cell is indicated by a(n) _____ .

3. A(n) _____ is any number that you enter or that results from a calculation.

EDITING AND FORMATTING A WORKSHEET

After a worksheet has been created, anything in it can be edited. Like word processors, spreadsheet programs are extremely accommodating when you want to make changes. To change a label or a date, you simply select its cell and make the desired changes. You can manually edit any part of a formula or function simply by selecting its cell and making your changes in the formula bar.

Spreadsheet programs make it easy to move, copy, or delete the contents of cells. You can also insert or delete rows and columns. You can add new sheets to a 3-D file or delete worksheets you no longer need. The data in a spreadsheet can also be sorted—or arranged—in various ways, such as in alphabetical or numerical order.

When you move formulas and data to a new location, the spreadsheet automatically adjusts the cell references for formulas based on that data. In Figure 14.9, for example, the second-quarter totals in cells D8 and D9 can be copied to create third-quarter totals without the necessity of reentering the cell references. In Figure 14.10, the second-quarter formulas were copied to create the third-quarter formulas. The spreadsheet program created the proper formulas automatically (based on the existing formulas), summing the third-quarter months.

Figure 14.9

Copying formulas.

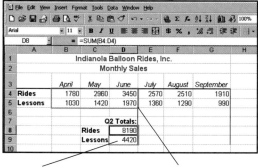

The formulas in these two cells,

which compute totals for these two ranges...

Figure 14.10

The copied formulas.

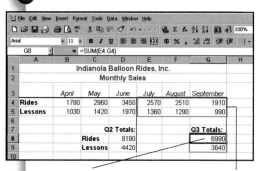

...were copied to these two cells.

The resulting formulas automatically adjust to compute the totals for these two ranges.

Relative and Absolute Cell References

The spreadsheet program changes the formulas when you copy them because it remembers that the formulas being copied will reference the same rows as the original but will automatically change the column reference when the formulas are moved to a new column. When they are used in formulas, cell references such as B4 or D7 are called **relative cell references.** In Figure 14.10, cell D8 contains the formula =SUM(B4:D4). When it is copied to

PRODUCTIVITY Tip

Automating Your Work With Macros

Although you may think your favorite software program saves you a great deal of time and energy, it could probably save you a great deal more if you used its most powerful tools—macros.

What Is a Macro?

Simply put, a macro is a list of commands, keystrokes, or other actions that has been saved and given a name. When you create a macro, you record a series of actions. When you replay the macro, it repeats those actions for you. You can use macros to automate nearly any task that requires multiple steps—no matter how many steps are involved.

Many commercial applications support macros, and some even feature an array of built-in, predefined macros that you can use right away or customize to suit your own work style. These applications usually allow you to create your own macros to automate tasks that you perform frequently or that require several steps (making them difficult to do manually).

Creating a Macro

Suppose, for example, that you are using a word processor to write a long report that contains many full-paragraph quotations. You want to format the quotations in italic, one point size smaller than the body text, and indented 1 inch from both the left and right margins. To format each quotation, you must take the following steps:

1. Select paragraph.
2. Change font size.
3. Apply italic.
4. Change left indent.
5. Change right indent.
6. Deselect paragraph.

If your word processor supports macros, however, you can create a new macro that includes these steps. Type a raw quotation, start the word processor's macro-recording feature, and perform the preceding steps while the recorder runs. You can then save the macro, give it a name (such as "Quotation"), and assign it to a shortcut key (such as Alt+1) or a toolbar button, depending on your program's macro capabilities. Afterward, you can run the macro with the click of a

mouse or by pressing a simple key combination instead of manually repeating all the steps to format each quotation.

Macros can be as simple or as complex as necessary, and you can create macros for nearly any task. In a spreadsheet, for example, you might create a macro that selects a column of data, applies a specific format, sorts the data, and inserts a function (like SUM) at the bottom. In a graphics program, you might create a macro that opens a group of image files, sizes them and adjusts their color settings, and prints them out on individual sheets, each identified by its file name. A macro can even include other macros, enabling you to perform multiple tasks at one time.

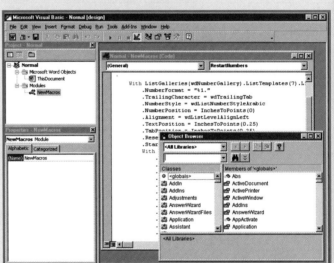

Editing a macro with Visual Basic for Applications.

In fact, macros have become so popular and powerful that many productivity applications feature built-in programming languages that you can use to create macros. These languages enable advanced users to incorporate real programming functions (such as variables and loops) into their macros to create "programs within programs." Microsoft Office's programs, for example, support an advanced macro language called Visual Basic for Applications (VBA). The programs in Lotus SmartSuite support LotusScript, and Corel's WordPerfect Office suite supports a language called PerfectScript.

247

cell G8, the program automatically changes the formula to =SUM(E4:G4) so that it adds the July, August, and September sales in row 4. This feature saves the time it would take you to type the formula. When you work with long lists of formulas, the time saved can be tremendous and you will make fewer keyboard mistakes.

Sometimes you do not want the formulas to change when you copy them. You want all the formulas, no matter where they are, to refer to a specific cell. For example, if the current interest rate is in cell A1 and several formulas are based on that rate, you want to be able to copy the formulas without the reference to A1 changing. In this case, you use an **absolute cell reference,** which is usually written using the dollar sign ($). For example, *A1* is a relative cell reference, and *A1* is an absolute cell reference. Figure 14.11 shows a projection for the third and fourth quarters. In this case, the user wanted to copy the formula from cell E8 to E9 to avoid retyping it and then edit it based on the previous year's experience. But both the projections for the third and fourth quarters needed to refer to cell E6. This reference was accomplished using absolute cell references.

Figure 14.11

Absolute cell references.

	A	B	C	D	E	F
1		Indianola Balloon Rides				
2		2nd Quarter Sales				
3		April	May	June	Q2 Sales	
4	Rides	1780	2960	3450	8190	
5	Lessons	1030	1420	1970	4420	
6	Total	2810	4380	5420	12610	
7						
8	Projected 3rd Quarter Sales				13114	
9	Projected 4th Quarter Sales				13619	
10						
11						

E8 = =E6+(E6*0.04)

The formulas in these two cells are based on an absolute cell reference.

NORTON ONLINE

Visit www.glencoe.com/norton/online/ for more information on **spreadsheet formats.**

Formatting Values, Labels, and Cells

Spreadsheet programs offer numerous formats specifically for numbers. Numbers can appear as dollars and cents, percentages, dates, times, and fractions. They can be shown with or without commas, decimal points, and so forth.

In addition to number formats, spreadsheets offer a choice of fonts and type styles, shadowed borders, and more. You can also create special effects by adding graphics, such as clip art, to your worksheets.

ADDING CHARTS

A popular feature of spreadsheet software is the ability to generate **charts** based on numeric data. Charts make data easier to understand—for example, when presenting data to an audience. You will often see charts in business presentations, yet you will rarely see the worksheets used to create the charts.

The worksheet in Figure 14.12 lists the total sales of various stereo components over a three-month period. Making quick conclusions based on this data is difficult. You must look carefully and do some mental arithmetic to determine which products sold best and which month had the best sales. But when the information is displayed in a chart, as in Figure 14.13, you can see easily which products have performed best and which month had the best sales results.

With modern spreadsheets, creating a chart is simple. The one in Figure 14.13 was created with just a few mouse clicks. Select the data you want to chart, select a chart type (bar chart, line chart, pie chart, or scatter chart, for example), and set the desired chart options. After the chart is created, you can continue to adjust its appearance using a set of special chart tools.

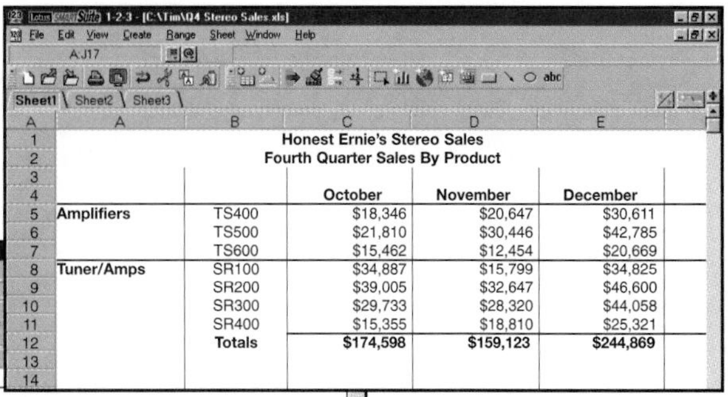

		October	November	December
Honest Ernie's Stereo Sales				
Fourth Quarter Sales By Product				
Amplifiers	TS400	$18,346	$20,647	$30,611
	TS500	$21,810	$30,446	$42,785
	TS600	$15,462	$12,454	$20,669
Tuner/Amps	SR100	$34,887	$15,799	$34,825
	SR200	$39,005	$32,647	$46,600
	SR300	$29,733	$28,320	$44,058
	SR400	$15,355	$18,810	$25,321
	Totals	$174,598	$159,123	$244,869

Figure 14.12
A spreadsheet containing data about stereo sales.

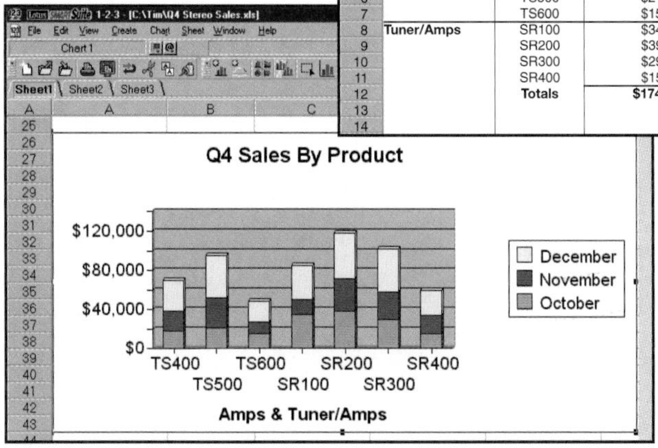

Figure 14.13
The data from Figure 14.12 is now summarized in a chart.

ANALYZING DATA IN A SPREADSHEET

You can use a worksheet to analyze data. This section discusses three useful techniques: what-if analysis, goal seeking, and sorting.

What-if analysis is the process of using a spreadsheet to test how alternative scenarios affect numeric results. All spreadsheets allow you to do simple what-if analyses. You can easily change one part of a formula or a cell that it refers to and see how that affects the rest of the worksheet. A more sophisticated type of what-if analysis is a table that automatically calculates the results based on any number of assumptions. Figure 14.14 shows such a table; it calculates the monthly mortgage payment for several possible interest rates.

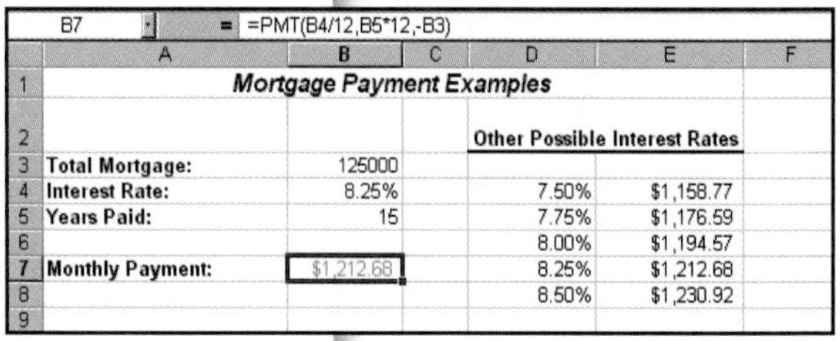

B7 = =PMT(B4/12,B5*12,-B3)

Mortgage Payment Examples				
			Other Possible Interest Rates	
Total Mortgage:	125000			
Interest Rate:	8.25%		7.50%	$1,158.77
Years Paid:	15		7.75%	$1,176.59
			8.00%	$1,194.57
Monthly Payment:	$1,212.68		8.25%	$1,212.68
			8.50%	$1,230.92

Figure 14.14
Monthly mortgage payments based on different interest rates.

What-if analysis is such an important tool that spreadsheets offer yet another way to do it. You can create several scenarios or versions of the same spreadsheet, each one containing different assumptions reflected in its formulas. In the mortgage loan example, you can create a best-case scenario that assumes you will find a house for $100,000 and an interest rate of 7.5%. Your worst-case scenario might be a house for $150,000 and an interest rate of 9%. Then you can create a report summarizing the different scenarios.

Goal seeking finds values for one or more cells that make the result of a formula equal to a value you specify. In Figure 14.15, cell B7 is the result of the Payment (PMT) formula. In this case, you know the maximum monthly payment you can afford is $1200, so you want cell B7 to be your starting point. The bank is offering an interest rate of 8.25% over 15 years. The total mortgage, cell B3, can be calculated from the monthly payment, years paid, and interest rate.

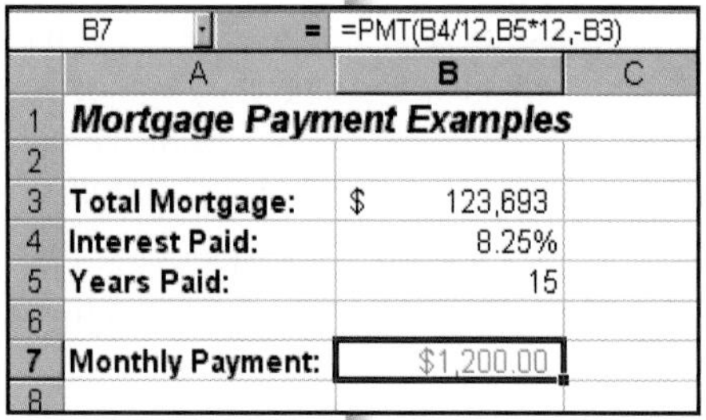

B7 = =PMT(B4/12,B5*12,-B3)

Mortgage Payment Examples	
Total Mortgage:	$ 123,693
Interest Paid:	8.25%
Years Paid:	15
Monthly Payment:	$1,200.00

Figure 14.15
The result of a goal-seeking operation.

Another data-analysis tool is sorting. When you **sort** data, you arrange it in a specific manner based on certain criteria, such as by date or dollar amount, or alphabetically. After data is sorted, it may be easier to perform calculations on the results.

Techview

MANAGING THE SMALL OR HOME OFFICE

Because resources are so limited for the small-business owner, application suites and a new breed of financial software are making it easy to run a small office/home office (SOHO). Instead of relying on outside accountants, marketers, designers, and other consultants, many SOHO workers can do many nontraditional chores—as well as their normal work—by using sophisticated software packages. These applications help small business owners solve various problems without making a large educational or monetary investment.

Application suites such as Microsoft Office, Corel's WordPerfect Office, and Lotus's SmartSuite include the following types of programs:

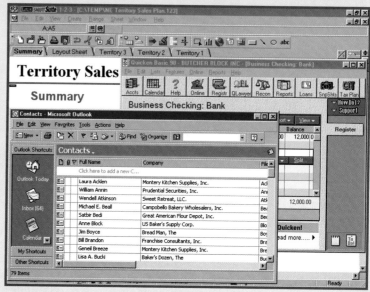

Small-business owners can use a wide range of software programs to simplify everything from sales to accounting.

◆ **Word Processor.** Most word processors include professional templates to give documents a clean look and help the user with spelling, grammar, and word choices. Word processors greatly simplify mass mailings and can print envelopes, brochures, and other complex documents. For SOHO workers who want to design their own Web pages, a word processor may be the only tool they need.

◆ **Spreadsheet.** Spreadsheets help managers tackle crucial financial tasks. The resulting files can be imported into many financial or accounting programs and can be useful to an accountant or consultant.

◆ **Database.** These packages enable the small-business owner to track products, orders, shipments, customers, and much more. When used as part of an application suite, the database program can provide much of the data required for invoices, receipts, form letters, and other mission-critical documents.

◆ **Presentation.** These programs help the user quickly create impressive presentations for use in slide shows in overheads and on the computer screen. Color graphics, animation, and concise text can help persuade clients and close sales.

◆ **E-Mail, Contact, and Schedule Management.** Even in a small office, time is valuable and people

cannot afford to confuse schedules. Programs like Microsoft Outlook and Lotus Organizer help people (individually and in groups) manage and coordinate their schedules, set appointments, and manage contacts. These programs offer e-mail software, making it even easier to send a message to someone from the contact list.

The specialty software market for small businesses is growing rapidly. Here are three examples of the types of special business-oriented programs targeted at small businesses:

◆ **Financial.** These inexpensive yet powerful packages can track inventories, billings, expenses, and much more. They can also help the user categorize income and expenses and do tax planning.

◆ **Business Planning.** New business-planning programs provide templates to help the user create business plans and customize documents by industry, product type, or market type. These programs can help the aspiring business owner find investors.

◆ **Tax Planning and Preparation.** Tax software enables business owners to prepare their own taxes without using an accountant or consultant. The user plugs in the numbers; the software does the rest.

LESSON QUIZ

True/False

Answer the following questions by circling True or False.

True   False   **1.** A spreadsheet and a worksheet are different names for the same item.

True   False   **2.** The active cell is indicated by a cell pointer.

True   False   **3.** A label is any number that you enter or that results from a computation.

True   False   **4.** A range is a group of contiguous cells.

True   False   **5.** After adding data to a worksheet, you must load it into a database program if you want to analyze the data.

Multiple Choice

Circle the word or phrase that best completes each sentence.

1. To navigate a worksheet, you should understand its system of _____ .
   A. cell addresses   **B.** spreadsheets   **C.** neither A nor B

2. _____ can help you make sense of a worksheet's contents.
   A. Cell pointers   **B.** Labels   **C.** Absolute cell references

3. A _____ can calculate numbers based on values or formulas in other cells.
   A. chart   **B.** cell reference   **C.** formula

4. _____ are the values that a function uses in its operation.
   A. Arguments   **B.** Formulas   **C.** Subroutines

5. In _____ , you arrange the data in a worksheet.
   A. what-if analysis   **B.** sorting   **C.** either A or B

LESSON LABS

If a spreadsheet is installed on your computer, complete the following exercise as directed by your instructor.

Practice using a worksheet:

A. In your worksheet's document area, type numbers in cells A1 through A5.

B. Using the mouse, select all the values in this range. (Click in cell A1. Then drag the mouse pointer down through cell A5.)

C. Click in cell A6 and type =**SUM(A1:A5)**. Press Enter. The total of the values in cells A1 to A5 should appear in cell A6. If it does not, ask your instructor for help.

D. Click in cell A3 and press Delete. The value in the cell disappears and the total in cell A6 changes.

E. Issue the Undo command. (There should be an Undo tool on the toolbar. If not, ask your instructor for assistance.) The value is returned to cell A3 and the total in cell A6 updates once more.

F. Click in cell B6 and type =**A6*0.05**. Press Enter. The formula's result appears in cell B6.

G. Close the spreadsheet program by clicking the Close button. If the program prompts you to save the worksheet, choose No.

VISUAL SUMMARY

LESSON 13: Word Processing and Desktop Publishing Software

Word Processing Programs and Their Uses

■ A word processor provides tools for creating, editing, and formatting text-based documents. Leading word processing programs include Microsoft Word, Corel WordPerfect, and Lotus WordPro.

The Word Processor's Interface

■ In a typical word processor interface, you will find a document area, menu bar, toolbars, rulers, scroll bars, and a status bar.

Entering and Editing Text

■ In the document window, a blinking insertion point shows you where characters will be placed as you type.

■ The Backspace and Delete keys let you remove characters quickly. An AutoCorrect feature can correct some errors as you type.

■ To perform most kinds of editing or formatting on text, you must first select the text; then any editing or formatting commands you issue are applied to all the selected text.

Formatting Text

■ Character formats include fonts, type size, type styles, and color.

■ Paragraph formats include line and paragraph spacing, indents and alignment, borders, and shading.

■ Document formats include margins, page size and orientation, headers, and footers.

Special Features of Word Processing Software

■ Word processors enable you to add graphics and sound files to your documents.

■ You can use a spell checker, grammar checker, and thesaurus to improve the language of a word-processed document.

■ Using mail merge, you can combine a form letter with contents from an address database and create a separate copy of the letter for each person in the database.

■ Templates are predesigned documents. They simplify document design, enabling you to create professional-looking documents simply by typing your text.

Desktop Publishing Software

■ Desktop publishing (DTP) software is specialized for designing and laying out long or complex documents. Documents created in DTP software are ready to be sent to a professional printer.

Converting Documents Into World Wide Web Pages

■ Word processing programs can create documents in HTML format, which are ready to be published as pages on the World Wide Web.

■ To create an HTML document in a word processor, create a document as you normally would. The word processor converts the document by inserting all the required HTML codes.

LESSON 14: Spreadsheet Software

Spreadsheet Programs and Their Uses

■ Spreadsheet programs provide tools for working with numerical data. Leading spreadsheet programs include Microsoft Excel, Corel Quattro Pro, and Lotus 1-2-3.

The Spreadsheet's Interface

■ In addition to standard interface components, a spreadsheet also provides a formula bar where you can enter, view, and edit data.

■ In a spreadsheet program, you work in a worksheet. Worksheets can lbe collected into groups called workbooks.

■ A worksheet contains a series of columns and rows. Each row-and-column intersection is called a cell. Cells contain the data in the worksheet.

■ Each cell is identified by a cell address, which is the combination of the cell's column letter and row number.

Entering Data in a Worksheet

■ You can enter text, values, dates, and formulas in the cells of a worksheet.

■ Formulas are used to perform calculations in the worksheet. Formulas can use cell references to use data in other cells.

■ A function is a predefined formula provided by the spreadsheet program.

Editing and Formatting a Worksheet

■ Spreadsheets provide many of the same formatting tools found in word processors.

■ You can select a contiguous group of cells, called a range, for formatting or editing.

■ Values and dates can be formatted in numerous ways.

Adding Charts

■ Spreadsheet programs provide charting tools, which let you create graphical representations of your data. To create a chart, select the data to be charted, select a chart type, and set the desired chart options. The spreadsheet program creates the chart for you.

Analyzing Data in a Spreadsheet

■ Spreadsheets are useful for analyzing your data. Analysis can help you reach a desired numeric result. What-if analysis lets you test different scenarios to see how each affects the results of a calculation. Goal seeking and sorting are other common data analysis tools found in spreadsheets.

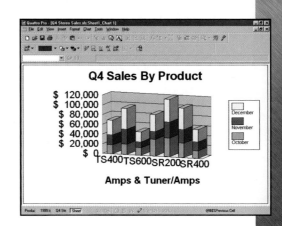

KEY TERMS

After completing this unit, you should be able to define the following terms.

3-D worksheet, *242*
absolute cell reference, *248*
alignment, *231*
argument, *245*
AutoCorrect, *228*
block, *228*
border, *231*
cell, *241*
cell address, *242*
cell pointer, *242*
cell reference, *245*
character formatting, *229*
chart, *248*
color separation, *236*
column, *232*
deselect, *228*
desktop publishing (DTP)
   software, *236*
document area, *226*
document formatting, *232*
document window, *226*
editing, *228*
font, *229*
footer, *232*
format, *229*
formula, *244*
formula bar, *241*

function, *245*
goal seeking, *249*
grammar checker, *234*
header, *232*
highlight, *228*
indent, *231*
insertion mode, *228*
kerning, *236*
label, *243*
landscape orientation, *232*
leading, *236*
line spacing, *230*
mail merge, *234*
margin, *230*
master page, *236*
monospace font, *229*
overtype mode, *228*
paragraph, *230*
paragraph formatting, *230*
paragraph spacing, *230*
point, *229*
portrait orientation, *232*
prepress control, *236*
proportional font, *229*
range, *245*
Redo, *228*
relative cell reference, *246*

rule, *231*
ruler, *227*
sans serif, *229*
section, *232*
serif, *229*
shading, *231*
sort, *249*
spell checker, *234*
spreadsheet, *241*
status bar, *227*
tab, *231*
table, *234*
tab stop, *231*
template, *235*
thesaurus, *234*
toolbar, *227*
tracking, *236*
type style, *230*
Undo, *228*
value, *243*
what-if analysis, *249*
word processing software, *226*
word processor, *226*
word wrap, *227*
workbook, *241*
worksheet, *241*

KEY TERMS QUIZ

Fill in each blank with one of the terms listed under Key Terms.

1. Word processors enable you to perform three basic types of formatting: _____ , _____ , and _____ .

2. In _____ , the new text you type writes over existing text.

3. _____ fonts have decorative curls at the ends of the strokes that make up each letter. _____ fonts do not.

4. _____ are the white borders around the edge of the page where text is not allowed to be typed.

5. You can divide a document into _____ and apply a different format to each.

6. _____ makes it easy to send the same letter to many people with the correct name and address printed on each letter.

7. _____ are like a pad of worksheets.

8. A column letter and row number combine to form a(n) _____ .

9. _____ are built-in formulas that perform specialized calculations automatically.

10. When you _____ data, you arrange it in a specific manner.

REVIEW QUESTIONS

In your own words, briefly answer the following questions.

1. In a word processor, what makes a block of text?

2. How does a grammar checker function in a word processor?

3. Which page orientation would you choose for a document containing a wide, eight-column table? Why?

4. What happens when you press Enter in a word processor?

5. Describe the advantages of using the templates provided by a word processor.

6. What is the difference between a spreadsheet and a worksheet?

7. Name the four kinds of data you can enter in a worksheet.

8. Describe the difference between an absolute cell reference and a relative cell reference.

9. How do spreadsheets perform calculations that involve dates?

10. Describe the purpose of goal seeking in a spreadsheet program.

DISCUSSION QUESTIONS

As directed by your instructor, discuss the following questions in class or in groups.

1. Do you think that using a spell checker and a grammar checker for all your final documents is a sufficient substitute for proofreading? Explain why.

2. What fundamental feature of spreadsheet software provides the real power behind its calculation capabilities? Briefly describe at least one common operation that demonstrates this capability.

ETHICAL ISSUES

Word processors and spreadsheets have made tools such as typewriters and ledger books obsolete. But like any powerful tool, they can be used and abused. With this thought in mind, discuss the following questions in class.

1. Word processors make it easy to create documents. They also make it easy to copy documents created by others. Copying other people's work is a growing concern because more people are downloading others' writings and research from the Internet and disks and then using them as their own. Would you use this tactic, say, to create a term paper for school? Do you think it is legally or morally right? Why or why not?

2. Spreadsheets give us fast access to numerical data and analysis. Some say that this access is partly to blame for our "numbers-oriented society," where companies are run by numbers with little apparent regard for issues like product quality, customer satisfaction, or loyalty to employees. Do you agree?

UNIT LABS

You and the Computer

Complete the following exercises using a computer in your classroom, lab, or home. You will need a word processor and spreadsheet installed on your computer. No other materials are needed.

1. **Get Charted.** Spreadsheet programs make it easy to create charts and provide lots of options for doing so. Take the following steps:

   A. Launch your spreadsheet program. A blank worksheet appears.

   B. In cells B1 through D1, type the words **January, February**, and **March**. These are the months whose sales figures you will chart.

   C. In cells A2 through A4, type the words **Widgits, Whatsits**, and **Whosits**. These are the products whose sales figures you will chart.

   D. In cells B2 through D4, type numerical values representing the monthly sales of each product. Then select cells A1 through D4.

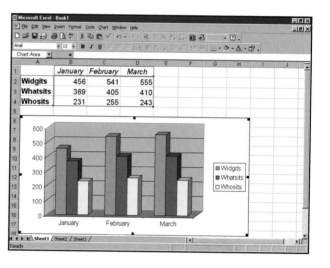

   E. Issue your spreadsheet's Chart command. It will provide you with instructions for picking a chart type and for specifying options for your charts. When you are done, your spreadsheet should display a chart. Close the spreadsheet program without saving the worksheet.

2. **Copy and Paste.** You can create documents in one application that contains data from a different application. Create a document now using your word processor and spreadsheet. Take the following steps:

   A. Launch your word processor and your spreadsheet. Each program will open in its own window. Switch to the word processor so that it becomes the active application.

   B. Type three short paragraphs of text, pressing Enter after each one. Move the insertion point to the beginning of the third paragraph and press Enter to create a blank paragraph. Press the up arrow button to move the insertion point to the blank paragraph.

   C. Switch to the spreadsheet program. Fill cells A1 through D5 with data of any kind. Now select the entire range.

   D. Issue the Copy command in your spreadsheet program. The cells' data is copied.

   E. Switch to the word processor and issue the Paste command. The data from the spreadsheet program appears in the word processor's document.

   F. In the word processor, select the spreadsheet's data and see what changes you can make to it. For example, can you format it, type over it, or delete it?

   G. Close both applications without saving either document.

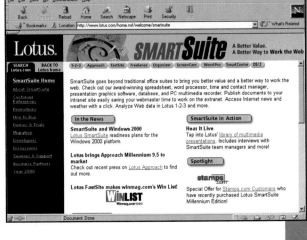

UNIT LABS

Internet Labs

To complete the following exercises, you will need a computer with an Internet connection and a Web browser. (For more information on using these tools, see "Prerequisites" at the front of this textbook.)

1. **Pick Your "Suite."** The most popular word processors and spreadsheet applications are available as part of larger "application suites." A suite is a collection of programs, such as a word processor, spreadsheet, database, presentation program, e-mail and contact management program, and more. Visit the Web sites of the three leading makers of application suites. Which one do you think would best suit your needs? Why?

   - Microsoft Corp.—**http://www.microsoft.com/** (Look for information on the Microsoft Office 2000 application suite.)

   - Corel Corp.—**http://www.corel.com/** (Look for information on the WordPerfect Office 2000 application suite.)

   - Lotus Development Corp.—**http://www.lotus.com/** (Look for information on the SmartSuite Millenium Edition application suite.)

2. **Find Some Fonts.** The Internet is a good place to find and acquire fonts. Some fonts can be downloaded from various Web sites at no cost. Other fonts can be purchased over the Web. Visit these Web sites and study the available fonts, but do not download any fonts without your instructor's permission.

   - Font Mania—**http://www.webfxmall.com/fonts/index1.html**

   - Microsoft Typography—**http://www.microsoft.com/typography/default.asp**

   - CNet—**http://www.cnet.com/** (Use the Search tool to search on the term "fonts.")

   - ZDNet—**http://www.zdnet.com/** (Use the Search tool to search on the term "fonts.")

IBE Labs

If you have the Interactive Browser Edition (IBE) CD-ROM for this textbook, you may complete the following interactive exercises using the instructions provided in the IBE.

1. **Crossword Puzzle.** Use the clues provided to complete the puzzle.

2. **Labeling.** Drag-and-drop pieces of a puzzle about interface components.

3. **Association Game.** Challenge your understanding of productivity software by arranging information correctly in a table.

4. **Format a Document.** Choose formatting options and see the results.

UNIT 8

Productivity Software, Part II

UNIT OBJECTIVES

Describe the basic purpose of presentation programs.

Explain the basic steps involved in creating slides.

Distinguish between a database and a database management system.

Identify five types of database structures.

Explain the basic steps involved in creating a database.

Define the term *enterprise software* and describe one way such software is used.

UNIT CONTENTS

This unit contains the following lessons:

Presentation Programs

OVERVIEW: Sharing Ideas and Information

If you have ever attended a seminar or lecture that included slides or overhead transparencies projected on a wall screen—or displayed on a computer screen or video monitor—then you probably have seen the product of a modern presentation program. Presentation programs enable the user to create and edit colorful, compelling presentations that can be displayed in various ways and used to support any type of discussion.

Presentation programs are used to produce a series of **slides**—single-screen images that contain a combination of text, numbers, and graphics (such as charts, clip art, or pictures), often on a colorful background. Slides can be simple or sophisticated. Depending on your needs, you can turn a basic slide show into a multimedia event using the built-in features of current presentation programs.

Presentation software is an important tool for anyone who must present information to a group. Sales and marketing professionals, for example, maintain several "stock" presentations that they can customize for different clients or products. Managers use slides to present information to employees, such as lists of benefits and responsibilities explained during new-hire orientation. Teachers and trainers commonly rely on slides in the classroom to serve as a roadmap for discussion.

OBJECTIVES

- Identify four interface elements found in most presentation programs.
- Describe the process of creating a presentation.
- Name three media sources that might be used in a multimedia presentation.
- List three ways that slides can be presented from a presentation program.

PRESENTATION PROGRAM BASICS

Before the first PC-based presentation programs were developed, creating a presentation could be a tedious and time-consuming ordeal. To start, you needed to create all the contents for your slides, which could entail handwriting the text or drawing graphics for each slide, then taking the materials to a professional print shop for typesetting. Creating the actual slides or overhead transparencies was a separate process, which could be as simple as using a photocopier or another specialized mechanical duplicating device to print the content onto transparency sheets, or hiring a photographer to create 35-mm slides of the content. The result was a set of hard-copy slides or overhead transparencies that could be used repeatedly—but could never be changed without going through the entire process again.

The process changed for the better, however, with the advent of computerized tools designed specifically to aid in slide creation. **Presentation programs** provide powerful design tools that make it easy for anyone to outline, create, edit, arrange, and display complex slide presentations. Because they provide functions—such as drag-and-drop, cut, copy, and paste, and formatting tools—found in most desktop applications, presentation programs are as familiar and comfortable to use as your favorite word processor.

The Presentation Program's Interface

The typical presentation program displays a slide in a large document window and provides a wide array of tools for designing and editing slides. Presentation programs provide many of the features found in word processors (for working with text), spreadsheets (for creating charts), and paint programs (for creating and editing simple graphics). You can add elements to the slide simply by typing, making menu or toolbar choices, and dragging. As you work on the slide, you see exactly how it will look when it is shown to an audience.

Figure 15.1 shows a slide designed in Microsoft PowerPoint 2000, a popular presentation program. Note that the status bar says that the presentation contains five slides. A presentation can contain a single slide or hundreds. Most presentation programs let you save a set of slides as a group in one file so that you can open the related slides and work with them together.

Visit **www.glencoe.com/norton/online/** for more information on popular **presentation programs.**

Figure 15.1
Interface features of Microsoft PowerPoint 2000, a popular presentation program.

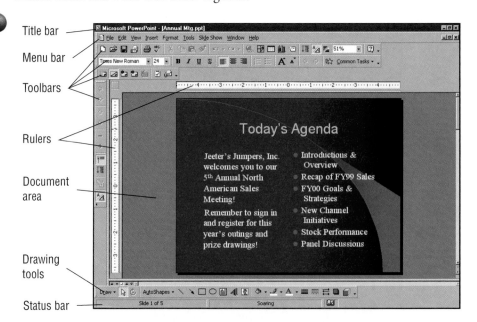

A windowed presentation program includes a menu bar, one or more toolbars (for managing files, formatting, drawing, and doing other tasks), rulers, slide-viewing or navigation buttons that let you move from one slide to another, a status bar, and other tools.

Creating a Presentation

Creating a presentation is simple; just choose the type of slide you want to create and then start adding the content. A complete presentation usually includes multiple slides arranged in a logical series. As you go, you can insert new slides anywhere, copy slides from other presentations, and reorder the slides.

You can create slides from scratch (starting with a blank slide), but it is easier and faster to work with one of the presentation program's many templates. Like a template in a word processor, a presentation template is a predesigned document that already has finished fonts, a layout, and a background. Your presentation program should provide dozens of built-in templates, as shown in Figure 15.2.

Most presentation programs provide a variety of templates.

Figure 15.2
Choosing a presentation template in PowerPoint.

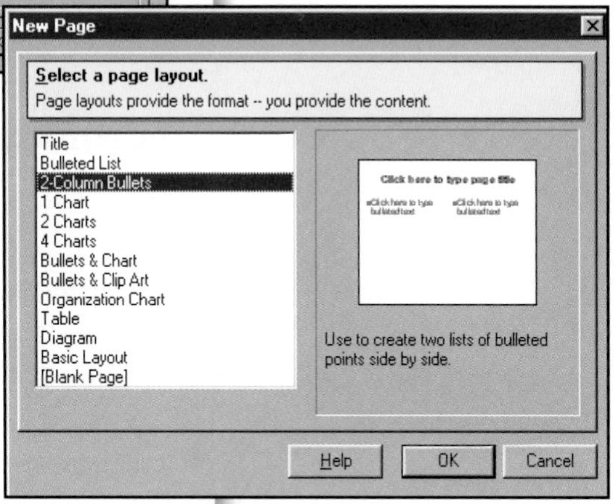

In preview mode, you can see how a template looks before you use it.

After you select a template, you can quickly assemble a presentation by creating individual slides. To create a slide, you can choose a slide type, as shown in Figure 15.3. Presentation programs provide several types of slides that can hold varying combinations of titles, text, charts, and graphics. You can choose a different type for each slide in your presentation, if you want.

After you select a slide type, the blank slide appears in the document window, ready for you to add text, charts, or graphics. The program provides special **text boxes** and **frames** (special resizable boxes for text and graphical elements) to contain specific types of content. These special boxes often contain instructions telling you exactly what to do. To add text to a text box, simply click in the box to place the insertion point there and then type your text, as shown in Figure 15.4 on page 262. The text is formatted automatically, but you can easily reformat the text later, using many of the same formatting options available in word processors.

Figure 15.3
Choosing a slide type in Lotus Freelance Graphics.

Adding charts, tables, clip art, or other graphics is nearly as easy (see Figure 15.5 on page 262). When you choose a slide type that contains a chart or table, for example, you can create the chart or table in a separate window and then insert it in the slide.

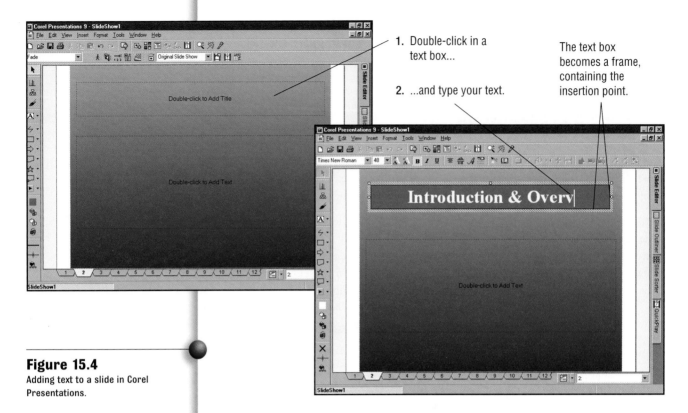

1. Double-click in a text box...

2. ...and type your text.

The text box becomes a frame, containing the insertion point.

Figure 15.4
Adding text to a slide in Corel Presentations.

To insert clip art or another type of graphic in a slide, you can select the appropriate image from your software's collection of graphics (as shown in Figure 15.6) or import an image file such as a scanned photograph or clip art. Built-in paint tools also enable you to draw simple graphics and add them to your slides. (These tools are handy if you want to add callouts to specific elements of a slide.)

Formatting Slides

Because presentation programs are like a combination of a word processor, spreadsheet, and paint program, you can easily format slides in many ways, including:

◆ **Formatting Text.** Formatting text in a presentation program is just like formatting text in a word processor. Text in slides is usually in the form of titles, headings, and lists. Although a text box can hold multiple paragraphs,

Figure 15.5
Creating a chart in PowerPoint.

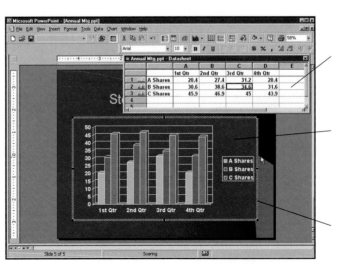

Enter data in this spreadsheet-style window...

...and it is reflected in the chart.

Each element in a slide is surrounded by a frame when you work on it.

Visit www.glencoe.com/norton/online/ for more information on **creating slides** for a presentation.

the paragraphs themselves are usually quite short. Most often, these paragraphs are formatted as bullets. To format text, you select it and then apply formats by using the toolbars or options from the Format menu.

◆ **Resizing Frames.** When you add a chart or graphic to a slide, you may need to resize it to allow better spacing for other elements on the slide. Sometimes it is necessary to resize text boxes, too, if you type more or less text than the box can hold by default. Resizing is easy using frames that surround most of the elements in a slide. To resize a frame, click it; several **handles** will appear around it, as shown in Figure 15.7. Handles are small boxes (usually white or black in color), which you can drag to resize the frame.

◆ **Adding Colors.** Colors enable you to create a wide range of moods for your presentations. Therefore, it is important to choose colors carefully. You should also make sure that the slides' colors complement one another and do not make text difficult to read (see Figure 15.8 on page 264).

◆ **Adding a Background or Shading.** You can add depth to a plain presentation by giving it a shaded background and by placing borders around certain elements. Borders separate different elements and help hold the viewer's attention on individual parts of the slide. Shaded backgrounds provide depth and can make static information appear dynamic. A **gradient fill,** as shown in Figure 15.9 on page 264, changes color as it moves from one part of the slide to another. This effect can almost make the slide appear as if it is in motion.

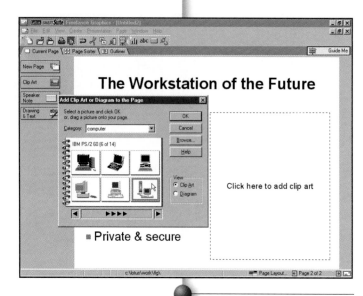

Figure 15.6
Selecting a graphic to insert into a slide.

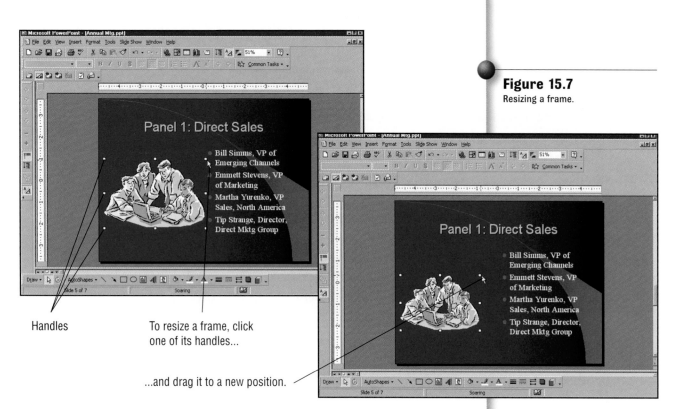

Figure 15.7
Resizing a frame.

Handles

To resize a frame, click one of its handles...

...and drag it to a new position.

Figure 15.8
Setting a color scheme for a presentation.

Figure 15.9
Borders and backgrounds can make a dull presentation more appealing.

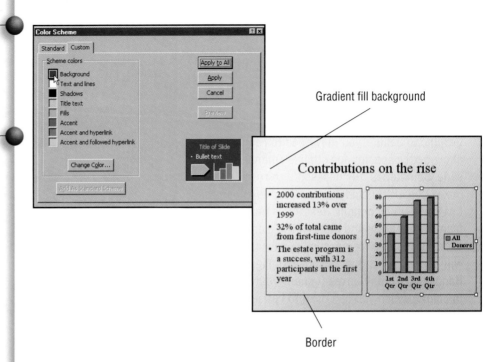

Gradient fill background

Contributions on the rise

- 2000 contributions increased 13% over 1999
- 32% of total came from first-time donors
- The estate program is a success, with 312 participants in the first year

Border

NORTON ONLINE

Visit **www.glencoe.com/norton/online/** for more information on **graphics and audio files** that you can download from the Internet for use in presentations.

Figure 15.10
Editing a presentation in the Outline view of Microsoft PowerPoint.

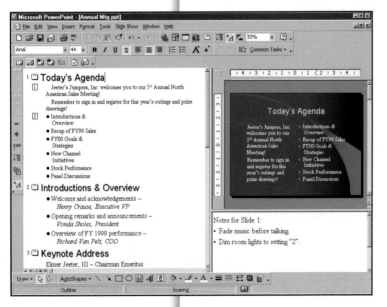

Special Features of Presentation Programs

In addition to the quick creation of dynamic and detailed slides, a presentation program can help you make your presentations lively and engaging and thus encourage your audience to pay attention and participate. Some special features found in presentation programs include the following:

◆ **Outlining.** Like any document with more than one part, a good presentation should be outlined (organized so information flows logically). An outlining tool enables you to organize your slides' contents as you create them by rearranging them and viewing them in order (see Figure 15.10).

◆ **Annotations.** Speakers often prepare a set of notes (called **annotations**) to accompany their slides. Using a presentation program, you can prepare notes for each slide as you create your presentation. You can set up notes so they are visible only to you, or you can print them with or without the actual slide.

◆ **Animation.** You can use animation tools to make text pop up or crawl onto the screen or to make slides "build" themselves by adding individual pieces of text that appear as you introduce them to the audience. You can also create animated **transitions,** a special effect that causes slides to blend together when you switch from one slide to the next. Popular transitions are the "fade" (where the first slide fades out and the next slowly appears) and the "blind" (where the first slide seems to disappear behind a closing Venetian blind and the next slide appears as the blind reopens).

◆ **Sound and Video.** Slide presentations can be full-fledged multimedia events. You can embed a sound or video object into a slide.

Techview

E-BOOKS: FLIPPING SWITCHES, NOT PAGES

As a student, you may get tired of lugging around a stack of books every day. Imagine having a single device, the size of a book, that can hold the contents of all your textbooks. Now imagine using this little system to read your favorite novels, reference book, or newspaper. This device is not a laptop computer. It is a new type of product called the electronic book or e-book, and it is designed to give you the feeling you are reading a real book instead of looking at a computer screen.

E-books try to mimic the feel of printed books in some way. They range in size from a paperback book to a notebook, with a surface occupied by a large LED display. You can easily "flip" through the e-book's pages or use hyperlinked contents or index entries to "jump" directly to a desired passage. The high-resolution screens are clear and can be viewed from various angles. Some e-books feature built-in dictionaries and let you annotate and search the online content.

Here is a look at a few of the e-book systems now on the market. You can expect these systems to evolve rapidly (assuming they become popular):

◆ **The EB Dedicated Reader.** Everybook, Inc.'s product attempts to duplicate the book-reading experience by providing two screens, separated by a spine. The product is about 8½ by 11 inches in size, and the two screens are full-color displays. The EB Dedicated Reader can store several books or magazines and lets you search and annotate text. The unit features a built-in modem that connects directly to the Everybook Store, an online outlet where you can download various publications. After a book is downloaded, you can print or fax individual pages.

◆ **Rocket eBook.** This product, from NuvoMedia, Inc., is about the size of a typical paperback book. The 3½- by 5-inch monochrome screen displays black text on a white background. The Rocket eBook features a touch-sensitive screen that you can control with your fingertip or by using a stylus (an electronic pen). This product can hold 4000 pages of text and graphics in its memory, which is enough space for several long books. Built-in features include a user's guide, a dictionary, search and bookmarking tools, annotation capability, and more. You can download content for the Rocket eBook to your PC from Internet sites, such as Barnes and Noble booksellers, and then transfer it to the eBook via a serial port connection. Each Rocket eBook uses a unique encryption code to ensure that its contents cannot be altered or transferred to another computer—even to another eBook.

◆ **The SoftBook Reader.** The SoftBook Reader, from SoftBook Press, features a 6- by 8-inch grayscale screen that is touch-sensitive for page turning and searching. The unit stores about 1500 pages of text and graphics. Memory upgrades can be installed to increase the SoftBook Reader's storage capacity to 50,000 pages. The unit features a built-in modem that connects the unit automatically to the SoftBook Press online bookstore, so you can download content directly to the SoftBook Reader.

Even though e-books are a new breed of product, publishers are jumping on board rapidly, making a wide range of printed products available in e-book format. E-book publishing partners include several large publishers of books, magazines, newspapers, and journals. E-book versions of the *Wall Street Journal*, the *New York Times*, and other newspapers are available, as are vertical publications such as technical manuals and dictionaries.

These partnerships and a wide variety of content, combined with attractive prices and ease of use, could finally make electronic publishing a successful reality for publishers of all types. With e-book prices ranging from about $200 up to $1500 (depending on model and features), there may soon be an e-book that fits nearly everyone's price range.

Despite their small size and light weight, e-books can store the contents of several large publications.

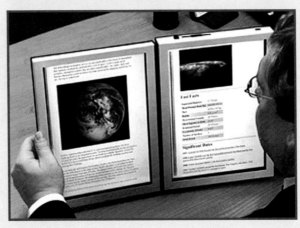

Then play the object by double-clicking its icon during a presentation. All the multimedia objects can be played directly from the computer if you have the appropriate sound and video display hardware.

◆ **Other Embedded Objects.** You can embed different types of objects, such as links to Web pages or other applications, in a presentation. When you click such a link in a slide, the Web page opens in a browser window or the other application launches.

◆ **Web Page Conversion.** Like word processors and other types of applications, presentation programs let you save your slides in HTML format for use as Web pages. While this is not the best technique for creating a personal home page, it is an easy way to make a presentation available online. Suppose, for example, that you are giving a presentation but some people cannot attend. By converting the presentation to HTML format and posting on the Internet or an intranet, you make the presentation available for those persons to view online. You can even embed navigation tools (such as forward and back buttons), hyperlinks, and other multimedia elements into an HTML presentation. Figure 15.11 shows a presentation created in Corel Presentation viewed in a browser window.

Figure 15.11
Viewing a presentation online and in HTML format. The presentation features navigation buttons and links. The viewer can zoom in or out on each slide, see the speaker's notes, and perform other actions.

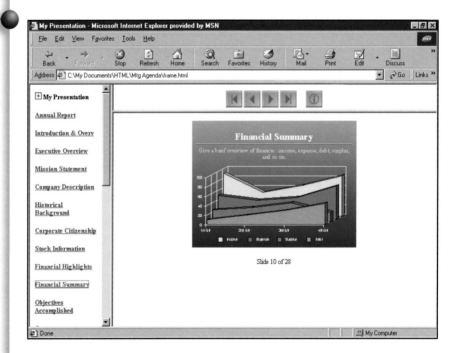

Self Check

Answer the following questions by filling in the blank(s).

1. A(n) _____ is a single-screen image that contains text and images, often on a colorful background.

2. A presentation _____ is a predesigned document with fonts, a layout, and a background.

3. You can resize a frame by dragging one of its _____ .

INTEGRATING MULTIPLE DATA SOURCES IN A PRESENTATION

In the days of manual presentations, a slide show typically contained two elements: the slides themselves and the speaker's voice. If the speaker wanted to add other types of data, they had to be incorporated separately, played on cue, and perfectly timed. Also, they might require the presenter to use other types of hardware—such as a tape player or VCR—during the presentation. If the separate media type (like a videotape) was viewed separately from the slides, it distracted the audience and created a potential stumbling block for the presenter.

Today's presentation programs enable you to incorporate many different types of media into a slide show. If you present the slides directly from the PC instead of having them printed and placing them on a slide or overhead projector, you can actually embed different media objects, such as audio files, QuickTime movies, or animation in your slides (see Figure 15.12). They can play without interrupting the flow of the presentation to start another application such as a tape player or VCR.

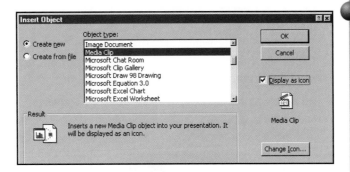

Figure 15.12
You can embed different types of objects in a presentation.

A media type can be any file that you store on the computer's disk. For example, it is possible to embed a link to a Word document, a Web page, an audio clip, or a full-motion video clip into a slide.

Figure 15.13 shows a slide as it appears in "slide show" mode on a computer screen. In other words, this screen is how the audience would see the slide in a presentation. In the slide's lower right corner, a small icon indicates that a sound file has been embedded as an audio object. By clicking the icon, the presenter can launch a player and play the sound file directly from the PC's disk.

This icon represents an embedded media object. Click it...

...and the appropriate player opens and plays the file.

Figure 15.13
Playing an embedded sound file from a slide. If the slide is being presented on a PC with a sound card and speakers, the audience will be able to hear the audio file as it plays. This technique works with many types of objects, from audio files to full-motion video.

267

PRESENTING SLIDE SHOWS

As mentioned earlier, presentations once required the use of a projector (slide or overhead) and a hard-copy version of the content, either on 35-mm slides or overhead transparencies. The presenter had to display each slide manually in a preset order. Jumping to a slide out of sequence meant quickly finding the right slide, pulling it, displaying it, and getting the presentation back on track. This tactic could be difficult when dealing with a large group of slides or an impatient audience.

Thanks to presentation programs, you can present your slides directly from the computer's disk, along with any audio or video files that you embed in your slides. Your audience can view slides in several ways:

◆ **On the PC's Screen.** If you are presenting slides to a few people, your PC's monitor might be adequate for an informal slide show. Of course, the larger the monitor, the better your audience can see the slides. Also, note that flat-panel monitors are not well suited for this purpose because of their limited viewing angle. If you want to show slides to more than three or four people at a time, consider a different display method.

◆ **On a Large-Format Monitor.** Large-format CRT and gas plasma monitors can display your slides at the proper resolution and large enough for a sizable audience to view comfortably. These devices are expensive and more difficult to transport than a standard monitor, but they may be the best solutions for some presentation settings (see Figure 15.14).

◆ **On a Television Screen.** Using a **PC-to-TV converter,** you can connect your computer to a standard television and view the PC's video output on the television monitor. While this solution may sound convenient, many compatibility issues must be considered (not all converters work with all televisions, for example), and televisions do not display images at the same resolution as a PC monitor. As a result, image quality may suffer when a PC-to-TV converter is used.

◆ **From a PC Projector.** Portable, high-resolution PC projectors are expensive, but they can display slides to a large audience. These projectors plug into one of the PC's ports and accept the system's video output. New-generation projectors can display crisp images in only semidarkened rooms, and a projector displays the image at the same resolution as the PC's monitor.

Figure 15.14
You can get the best results from your slide shows if you present them directly from the PC's disk using a display device that is appropriate for the audience and room size.

Regardless of the method you use to project your slides, navigating a slide show is a simple process. You can move from one slide to the next by clicking the mouse button or pressing Enter. Or you can automate the presentation by setting a display time for each slide. Presentation programs make it easy to take slides out of sequence or rearrange slides during a presentation. You can even use the program's drawing tools to draw on a slide while it is being displayed.

PC-to-TV Converters

The idea of hooking your PC to a television may seem strange, but for many types of presentations, television is an ideal solution. How do you get your PC to "talk" to your television? Some new PCs, especially higher-end laptops, have "TV-Out" plugs as a standard feature. If your PC does not have a TV-Out plug, you need a PC-to-TV converter—a small box that connects to your PC's video port and translates the video signal into a television signal.

First, the Problems

The conversion process is not always simple and may not provide the image quality you need for several reasons:

◆ **Signal Format.** The converter must change the PC's signal into one the television understands.

◆ **Resolution.** If your PC display is set to a higher resolution than the television uses, the converter must adjust the number of vertical lines to fit a television. This adjustment can reduce image quality.

◆ **Scan Rate.** Televisions and PC monitors create images by drawing dots on the screen, at a fixed rate called the scan rate. Scan rates differ for televisions and PCs, and a converter must compromise between those rates.

◆ **Interlacing.** A television creates an interlaced picture by alternating between the odd and even horizontal lines that make up the picture. The converter must change the PC's noninterlaced signal into an interlaced signal for the television.

◆ **Picture Ratio.** Televisions draw a picture a little larger than their own screen, resulting in a slight loss around the edges of the image called an overscan. Every television has a slightly different overscan, so you could lose part of your PC's image on the television.

Making a Smooth Conversion

Converters provide a wide range of options. Here are a few points to consider:

◆ **Picture Resolution.** Make sure that your converter can handle the resolution you want to use.

◆ **Color.** Your converter must be able to accept the number of colors that your video card sends.

A PC-to-TV converter can be an affordable alternative to PC projectors or large monitors.

◆ **Video Out Frequency.** The standard VGA and SVGA video card puts out a signal that refreshes the screen sixty times per second. However, many video cards and monitors can refresh at much higher rates, which produces a flicker-free picture on your monitor. Make sure your converter can accept the frequency that your video card uses.

◆ **Flicker Filters.** Since PCs use a noninterlaced picture while televisions use interlacing, the conversion of one to the other may result in an image that flickers. Choose a converter that eliminates flicker.

The Shape of Conversions to Come

As computers and televisions become more high-tech, the need for converters may be eliminated. Here are a few improvements to look forward to:

◆ **100 Hz Television.** These televisions draw their pictures twice as fast as a standard television. The result is a picture similar to that of a PC.

◆ **S-Video.** This method combines and sends signals to reduce errors introduced by converting PC to TV signals, resulting in a clearer picture.

◆ **High Definition Television (HDTV).** HDTV is still in the early stages of its release, but when it comes, the need for converters will be eliminated. HDTV has a digital noninterlaced picture with twice the vertical resolution of current television. The resulting picture is as clear as a PC.

LESSON QUIZ

True/False

Answer the following questions by circling True or False.

True   False   **1.** Before you can display a presentation, you must print it out and convert the hard copy into transparencies for use on a projector.

True   False   **2.** As you create a slide presentation, you can rearrange slides in any order.

True   False   **3.** To resize a frame, click it and drag one of its handles.

True   False   **4.** Annotations are notes that accompany slides in a presentation.

True   False   **5.** If you display a presentation from disk, you can show it only on your PC's monitor.

Multiple Choice

Circle the word or phrase that best completes each sentence.

1. You use a presentation program to produce a series of _____ .

   A. objects   **B.** frames   **C.** slides

2. A presentation _____ is a predesigned document, with fonts, a layout, and a background.

   A. format   **B.** template   **C.** program

3. When you add text to a slide, you insert it in a _____ .

   A. text box   **B.** handle   **C.** chart

4. A _____ changes color as it moves from one part of the slide to another.

   A. background   **B.** border   **C.** gradient fill

5. A(n) _____ is a special effect that causes slides to blend together when you switch from one slide to the next.

   A. annotation   **B.** video   **C.** transition

LESSON LABS

Complete the following exercises as directed by your instructor.

1. Explore your presentation program's interface. When you launch the program, it will open with a new, blank slide ready for you to design. Review the program's interface closely and identify the title bar, menu bar, toolbars, rulers, scroll bars, status bar, and insertion point.

2. Follow your instructor's directions to view the list of templates provided by your presentation program. Review the templates and their basic appearance. Now, list the template you would

choose if you had to give the following types of presentations:

Presentation	Template
Lecture on the Civil War	_____
Motivational Speech	_____
Pitch to prospective investors	_____
Orientation for new employees	_____

Database Management Systems and Enterprise Software

OVERVIEW:
The Mother of All Computer Applications

Before a computer can compute, it needs some base of information—a database. People have the same need for data, of course, and maintain their own databases. For example, an address book, a company's phone book, a library's card catalog, and an instructor's list of students are all organized lists of data.

Given the prevalence of databases in your daily life, it should not surprise you to learn that many of the early attempts to build and program computers grew out of a need to store and manipulate large lists of data. While computers today perform tasks well beyond the simple tabulating and sorting of early computers, the need for an organized data source still exists. For example, a word processor maintains several databases. These databases include a dictionary of words for the spell checker and thesaurus, a list of available fonts, data for mail merges, user preferences, and other types of data.

Practically every application— even if it has nothing to do with words or organized lists—has grown from earlier programs that stored and processed data. In the case of large commercial applications (such as facilities management or sales support software), the perceived size, complexity, function, and appearance of the software may make the software look completely different from the more common word processor style of productivity applications, but there is still a database at the heart of each operation.

OBJECTIVES

- Define the terms *database* and *database management system (DBMS)*.
- List three tasks that a DBMS enables users to do.
- Differentiate between flat-file databases and relational databases.
- List three steps needed to create a database.
- Explain the purpose of filters and forms.
- List three examples of query languages.

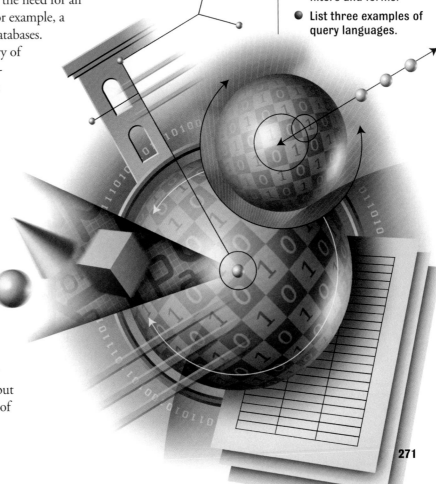

271

DATABASES AND DATABASE MANAGEMENT SYSTEMS

To make large collections of data useful, individuals and organizations use computers and an efficient data management system. Like a warehouse, a **database** is a repository for collections of related data or facts. A **database management system (DBMS)** is a software tool that allows multiple users to store, access, and process data or facts into useful information.

Database management is one of the primary reasons people use computers. Many large companies and organizations rely heavily on a commercial or custom DBMS to handle immense data resources. Such organizations require sophisticated systems to accommodate their data management needs. Often, a DBMS is custom-programmed to fit the exact needs of a company and may be designed to run on a large mainframe computer system.

A DBMS is an equally vital tool for people and organizations that use networks and stand-alone personal computers. In these cases, the DBMS is often a commercial software product sold by the same companies that offer popular spreadsheets and word processing software.

Personal computers have brought database management to the desktops of individuals in businesses and homes. Although the casual computer user may not need an inventory-tracking system, home users utilize commercial DBMS products to maintain address lists of friends and business contacts, manage household purchases and budgets, organize music CD and video libraries, and store data for home businesses.

These types of software may not be referred to as database or database management programs; instead they are called personal information managers, personal organizers, and other names. Behind their interfaces, however, these PC programs have the heart of a database management system. For example, Figure 16.1 shows the popular personal accounting package Quicken. With Quicken, you can manage your checkbook, bank accounts, calendar, taxes, and more. To store and retrieve these different types of data, Quicken uses a database and data management capabilities.

Microsoft Outlook, shown in Figure 16.2, is another example of a popular personal information manager that uses databases. With applications such as Outlook, you can store and manage your schedules, e-mail addresses, news sources, and other types of information.

A dedicated DBMS makes it possible to do many routine tasks that would otherwise be tedious, cumbersome, and time-consuming without the services of a computer. For example, a DBMS can do the following:

◆ Sort thousands of addresses by ZIP Code prior to a bulk mailing.

◆ Find all records of New Yorkers who live in boroughs outside Manhattan.

Figure 16.1

Quicken uses a database to store and manage your personal finances.

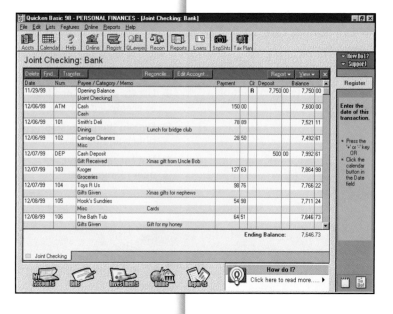

- Print a list of selected records, such as all real estate listings that closed escrow last month.

- Invoice a customer's new car lease, adjust the dealership's inventory, and update the service department's mailing list merely by entering the data for a single sales transaction.

In other words, a DBMS not only stores information, it provides mechanisms for retrieving that information easily based on whatever criteria you specify. The DBMS can sift easily through thousands or even millions of pieces of data, returning only the data you need.

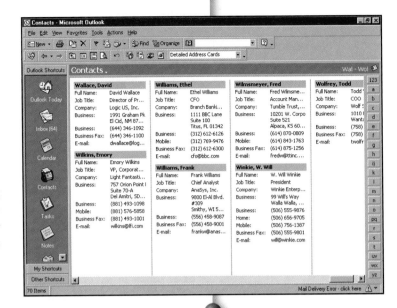

Figure 16.2
Microsoft Outlook uses databases to help you manage information such as addresses, phone numbers, schedules, and more. Outlook also provides e-mail, newsreading, and other functions, but at its core is a complex database and database management system.

The Database

A database contains a collection of related items or facts arranged in a specific structure. The most obvious example of a noncomputerized database is a telephone directory. Telephone companies now use an electronic database program to produce their printed phone books. Sometimes you will see a specialized phone book that is sorted not only by last name, but by other items such as phone number or street address. These books are easy to produce because the telephone company's electronic database can sort and organize the data in many different ways. (You learned about sorting in the discussion of spreadsheet programs in Unit 7.) Database programs can also sort lists of data, arranging them in alphabetical, numeric, or chronological order.

Before learning more about the powers of electronic databases, you need to learn about how data is organized within a database and some of the more common terms. You also need to know that, while there are some standard and accepted database terms, they are not always used or used correctly. To help you visualize how a database stores data, think about a typical address book like the one shown in Figure 16.3.

Three of the most important terms to know about databases are listed below:

- **Fields.** Notice in Figure 16.3 that each piece of information in the address book is stored in its own location, called a **field.** For example, each entry has a field for First Name and another field for Last Name, as well as fields for

Figure 16.3
Data is stored in tables. A table is divided into records, and each record is divided into fields.

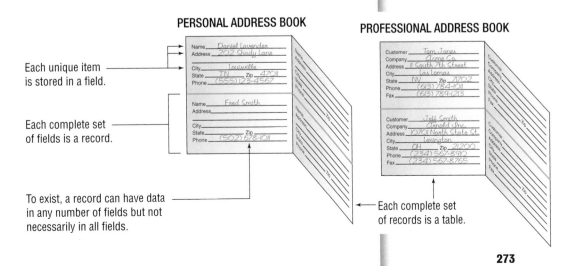

Each unique item is stored in a field.

Each complete set of fields is a record.

To exist, a record can have data in any number of fields but not necessarily in all fields.

PERSONAL ADDRESS BOOK

PROFESSIONAL ADDRESS BOOK

Each complete set of records is a table.

Address, City, State, ZIP Code, and Phone Number. Each unique type of information is stored in its own field.

◆ **Records.** One full set of fields—that is, all the related information about one person or object—is called a **record**. Therefore, all the information for the first person is record 1, all the information for the second person is record 2, and so on.

◆ **Tables.** A complete collection of records makes a table.

Figure 16.4

A database consists of tables and all the supporting documents.

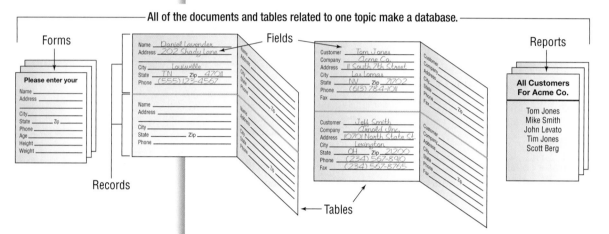

Figure 16.4

A database consists of tables and all the supporting documents.

Once you have a structure for storing data (whether it is a printed address book, phone book, or electronic table), you can enter and view data, create reports, and perform other tasks with the data. For example, you might create a customer report that lists customers by ZIP Code. These extra tools, along with the tables, combine to form a database, as shown in Figure 16.4.

Now that you have a better understanding of database terms, you can begin exploring an electronic database. Figure 16.5 shows a customer information table as it appears in the popular PC database application, Lotus Approach.

Notice that the table arrangement consists of a set number of named columns (fields) and an arbitrary number of unnamed rows (records). The table organizes each record's data by the same set of fields, but the table can store any number of records. For example, if you are storing employee data, theoretically, you can have an unlimited number of employees. But there are a finite number of "facts" or fields about each employee. The only limit is the storage capability of the disk. Any one record in the table does not necessarily have data in every field. For a record to exist, however, it must have data in at least one field. For example, an employee must have a name. It is not an optional fact about an employee. Therefore, it will always be present in the record for each employee.

Figure 16.5

A customer information table in Lotus Approach.

The order of fields in a table strictly defines the location of data in every record. For example, a phone number field must contain a record's phone

number—it cannot contain a person's name or ZIP Code. Similarly, the set of fields in any one table provides a sensible definition of the database for those who must access its data. For instance, you would expect to find the part number for a radiator in an inventory of auto parts, but you should not expect to view an employee's payroll record in the same table.

Flat-File and Relational Database Structures

Many early database applications and some current low-end applications could access and manipulate only one table at a time. Each table was stored in its own file, as were any related documents. In these cases, there was no reason to use the term *table* because the table and the database were one and the same. Very often, the table was simply called a file or just "the database."

To be more precise, however, a database file that consists of a single data table is called a **flat-file** (or sequential file) **database.** Flat-file databases are useful for certain single-user or small-group situations, especially for maintaining lists such as address lists or inventories. Data that is stored, managed, and manipulated in a spreadsheet is similar to a flat-file database. (Notice that the table in Figure 16.5 looks like a spreadsheet. If this table were stored by itself or not associated with any other database tables, it would be a flat-file database.)

Although easy to learn and use, flat-file database systems can be difficult to maintain and limited in their power. When numerous files exist (one for each table or related document), there is often a lot of data redundancy, which increases the chance for errors, wastes time, and uses excess storage space. Adding, deleting, or editing any field requires that you make the same changes in every file that contains the same field.

In a **relational database**—a database made up of a set of tables—a common field existing in any two tables creates a relationship between the tables. As shown in Figure 16.6, a Customer ID Number field in both the Customers table and the Orders table links the two tables, while a Product ID field links the Orders and Products tables.

The relational database structure is easily the most prevalent in today's business organizations. In a business, a typical relational database would likely contain data tables such as the following:

- Customer information
- Order information
- Employee information
- Inventory information
- Vendor information

Multiple tables in this kind of database make it possible to handle many data management tasks, for example:

- The customer, order, and inventory tables can be linked to process orders and billing.

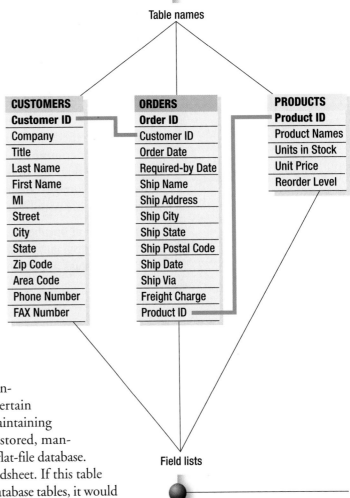

Table names

CUSTOMERS		ORDERS		PRODUCTS
Customer ID		**Order ID**		**Product ID**
Company		Customer ID		Product Names
Title		Order Date		Units in Stock
Last Name		Required-by Date		Unit Price
First Name		Ship Name		Reorder Level
MI		Ship Address		
Street		Ship City		
City		Ship State		
State		Ship Postal Code		
Zip Code		Ship Date		
Area Code		Ship Via		
Phone Number		Freight Charge		
FAX Number		Product ID		

Field lists

Figure 16.6
Linked fields in relational database tables.

◆ The vendor and inventory tables can be linked to maintain and track inventory levels.

◆ The order and employee tables can be linked to control scheduling.

Other Database Structures

Although this chapter focuses on the relational database model, other database structures are used. Some of these structures are older than the relational model and are more commonly used on mainframe systems, while others are new. Regardless of their age or likely location, you may run into these database structures on a PC; understanding them helps you to see the advantages and disadvantages of the more popular relational model.

◆ **Hierarchical Databases.** The **hierarchical database** is an older style of database, originally developed on mainframe computers. As shown in Figure 16.7, the tables are organized into a fixed treelike structure, with each table storing one type of data. The trunk table (also called the main table), stores general information—for example, a list of open projects. Any field in that table may reference another table that contains subdivisions of data—such as all the vendors or personnel working on a particular project. Each one of those tables may, in turn, reference other tables that store even finer subdivisions of data, like vendor credit or employee data. The relationship between tables is said to be a **parent-child relationship,** with any child table relating to only one parent table. This arrangement is also called a **one-to-many relationship** because each parent table may have many child tables, but each child has only one parent.

Because their relationships are fixed, hierarchical databases require little duplicated data and may locate data quickly. However, the tables' fixed relationships limit the flexibility of the database, making some kinds of queries or reports difficult or impossible. As a result, this type of structure is used more often when the database is embedded within another application and always accessed in the same way.

◆ **Network Databases.** The **network database** model is similar to the hierarchical structure except that any one table can relate to any number of other tables (see Figure 16.8). The network database's tables, therefore, are said to have a **many-to-many relationship.** As a result, no tiers or inherent hierarchy exists within the database. In principle, a network database works like a fixed version of the more flexible relational database. Like the hierarchical structure, the network database is used in older (primarily mainframe) systems and is best suited for embedded applications where the demands on the database are fixed.

◆ **Object-Oriented Databases.** The **object-oriented database (OODB),** which was first developed in the late 1980s, groups data items into complex items called objects. These objects, which parallel the object structures used in

Figure 16.7
Linked tables in a hierarchical database.

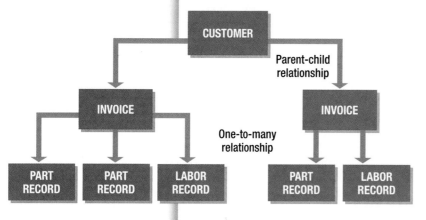

CUSTOMER

Parent-child relationship

INVOICE

One-to-many relationship

INVOICE

PART RECORD   PART RECORD   LABOR RECORD

PART RECORD   LABOR RECORD

NORTON
ONLINE

Visit **www.glencoe.com/norton/online/** for comparisons of different types of **databases.**

object-oriented programming, can represent anything: a product, an event, a customer complaint, or even a purchase. An object is defined by its characteristics, attributes, and procedures. An object's characteristics can be text, sound, graphics, and video. Examples of attributes might be color, size, style, quantity, and price. A procedure refers to the processing or handling associated with an object.

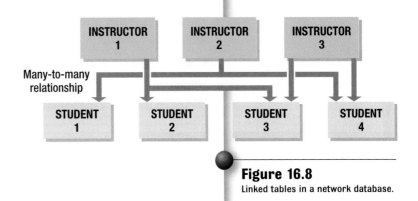

Figure 16.8
Linked tables in a network database.

The DBMS

As you have seen, a database is basically a collection of data. A database management system is a program, or collection of programs, that allows any number of users to access and modify the data in a database. A DBMS also provides tools that enable users to construct special requests (called queries) to obtain selected records easily from the database.

Perhaps the biggest asset of a DBMS is its ability to provide quick access and retrieval from large databases. Because database files can grow extremely large (many gigabytes—millions of records—on large systems), recalling data quickly is not a trivial matter. A DBMS, especially when it is running on powerful hardware, can find any speck of data in an enormous database in minutes—sometimes even in seconds or fractions of a second.

Data management tasks fall into one of three general categories:

◆ Entering data into the database

◆ Sorting the data—that is, arranging or reordering the database's records

◆ Obtaining subsets of the data

Equally important, a DBMS provides the means for multiple users to access and share data in the same database by way of networked computer systems.

Many different DBMS programs are available. Enterprise-level products, such as Oracle, DB2, and Sybase, are designed to manage large corporate or special-purpose database systems. Programs such as Microsoft Access, Corel's Paradox, and Lotus Approach are popular among individual and small-business database users.

WORKING WITH A DATABASE

The DBMS interface presents the user with data and the tools required to work with the data. You work with the interface's tools to perform data management functions:

◆ Creating tables   ◆ Sorting records

◆ Entering and editing data   ◆ Querying the database

◆ Viewing data   ◆ Generating reports

Creating Database Tables

The first step in building any database is to create one or more tables. As you know, tables hold the raw data that the DBMS will work with. To create a new database, you must first determine what kind of data will be stored in each table. In other words, you must define the table's fields with a three-step process:

1. Name the field.   **2.** Specify the field type.   **3.** Specify the field size.

When naming the field, indicate as briefly as possible what the field contains. Figure 16.9 shows a database table with clearly named fields.

Figure 16.9
Clearly named fields.

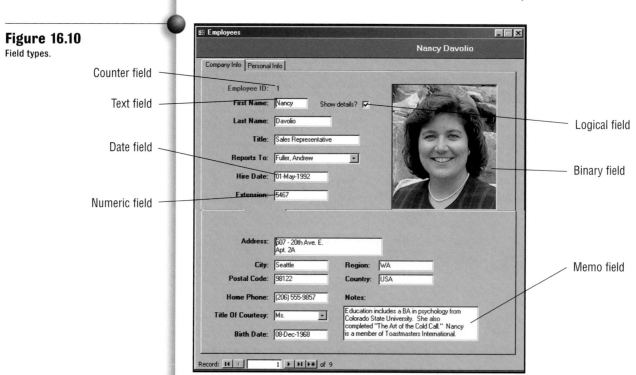

	Stock No	Vendor No	Equipment Class	Model	Part No	Description
1	900.00	3,820.00	Vehicle	DV-100	T-5100	Underwater Diver Vehicle
2	912.00	2,014.00	Vehicle	18-DV	7160-00	Underwater Diver Vehicle
3	1,313.00	3,511.00	Air Regulators	MK-200/G200	12-200-000	Regulator System
4	1,314.00	5,641.00	Air Regulators	TR-200	6832-14A	Second Stage Regulator
5	1,316.00	3,511.00	Air Regulators	MK-10/G200 B	12-502-000	Regulator System

Field name

Specifying the field type requires knowledge of what kind of data the DBMS can understand. Most modern database systems can work with seven predefined field types. Figure 16.10 shows examples of each of these field types.

Text fields (also called character fields or alphanumeric fields) accept any string of alphanumeric characters that are not used in calculations. Such an entry might be a person's name, a company's name, an address, a phone number, or any other textual data. Text fields also typically store entries consisting of numbers, such as phone numbers or ZIP Codes not used in calculations.

Numeric fields store purely numeric data. The numbers in a numeric field might represent currency, percentages, statistics, quantities, or any other value that can be (but is not necessarily) used in calculations. The data itself is stored in the table strictly as a numeric value, even though the DBMS can display the value with formatting characters such as dollar or percent signs, decimal points, or commas.

A **date field** or **time field** stores date or time entries. This field type converts a date or time entry into a numeric value, just as dates and times are stored internally as serial numbers in spreadsheet cells. In most database systems, a date value

Figure 16.10
Field types.

Counter field
Text field
Date field
Numeric field
Logical field
Binary field
Memo field

represents the number of days that have elapsed since a specific start date. When you enter a date in a date field, the DBMS accepts your input, displays it in the format of a date (such as 9/9/2003), and converts it to a number (such as 37873) that it stores in the database. Date and time fields typically include automatic error-checking features. For instance, date fields can verify a date's accuracy and account for the extra day in a leap year. Date and time fields are quite handy for calculating elapsed time periods, such as finding records for invoices thirty-one days overdue.

Logical fields (also called Boolean fields) store one of only two possible values. You can apply almost any description for the data (yes or no, true or false, on or off, and so forth). For example, a Catalog field in a Customer table can tell a customer service representative whether a customer has ordered a new catalog (Yes) or not (No).

Binary fields store binary objects, or BLOBs. A **BLOB (Binary Large OBject)** can be a graphic image file such as clip art, a photograph, a screen image, a graphic, or formatted text. A BLOB can also be an audio file, video clip, or other object, as shown in Figure 16.11.

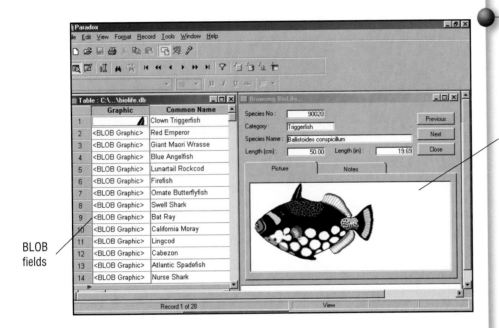

BLOB fields

Binary field containing a graphic

Figure 16.11
Binary fields allow graphic images and other nontext items to be stored in a database.

In some DBMSs, **counter fields** (sometimes called autonumber fields) store a unique numeric value that the DBMS assigns to each record. Because it is possible for two records to have identical data in some tables (such as two employees with the same name), a counter field ensures that every record will have a completely unique identification. Counter fields may also be used for creating records that number sequentially, such as invoices.

Because most field types have fixed lengths that restrict the number of characters in an entry, **memo fields** (also called description fields) provide fields for entering notes or comments of any length.

After the table has been set up, data can be entered. In most cases, entering data is a matter of typing characters at the keyboard. Entering data in a database table is much like entering data in a spreadsheet program. The process can have more pitfalls than you might expect, however, especially if it is being carried out by someone other than the user who set up the tables. For example, the DBMS might not handle a number correctly if the user enters it with a dollar sign—even though the number will be displayed as a dollar amount. If the data is entered with an inconsistent mix of upper- and lowercase letters, the DBMS may not be able to sort the data or locate specific records.

Most DBMSs allow you to create a data entry **form** to make data entry easier (see Figure 16.12). The form is nothing more than a custom view of the table that typically shows one record at a time and includes special controls and labels that make data entry less confusing. For example, you can include controls that automatically move the insertion point to the next field when the typist presses the Enter or Tab key, or you can convert all the input into capital letters to maintain data consistency. You can even direct input into multiple tables, which really makes life easier for a typist who does not know about the underlying structure of the DBMS and database tables.

The techniques you can employ to control data entry have different names and different capabilities, depending on the specific DBMS product. Some products call these controls **masks;** others call them **pictures** or **field formats.** Regardless of the name, the device accepts only valid characters and controls the entry's display format. For example, you can set up a State field so that a state's two-letter code appears uppercase (TN), no matter how the data is typed (tn, Tn, tN, or TN). A phone number field's entry can be controlled in a similar manner. Even though the user types only the phone number's ten digits, it appears with the area code enclosed in parentheses, a space, and a hyphen following the prefix—for example, (818) 555-1234.

Figure 16.12
Forms make data entry easier.

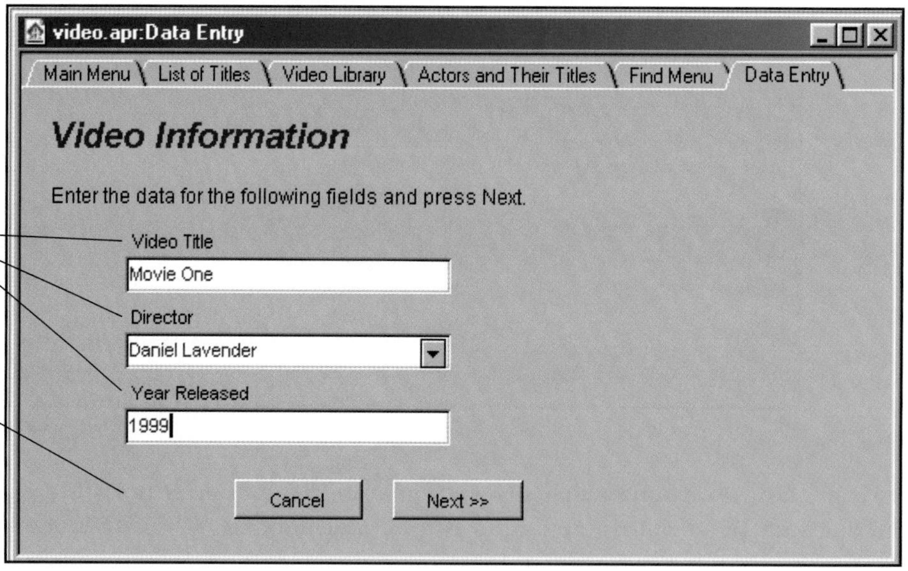

Understandable labels

Form

Viewing Records

The way data appears on screen contributes to how well users can work with it. You have already seen examples of data presented in two-dimensional, worksheet-style tables. With many DBMS products, the table view (sometimes called the datasheet view) is what you use to create a database table and to modify field specifications. This view is also suitable for viewing lists of records that you group together in some meaningful way, such as all customers who live in the same city.

Sometimes viewing the entire table is unwieldy because there are too many entries. **Filters** are a DBMS feature for displaying a selected list or subset of records from a table. The visible records satisfy a condition that the user sets. It is called a filter

Norton Notebook

DATA WAREHOUSES, PART II

In Part I of this discussion (in Lesson 10), you learned that many companies use large storage systems to create data warehouses that can store enormous amounts of data. The hardware portion of the data warehouse may be a mainframe system or a RAID disk array, providing gigabytes or terabytes of storage space.

On the software side are the DBMS and tools that enable users to add and work with data in the database, converting it into useful information. The process of searching and sorting data to find relationships within it is called data mining, and it is possible only with the proper tools and approach to managing large volumes of data.

Many corporate data warehouses are based on large-scale enterprise DBMS software packages. These applications—developed by companies such as IBM, Oracle, Sybase, and Informix—can manage relational databases with hundreds of unique tables and millions of individual records. An enterprise-level DBMS provides programming-style tools that allow database managers or developers to create customized forms and reports and to set up queries to find the tiniest, most unique pieces of data from the system.

Because these systems are network-enabled, they provide data access to users in wide-ranging locations. Users in remote offices can access the centralized data warehouse from their location and work with data in real time using a network connection or the Internet.

You may have accessed a data warehouse without even realizing it. For example, if you have ever logged onto the Federal Express Web site (**www.fedex.com/**) and tracked the location of a package, then you have tapped into the company's database. By using Web-enabled tools to create forms that customers can use in their Web browser, Federal Express (and many other companies) has provided its clients with a simplified "front end" into its database.

Such forms enable you to create a database query, such as *What is the status of the package whose tracking number is 812371566015?* The DBMS can (with the use of internal indexes) sift through the millions of packages stored in the

database and return the one record related to your package, within seconds. The result of the query is the package's current location in the system and its anticipated delivery date and time—or news that the package has already been delivered. These forms accept only certain types of input and therefore enable you to view only the data from a given set of fields for a single record. This limitation provides you the information you need without jeopardizing the security of the database.

An important step in making all the data useful is called data scrubbing. Data scrubbing or data validation is the process of safeguarding against erroneous data or duplicate data. In the case of Federal Express's database, for example, imagine the problems that could result if multiple packages were assigned the same tracking number. A data-scrubbing procedure prevents this mishap from occurring.

Data scrubbing can be handled in many ways. During the data-entry process, for example, the DBMS may refuse to accept data that does not conform to a certain format, that is not spelled in a specific way, or that is duplicated in a different record. Masks may also be applied, for instance, to ensure that all customer IDs, ZIP Codes, and telephone numbers are formatted in the same manner. This safeguard guarantees consistency throughout the database.

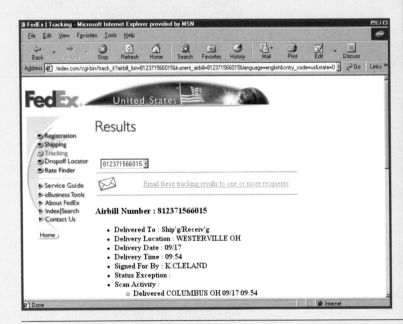

The results of a package-tracking query at the Federal Express Web site.

Figure 16.13

When you view a data table in datasheet view, you can see all records and fields at the same time—or as many as will fit on the screen.

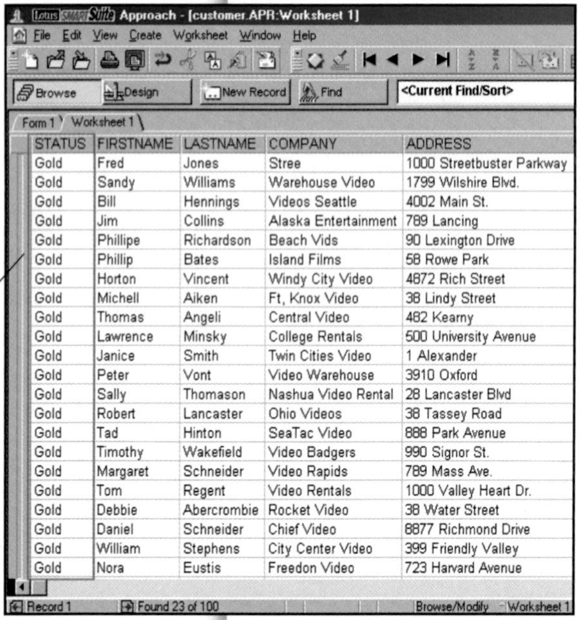

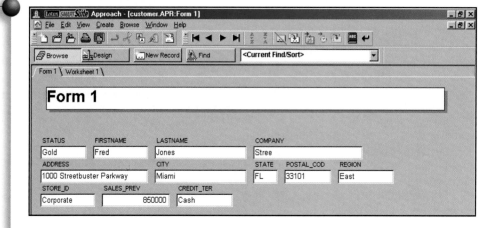

Filtered column

because it tells the DBMS to display those records that satisfy the condition while hiding—or filtering out—those that do not. For example, you can create a filter that displays only those records that have the data "Gold" in the Status field, as shown in Figure 16.13.

As shown in Figure 16.14, a DBMS also allows you to create forms for viewing records. These forms are similar in design to those used in data entry, but they are used to display existing data instead of receiving new data. By using forms, you can create simple, easily understood views of your data that show just one record at a time. You can also create complex forms that display related information from multiple tables.

Sorting Records

One of the most powerful features of a DBMS is the ability to sort a table of data, either for a printed report or for display on the screen. Sorting arranges records according to the contents of one or more fields. For example, in a table of products, you can sort records into

Figure 16.14

This form lets the user work with information for a single record.

numerical order by product ID or into alphabetical order by product name. To obtain the list sorted by product name, you define the condition for the Product Name field that tells the DBMS to rearrange the records in alphabetical order for this data (see Figure 16.15). You can sort the same list on another field, such as Supplier, as shown in Figure 16.16.

When sorting records, one important consideration is determining the sort order. An ascending sort order arranges records in alphabetical order (from A to Z), numerical order (from 0 to 9), or chronological order (from 1/1/1900 to 12/31/1999). For example, if you base an ascending sort on a Last Name field, the records will be arranged in alphabetical order by last name. Conversely, a descending sort order arranges records in the opposite order—that is, from Z to A, or from 9 to 0.

Here the records are sorted according to entries in this field.

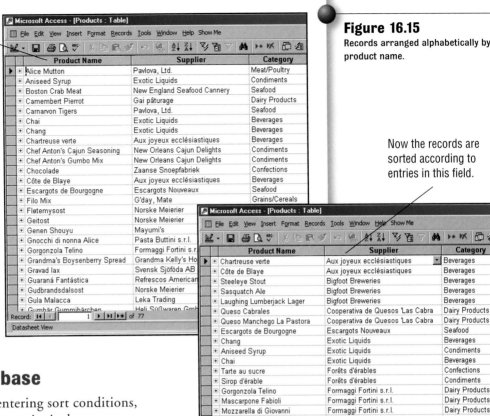

Figure 16.15
Records arranged alphabetically by product name.

Now the records are sorted according to entries in this field.

Figure 16.16
The records have now been arranged alphabetically according to the contents of the Supplier field.

Querying a Database

In a manner similar to entering sort conditions, you can enter expressions or criteria that

◆ Allow the DBMS to locate records.

◆ Establish relationships or links between tables to update records.

◆ List a subset of records.

◆ Perform calculations.

◆ Delete obsolete records.

◆ Perform other data management tasks.

Any of these types of requests is called a **query,** a user-constructed statement that describes data and sets criteria so that the DBMS can gather the relevant data and construct specific information. In other words, a query is a more powerful type of filter that can gather information from multiple tables in a relational database.

For example, a sales manager might create a query to list orders by quarter. The query can include field names such as CUSTOMER and CITY from a Customers table, and ORDER DATE from an Orders table. To obtain the desired information, the query requires the specific data or criteria that will isolate those records (orders received during a given period) from all the records in both tables. In this case, the sales manager includes a range of dates during which the orders would ship.

Some database systems provide special windows or forms for creating queries. Generally, such a window or form provides an area for selecting the tables the query will work with and columns for entering the field names where the query will obtain or manipulate data.

Because nearly all databases are designed and built using accepted terms and structures, it should be possible to generate a single language that can, in theory, query any database. If such a language were developed, a user who knew the language

Figure 16.17

This SQL query opens the Employees table and extracts a list of all employees whose hire date is after 01/01/1993.

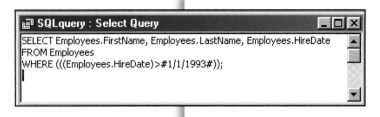

```
SQLquery : Select Query                                    _ □ X

SELECT Employees.FirstName, Employees.LastName, Employees.HireDate
FROM Employees
WHERE (((Employees.HireDate)>#1/1/1993#));
```

could query any database, regardless of who created the database or what software was used in the creation. Mainframe database developers created the Structured English QUEry Language (SEQUEL) in the mid 1970s to solve this dilemma. SEQUEL, and its later variant **SQL,** are English-like query languages that allow the user to query a database without knowing much about the underlying database structure (see Figure 16.17).

Because SQL is such a powerful tool, some PC-based database management systems now enable users to perform SQL queries. Because each DBMS application has its own special features, however, developers have a tendency to create "dialects" of SQL that do not quite meet the standard for a universal database querying language. Sometimes the developers add commands; other times they limit the commands or some of the command options. Nevertheless, SQL is useful and you may see it from time to time, especially if you are using a relational DBMS such as Oracle or DB2, or a more recent PC-based DBMS such as Microsoft Access.

```
Use Employees
List FirstName, LastName for HireDate >"01/01/93"
```

Figure 16.18

An Xbase query to generate a list of employees hired after 01/01/1993.

NORTON ONLINE

Visit **www.glencoe.com/norton/online/** for more information on **database query languages.**

In addition to SQL, PC-based databases sometimes use a query/programming language called **Xbase** (see Figure 16.18). Xbase is a generic query language derived from the query/programming language used in the Dbase family of database products developed by Ashton Tate. Like SQL, Xbase is somewhat English-like, but it is more complicated because its commands cover the full range of database activities, not just queries. As with SQL, software developers have a tendency to create dialects of Xbase to suit their software's needs, so each version of Xbase may be a little different from its peers.

For those users who prefer a graphic interface when querying a database, some programs provide an interface, like a form or a grid, that collects the facts about a query from the user and composes the SQL or query statements behind the scenes. This feature allows a user to **query by example (QBE)** or to perform "intuitive" queries. With QBE, you specify the search criteria by typing values or expressions into the fields of a QBE form or grid (see Figure 16.19).

Figure 16.19

A QBE query to generate a list of employees hired after 01/01/1993.

Field:	LastName	FirstName	HireDate
Table:	Employees	Employees	Employees
Sort:			
Show:	☑	☑	☑
Criteria:			>#1/1/93#
or:			

```
Hire Dates Post 1-1-93 : Sele...   _ □ X
     Last Name   First Name   Hire Date
►    Peacock     Margaret     03-May-93
     Buchanan    Steven       17-Oct-93
     Suyama      Michael      17-Oct-93
     King        Robert       02-Jan-94
     Callahan    Laura        05-Mar-94
     Dodsworth   Anne         15-Nov-94
*
Record: I◄  ◄         1  ►  ►I ►* of 6
```

Figure 16.20

The results of the SQL, Xbase, or QBE query showing a list of employees hired after 01/01/1993.

Whether a DBMS uses SQL, Xbase, or QBE, or offers all three, the results of a query are always the same (see Figure 16.20).

Generating Reports

Not all DBMS operations have to occur on screen. Just as forms can be based on queries, so can reports. A **report** is printed information that, like a query result, is assembled by gathering data based on user-supplied criteria. In fact, report generators in most DBMSs create reports from queries.

Reports can range from simple lists of records to customized formats for specific purposes, such as invoices. Report generators can use selected data and criteria to carry out automated mathematical calculations as the report is printed. For example, relevant data can be used to calculate subtotals and totals for invoices or sales summaries. Reports are also similar to forms because their layout can be customized with objects representing fields and other controls, as shown in Figure 16.21.

Listing of Customer Dive Shops Worldwide

Marine Adventures and Sunken Treasures

Bahamas

Customer No.	Name	Street	City	State/Prov.	ZIP/Postal Code
1,231.00	Unisco	PO Box Z-547	Freeport		
2,163.00	SCUBA Heaven	PO Box Q-8874	Nassau		
2,165.00	Shangri-La Sports Center	PO Box D-5495	Freeport		
5,384.00	Tora Tora Tora	PO Box H-4573	Nassau		

Belize

Customer No.	Name	Street	City	State/Prov.	ZIP/Postal Code
1,984.00	Adventure Undersea	PO Box 744	Belize City		

Bermuda

Customer No.	Name	Street	City	State/Prov.	ZIP/Postal Code
6,215.00	Underwater SCUBA Comp	PO Box Sn94	Somerset		SXBN
6,582.00	Norwest'er SCUBA Ltd.	PO Box 6834	Paget		PSBZ

British West Indies

Customer No.	Name	Street	City	State/Prov.	ZIP/Postal Code
1,354.00	Cayman Divers World Unl.	PO Box 541		Grand Cayman	
3,151.00	Fisherman's Eye	PO Box 7542		Grand Cayman	
5,163.00	Safari Under the Sea	PO Box 7456		Grand Cayman	

Canada

Customer No.	Name	Street	City	State/Prov.	ZIP/Postal Code
1,551.00	Marmot Divers Club	827 Queen St.	Kitchener	Ontario	G3N 2E1
2,156.00	Davy Jones' Locker	246 S. 16th Place	Vancouver	British Columbia	K8V 9P1
4,531.00	On-Target SCUBA	7-73763 Nakanawa	Winnipeg	Manitoba	J2R 5T3

Figure 16.21
This polished-looking summary is a relatively simple database report.

Self Check

Answer the following questions by filling in the blank(s).

1. A(n) _____ is a repository for collections of related data or facts.

2. A database file that contains a single data table is called a(n) _____ .

3. In a table, a(n) _____ field accepts alphanumeric entries that are not used in calculations.

ENTERPRISE SOFTWARE

Technically, an enterprise can be any organization. In practice, however, the term **enterprise** refers to organizations with large hardware and software applications used by hundreds or thousands of people. Sometimes these applications look very much like the DBMS that drives them, as in inventory management programs; other times the underlying database is mostly hidden, as in order entry or facilities management systems. These large-scale applications are often categorized as **enterprise software.**

Because enterprise systems are usually large-scale, it is tempting to think of them as mainframe tools and not a major concern for PC users. Today's PCs are as powerful as mainframes were a few years ago, and many large-scale DBMS applications—such as Oracle, Informix, Microsoft SQL Server, and Sybase—are now available for stand-alone PCs or PC-based networks. So it is possible that, in a business or educational environment, you might run into enterprise software, particularly if a network is used. Even if a PC does not have a huge application running on it, the system may have a software interface that allows the PC to work with a large application on another PC, network server, or mainframe (see Figure 16.22 on page 286).

NORTON
ONLINE

Visit **www.glencoe.com/norton/online/** for more information on **commercial database reporting tools** and **enterprise-level database products.**

Meeting the Needs of Many Users

Enterprise applications often meet the needs of many users at the same time, sometimes over a wide area. It is possible for two users with identical software to access the same data source and perform the same tasks, even if they are on opposite sides of town—or opposite sides of the world. It is also possible for the users to have slightly different software interfaces for performing different tasks, but all joined to one central data source, as shown in Figure 16.23.

For example, companies use one type of enterprise software, called an electronic document management (EDM) system, to track documents, keep related ideas together, and aid in facilities management. Using such an application, a maintenance worker can display line drawings of a factory floor to see what changes are necessary for an impending project. The same software also allows a secretary to record text notes from a project meeting and link them to the line drawings of the factory floor. Engineers using the software can add redline corrections to the factory floor drawings, and project supervisors can display the meeting notes. As work on the project progresses, an engineer may use the software to add a bill of materials while a company purchaser tracks inventory as it is consumed.

Figure 16.23
Enterprise software allows different users to share the same data, even on opposite sides of the world.

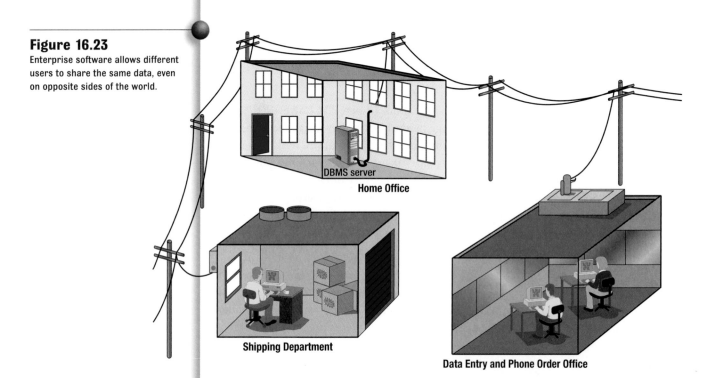

The idea of one application meeting the needs of many diverse users applies even if the work is different from one user to the next. Consider an EDM system that is used to manage patient records in a hospital. A receptionist may use the software to record appointments and patient insurance claims, while a doctor may use the same patient records to find X rays and medical histories. In another part of the hospital, an administrator can monitor the number of beds in use and determine staffing needs accordingly. In other words, enterprise software can be big and each interface may look a little different depending on the needs of the particular user, but it is all tied together (see Figure 16.24).

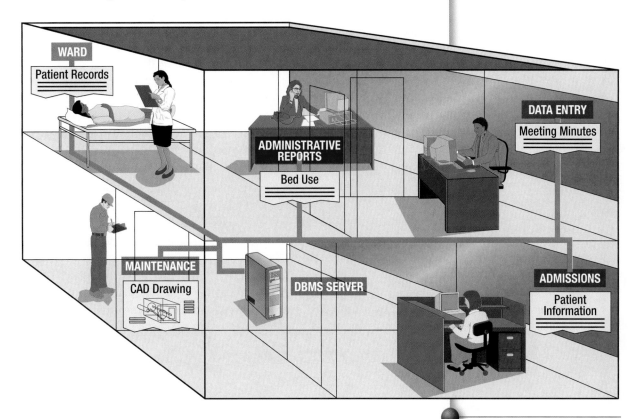

Figure 16.24
Different users with different needs have a unique interface for accessing the underlying database.

The Database Behind the Scenes

Regardless of the tasks performed by a particular piece of enterprise software, there is a good chance that a database is at the heart of the application. Consider again the EDM facilities management application. The factory drawings used by the maintenance worker are all indexed in a database and are retrieved based on a simple query. The secretary adding meeting notes may be typing in a text editor, but a database is used to link that text with a particular project. Likewise, the engineer's bill of materials is drawn out of a list of parts used in a project, and the bill of materials itself represents another list to be stored. Even the purchaser who tracks and orders supplies uses the database to find out what materials have been used and what is needed.

The fact that a database lurks at the heart of most enterprise software does not mean the software looks or acts like a database—at least, not from the end user's perspective. In fact, most of the development tools used to create interfaces for these large-scale applications help the developer create non-technical interfaces that hide the underlying database. Often these screens attempt to duplicate existing paper forms that the user once filled out by hand.

COMPUTERS
in your career

Database-Related Jobs

Database technologies touch the work lives of millions of people each day. You do not have to be a database expert, however, to work with a database management system or enterprise software application. As described in this unit, many people work with databases every day without even realizing it.

◆ **Secretaries, Clerks, Data-Entry Specialists, and Telemarketers.** Most computer users do not work with a true DBMS on a daily basis. Instead, most work with a front-end program, such as a contact management, order-entry, or accounts payable/receivable system, that acts as an intermediary between the user and the actual database.

◆ **Help Desk and Product Support Specialists.** Persons who work at call centers or help desks interact with large databases of product and customer information and continuously add and edit information about customer complaints, problems, and suggestions. By drawing from the information stored in a help desk's database, product designers can find unpopular features in their products and fix those problems in new versions.

◆ **Software Engineers.** Some commercially developed software uses a DBMS to store the data relevant to that software. Software engineers design, develop, and test these applications. Other software engineers design, develop, and test the DBMS application itself. Software engineering is one of the fastest growing careers in the computer industry.

◆ **Database Programmers and Developers.** The demand for experienced database professionals is high, especially for high-end users who can develop forms and set up complex relational databases. Database developers create custom tools for corporate databases, create special front ends and order-entry tools, generate complicated queries, develop report-generation macros, and more. These developers are skilled in programming languages such as COBOL, Visual Basic, Java, and C, as well as database query languages such as SQL. They are familiar with powerful databases such as Sybase, DB2, Oracle, and others.

◆ **Database Administrators.** Database administrators typically lay out, design, and construct corporate databases using the DBMS software. After the corporate databases are constructed, database administrators are called upon to develop backup, load, and unload strategies. They are often involved with altering the database based on system enhancements and upgrades to the DBMS software.

◆ **System Analysts.** Many organizations hire system analysts to review and update the operation of their enterprise applications. The analyst must be well-versed in database concepts and terminology and must understand how the organization uses its DBMS and data tables to store, retrieve, and manage data. Analysts frequently assist managers in designing queries and reports that draw data from the database or in creating forms that make data input easier or more efficient.

LESSON QUIZ

True/False

Answer the following questions by circling True or False.

True   False   **1.** A database is a software tool that allows users to store, access, and process data or facts into useful information.

True   False   **2.** A record is a full set of fields about one person or object.

True   False   **3.** Once the structure of a database is established, you can place any type of information you want into any field.

True   False   **4.** A flat-file database uses only one data table.

True   False   **5.** To create a new database, you must first define its fields.

Multiple Choice

Circle the word or phrase that best completes each sentence.

1. A _____ is an example of a database.
   A. telephone book   **B.** video library   **C.** both A and B

2. A _____ is a complete collection of records.
   A. table   **B.** field   **C.** DBMS

3. A _____ database is made up of a set of tables where a common field in any two tables creates a relationship between the tables.
   A. flat-file   **B.** network   **C.** relational

4. A(n) _____ stores a unique numeric value that is assigned to each record.
   A. counter field   **B.** table   **C.** object

5. A _____ tells the DBMS to display records that satisfy a condition while hiding those that do not.
   A. form   **B.** filter   **C.** report

LESSON LABS

Complete the following exercises as directed by your instructor.

1. Determine whether a database management program is installed on your computer. If you have an application suite (such as Microsoft Office, Corel WordPerfect Office, or Lotus SmartSuite) installed, a database application may be installed as part of the suite. Otherwise, a stand-alone DBMS package may be installed. Locate your DBMS and launch it. What steps must you take to start the program?

2. Create a sample database by using a database application, a spreadsheet program, or your word processor's table feature.

   A. Launch the program.

   B. Set up the following field names: Last Name, First Name, Street Address, City, State, ZIP Code, and Phone Number. If you are using a database program, you may need to specify whether these fields should be text, numeric, or other types of fields.

   C. Enter data in each field for six people. When you are finished, save the new file to disk. Name it *My First Database*. Then close the program.

LESSON 15: Presentation Programs

Presentation Program Basics

- Presentation programs enable you to create a series of slides that can be used to support a discussion.

- A presentation can be saved as a single file containing one slide or many slides that are used together.

- Slides can include different types of text, charts, tables, and graphics.

- Most presentation programs provide templates, which are pre-designed slides.

- Slides can be formatted with different fonts, colors, backgrounds, and borders. Using frames, you can resize many of the elements in a slide.

- Presentation programs provide several special features that enable you to add annotations to your slide show, create animations within slides, convert a slide to an HTML document, and more.

Integrating Multiple Data Sources in a Presentation

- You can add different media types, such as audio or video files, to your slides.

- If you present your slide show directly from your PC's disk (and if the system is connected to a suitable video and audio output device), you can present its multimedia elements.

Presenting Slide Shows

- You can print your slides and present them using a slide projector or overhead projector.

- An efficient way to present a slide show is to display the slides directly from the PC's disk. This technique enables you to present slides out of order or even mark slides as they appear on the screen.

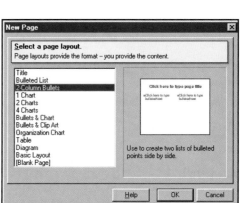

- Depending on the size of your audience and room, you can display slides on the PC's monitor, project them onto a screen, or connect the PC to a television or larger display.

- You can move from one slide to the next manually, or you can automate the presentation so that each slide appears on screen for a set amount of time before being replaced by the next slide.

LESSON 16: Database Management Systems and Enterprise Software

Databases and Database Management Systems

- A database is a repository for collections of related data or facts.

- A database management system (DBMS) is a software tool that enables many users to add, view, and work with the data in a database.

- Flat-file databases are two-dimensional tables of fields and records. They cannot form relationships with other tables.

- Relational databases are powerful because they can form relationships among different tables.

Working With a Database

- To create a database, you must first set up its tables and define the types of fields each table will contain.

- A DBMS provides tools that can validate data as it is entered and thus ensure the data is in the correct format.

- Forms are custom screens for displaying and entering data that can be associated with database tables and queries.

- Filters let you browse through selected records that meet a set of criteria.

- Sorting arranges records in a table according to specific criteria.

- Queries are user-constructed statements that set conditions for selecting and manipulating data.

- Reports are user-generated sets of data usually printed as a document.

Enterprise Software

- Enterprise software is any large-scale application based on a DBMS. This type of software is called enterprise software because it is suited to the needs of large organizations with extensive hardware and software.

- Enterprise software can be tailored to meet the needs of many different users in different locations.

- In an enterprise setting, different users may be provided with different interfaces to the core database, enabling each person to view and work with only the type of information that meets that person's specific needs.

UNIT REVIEW

KEY TERMS

After completing this unit, you should be able to define the following terms.

annotation, *264*
binary field, *279*
binary large object (BLOB), *279*
counter field, *279*
database, *272*
database management system (DBMS), *272*
date field, *278*
enterprise, *285*
enterprise software, *285*
field, *273*
field format, *280*
filter, *280*
flat-file database, *275*
form, *280*
frame, *261*
gradient fill, *263*
handle, *263*
hierarchical database, *276*
logical field, *279*
many-to-many relationship, *276*
mask, *280*

memo field, *279*
network database, *276*
numeric field, *278*
object-oriented database (OODB), *276*
one-to-many relationship, *276*
parent-child relationship, *276*
PC-to-TV converter, *268*
picture, *280*
presentation program, *260*
query, *283*
query by example (QBE), *284*
record, *274*
relational database, *275*
report, *285*
slide, *259*
SQL, *284*
text box, *261*
text field, *278*
time field, *278*
transition, *264*
Xbase, *284*

KEY TERMS QUIZ

Fill in each blank with one of the terms listed under Key Terms.

1. A(n) _____ enables you to create colorful slides.

2. A(n) _____ is designed to hold text content in a slide.

3. You can prepare a set of notes, called _____ , to accompany your slides.

4. Using a(n) _____ , you can connect your computer to a television.

5. In a database table, each row represents a(n) _____ .

6. In a(n) _____ , tables are organized in a fixed, treelike structure.

7. In a(n) _____ relationship, any table can relate to any number of other tables.

8. A(n) _____ groups data items into objects.

9. _____ store a unique numeric value that the DBMS assigns for every record.

10. A(n) _____ displays a selected list or subset of records from a table.

REVIEW QUESTIONS

In your own words, briefly answer the following questions.

1. How do you add text in a text box when creating a slide?
2. What effect can you use to make a slide appear as if it were in motion?
3. What can you do with a slide if you save it in HTML format?
4. Your audience can view slides in one of four ways. List them.
5. What is the difference between a database and a database management system?
6. In a database table, what does each column represent?
7. In an object-oriented database, what can an object represent?
8. You can use the tools of a DBMS to perform six important data management functions. List them.
9. What is a form?
10. What does the abbreviation QBE stand for?

DISCUSSION QUESTIONS

As directed by your instructor, discuss the following questions in class or in groups.

1. Suppose that you were asked to give a presentation on a subject you understand well. To support your presentation, you must prepare a twenty-minute slide show using presentation software. Describe the slide presentation you would create. How many slides would you use? How would you organize them? What types of content would you use in each? What features of the presentation program would you use to enhance the presentation?

2. Describe a scenario in which a large organization might use a database management system. What types of tables would the organization's database contain? What kinds of relationships would exist among the tables? What types of forms would be needed, and by what users? What types of queries and reports would managers want to run on this database?

 ETHICAL ISSUES

Businesses and governments now maintain huge databases filled with information about individuals. With this thought in mind, discuss the following questions in class.

1. You submit information about yourself whenever you apply for a credit card, subscribe to a magazine, or register a product that you have purchased. Should businesses and government agencies be allowed to keep this data permanently? How much information should they be allowed to collect about individuals? Do you feel the practice of maintaining personal data is wrong or should be illegal? Why or why not?

2. Credit agencies and banks commonly sell information about their customers, which is then used to create direct-marketing lists. Some people feel that banks and credit agencies thus profit by selling individuals' private information, leading to an erosion of personal privacy. Do you share this view? Why or why not?

UNIT LABS

You and the Computer

Complete the following exercises using a computer in your classroom, lab, or home. No other materials are needed.

1. **Create a Presentation.** This exercise assumes that you have a presentation program installed on your computer. If you do, launch the program (with your instructor's help, if necessary) and create a single slide. Use a template to design the slide, and choose a slide format that provides a title and a text box. Make the slide about yourself, as if you were going to use it to introduce yourself to a group of people during a presentation.

2. **Design a Database.** You can create an outline for a database by using a word processor. Imagine that you own a small business that sells gourmet coffees. You want to create a database system to store information about products, vendors, customers, employees, accounts paid and received, and so on. Open your word processor and, in a blank document, list the tables you would include in your database. Under the name of each table, create a list of the fields the table should contain. Use your word processor's drawing tools to show the relationships between the tables. When you are finished, print the document and save the file under the name "Design." Close the word processor.

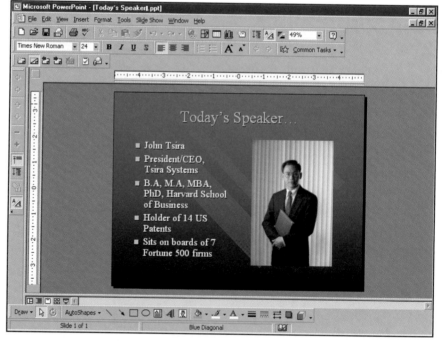

Internet Labs

To complete the following exercises, you need a computer with an Internet connection and a Web browser. (For more information on using these tools, see "Prerequisites" at the front of this textbook.)

1. **Which Presentation Program Is Right for You?** Visit the following Web sites and gather information about the presentation programs offered by these vendors:

   - Microsoft PowerPoint—
   http://www.microsoft.com/office/powerpoint/

   - Corel Presentations—
   http://www.corel.com/Office2000/standard.htm#presentations

   - Lotus Freelance Graphics—
   http://www.lotus.com/home.nsf/welcome/freelance/

   - Harvard Graphics—**http://www.harvardgraphics.com/**

If you want to look for more products or options, visit a Web search engine (such as Yahoo! at **http://www.yahoo.com/**, Alta Vista at **http://www.altavista.com/**, or The Big Hub at **http://www .thebighub.com/**) and search on the terms *presentation program* and *slide*. When you are done, launch Notepad and write a one-page paper summarizing your findings and explaining which presentation program you would purchase. Give your reasons for choosing that program. Print the paper and give a copy to your instructor.

2. **Discover Enterprise Databases.**
Several PC-based database management products are available, but if you work for a large corporation, chances are you will use an enterprise application based on a large-scale DBMS. Visit the following Web sites for information about some of these enterprise-level database programs:

- IBM DB2—**http://www .software.ibm.com/data/db2/**

- Oracle—**http://www.oracle.com/**

- Microsoft SQL Server—**http://www.microsoft.com/**

- Sybase—**http://www.sybase.com/**

- Informix—**http://www.informix.com/**

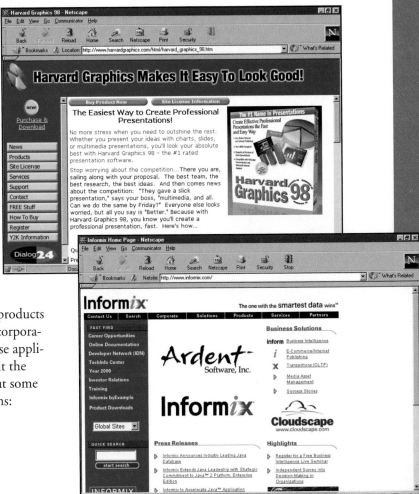

IBE Labs

If you have the Interactive Browser Edition (IBE) CD-ROM for this textbook, you may complete the following interactive exercises using the instructions provided in the IBE.

1. **Presentation Programs or Databases?** Determine which type of software should be used for specified needs.

2. **Labeling.** Create a chart that shows how to build a slide presentation.

3. **Scavenger Hunt.** Answer questions to find a clue toward solving the puzzle.

4. **Database Queries.** Test your knowledge of how a database processes queries.

UNIT 9

Networks and Data Communications

UNIT OBJECTIVES

Describe the benefits of using a network.

Identify the media and topologies commonly used in networks.

Name the primary methods used in data communications.

Describe four types of digital telephone services.

Name one way to set up a home network.

UNIT CONTENTS

This unit contains the following lessons:

Networking Basics

OVERVIEW:
Sharing Data Anywhere, Anytime

When PCs first appeared in businesses—and software programs were designed for a single user—there were few obvious advantages to connecting PCs, and the technology was not adequate for doing so. As computers spread throughout business, and as developers began offering complex software designed for multiple users, many organizations quickly learned the importance of connecting PCs. **Data communications,** the electronic transfer of information between computers, became a major focus of the computer industry. The rapid growth of the Internet also spurred the spread of data communications. Networking technology has thus become the most explosive area of growth in the entire computer industry. The demand for larger, faster, higher-capacity networks has increased as businesses have realized the value of networking their computer systems.

Networks come in many varieties. When most people think of a network, they imagine several computers in a single location sharing documents and devices such as printers. Networks can include all the computers and devices in a department, a building, or multiple buildings spread over a wide geographic area. By interconnecting many individual networks into a massive single network (like the Internet), people around the world can share information as though they were across the hall from one another. The information they share can be much more than text documents. Many networks carry voice, audio, and video traffic, enabling videoconferencing and types of collaboration that were not possible just a few years ago.

OBJECTIVES

- List the four benefits of using a network.
- Differentiate between LANs and WANs.
- Identify three common network topologies.
- Name four common network media.
- List four examples of network operating system software.

THE USES OF A NETWORK

The word *network* has several definitions. The most commonly used meaning describes the methods people use to maintain relationships with friends and business contacts. Applied to computers, the term has a similar definition. A **network** is a way to connect computers so that they can communicate, exchange information, and share resources in real time. Networks enable multiple users to access shared data and programs instantly. This capability frees individual users from keeping separate copies of data and programs on their own computers.

In business, networks have revolutionized the use of computer technology. Today, fewer organizations use a centralized system (such as a mainframe and terminals) to enable data communication. While a mainframe system and its terminals do constitute a network, such systems do not allow the flexibility of PC-based networks, which are increasingly common in organizations of all sizes. In these settings, almost every employee has a personal computer connected to the network, as shown in Figure 17.1. In education, schools have also shifted to strategies built around networked personal computers.

Whatever the setting, networks provide tremendous benefits. Four of the most important benefits are listed below:

◆ Simultaneous access to critical programs and data

◆ Sharing of peripheral devices, such as printers and scanners

◆ Streamlined personal communications

◆ Easier backup process

The following sections examine each of these advantages in more detail.

Simultaneous Access

It is a fact of business computing that multiple employees often need access to the same data at the same time. A good example is a quarterly sales report, which needs to be viewed and updated by several managers in an organization. Without a network that enables file sharing, workers typically keep separate copies of data on different disks, and universally updating the data becomes difficult. As soon as a change is made to the data on one machine, a discrepancy arises and it can be hard to tell which set of data is correct.

Businesses can solve this problem by determining which data is used by more than one person, then storing that data on a **network server** (or just **server**)—a central computer that provides a storage device and other system resources that all users can share. If the server stores data files for users to access, it is commonly called a **file server.** The business can store a single master copy of a data file on the server, which employees can access whenever they want (see Figure 17.2).

To protect the integrity of the data, managers can determine which users can update the data by granting two basic types of access to it:

◆ **Read-Only.** Some users are entitled only to read data stored on a shared device. This type of access is

NORTON
ONLINE

Visit **www.glencoe.com/norton/online/** for more information on **networks**.

Figure 17.1
Most offices have a PC on nearly every desk. The computers are connected to form a network.

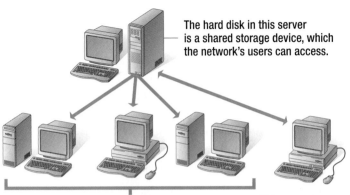

The hard disk in this server is a shared storage device, which the network's users can access.

Figure 17.2
Users can share data stored on a central file server.

To protect the shared data, these users can access the files but cannot make changes to them. This type of access privilege is called "read-only" access.

This user can open the files, make changes to them, and save the changes on the server. All users see the changes that this user makes to the shared data. This type of access privilege is called "read/write" access.

called **read-only access** because the users can read (retrieve) data but cannot write changes to the master data files. This type of protection prevents unwanted changes from being made to the data.

◆ **Read/Write.** Some users may be allowed to open shared files from the network server and to make changes to those files. Because these users can save changes to the shared files, they have **read/write access**. When such users make changes to the files, the updated data can be viewed by all users. To enable users to read and write files, network managers can assign different types of access rights to each user. There are various levels of access rights, each one granting a unique set of privileges to users. If a user has write access to certain files, he or she can open, change, and save those files but may not be able to delete or move the files. With supervisor rights, however, the user can perform any task on the files, including copying, moving, and deleting. Network managers can assign specific access rights to each user on the network on a per-drive, per-folder, or per-file basis.

In addition to using many of the same data files, most office workers also use the same programs. In an environment where PCs are not networked, a separate copy of each program must be installed on every computer. This setup can be an expensive proposition, from two points of view. First, the cost of purchasing software can be high. Second, multi-user installation and configuration can be time- and labor-intensive—and maintaining many separate installations of a program is an ongoing expense. There are two basic solutions to this problem:

◆ **Site Licenses.** One solution to this problem is to purchase a **site license** for an application. Under a site license, a business purchases a single copy (or a few copies) of an application, then pays the developer for a license to copy the application onto a specified number of computers. Under a site license, each user has a complete, individual copy of the program running on his or her PC, but the business generally pays less money than it would by purchasing a complete copy of the software for each user.

◆ **Network Versions.** Another solution is to connect users' computers to a central network server, and enable users to share a **network version** of a program. In a network version, only one copy of the application is stored on the server, with a minimum number of supporting files copied to each employee's computer. When employees need to use a program, they simply

load it from the server into the RAM of their own desktop computers, as shown in Figure 17.3. In some networks, and with certain types of programs, the user's computer handles all the processing tasks required by the application, even though the application's core files are stored on the network. In other cases, the network server also handles some or all of the processing tasks. In these cases, the network server may be called an **application server** because it handles some application processing as well as storage.

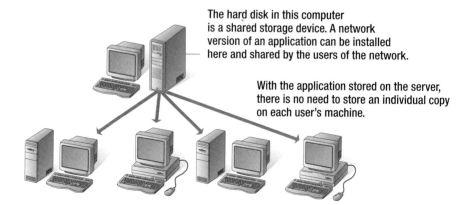

The hard disk in this computer is a shared storage device. A network version of an application can be installed here and shared by the users of the network.

With the application stored on the server, there is no need to store an individual copy on each user's machine.

Figure 17.3
Using a network version of an application.

Note, however, that these strategies are not always less expensive than purchasing individual copies of software for each user. Depending on the type of software being used and the number of people using it, licensing can cost about the same, whether the application is installed on each user's computer or run through the network. In some large, busy installations, the cost of the network itself—particularly of providing adequate bandwidth for many users—can exceed the costs of purchasing many copies of the software. In such cases, the network's real advantage is that it allows the applications to be managed centrally (at the server) instead of on many individual computers.

Figure 17.4
Groupware products give users access to shared documents, e-mail, scheduling tools, and other resources.

Some software designed for networks is classified as **groupware** (see Figure 17.4). This type of software includes scheduling software, e-mail, and document-management software. Groupware allows multiple users on a network to cooperate on projects. Users can work on the same documents, share their insights, and keep each other abreast of their schedules so that meetings can be set up easily. Lotus Notes, Microsoft Exchange, and Novell Groupwise are perhaps the best-known examples of groupware.

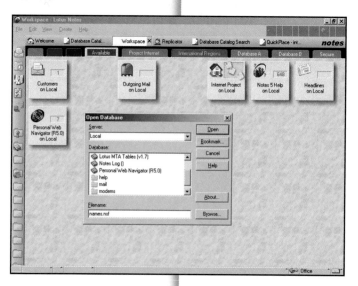

Shared Peripheral Devices

Perhaps the best incentive for small businesses to link computers in a network is to share peripheral devices, especially expensive devices such as high-volume laser printers. Although printer costs have fallen considerably over the years, it still is not cost-effective for each user in an organization to have his or her own printer. Aside from the duplicated cost of purchasing multiple printers, maintenance contracts and other factors (such as the cost of supplies) increase the overall cost of ownership.

Sharing a laser printer on a network makes the cost much less prohibitive and also centralizes management of the printer.

By using a process called **spooling,** multiple users can send print jobs to a printer simultaneously. When users send documents (known as **print jobs**) to a networked printer, each job is stored temporarily on the file server. As the printer finishes printing the current job, the file server sends the next job to the printer so that it can be printed. Typically, a banner page (a special page that identifies the print job's owner) is printed at the beginning of a new job to separate print jobs so they can be identified easily and routed accordingly. An added advantage to spooling is that it allows a user to continue working while the document is printing rather than waiting for the computer to finish sending the print job to the printer.

Personal Communications

One of the most far-reaching applications of data communications is **electronic mail (e-mail),** a system for exchanging written messages (and increasingly, voice and video messages) through a network. E-mail is somewhat of a cross between the postal system and a telephone answering system.

In an e-mail system, each user has a unique identifier, typically referred to as an e-mail address. To send someone an e-mail message, you must use a special e-mail program that works with the network to send and receive messages. You enter the person's e-mail address and then type the message. When you are finished, you click the program's send icon and the message is sent to the e-mail address. When the message's recipient accesses the e-mail system, it reports that mail has arrived. Some systems notify the recipient as each message arrives by flashing a message on the computer screen or by beeping. After reading the message, the recipient can save it, delete it, forward it to someone else, or respond by sending a reply message. Figure 17.5 shows the process for sending and receiving e-mail.

Visit **www.glencoe.com/norton/online/** for more information on **e-mail.**

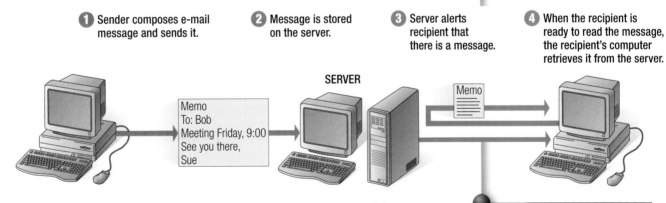

1 Sender composes e-mail message and sends it.

2 Message is stored on the server.

3 Server alerts recipient that there is a message.

4 When the recipient is ready to read the message, the recipient's computer retrieves it from the server.

SERVER

Memo
To: Bob
Meeting Friday, 9:00
See you there,
Sue

Memo

Figure 17.5
Sending and receiving e-mail over a typical network.

In addition to sending text messages, many e-mail systems allow you to attach data files—such as spreadsheet files or word-processed documents—to a message (see Figure 17.6 on page 302). This feature allows people to share files even when they do not have access to the same storage devices. For example, a local area network may also have a connection to a large information network, such as America Online or the Internet. In this case, the person on the local network can share files with anyone on the large information network simply by attaching data files to e-mail messages.

E-mail is both efficient and inexpensive. Users can send written messages without worrying about whether the other user's computer is currently running. On

Figure 17.6

Attaching a document to an e-mail message is a simple way to trade files with other people.

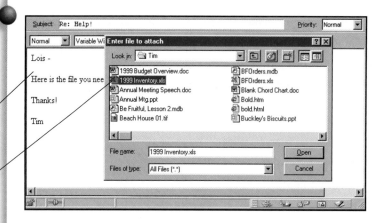

The user creates a message in this window.

In this dialog box, the user selects a file to attach to the message.

NORTON
ONLINE

Visit **www.glencoe.com/norton/online/** for more information on **video-conferencing.**

centralized networks, the message is delivered almost instantaneously, and the cost of sending the message is negligible. E-mail has provided the modern world with an entirely new and immensely valuable form of communication.

In addition to e-mail, the spread of networking technology is adding to the popularity of teleconferencing and videoconferencing. A **teleconference** is a virtual meeting in which a group of people in different locations conduct discussions by typing messages to each other. Each message can be seen by all the other people in the teleconference. Teleconferencing software has become more sophisticated, with features such as a shared scratch pad where diagrams or pictures can be drawn or electronically pasted.

Networking technologies have also boosted the popularity of collaborative software, which allows users to connect with one another over LAN or modem links so that they can see what is happening on other users' computers. It lets people send messages, exchange files, and sometimes even work on the same document at the same time.

If users have the necessary hardware (a PC video camera, microphone, and speakers) and software, they can see and speak to each other as they meet online instead of merely typing messages. This process is known as **videoconferencing** (see Figure 17.7).

In videoconferencing, the audio and video signals are transmitted across the network's (or Internet's) connections between the participants' computers. Special videoconferencing software such as CU-SeeMe enables two users to conduct a point-to-point videoconference, or allows three or more users to conduct a multi-point videoconference.

Figure 17.7

Participating in an online video-conference.

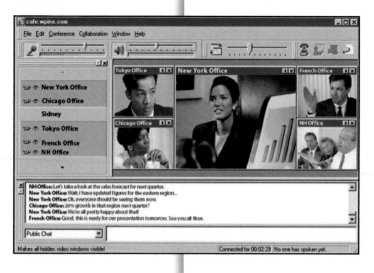

Easier Backup

In business, data is extremely valuable, so making sure that employees back up their data is critical. One way to address this problem is to keep all valuable data on a shared storage device that employees access through a network. Often the person managing the network has the responsibility of making regular backups of the data on the shared storage device from a single, central location (see Figure 17.8). Also available is network backup software that enables backups to be made of files stored on employees' hard drives. With this method, files do not have to be copied to the central server before they can be backed up.

HOW NETWORKS
ARE STRUCTURED

To understand the different types of networks and how they operate, it is important to know something about how networks are structured. There are two main types of networks, distinguished mainly by geography: local area networks (LANs) and wide area networks (WANs). Some networks use servers (server-based networks) and some do not (peer-to-peer networks). These terms are all defined in detail in the following sections.

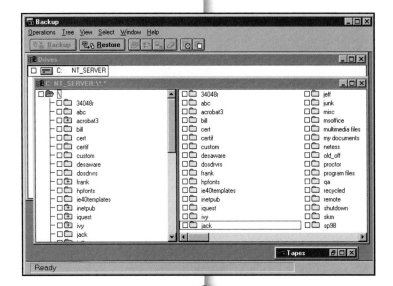

Local Area Networks (LANs)

A **local area network (LAN)** is a network of computers located relatively near each other and connected in a way that enables them to communicate with one another (by a cable, an infrared link, or a small radio transmitter). A LAN can consist of just two or three PCs connected together to share resources, or it can include hundreds of computers of different kinds. Any network that exists within a single building, or even a group of adjacent buildings, is considered a LAN.

It is often helpful to connect different LANs together. For example, two different departments in a large business may each have its own LAN, but if there is a need for data communications between the departments, then it may be necessary to create a link between the two LANs. To understand how this is possible, you need to understand how networks transmit data and how different types of networks can share data.

Figure 17.8
Backup systems like this one can be used to back up a server and individual personal computers on the network.

On a network, data is broken into small groups called packets—before being transmitted from one computer to another. A **packet** is a data segment that includes a header, payload, and control elements that are transmitted together (see Figure 17.9). The receiving computer reconstructs the packet into the original structure.

The payload is the part of the packet that contains the actual data being sent. The header contains information about the type of data in the payload, the source and destination of

Figure 17.9
An e-mail message divided into packets.

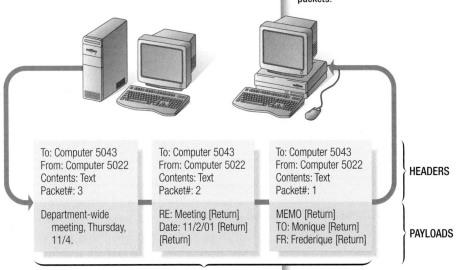

the data, and a sequence number so that data from multiple packets can be reassembled at the receiving computer in the proper order. Each LAN is governed by a **protocol,** which is a set of rules and formats for sending and receiving data, and an individual LAN may utilize more than one protocol. Some of the most common protocols in use today include the following:

◆ **TCP/IP.** Originally associated with UNIX hosts, TCP/IP is the protocol of the Internet and is required on every client machine for direct communication across the Internet to occur. TCP/IP is now the default networking protocol of Windows 2000 and many other operating systems. (You will learn more about TCP/IP in Unit 10, "The Internet and Online Resources.")

◆ **IPX/SPX.** A proprietary protocol of Novell, IPX/SPX has been used in most versions of the NetWare network operating system for networking offices throughout the world.

◆ **NetBEUI.** A relatively simple protocol that has no real configurable parameters, NetBEUI sends messages through broadcasts to every computer that can receive it. It is an excellent protocol for networking small offices or homes, but it does not expand well into larger environments. NetBEUI was the default networking protocol in Windows 3.11, Windows 95, and other Microsoft client operating systems.

◆ **DLC.** Originally a protocol used with large mainframe computer systems, DLC is now used to control communications with network printers. It allows the printers to be configured remotely and to send status messages.

If two LANs are built around the same communication rules, then they can be connected with one of two devices:

◆ **Bridge.** A **bridge** is a device that looks at the information in each packet header and forwards data that is traveling from one LAN to another.

◆ **Router.** A **router** is a more complicated device that stores the routing information for networks. Like a bridge, a router looks at each packet's header to determine where the packet should go and then determines a route for the packet to take and thus reach its destination.

If you need to create a more sophisticated connection between networks, you need a **gateway,** a computer system that connects two networks and translates information from one to the other. Packets from different networks have different kinds of information in their headers, and the information can be in various formats. The gateway can take a packet from one type of network, read the header, and then encapsulate the entire packet into a new one, adding a header that is understood by the second network (see Figure 17.10 on page 306).

Wide Area Networks (WANs)

Typically, a **wide area network (WAN)** is two or more LANs connected together, generally across a wide geographical area. For example, a company may have its corporate headquarters and manufacturing facility in one city and its marketing office in another. Each site needs resources, data, and programs locally, but it also needs to share data with the other site. To accomplish this feat of data communication, the company can attach routers connected over public utilities (such as telephone lines) to create a WAN. Note, however, that a WAN does not have to include any LAN systems. For example, two distant mainframe computers can communicate through a WAN, even though neither is part of a local area network.

Geographical distance aside, the chief distinction between a WAN and a LAN is the cost associated with transmitting data. In a LAN, all components are typically owned by the organization that uses them. For instance, if a company connects its networked PCs with cable, it owns the cabling and therefore pays a fixed cost to transmit data across the network. To transmit data across great distances, however, WAN-based

NORTON
ONLINE

Visit **www.glencoe.com/norton/online/** for more information on **protocols, bridges, routers,** and **gateways.**

Norton Notebook

CERTIFICATION PROGRAMS

With the networking boom that began in the late 1980s, thousands of organizations decided to invest in network systems. System administrators—who were responsible for everything from hardware maintenance to employee training—quickly realized that a high level of special expertise was required to run business networks. As a result, the demand for networking experts exploded.

This new generation of network administrators needed not only an in-depth understanding of computers and general networking technologies, they also needed training in the specific systems used by their new employers. To solve this problem and to provide networking professionals with verifiable credentials, the makers of many networking technologies began offering "certification" programs. Graduates are certified to have a given level of expertise and training in one or more technologies.

If a career in network design or administration appeals to you, then you should consider getting certified in one or more popular networking technologies. The programs can be expensive and a great deal of study is required, but certified professionals will assure you that the rewards are well worth the investment. Here are a few certification programs to consider:

◆ **CompTIA Certifications.** The Computer Technology Industry Association provides four certification programs, ranging from the A+ program for entry-level technicians to the Network+ program for network administrators. These programs can provide a foundation for more specialized training and certifications offered by specific technology vendors. For information, visit **www.comptia.org/** and click the Certification link.

◆ **Novell Certification.** Novell, Inc., was one of the first technology vendors to offer certification training on its networking products, and Novell certifications continue to be valued by experienced network managers. Novell offers a wide variety of certifications, including the basic Certified Novell Administrator (CNA) program, the general Certified Novell Engineer (CNE) program, and the advanced-level Master CNE program, among others. For information, visit **www.cnenet.novell.com/**.

◆ **Microsoft Certification.** You can earn certification on many of Microsoft's professional products, including its applications, database systems, and programming languages as well as networking technologies using Windows NT, BackOffice, and

The Web is an excellent resource for learning more about network training and certification programs.

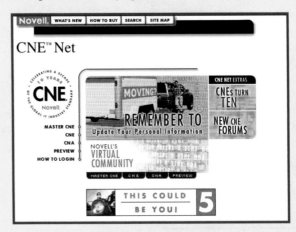

other products. The Microsoft Certified Professional (MCP) program provides training and testing, and graduates are prized for their expertise. For information, visit **www.microsoft.com/mcp/**.

◆ **Cisco Certification.** Cisco Systems, Inc. produces bridges, routers, and many other types of networking hardware and software. Cisco also provides certification training in several areas of networking technologies. The Cisco Certified Internetwork Expert (CCIE) program provides high-level training for current networking professionals. You must have a high level of networking expertise before enrolling in these programs. For information, visit **www.cisco.com/warp/public/10/wwtraining/**.

Before enrolling in any certification program, be sure to check its prerequisites. Many programs require trainees to demonstrate a certain level of understanding or expertise in the targeted technology before being accepted into the program.

Most certification programs require participants to pass one or more exams to earn a certification. In some programs, this requirement includes attending training classes or seminars, while others offer tests to anyone who wants to take them.

Costs vary widely, depending on the courses' offerings. A test-only certification (where you study on your own and then take an exam) may cost a few hundred dollars per exam. Seminar-based courses can take weeks or months to complete and cost hundreds or thousands of dollars.

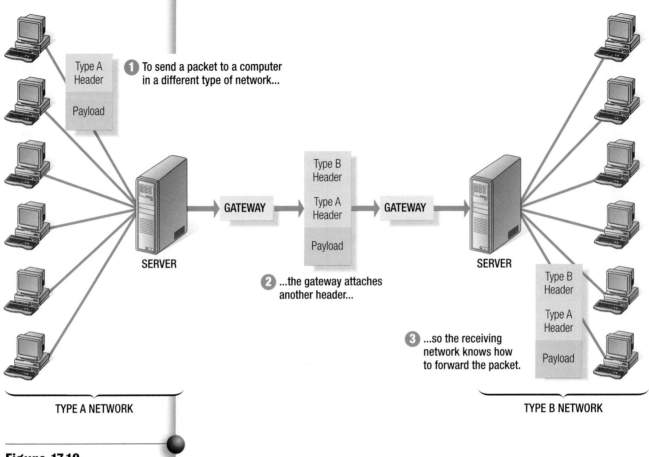

① To send a packet to a computer in a different type of network...

Type A Header

Payload

GATEWAY

Type B Header

Type A Header

Payload

② ...the gateway attaches another header...

GATEWAY

SERVER

③ ...so the receiving network knows how to forward the packet.

Type B Header

Type A Header

Payload

SERVER

TYPE A NETWORK

TYPE B NETWORK

Figure 17.10
How a gateway forwards a packet from one type of network to a different type of network.

organizations typically lease many of the components used for data transmission—such as high-speed telephone lines or wireless technologies such as satellites.

Server-Based Networks

Describing a network as a LAN or a WAN gives you a sense of the physical area the network covers. However, this classification does not tell you anything about how individual computers on a network, called **nodes,** interact with one another.

Many networks include not only nodes but also a central computer with a large hard disk used for shared storage. As you saw earlier, this central computer is known as the file server, network server, application server, or just the server. Files and programs used by more than one user (at different nodes) are often stored on the server.

One relatively simple implementation of a network with nodes and a file server is a **file server network** (see Figure 17.11). This arrangement allows each node to have access to the files on the server but not necessarily to files on other nodes. When a node needs information from the server, it requests the entire file containing the information. In other words, the file server is used simply to store files and to forward (or send) them to nodes that request them.

Figure 17.11
A simple LAN with a file server.

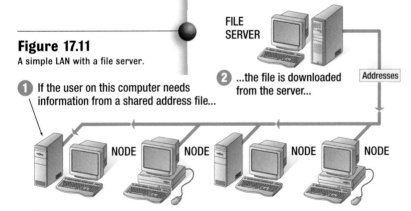

FILE SERVER

② ...the file is downloaded from the server...

Addresses

① If the user on this computer needs information from a shared address file...

NODE NODE NODE NODE

③ ...and this computer searches the file for the desired information.

Client/Server Networks

One popular type of server-based network is **client/server** computing, a hierarchical strategy in which individual computers share the processing and storage workload with a central server. This type of arrangement requires specialized software for both the individual node and the network server. It does not, however, require any specific type of network. Client/server software can be used on LANs or WANs, and a single client/server program can be used on a LAN where all the other software is based on a simple file server relationship.

The most common example of client/server computing involves a database that can be accessed by many different computers on the network. The database is stored on the network server. Also stored on the server is the server portion of the database management system (DBMS), the program that allows users to add information to, or extract it from, the database. The user's computer (which can be called the node, workstation, or client) stores and runs the client portion of the DBMS.

Now, suppose that two users want information from the database. For example, suppose that the database is a list of customer purchases. The first user needs to know the names of customers in the Wichita area who made purchases of more than $500, and the second user wants a total of purchases made during the month of July. Using their client software to describe the information they need, each user sends a request to the server. The server software searches the database, collects the relevant customer names, and sends them back to the first client. It then searches the database for the information requested by the second user, using some of the same entries. For each user, the client software presents the information in a way that makes sense. This process is shown in Figure 17.12.

Client/server software is valuable to large, modern organizations because it distributes processing and storage workloads among resources efficiently: users get the information they need faster. Client/server computing is also a commonly used model on the Internet. Users typically have client software that provides an easily used interface for interacting with this giant WAN. Other types of processing, such as receiving, storing, and sending e-mail messages, are carried out by remote computers running the server part of the relevant software.

NORTON
ONLINE

Visit **www.glencoe.com/norton/online/** for more information on **client/server** technology and **peer-to-peer networks**.

Figure 17.12
Distribution of processing in a client/server computing model.

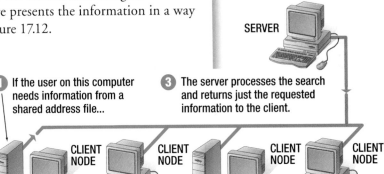

SERVER

1 If the user on this computer needs information from a shared address file...

3 The server processes the search and returns just the requested information to the client.

CLIENT NODE   CLIENT NODE   CLIENT NODE   CLIENT NODE

2 ...the database search is composed on the client computer, where the user interface for the database software is running.

Peer-to-Peer Networks

In a **peer-to-peer network,** (sometimes called a workgroup), all nodes on the network have equal relationships to all others, and all have similar types of software that support the sharing of resources (see Figure 17.13 on page 308). Typically, each node has access to at least some of the resources on all other nodes, so the relationship is nonhierarchical. If they are set up correctly, many multi-user operating systems give users access to files on hard disks and to printers attached to other computers in the network.

In addition, some high-end peer-to-peer networks allow **distributed computing,** which enables users to draw on the processing power of other computers in the network. Users can transfer tasks that take a lot of CPU power—such as creating computer software—to available computers, leaving their own machines free for other work.

Peer-to-peer LANs are commonly set up in small organizations (fewer than twenty-five nodes) or in schools, where the primary benefit of a network is shared storage and printers or enhanced communications. Where large databases or many users are involved, LANs are more likely to be set up in a client/server relationship.

A peer-to-peer network can also include a network server. In this case, a peer-to-peer LAN is similar to a file server network. The only difference between them is that the peer-to-peer network gives users greater access to the other nodes than a file server network does.

Figure 17.13
A peer-to-peer network.

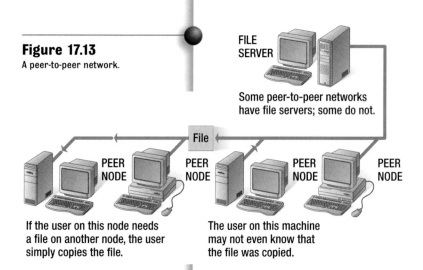

FILE SERVER

Some peer-to-peer networks have file servers; some do not.

File

PEER NODE   PEER NODE   PEER NODE   PEER NODE

If the user on this node needs a file on another node, the user simply copies the file.

The user on this machine may not even know that the file was copied.

Self Check

Answer the following questions by filling in the blank(s).

1. A(n) _____ is a central computer that provides storage and other resources that users can share.

2. _____ is a system for exchanging written messages over a network.

3. A(n) _____ is a small network that does not necessarily use a server.

NETWORK TOPOLOGIES FOR LANS

In addition to the size of a network and the relationship between the nodes and the server (if any), another distinguishing feature among LANs is the **topology**— the physical or logical layout of the cables and devices that connect the nodes of the network. There are three basic topologies: bus, star, and ring. Another, less common type of physical topology is the mesh topology. Network designers consider several factors when determining which topology or combination of topologies to use: the type of computers currently installed, the type of cabling (if any) currently in place, the cost of the components and services required to implement the network, the distance between each computer, and the speed with which data must travel around the network.

Figure 17.14
A LAN with bus topology.

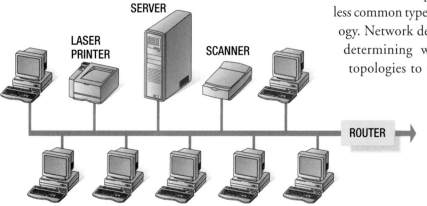

SERVER

LASER PRINTER

SCANNER

ROUTER

The Bus Topology

A **bus network** uses a single conduit to which all the network nodes and peripheral devices are attached (see Figure 17.14). Each node is connected in series to a single cable. At the cable's start and end points, a special device called a terminator is attached. A terminator stops the network signals so they do not bounce back down the cable.

NORTON
ONLINE

Visit **www.glencoe.com/norton/online/** for more information on **topologies**.

The bus topology has inherent disadvantages. Keeping data transmissions from colliding requires some extra circuitry and software. A broken connection can bring down (or "crash") all or part of the network, rendering it inoperable so that users cannot communicate until the connection is repaired. The primary advantage of the bus topology is that it uses the least amount of cabling of any topology.

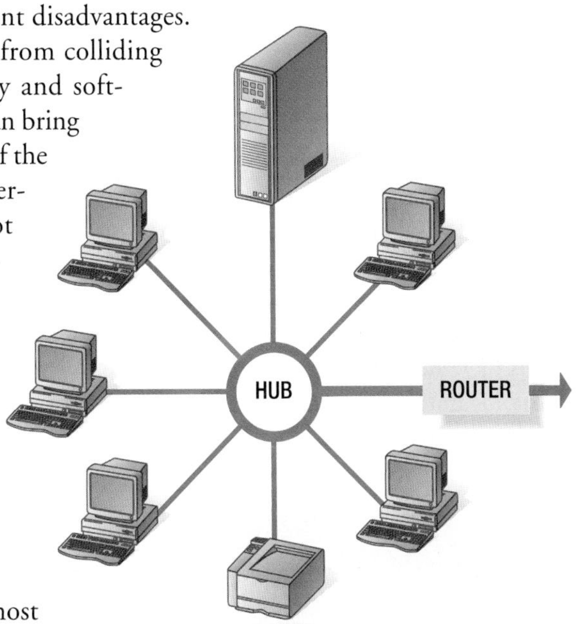

HUB   ROUTER

LASER
PRINTER

Figure 17.15
A LAN with star topology.

The Star Topology

The **star network** is the most common topology in use today. In a star network, a device called a **hub** is placed in the center of the network; that is, all nodes are connected to the central hub and communicate through it. Groups of data are routed through the hub and sent to all the attached nodes, thus eventually reaching their destinations.

Some hubs—known as intelligent hubs—can monitor traffic and help prevent collisions. In a star topology, a broken connection (between a node and the hub) does not affect the rest of the network. If you lose the hub, however, all nodes connected to that hub are unable to communicate. Figure 17.15 shows the star topology.

Figure 17.16
A LAN with ring topology.

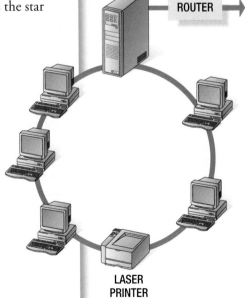

ROUTER

The Ring Topology

The **ring topology** connects the nodes of the network in a circular chain, with each node connected to the next. The final node in the chain connects to the first to complete the ring, as shown in Figure 17.16. With this methodology, each node examines data sent through the ring. If the data—known as a **token**—is not addressed to the node examining it, that node passes it along to the next node in the ring.

The ring topology has a substantial advantage over the bus topology. There is no danger of collisions because only one packet of data may traverse the ring at a time. As with the bus topology, however, if the ring is broken, the entire network is unable to communicate until the ring is restored.

LASER
PRINTER

The Mesh Topology

The **mesh topology** is the least used network topology and the most expensive to implement. In a mesh environment, a cable runs from every computer to every other computer. If you have four computers, you must have six cables—three coming from each computer to the other computers. The big advantage to this arrangement is that data can never fail to be delivered; if one connection goes down, there are other ways to route the data to its destination. Impractical for most workplace environments, the mesh topology is ideal for connecting routers on the Internet to make sure that data always gets through.

NETWORK MEDIA AND HARDWARE

No matter what their structure, all networks rely on media to link their nodes and/or servers together. You may recall that when referring to data storage, the term *media* refers to materials for storing data, such as magnetic disks and tape. In network communications, however, the term refers to the wires, cables, and other means by which data travels from its source to its destination. The most common media for data communication are twisted-pair cable, coaxial cable, fiber-optic cable, and wireless links.

NORTON ONLINE

Visit www.glencoe.com/norton/online/ for more information on **network media**.

Figure 17.17
Shielded (top) and unshielded (bottom) twisted-pair wire are the most common media for computer networks.

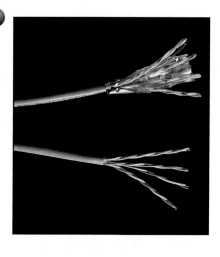

Twisted-Pair Cable

Twisted-pair cable normally consists of two wires individually insulated in plastic, then twisted around each other and bound together in another layer of plastic insulation. Except for the plastic coating, nothing shields this type of wire from outside interference, so it is also called unshielded twisted-pair (UTP) wire. Some twisted-pair wire is also encased in a metal sheath and therefore is called shielded twisted-pair (STP) wire. Figure 17.17 shows what UTP and STP look like.

Indoor wiring for telephones uses twisted-pair wire, so this type of wire is often called telephone wire. Because it was readily available and inexpensive, telephone wire gained early favor as a conduit for data communications. Today, however, most twisted-pair wire used for network communication is made to more demanding specifications than voice-grade telephone wire.

Sometimes network media are compared by the amount of data they can transmit each second. The difference between the highest and lowest frequencies of a transmission channel is known as **bandwidth.** Simply stated, the higher a medium's bandwidth, the more data it can transmit at any given time. As more users transmit data over a network, however, the bandwidth decreases, thereby slowing down all transmissions. Bandwidth is expressed in cycles per second (hertz) or in bits per second. Twisted-pair wire was once considered a low-bandwidth medium, but networks based on twisted-pair wires now support transmission speeds up to 1 gigabit per second (Gbps), and even faster speeds are on the horizon.

Coaxial Cable

Coaxial cable, sometimes called **coax** (pronounced "co-axe"), is similar to the cabling used in cable television systems. There are two conductors in coaxial cable. One is a single wire in the center of the cable, and the other is a wire mesh shield that surrounds the first wire, with an insulator between (see Figure 17.18).

Because it supports transmission speeds up to 10 Mbps, coaxial cable can carry more data than older types of twisted-pair wiring. However, it is also more expensive and became less popular when twisted-pair technology improved. Two types of coaxial cable are used with networks: thick and thin. Thick coax is the older standard and is seldom installed in new networks.

Fiber-Optic Cable

A **fiber-optic cable** is a thin strand of glass that transmits pulsating beams of light rather than electric frequencies (see Figure 17.19). When one end of the strand is exposed to light, the strand carries the light all the way to the other end—bending around corners along the way. Because light travels at a much higher speed than electrical signals, fiber-optic cable can easily carry data at more than a billion bits per second. Because of improvements in transmission hardware, however, fiber-optic cable transmission speeds have drastically improved and now approach 100 Gbps. Fiber-optic cable is also immune to the electromagnetic interference that is a problem for copper wire. Fiber-optic cable also offers extraordinary bandwidth. It is not only extremely fast and can carry an enormous number of messages simultaneously, but fiber-optic cable is a very secure transmission medium.

The disadvantages of fiber-optic cable are its cost relative to twisted-pair and coax, and the difficulty associated with its installation. Special equipment is required to cut the cable and install connectors; as a result, fiber-optic line can be difficult to splice. Also, great care must be taken when bending fiber-optic cable. As costs have come down, however, fiber-optic cable has become increasingly popular, and it is now revolutionizing several communications industries. Telephone and cable television companies have been moving from twisted-pair wire and coaxial cables to fiber-optic cables.

Wireless Links

Today, wireless communication competes with twisted-pair, coaxial, and fiber-optic cable. The advantage of wireless communication is the flexibility that it offers in terms of the network layout. **Wireless communication** relies on radio signals or infrared signals for transmitting data.

There are four common uses of wireless communication in networks:

◆ Office LANs can use radio signals to transmit data between nodes.

◆ Laptops can be equipped with cellular telephone equipment and a modem so that businesspeople can stay in touch with the office network when they travel.

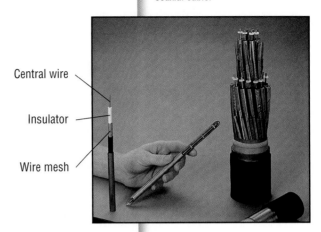

Figure 17.18
Coaxial cable.

Central wire

Insulator

Wire mesh

Figure 17.19
Fiber-optic cable.

Strands of glass

◆ Corporate WANs often use microwave transmission to connect two LANs within the same metropolitan area. If a company has buildings on opposite sides of town, it can set up a microwave antenna on top of each to transmit data back and forth quickly (see Figure 17.20). This type of communication, however, requires an unobstructed line of sight between the two antennas.

◆ WANs that cover long distances often use satellites and microwave communication. Television and telephone companies have used satellites for many years, but big businesses also use them for their computer networks.

The Network Interface Card, Network Protocols, and Cabling Specifications

Cables are used to link a network together in a topology, as described earlier. When cables cannot be used, a wireless implementation may be an alternative. Regardless of the wiring and topology, each computer on the network still needs a hardware component to control the flow of data. The device that performs this function is the **network interface card (NIC),** commonly called a network card. This printed circuit board fits into one of the computer's expansion slots and provides a port on the back of the PC, where the network cable can be attached. Network software works with the operating system and tells the computer how to use the NIC. Both the network software and the NIC must adhere to a network protocol, discussed earlier.

Another critical specification of a network is the cabling equipment (also called the network technology) used to create a LAN. The most common types of network technology include Ethernet (which also includes Fast Ethernet) and Token Ring. Each is designed for a certain kind of network topology and has certain standard features.

Ethernet

Currently, **Ethernet** is the most common network technology used. Ethernet was originally designed for a bus topology and thick coaxial cable, but most new network installations use an Ethernet star topology with either twisted-pair or fiber-optic cables as the medium. A new technology for implementation in home networks uses the preexisting telephone wiring in the house to provide a network medium for interconnecting computers and other "smart" (network-aware) devices, including smart appliances. This technology is easy to integrate because it does not require installation of new media and does not affect voice calls; you can continue to use the home network even while making telephone calls. Intel's AnyPoint product is one of the leaders in this new technology field. In addition, a new home network uses the installed electrical wiring.

With Ethernet, if two nodes transmit simultaneously, the collision is detected and they retransmit one at a time. This approach to network communications is called carrier sense multiple access/collision detection (CSMA/CD). As you might guess, collisions are few in a small network. On a large network, access time can become noticeably delayed as collisions become more prevalent.

The original implementations of Ethernet, which used coaxial cable, were called 10Base-5 and 10Base-2. The most popular implementation of Ethernet—called 10Base-T—uses a star topology and twisted-pair wires and can achieve transmission speeds up to 10 Mbps.

Fast Ethernet

Also known as **Fast Ethernet,** 100Base-T is available using the same media and topology as Ethernet, but different network interface cards are used to achieve speeds of up to 100 Mbps. Other implementations of Ethernet are pushing transmission speeds even higher.

Token Ring

IBM's network technology is the **Token Ring.** The controlling hardware in a Token Ring network transmits an electronic token—a small set of data—to each node on the network many times each second if the token is not already in use by a specific node. A computer can copy data into the token and set the address where the data should be sent. The token then continues around the ring, and each computer along the way looks at the address until the token reaches the computer with the address that was recorded in the token. The receiving computer then copies the contents of the token and sends an acknowledgment to the sending computer. When the sending computer receives the acknowledgment from the receiving computer, it resets the token's status to "empty" and transmits it to the next computer in the ring.

The hardware for a Token Ring network is expensive; Token Ring adapter cards can cost as much as five times more than other types of network adapters. Token Ring networks once operated at either 4 or 16 megabits per second, but like Ethernet, new technology has pushed the transmission rate up to 100 megabits per second.

NETWORK SOFTWARE

Most of the networking terms you have seen so far—with the exception of the protocols discussed in the previous section—have referred to hardware. As with every other part of the computer system, however, there must be software to control the hardware. The group of programs that manages the resources on the network is often called the **network operating system (NOS).**

Network operating systems can range in size from Windows 95 (which allows you to connect several computers into a peer-to-peer network) to Windows 2000, NetWare, and Banyan Vines (which allows the world to be networked within a single enterprise). Some of the popular network operating systems include:

◆ **Novell NetWare.** One of the most popular network operating systems in terms of number of installations, NetWare (developed by Novell, Inc.) can be used to run networks with different topologies, including Ethernet and Token Ring. NetWare also includes support for various hardware platforms, such as Mac, PC, and UNIX hosts and servers.

◆ **Microsoft Windows NT Server 4.0.** Microsoft Windows NT Server 4.0 provides a graphical, Windows 9x–style user interface and is ideal for administering small

Visit **www.glencoe.com/norton/online/** for more information on **network operating systems.**

Figure 17.21

The graphical interface in Windows NT Server 4.0 resembles the Windows 9x operating systems.

and medium-sized networks. Many companies that have invested in Microsoft Windows 3.11, Windows 95, and Windows 98 use Windows NT Server as their NOS. An example of the interface is shown in Figure 17.21. Windows NT Server also operates with many other network operating systems.

◆ **Microsoft Windows 2000.** Available in four variations (Professional, Server, Advanced Server, and Data-Center), Microsoft Windows 2000 is the latest release of—and a radical departure from—Windows NT. Windows 2000, shown in Figure 17.22, adds an enterprise directory model known as Active Directory while maintaining the graphical user interface. With these features and scalability/expandability, it is ideal for administering networks ranging from small to enterprise-wide.

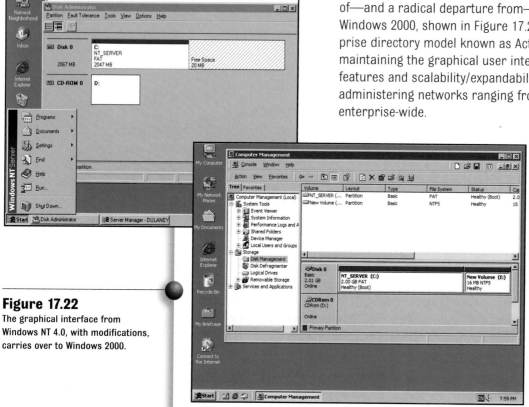

Figure 17.22

The graphical interface from Windows NT 4.0, with modifications, carries over to Windows 2000.

◆ **Banyan VINES.** The VINES NOS is commonly found in installations that have large network infrastructures, such as the U.S. Marine Corps, because VINES can update user information on multiple servers connected to each other on the same network.

Figure 17.23

The AppleShare NOS allows networking between Macintosh machines.

◆ **AppleShare.** AppleShare is used by Apple Macintosh users to network with one another (see Figure 17.23). AppleShare provides access to shared resources, such as printers and storage devices, and to centralized servers. In many installations, you will find networks comprising AppleShare networks alongside servers running other network operating systems, such as Windows NT Server.

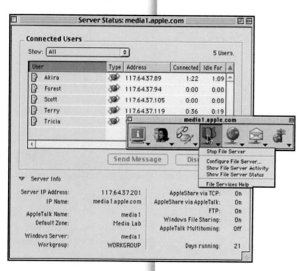

◆ **Linux.** Linux has garnered a large share of the small business and home market for providing Internet and networking services. An open operating system, it is a cost-effective alternative to other operating systems for sharing files, applications, printers, modems, and Internet services.

Techview

AVOIDING A TANGLED MESS

You may think that setting up a network is simple once you have selected the type of network, server, operating system, and other options you need. However, that is only the beginning.

Two of the most time-consuming and costly chores in networking involve choosing the type of wiring that will connect the nodes and servers, and deciding on the most efficient means of running the cable. These issues can be so confusing and costly that many companies have been created to deal with network cabling.

To show how troublesome network cabling issues can become, suppose that you have a warehouse that is 100 feet long and you want to install a network of eleven computers, all lined against one wall. This arrangement places the PCs 10 feet apart, which is the perfect spacing for cubicles.

If you want to use a bus topology, a terminator is placed on the first and last PCs, and ten 10-foot cables are run from one computer to the next. This method means that 100 feet of cable must be purchased and installed.

If you choose a ring or star topology for your network, however, your cabling requirements may increase dramatically. But the additional cabling and equipment (such as a hub) may make your network easier to manage. For instance, it can be easier to add new users to a star network than to a bus network. In such cases, the additional cabling requirements may well be worth the time and expense. Depending on the specific implementation you choose (that is, where you place the hub within the room), your star network may require two or three times more cable than a basic bus network.

There are additional factors to consider. Here are just a few questions networking experts must answer:

◆ Is the network being installed in an existing building, or is it being added to a building under construction? It is always easier to work within a building under construction than to have to drill through walls and run cable in an existing building. For example, many historical buildings such as courthouses have brick walls internally and restrictions (by historical societies) on work that can be done. In such cases, creative alternatives have to be considered.

◆ Can cabling run through the walls or must it run through ceilings? If the cabling will be run through the ceiling, the price of the material triples. Why? Fire codes prevent running ordinary networking cable in places where it can catch fire without being readily seen because of the noxious fumes given off during the burning.

◆ Will conduit be required to encase the cabling? Will you need to use wall plates, wiring closets, and the like?

◆ How much cabling will be exposed? Are there danger zones where people may trip over or drop items on the cabling or connectors?

◆ What if the company wants to be able to rearrange itself on short notice, moving offices, desks, and computers at will? This option can immediately rule out star and bus topologies because the network cannot be brought down every time someone changes an office.

The picture is further complicated when the network must span multiple buildings or several floors of a building.

Cabling is a major concern when setting up any network.

LESSON QUIZ

True/False

Answer the following questions by circling True or False.

True   False   **1.** A network is a way to connect computers so they can communicate, exchange information, and share resources.

True   False   **2.** If network users can open shared files but cannot make changes to those files, they have read-only access.

True   False   **3.** When a user sends a document to a network printer, the document is called a banner page.

True   False   **4.** On a network, data is transmitted in small groups called packets.

True   False   **5.** Distributed computing means getting another computer on the network to do some or all of your processing.

Multiple Choice

Circle the word or phrase that best completes each sentence.

1. _____ is one of the benefits of using a network.
   A. Simultaneous access to programs and data
   B. The ability to share peripheral devices
   C. Both A and B

2. If a server stores data files for users to access, it is commonly called a(n) _____ .
   A. file server   **B.** application server   **C.** both A and B

3. CU-SeeMe is an example of _____ software.
   A. teleconferencing   **B.** videoconferencing   **C.** network operating system

4. A _____ is a networking device that stores the addressing information of each computer on each of the LANs it connects.
   A. bridge   **B.** router   **C.** server

5. A _____ network places a hub in the center of the network nodes.
   A. bus   **B.** ring   **C.** star

LESSON LABS

Complete the following exercises as directed by your instructor.

1. View your network adapter card settings. Right-click the Network Neighborhood icon on the desktop, then choose Properties from the shortcut menu. When the Properties dialog box opens, click the Configuration tab and double-click the network adapter that appears. The card's properties will appear. Write down the settings and close all dialog boxes.

2. View your network protocol settings. Right-click the Network Neighborhood icon on the desktop, then choose Properties from the shortcut menu. When the Properties dialog box appears, click the Configuration tab, select a protocol from the list, and click the Properties command button. Do not make any changes. Write down the settings and close all dialog boxes.

Networking at Home & Abroad

OVERVIEW:
The Local and Global Reach of Networks

Networks were once used mainly by educational, military, and government institutions, but today networks span the globe and reach into the average home. For many small businesses, networking means connecting several workstations to allow workers to collaborate and share data. Small businesses often establish connections to the Internet, enabling users to browse the World Wide Web and exchange e-mail.

Medium- to large-size businesses typically use a network to interconnect users for the same reasons as small businesses, but they often use a WAN to interconnect various departments or divisions separated by different buildings, regions, or even continents. Many of these businesses use a direct connection to the Internet to provide Internet access to their users.

Even a home computer user can be part of a truly global network. A dial-up connection to the Internet makes your home computer one of the millions of nodes on the vast Internet network. You can share files, collaborate, communicate, and conference with people on the other side of the globe.

This lesson examines the most common technologies used for interconnecting computers to large private networks, and to public networks such as the Internet.

OBJECTIVES

- Explain how computer data travels over telephone lines.
- Explain a modem's function.
- List four features you should consider when evaluating modems.
- Differentiate four types of digital telephone services.
- Describe one potential use for a home network.

DATA COMMUNICATIONS OVER STANDARD TELEPHONE LINES

Network hardware and software offer a way to establish ongoing data communications, generally over media (twisted-pair wire, coaxial cable, fiber-optic cable, and so forth) specifically set up for the network and known as dedicated media. The alternative to using dedicated media is to use the telephone system—called the **plain old telephone system (POTS)** for data communication. This option is possible because the telephone system is really just a giant electronic network owned by the telephone companies.

Although it is designed to carry two-way electronic information, the network of telephone lines is significantly different from a typical computer network. Remember, the telephone system was originally designed to carry voice messages, which are analog signals. Increasingly, however, telephone lines are being used to send digital data. The reason for this trend is simple. By connecting your computer to the telephone, potentially you can send data to anyone else in the world who has a computer and telephone service, and you do not need to set up a network to do it. You simply pay the telephone company for the time you spend connected to the other computer. This trend has important implications for users as well as for telephone companies. Typically, the analog lines that carry voice signals are not very well suited for carrying data because the limit for transmission speeds over analog lines is only about .005 as fast as a 10Base-T Ethernet network. As a result, the telephone companies now offer digital lines specifically designed for data communications.

Soon after the introduction of the PC, users recognized the value of trading data and software over telephone lines. In response to this user demand, Hayes Microcomputer Products, Inc., developed the first modem for personal computers, the Smartmodem. Introduced in 1978, the modem connected a computer to a standard telephone line and allowed the transmission of data. This technological innovation started an explosion of digital connectivity for both businesses and individual users.

Modems

Although digital telephone lines are gaining popularity, most people still have analog telephone lines attached to their homes and businesses. Attaching a computer to an analog telephone line requires a modem, so it is important to know something about how modems work and what to look for when you buy one.

In standard telephone service, a telephone converts the sound of your voice into an electric signal that flows through the telephone wires. The telephone at the other end converts this electric signal back into sound so that the person you are talking to can hear your voice. Both the sound wave and the telephone signal are analog signals; they vary continuously with the volume and pitch of the speakers' voices. Because a computer's "voice" is digital—consisting of on/off pulses representing 1s and 0s—the device called a modem (short for modulator-demodulator) is needed to translate these digital signals into analog signals that can travel over standard telephone lines. In its modulation phase, the modem turns the computer's digital signals into analog signals. In its demodulation phase, the reverse takes place and analog signals are converted into digital signals. Figure 18.1 shows how computers communicate through modems and a telephone connection.

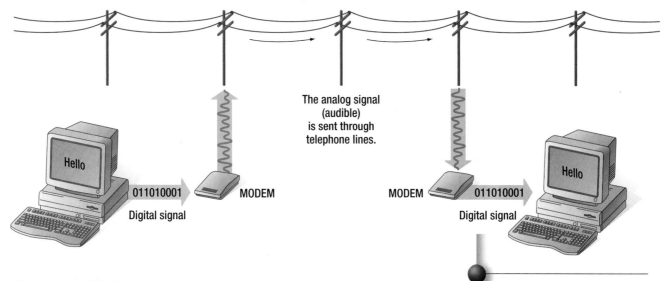

The analog signal (audible) is sent through telephone lines.

Hello

011010001 → MODEM

Digital signal

MODEM → 011010001

Digital signal

Hello

Choosing a Modem

A modem can be a simple circuit board—an expansion card—that plugs into one of the PC's expansion slots, or it can be an external device that plugs into a serial port. An emerging technology that is too new to have widespread use is the software modem. The software modem relies on the capabilities of today's faster computers to perform much of the communications work normally handled by a hardware modem. In effect, a software modem replaces most of the hardware in a hardware modem with an application program. The advantage is that the modem can be upgraded easily to accommodate new standards and speeds by simply updating the modem software.

Until a few years ago, choosing a modem was a difficult task. The modem industry, like the computer telecommunications industry in general, is plagued by a bad case of alphabet soup addiction—a dizzying array of specifications, abbreviations, and numbers that can confuse even the most experienced computer users. Terms such as V.22, V.32, V.32bis, V.34bis, V.34, V.42bis, V90, K56Flex, CCITT, MNP4, and MNP5 are just a few that you will encounter. This confusion is due to the proliferation of new standards; telecommunications technology improves so swiftly that companies continually develop products that exceed the capabilities of existing ones.

Fortunately, modem buying is much easier today because most newer modems support the most current standards and also the old ones. This feature enables almost all modems to exchange data with one another.

When you buy a modem, you should consider the following four factors:

◆ **Transmission Speed.** A modem's transmission speed (the rate at which it can send data) is measured in **bits per second (bps)**.

◆ **Data Compression.** Modern modems typically use data compression technologies to shrink the size of data before transmitting it over the telephone line. This method enables the modem to send and receive more data in less time than is possible when dealing with uncompressed data. Many different data compression schemes have been introduced over the years, and the newest modems are compatible with all of them. Today, if you purchase a 56K modem (one that transmits data at a rate of 56 kilobits per second), it will most likely use the V.90 data compression standard.

◆ **Error Correction.** Data moves through the line so quickly that even the smallest amount of static can introduce significant errors. Noise you could not

Figure 18.1
How modems connect computers through telephone lines.

NORTON
ONLINE

Visit **www.glencoe.com/norton/online/** for more information on **data compression**.

hear if you were using the telephone line for a conversation can wreak havoc with computer data. As a result, modems and communications software use **error-correction protocols** to recover from transmission errors. These protocols enable a modem to detect errors in the data it is receiving and to request that error-ridden data be re-sent from its source.

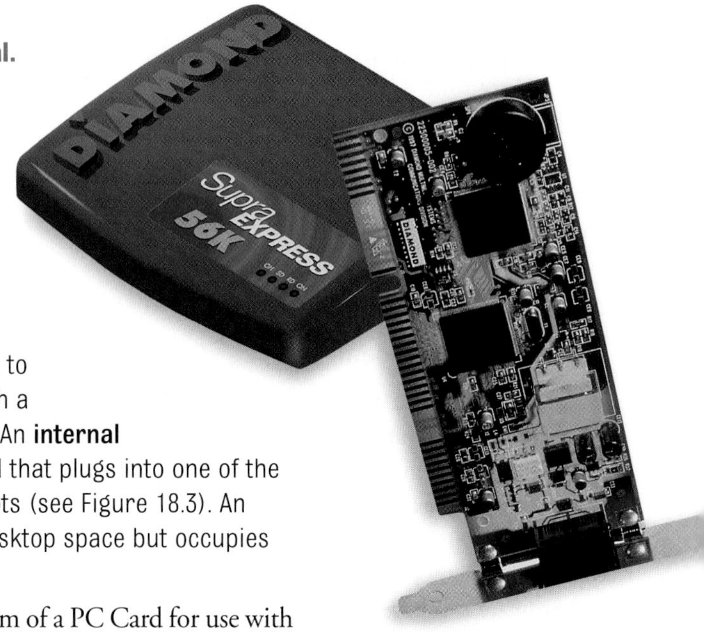

◆ **Internal Versus External.** An **external modem** is a box that houses the modem's circuitry outside the computer (see Figure 18.2). It connects to the computer using a serial cable connected through a serial port and to the telephone system with a standard telephone jack. An **internal modem** is a circuit board that plugs into one of the computer's expansion slots (see Figure 18.3). An internal modem saves desktop space but occupies an expansion slot.

Modems also come in the form of a PC Card for use with laptop computers (see Figure 18.4). Some use standard telephone lines, but others include a cellular phone, which enables completely wireless transmissions. These types of expansion devices for notebook computers were formerly referred to as PCMCIA cards, but now are referred to as simply PC Cards.

Another type of modem that is increasing in use is the cable modem. This device performs a function similar to a typical modem except that it connects the computer to the Internet through the cable TV system. Cable modems typically support downstream (from the Internet to your computer) transmission speeds of 10 Mbps. This feature enables your cable TV provider to offer Internet access at significantly higher transmission speeds than you could achieve with a dial-up modem. One common complaint with early implementations was that transfer speed reduced considerably as more users accessed the Internet through a given cable system, but advances in technology and bandwidth expansion by the cable TV companies have addressed those problems in many localities.

Most modems used with personal computers can also emulate a fax machine. Called **fax modems,** these devices can exchange faxes with any other fax modem or fax machine. With the proper software, users can convert incoming fax files into files that can be edited with a word processor—something that stand-alone fax machines cannot do.

Uses for a Modem

File transfer is the general term used to describe sending a file to a remote computer, whether the transfer occurs through the telephone lines or through a network. The act of sending a file to another user or to a network is known as **uploading** the file. Copying a file from a remote computer is known as **downloading** the file. For a file to be transferred from one computer to another through a pair of modems,

Figure 18.2
On the back of this external modem are connections for attaching it to the computer, a telephone jack, and a telephone. There is also a plug for a power cord because external modems require their own power supply.

Figure 18.3
An internal modem plugs into one of the computer's expansion slots. When it is installed, all you can see is the metal edge with the two telephone jacks. One jack is used to attach the modem to the telephone jack on the wall. The other can be used to connect a telephone, so you can still use the telephone line for calls even though the line goes through the modem.

Figure 18.4
This notebook computer is equipped with a modem in the form of a PC Card. The modem comes equipped with a cellular unit so the user can log into a network without using a telephone line.

both computers must use the same file transfer protocol (FTP)—the set of rules or guidelines that dictate the format in which data will be sent. The most common file transfer protocols for modems are called Kermit, Xmodem, Ymodem, and Zmodem.

One of the important functions of the file transfer protocol is to check for errors as a file is sent. Normally, modem communication is **full-duplex,** which means data can travel in both directions at the same time (see Figure 18.5). Sometimes, however, modem communication can be **half-duplex,** which means that data can be sent in both directions but only one direction at a time. In either type of communication, the receiving computer can respond to the sender and verify that the data it received contained no errors. If there are errors, the computer sending the data retransmits whatever portion is incorrect. Each file transfer protocol uses its own method to check for errors. Some are more efficient than others and therefore can transmit data faster.

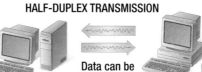

FULL-DUPLEX TRANSMISSION

Data can be sent in both directions at the same time.

HALF-DUPLEX TRANSMISSION

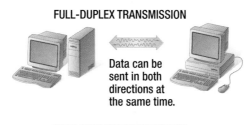

Data can be sent in both directions but only one direction at a time.

Figure 18.5
Most modern modem and network connections are full-duplex. However, computers are occasionally connected using half-duplex transmission.

Connections With Office Networks

More and more people are **telecommuting:** working at home or on the road and using telecommunications equipment—telephones, modems, fax machines, and so forth—to stay in touch with the office (see Figure 18.6). The advantages of telecommuting over working in an office can be compelling. The telecommuter is spared the time and expense of traveling to work.

For the telecommuter, setting up a home office almost always requires a computer and a modem. With the right software, the home user can then dial into the office network and upload or download files at any time. Dialing into the network has the same effect as logging into it at the office, except that transmitting files is slower.

NORTON

ONLINE

Visit **www.glencoe.com/norton/online/** for more information on **telecommuting.**

Figure 18.6
Home offices now have access to multifunction machines, such as this model, which can act as a printer, copier, fax machine, and scanner.

Answer the following questions by filling in the blank(s).

1. The term modem is short for _____ .

2. A modem's transmission speed is measured in _____ .

3. The act of sending a file to another user is known as _____ the file.

USING DIGITAL TELEPHONE LINES

As you learned earlier, standard telephone lines transmit analog signals in which sound is translated into an electrical current. As a result, you need a modem to translate data into a form that can be sent over the telephone lines. In addition, telephone lines operate at about 3100 Hz, which means that data has to be compressed to travel at more than about 2400 bps. Data compression has become quite sophisticated, so modems can often transmit data at rates as high as 56 Kbps (56,000 bps). Nevertheless, this volume can create a severe bandwidth bottleneck because typical network transmission speeds are at least 10 Mbps (10,000,000 bps)—about 200 times as fast.

Figure 18.7

When sending data, a computer transmits a digital signal to a modem, which transmits an analog signal to the switching station, which transmits a digital signal to another switching station. This process is then reversed until it reaches the receiving computer.

The telephone companies recognized this problem several years ago and began the long process of converting an analog system into a digital system. The massive data channels that connect major geographical regions are already digital, but the telephone lines running under or above most city streets are still analog. This combination of digital and analog lines makes for an extremely confusing system, especially when you are transmitting data through a modem (see Figure 18.7). However, when the telephone companies complete the transition and digital lines are installed to every building, the data transmission system will be a lot simpler. The transformation from analog to digital lines will affect most users in three simple ways:

◆ You will need a different phone—a digital one that translates your voice into bits rather than an analog signal.

◆ You will not need a modem to send data. Instead, you will use an adapter that simply reformats the data so that it can travel through the telephone lines.

◆ You will be able to send data much more quickly.

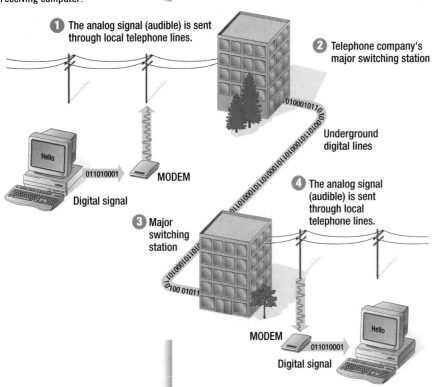

❶ The analog signal (audible) is sent through local telephone lines.

❷ Telephone company's major switching station

0100010110

Underground digital lines

Hello

011010001 MODEM

Digital signal

❸ Major switching station

❹ The analog signal (audible) is sent through local telephone lines.

Hello

MODEM 011010001

Digital signal

ISDN, T1, and T3

Many different kinds of digital services are offered by the phone companies. Some of the best known are called ISDN, T1, and T3. Of these, ISDN received the most attention in the past few years because it was the most affordable and the one most likely to make its way into homes and small businesses. **ISDN, which stands for integrated services digital network,** is a system that replaces all analog services with digital services (see Figure 18.8).

When most people talk about ISDN, they are referring to a particular level of service called BRI (basic rate ISDN). BRI provides three communication channels on one line—two 64 or 56 Kbps data channels and one 19 Kbps channel that is used to set up and control calls. The two data channels can carry voice or data and they can be used simultaneously, so you can transmit data and carry on a conversation at the same time on the same line. Also, the channels can be combined so that BRI service can be used to transmit data at rates as high as 128 Kbps without compression.

Some telephone companies now offer BRI service in some locations—especially in large metropolitan areas. Installation can be expensive, but the cost of service is slowly coming down to compete with the basic rates offered for analog lines.

A higher level of service for ISDN is called primary rate ISDN, or PRI. In the United States, PRI provides twenty-four channels at 64 Kbps each, a total bandwidth of 1.544 Mbps. This level of bandwidth is also known as **T1** service. In Europe, PRI service provides thirty-one data channels.

Although it is not specified by the ISDN standard, it is also possible to purchase lines from telephone companies that offer even more bandwidth. For example, a **T3** line offers 672 channels of 64 Kbps each (plus control lines) for a total of 44.736 Mbps. Many telephone companies also offer services between the levels of BRI and PRI. Different businesses have all kinds of different needs for bandwidth, so telephone companies try to be as flexible as possible in their offerings.

The ISDN adapter provides the link to digital local telephone lines.

Digital connection between major switching stations

Digital local telephone lines

ISDN ADAPTER

Figure 18.8
With local digital telephone lines, data transmissions can remain in a digital format from the sending computer to the receiving computer.

NORTON
ONLINE

Visit **www.glencoe.com/norton/online/** for more information on **ISDN**.

DSL Technologies

One of the latest developments in connectivity is **digital subscriber line (DSL).** DSL is rapidly outpacing ISDN in areas where DSL is available because it is typically less expensive in terms of hardware, setup, and monthly costs. In fact, many local telephone companies are opting to develop DSL in their markets and are foregoing ISDN altogether.

Two key points that make DSL so attractive are its speed and its medium. DSL can achieve theoretical speeds up to 52 Mbps, a huge speed advantage over the fastest dial-up modems or even some digital connections. The second advantage is that DSL can use POTS lines, the standard copper wire used for telephone communications

COMPUTERS
in your career

Careers in Networking

Two of the most popular (and best-paying) computer-related fields are networking and data communications. Most large organizations have existing networks that must be maintained, repaired, and updated as the company grows or shrinks. When companies merge, networks must be combined to create a seamless interface for the organization. Many times two or more networks that use different topologies, network operating systems, and protocols must be combined into one large network.

As these networks are merged, there must be a limited amount of downtime so employees can continue processing data for the company. People interested in careers relating to networking and data communications must be educated in a wide range of computing and networking topics.

Some of the careers relating to networking and data communications are listed below:

◆ **Network Administrators.** These individuals are responsible for managing a company's network infrastructure. Some of the jobs in this field include designing and implementing networks, setting up and managing users' accounts, installing and updating network software and applications, and backing up the network. To succeed as a network administrator, you should gain experience in the major network operating systems, including Novell NetWare, Windows NT 4.0 Server, and Windows 2000 Server. You also should have experience with major operating systems, such as Windows 98, MS-DOS, Apple Macintosh, and UNIX. You might also consider becoming certified by Novell or Microsoft.

Networking is one of the most rapidly growing fields in the computing industry.

◆ **Information Systems (IS) Managers.** IS managers are responsible for managing a team of information professionals, including network administrators, software developers, project managers, and other staff. Jobs in the IS management field differ according to the needs of the company, but many IS managers maintain project lists, oversee project management, perform database administration, and possibly do some programming. IS managers should possess experience and skills in a wide range of networking and computing areas, including network operating system experience, operating system experience, relational database knowledge, and staff management abilities.

◆ **Data Communications Managers.** These managers are responsible for setting up and maintaining Internet, intranet, and extranet sites. Often they are also responsible for designing and establishing an organization's telecommuting initiative. This task often requires experience with several technologies, including networking, data communications, remote access software, and Internet technologies. If you are interested in a career in data communications, you should learn as much as you can about these technologies.

in most homes and businesses today. The typical home computer user can connect to the Internet or a private network through DSL at high transmission speeds, often for a cost that is competitive with standard dial-up connections.

There are several types of DSL available in different markets, each offering different capabilities and rates:

◆ Asymmetrical DSL (ADSL) uses discrete multitone (DMT) or carrierless amplitude phase (CAP) modulation.

◆ Rate adaptive DSL (RADSL) adjusts the speed based on signal quality.

◆ High-bit-rate DSL (HDSL) allows the telephone company to provide T1 speeds at a lower cost than T1 but requires two wire pairs.

◆ ISDN DSL (IDSL) uses existing ISDN facilities.

◆ Symmetric DSL (SDSL), a version of HDSL, uses a single pair of wires and provides slower transfer rates than HDSL.

◆ Very-high-bit-rate DSL (VDSL) provides a high bandwidth with a commensurate cost and is geared primarily toward LAN and WAN connectivity.

The actual performance you can achieve with DSL depends on the type of DSL and the distance between the DSL modem and the telephone company's switch. Table 18.1 summarizes the various DSL transmission rates and distances.

Visit **www.glencoe.com/norton/online/** for more information on **DSL**.

Table 18.1	DSL Transmission Specifications			
Type of Service	**Upstream**	**Downstream**	**Pairs**	**Cable Distance (Feet)**
ADSL	1 Mbps	8 Mbps	1	12,000
DSL Lite	512 Kbps	1.544 Mbps	1	18,000
HDSL	1.544 Mbps	1.544 Mbps	2	12,000
	2.048 Mbps	2.048 Mbps	3	12,000
IDSL	128 Kbps	128 Kbps	1	18,000
RADSL	90 Kbps	610 Kbps	1	18,000
	1.088 Mbps	7.168 Mbps	1	25,000
SDSL	1.544 Mbps	1.544 Mbps	1	10,000
VDSL	1.6 Mbps	12.96 Mbps	1	3,000
	2.3 Mbps	25.82 Mbps	1	3,000
		51.84 Mbps	1	1,000

ATM

DSL, ISDN, T1, and T3 can all be used effectively to set up WANs as long as the networks are used primarily for transferring the most common types of data—files, e-mail messages, and so on. However, these types of services are not always well suited for transmitting live video and sound. As a result, communications companies offer a service called **ATM**, which stands for **asynchronous transfer mode.**

ATM is a protocol designed by the telecommunications industry as a more efficient way to send voice, video, and computer data over a single network. It was

originally conceived as a way to reconcile the needs for these different kinds of data on the telephone system, but the proponents of ATM argue that it can also be implemented on computer LANs and WANs. In fact, ATM is a network protocol, and therefore it is similar to Ethernet and Token Ring.

To understand the significance of ATM, you need to know how most telephone lines work. With a **circuit-switched** line, you call a number, the telephone system connects you, and you have complete access to that connection until you hang up. This arrangement is vastly different from most computer networks, which transmit packets of data and are therefore referred to as **packet-switched** systems. In circuit-switched lines, you and the person at the other end of the line have a fixed amount of bandwidth available. Even if you do not say anything to each other—or in the case of modem transmission, if you do not send any data—the bandwidth is still available.

This type of communication can be inefficient because data communication tends to be erratic. For example, consider two office LANs connected using the telephone system. Every few minutes, a person in one office might send a file to a person in another office. During this time—maybe just a few seconds—the necessary bandwidth is high. During the remaining time, however, no bandwidth is required at all. Yet the telephone line remains active, reserving the same amount of bandwidth.

Table 18.2	Digital Telephone Services	
Service	**Speeds Available**	**Description**
DSL	90 Kbps to 51.84 Mbps	Offers high-speed transmission rates and can utilize existing POTS lines (copper telephone wiring common in most telephone installations).
ISDN	BRI = 128 Kbps PRI = 1.544 Mbps	BRI is a dial-up digital service (called dial-up because the line is open only when you make a call). Service is relatively inexpensive, but user pays for usage and long distance. PRI is a continuous, or dedicated, connection.
T1	1.544 Mbps	Can refer to several types of service, including PRI and private, leased lines between two points (usually to form a WAN).
Fractional T1	64K and up	A fraction of a T1 line is leased between two points.
T3	44.736 Mbps	Service equivalent to twenty-eight T1 lines. Requires that fiber-optic cable be installed.
Frame Relay	56 Kbps to 1.536 Mbps	A fast, packet-switching technology. Signal is carried to a frame relay circuit at the telephone company's branch office. Groups of data are encapsulated in packets and forwarded to their destination. Frame relay service typically implies a permanent virtual circuit between two points (usually to form a WAN). However, frame relay switches can also be used with dial-up ISDN lines.
SMDS	1.17 Mbps to 34 Mbps	Switched multimegabit digital service is another fast, packet-switching technology, similar to frame relay service but catering to higher-end users.
ATM cell relay	51.84 Mbps to 10,000 Mbps	Another switching technology. Because it is fast, flexible, and well-suited for all types of data (including sound and video), ATM may become the technology used for backbones in the telephone company branch offices.

Clearly, voice and data have different bandwidth requirements. Other types of communication, such as transmission of a digital video signal, have still different types of requirements. ATM addresses the needs of different kinds of communication by providing different kinds of connections and bandwidth on demand. Rather than reserving a fixed amount of bandwidth whether data is being transmitted or not, an ATM network transmits packets, known as cells, that include information about where they should go, what type of data is included, and what order the packets should follow. Cells can be sent in clumps, by different routes if necessary, even out of order (because the packet includes enough information to put the data back into the proper order). Unlike standard telephone transmission, which is based on circuit switching, ATM is based on cell switching.

Because the volume of cells being transmitted can vary with the bandwidth of the incoming signal, ATM is considered an ideal way to combine voice, data, and video transmission on the same high-bandwidth network. As a result, it is one of the most widely used industry buzzwords of the decade. Whether it will capture the telecommunications and data communications industries, however, is yet to be determined. Table 18.2 summarizes some of the common digital services.

Cable Modem Connections

As explained briefly in this lesson, a cable modem is a relatively new technology that enables home computer users to connect to the Internet through their cable TV connection with higher speeds than those offered by dial-up connections (see Figure 18.9). However, cable modems are also finding acceptance in small- to medium-sized businesses as an alternative to other technologies such as DSL and ISDN. Under the best conditions, cable modems can achieve downstream speeds of about 27 Mbps, a substantial increase over dial-up connections, ISDN, and some types of DSL.

In a typical cable network, a head end serves as the primary point where the television signals enter the system through satellite and standard over-the-air broadcast means. The head end is also where the dedicated Internet connection occurs,

Figure 18.9
A cable modem system combines a typical cable television network with a wide area network, which is connected to the Internet.

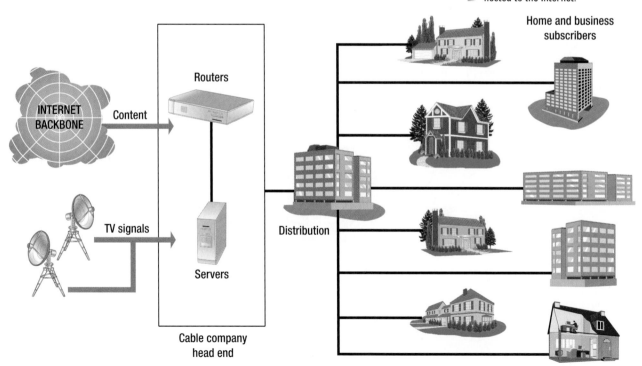

327

connecting the cable TV network to the Internet. From the head end, the network branches out to subscriber locations using combinations of fiber-optic and copper cable, typically terminating at each end-user location as coax cable. Because a transmission must often traverse several miles from the head end to the end user, amplifiers are used to restore the signal strength. The greater the distance from the head end, the more amplifiers are required.

As with other communications technologies, selecting a cable modem is not a "cut-and-dried" process. In fact, the selection will probably be decided by the cable provider, who most often supplies the cable modem, configures it, and installs it. As the technology in implementation grows and standards gel, it is likely that televisions with integrated modems will be sold.

What lies ahead for cable modem technology is not clear today because competing technologies such as DSL are gaining in popularity. Cable services have struggled to overcome problems with the technology, most notably a significant impact on overall performance as utilization goes up. Whether cable Internet access is or becomes available in a given area really depends on the race between cable companies and telecommunications providers to implement their high-speed technologies.

NETWORKS IN THE HOME

Home networking is becoming more popular as the number of homes with multiple computers increases, along with the number of people who telecommute. Networks offer essentially the same advantages to home users as to a business. They enable you to share resources such as printers, disk space, and backup systems more efficiently, something that is often more important for home users than for business users because of the difference in budgets. Another use for home networks is network-based gaming. More and more games are network-integrated, enabling users to play against other users on the network or on the Internet. The introduction of Internet connection sharing in Windows 98 and Windows 2000 adds another benefit: sharing a single dial-up connection to the Internet among multiple home computers (see Figure 18.10).

As the market for home networking has grown, so has the choice of technologies. Like any business, a home can be a good target for standard networks using twisted-pair cable and hubs. This type of network installation requires installation of additional cable, which is not difficult if all the computers share the same room or in cases where cable can be installed during construction of the home. Where only a few computers are involved in the same room, coaxial cable is a quick and easy solution. When computers are located in different rooms, however, adding cable dedicated to networking is not always practical because of cost and difficulty of installation.

NORTON
O N L I N E

Visit **www.glencoe.com/norton/online/** for more information on **cable modems**.

Figure 18.10

Millions of homes now have multiple PCs. New technologies enable families to create networks within the home using existing media (such as telephone lines) and existing operating systems (such as Windows).

To overcome this problem, network solutions based on existing telephone lines are finding success in the market. Intel's AnyPoint network is a good example of this type of technology (see Figure 18.11). AnyPoint uses the existing telephone lines in the house and enables homeowners to network a computer in any room with an existing telephone line easily and quickly. These technologies piggyback the network signal on the telephone cable without affecting voice traffic, so you can continue to use the telephone for calls. You can even use a dial-up connection through the telephone lines to connect to the Internet while you share files and printers through the telephone lines locally.

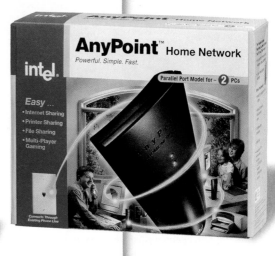

Figure 18.11
Products like Intel's AnyPoint home network system make it easy to set up a fully functioning network at home.

Another technology with some success in the home networking market—primarily for implementation in existing structures—is wireless networking. Some solutions use infrared technology while others use some form of radio transmission such as spread-spectrum technology. Wireless solutions are most useful in installations where installing cable is impractical, such as in concrete or masonry structures.

Most home networking requirements are not as extensive as those for a business or large organization. All of the operating systems targeted for the home user, particularly Windows 95, Windows 98, and the Mac operating systems, provide built-in networking capabilities (see Figure 18.12). Beyond the operating system included with the computers, there are generally no other applications required to enable or configure networking in a home network.

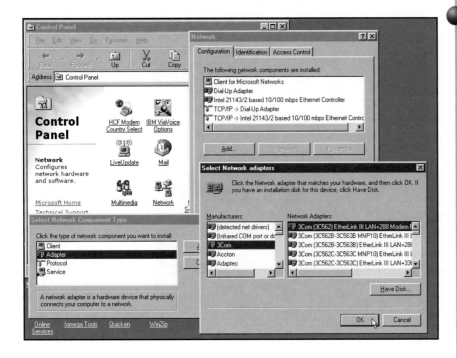

Figure 18.12
Operating systems like Windows 98 make it easy for small businesses and home users to set up and manage small networks.

Visit **www.glencoe.com/norton/online/** for more information on **home networking** technologies.

The Network Comes Home

It's not too unrealistic to assume that in the next decade most homes will have a high-speed connection to the Internet and receive services like video-on-demand, interactive television, and other new services through a common connection.

Within another decade, most home devices will be integrated into the network, enabling technicians to troubleshoot and possibly to repair appliances remotely. Your washing machine will talk to your dryer to tell it what type of load to expect next. Your oven will coordinate with your microwave to make sure everything is ready for dinner at the same time.

Higher bandwidth will enable you to monitor your home visually from work (assuming you still work outside the home) and control essentially the entire household remotely. Your home computer will monitor the temperature, humidity, and other environmental factors and adjust the thermostats accordingly.

What will this brave new world cost? Financially, probably little. It is likely that high-speed access itself will be based on a flat-rate monthly fee, much like unlimited dial-up Internet access today. While the service providers will not be making much profit in providing a high-speed connection to your home, they will be actively marketing other services for a fee.

Where providers will reap a profit is in charges for specific services such as video-on-demand, customized music stations, home security monitoring, entertainment and gaming, and other services. Like today's telephone system in the United States, you will pay a flat monthly fee to make all the local calls you want, but when you need extra services (such as long distance), you pay for it.

The costs of this new technology and the benefits it can bring are not just monetary, however. Throughout this tapestry runs the thread of reduced privacy. As you open your home to technology and connectivity, you also open it to hackers.

If you can monitor your home from the office, you can bet that hackers will be trying to break into your home to snoop on you. Not only will you have to be concerned with protecting your data at the office, you will also have to keep a wary eye on what information you store on your home computers. Companies that focus on providing secure home- computing environments will see considerable financial success in the coming decades.

Your home appliances, PC, and utilities will communicate with one another through a home network.

LESSON QUIZ

True/False

Answer the following questions by circling True or False.

True   False   **1.** You do not need a modem to connect a computer to an analog telephone line.

True   False   **2.** The expression Kbps stands for "thousand bits per second."

True   False   **3.** File transfer refers to the process of sending a file to a remote computer.

True   False   **4.** Basic rate ISDN service provides thirteen communication channels.

True   False   **5.** With a circuit-switched line, users always have a fixed amount of bandwidth available, even when they are not actually using the line.

Multiple Choice

Circle the word or phrase that best completes each sentence.

1. You should consider _____ when purchasing a modem.
   A. transmission speed   **B.** error correction   **C.** both A and B

2. The abbreviation *bps* stands for _____ .
   A. baud per second   **B.** bits per second   **C.** bytes per second

3. A(n) _____ enables a modem to determine whether data has been corrupted (for example, by noise in the telephone line) and to request that it be retransmitted.
   A. error-protection protocol   **B.** file transfer protocol   **C.** neither A nor B

4. _____ service offers a total of 44.736 Mbps of bandwidth.
   A. ISDN   **B.** T1   **C.** T3

5. In a cable network, the _____ is where the cable TV network connects to the Internet.
   A. head end   **B.** switching station   **C.** modem

LESSON LABS

Complete the following exercises as directed by your instructor.

1. Determine what type of modem is in your computer and view its settings. Click the Start button to open the Start menu, then click Settings, Control Panel. When the Control Panel dialog box opens, double-click the Modems icon. The Modems Properties dialog box opens. If any modems are listed, select them one at a time and click the Properties button. Review and write down the properties for each modem. Be careful not to change any settings. Close all dialog boxes.

2. HyperTerminal is a Windows utility that enables your computer to "call" another computer directly and exchange data over a telephone line. Click the Start button; then choose Programs, Accessories, Communications, HyperTerminal. When the HyperTerminal program group appears, double-click the HyperTerminal icon. When the New Connection window opens, click the Help menu, then choose Help Topics. Read the help topics, and then close all windows.

LESSON 17: Networking Basics

The Uses of a Network

■ A network is a way to connect computers for communication, information exchange, and resource sharing.

■ The four most compelling benefits of networking are simultaneous access to programs and data, peripheral sharing, streamlined communications, and easier backups.

■ Many networks are built around a central computer called a network server, which provides a storage device and other resources that users can share.

■ E-mail, videoconferencing, and teleconferencing are examples of the personal communications that can be conducted over a network or the Internet.

How Networks Are Structured

■ Networks can be categorized in different ways, such as by geography (how much terrain they cover) or by the use or absence of a central server.

■ A local area network (LAN) consists of computers that are relatively near one another. A LAN can have a few PCs or hundreds of them in a single building or scattered throughout several buildings.

■ LANs can be connected by a bridge or router to create a much larger network that covers a larger geographic area. To connect LANs, a gateway may be required to enable them to share data in a way that the different LANs can understand.

■ A wide area network (WAN) is the result of connecting LANs through public utilities.

■ Many networks are built around a central server. The PCs that connect to the server are called nodes. In a file server network, the server provides storage and file-sharing services for the nodes. In a client/server network, nodes and the server share the storage and processing chores.

■ A peer-to-peer network is a small network that usually does not include a central server. In a peer-to-peer network, users can share files and resources on all the network's nodes.

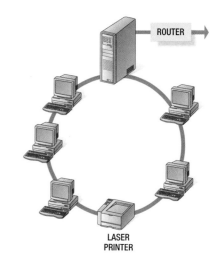

Network Topologies for LANs

■ A topology is the physical layout of the cables and devices that connect the nodes of a network. The three basic topologies are bus, star, and ring. These topologies are so named because of the shape of the network they create.

Network Media and Hardware

■ When used in the context of networks, the term *media* refers to the wires, cables, and other means by which data travels from its source to its destination.

■ The most common media for data communications are twisted-pair wire, coaxial cable, fiber-optic cable, and wireless links.

■ The performance of network media is evaluated by the amount of data they can transmit each second. This value is called bandwidth. The higher a network's bandwidth, the more data it can carry.

- Inside each network node, a network interface card provides a connection point for the network cable.

- To communicate with other parts of the network, each computer must follow a network protocol—a language computers use for communicating data. TCP/IP, IPX/SPX, and NetBEUI are examples of network protocols.

- The most common types of network technology include Ethernet, Fast Ethernet, and Token Ring.

Network Software

- A network operating system is the group of programs that manages the resources on a network.

LESSON 18: Networking at Home and Around the World

Data Communications Over Standard Telephone Lines

- Networks (especially the Internet and large WANs, with nodes spread over a large geographic area) commonly transmit data across telephone lines.

- Although telephone companies are offering more digital lines (which are better suited to data transmission), most homes and businesses are still served by analog telephone lines.

- To transfer digital data over analog telephone lines, computers must use modems. When a computer sends data, its modem translates digital data into analog signals for transmission over standard telephone lines. At the receiving end, the computer's modem converts the analog signals back into digital data.

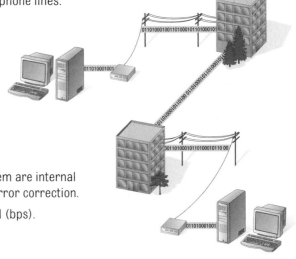

- The most important factors to consider when choosing a modem are internal versus external, transmission speed, data compression, and error correction.

- Modem transmission speeds are measured in bits per second (bps). Currently, the preferred standard for modems is 56.6 Kbps.

Using Digital Telephone Lines

- Using digital connections, business networks and homes can transmit data many times faster than is possible over standard telephone lines. In areas where digital connection is not possible, homes and businesses are connected with standard analog lines, but high-speed digital lines are run between the telephone company's switching stations.

- The most popular digital telephone services are integrated services digital network (ISDN), T1, T3, and DSL. They offer faster data transfer rates and higher bandwidths than standard telephone lines.

Networks in the Home

- New technologies enable homeowners to set up home networks to connect multiple computers. Home networks typically operate on existing media such as the home's telephone lines or cable wiring.

UNIT REVIEW

KEY TERMS

After completing this unit, you should be able to define the following terms.

application server, *300*
asynchronous transfer mode (ATM), *325*
bandwidth, *310*
bits per second (bps), *319*
bridge, *304*
bus network, *309*
circuit-switched, *326*
client/server, *307*
coaxial (coax) cable, *311*
data communications, *297*
digital subscriber line (DSL), *323*
distributed computing, *307*
downloading, *320*
electronic mail (e-mail), *301*
error-correction protocol, *320*
Ethernet, *312*
external modem, *320*
Fast Ethernet, *313*
fax modem, *320*
fiber-optic cable, *311*
file server, *298*

file server network, *306*
file transfer, *320*
full-duplex, *321*
gateway, *304*
groupware, *300*
half-duplex, *321*
hub, *309*
integrated services digital network (ISDN), *323*
internal modem, *320*
local area network (LAN), *303*
mesh topology, *310*
network, *298*
network interface card (NIC), *312*
network operating system (NOS), *313*
network server, *298*
network version, *299*
node, *306*
packet, *303*
packet-switched, *326*
peer-to-peer network, *307*
plain old telephone system (POTS), *318*

print job, *301*
protocol, *303*
read-only access, *299*
read/write access, *299*
ring topology, *309*
router, *304*
server, *298*
site license, *299*
spooling, *301*
star network, *309*
T1, *323*
T3, *323*
telecommuting, *321*
teleconference, *302*
token, *309*
Token Ring, *313*
topology, *308*
twisted-pair cable, *310*
uploading, *320*
videoconference, *302*
wide area network (WAN), *304*
wireless communications, *311*

KEY TERMS QUIZ

Fill in each blank with one of the terms listed under Key Terms.

1. A system for transmitting written messages through a network is known as

   _____ .

2. A(n) _____ is a network of computers that serves users located relatively near each other.

3. You can connect computers together to communicate and exchange information by using a(n) _____ .

4. The physical layout of wires and devices that connect the network's nodes is called the _____ .

5. Copying a file from a remote computer is called _____ .

6. _____ uses light to transmit data from one point to another.

7. The group of programs that manages the resources on the network is known as the _____ .

8. A star network features a device called a(n) _____ at its center.

9. The individual computers on a network are called _____ .

10. The act of sending a file to another user or to a network is called _____ .

REVIEW QUESTIONS

In your own words, briefly answer the following questions.

1. List and describe the benefits that networks provide.

2. How do networks help businesses save money?

3. Describe how an e-mail system is a combination of the postal system and a telephone answering system.

4. What are the four types of data communications media that link networks?

5. Describe the method used in Ethernet networks to detect collisions.

6. What are the three most common types of network technologies?

7. What purpose does a modem serve?

8. What factors should you consider when purchasing a modem?

9. If digital telephone lines replace analog telephone lines, how will data communications be simplified?

10. If your home has multiple computers, what are the advantages of connecting them in a network?

DISCUSSION QUESTIONS

As directed by your instructor, discuss the following questions in class or in groups.

1. As a group, create a list of ways in which companies can save money by setting up a network.

2. How practical are home networks? Do you think there is a real use for connecting PCs, home appliances, utilities, and so on? Or is the notion of home networking just another way for technology companies to profit? Share your views with the group.

ETHICAL ISSUES

Networks give us more choices and freedom in the workplace, but they can also be misused. With this thought in mind, discuss the following questions in class.

1. Telecommuters enjoy working at home because it gives them more control over their schedules while removing the distractions that are part of the workplace. Realizing that they are no longer under the watch of their supervisor, however, some workers abuse their telecommuting privileges. What are the risks to business of allowing employees to telecommute? At what point is an employee abusing the freedom afforded by telecommuting?

2. It is estimated that most occurrences of hacking are conducted by employees who pilfer data from their employers' networks and then sell or misuse the information. How far should companies go to prevent such abuse? What kinds of punishments are appropriate?

UNIT LABS

You and the Computer

Complete the following exercises using a computer in your classroom, lab, or home. No other materials are needed.

1. **Check Your File-Sharing Settings.** If your computer is connected to a network, you can configure settings that enable others to use files that are saved on your hard disk. To check this setting, take the following steps:

   A. Click the Start button to open the Start menu, then choose Settings, Control Panel. The Control Panel window opens.

   B. Double-click the Network icon. The Network dialog box opens.

   C. Click the File and Print Sharing button. The File and Print Sharing dialog box appears.

   D. See whether the "I want to be able to give others access to my files" check box is selected. If it is, other users on the network may be able to access certain areas of your PC's disk. (*Note:* Do not make any changes to this dialog box.)

   E. Click Cancel twice, then close the Control Panel window.

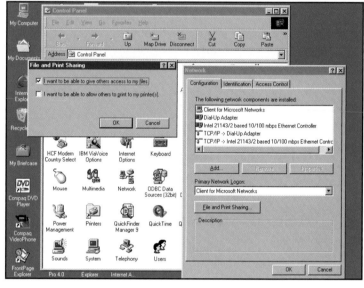

2. **Check Your Network.** If your computer is connected to a network, you can use Windows tools to view the other nodes and servers that are also connected to the network. Take the following steps:

   A. On the Windows desktop, double-click the Network Neighborhood icon. The Network Neighborhood window opens.

   B. Double-click the Entire Neighborhood icon. If your PC is part of a network, it should expand to display a list of all the PCs, servers, and other devices connected to the network.

   C. Right-click any item in the list, then choose Properties from the shortcut menu. Review the properties of several parts of the network. Do not make any changes to any of the settings or information.

   D. When you are done, close any dialog boxes that may be open, then close the Network Neighborhood window.

Internet Labs

To complete the following exercises, you need a computer with an Internet connection and a Web browser. (For more information on using these tools, see "Prerequisites" at the front of this textbook.)

1. **Network Operating Systems.** Visit the following Web sites and gather as much information as you can about each company's network operating system:

- Apple Computer, Inc., makers of AppleShare—**www.apple.com/**

- Artisoft, Inc., makers of LANtastic—**www.artisoft.com/**

- Microsoft Corp., makers of Windows 98, Windows 2000, and Windows NT—**www.microsoft.com/**

- Novell, Inc., makers of NetWare—**www.novell.com/**

If you want more information about specific network operating systems, visit your favorite search engine (such as Alta Vista, *The Big Hub,* Yahoo!, etc.), and search on the term *network operating system.* When you are finished, assume that you own a business with about fifty employees, all using PCs. Which network operating system would you choose, based on the information you found on the Internet? Be prepared to explain your choice to the class.

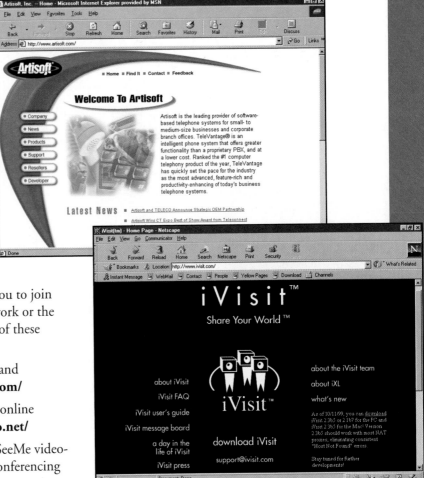

2. **Check Videoconferencing.** Several affordable videoconferencing applications are available, all of which enable you to join online videoconferences on a private network or the Internet. You can learn more about some of these products at these Web sites:

- iVisit, makers of the iVisit video chat and conference application—**www.ivisit.com/**

- VDOnet, makers of the VDO line of online communications products—**www.vdo.net/**

- White Pine Software, makers of CU-SeeMe videoconferencing client, as well as video conferencing server applications and other online communications applications—**www.wpine.com/**

IBE Labs

If you have the Interactive Browser Edition (IBE) CD-ROM for this textbook, you may complete the following interactive exercises using the instructions provided in the IBE.

1. **Trivia.** Choose a category; then test your knowledge.

2. **Labeling.** Label a diagram on digital phone lines.

3. **Ask an Expert.** Compare how your recommendations match up with the expert's.

4. **Home Network.** Step through the decisions required to set up a home network.

UNIT 10

The Internet and Online Resources

UNIT OBJECTIVES

List two reasons for the Internet's creation.

Describe the parts of an Internet address.

Name five major features of the Internet.

List two ways in which a PC can access the Internet.

UNIT CONTENTS

This unit contains the following lessons:

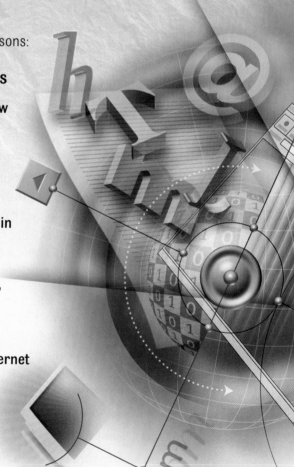

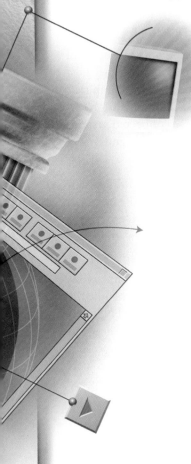

LESSON 19

Internet Basics

OVERVIEW:
A Growing Influence in Our Lives

By the time it started becoming a household word in the early 1990s, the Internet had existed for more than thirty years. Relatively few people knew what it was, and even fewer had actually used it. By 1994, when people began "surfing the Internet" in large numbers, its potential was only beginning to be understood. Today, the Internet is a constant in the lives of millions of people around the world, and its reach and usefulness seem almost unlimited.

In fact, the Internet may be one of the most important factors shaping the near future. Its existence has already changed the way many people work, communicate, and do business. The Internet has enabled us to access nearly any kind of information from a PC, and it has freed us from many kinds of chores. It has given us a new place to shop, study, work, and socialize.

As the "information society" moves forward, an understanding of the Internet may become as important as a college degree, depending on the type of career you want to pursue. Certainly, as a tool for personal communication, research, commerce, and entertainment, the Internet is an indispensable asset you should master. If you use it as a business tool, the Internet will probably be as essential to your job as a word processor, spreadsheet, or any other type of computer application.

This unit introduces you to the basic structure and features of the Internet. It shows you how individuals and businesses can connect to the Internet.

OBJECTIVES

- Name the two organizations that created the network now known as the Internet.
- Explain, in basic terms, the importance of TCP/IP to the Internet.
- Describe the basic structure of the Internet.
- List the eight major services that the Internet provides to its users.
- Identify two key Internet-related features found in many software applications.

THE INTERNET: THEN AND NOW

No introduction to the Internet is complete without a short review of its history. Even though today's Internet bears little resemblance to its forebear of thirty years ago, it still functions in basically the same way. As you will see in the next few pages, the Internet has evolved into something different than the special-purpose, restricted-use network its planners originally envisioned.

The Beginning: A "Network of Networks"

The seeds of the Internet were planted in 1969, when the Advanced Research Projects Agency (ARPA) of the U.S. Department of Defense began connecting computers at different universities and defense contractors. The goal of this early project was to create a large computer network with multiple paths—in the form of telephone lines—that could survive a nuclear attack or other disaster. If one part of the network were destroyed, other parts of the network would remain functional because data could continue to flow through the surviving lines. ARPA also wanted users in remote locations to be able to share scarce computing resources.

Soon after the first links in **ARPANET** (as this early system was called) were in place, the engineers and scientists who had access to this system began exchanging messages and data that were beyond the scope of the Defense Department's original objectives. People also discovered that they could play long-distance games and socialize with other people who shared their interests. The users convinced ARPA that these unofficial uses were helping to test the network's capacity.

At first, ARPANET was basically a wide area network serving only a handful of users, but it expanded rapidly. Initially, the network included four primary host computers. A **host** is like a network server, providing services to other computers that connect to it. ARPANET's host computers (like those on today's Internet) provided file transfer and communications services and gave connected systems access to the network's high-speed data lines. The system grew quickly and spread widely as the number of hosts grew.

The network jumped across the Atlantic to Norway and England in 1973, and it never stopped growing. In the mid-1980s, another federal agency, the National Science Foundation (NSF), joined the project after the Defense Department dropped its funding. NSF established five "supercomputing centers" that were available to anyone who wanted to use them for academic research purposes.

The NSF expected the supercomputers' users to use ARPANET to obtain access, but the agency quickly discovered that the existing network could not handle the load. In response, the NSF created a new, higher capacity network, called **NSFnet,** to complement the older and by then overloaded ARPANET. The link between ARPANET, NSFnet, and other networks was called the **Internet.** (The process of connecting separate networks is called **internetworking.** A collection of "networked networks" is described as being internetworked, which is where the Internet—a worldwide network of networks—gets its name.)

NSFnet made Internet connections widely available for academic research, but the NSF did not permit users to conduct private business over the system. Therefore, several private telecommunications companies built their own network backbones that used the same set of networking protocols as NSFnet. Like a tree's trunk or an animal's spine, a network **backbone** is the central structure that connects other elements of the network (see Figure 19.1). These private portions of the

NORTON ONLINE

Visit **www.glencoe.com/norton/online/** for more information on the **history of the Internet.**

Internet were not limited by NSFnet's "appropriate use" restrictions, so it became possible to use the Internet to distribute business and commercial information.

Interconnections (known as gateways) between NSFnet and the private backbones allowed a user on any one of them to exchange data with all the others. Other gateways were created between the Internet and other networks, large and small, including some that used completely different networking protocols.

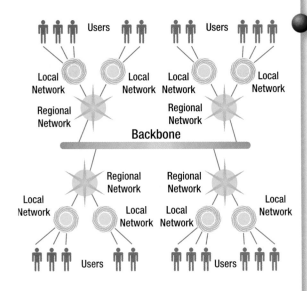

The original ARPANET was shut down in 1990, and government funding for NSFnet was discontinued in 1995, but the commercial Internet backbone services have easily replaced them. By the early 1990s, interest in the Internet began to expand dramatically. The system that had been created as a tool for surviving a nuclear war found its way into businesses and homes. Now, advertisements for movies are far more common online than collaborations on physics research.

Today: Still Growing

Today, the Internet connects thousands of networks and more than 100 million users around the world. It is a huge, cooperative community with no central ownership. This lack of ownership is an important feature of the Internet, because it means that no single person or group controls the network. Although there are several organizations (such as The Internet Society and the World Wide Web Consortium) that propose standards for Internet-related technologies and guidelines for its appropriate use, these organizations almost universally support the Internet's openness and lack of centralized control.

As a result, the Internet is open to anyone who can access it. If you can use a computer and if the computer is connected to the Internet, you are free not only to use the resources posted by others, but to create resources of your own; that is, you can publish documents on the World Wide Web, exchange e-mail messages, and perform many other tasks.

This openness has attracted tens of millions of users to the Internet. As of this writing, it was estimated that more than fifty countries had Internet access, and that more than 300 million people will have access to the Internet by the end of the year 2000. The number of actual users continues to climb dramatically, as shown in Figure 19.2.

Users are going online for a wide variety of reasons. A 1999 survey by Odyssey, L.P., showed that home computer users spent more than fifteen hours per week using the Internet and online services. In total, home users worldwide spent more than 1 billion hours each week using their computers, and more than half that time was spent online. Table 19.1 on page 342 shows the kinds of online activities people were most commonly engaged in as of July 1999.

Figure 19.2
The number of Internet users is expected to continue its dramatic increase for the foreseeable future.

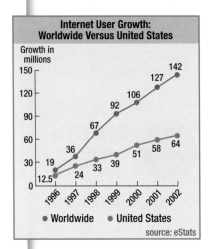

Table 19.1	Online Activities, Ranked by Popularity*

Activity	Percentage of Households Engaged in This Activity
E-mail	85
Research	78
Education	71
General surfing	67
News	67
Products/services	58
Health information	52
Investment information	49
Games	48
Shopping	48

*Includes Internet, WWW, and commercial online services as of July 1999.
Source: *Copyright 1999 internet.com Corporation. All rights reserved.*
Reprinted with permission from http://cyberatlas.internet.com

HOW THE INTERNET WORKS

The single most important fact to understand about the Internet is that it can potentially link your computer to any other computer. Anyone with access to the Internet can exchange text, data files, and programs with any other user. For all practical purposes, almost everything that happens across the Internet is a variation of one of these activities. The Internet itself is the pipeline that carries data between computers.

TCP/IP: The Universal Language of the Internet

The Internet works because every computer connected to it uses the same set of rules and procedures (known as protocols) to control timing and data format. The protocols used by the Internet are called **Transmission Control Protocol/Internet Protocol,** universally abbreviated as **TCP/IP.**

The TCP/IP protocols include the specifications that identify individual computers and that exchange data between computers. They also include rules for several categories of application programs, so programs that run on different kinds of computers can talk to one another. For example, someone using a Macintosh computer can exchange data with a UNIX computer on the Internet.

TCP/IP software looks different on different kinds of computers, but it always presents the same appearance to the network. It does not matter if the system at the other end of a connection is a supercomputer, a pocket-size personal communications device, or anything between; as long as it recognizes TCP/IP protocols, it can send and receive data through the Internet.

Routing Traffic Across the Internet

Most computers are not connected directly to the Internet. Rather, they are connected to smaller networks that connect to the Internet backbone through gateways.

NORTON
ONLINE

Visit **www.glencoe.com/norton/online/**
for more information on **TCP/IP.**

That fact is why the Internet is sometimes described as "a network of networks." Figure 19.3 shows a typical Internet connection.

The core of the Internet is the set of backbone connections that tie the local and regional networks together and the routing scheme that controls the way each piece of data finds its destination. In networking diagrams, the Internet backbone is often portrayed as a big cloud because the routing details are less important than the fact that the data passes through the Internet between the origin and the destination.

A description of the basic model for most Internet tools follows. A client application on a user's computer requests data through the network from a server. As you learned in Unit 9, a server is a powerful computer, generally containing a large hard disk, that acts as a shared storage resource. In addition to containing stored files, a server may also act as a gatekeeper for access to programs or data from other computers. The Internet includes many thousands of servers, each with its own unique address. These servers, in tandem with routers and bridges, do the work of storing and transferring data across the network.

Figure 19.3
In a typical Internet connection, individual computers connect to a local or regional network, which is connected in turn to the Internet backbone via a gateway.

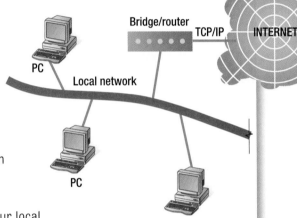

Because the Internet creates a potential connection between any two computers, however, the data may be forced to take a long, circuitous route to reach its destination. Suppose, for example, that you request data from a server in another state:

1. Your request must be broken into packets. (For a detailed explanation of packets, see Lesson 17, "Networking Basics.")

2. The packets are routed through your local network, and possibly through one or more subsequent networks, to the Internet backbone.

3. After leaving the backbone, the packets are then routed through one or more networks until they reach the appropriate server and are reassembled into the complete request.

4. Once the destination server receives your request, it begins sending you the requested data, which winds its way back to you—possibly over a different route.

Between the destination server and your PC, the request and data may travel through several different servers, each helping to forward the packets to their final destination.

Addressing Schemes—IP and DNS Addresses

Internet activity can be defined as computers communicating with one another using the common "language" of TCP/IP. Examples include the following:

◆ A client system (such as your home computer) communicating with an Internet server.

◆ An Internet server computer communicating with a client computer.

◆ Two server computers communicating with one another.

◆ Two client computers communicating via one or more servers.

The computer that originates a transaction must identify its intended destination with a unique address. Every computer on the Internet has a four-part numeric address, called the **Internet protocol address (IP address),** which contains routing information that identifies its location. Each of the four parts is a number between 0 and 255, so an IP address looks like this: 205.46.117.104

Computers have no trouble working with long strings of numbers, but humans are not so skilled. Therefore, most computers on the Internet (except those used exclusively for internal routing and switching) also have an address called a **domain name system (DNS) address**—an address that uses words rather than numbers.

Domains and Subdomains

DNS addresses have two parts: a host name (a name for a computer connected to the Internet) followed by a **domain** that generally identifies the type of institution that uses the address. This type of domain name is often called a **top-level domain.** For example, many companies have a DNS address whose first part is the company name, followed by ".com"—the now-overused marketing gimmick. Table 19.2 lists the most common types of Internet domains used within the United States.

Table 19.2	Internet Domains	
Domain	**Type of Organization**	**Example**
.com	Business (commercial)	ibm.com (International Business Machines Corp.)
.edu	Educational	centre.edu (Centre College, Danville, KY)
.gov	Government	whitehouse.gov (The White House)
.mil	Military	navy.mil (The United States Navy)
.net	Gateway or host (or business/commercial)	mindspring.net (Mindspring, a regional Internet service provider)
.org	Other organization (typically nonprofit)	isoc.org (The Internet Society)

Some large institutions and corporations divide their domain addresses into smaller **subdomains.** For example, a business with many branches might have a subdomain for each office—such as boston.widgets.com and newyork.widgets.com. You might also see some subdomains broken into even smaller sub-subdomains, like evolution.genetics.washington.edu.

In 1996, the Internet Assigned Numbers Authority (IANA) and the Internet Society began an organized movement to create an additional set of top-level Internet domain names. This action was necessary because many companies and private groups were finding it difficult to devise a suitable domain name for their Internet sites. There was only so much room in the "com" domain, and some companies found that their name or product name was already being used in someone else's Internet address.

The group's goal was to expand the list of top-level domains to make it easier for organizations of all kinds to create an Internet domain for themselves. Together with representatives of several agencies interested in the management of the global domain name system, the group developed the Generic Top-Level Domain Memorandum of Understanding (abbreviated as gTLD-MoU). This memorandum spells out proposals for the future management of Internet domains and proposes seven new top-level domain names for future use (see Table 19.3).

Outside the United States (although many institutions and businesses in the United States are starting to use this same address scheme), domains usually identify the country in which the system is located, such as .ca for Canada or .fr for France. Sometimes,

Visit **www.glencoe.com/norton/online/** for more information on **IP addresses, domains** and the **domain name system.**

a geographic domain address will also include a subdomain that identifies the district within the larger domain. For example, Mindlink is a commercial Internet service provider in the Canadian province of British Columbia. Its DNS address is mindlink.bc.ca. Some United States institutions such as colleges and elementary schools use the same expanded address scheme. For example, some community colleges include *cc* in their DNS address, whereas some schools include *K12* in their address.

Table 19.3	Additional Proposed Top-Level Domain Names

Domain	Type of Organization
.firm	Businesses or firms (equivalent to .com)
.shop	Business that offer items for purchase over the Internet
.web	Organizations involved in Web-related activities
.arts	Organizations promoting artistic or entertainment activities over the Internet
.rec	Organizations promoting recreational activities over the Internet
.info	Organizations that provide informational services over the Internet
.nom	Individual, family, or personal "nomenclature" (such as a personalized Internet address)

MAJOR FEATURES OF THE INTERNET

The technical details that make the Internet work are only part of the story. The reason that so many people use the Internet has more to do with content than connectivity. A huge amount of information is available today through the Internet.

As a business tool, the Internet has many uses. Electronic mail is an efficient and inexpensive way to send and receive messages and documents around the world within minutes. The World Wide Web is becoming both an important advertising medium and a channel for distributing software, documents, and information services. As channels for business research, the databases and other information archives that exist online are often better and more up-to-date than any library. The Internet has also created hundreds of "virtual communities" made up of people who share an interest in a technical discipline, hobby, or political or social movement.

To use any of these services, you need a computer that is connected to the Internet in some way. Most individual users connect their computer's modem to a telephone line and set up an account with an **Internet service provider (ISP),** which provides local or regional access to the Internet backbone. Many other users connect to the Internet through a school or business LAN. These methods of connecting to the Internet are discussed later in this unit. The following sections introduce some of the most popular features of the Internet.

The World Wide Web

The **World Wide Web** (the **Web** or **WWW**) was created in 1989 at the European Particle Physics Laboratory in Geneva, Switzerland, as a method for incorporating footnotes, figures, and cross-references into online hypertext documents. A hypertext document is a specially encoded file that uses the **hypertext markup language (HTML).** This language allows a document's author to embed **hypertext links** (also called **hyperlinks** or just **links**) in the document. Hypertext links are the foundation of the World Wide Web.

As you read a hypertext document—more commonly called a **Web page**—on screen, you can click a word or picture encoded as a hypertext link and immediately jump

NORTON
ONLINE

Visit **www.glencoe.com/norton/online/** for more information on **HTML** and the **World Wide Web**.

to another location within the same document or to a different Web page (see Figure 19.4). The second page may be located on the same computer as the original page or anywhere else on the Internet. Because the user does not have to learn separate commands and addresses to jump to a new location, the World Wide Web organizes widely scattered resources into a seamless whole.

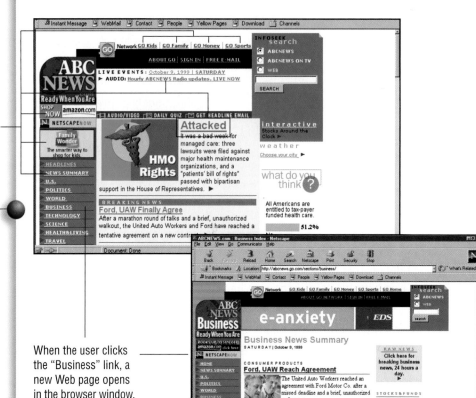

Examples of hyperlinks

Figure 19.4
This is an example of a typical Web site. The user can click one of the hyperlinked text lines or images to jump to a different location in the same site, or to a different site on the Web.

When the user clicks the "Business" link, a new Web page opens in the browser window.

A collection of related Web pages is called a **Web site.** Web sites are housed on **Web servers,** Internet host computers that often store thousands of individual pages. Copying a page onto a server is called **posting** the page, but the process may also be referred to as publishing or uploading. (The term *posting* is also used when other types of documents are placed on Internet host computers, such as posting an article in a newsgroup.)

Popular Web sites (such as those managed by CNN, USA Today, and ESPN) receive millions of **hits** or **page views** every day. When you visit a Web page—that is, download a page from the Web server to your computer for viewing—the act is commonly called "hitting" the Web site. Many Web masters measure their sites' success by the number of hits they receive in a given timeframe (see Figure 19.5). A **Web master** is a person or group responsible for designing and maintaining a Web site.

Figure 19.5
Many Web pages feature a hit counter, like this one, to display the number of times the page has been viewed.

You are visitor Number 138428 to this page!

Web pages are now used to distribute news, interactive educational services, product information and catalogs, highway traffic reports, and live audio and video, among many other items. Interactive Web pages permit readers to consult databases, order products and information, and submit payment with a credit card or other account number.

You may hear the terms *World Wide Web* and *Internet* used interchangeably, as though they are the same. However, the Web is simply one part of the Internet— a type of service available to persons who can access the Internet's resources.

Web Browsers and HTML Tags

The Web was an interesting but not particularly exciting tool used by scientific researchers—until 1993, when Mosaic, a point-and-click Web browser, was developed at the National Center for Supercomputing Applications (NCSA) at the University of Illinois. A **Web browser** (or **browser**) is a software application designed to find hypertext documents on the Web and then open the documents on the user's computer. A point-and-click browser provides a graphical user interface that enables the user to click graphical objects and hyperlinks. Several text-based Web browsers are also available and are used in non-GUI operating systems, such as certain versions of UNIX. Mosaic and the Web browsers that have evolved from it have changed the way people use the Internet. The most popular browsers are Microsoft's Internet Explorer and Netscape Navigator.

A Web browser displays a Web page as specified by the page's underlying HTML code. The code provides the browser with the following information:

◆ The fonts and font sizes used in the page

◆ Where and how to display graphical images

◆ Whether sound, animation, or other special types of content are included in the page and how to display them

◆ The location of hypertext links and where to go if the user clicks a link

◆ Whether special programming codes, which the browser needs to interpret, are used in the page

To format a document in HTML, a designer places **HTML tags** throughout the document. The tags, which are enclosed in angle brackets (<>), tell the browser how to display individual elements on the page. (The HTML codes are hidden unless you display them in the browser window or in another application.)

HTML tags are placed around the portions of the document they affect. Therefore, most tags have a starting tag, such as <H1>, and an ending tag, such as </H1>. A slash indicates an ending tag. The formatting begins with the starting tag and continues to the ending tag. This placement of tags permits precise formatting control within a document (see Figures 19.6 and 19.7). Tags can also be grouped: multiple starting and ending tags can be placed around the same portion of a document.

Figure 19.6
A simple HTML document. The "strong" tag tells the browser to display the enclosed text in a bold font.

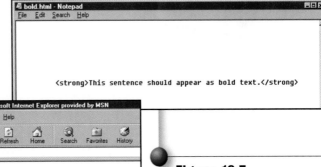

Figure 19.7
The document, opened in a Web browser. The text appears in bold.

HTTP and URLs

The internal structure of the World Wide Web is built on a set of rules called **Hypertext transfer protocol (HTTP).** HTTP uses Internet addresses in a special format, called a **uniform resource locator (URL).** URLs look like this:

type://address/path/

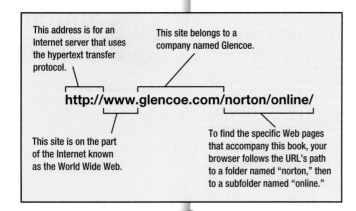

This address is for an Internet server that uses the hypertext transfer protocol.

This site belongs to a company named Glencoe.

http://www.glencoe.com/norton/online/

This site is on the part of the Internet known as the World Wide Web.

To find the specific Web pages that accompany this book, your browser follows the URL's path to a folder named "norton," then to a subfolder named "online."

Figure 19.8
Parts of a typical URL.

In a URL, *type* specifies the type of server in which the file is located, *address* is the address of the server, and *path* is the location within the file structure of the server. The path includes the list of folders (or directories) where the desired file is located. Consider the URL for this book's Web site—http://www.glencoe .com/norton/online/—as shown in Figure 19.8.

If you were looking for a document named *Welcome* at this Web site, its URL might be the following:

http://www.glencoe.com/norton
/online/welcome.html

Files in other formats may also have URLs. For example, look at the URL for the SunSite FTP archive of PC software at the University of North Carolina:

ftp://sunsite.unc.edu/pub/micro/pc-stuff/

Note that when a URL ends with a folder name rather than a file, the URL includes a final slash (/). Because they lead to specific documents on a server's disk, URLs can be extremely long. But every single document on the World Wide Web has its own unique URL (see Figure 19.9).

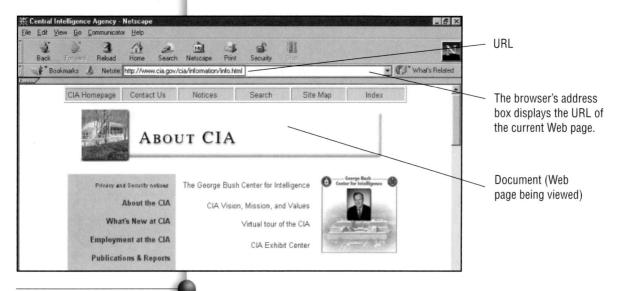

URL

The browser's address box displays the URL of the current Web page.

Document (Web page being viewed)

Figure 19.9
Each Web page has its own unique URL, which directs your browser to the document's location.

As shown in Figure 19.10, you use URLs to navigate the Web in two ways:

A. Type the URL for a Web site in the address box of your browser. For example, if you want to visit the Web site of the Internal Revenue Service, click in the browser's address box (to place an insertion point there) and type as follows:

http://www.irs.gov/

B. Click a hyperlinked word or image, and your browser automatically finds and loads the Web page indicated by the hyperlink. (When you point to a hyperlink, the browser's status bar displays the URL that the link leads to.)

Home Pages

You probably have heard the term **home page** used to reference a page named index.htm on a Web site. This term is important and actually has two meanings:

NORTON
ONLINE

Visit **www.glencoe.com/norton/online/** for more information on **HTTP** and **URLs**.

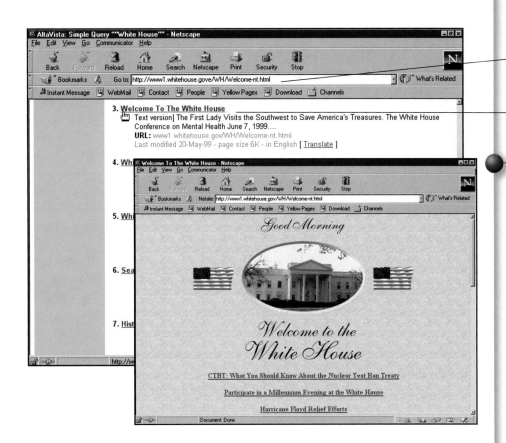

You can type the desired Web page's URL here, and then press Enter.

You can click a hyperlink.

Figure 19.10
You can move from one Web page to another by specifying a URL or clicking a hyperlink. Both navigation methods take you to the same place.

◆ **Personalized Start Page.** On your computer, you can choose a Web page that opens immediately when you launch your Web browser by using a command in your browser to specify the URL for the desired page. This **personalized start page** can be on your computer's hard drive or a page from any Web site. For example, if you want to see today's copy of USA Today Online when you launch your browser, use the address **http://www.usatoday.com/** as your personal home page.

◆ **Web Site Home Page.** A Web site's primary page is also called its home page. This page is the first one you see when you type the site's basic URL. From this page, you can navigate to other pages on the Web site (and possibly to other sites). For example, if you type the URL **http://www.cnn.com/** into your browser's address box, the CNN home page opens in your browser window.

Choosing a start page is a personal decision, based on the kinds of information you want to see when you open your browser. You can use a word processor or HTML editor to create your own personalized start page containing links to your favorite Web sites.

Helper Applications and Multimedia Content

As versatile as they are, Web browsers alone cannot display every type of content now available on the Web, especially multimedia content. Many Web sites now feature audio and video content, including full-motion animation and movies. These large files require special applications in order to be played in real time across the Web. Because these applications help the browser by being "plugged in" at the right moment, they are called **helper applications** or **plug-in applications.**

Plug-ins are used to support several types of content, including **streaming audio** and **streaming video.** Streaming technology works by sending the audio or video

Visit **www.glencoe.com/norton/online/** for more information on **helper applications** for browsers, **streaming audio,** and **streaming video.**

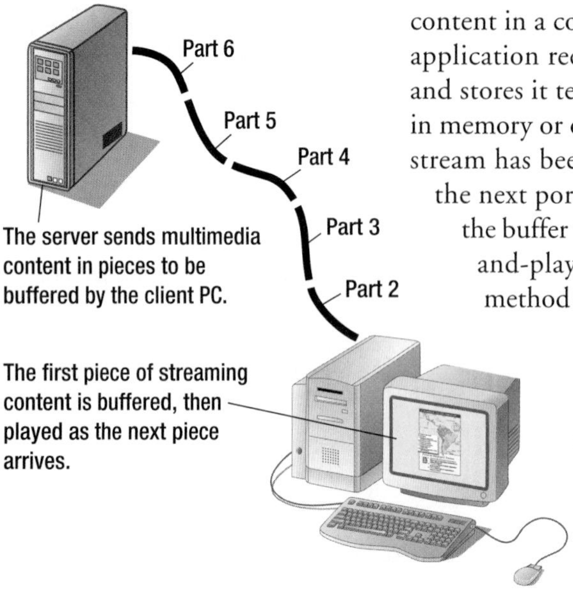

Figure 19.11
By streaming audio and video content from the server to the client (the user's PC), multimedia plug-in applications enable you to watch movies and listen to high-quality audio.

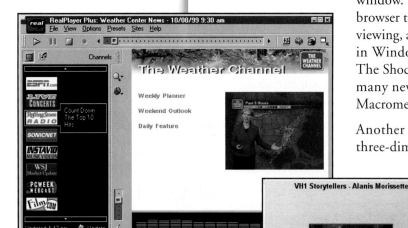

Part 6
Part 5
Part 4
Part 3
Part 2

The server sends multimedia content in pieces to be buffered by the client PC.

The first piece of streaming content is buffered, then played as the next piece arrives.

content in a continuous stream. The plug-in application receives a portion of the stream and stores it temporarily in a buffer (an area in memory or on disk). After a portion of the stream has been buffered, it is played while the next portion of the stream is stored in the buffer (see Figure 19.11). This buffer-and-play technique is an effective method for playing a large file quickly without waiting for the entire file to download. Multimedia plug-in applications also use file compression to move the process even faster. Even so, multimedia files can take much longer to download than typical HTML documents.

There is a tremendous array of multimedia content available on the Web. For example, sites like broadcast.com, netradio.com, and even Microsoft provide access to radio stations from around the world in addition to Internet-only radio. Television channels such as CNN and The Weather Channel also deliver their audio and video content over the Web. Using plug-in applications such as Microsoft's Windows Media Player, Apple's QuickTime Player, or RealNetworks' RealPlayer, you can play any of these sources on your desktop (see Figure 19.12).

One of the most commonly used plug-in applications is made by Macromedia, Inc. This tool, called Shockwave, enables Web designers to create high-quality animation or video, complete with audio, that plays directly within the browser window. These types of animation do not require the browser to **spawn** (launch) an external application for viewing, as is the case with multimedia types displayed in Windows Media Player, QuickTime, and others. The Shockwave Player is essential if you want to view many newer Web sites and is available free from the Macromedia Web site (**www.macromedia.com/**).

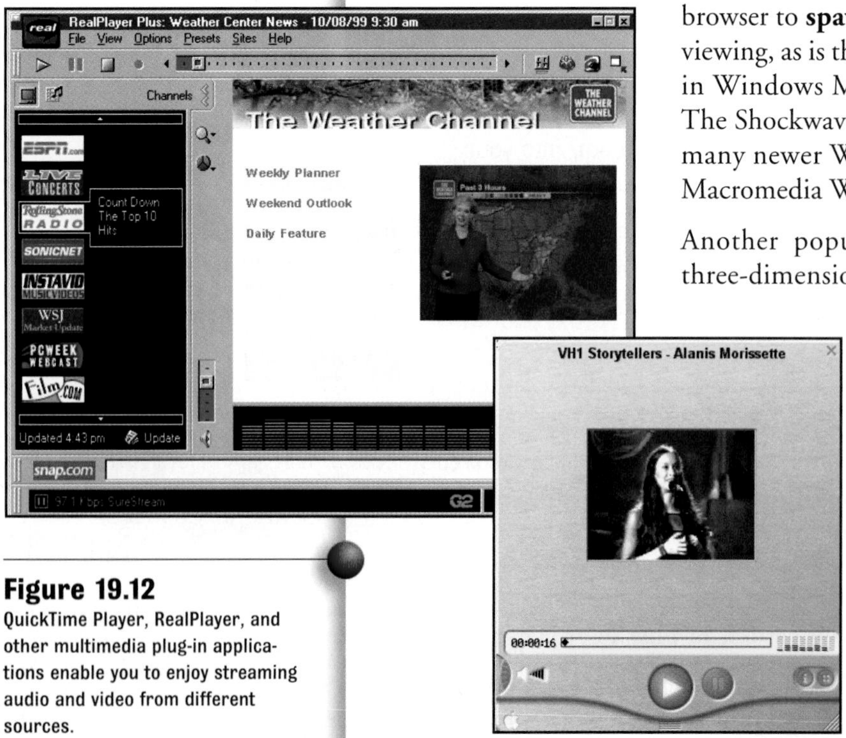

Another popular type of multimedia content is three-dimensional (3-D) animation. By using a plug-in application to add 3-D viewing capabilities to your browser, you can visit 3-D worlds filled with buildings, landscapes, and animated characters, and navigate them as you would a video game. Using 3-D technology over the Web, manufacturers enable customers to take a close look at products, view the interiors of cars and buildings, and play games. With technologies such as **virtual reality modeling language (VRML),** Web designers

Figure 19.12
QuickTime Player, RealPlayer, and other multimedia plug-in applications enable you to enjoy streaming audio and video from different sources.

PRODUCTIVITY Tip

Portals: Your Own Front Door to the Web

A Web portal is a free, personalized start page, hosted by a Web content provider, that you can personalize in several ways. Your personalized portal can provide various content and links that simply cannot be found in typical corporate Web sites. By design, a portal offers two advantages over a typical personal home page:

◆ **Rich, Dynamic Content.** Your portal can include many different types of information and graphics, including news, sports, weather, entertainment news, financial information, multiple search engines, chat room access, e-mail, and more. If you leave your browser open for long periods, you can refresh the page and view any updated content that may have changed since you last checked it.

◆ **Customization.** You can customize a portal page by selecting the types of information you want to view. Many portal sites allow you to view information from specific sources, such as CNN, Time, Slate, the Weather Channel, and others. Some portals even provide streaming multimedia content, such as sound bites, music videos, or news clips. You also can choose the hyperlinks that will appear in your portal, making it easy to jump to other favorite sites. Most portal sites let you change your custom selections whenever you want.

To set up a portal, visit a site that provides portal services; several are listed at the end of this feature. Look for a link such as "Personalize," "My . . . ," or "Make This Your Home Page." Click the link and a list of instructions and options will appear. Pick the options you want and follow the directions to save your selections.

Explore several portal sites to find the options you like best. As you customize your portal, remember two points:

The Microsoft Network (MSN) is one of several Web sites offering portal services. You can select from a list of options to customize your own portal.

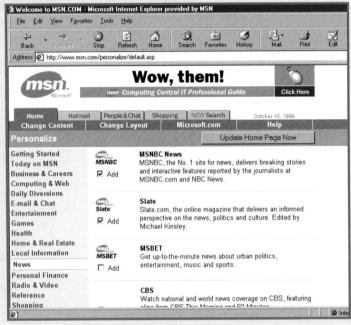

◆ The more options you choose, the longer the portal page will take to open in your browser. Be selective.

◆ To save your preferences and use them in the future, your portal will create a cookie and leave it on your computer's disk. A cookie is a small file that contains setting information, and it must reside on your system. Be careful not to delete this cookie, or your portal's settings will be lost. Cookies are not harmful to your system, and the portal provider will not use the cookie to retrieve personal information from your computer.

Here are a few Web sites that provide portal services. Remember, the list is growing and options change constantly, so look at several sites before choosing one.

Microsoft Network—**http://www.msn.com/**
Netscape Netcenter—**http://www.netscape.com/**
Excite—**http://www.excite.com/**
Yahoo—**http://www.yahoo.com/**
Snap—**http://www.snap.com/**

NORTON ONLINE

Visit **www.glencoe.com/norton/online/** for more information on **Web portals**.

are creating virtual worlds for Web users to explore (see Figure 19.13). To visit VRML-enabled Web sites, you need either a VRML browser or a VRML plug-in application (the more common choice) for your standard browser. Several VRML plug-ins are available free, including Live3D, Cosmo Player, and others.

Finding Content With a Search Engine

Without a directory of some sort to help you find the right information on the Web, you could literally spend hours going from one Web site to another trying to find what you need. Fortunately, several specialized Web sites, called **search engines,** use powerful data-searching techniques to discover the type of content available on the Web. By using a search engine and specifying your topic of interest, you can find the right site or information. For example, if you need to find information on Aristotle, you can visit a search engine site such as Alta Vista or Lycos and type *Aristotle* in the site's Search box. The engine will provide you with a list of sites that should match your criterion (see Figure 19.14). For more detailed instructions on using search engines, see Appendix B, "Using Web-based Search Tools." Table 19.4 lists a few of the most popular search engines on the Web.

Figure 19.14
The Alta Vista search engine found more than 92,000 Web pages containing information relating to the term *Aristotle.*

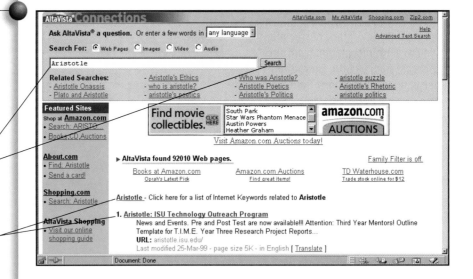

Type a term in the Search For box; then click the Search button.

You can click a category or site to jump to it.

Visit **www.glencoe.com/norton/online/** for more information on **search engines** and **e-mail.**

Electronic Mail (E-Mail)

To create, send, and receive e-mail, you need an **e-mail program** (also called an **e-mail client**) and an Internet connection through an ISP or LAN. Most e-mail programs permit users to attach data files and program files to messages. For example, you can send a message to a friend and attach a word processing document or some other file to the message. The recipient can then open and use the document on his or her computer. Popular Internet e-mail programs include Eudora, Microsoft Outlook, and Netscape Messenger, among others.

Table 19.4 **Popular Web Search Engines**

Name	URL	Name	URL
Alta Vista	http://www.altavista.com/	Yahoo!	http://www.yahoo.com/
Excite	http://www.excite.com/	Google	http://www.google.com/
Hotbot	http://www.hotbot.com/	Metacrawler	http://www.metacrawler.com/
Snap	http://www.snap.com/	Dogpile	http://www.dogpile.com/
The Big Hub	http://www.thebighub.com/	Mining Co.	http://www.miningco.com/
Webcrawler	http://www.webcrawler.com/	Pathfinder	http://www.pathfinder.com/

E-Mail Addresses

If you have an account with an ISP or if you are a user on a corporate or school LAN, then you can establish an **e-mail address.** This unique address enables other users to send messages to you and enables you to send messages to others.

As mentioned earlier, DNS addresses and numeric IP addresses identify individual computers on the Internet. Any single computer might have many separate users, however, and each user must have an account on that computer. A user can set up such an account by specifying a unique **user name.** Some of the largest domains, such as America Online (aol.com) may have millions of different users, each with his or her own user name.

When you send a message to a person rather than a computer, you must include that person's user name in the address. The standard format is the user name first, separated from the DNS address by an "at" symbol (@). For example, suppose you have a friend named John Smith who works (and has an e-mail account) at a company called Widgets, Inc. If the company's DNS address is widgets.com, then John Smith's e-mail address might be

jsmith@widgets.com

You read this address as "J Smith at widgets dot com." Figure 19.15 shows how addresses are used in e-mail programs.

When you send an e-mail message, the message is stored on a server until the recipient can retrieve it. This type of server is called a **mail server.** Many mail servers use the **post office protocol** and are called **POP servers.** Nearly all ISPs and corporate LANs maintain one or more mail servers.

Encryption tool

Sender's address

Recipient's address

Toolbar for formatting message.

Figure 19.15
User addresses enable people to send and receive e-mail messages over the Internet. Most e-mail programs provide tools for formatting messages and encoding them for security.

Listserv Systems

Besides the one-to-one messages that are popular on both the Internet and LAN e-mail systems, Internet e-mail is also used for one-to-many messages, in which the same set of messages goes to a list of many names. One type of mailing list that uses e-mail

NORTON ONLINE

Visit **www.glencoe.com/norton/online/** for more information on **listserv** systems.

is an automated list server, or **listserv.** Listserv systems allow users on the list to post their own messages, so the result is an ongoing discussion. Hundreds of mailing-list discussions are in progress all the time on a huge variety of topics. For example, there are mailing lists for producers of radio drama, makers of apple cider, and members of individual college classes who want to keep up with news from their old classmates.

Self Check

Answer the following questions by filling in the blank(s).

1. The network that eventually became the Internet was first called _____ .

2. Every computer on the Internet has a numeric address called its _____ .

3. Hypertext links are more commonly called _____ .

News

In addition to the messages distributed to mailing lists by e-mail, the Internet also supports a form of public bulletin board called **news.** As of this writing, there were more than 45,000 **newsgroups,** each devoted to discussion of a particular topic. Many of the most widely distributed newsgroups are part of a system called **Usenet,** but others are targeted to a particular region or to users connected to a specific network or institution, such as a university or a large corporation.

To participate in a newsgroup, users post **articles** (short messages) about the newsgroup's main topic. As users read and respond to one another's articles, they create a **thread** of linked articles. By reading the articles in a thread, you can see the message that initiated the discussion and all the messages that have been posted in response to it.

A **newsreader** program—the client software—obtains articles from a **news server,** a host computer that exchanges articles with other servers through the Internet. Because these servers use the **network news transfer protocol,** they are sometimes called **NNTP servers.** To participate in newsgroups, you must run a newsreader program to log on to a server. Most ISPs provide access to a news server as part of an Internet account.

To see articles that have been posted about a specific topic, you can **subscribe** to the newsgroup that addresses that topic. Newsgroups are organized into major categories, called domains, and categorized by individual topics

Table 19.5	Common Usenet Domains

Domain	Description
comp	Computer-related topics
sci	Science and technology (except computers)
soc	Social issues and politics
news	Topics related to Usenet
rec	Hobbies, arts, and recreational activities
misc	Topics that do not fit into one of the other domains

The most important alternative topics include the following:

Domain	Description
alt	Alternative newsgroups
bionet	Biological sciences
biz	Business topics, including advertisements
clari	News from the Associated Press and Reuters, supplied through a service called Clarinet
k12	Newsgroups for primary and secondary schools

within each domain. There are several major domains within the Usenet structure and many more alternative domains. Table 19.5 lists the major Usenet domains.

The name of a newsgroup begins with the domain, followed by one or more words that describe the group's topic, such as alt.food. Some topics include separate newsgroups for related subtopics, such as alt.food.chocolate. Newsgroup names can be quite long. As Figure 19.16 shows, subscribing to a newsgroup is a three-step process. Figure 19.17 shows a series of articles and responses that make up a thread.

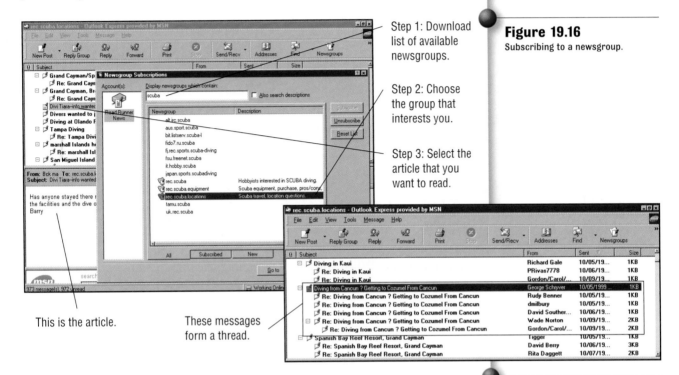

Step 1: Download list of available newsgroups.

Step 2: Choose the group that interests you.

Step 3: Select the article that you want to read.

This is the article.

These messages form a thread.

Figure 19.16
Subscribing to a newsgroup.

Figure 19.17
A series of articles and responses create a thread, or ongoing discussion, in a newsgroup.

To subscribe, you must download a list of available newsgroups from the server, choose the groups that interest you, and select articles. In most newsreaders, you can choose to reply to an article by posting another article to the newsgroup or by sending a private e-mail message to the person who wrote the original article.

Newsgroups are a relatively fast way to distribute information to potentially interested readers, and they allow people to discuss topics of common interest. They can also be a convenient channel for finding answers to questions. Many questions are asked again and again, so it is always a good idea to read the articles that other people have posted before you jump in with your own questions. Members of many newsgroups post lists of **frequently asked questions (FAQs)** and their answers every month or two.

Remember that, although newsgroups can be a source of information, there is no fact-checking process for newsgroups. Thus, newsgroups are also one of the biggest sources of misinformation and rumors on the Internet. Be careful about the information you choose as reliable. To combat this problem, some newsgroups are overseen by a **moderator**—someone who sorts through articles before they are posted and weeds out those that are obviously meant to misinform, spread rumors, or insult someone.

Telnet—Remote Access to Distant Computers

Telnet is the Internet tool for using one computer to access a second computer. Using Telnet, you can send commands that run programs and open text or

Visit **www.glencoe.com/norton/online/** for more information on Internet newsgroups.

Figure 19.18

A Telnet connection to a library catalog. The user is searching for magazine and journal articles on the subject of hypertension.

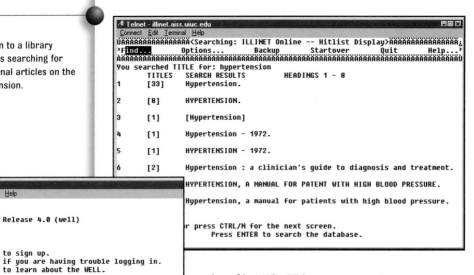

```
Telnet - illinet.aiss.uiuc.edu                              _ □ ×
Connect  Edit  Terminal  Help
ŪĀĀĀĀĀĀĀĀĀĀĀĀĀĀĀ<Searching: ILLINET Online -- Hitlist Display>ĀĀĀĀĀĀĀĀĀĀĀĀĀĀ¿
³Find...        Options...      Backup      Startover      Quit       Help...³
ĀĀĀĀĀĀĀĀĀĀĀĀĀĀĀĀĀĀĀĀĀĀĀĀĀĀĀĀĀĀĀĀĀĀĀĀĀĀĀĀĀĀĀĀĀĀĀĀĀĀĀĀĀĀĀĀĀĀĀĀĀĀĀĀĀĀĀĀĀĀĀĀĀÛ
You searched TITLE for: hypertension
        TITLES   SEARCH RESULTS        HEADINGS 1 - 8
1       [33]     Hypertension.

2       [8]      HYPERTENSION.

3       [1]      [Hypertension]

4       [1]      Hypertension - 1972.

5       [1]      HYPERTENSION - 1972.

6       [2]      Hypertension : a clinician's guide to diagnosis and treatment.

        HYPERTENSION, A MANUAL FOR PATENT WITH HIGH BLOOD PRESSURE.

        Hypertension, a manual for patients with high blood pressure.

 r press CTRL/N for the next screen.
        Press ENTER to search the database.
```

Figure 19.19

A Telnet connection to an online conference service.

```
Telnet - well.com                                           
Connect  Edit  Terminal  Help

UNIX(r) System V Release 4.0 (well)

This is the WELL

Type   newuser   to sign up.
Type   trouble   if you are having trouble logging in.
Type   guest     to learn about the WELL.

If you already have a WELL account, type your username.

login: █
```

data files. The Telnet program is a transparent window between your own computer and a distant host system—a computer that you are logging on to. The computer is in a different physical place, but it is as if you are sitting in front of it and operating it. A Telnet connection sends input from your keyboard to the host and displays text from the host on your screen.

Connecting to a Telnet host is easy; enter the address, and the Telnet program sets up a connection. When you see a log-on message from the host, you can send an account name and password to start an operating session. Access to some Telnet hosts is limited to users with permission from the owner of the host, but many other hosts offer access to members of the general Internet public.

Telnet connections are useful for many purposes. For example, Figure 19.18 shows a Telnet connection to a library's online catalog. You can obtain information about books in the library's collection over the Internet as easily as you could from the library's own reference room. Another common use for Telnet is to provide access to online conferences that are not part of Usenet, such as the one in Figure 19.19.

FTP

You can use Telnet to operate a distant computer by remote control through the Internet, but sometimes there is no substitute for having your own copy of a program or data file. **File transfer protocol (FTP)** is the Internet tool used to copy files from one computer to another.

When a user has accounts on more than one computer, FTP can be used to transfer data or programs between them. Public FTP archives will permit anyone to make copies of their files. These **FTP sites** are housed on **FTP servers**—archives often containing thousands of individual programs and files. Anyone can download and use these files by using special **FTP client software** (see Figure 19.20). Because these public archives usually require visitors to use the word "anonymous" as an account name, they are known as **anonymous FTP archives.**

Figure 19.20

Here is a popular FTP client program named WS_FTP LE. It is being used to transfer a file named assist.exe from Microsoft's anonymous FTP site (the remote site) to the user's computer (the local system).

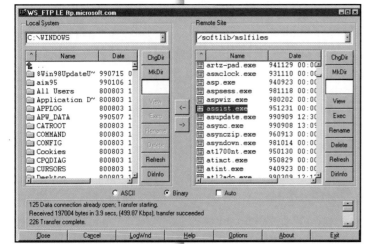

It is not always necessary to use an FTP client to download files from an FTP site. Web browsers also support FTP. In fact, if you visit a Web site such as Microsoft (**www.microsoft.com/**) or Macromedia (**www.macromedia.com/**), you can download programs and data files directly onto your computer through your Web browser. This type of file transfer usually is an FTP operation and is available through many different Web sites.

FTP sites provide access to many different types of files. You can find information of all kinds, from weather maps to magazine articles, housed on these systems. Computer hardware and software companies frequently host their own FTP sites, where you can copy program updates, bug solutions, and other types of software.

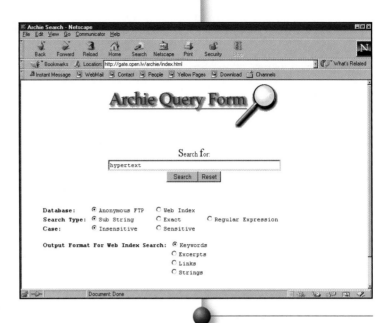

Figure 19.21
Web sites like this one enable you to use Archie to search for files on the Internet. Here, the user is searching for files related to the keyword *hypertext*.

Although FTP is easy to use, it can be hard to find a file that you want to download. One way to find files is to use **Archie,** the searchable index of FTP archives maintained by McGill University in Montreal. (Archie is a nickname for archives.) The main Archie server at McGill gathers copies of the directories from more than 1000 other public FTP archives every month and distributes copies of those directories to dozens of other servers around the world. When a server receives a request for a keyword search, it returns a list of files that match the search criteria and the location of each file. Many FTP client programs provide Archie search tools, and some Web sites enable you to conduct Archie searches through your Web browser (see Figure 19.21).

Internet Relay Chat (IRC)

Internet relay chat (IRC), or just **chat,** is a popular way for Internet users to communicate in real-time with other users. Real-time communication means communicating with other users in the immediate present. Unlike e-mail, chat does not require a waiting period between the time you send a message and the time the other person or group of people receives the message. IRC is often referred to as the "CB radio" of the Internet because it enables a few or many people to join a discussion.

IRC is a multi-user system where people join channels to talk publicly or privately. **Channels** are discussion groups where chat users convene to discuss a topic. Chat messages are typed on a user's computer and sent to the IRC channel, where all users who have joined that channel receive the message. Users can then read, reply to, or ignore that message or create their own message (see Figure 19.22).

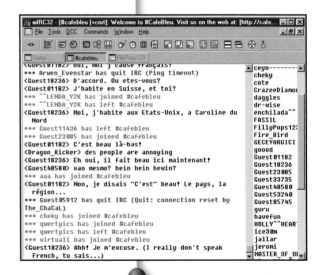

Figure 19.22
A chat in progress. In this chat program (mIRC), the discussions appear in the lefthand pane, and the participants' names appear on the right.

IRC became popular in the news during the 1991 Persian Gulf War. Updates from around the world came across the wire, and most IRC users who were online at the time gathered on a single channel to read those reports. Similarly, live reports of the coup attempt against Boris Yeltsin in September 1993 were communicated by Moscow IRC.

Figure 19.23

Many Web sites, including MSN, CNN, and others, provide chat rooms for visitors. At these sites, you can chat without navigating channels or using special chat software.

Visit **www.glencoe.com/norton/online/** for more information on **Telnet**, **FTP**, **Archie**, and **IRC**.

Another twist on chat is **instant messenger** software. Using instant messenger software—like America Online's Instant Messenger, Microsoft's MSN Messenger Service, or Mirabilis' ICQ, you can set up "buddy lists" of people with whom you like to chat. When you and a buddy are online at the same time, you can open a new window on your computer and begin a private chat session. For example, ICQ can notify you when a buddy goes online, so you can begin chatting. Instant messenger applications are gaining popularity because they give users more control over their chatting environment than traditional IRC channels, which are open to anyone who wants to join. Chat rooms are also an increasingly popular addition to Web sites, which makes it possible to participate in chat sessions directly within a Web browser window without installing or running special chat software (see Figure 19.23).

ONLINE SERVICES

An **online service** is a company that offers access, generally on a subscription basis, to e-mail, discussion groups, databases on various subjects (such as weather information, stock quotes, newspaper articles, and so on), and other services ranging from electronic banking and investing to online games. Online services also offer access to the Internet, functioning as an ISP to their subscribers. The most popular online services are America Online, CompuServe, and Prodigy.

In addition to Internet access, online services offer other features that typical ISPs do not. For example, America Online has become famous for its casual chat rooms, and CompuServe is probably best known for its discussion forums geared to technically oriented users. These activities do not take place on the Internet, where everyone can access them. Rather, these services are provided only for the online services' subscribers. Discussion groups hosted by online services are often monitored by a **system operator,** or **sysop,** who ensures that participants follow the rules. Users typically pay by the month; the subscription allows them to use the service for a limited number of hours per month. If they use the service for more time, they pay by the hour. Subscriptions with unlimited hours are also available.

Although the biggest online services are general in content and offer many features, others are much more specialized, offering access to specific databases. Perhaps the best known is LEXIS-NEXIS, a company that sells access to its two databases. LEXIS© is a legal database that researchers can use to find specific laws and court opinions. NEXIS© is a bibliographic database that contains information about articles on a wide range of topics.

INTERNET-RELATED FEATURES IN APPLICATION PROGRAMS

To access most of the services on the Internet, you can use stand-alone applications such as the Web browsers, e-mail clients, and other types of software described so far. However, many popular productivity applications now feature various Internet-related tools. These features enable you to perform two types of tasks:

- Retrieve content from the Internet as though it were just another disk on your computer.
- Create content for posting on the Web or sending to another person as an e-mail message.

Retrieving Content

By creating Internet-aware applications, software designers try to make the Internet as accessible and useful as your computer's hard disk. Applications enable you to access the Web without manually switching to a browser, for example, or load a document from the Internet as though it were on your hard disk.

Various products take different approaches to this type of content retrieval. In several members of Microsoft's Office 2000 suite, for example, a Web toolbar is available. You can use this toolbar to quickly launch your Web browser and visit a specified site. Lotus' SmartSuite features the SmartCenter, which lets you jump from applications directly to Web sites, download files, and more (see Figure 19.24).

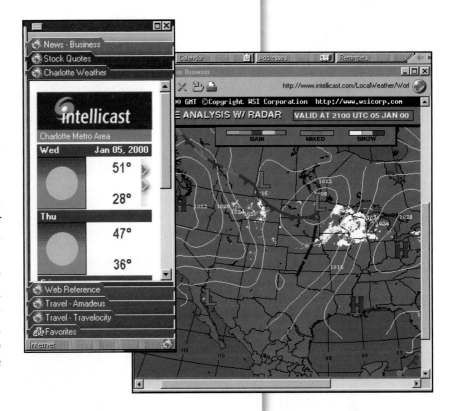

Figure 19.24
Accessing the Web through Lotus SmartCenter's custom browser window.

Creating Content

Many of today's popular productivity applications feature tools that enable you to convert existing documents into HTML-format files. Specifically, three types of tools free you from learning to use HTML tags or manually embedding them in documents:

- **Save As HTML Command.** By using the program's Save As HTML (or save as Web page) command, you can convert an existing document into an HTML file, ready to be posted on a Web server. You can then view your HTML page in your browser, just as you can view the original document in the word processor. Today's application programs can retain most, if not all, of the formatting applied to the original document, so the HTML file will resemble the original.

- **Web Templates.** Many applications now provide Web templates, which are predesigned Web pages. You can create entire Web sites from templates, with hyperlinks connecting all the pages in a logical organization. Templates include preselected fonts, backgrounds, color schemes, and more.

- **Wizards.** A Web-design wizard is a utility that literally walks you through the process of creating a Web page or site. A wizard appears as a series of dialog boxes that ask questions and prompt you to make choices. When you are done, a nearly complete Web page is ready for you to add content (see Figure 19.25 on page 360). Wizards are especially useful because they help you avoid common mistakes in design, setting up links, and performing other tasks.

NORTON
ONLINE

Visit **www.glencoe.com/norton/online/** for more information on **Internet** features in popular application programs.

Figure 19.25
The Web Page Wizard in Microsoft
Word 2000.

Many popular applications now feature an e-mail command that enables you to export the current document as the body of an e-mail message or as an attachment to a message. This feature eliminates copying or pasting the document or searching for the file by using operating system tools.

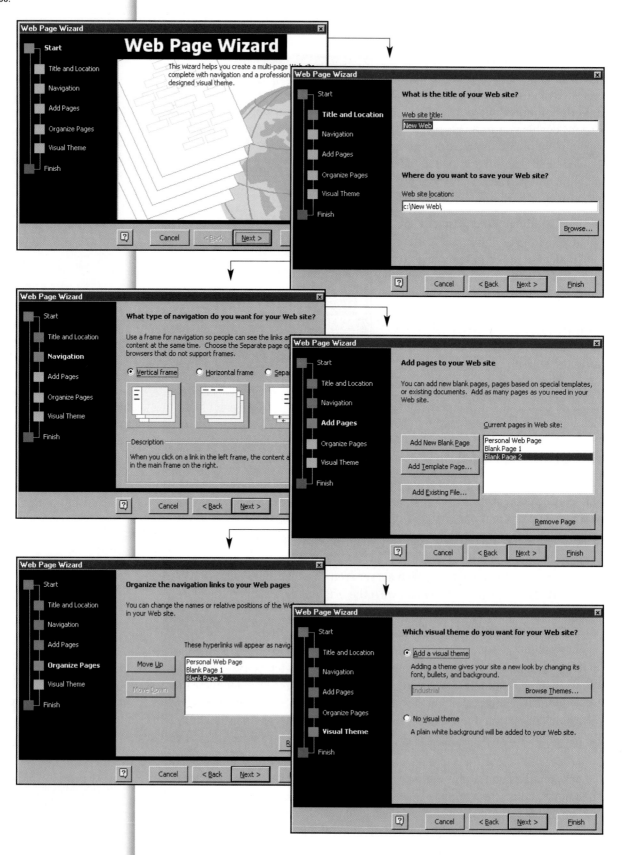

Norton Notebook

MINDING YOUR MANNERS ONLINE

Although there is no set of written rules governing behavior on the Internet, the wise user participates in an honor system. On the Internet, appropriate behavior is called netiquette, a combination of *Internet etiquette*. Netiquette is crucial for keeping the Internet a civil place because the Internet is not policed or run by a single person or group. The basic rules of netiquette are as follows:

◆ **Behave As Though You Are Communicating in Person.** When communicating with someone online, act as if you are talking to that person face to face.

◆ **Remember That Your Words Are Open to Interpretation.** If you post jokes, sarcasm, or other attempts at humor, do not be surprised if someone is offended. Word your postings clearly and carefully, and use appropriate language.

◆ **Do Not "Shout" Online.** Typing in ALL CAPITAL LETTERS is like shouting and is considered rude.

◆ **Do Not "Flame" Other Users.** In 'Net-speak, a flame is a posting that contains insults or other derogatory content. Flamers can be shut out of listservs and chat rooms, and other users can block a flamer's messages from the e-mail and news accounts.

◆ **Do Not Send Spam.** Spam is the online equivalent of junk mail—uninvited messages, usually of a commercial nature. Most ISPs have strict spam policies. If you are caught distributing uninvited messages to multiple recipients (especially if the messages contain commercial, libelous, or vulgar content), your ISP may cancel your account.

◆ **Do Not Distribute Copyrighted Material.** Usenet newsgroups and many private Web pages are filled with copyrighted and trademarked text and graphics, posted without the owner's permission. Do not be fooled into thinking that text or images are "in the public domain" because you found them on the

Most ISPs provide an appropriate-use policy on their Web site or in their printed documentation. This example is posted on the Web site of Road Runner, an ISP in Charlotte, North Carolina.

> **TIME WARNER CABLE** — CHARLOTTE, NORTH CAROLINA
>
> **ROAD RUNNER ACCEPTABLE USE POLICY**
>
> Road Runner seeks to create and foster an on-line community that can be used and enjoyed by all its members. To further that goal, Road Runner has developed an Acceptable Use Policy with standards for using the service. Although much of what is included here is common sense, Road Runner takes these issues very seriously and will enforce these rules to ensure that an enjoyable environment is provided to all its subscribers.
>
> Road Runner therefore reserves the right to remove any content posted to its system which it deems offensive, inappropriate, or in violation of its policies. Road Runner also reserves the right to suspend or cancel a subscriber's account for engaging in inappropriate conduct. (Subscribers, of course, also remain legally responsible for any such acts). In using Road Runner, subscribers accept these restrictions as well as those set forth in the Subscription Agreement and agree to use the system only for lawful purposes.
>
> In addition, subscribers agree not to use or allow others to use Road Runner:
>
> - to post or transmit hate speech, threats of physical violence, or harassing content;
> - to post or transmit material in violation with copyright laws;
> - to post or transmit content that is legally obscene or violates child pornography statutes; that contains graphic visual depictions of sexual acts, or visual depictions of sexually explicit conduct involving children, or that contains depictions of children, the primary appeal of which is prurient;
> - to post or transmit other sexually oriented material that, in the specific context, is offensive or inappropriate;

Internet. Copyrights still apply; copyright infringement is illegal and can lead to prosecution.

◆ **Do Not Be a Coward.** As a general rule, you should never conceal your identity on the Internet. If you choose to use a screen name, do not hide behind it to misbehave.

Always check the rules when you go online. Nearly all ISPs post an appropriate use policy on their Web site that lists guidelines for acceptable behavior on the Internet. This document may be a simple disclaimer or may take the form of an FAQ. If you violate these guidelines and are reported to the ISP, your account may be dropped. Look for an FAQ before using chat rooms, listservs, message boards, newsgroups, and other Internet services, especially moderated ones.

Even though you cannot be seen on the Internet, you can still be identified. Conscientious users of e-mail and newsgroups commonly forward flames or inappropriate postings to the poster's ISP. If an ISP collects enough complaints about an account holder, it can cancel that person's account. In cases where libel, copyright infringement, or other potential crimes are involved, the ISP may also turn the poster over to the authorities. In one such case (in December 1999), a Florida teenager posted a threatening chat-room message to a Colorado student. Even though the poster had used an alias to hide his identity, federal agents were able to track him down and arrest him.

NORTON ONLINE

Visit **www.glencoe.com/norton/online/** for more information on **netiquette**.

LESSON QUIZ

True/False

Answer the following questions by circling True or False.

True   False   **1.** The Internet is so named because it is a collection of "networked networks."

True   False   **2.** Even if they use TCP/IP protocols, different types of computers cannot exchange data over the Internet.

True   False   **3.** .com and .edu are examples of subdomains.

True   False   **4.** Most individual users connect to the Internet through an ISP.

True   False   **5.** HTML tags are optional components of a Web page.

Multiple Choice

Circle the word or phrase that best completes each sentence.

1. The internal structure of the World Wide Web is based on the _____ .

    A. hypertext markup language   **B.** hypertext transfer protocol   **C.** uniform resource locator

2. Windows Media Player is an example of a(n) _____ .

    A. Web browser   **B.** HTML converter   **C.** helper application

3. To send and receive e-mail messages, you must have a(n) _____ .

    A. e-mail client   **B.** e-mail address   **C.** both A and B

4. In newsgroups, a series of related articles and responses is called a _____ .

    A. newsreader   **B.** Usenet   **C.** thread

5. The _____ is the Internet tool used to copy files from one computer to another.

    A. World Wide Web (WWW)   **B.** file transfer protocol (FTP)   **C.** Usenet

LESSON LABS

Complete the following exercises as directed by your instructor.

1. Determine whether a Web browser is installed on your system. Open the Start menu, point to Programs, and search the Programs menu for an application such as Microsoft Internet Explorer or Netscape Navigator. If you find a browser, click its name in the Programs menu to launch the application. Note what happens after you launch the browser and write it down. What appears on the screen?

2. Determine what other types of Internet applications are installed on your system. (You may need your instructor's help to do this exercise.) Check the Programs menu as you did in Lesson Lab 1. Also, click the Accessories option in the Programs menu; then click Internet Accessories. What other programs are available? An e-mail client or a newsreader? List the applications and their location in your menu system.

LESSON 20

Getting Online, Working Online

OVERVIEW:
Joining the Internet Phenomenon

As more businesses and people join the Internet community, they are finding that the Internet is enhancing their work lives. Thanks to communication technologies, many businesspeople now work from home instead of commuting to an office or factory each day. The World Wide Web is also used at the corporate level to sell products, provide customer services, and support business partnerships among various companies.

This lesson provides an overview of the options for connecting a computer to the Internet and shows you how the Internet, intranets, and extranets are affecting the workplace and the way we conduct business transactions.

OBJECTIVES

- List six ways to connect a computer to the Internet.
- Identify three kinds of high-speed data links commonly used to connect individuals and small businesses to the Internet.
- Describe the process of connecting a PC to the Internet through an ISP account.
- List four types of firewalls and explain why businesses use them.
- Define the terms *intranet* and *extranet*.
- Explain what is meant by e-commerce and how it affects consumers and businesses.

363

ACCESSING THE INTERNET

There are many ways to obtain access to the Internet. The method varies according to the type of computer system being used.

Direct Connection

In a **direct connection,** Internet programs run on the local computer, which uses the TCP/IP protocols to exchange data with another computer through the Internet. An isolated computer can connect to the Internet through a serial data communications port using either **serial line interface protocol (SLIP)** or **point-to-point protocol (PPP),** two methods for creating a direct connection through a telephone line. This type of connection is an option for a stand-alone computer that does not connect to the Internet through an Internet service provider, as discussed later. However, direct connections are uncommon.

Remote Terminal Connection

A **remote terminal connection** to the Internet exchanges commands and data in ASCII text format with a host computer that uses UNIX or a similar operating system. The TCP/IP application programs and protocols all run on the host. Because the command set in UNIX is called a shell, this kind of Internet access is known as a **shell account.** Again, this type of connection works for some types of stand-alone computers but is uncommon.

Gateway Connection

Even if a local area network does not use TCP/IP commands and protocols, it may still be able to provide some Internet services, such as e-mail or file transfer. Such networks use gateways that convert commands and data to and from TCP/IP format.

Although it is possible to connect a local network directly to the Internet backbone, it is usually not practical (except for the largest organizations) because of the high cost of a backbone connection. Many businesses and most individual users obtain access through an Internet service provider (ISP), which supplies the backbone connection. ISPs offer several kinds of Internet service, including inexpensive shell accounts; direct TCP/IP connections using SLIP or PPP accounts; and full-time, high-speed access through dedicated data circuits.

Connecting Through a LAN

If a local area network uses TCP/IP protocols for communication within the network, it is a simple matter to connect to the Internet through a router, another

Visit **www.glencoe.com/norton/online/** for more information on **SLIP** and **PPP**.

Figure 20.1
If a LAN does not use TCP/IP protocols, it can connect to the Internet through a router and a gateway. However, if a LAN uses TCP/IP protocols, it does not require a gateway to connect to the Internet; just a router is needed.

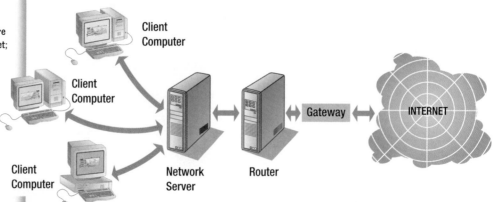

computer that stores and forwards data to other computers on the Internet. If the LAN uses a different kind of local protocol, a gateway converts it to and from TCP/IP (see Figure 20.1). When a LAN has an Internet connection, that connection extends to every computer on the LAN. This type of connection is commonly used by businesses to provide the LAN's users with Internet access.

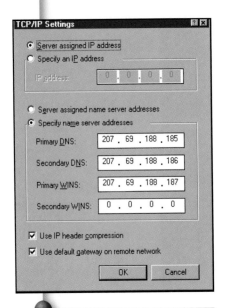

Connecting Through a Modem

If there is no LAN on site, an isolated computer can connect to the Internet through a serial data communications port and a modem and by using either a shell account and a terminal emulation program or a direct TCP/IP connection with a SLIP or PPP account. Again, ISPs provide these types of services for home users and businesses who want to connect to the Internet.

Most individual users connect to the Internet by using a telephone line; a 28.8 Kbps, 33.6 Kbps, or 56 Kbps modem; and a SLIP or PPP account. Using settings provided by the ISP, the user can configure the PC's operating system to dial into one of the ISP's server computers, identify itself as the customer's computer, and gain access to Internet services (see Figure 20.2). Depending on the ISP, the customer's computer may be assigned a permanent IP address, or its IP address may change each time it logs on to the ISP's server.

Figure 20.2
Configuring settings in Windows 98 for an Internet connection through an ISP. When you set up an ISP account, the ISP should provide you with all the instructions and settings you need. A typical account configuration takes only a few minutes using tools in your operating system or provided by the ISP.

High-Speed Data Links

Modem connections are convenient, but their capacity is limited to the relatively low data-transfer speed of a telephone line. A 56 Kbps modem is fine for text, still images, and low-quality streaming multimedia, but it is really not practical for huge digital audio and video files. When many users are sharing an Internet connection through a LAN, the connection between the network and the ISP must be adequate to meet the demands of many users at the same time. Fortunately, dedicated high-speed data circuits are available from telephone companies, cable TV services, and other suppliers. Using fiber optics, microwave, and other technologies, it is entirely practical to establish an Internet connection that is at least ten times as fast as a modem link.

ISDN Service

For small businesses and individual users, integrated services digital network (ISDN) is an attractive alternative. ISDN is a digital telephone service that combines voice, data, and control signaling through a single circuit. An ISDN data connection can transfer data at up to 128,000 bits per second. Most telephone companies offer ISDN at a slightly higher cost than the conventional telephone service that it replaces, and costs are coming down as more homes and businesses obtain ISDN connections.

ISDN service operates on standard telephone lines but requires a special modem (see Figure 20.3) and phone service, which add to the cost of the service. Even so, the benefits of ISDN are substantial. For example, you can connect a PC, telephone, and fax into a single ISDN line and use them simultaneously. Many ISPs and local telephone companies that also offer Internet access services support ISDN connections.

Figure 20.3
Many ISDN modems use data compression technologies to double the data transfer rates of a basic ISDN line.

*x*DSL Services

The abbreviation DSL stands for digital subscriber line, and several versions of DSL technology are available for home and business use. In fact, the abbreviation often begins with an *x* (*x*DSL) because there are various types of DSL service, each providing a different level of service, speed, bandwidth, and distance. Table 20.1 lists the most well-known varieties of *x*DSL and their basic capabilities.

Note that the transmission speeds given in Table 20.1 are typical ranges. Transmission speeds can vary greatly and are affected by several factors, including distance, wire and equipment type, service provider capabilities, and more. Also note that different providers may use DSL terms differently and apply different usage standards in delivering DSL services. This variation can create great confusion among customers and has slowed DSL's acceptance.

Table 20.1	*x*DSL Services
Service	**Data Transmission Rate**
DDSL (dedicated digital subscriber line)	160 Kbps (downloading and uploading)
SDSL (symmetric digital subscriber line)	1.544 Mbps (downloading and uploading)
ADSL (asymmetric digital subscriber line)	1.5 Mbps to 9 Mbps (downloading); 16 Kbps to 640 Kbps (uploading)
HDSL (high-data-rate digital subscriber line)	1.544 Mbps to 2 Mbps (uploading and downloading)
VDSL (very-high-rate digital subscriber line)	13 Mbps to 52 Mbps (downloading); 1.5 Mbps to 2.3 Mbps (uploading)

DSL services are not yet widely available, but they can be less expensive than ISDN service. DSL is gaining popularity among small businesses that need to connect a LAN to the Internet and provide users with rapid data-transfer rates and continuous service. Some DSL services also enable simultaneous data, voice, and fax transmissions on the same line.

Cable Modem Service

Many cable companies now use a portion of their network's bandwidth to offer Internet access through existing cable television connections. Cable modem service took some time to get off the ground because it required cable systems to set up local Internet servers (to provide access to the Web, e-mail, and news) and to establish connections to the Internet backbone. As the infrastructure grows, however, cable modem services will arrive in cities around the United States.

Cable television systems send data to users over coaxial cable, which can transmit data as much as 100 times faster than common telephone lines and at a much greater bandwidth. Cable can transmit not only data but also streaming audio and video simultaneously, at a much higher speed than is possible over standard telephone lines. Because of cable's enhanced bandwidth, Internet data can be transmitted on its own channel, separate from the audio, video, and control signals used for television programming. A user can surf the Internet and watch television at the same time, over the same cable connection, without the two data streams interfering with one another.

NORTON
ONLINE

Visit www.glencoe.com/norton/online/ for more information on **ISDN service**, *x*DSL services, and **cable modems**.

To work with a cable modem (see Figure 20.4), the user's PC needs a network interface card and access to a cable television outlet (the kind found in many homes). The cable connection is extended to the modem, which is then connected to the network interface card. As a result, the computer becomes part of a wide area network using TCP/IP protocols and whose users share access to the Internet via a dedicated connection.

Cable modem service does not require the use of a standard modem. If the user's PC also has a standard modem installed, it can be used for other purposes, such as faxing.

CONNECTING A PC TO THE INTERNET

Connecting a desktop computer to the Internet actually involves two separate issues: software and the network connection. The industry has developed a standard interface called Windows Sockets, or **Winsock,** which makes it possible to mix and match application programs from more than one developer and to allow those applications to work with any type of network connection. Figure 20.5 shows how applications, the Winsock interface, and network drivers fit together.

Many companies offer suites of Internet access tools. These packages usually contain client programs for e-mail, Telnet, FTP, and other applications, along with a World Wide Web browser and software for connecting to a network using dial-up modem connections, connection through a LAN, or both. In addition, some packages include sign-up utilities that will work with one or more Internet service providers who offer modem access through local telephone numbers in most major metropolitan areas.

The all-in-one-box approach has several advantages. In most cases, the applications in a suite share a common interface design, so they are easy to learn and use. Because all the applications come from the same source, there is a single point of contact for technical support and product upgrades. If a suite includes an account with a particular ISP, most likely the service provider has worked with the software developer to make sure that there are no incompatibilities between the software and the network.

Figure 20.4
Cable modems provide fast data-transfer speeds at costs comparable to a standard ISP account.

NORTON ONLINE

Visit **www.glencoe.com/norton/online/** for more information on **Winsock.**

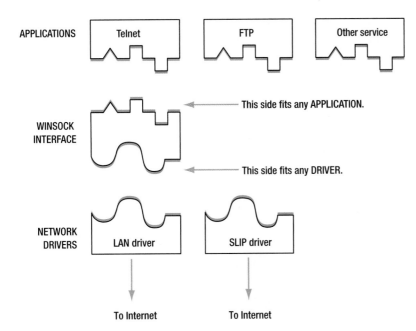

Figure 20.5
How Winsock provides an interface between applications and networks.

Answer the following questions by filling in the blank(s).

1. The serial line interface protocol is one method for creating a(n) _____ over a telephone line.

2. The abbreviation DSL stands for _____ .

3. Using a(n) _____ connection, you can surf the Internet and watch television at the same time.

WORKING ON THE INTERNET

The increased use of the Internet and the World Wide Web places networks at even greater risk of undesirable intrusion. Many organizations publish information on the Web, whereas others have employees who pass information to the Internet from the company network or download material from the Internet.

Not that long ago, the Internet was the exclusive province of educators, scientists, and researchers. That situation has changed, and today companies and individuals all over the world are eagerly stampeding into cyberspace. The legal, procedural, and moral infrastructure for this volume of activity simply does not exist yet. Companies and individuals must remain cautious while the standards are still being defined.

NORTON
ONLINE

Visit **www.glencoe.com/norton/online/** for more information on **firewalls**.

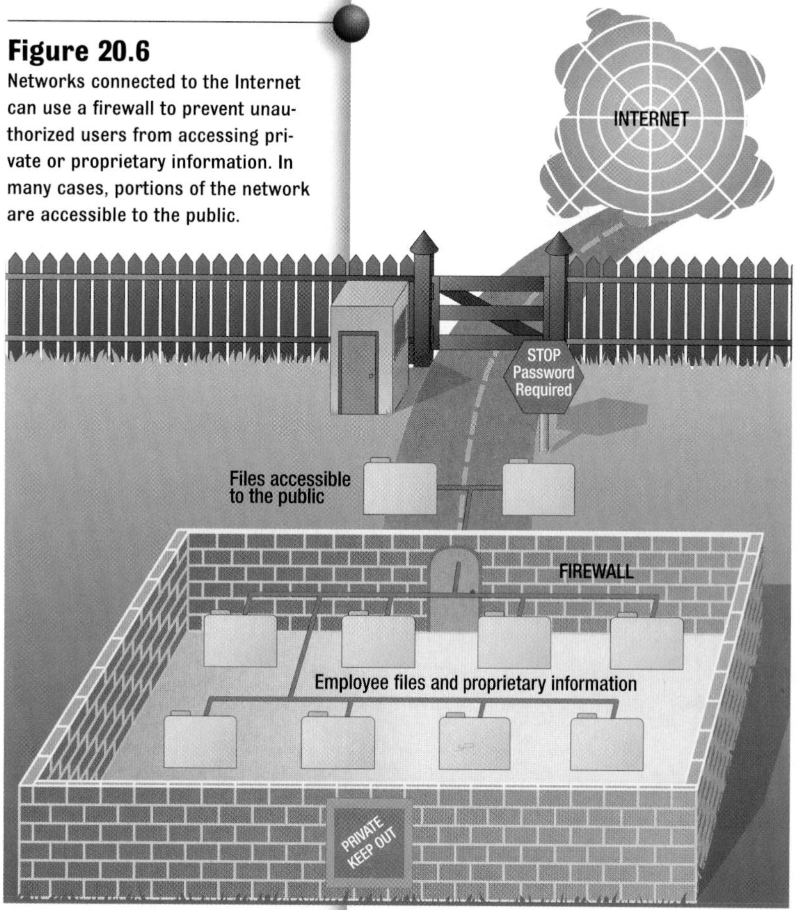

Businesses and Firewalls

With millions of Internet users able to pass information to and take information from the network, the security of business networks is a major concern. Many businesses set up **firewalls** to control access to their networks by persons using the Internet (see Figure 20.6). Firewalls act as barriers to unauthorized entry into a network that is connected to the Internet, allowing outsiders to access public areas but preventing them from exploring proprietary areas of the network.

A firewall system can be hardware, software, or both. A firewall basically works by inspecting the requests and data that pass between the private network and the Internet. If a request or data does not pass the firewall's security inspection, it is stopped from traveling any further.

Network managers can use various methods for creating firewalls and typically use a combination of techniques. Table 20.2 on page 370 lists some of the most common firewall methodologies.

Figure 20.6
Networks connected to the Internet can use a firewall to prevent unauthorized users from accessing private or proprietary information. In many cases, portions of the network are accessible to the public.

INTERNET

STOP
Password
Required

Files accessible
to the public

FIREWALL

Employee files and proprietary information

PRIVATE
KEEP OUT

Techview

FREEBIES ON THE WEB

If you set up an account with an Internet service provider, you will probably install software, such as a Web browser, an e-mail client, and a newsreader. Many users also install a separate FTP client and Telnet software. All you need, however, is a current version of a Web browser to surf the Web, send and receive e-mail, chat, participate in newsgroup discussions, and more. In fact, you do not necessarily need an account with an ISP or online service to access these features; you can log on to the Web from a computer at a library or your school's computer center, for example. Here are a few of the free services you can access through the Web.

E-Mail

By visiting Web sites like Hotmail, Mail.com, Yahoo!, and others, you can set up a free e-mail account. You must register for the account by creating a user name and password; the service creates a complete e-mail address for you, such as **yourname@hotmail.com**.

You can send and receive e-mail from these sites, and several offer other useful personalization features. However, some free Web-based e-mail services will store your messages for only a certain amount of time and then automatically delete them. Some will also cancel your account if you do not use it for a given amount of time. But if you use e-mail regularly and want to access your mail from any browser (without having to log on to your ISP account), Web-based mail is a big time-saver.

Mail.com is only one source of free e-mail on the World Wide Web.

Many Web sites, including The Microsoft Network, offer free personal Web pages and design services.

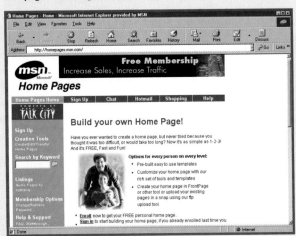

Personal Web Pages

Nearly every ISP provides space on its Web servers where clients can create and post personal Web pages. This service is almost always free. As part of the service, ISPs provide online design tools that make it easy to create a personal Web site.

But you do not even need an ISP to get a free Web page. Again, Web sites such as the Microsoft Network, America Online, Yahoo!, and many others provide this kind of service. You simply register for the service, select a URL for your site, and post your Web pages. Free design tools are usually available also.

Chat

It is no longer necessary to log on to an IRC chat channel to participate in a chat room discussion, nor do you have to join an online service like AOL or Prodigy to take advantage of their chat rooms. Now you can access chat in real time through various sources.

Many large Web sites, such as CNN, About.com, Snap, and others, offer Web communities that are basically chat rooms. At these sites, you can register for a user name and a password and choose from dozens of different communities to join. Web-based communities usually conduct chat sessions right in your browser window, although some communities spawn a separate window to contain the chat.

Table 20.2 **Common Firewall Methodologies**

Method	Description
Proxy server	A proxy server is like a "second server" and hides the actual network server from the Internet. The proxy server examines every packet that enters and leaves the network via the Internet, stopping any data that does not meet security criteria. For example, an administrator can set up a proxy server to block user access to certain types of Web sites.
Packet filter	A packet filter inspects (or filters) each packet of data that enters or leaves the network via a router. The filter uses a set of security rules defined by the organization's network administrator. If any packet does not pass the inspection, it is not allowed to continue.
Application gateway	An application gateway imposes special security restrictions on specific Internet services such as e-mail, FTP, and so on. An application gateway is an effective method for stopping intrusions to private networks.
Circuit gateway	A circuit gateway imposes security restrictions on specific connections, such as a TCP/IP connection between a network server and a remote computer.

NORTON ONLINE

Visit **www.glencoe.com/norton/online/** for more information on **intranets** and **extranets**.

Even if a company does not make any portion of its network available to Internet users, it can allow employees to access the network over the Internet. This capability is important for **telecommuters,** or people who work from home or a remote location rather than the office. In these situations, firewalls can ensure that only authorized users can access the network over the Internet.

Intranets and Extranets

Before the advent of the World Wide Web, most corporate networks were bland environments that basically supported file sharing and e-mail. However, corporate and academic networks are being configured more frequently to resemble the Internet. This setup enables users to work in a Weblike graphical environment using a Web browser as their interface to corporate data. Two common types of "corporate spin-offs" of the Web are called intranets and extranets. These systems are designed to support data sharing, scheduling, and workgroup activities within an organization.

An **intranet** is a LAN or WAN that uses TCP/IP protocols but belongs exclusively to a corporation, school, or organization. The intranet is accessible only to the organization's workers. If the intranet is connected to the Internet, then it is secured by a firewall to prevent unauthorized users from gaining access to it.

An **extranet** is an intranet that can be accessed by outside users over the Internet. To gain entrance to the extranet's resources, an external user (such as a telecommuter or business partner) typically must log on to the network by providing a valid user ID and password.

Intranets and extranets are popular for several reasons:

◆ Because they use standard TCP/IP protocols rather than the proprietary protocols used by network operating systems, they are simpler and less expensive to install and configure.

◆ Because they enable users to work in standard (and usually free) Web browsers, they provide a consistent, friendly interface.

◆ Because they function readily with firewalls and other standard Internet security technologies, they provide excellent security against infiltration, viruses, theft, and other problems.

Issues for Business Users and Telecommuters

Whether you use the entire Web in your work or use only your company's network via an Internet connection, you need to consider some issues as you work online. Here are just three:

◆ **Ownership.** Many Internet users assume incorrectly that all the data available on the Internet is free and available for use by anyone else. In fact, any piece of text or graphics that you retrieve from the Internet may be covered by trademark or copyright law, making it illegal to reuse it without the owner's consent. This issue is especially important for persons who access the Internet over a corporate network because their employers become involved in cases where copyrights or trademarks are violated.

◆ **Libel.** On the Internet, "private" communications (such as e-mail messages) can be quickly forwarded far beyond their intended readership, which amounts to publication. If messages are sent through an employer's network, the employer may become involved if the sender is accused of libel.

◆ **Appropriate Use.** When using a business network to access the Internet, users must be careful to use network resources appropriately. For example, do not access recreational newsgroups over the company's Internet connection or download obscene or pornographic images from adult-oriented Web sites.

Employees also need to protect corporate property—such as trade secrets, telephone lists, personnel records, and product specifications—stored on the network. Suppose, for example, that someone calls you at your office accidentally, intending to call one of your coworkers. To ensure that this person has the correct telephone number, you agree to e-mail your corporate phone directory. This simple favor can become a major headache if the caller turns out to be a telemarketer or recruiter who then starts calling everyone on the list.

COMMERCE ON THE WORLD WIDE WEB

The World Wide Web has become a global vehicle for **electronic commerce (e-commerce),** creating new ways for businesses to interact with one another and their customers. In simple terms, e-commerce means doing business online. In 1997, an ActivMedia study estimated that more than $24 million in sales were conducted over the World Wide Web. A more recent survey by Goldman, Sachs, & Co. says that $39 billion in e-commerce was done in 1998, with another $114 billion in 1999. Looking forward, the survey predicted that e-commerce sales will total $1.5 trillion by the year 2004.

E-Commerce at the Consumer Level

There are tens of thousands of Web sites devoted to e-commerce at the consumer level (see Figure 20.7), ready to give consumers information about products and services, take orders, receive payments, and provide on-the-spot customer service.

Figure 20.7

Like many other e-commerce sites that target consumers, amazon.com offers browsing, extensive help systems, secure purchasing, online customer service, and other features.

Figure 20.8

An example of an electronic shopping cart at the PC Connection Web site. This user is preparing to purchase a memory upgrade for a computer. The cart shows the product, model information, price, quantity, in-stock status, shipping charges, and more.

Using an e-commerce site is like browsing through an online catalog. More sophisticated sites allow you to search for specific products, look for certain features, and compare prices. They provide an electronic "shopping basket" or "shopping cart" where you can temporarily store information about items you want to buy (see Figure 20.8). You can select an item, store it in the basket, and continue shopping until you are ready to purchase.

When you are ready to make your purchase, you can pay for it in several ways:

◆ **One-Time Credit Card Purchase.** If you do not want to set up an account with the seller, you can provide your personal and credit card information each time you make a purchase.

◆ **Set Up an Online Account.** If you think you will make other purchases from the online vendor, you can set up an account at the Web site (see Figure 20.9). The vendor stores your personal and credit card information on a

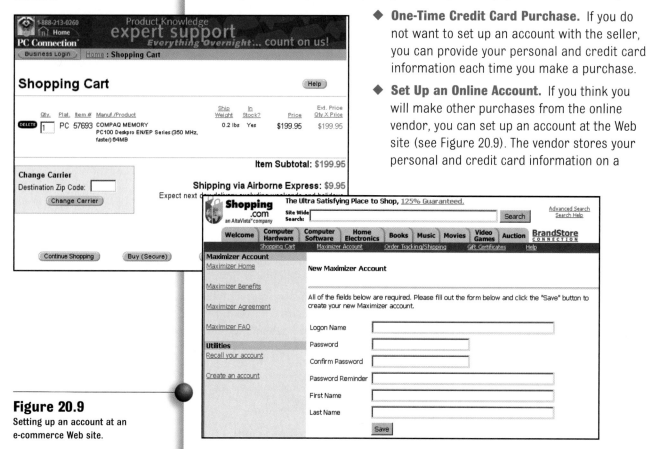

Figure 20.9

Setting up an account at an e-commerce Web site.

secure server, then places a special file (called a **cookie**) on your computer's disk. Later, when you access your account again by typing a user ID and password, the site uses information in the cookie to access your account. Online accounts are required at some vendors' Web sites, such as brokerage sites that provide online investing services.

◆ **Use Electronic Cash. Electronic cash** (also called **digital cash**) has been available since 1996 but has not yet gained wide public acceptance for online shopping. Electronic cash takes the form of a redeemable electronic certificate, which you can purchase from a bank that provides electronic cash services. Not all e-commerce Web sites accept digital cash yet.

◆ **Use an Electronic Wallet.** An **electronic wallet** is a program on your computer that stores credit card information, a digital certificate that verifies your identity and shipping information. (A different version, called a **thin wallet,** stores the information on a server owned by your credit card company rather than on your computer.) Like electronic cash, electronic wallets are not yet widely accepted by e-commerce Web sites, but their popularity is growing.

Security

Until 1998, e-commerce was slow to gain acceptance among consumers, who were concerned about security. Many people feared that it was not safe to provide personal or credit card information over the Internet. That fear has almost been eliminated, however, with the advent of security measures and improved public perception.

Reputable e-commerce Web sites (especially those run by well-known companies) use sophisticated measures to ensure that customer information cannot fall into the hands of criminals. One measure is providing **secure Web pages** where customers can enter personal information, credit card and account numbers, passwords, and other information. When using an e-commerce site, you can tell if the current page is secure in two ways (see Figure 20.10):

◆ **Check the URL.** If the page's URL begins with https:// or ends with shtml, then the page is secure. In both cases, the letter *s* indicates security measures.

◆ **Check Your Browser's Status Bar.** If you use Microsoft Internet Explorer or Netscape Navigator, a small padlock symbol will appear in the browser's status bar when a secure Web page is open.

Web masters can provide secure Web sites in several ways. One way is to encode pages using **secure sockets layer (SSL)** technology, which encrypts data. (**Encryption** technology secures data by converting it into a code that is unusable by anyone who does not possess a key to the code.) If a Web page is protected by SSL, its URL will begin with https:// rather than http://. Another way to protect data sent over the Internet is by using the **secure HTTP (S-HTTP)** protocol. Whereas SSL can encode any amount of data, S-HTTP is used to encode individual pieces of data.

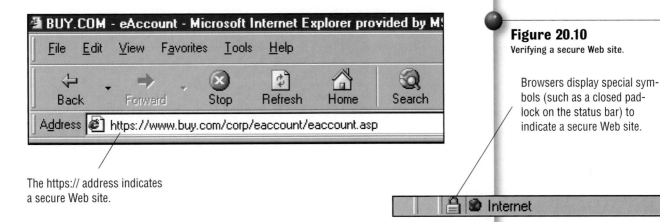

The https:// address indicates a secure Web site.

Figure 20.10
Verifying a secure Web site.

Browsers display special symbols (such as a closed padlock on the status bar) to indicate a secure Web site.

E-Commerce at the Business Level

When viewed beyond the perspective of individual consumer transactions, e-commerce is an entirely different way for companies to conduct business. Using powerful Web sites and online databases, companies not only sell goods to individual customers, but track inventory, order products, send invoices, and receive payments. Using e-commerce technologies (ranging from LANs to supercomputers), companies are rapidly forming online partnerships to collaborate on product designs, sales and marketing campaigns, and more. Corporate extranets have become an important part of corporate-level e-commerce by giving companies access to vital information on one another's networks.

COMPUTERS
in your career

Career Opportunities and the Internet

Many careers are associated with the Internet, including network administrators, information system professionals, and data communications managers. Aside from careers that focus on architecture and administration of the Internet, many other professions require not only a working knowledge of the Internet but a mastery of the tools used to create and distribute content across it. Here are a few such careers:

◆ **Web Designers and Web Masters.** Corporate Web, intranet, and extranet sites are developed, designed, and maintained most often by teams of professionals. At the helm of such teams are experienced designers and Web masters. Web designers bring various traditional design skills to the table—such as experience with graphics, text design, and layout—but they are also skilled with HTML tools and scripting languages. Web masters often provide more technical skills required for high-level network support. One or both of these leaders must also have management skills to direct and coordinate the efforts of a design team.

◆ **Multimedia Developers.** As more people connect to the Internet, companies face increasing competition to provide highly visual, interactive content to capture and retain visitors to their Web sites. This need has already driven up the demand for multimedia developers who can design content for the Internet, particularly the Web. To become marketable in this field, you need a thorough background in multimedia authoring and distribution. These specialists also benefit from programming skills, using languages such as Java, VisualBasic, and others that are widely used on the Internet.

◆ **Programmers.** Programmers are finding all sorts of opportunities in Internet development because Web sites are commonly used to support high-level functions such as interactivity, searches, data mining, and more. To get involved in Internet-related products, these programmers learn a wide variety of languages, including Perl, VisualBasic, Java, C++, and others.

◆ **Writers and Editors.** Just as the Internet has changed the way multimedia content is delivered, it has also changed the way books, periodicals, and other printed media are delivered and viewed by consumers. Most publishing houses and newspapers require their writers and editors to work electronically and to deliver manuscript and articles via the Internet or other network. Many writers must also know how to create content for the Internet and be familiar with HTML. Similarly, editors should know how to work with HTML documents and how to deliver these pages to an Internet site for publication.

Web site design is often done by teams of people, which may include graphic artists, writers and editors, formatters, researchers, programmers, and professionals with expertise in other disciplines.

LESSON QUIZ

True/False

Answer the following questions by circling True or False.

True   False   **1.** Remote terminal connections can be used only with supercomputers.

True   False   **2.** To use ISDN service at home, you must replace your standard telephone lines with special ISDN-only lines.

True   False   **3.** A firewall can control access to a corporate network by someone using the Internet.

True   False   **4.** An intranet can be accessed by anyone over an Internet connection.

True   False   **5.** In simple terms, e-commerce means conducting business online.

Multiple Choice

Circle the word or phrase that best completes each sentence.

1. You can set up a direct connection to the Internet over a telephone line by using _____ .
   A. serial line interface protocol   **B.** point-to-point protocol   **C.** either A or B

2. _____ is one type of high-speed data link.
   A. 56 Kbps   **B.** ISDN   **C.** Winsock

3. To work with a cable modem, your PC needs a(n) _____ .
   A. network interface card   **B.** *x*DSL connection   **C.** neither A nor B

4. You can pay for online transactions by using a(n) _____ .
   A. credit card   **B.** cookie   **C.** SSL connection

5. If a Web page's URL includes _____ , the page is secure.
   A. https   **B.** shtml   **C.** either A or B

LESSON LABS

Complete the following exercises as directed by your instructor.

1. Determine whether your computer has a modem. Click the Start button; then click Settings. When the Settings submenu appears, click Control Panel to open the Control Panel dialog box. If you see a Modems icon, double-click it to open the Modem Properties dialog box. Write down the information about your modem. Close the Modem Properties dialog box, but leave the Control Panel dialog box open for the next exercise.

2. Use the Control Panel dialog box to see whether your PC has a network interface card installed. Double-click the System icon to open the System Properties dialog box. Click the Device Manager tab; then click the plus sign (+) next to Network adapters. If any adapters are installed, the list expands to show them. Select each adapter in turn, and click Properties to display the Properties dialog box. Write down the information for each adapter, and then click Cancel.

LESSON 19: Internet Basics

The Internet: Then and Now

- The Internet was created for the U.S. Department of Defense as a tool for communications. Today, the Internet is a network of interconnected networks.

- The Internet carries messages, documents, programs, and data files that contain every imaginable kind of information for businesses, educational institutions, government agencies, and individuals.

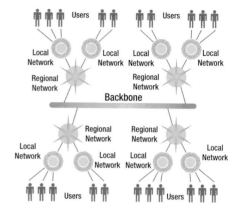

How the Internet Works

- All computers on the Internet use TCP/IP protocols. Any computer on the Internet can connect to any other computer.

- Individual computers connect to local and regional networks, which are connected together through the Internet backbone.

- A computer can connect directly to the Internet, or as a remote terminal on another computer, or through a gateway from a network that does not use TCP/IP.

- Every computer on the Internet has a unique numeric IP address, and most also have an address that uses the domain name system.

Major Features of the Internet

- The World Wide Web combines text, illustrations, and links to other files in hypertext documents.

- Electronic mail systems enable you to exchange messages with any other user anywhere. You can also attach document or program files to e-mail messages.

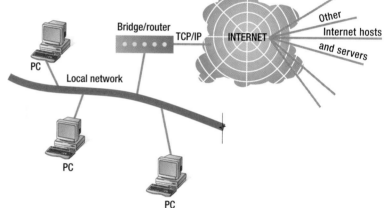

- Telnet allows a user to operate a second computer from his or her machine.

- FTP is the Internet tool for copying data and program files from one computer to another.

- News and mailing lists (listservs) are public conferences distributed through the Internet and other electronic neworks.

- Chats are public conferences, conducted in real time, where people join channels to discuss topics of interest.

Online Services

- In addition to Internet access, online service companies offer a wide variety of other features, such as e-mail, discussion groups, stock quotes, news, and online games.

Internet-Related Features in Application Programs

- Internet tools and services are commonly added to popular application programs such as word processors and spreadsheets. Such features enable you either to create content for the Internet or to access content from the Internet.

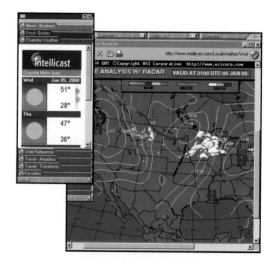

LESSON 20: Getting Online, Working Online

Accessing the Internet

- Users can connect to the Internet through a direct connection, local area network, high-speed data link, and other means.

- Individuals and small businesses access the Internet most commonly by setting up an account with an Internet service provider and using a telephone line and modem.

- High-speed data links such as ISDN and xDSL are more expensive options, but they provide much faster service than standard telephone line connections over a modem.

- Cable modems are quickly becoming a popular high-speed connection because they use coaxial cable already installed in many homes.

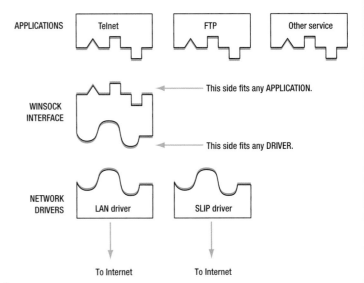

Connecting a PC to the Internet

- The Winsock standard specifies the Windows interface between TCP/IP applications and network connections. Users can mix and match Winsock-compatible applications and ensure they will work with the user's network connection to access the Internet.

- Internet application suites are available from many suppliers; they combine a full set of applications and drivers in a single package.

Working on the Internet

- By connecting their networks to the Internet, companies are creating new ways to conduct business and for employees to work. Telecommuters work from remote locations by connecting to the company network via the Internet.

- Businesses that connect their networks to the Internet can use firewalls to prevent unauthorized users from accessing proprietary information.

- Intranets and extranets are internal networks based on TCP/IP and support the use of Web browsers.

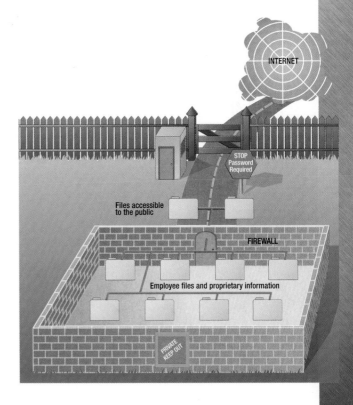

Commerce on the World Wide Web

- The act of conducting business online is called e-commerce.

- At the consumer level, it is possible to buy a wide range of goods and services at Web sites. Many such sites accept different forms of payment online and provide a secure environment for transactions.

- At the corporate level, e-commerce technologies enable companies to form online partnerships, conduct business transactions online, and collaborate on projects.

KEY TERMS

After completing this unit, you should be able to define the following terms.

anonymous FTP archive, *356*
Archie, *357*
ARPANET, *340*
article, *354*
backbone, *340*
browser, *347*
channel, *357*
chat, *357*
cookie, *372*
digital cash, *372*
direct connection, *364*
domain, *344*
domain name system (DNS)
    address, *344*
electronic cash, *372*
electronic commerce
    (e-commerce), *371*
electronic wallet, *372*
e-mail address, *353*
e-mail client, *352*
e-mail program, *352*
encryption, *373*
extranet, *370*
file transfer protocol (FTP), *356*
firewall, *368*
frequently asked questions (FAQs), *355*
FTP client software, *356*
FTP server, *356*
FTP site, *356*
helper application, *349*
hit, *346*
home page, *348*
host, *340*

HTML tag, *347*
hyperlink, *345*
hypertext link, *345*
hypertext markup language (HTML), *345*
hypertext transfer protocol (HTTP), *347*
instant messenger, *358*
Internet, *340*
Internet protocol (IP) address, *344*
Internet relay chat (IRC), *357*
Internet service provider (ISP), *345*
internetworking, *340*
intranet, *370*
link, *345*
listserv, *354*
mail server, *353*
moderator, *355*
network news transfer protocol
    (NNTP), *354*
news, *354*
newsgroup, *354*
newsreader, *354*
news server, *354*
NNTP server, *354*
NSFnet, *340*
online service, *358*
page view, *346*
personalized start page, *349*
plug-in application, *349*
point-to-point protocol (PPP), *364*
POP server, *353*
posting, *346*
post office protocol, *353*
remote terminal connection, *364*

search engine, *352*
secure HTTP (S-HTTP), *373*
secure sockets layer (SSL), *373*
secure Web page, *373*
serial line interface protocol (SLIP), *364*
shell account, *364*
spawn, *350*
streaming audio, *349*
streaming video, *349*
subdomain, *344*
subscribe, *354*
system operator (sysop), *358*
telecommuter, *370*
Telnet, *355*
thin wallet, *372*
thread, *354*
top-level domain, *344*
Transmission Control Protocol/
    Internet Protocol (TCP/IP), *342*
uniform resource locator (URL), *347*
Usenet, *354*
user name, *353*
virtual reality modeling language
    (VRML), *350*
Web browser, *347*
Web master, *346*
Web page, *345*
Web server, *346*
Web site, *346*
Winsock, *367*
World Wide Web (the Web or WWW), *345*

KEY TERMS QUIZ

Fill in each blank with one of the terms listed under Key Terms.

1. The process of connecting separate networks is called _____ .

2. In addition to an IP address, most computers on the Internet also have a(n) _____ .

3. A(n) _____ provides local or regional access to the Internet backbone.

4. The term _____ is used when documents are placed on Internet host computers.

5. To format a Web page, the designer places _____ throughout the document.

6. A(n) _____ is the Web page that opens when you launch your Web browser.

7. Web sites like Alta Vista and The Big Hub are examples of _____ .

8. To combat misinformation and rumors, some Internet newsgroups are overseen by a(n) _____ .

9. A business can set up a(n) _____ to control access to its network by persons using the Internet.

10. Many e-commerce Web sites provide _____ , where customers can enter personal information without fear that it will be stolen.

REVIEW QUESTIONS

In your own words, briefly answer the following questions.

1. What is an Internet host?

2. What is the most popular reason people use the Internet?

3. Why is the Internet sometimes described as "a network of networks"?

4. How do most individual computer users connect to the Internet?

5. What is the difference between a Web page and a Web site?

6. Name the parts of a URL.

7. There is a potential drawback to relying on Internet newsgroups as sources of information. Describe the problem and possible solutions.

8. List three technologies people can use to gain high-speed access to the Internet.

9. In basic terms, what does a firewall do?

10. What is the difference between an intranet and an extranet?

DISCUSSION QUESTIONS

As directed by your instructor, discuss the following questions in class or in groups.

1. Despite the promise that the Internet will perhaps be as universal one day as radio and television, how do you feel about the growing "commercialization" of the Internet? Do you think the motive to use the Internet as a vehicle for profit will have a negative impact on it as a rich source of information?

2. Discuss your view of the Internet's value to individual users. How important do you think the Internet is to casual home users? Support your opinion.

 ETHICAL ISSUES

Despite all the conveniences it offers to users, the Internet is filled with pitfalls. With this thought in mind, discuss the following questions in class.

1. People can shop, pay bills, communicate, play, study, and work online. Web designers, Internet marketers, ISPs, and other companies encourage us to use the Internet as much as possible, for any reason. In simple terms, can Internet use be bad? At what point do we become too dependent on the Internet? At what point does Internet use interfere with normal routines?

2. In the summer of 1999, a large bank fired several workers for using the company network to download pornography from the Web. The workers had also used the company's e-mail system to send copies of the images to one another and to friends outside the company. In your view, was the company too harsh in its punishment? Why? Do you believe the workers did anything illegal or potentially harmful? Support your position.

UNIT LABS

You and the Computer

Complete the following exercise using a computer in your classroom, lab, or home.

Telnet. Take the following steps to learn about your Telnet software—which is built right into your Windows operating system:

A. Click the Start button to open the Start menu; then click Programs. In the Programs menu, click the MS-DOS Prompt icon. An MS-DOS Prompt window appears on your desktop. A blinking cursor appears in the window, where you can type commands.

B. Type **TELNET** and press Enter. A Telnet window opens on your desktop.

C. Click Help on the menu bar to open the Help menu; then click Contents.

D. In the Telnet Help window, click various help topics and read the information that displays for each one.

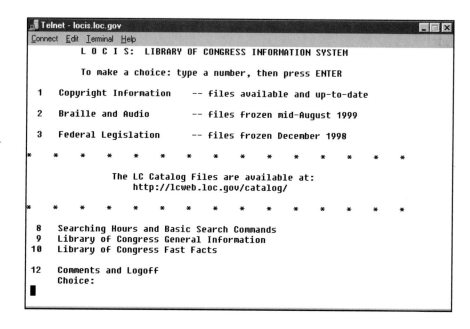

If your computer has an Internet connection, take the following steps to visit a Telnet site. Otherwise, close the Telnet and MS-DOS Prompt windows by clicking the Close buttons on their title bars.

A. On the Telnet menu bar, click Connect to open the Connect menu; then click Remote System. The Connect dialog box opens.

B. In the Host Name box, type one of the following Telnet addresses:

- **locis.loc.gov**—to learn about the Library of Congress.
- **uwmcat.lib.uwm.edu**—to browse the collections at the University of Wisconsin Library.
- **ajb.dni.us**—to search for job listings in the America's Job Bank database.

C. From the Port drop-down list, select *telnet*. From the TermType drop-down list, select *vt100*. (Your instructor may direct you to select different options.)

D. Click Connect. If your connection is successful, the Telnet window will change to display the opening screen of the Telnet site. If not, repeat steps A and B, using a different address.

E. Follow the instructions to log into the site and explore. When you are finished, close the Telnet and MS-DOS Prompt windows by clicking the Close buttons on their title bars. Your Telnet connection will be closed.

Internet Labs

To complete the following exercises, you need a computer with an Internet connection and a Web browser. (For more information on using these tools, see "Prerequisites" at the front of this textbook.)

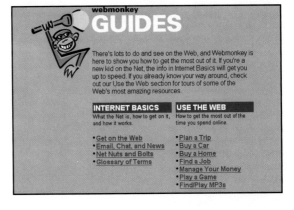

1. **Learn More About the Internet.** One of the best places to learn about the Internet is on the Internet. Dozens of authoritative Web sites provide information on the history of the Internet and technical issues, and tutorials for using the Web, Internet-related software, and more. To find more basic information about the Internet, visit these Web sites:

   - Webmonkey Guides—**http://www.hotwired.com/webmonkey/guides/**

   - An Overview of the Web—**http://www.imaginarylandscape.com/helpweb/www/oneweb.html**

   - NewbieNet—**http://www.newbie.net/**

   - Internet 101—**http://www2.famvid.com/i101/**

2. **Set Up a Free E-Mail Account.** Even if you do not have an ISP account, you can still use e-mail, if you can use a computer with access to the World Wide Web. Visit these sites to learn more about free e-mail accounts. Pick a provider, then follow the directions on that site to set up an account. Remember to write down your user name and password.

   - Hotmail—**http://www.hotmail.com/**

   - Mail.com—**http://www.mail.com/**

   - E-Mail.com—**http://www.email.com/**

IBE Labs

If you have the Interactive Browser Edition (IBE) CD-ROM for this textbook, you may complete the following interactive exercises using the instructions provided in the IBE.

1. **Crossword Puzzle.** Use the clues provided to complete the puzzle.

2. **Labeling.** Create a chart to show how computers access the Internet.

3. **What's Your Recommendation?** Based on the scenarios provided, you must set up domain names for businesses.

4. **Home Network.** This activity focuses on how data flows from one computer to the next via the Internet.

UNIT 11

Computer Graphics and Design

UNIT OBJECTIVES

Describe the impact of computers on graphics and design.

List two key uses for graphics software.

Identify eight primary graphics file formats.

List six important types of graphics software.

UNIT CONTENTS

This unit contains the following lessons:

Lesson 21: Working With Images

Lesson 22: Graphics Software

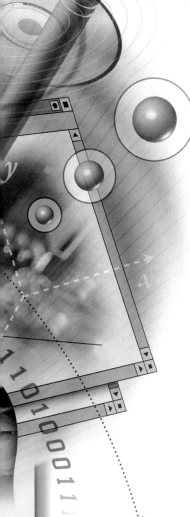

Working With Images

OVERVIEW:
Graphics, Graphics Everywhere

You may not realize how much of the imagery you see is created on a computer. From postage stamps to magazine illustrations, from billboards to television programs, all kinds of graphics are created and edited using computers and graphics software. Graphics programs—and the designers who use them—have become so polished that it is often impossible to tell a photograph or hand-drawn illustration from a computer-generated graphic.

With the computer's capability to mimic traditional artists' media, graphics software allows artists to do with a computer what they once did with brushes, pencils, and darkroom equipment. Similarly, architects and engineers now do most of their design and rendering work on computers—even though many were trained in traditional paper-based drafting methods. By using the computer, they produce designs and renderings that are not only highly accurate but also aesthetically pleasing.

Graphics software has advanced a great deal in a short time. In the early 1980s, most graphics programs were limited to drawing simple geometric outlines, usually in one color. Today, graphics software offers advanced drawing and painting tools and almost unlimited color control. You can see the products of these powerful tools everywhere you look. Their results can be subtle or stunning, obviously artificial, or amazingly lifelike.

OBJECTIVES

- Identify three computer platforms widely used in graphic design.
- Define the terms *bitmap* and *vector*, and differentiate these file types.
- List all the standard file formats for bitmap and vector images.
- Identify four ways to load graphic files into a computer.
- Discuss the various copyright issues that arise from the use of computer graphics.

COMPUTER PLATFORMS
USED FOR GRAPHICS

In today's publishing and design industries, it is not uncommon for an artist to create a graphic on a Windows-based PC, take the resulting file to a Macintosh computer to manipulate the graphic further, and then bring the file back to the PC for finishing touches or placement into a document. It is also common to do the opposite—create on a Macintosh, move the work to a Windows-based PC for enhancement, and then return to the Macintosh. Traditional artists must know the capabilities of their brushes and cameras, and today's computer-based artist must have a wide-ranging knowledge of graphics software, the hardware platforms on which it runs, and the formats in which the data can be stored.

Macintosh Computers

In 1984, the introduction of the Apple Macintosh computer and a modest piece of software known as MacPaint ushered in the era of "art" on the personal computer. With a pointing device and a black-and-white WYSIWYG (pronounced *wizzy wig*) monitor that displayed images as they would appear in print, the Macintosh computer allowed users to manipulate shapes, lines, and patterns with great flexibility. (The acronym **WYSIWYG** stands for "What You See Is What You Get" and is used to describe monitors and software that display documents as they will appear when printed.)

Figure 21.1
Some of the most sophisticated design and illustration tools were originally created specifically for the Macintosh platform. Today, almost all important graphics software is available for both Windows-based PCs and Macintosh computers.

Graphic artists also appreciated the Macintosh's easy-to-use graphical interface, with enhancements such as sophisticated typefaces and the capability to magnify images and undo mistakes. Within a few years, the graphics world had embraced the Macintosh as a serious production tool (see Figure 21.1). With the release of more powerful graphics software and the advent of the **Postscript** page-description language—which enabled accurate printing of complex images—the Macintosh became the tool of choice for a new breed of computer artists.

Windows-Based PCs

In the late 1980s, Microsoft's Windows brought many of the same capabilities to IBM PCs and compatibles, greatly expanding that market for graphics software. PC hardware was also becoming more graphics-capable, with the advent of high-resolution, high-color monitors and video cards. Today, PCs and Macintosh systems provide basically the same capabilities when it comes to running graphics software. A wide array of graphics programs is now available for both platforms.

UNIX-Based Workstations

Another important platform for computer graphics is the class of machines known as workstations. These specialized, single-user computers possess extremely powerful and fast CPUs, large-capacity hard disks, high-resolution displays, sophisticated video cards, and lots of RAM. Many workstations run UNIX; some artists use graphics software written especially for the workstation. Professional graphic artists and designers typically use workstations made by Sun Microsystems and SGI. Because of their expense, workstations typically are reserved for the most demanding graphics projects, such as complicated animation, high-resolution mapping, technical drafting, and cinematic special effects.

In recent years, the price of workstations has dropped dramatically, making their power more accessible to the average graphics user. Macintosh- and Windows-based computers have become much more powerful, however, greatly shrinking the gap between workstations and personal computers. This increase in power has encouraged UNIX software manufacturers to offer UNIX software in PC formats as well. In fact, moviemakers now frequently use PCs and PC-based software to create special effects and animation for movies—a domain once held exclusively by the workstation (see Figures 21.2 and 21.3).

Figure 21.2
Many movies, television programs, and commercials rely heavily on computer-generated special effects. Before being transferred to film, these virtual landscapes and characters are created on workstations and personal computers in a wide variety of commercial and proprietary software.

Figure 21.3
Today, the majority of advertisements, magazine covers, and posters are created using graphics software.

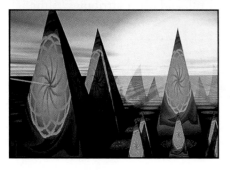

Computer Graphics and Design

TYPES OF GRAPHICS FILES

Graphics files are composed of one of the following two features:

◆ A grid whose cells are filled with a color, called a **bitmap** (see Figure 21.4). The individual cells in the grid can all be filled with the same color or each cell can contain a different color. The term **raster** is sometimes used to describe bitmap images. Bitmap images may also be referred to as bitmapped images.

◆ A set of **vectors,** which are mathematical equations describing the size, shape, thickness, position, color, and fill of a closed graphical shape or of lines (see Figure 21.5).

Some types of graphics programs work with bitmaps; others work with vectors. Each category has advantages and disadvantages. Whether you use a bitmap- or vector-based program depends on what you are trying to do. For example, if you want to be able to retouch a photo, create seamless tiling textures for the Web or for 3-D surfaces, or create an image that looks like a painting, you will choose bitmap-based software (see Figure 21.6).

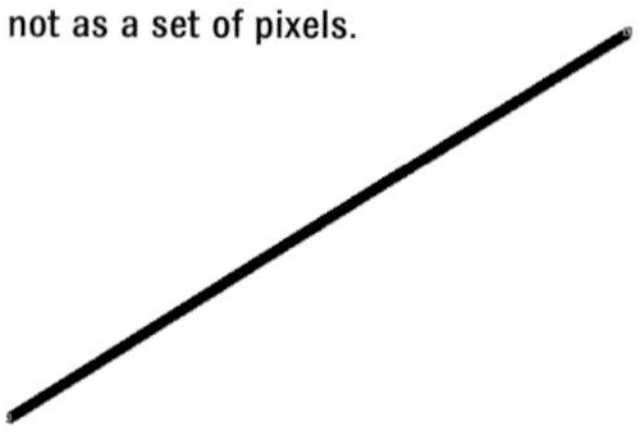

Vector-based software is your best choice if you want the flexibility of resizing an image without degrading its sharpness, the ability to reposition elements easily in an image, or the ability to achieve an illustrative look as when drawing with a pen or pencil. If you need both capabilities, some graphics software allows you to create art that takes advantage of each kind of program.

Working With Bitmaps

When you use bitmap-based graphics software, you are using the computer to change the characteristics of the pixels that compose an image. Manipulating pixels can become complex. For example, an 8- by 10-inch black-and-white image—if displayed at a typical screen resolution of 72 pixels per inch (ppi)—is a mosaic of 414,720 pixels, as shown in Figure 21.7.

The computer must remember the precise location of each and every pixel as they are viewed, moved, or altered. If you decide that the same 8- by 10-inch piece of artwork must have up to 256 colors in its makeup (which is considered minimal with today's technology), then the computer must keep track of the 414,720 pixels multiplied by the 8 bits per pixel that are necessary to identify 256 different colors. The computer must keep track of 3,317,760 bits for one color image (see Figure 21.8).

Working With Vectors

Strictly speaking, vectors are lines drawn from one point to another, as shown in Figure 21.9. Vector-based software can use mathematical equations to define the thickness and color of a line, its pattern or fill, and other attributes. Although a

Figure 21.4
If you magnify a bitmap, you can see its individual pixels.

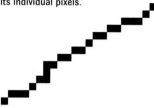

Figure 21.5
This vector is defined as a line stretching between two endpoints, not as a set of pixels.

Figure 21.6
This text has been generated with a bitmap-based paint program, so the text is actually composed of tiny blocks, called pixels. The text is a simple bitmap image.

Congratulations!

enable users of one program to work with files created in other programs. Only a handful of common file formats, such as **Data Exchange Format (DXF)** and **Initial Graphics Exchange Specification (IGES),** exist for vector graphics. These "universal" formats should enable you to create a vector file in one program, such as AutoCAD, and use it in another program, such as CorelDRAW or Visio.

Self Check

Answer the following questions by filling in the blank(s).

1. Because of their expense, _____ computers are typically reserved for the most demanding graphics projects.

2. Bitmap-based graphics software uses the computer to manipulate _____ .

3. A(n) _____ is a standardized method of encoding data for storage.

GETTING IMAGES INTO YOUR COMPUTER

The majority of graphics programs allow the user to create images from scratch, building simple lines and shapes into complex graphics. But you do not always start from scratch; it is common to begin with an existing image, which you can edit or enhance using graphics software. There are several ways to get images into a computer for editing. Four of the most commonly used methods are scanners, digital cameras, clip art, and electronic photographs.

Visit www.glencoe.com/norton/online/ for more information on **scanners**.

Scanners

A scanner is a little bit like a photocopy machine, except that instead of copying the image to paper, it transfers the image directly into the computer (see Figure 21.11). If the image is on paper or a slide, a scanner can convert it into a digital file that a computer can manipulate. The scanner is an input device attached to the computer by a cable and controlled by software. This software may accompany the scanner or it may be included with a graphics program. The result of scanning an image is a bitmap file (although software tools are available for translating these images into vector formats).

Digital Cameras

Digital cameras provide another way to import images into a computer. They store digitized images (in on-board flash memory, and on removable media such as a PC card, floppy disk, or disk cartridge) for transfer into a computer. Many are small and easy to use and include software and cables or infrared connections for the transfer process. The resulting file is generally a bitmap. Once on disk, digital images can be copied, edited, printed, or used in World Wide Web pages or other documents.

Figure 21.11
A scanner is a valuable tool for graphic artists because it allows them to convert printed images into bitmap files that can be stored on a computer and manipulated with graphics software.

Techview

Digital cameras are rapidly increasing in popularity, to the point that many professional photographers now use digital equipment almost exclusively. As prices drop and more models become available, digital cameras are also finding their way into an ever-increasing number of homes.

Photography the Old Way

Traditional cameras work by exposing a piece of film (celluloid covered with a light-sensitive emulsion, such as silver nitrate) to light for a fixed amount of time. The film reacts to the light that passes through the camera's lens, "capturing" reflected images.

The biggest advantage of traditional photography is that, depending on the equipment and conditions, a photograph can have almost infinite resolution. That is, its quality is not limited by the finite number of "dots" that comprise the image.

Traditional photography also has some drawbacks. Film must be processed before the results can be seen. Great care must be taken to preserve the negative image produced on the film. It can be extremely difficult to modify a film-based photograph, using traditional processing methods. Finally, film processing and printing can be a slow, expensive process.

And the New Way

Instead of using only a lens to capture light, most digital cameras use a charge-coupled device (CCD) to convert light into a digital image. CCDs are commonly used on scanners and video cameras as well as digital cameras.

After capturing an image, a digital camera stores it in a special type of memory or on a magnetic disk. Manufacturers have developed a variety of storage technologies. Some cameras use a standard 3.5-inch floppy disk for storage. Other cameras use PC Cards or special "memory sticks" to hold photos; these devices use flash memory to store data even when the camera is turned off.

Digital cameras can store photos in a variety of formats, which may require different amounts of storage and provide varying resolutions. Most digital cameras can store images in high-resolution JPEG or TIFF formats, but these formats consume a great deal of storage space.

The biggest advantage of digital photography is convenience. Many cameras provide LCD screens so you can review a picture right after taking it. This lets you decide whether you want to keep or delete the picture. Instead of taking film to a developing lab, you can copy the images to a PC and print them out.

Printing is both the biggest blessing and biggest curse of digital photography. Even though digital cameras store pictures at very high resolutions (millions of pixels per image), the printed image's quality is restricted to the printer's quality. So, if you use a color ink jet printer with a resolution of 300×600 dpi, that's as good as your images will look. For best results when printing digital photographs, use premium-quality photo printing paper, which is available at any office supply store.

A digital camera stores the image as a bitmap file rather than an exposed piece of film.

You can use color laser printers for higher-resolution printing, but they are very expensive. A less expensive option is the snapshot printer, which offers near-photographic resolution, but snapshot printers are slow and most print only small formats.

Even so, digital cameras are a boon to many people. You can use digital photos in Web pages and documents. Using PhotoCD or a CD-R device, you can store hundreds of photos on a single disk. And, in spite of their limited resolution, home-printed photos are faster and cheaper than professionally printed photos from film.

Digital cameras are available from a wide range of manufacturers. You can buy a basic camera for around $100. Professional-grade digital cameras can cost tens of thousands of dollars.

Clip Art

The term **clip art** originated with large books filled with page after page of professionally created drawings and graphics that could be cut out, or "clipped," from the pages and glued to a paper layout. Today, clip art provides an easy way to enhance digital documents. It is commonly available on CD-ROM or diskettes, or via commercial online services. Many word processing and presentation programs also feature a selection of clip art, as shown in Figure 21.12, although the choices may be limited unless the program is stored on a compact disk. Clip art can be found in both bitmap and vector formats. The variety of clip art is huge, ranging from simple line drawings and cartoons to lush paintings and photographs.

Electronic Photographs

Graphic artists commonly use traditional photos that have been converted into digital format by scanning. Digitizing a photo always involves some type of scanner, but the process has become sophisticated in recent years, ensuring high-resolution, professional-quality digital images. Photos are often digitized at special processing labs that scan the images and save the resulting files in a format called PhotoCD (see Figure 21.13). Kodak created the PhotoCD (PCD) format as a standard way of recording photographic images and storing them on a compact disk.

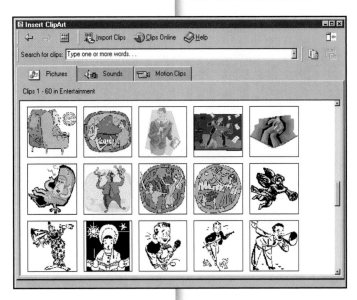

Figure 21.12
Many newer application programs provide built-in libraries of clip art. You can also purchase large collections of clip art or download clip art from various online sources.

The PhotoCD offers many advantages. First, it provides a convenient storage medium for photos. Second, PhotoCD software makes it easy to view and select photos quickly from disk. Third, many PhotoCDs store the images at several different resolutions, making them available for different purposes. A magazine, for example, requires much higher-resolution images than a newspaper or a Web page.

COPYRIGHT ISSUES

The ease with which computer users can acquire and manipulate images has brought another issue to the fore—copyright. Although clip art is often licensed for unlimited use, most pieces of artwork (drawings, backgrounds, buttons, animation, and photos) that you see in print or on the Internet are not. Instead, they are owned by the creator or publisher of the artwork. Artwork may have also been licensed for publication or displayed in a specific place for a limited number of times.

If you scan a photograph from a magazine, place it in your work, and sell it to someone else, you are infringing on a copyright and can be fined or prosecuted. This restriction applies even if you edit the image; making changes to someone else's work does not make you the owner. If you want to use an image you did not create solely on your own, and it is not part of a clip art package, you must contact the copyright holder for permission.

Figure 21.13
The computer shown here is used to convert pictures into a digital format and store them on PhotoCDs.

Norton Notebook

GRAPHICS PIRACY ON THE INTERNET

One reason the World Wide Web has become so popular is its support of graphics in Web pages. By adding all sorts of images to HTML documents, Web designers make their sites more attractive and appealing to visitors. Similarly, Internet services such as FTP and newsgroups enable users to find, download, and exchange files of all types quickly, including graphics.

This easy access to images, however, has also created a cottage industry of graphics piracy because some Internet users gather large quantities of images and distribute them online. The primary purpose of hundreds of Web sites and Usenet newsgroups is to provide users with a place to find, exchange—and sometimes even purchase—illegally obtained graphics.

The Internet provides a seemingly limitless number of pirated images, including clip art, electronic photographs, scanned artwork and photographs, video clips, and more. As you might imagine, the subject matter of these images runs the gamut from family-oriented cartoons, to celebrity images, to pornography.

Although a small percentage of these online graphics are homemade (created by the person distributing them), the vast majority are illegally acquired by scanning or copying from digital sources. You can easily find images scanned directly from popular magazines, clips pirated from videotapes, and still images captured from television shows and movies.

The real problem is that pirates distribute these copyrighted graphics freely, ignoring the rights of the images' actual owners. The most daring pirates scan images from popular magazines, and then attempt to sell them over Web sites, through newsgroups, or on CD-ROM as though this were perfectly legal.

Ignorance Is No Excuse

Many graphics pirates take up this practice because they do not understand copyright laws or the possible consequences of their actions. They believe that once an image has been digitized, it enters the public domain—in other words, it is the property of no one and free for anyone to use. Some graphics pirates believe that by making a small change to an image (such as adding a name or logo), they are making it their personal property. However, the pirates are wrong in both cases.

Photographic images, illustrations, and other types of graphics are indeed protected—in the United States, at least—by copyright laws that strictly limit the way they can be reused.

Staying Out of Trouble

Here are some steps you can take to make sure you are handling electronic graphics properly:

◆ **Consider the Source.** If you find images of any kind on a Web site or newsgroup, consider them suspect. If you need electronic images for a document of your own, especially if you want to sell the document, look for sources of license-free images (you do not need to pay a license fee to use them) or be ready to pay a fee for an image from a legitimate source.

◆ **Get Proof and Permission.** Regardless of where you obtain an image, the distributor should be willing and able to provide proof of ownership of the image and to grant or deny permission to use it, regardless of whether a fee is involved. If you cannot obtain this type of documentation in writing (not over e-mail or on a Web page), then do not use the image.

◆ **Never Upload Images to Newsgroups or the Web.** Whether you illegally scan published images or acquire images from a legitimate source, resist the urge to put them on the Internet. Even if you own an image or have the right to use it commercially, you can assume that once it is on the Internet, it will be copied and distributed in ways you never intended.

◆ **Know What You Are Doing.** If you get involved in electronic graphics, become acquainted with copyright laws and the protections in place to safeguard the rights of copyright holders.

NORTON ONLINE

Visit **www.glencoe.com/norton/online/** for more information on **graphics piracy.**

LESSON QUIZ

True/False

Answer the following questions by circling True or False.

True   False   **1.** In 1984, the IBM-PC ushered in the era of "art" on the personal computer.

True   False   **2.** Vector images use groups of dots to define entities.

True   False   **3.** A typical screen resolution is 72 pixels per inch.

True   False   **4.** If a file format works with a given program, the two are said to be compatible.

True   False   **5.** Clip art is available only in large books.

Multiple Choice

Circle the word or phrase that best completes each sentence.

1. A _____ image is a grid whose cells are filled with color.
   A. bitmap   **B.** vector   **C.** workstation

2. A file format is _____ .
   A. always proprietary   **B.** a standardized method of encoding data for storage   **C.** neither A nor B

3. Data Exchange Format (DXF) is a _____ .
   A. bitmap graphics file format   **B.** vector graphics file format   **C.** both A and B

4. A(n) _____ can convert a printed image into digital format.
   A. photocopy machine   **B.** electronic photograph   **C.** scanner

5. _____ is often licensed for unlimited use.
   A. A bitmap   **B.** Clip art   **C.** Copyright

LESSON LABS

Complete the following exercises as directed by your instructor.

1. To find out if there are any images on your hard disk, launch Windows Explorer and select the icon for your hard disk. On the menu bar, click Tools, and point to Find; then click Files or Folders. The Find dialog box appears. Type ***.gif, *.jpg** in the Named box. In the Look in box, select the icon for your hard disk; then check the Include subfolders check box. Click Find Now. If Windows finds any files, they will appear in the bottom half of the dialog box. Close the Find dialog box.

2. Here is an easy way to learn about incompatibility between files and programs. Launch Notepad by clicking the Start button, pointing to Programs, and pointing to Accessories; then click Notepad. On the menu bar, click File, then click Open. In the Open dialog box, click the Files of Type drop-down arrow and choose All Files. Next, browse your disk for a file with an extension such as .gif, .jpg, or .tif. Select the file, if there is one. Then click Open. What happens? Close Notepad.

LESSON 22

Graphics Software

OBJECTIVES

- List five types of graphics software and their uses.
- Differentiate the way bitmap- and vector-based graphics programs work.
- Describe four methods for creating 3-D computer models.
- Identify three important categories of computer-generated animation.
- Name five graphic elements commonly found in Web pages.

OVERVIEW: The Tools of the Trade

Creating a digital image or manipulating an existing one can involve a complex array of processes. Since even the most sophisticated graphics program cannot perform all the operations that may be required for some types of graphics, designers frequently use more than one of the five major categories of graphics software to achieve their goals:

- ► Paint programs
- ► Photo-manipulation programs
- ► Draw programs
- ► Computer-Aided Design (CAD) programs
- ► 3-D modeling and animation programs

Of the five, the first two are bitmap-based paint programs; the rest are vector-based draw programs. This lesson will help you understand how artists use each type of program and why.

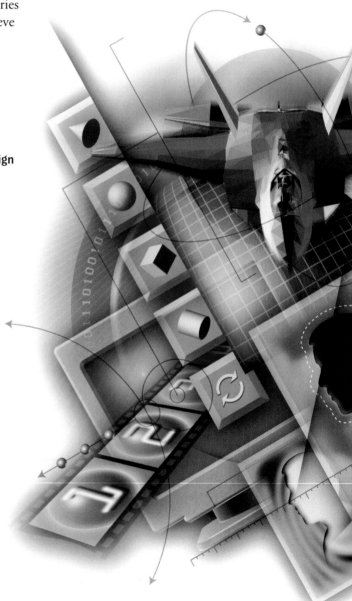

PAINT PROGRAMS

Paint programs are bitmap-based graphics programs. You may already be familiar with a paint program, like Windows Paint, or you may have used similar bitmap-based tools in a word processor to draw simple shapes or lines in a document. Paint programs range from the very simple (with only a handful of tools) to the very complex, with tools that have names like paintbrush, pen, chalk, watercolors, airbrush, crayon, and eraser. Because paint programs keep track of each and every pixel placed on a screen, they can also perform tasks that are impossible with traditional artists' tools—for example, erasing a single pixel or creating instant copies of an image.

Paint programs lay down pixels in a process comparable to covering a floor with tiny mosaic tiles. Changing an image created with a paint program is like scraping tiles off the floor and replacing them with different tiles. This dot-by-dot approach allows a high degree of flexibility, but it also has a few drawbacks. For example, once you create a circle or make an electronic brush stroke, you can erase or tinker with the individual pixels, making minor adjustments until the image is exactly what you want (see Figure 22.1). On the other hand, you cannot change the circle or stroke as a whole, especially if you have painted over it, because the software does not recognize bitmaps as a circle or brush stroke after they are created. They are simply a collection of pixels.

Although there are exceptions, most paint programs are also not well suited to handling text. Even though many provide an easy way to add text to an image, the text becomes just another collection of pixels after it is placed. If you misspell a word, you cannot simply backspace over the faulty text and retype it, as you would in a word processor. Instead, you must select the word (or a portion of it), delete the selected portion, and replace it.

This process can be difficult if you place the text over another part of the image. Many newer paint programs enable you to layer a new part of an image over existing parts, leaving the older parts intact if you move or erase the new part. In these cases, you can delete or edit text without affecting the rest of the image. If your paint program does not provide layering, however, existing portions of the image are replaced by—that is, their pixels are recolored with—any new part that you add to the image (see Figure 22.2).

These limitations aside, paint programs provide the tools for creating some spectacular effects. More sophisticated paint programs can make brush strokes that appear thick or thin, soft or hard, drippy or neat, opaque or transparent. Some programs allow you to change media with

Figure 22.1

This circle was created using a paint program. As you zoom into the circle, making it larger on the screen, you can see the pixels that comprise it.

The last *m* should be an *e*.

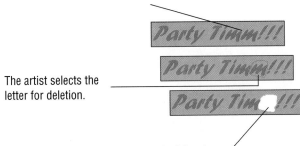

The artist selects the letter for deletion.

When the letter is deleted, so is the background.

Figure 22.2

This text was drawn in a paint program that does not allow layering. To correct the misspelling, the artist must select the letter *m* and delete it. However, because the letters replaced the background color instead of being layered on top of it, the deletion also removes part of the background.

a mouse click, turning your paintbrush into a chalk or a crayon or giving your smooth "canvas" a texture like rice paper or an eggshell (see Figure 22.3).

Unusual special effects abound in paint programs. For example, you can convert an image in any number of bizarre ways. Paint programs let you distort a person's features, break a statue into hundreds of tiles, swirl an image as though it is being pulled into a whirlpool, and much more. For example, Figure 22.4 shows an image before and after the Mosaic effect is applied in a paint program. Many different paint packages are available, including Adobe Photoshop, Jasc Software's PaintShop Pro, and MetaCreations' Painter, to name a few.

Figure 22.4
A photographic image, before and after distortion by the Mosaic filter in a paint program.

PHOTO-MANIPULATION PROGRAMS

When scanners made it easy to transfer photographs to the computer at high resolution, a new class of software was needed to manipulate these images on the screen. Cousins to paint programs, **photo-manipulation programs** now take the place of a photographer's darkroom for many tasks. Although used most often for simple jobs such as sharpening focus or adjusting contrast, photo-manipulation programs are also used to modify photographs in ways far beyond the scope of a traditional darkroom. The picture shown in Figure 22.5, for example, has obviously been subjected to electronic manipulation.

Because photo-manipulation programs (like paint programs) edit images at the pixel level, they can control precisely how a picture will look. They are also used to edit nonphotographic images and to create images from scratch. This is why

some artists put photo-manipulation programs in the same category as paint programs. The advent of photo-manipulation programs has caused an explosion in the use of computers for modifying images. Adobe Photoshop, Corel Photo Paint, and Ulead's PhotoImpact are some popular photo-manipulation programs.

Figure 22.5
This image demonstrates how a photo-manipulation program can be used to combine a traditional photograph with computer-generated graphics effects.

Photo-manipulation programs can accomplish some amazing feats. After a photograph has been brought into the computer, usually by scanning or from a digital camera or PhotoCD, the artist can change or enhance the photo, down to individual pixels, at will. For example, if a photo has dust spots or someone's eyes look red from a flash, the artist can draw the right number of appropriately colored pixels delicately into the affected areas to correct the problem (see Figure 22.6). Photo-manipulation programs are frequently used to correct color and brightness levels in photographs, to apply special effects, and to combine different parts of images seamlessly so they look like a complete image.

White lines come from scratches on the original film.

Using the airbrush tool, the artist can blend them into the background.

Figure 22.6
Repairing a scratched image with an airbrush tool.

Visit **www.glencoe.com/norton/online/** for more information on **photo-manipulation programs.**

Photo-manipulation programs also contain tools that can alter the original image drastically, in effect causing photos to lie (see Figure 22.7). For example, if a photograph of a group of people has been scanned into the computer, special tools can erase the pixels that form the image of one of these people and replace them with pixels from the background area—effectively removing the person from the photo.

Figure 22.7
The keyhole in this photo has been partially erased and replaced with parts of a new background—the cow.

DRAW PROGRAMS

Draw programs are vector-based graphics programs that are well suited for work when accuracy and flexibility are as important as coloring and special effects. Although they do not possess the pixel-pushing capability of paint programs, draw programs can be used to create images with an "arty" look and have been adopted as the primary tool of many designers. You see the output of draw programs in everything from cereal box designs to television show credits. CorelXARA, CorelDraw, and Adobe Illustrator are popular PC drawing programs.

Draw programs work by defining every line as a mathematical equation, or vector. They are sometimes referred to as object-oriented programs because each item drawn—whether it is a line, square, rectangle, or circle—is treated as a separate and distinct object from all the others. (Some designers and draw programs use the term *entity* rather than *object,* but the concept is the same.) All objects created in modern draw programs consist of an outline and a fill. The fill can be nothing at all, a solid color, a vector pattern, a photo, or something else. For example, when you draw a square with a draw program, the computer remembers it as a square of a fixed size at a specific location, that may or may not be filled—not as a bunch of pixels in the shape of a square.

Draw programs offer two big advantages over paint programs. First, when objects are created, they remain objects to the computer. After you draw a circle, you can return to it later and move it intact by dragging it with the mouse, even if it has been covered with other shapes or lines. You can change the circle's shape into an oval, change the size of the circle, or change its color, or you can fill its interior with a color, a blend of colors, or a pattern (see Figures 22.8 and 22.9). You can make these changes without affecting any other objects in the drawing.

Figure 22.8
Simply by clicking and dragging in a draw program, you can change a circle into an oval. You can use similar techniques to change squares to rectangles and to modify other shapes.

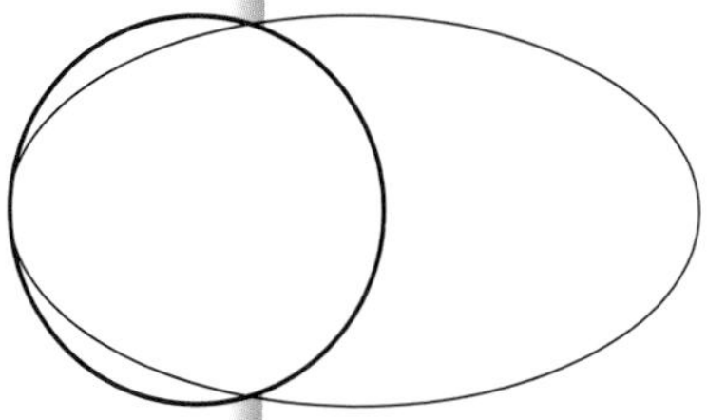

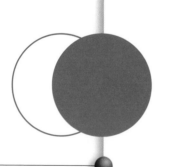

Figure 22.9
Because this circle was created with a draw program, it can be filled with a color (green, in this case), moved, and copied.

Another advantage draw programs have is the ability to resize images easily, without degrading their sharpness or focus, so that they match the size of the paper on which they will be printed. Because bitmap images are a grid of dots, they can be difficult to resize accurately while retaining their clarity. This characteristic is why paint programs are often described as being **resolution-dependent;** the image's appearance may change depending on the resolution at which it is displayed.

Vector graphics, on the other hand, are much easier to resize. The software mathematically changes all the objects so they appear larger or smaller. Similarly, many draw programs can scale objects—increasing or reducing size by a certain factor or in relation to other objects in the drawing. With scaling, there is no change in the resolution, so there is no loss in the image's quality. Draw programs are described as being **resolution-independent;** the image looks the same no matter what its resolution.

Draw programs are also superior to paint programs in their handling of text, as shown in Figure 22.10.

The distinction between draw programs and paint programs is blurring quickly. Attributes of paint programs have been incorporated into draw programs, and vice versa, producing some software packages that can be used to handle almost any task involving graphics. For example, most draw programs now include the capability to import photos or art created with paint programs, although for the most part they lack the capability to edit them at the pixel level.

HAPPY BIRTHDAY!

the road less traveled

COMPUTER-AIDED DESIGN PROGRAMS

Computer-Aided Design (CAD), also called Computer-Aided Drafting or Computer-Aided Drawing, is the computerized version of the hand-drafting process that used to be done with a pencil and ruler on a drafting table. Over the last fifteen years, the drafting process has been almost completely computerized because CAD programs have become easier to use and offer a wider array of features. CAD is used extensively in technical fields, such as architecture, and in mechanical, electrical, and industrial engineering. CAD software is also used in other design disciplines, such as textile and clothing design, product and package design, and others.

CAD programs have been created for many different computer platforms. Some of the most powerful CAD tools—such as Pro/ENGINEER by Parametric Technology Corp.; AutoCAD by Autodesk, Inc.; and MicroStation by Bentley Systems, Inc.—are available for the PC, workstation, and even larger-scale platforms.

CAD Precision

Unlike drawings made using paint or drawing programs, CAD drawings are usually the basis for the actual building or manufacturing process of, for example, houses, engine gears, or electrical systems. To satisfy the rigorous requirements of manufacturing, CAD programs provide a high degree of precision. If you want to draw a line that is 12.396754 inches long or a circle with a radius of .90746 centimeters, a CAD program can fulfill your needs. CAD programs are so precise, in fact, that they can produce designs accurate to the micrometer—or one-millionth of a meter.

This accuracy also extends to the other end of the scale. Not only can you design the tiniest object in a CAD program, you can also design the largest objects in full scale. In the CAD program's database, the measurements of each line are identical to their actual measurements in real life. Therefore, if you want to draw a full-scale, three-dimensional version of the Earth, you can do it. (In fact, it has already been done, as shown in Figure 22.11.)

Figure 22.10
Draw programs make it easy to color text. Lines of text can be bent or distorted. Text can also be forced to follow a curvy line.

NORTON ONLINE

Visit **www.glencoe.com/norton/online/** for more information on **draw programs** and **CAD products**.

Figure 22.11
You cannot tell from the computer screen, but in the AutoCAD database, this three-dimensional image of Earth is in full scale. If you had a sheet of paper large enough, you could print this drawing, and it would be the same size as the Earth.

CAD programs achieve such a great degree of accuracy in three ways:

1. CAD programs are vector-based. As you learned earlier, a vector-based program recognizes objects not just as a fixed series of pixels but according to variable starting and ending points, thickness, weight, and other attributes.

2. CAD programs generally do not store objects as objects; rather, they store the object's attributes in a database. (In fact, CAD programs are actually database programs; the information in the database tells the program how to re-create objects on screen and on paper.)

3. CAD programs are math-based and take advantage of the computer's floating-point math processor to perform calculations. As a result, CAD programs can easily recognize large or small objects and instantly scale the image to fit on the screen or on paper and in proportion to other objects.

Layers and Dimensions

Another important feature of CAD programs is their ability to define **layers,** which are like transparent layers of film that you can place on top of each other. Layers permit CAD users to organize complex drawings. For example, a structural engineer designing an office building might create layers such as electrical, plumbing, structural, and so on. The engineer can then show and hide these individual layers while different parts of the building are designed. The concept of layering has become so useful to designers that many paint and draw programs now provide layering capabilities that function in much the same manner as CAD layers.

All CAD programs have the ability to add dimensions to a drawing. Remember, CAD programs store information about each object in the drawing, including its size and scale. **Dimensions** are notations showing the measurements of an object and are usually placed on their own layer. Dimensioning is essential to the process of actually building or manufacturing the object being drawn. Most CAD programs can also perform calculations on drawings. For example, they can calculate the area of a living room or the volume of a storage tank.

Finally, because CAD drawings are created from a database of attributes, designers can use the information in other ways. If you design a complete building in a CAD program, for example, you can use the database to create lists of materials required for construction. Special software enables contractors to use this database information to create cost estimates and schedules.

Figure 22.12
A 3-D wireframe model.

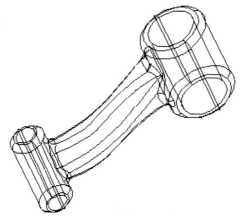

CAD and 3-D Design

You can also thank the CAD world for the 3-D craze that has swept through the design industry since the early 1990s. Three-dimensional design started in CAD programs during the late 1980s as a way to allow designers to view their designs from all possible angles on screen. Today, most CAD programs provide different ways to design, display, animate, and print 3-D objects, called **models.** For example,

wireframe models represent 3-D shapes by displaying their outlines and edges (see Figure 22.12). Many CAD programs also work with **solid models,** which work by giving the user a representation of a block of solid material. The user can then use different operations (cutting, adding, combining, and so on) to shape the material and create a finished model. Once a model is finished, CAD programs can **render** the image, shading in the solid parts and creating output that looks almost real. Figure 22.13 shows a rendered image of the wireframe model from Figure 22.12. A solid model would look the same.

In the early days of 3-D design, the designer would create the raw three-dimensional models in a CAD program and then export the files into a special rendering and animation program to add lighting, shading, surface features, and more. Now, however, higher-end CAD programs include these capabilities, freeing the user from relying on multiple programs—except when special effects or complicated animation is required.

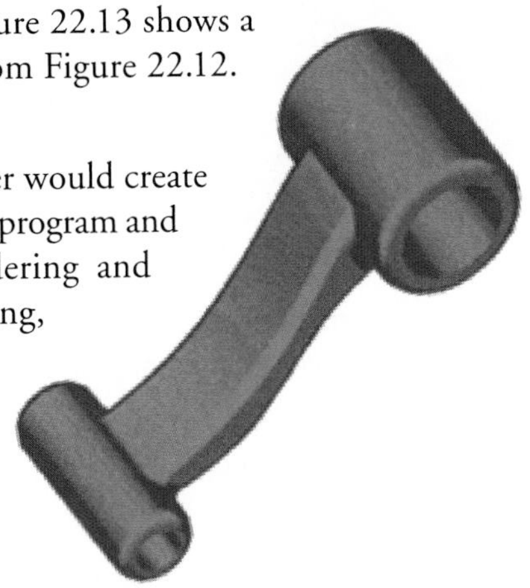

Figure 22.13
A rendering of the 3-D wireframe model. If the model had been solid rather than wireframe, the rendering would look almost the same.

Self Check

Answer the following questions by filling in the blank(s).

1. Paint programs are _____ -based graphics programs.

2. In a(n) _____ graphics program, the appearance of an image may change depending on the resolution at which it is displayed.

3. CAD users can organize complex drawings by using _____ .

3-D MODELING PROGRAMS

Whether you are aware of it or not, you are constantly exposed to elaborate 3-D imaging in movies, television, and print. Many of these images are now created with a special type of graphics software, called **3-D modeling software,** which enables users to create electronic models of three-dimensional objects without using CAD software. Fast workstations or PCs coupled with 3-D modeling programs can lend realism to even the most fantastic subjects. Professional 3-D designers use sophisticated, expensive 3-D modeling programs such as 3-D Studio MAX, Electric Image, SoftImage, Ray Dream Designer, and LightWave 3D.

There are four different types of 3-D modeling programs, and each uses a different technique to create three-dimensional objects:

◆ **Surface modelers** build objects by stretching a surface—like a skin—over an underlying wireframe structure (see Figure 22.14 on page 402).

◆ **Solid modelers** use the same technique as surface modelers but also understand thickness and density (see Figure 22.15 on page 402). This capability can be important if you need to punch a hole through an electronic object.

NORTON
ONLINE

Visit **www.glencoe.com/norton/online/** to find galleries of 3-D images.

Figure 22.14

This gear is an example of a CAD model rendered with surface modeling techniques.

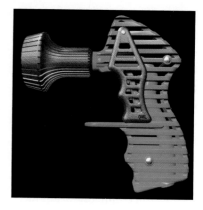

Figure 22.15

This CAD model of a spray nozzle for a hose was created using solid modeling techniques.

◆ **Polygonal modelers** combine many tiny polygons to build objects—similar to the way one would build a geodesic dome out of many perfectly fitted triangles (see Figure 22.16).

◆ **Spline-based modelers** build objects, either surface or solid, using mathematically defined curves that are rotated on an axis to form a 3-D shape.

Figure 22.16

This model shows how polygonal modeling techniques can be used.

Regardless of the method used to create them, 3-D objects can be modified to any shape using electronic tools akin to those used in woodworking. Wood can be cut, drilled, shaped, and sanded, and objects created with a 3-D modeling program can be changed or molded. For example, holes can be drilled into computer-based 3-D objects, and corners can be made round or square by selecting the appropriate menu item. Three-dimensional objects can also be given realistic textures and patterns; they can be animated or made to fly through space.

ANIMATION

An outgrowth of the 3-D explosion is computer-based animation. Since the creation of filmmaking, animation was possible only through a painstaking process of hand-drawing a series of images (called cels), as shown in Figure 22.17, and then filming them one by one. Each filmed image is called a **frame.** When the film is played back at high speed (usually around thirty frames per second for high-quality animation), the images blur together to create the illusion of motion on the screen. The process of manually creating a short animation—even just a few seconds' worth—can take weeks of labor.

Computer-generated imagery (CGI) has changed the world of animation in many ways. Although computer animation works on the same principles as traditional

Figure 22.17

Images from a traditional, manually drawn animation. Although computers speed up the animation process tremendously, they still work on the same idea: generate hundreds or thousands of individual images, and then display them in rapid succession to create the illusion of motion.

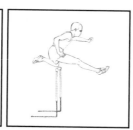

PRODUCTIVITY Tip

Drawing Tools for Everyone

A popular piece of computing wisdom tells us: "Having a word processor does not make you a writer." Similarly, owning some graphics software cannot make you an artist. But it cannot hurt, especially if you need to create graphics for reports, Web pages, or other projects. Even if you have no artistic skills, you can create effective graphics with basic, inexpensive (or free) software. Paint and draw programs have become so sophisticated and simple to use that you really do not need to be an artist to achieve professional-looking results.

If your graphics needs are simple, start by trying some inexpensive shareware programs. You can obtain a shareware program for free, initially, and can easily download one from Web sites like **www.download.com/**, **www.shareware.com/**, and many others. If you decide to keep the program after trying it, register your copy and pay the fee required by the developer, usually just a few dollars. With some practice, you may be ready to try a full-featured commercial program.

For simple drawings (such as plain geometric shapes and line drawings), start with Windows Paint, which comes with every copy of Windows. You can also find basic drawing tools in word processing programs. If your needs are more complex, try the shareware version of a paint program such as LView (available at **www.lview.com/**) or PaintShop Pro (available at **www.jasc.com/**). Such programs offer the following features:

◆ **Rich Drawing Tools.** Many inexpensive programs provide a wide array of drawing tools, including brushes, chalk, pencils, airbrushes, and more.

◆ **Photo-Manipulation Features.** If you can save your scanned photos or digital pictures to a common file format (such as JPEG or TIFF), you can edit them, change color settings, make contrast and brightness corrections, and hide flaws.

◆ **Support for Multiple File Formats.** Even shareware paint programs support most commonly used file formats, such as JPEG, PCX, TIFF, and many others.

If you need to create more accurate, easily scalable drawings and want an illustrated "look" to your work, then you should get a draw program. Instead of spending several hundred dollars for a draw package, try a low-cost program such as CorelXARA (available from online vendors such as **www.i-us-com/** or **www.corel.com/**), Visio,

Shareware versions of products like PaintShop Pro are popular because they provide professional-quality features at low cost.

or an older version of CorelDRAW. You can also download trial versions of powerful draw programs like Adobe Illustrator (at **www.adobe.com/**) and CorelDRAW (at **www.corel.com/**). Unlike shareware products, trial products may have some disabled features or they may expire after a certain time. These programs are packed with features, such as:

◆ **Drag-and-Drop Editing.** You can move, copy, reshape, scale, and distort shapes simply by clicking and dragging. This capability eliminates the need to navigate menus and provides instant results.

◆ **High Resolution and Color Depth.** Even inexpensive draw programs can save files at high resolutions and in 16 million colors.

◆ **Sophisticated Text Handling.** Most draw programs provide outstanding text features, allowing you to create special text effects, shows, 3-D text, and more. Because text is made of vectors, edges are clean when viewed on the screen and in print.

Low-cost and shareware CAD and 3-D modeling programs are available. If you are just beginning to experiment with computer graphics, however, you may want to delay installing or purchasing such programs. Start with the basics and work your way up. You will be amazed at the results you can get with a little practice and patience.

animation (a sequence of still images displayed in rapid succession), computer animators now have highly sophisticated tools that take the drudgery out of the animation process and allow them to create animation more quickly than ever. Computer animators also have the advantage of being able to display their animation on the computer screen or output them to CD-ROM, videotape, or film.

An added bonus of computer animation is the ability to animate three-dimensional characters and create **photorealistic** scenes. (The computer-generated image looks so realistic that it could be mistaken for a photograph of a real-life object.) These capabilities make computer-generated characters difficult to distinguish from real ones. Some examples are the dinosaur in *Godzilla,* the space ships in *Galaxy Quest,* and the eerie landscapes of *The Matrix.* Using computers and special animation software, artists and designers can create many types of animation, from simple perspective changes to complex full-motion scenes that incorporate animated characters with real-life actors and sound (see Figure 22.18).

Figure 22.18
Computer-generated animation is often so lifelike that it is hard to distinguish from the real thing.

Fly-Bys and Walk-Throughs

Architects and engineers frequently use the computer to take clients on a virtual tour of construction projects long before the actual construction has started. Using three-dimensional computer models created in a CAD program or 3-D modeling software such as 3D Studio MAX, designers can create lifelike simulations of the finished project—whether it's a hotel or a factory—complete with finishing touches such as carpeting, lighting, landscaping, and people.

One of the simplest forms of computer animation is the **fly-by.** In a fly-by, the designer sets up an exterior view of a three-dimensional model, which may be of a human-made structure (like a building or a stadium) or a natural one (such as a canyon or storm). The view is provided by one of the software "cameras" in the CAD or 3-D software. This type of software can provide many cameras, so the user can change views of a project at any time during the design process or even see multiple views at once on the screen. The designer then plots a motion path for the camera—that is, a line along which the camera travels. The motion path may take the camera around, over, or through the building, providing a "flying" effect or bird's-eye view. An example is shown in Figure 22.19. The designer then sets the camera in motion; as the camera travels along its path, the software captures still images (frames) of the scene as if it were being recorded by a real camera.

Figure 22.19
A 3-D fly-by can provide a bird's-eye view of a scene.

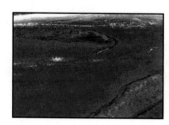  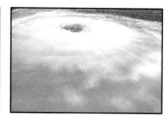 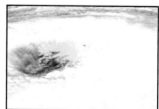

A **walk-through** operates on the same principle as a fly-by but is used to capture moving interior shots of a building or scene. If you have ever played a video game in which you control a character's movements through a 3-D scene (as in *Doom* or *Riven*), you are controlling a walk-through.

Walk-throughs and fly-bys can be preset by the designer. Using sophisticated software, however, designers can also do free-form walk-throughs and fly-bys in real time, controlling the camera's motion and angle as they go. Fly-bys and walk-throughs are considered simple forms of animation because the character (in this case, the building) does not move. Instead, the camera's ever-changing perspective creates the sense of motion through the scene.

Fly-bys and walk-throughs can be output from the computer onto videotape or compact disk, but this is a static method of giving a virtual tour; that is, you cannot deviate from the tour's route after it has been recorded. Therefore, many designers like to conduct virtual tours at the computer, enabling the virtual visitor to take charge of the tour. The visitor can wander through the design freely, enter any room at will, take the elevator or the stairs, and even open drawers and cabinets in the virtual furniture!

Character Animation

The type of computer-based animation receiving the most attention today is **character animation:** the art of creating a character (such as a person, an animal, or even a nonorganic item, such as a box or a car) and making it move in a lifelike manner. The basic techniques of character animation have not changed much from the drawing board to the computer. The process still involves drawing the character in a sequence of positions—one position per frame of film, and each one at a slightly more advanced position than the preceding one—until the entire movement is achieved.

If a character must walk from point A to point B, for example, the designer starts by drawing the character at the starting point and then again at the ending point of the walk. These two points are called the **keyframes** because they represent the most important focal points in the action. Next, the designer creates all the frames that show the character moving between points A and B; these frames are called **tweens** (short for *between* because these frames are positioned between the keyframes).

Computers have greatly simplified character animation in several ways. First, instead of drawing the character multiple times, the computer animator needs to draw it only once; the computer can duplicate the character as often as it is required. Instead of drawing a flat, two-dimensional character, many computer artists create complete three-dimensional characters that can be bent, twisted, and viewed from any angle.

To create a motion sequence, the animator needs to create only the keyframes. The character is set up in the beginning position and the ending position. The computer can then perform all the "tweening" by calculating the types of movements required to get the character from the first position to the last one (see Figure 22.20). The animator can tweak individual tweens to obtain the right effect. Animation software offers various tools to assist in the animation process and make the results more realistic.

NORTON
ONLINE

Visit **www.glencoe.com/norton/online/** for more information on **character animation**.

Figure 22.20
This animation cycle shows the beginning and ending keyframes and some of the tweens that fall between them.

 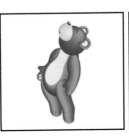 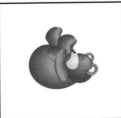  

Computer Graphics in Film and Games

It should come as no surprise that the majority of modern video games are filled
with computer-generated imagery, animation, backgrounds, and special effects.
Large studios now exist at companies such as Sega, Nintendo, and other interactive game designers where artists and animators use the latest technology to create
the most realistic, action-packed gaming experiences.

Game designers and filmmakers use many of the same techniques to create characters and backgrounds for viewing. Using 3-D modeling software, animation
tools, and scripting software, these designers create not only the graphics but also
the action sequences through which the characters and players move. Using tools
such as Macromedia Director and Authorware, game designers can create scripts
that tell the computer which graphics to display, which user commands to accept,
and much more.

Game makers and filmmakers rely heavily on computer-aided **compositing** techniques to blend computer-generated imagery and filmed or videotaped images of
real characters and objects (see Figure 22.21). Using compositing tools, designers
can add characters and objects to scenes that did not originally contain them. In
the recent re-release of the *Star Wars* movie, for example, special effects artists at
LucasFilms used these techniques to add familiar characters to previously unused
scenes, enhancing the movies' plot and extending its length.

Figure 22.21
Using compositing techniques, game
makers and filmmakers can add
characters and objects where they
previously did not exist.

GRAPHICS AND THE WORLD WIDE WEB

Perhaps even more than 3-D design and animation, the World Wide Web has
aroused intense curiosity and interest in computer graphics because nearly anyone
can create and post a Web page and because the World Wide Web can support many
types of graphics. By using basic paint and draw software as described earlier in this
unit, it is easy to create or edit graphics for use on a Web page. Such graphics include
simple items like bullets and horizontal rules, more complicated images such as
logos, and complex artwork and photographs. If you have spent any time surfing
the Web, you may agree that graphics elements truly enhance the viewing experience and can make even a simple page look elegant (see Figure 22.22).

Adding Graphics to a Web Page

Although a Web page might look like one big graphic, most pages are actually collections of graphics and text elements combined by the browser according to HTML
tags embedded in the page's content. If any navigation buttons, icons, bullets, bars,

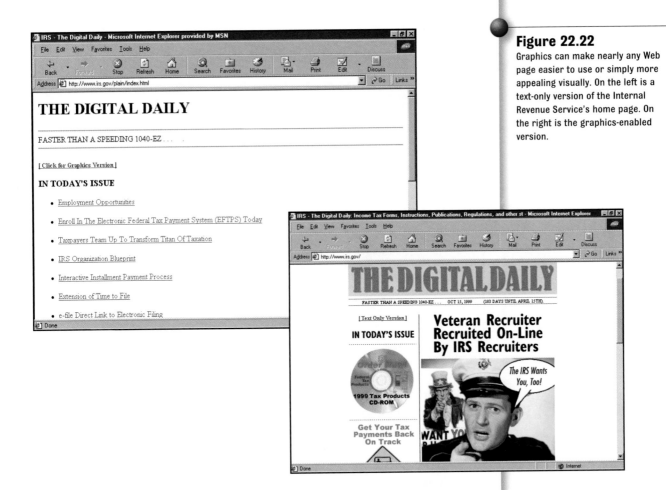

Figure 22.22
Graphics can make nearly any Web page easier to use or simply more appealing visually. On the left is a text-only version of the Internal Revenue Service's home page. On the right is the graphics-enabled version.

or images appear on the page, they are separate graphics files that are being displayed at the same time. When a Web designer creates a Web page, he or she usually begins by adding the text elements to an HTML-format file. By surrounding the text elements with special codes—called HTML tags—the designer can cause different pieces of text to be displayed in different ways by the Web browser. Tags tell the browser what information to display and how to display it.

The designer can also add tags that tell the browser to display graphics, as shown in Figure 22.23 on page 408, and a single Web page can hold many individual graphics. On the Web server, the designer must store all the graphics files required by the Web page. When the user's browser encounters the tags for a graphic, the server sends the graphics file to the browser. The HTML tags help the browser organize the graphics, text, and other design elements on the page.

The designer can use various methods to incorporate graphics in a Web page. They can be placed almost anywhere on the page, aligned in different ways, sized, incorporated in tables, and used as backgrounds. Graphics files are used to create buttons and bullets, horizontal rules, navigational tools, and much more.

Image Quality

As you learned earlier in this unit, computers can display graphics at various resolutions and color depths. Whenever possible, designers use graphics of the highest possible resolution and color depth. On an interactive medium such as the World Wide Web, however, image quality often must be sacrificed to reduce file size and download times.

NORTON
ONLINE

Visit www.glencoe.com/norton/online/ for more information on **controlling image quality** in **Web graphics**.

These tags in the HTML file...

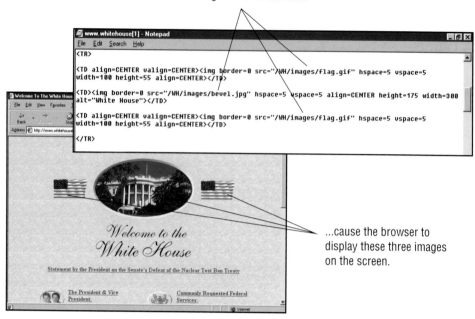

Figure 22.23

These two screens show a Web page's source code and the results in a browser. On the top, you can see the tags that format text and display graphics. On the bottom, you can see how the browser interprets the tags and displays the information.

...cause the browser to display these three images on the screen.

Remember that whenever your browser encounters a graphic in a Web page, it must download the graphic file from the Web server to your disk and then display it on screen. If the file is large or if the page contains many graphics, download time can be annoyingly slow. Web users frequently exit from a site before the page finishes downloading because the page is so graphics-intensive that it takes a long time to download. Therefore, Web designers have adopted a few standards to ensure that their pages download as quickly as possible from the server to the user's disk:

◆ **Resolution.** Web graphics are typically saved and displayed at a resolution of 72 pixels per inch (ppi), even though it is possible to save pictures at a much higher resolution, because monitors have a fixed display resolution of 72 ppi. As Figure 22.24 demonstrates, higher-resolution settings do not necessarily improve the appearance of an image when displayed on a standard monitor. Higher-resolution images also require more storage space and take longer to download to the user's computer.

◆ **Color Depth.** Although most computer screens can display colors of up to 24 or even 32 bits (called true color), the files that take advantage of these color

Figure 22.24

These three images were saved at different resolutions: 72 ppi, 144 ppi, and 244 ppi, from left to right. Note that the quality of the image does not improve much with the change in resolution.

settings can be large. Generally, Web designers use only two file formats—GIF and JPEG—which have specific color settings and specific uses. The maximum color depth for a GIF file is 8 bits, or 256 colors. JPG images are always 24-bit images that can display millions of colors.

◆ **Image Size.** Although it is possible to save images that are larger than the user's display space, Web designers avoid this practice. When a Web page requires large graphics, designers try to ensure that the image is not so large that it will run off the edge of the user's screen at 800 × 600 screen resolution.

File Formats

To maintain compatibility with the visitor's browser, designers create Web-page graphics in two file formats: GIF and JPG. Although just about any graphics file format can be used on a Web page, browsers support only the GIF, JPG, and PNG file formats without requiring the use of special plug-in software. Generally, browsers can open and view images in GIF, JPG, and PNG formats directly in the browser window, although PNG-format images are not commonly used. (For descriptions of various file formats, refer back to Table 21.1 on page 388.)

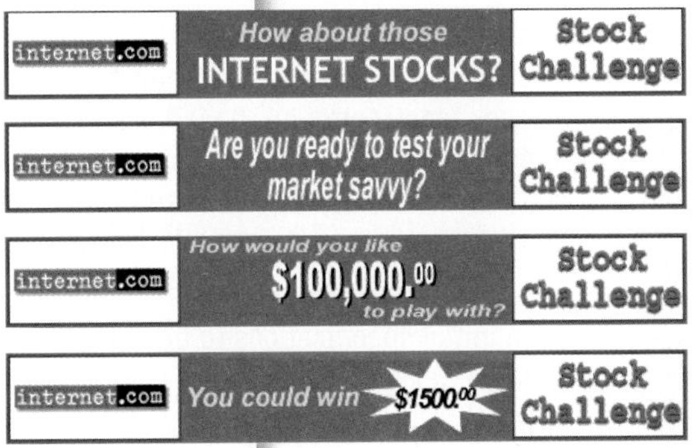

Using a variation of the GIF file, designers can easily add variety and movement to Web pages. The **animated GIF** file is simply a set of images, saved together in a single GIF-format file. When opened in a browser, the file's different images are displayed one after another, in a cycle (see Figure 22.25). The designer can set the order for the images to display and the amount of display time for each image. The result is a mini-animation. Animated GIFs are frequently used in advertising banners and other graphics elements to attract the user's attention.

Figure 22.25
When displayed in succession, these images create a simple animation. They are saved together in a special animated GIF file, which a browser can display.

Designers can also make animation available through plug-ins. Macromedia's Flash and Shockwave plug-ins, for example, have become popular methods for viewing animation in Web pages. The user must install the Flash and Shockwave plug-in software. When the browser encounters a Shockwave-format file in a Web page, it can download the file and play it back. Plug-ins such as Shockwave provide additional capabilities; for example, designers can create interactive animation, such as games, that allow the user to interact with the animation and change its direction or outcome (see Figure 22.26).

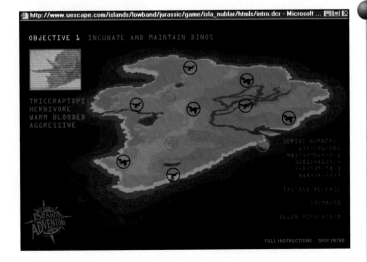

Figure 22.26
Plug-ins such as Shockwave not only make it possible to view animation on the Web but to play interactive games as well. This site features a Shockwave game based on the movie *Jurassic Park*.

COMPUTERS
in your career

Computer Graphics and Design

Few areas of computing are as wide open as the field of computer graphics. If you are an artist or aspire to be a designer, consider adding computer-based design tools to your list of skills. By transferring their drawing and design skills to the computer, many of today's professional graphic artists have greatly expanded their portfolios and client lists. Here are just a few areas where computer-based graphics are used routinely:

◆ **Web Page Designers.** No Web site is complete unless it is graphically rich and filled with navigation tools. Web designers use programs such as Adobe Photoshop, Adobe Illustrator, and many others to create graphics for their pages. Good designers bring a sense of color and balance to the Web page and use graphics to enhance the site's message as well as to make it more visually appealing and easier to navigate.

◆ **Architects and Engineers.** If you have studied drafting, you can apply that skill to computer-aided drafting tools and find a career in architecture or engineering as a designer or drafter. (In fact, nearly all drafting classes teach computer-based drafting as well as manual drafting skills.) Computer drafting tools are used in a huge array of design fields, from building and construction to aerospace and product packaging. In the world of computer design, you are limited only by your imagination and willingness to learn, as you can work in 2-D, 3-D, animation, programming, and many other segments of the field.

◆ **Product Designers.** From shampoo bottles to automobiles, from initial specifications to modeling and visualization, most product design is done on the computer.

◆ **Advertising Designers.** Computer graphics have exploded in popularity among advertising agencies, which use computers to create everything from magazine ads to program-length television infomercials. Advertisers are continually pushing the envelope in computer-based and character animation as they seek to give personality to the items they hope to sell.

◆ **Game Designers and Filmmakers.** These fields are perhaps at the pinnacle of computer graphics today because they use the most sophisticated tools available to create complex effects for use in video games and movies. These designers use every tool available to obtain the desired results, from simple paint packages to advanced particle-generating effects software, as well as high-end workstations.

◆ **Animators.** Until a few years ago, animation was done almost exclusively by hand. Today's animators use a wide variety of computerized systems to create animation—from the simple, two-dimensional cartoons you see on Saturday-morning television to complex 3-D animation of normally inanimate objects (such as dancing cereal boxes). Professional animators work on all different platforms and use out-of-the-box software as well as sophisticated custom programs that make computer-generated animation seem as realistic as possible.

Computer hardware and graphics software are used in almost every design field.

LESSON QUIZ

True/False

Answer the following questions by circling True or False.

True   False   **1.** Paint programs are vector-based.

True   False   **2.** Draw programs are sometimes called object-oriented programs.

True   False   **3.** CAD drawings are used as the basis for building and manufacturing because of their layers.

True   False   **4.** A spline-based modeler uses curves rotated on an axis to form 3-D shapes.

True   False   **5.** Fly-bys depict interior scenes and walk-throughs depict exterior scenes.

Multiple Choice

Circle the word or phrase that best completes each sentence.

1. _____ programs edit images at the pixel level.
 A. Paint   **B.** Photo-manipulation   **C.** Both A and B

2. Vector-based programs are described as being _____ .
 A. resolution-dependent   **B.** resolution-independent   **C.** modeling programs

3. _____ are notations showing the measurements of objects in a drawing.
 A. Layers   **B.** Splines   **C.** Dimensions

4. The images that make up an animation are called _____ .
 A. objects   **B.** vectors   **C.** frames

5. A Web designer can use _____ to tell a browser to display an image.
 A. HTML tags   **B.** color depth   **C.** both A and B

LESSON LABS

Complete the following exercises as directed by your instructor.

1. If your computer came with Windows 95 or Windows 98 installed, it may have one or more graphics programs such as Windows Paint, Microsoft Image Composer, or some other program installed. Check your Programs menu for programs that might be used for graphics. If the product's name does not make its use clear, ask your instructor for help. List the graphics programs installed on your system.

2. Launch Windows Paint and draw a picture. Windows Paint is a basic bitmap-based paint program that is almost always installed with Windows. To launch the program, click the Start menu, point to Programs, and point to Accessories; then click Windows Paint. Experiment with the program's drawing tools to create a simple image. Print and save the image, if your instructor approves; then close Paint.

LESSON 21: Working With Images

Computer Platforms Used for Graphics

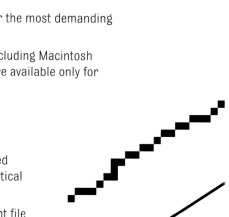

- Today, almost all commercial graphics work, design, and illustration is done on the computer rather than by hand. Designers need to be as skilled with computers and software as they are with artistic techniques.

- The era of art on personal computers was started in 1984, with the release of the first Apple computers. Their use of pointing devices, the WYSIWYG interface, and graphics programs made Apple and Macintosh computers a good choice for artists and designers.

- With the advent of Windows, IBM-compatible PCs caught up with the Macintosh in terms of graphics performance. Today, PCs are also used extensively in the graphics and design fields.

- Because of their power and expense, workstations are reserved for the most demanding graphics applications.

- Graphics software is available for different computer platforms, including Macintosh computers and IBM-compatible PCs. Some graphics applications are available only for workstations.

Types of Graphics Files

- Graphics files fall into one of two basic types: bitmap and vector.

- Bitmap graphics define images as a grid of cells, with each cell filled with a color. Vectors define objects in a drawing by using mathematical equations to pinpoint their location and other features.

- A file format is a means of encoding data for storage. Many different file formats are used with graphics.

- Common bitmap file formats are BMP, PICT, TIFF, JPEG, and GIF.

- Not all file formats work in all programs, a problem called incompatibility. To solve this problem, developers have created universal file formats that are compatible across various software applications.

Getting Images Into Your Computer

- Scanners enable the user to digitize hard-copy images such as photographs so they can be stored and edited in a computer.

- Digital cameras are gaining popularity among professional and casual photographers. A digital camera stores images in its memory or on a disk until they can be loaded into a computer.

- Clip art and electronic photographs are images that are already available in digital form. These images cover a wide range of subjects, from cartoons to business. Clip art can include sketches and drawings as well as high-quality photographs.

Copyright Issues

- Copyright is an important concern if a designer wants to reuse art created by someone else.

- Copyright laws govern the way images can be reused and distributed and thus protect the rights of the images' owner.

LESSON 22: Graphics Software

Paint Programs

- Paint programs work with bitmap images and manage the individual pixels that make up an image.
- Paint programs include various tools and can be used to add special effects to an image.

Photo-Manipulation Programs

- Photo-manipulation programs work with bitmap images and are widely used to edit digitized photographs.
- You can use a photo-manipulation program to repair problems with an image, such as adjusting colors or hiding mistakes.
- Powerful photo-manipulation programs can produce sophisticated effects, such as combining multiple images into a seamless whole, hiding parts of an image, creating text, and more.

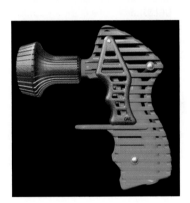

Draw Programs

- Draw programs work with vectors and give the designer a great deal of flexibility in editing an image.
- Objects created in a draw program can be altered easily and without loss of image quality.
- Draw programs work well with text.

Computer-Aided Design Programs

- Computer-Aided Design (CAD) software is used in technical design fields to create models of objects that will be built or manufactured.
- CAD software allows users to design objects in three dimensions (3-D), and can produce 3-D wireframe and solid models.

3-D Modeling Programs

- Three-dimensional (3-D) modeling programs are used to create spectacular visual effects.
- Three-dimensional modeling programs work by creating objects via surface, solid, polygonal, or spline-based modeling.

Animation

- Computers are used to create animation for use in various fields, including games and movies.
- Fly-bys and walk-throughs are basic types of computer animation.
- Character animation is the art of creating a character and making it move in a lifelike manner.
- Compositing tools allow game makers and filmmakers to add characters and objects to scenes that did not originally contain them.

Graphics and the World Wide Web

- The GIF and JPEG image formats are the most widely used formats on the World Wide Web.
- Animation can be added to a Web page by using simple animated GIF images or plug-in software such as Flash or Shockwave.

UNIT REVIEW

KEY TERMS

After completing this unit, you should be able to define the following terms.

3-D modeling software, *401*
animated GIF, *409*
bitmap, *386*
BMP, *388*
character animation, *405*
clip art, *391*
compatible, *388*
compositing, *406*
Computer-Aided Design (CAD), *398*
Computer-Generated Imagery (CGI), *402*
Data Exchange Format (DXF), *389*
dimension, *400*
draw program, *398*
file format, *387*
fly-by, *404*
frame, *402*
GIF, *388*
incompatible, *388*
Initial Graphics Exchange Specification
   (IGES), *389*
JPEG, *388*
keyframe, *405*
layer, *400*

model, *400*
paint program, *395*
photo-manipulation program, *396*
photorealistic, *404*
PICT, *388*
PNG, *388*
polygonal modeler, *402*
Postscript, *384*
raster, *386*
render, *401*
resolution-dependent, *398*
resolution-independent, *398*
solid model, *401*
solid modeler, *401*
spline-based modeler, *402*
surface modeler, *401*
TIFF, *388*
tween, *405*
vector, *386*
walk-through, *404*
wireframe model, *401*
WYSIWYG, *384*

KEY TERMS QUIZ

Fill in each blank with one of the terms listed under Key Terms.

1. Paint and photo-manipulation programs work with _____ images.

2. A 3-D modeling program that lets you work with a block of material is known as a(n) _____ .

3. With CAD programs, you can create various types of _____ to represent 3-D objects.

4. You can also _____ a solid-looking representation of an object using a CAD program.

5. Someone with no art training can use _____ as an easy way to start or enhance digital artwork.

6. If a file format and program do not work together, they are said to be _____ .

7. Graphics files are composed of either bitmaps or a set of _____ .

8. A(n) _____ graphics program displays images the same way, regardless of the monitor you are using.

9. A computer-generated object that looks like a photograph of a real object is said to be _____ .

10. By using a(n) _____ that plays in a cycle, you can easily add an animation to a Web page.

REVIEW QUESTIONS

In your own words, briefly answer the following questions.

1. What two products ushered in the era of "art" on personal computers?

2. How are workstation computers typically used in graphics, and why are they often reserved for those uses?

3. Draw programs enable the user to work with what kind of images?

4. What device can be used to convert images on paper into a digital graphics file?

5. Where does the term *clip art* come from?

6. What limitations are there with bitmap-based paint programs?

7. Why are CAD programs so accurate?

8. Name the four types of 3-D modelers described in this unit.

9. What is the difference between a fly-by and a walk-through?

10. What are compositing tools used for?

DISCUSSION QUESTIONS

As directed by your instructor, discuss the following questions in class or in groups.

1. What tools and techniques that were not required by graphic artists and illustrators in the past do you think today's designers must know and understand to be productive?

2. In what areas of our lives do you think we will see more sophisticated graphics?

 **ETHICAL ISSUES**   Computers and graphics software provide powerful creative tools to artists and designers, but is there a downside to the explosion of computer graphics? With this question in mind, discuss the following questions in class.

1. Magazines commonly retouch photographs before printing them, especially on covers. In some cases, editors make the subjects look very different from what they look like in reality, and not always for the better. Should this type of retouching be regulated, or do you see it as harmless? Support your position.

2. It is increasingly common to find copyrighted images being used on Web sites, distributed in newsgroups and chat rooms, and in other places. Often, these images are used without the knowledge or permission of the owner. Do you believe that once an image is digitized, it enters the public domain and no longer belongs to its creator? Why or why not?

UNIT LABS

You and the Computer

Complete the following exercises using a computer in your classroom, lab, or home. No other materials are needed.

1. **Check Your Settings.** The way your PC displays graphics depends a great deal on your monitor's settings. You can easily check your settings and change them if you need better graphics performance. In this exercise, you will learn how to check monitor settings, but do not change them without your instructor's permission. Take the following steps:

   A. Click the Start button, and point to Settings. Click Control Panel to open the Control Panel window.

   B. Double-click the Display icon. The Display Properties dialog box opens.

   C. Click the Settings tab. Check the settings in the Colors and Screen Area boxes and write them down.

   D. To see the other available color settings for your system, click the Colors drop-down arrow. Review the settings and write them down. (Is your system set to the highest possible color setting?) Then click outside the list to close it without changing anything.

   E. To see the other available resolution settings for your monitor, drag the Screen Area slider control to the right and left. It should display the available settings. Return the slider to its original position.

   F. Click Cancel to close the Display Properties dialog box; then close the Control Panel window.

2. **Learn About Your Clip Art.** If your computer has a newer version of a word processor installed, then it probably has some clip art also installed. The application's online help system can tell you how to access your clip art and how to use it in documents. Launch your word processor; then open its online help system. (You can usually do this by clicking the Help menu, and then clicking the Help or Contents option. For specific directions, ask your instructor.) In the help system's window, use a Search or Index tool to look for the term *clip art*. Then follow the help system's directions to open a document and insert a piece of clip art.

Internet Labs

To complete the following exercises, you need a computer with an Internet connection and a Web browser. (For more information on using these tools, see "Prerequisites" at the front of this textbook.)

1. **Find Some Interesting Software.** Many graphics software makers have Web sites where you can get information about their products, including prices, features, reviews, and more. Some vendors let you download free trial versions or shareware versions of their applications. Visit these Web sites for information on a few graphics programs, but do not download any software without your instructor's permission.

- **Adobe Systems, Inc.**—Adobe makes graphics and desktop publishing programs like Illustrator, Photoshop, PageMaker, and others. Visit **http://www.adobe.com/** and click the Products link.

- **JASC, Inc.**—JASC makes the popular PaintShop Pro paint program as well as other graphics and Web design tools. Visit **http://www.jasc.com/** and click the Products link.

- **Visio Corp.**—Visio produces various drawing tools that make it easy for people without design training to create intricate, accurate technical drawings. Visit **http://www.visio.com/** and click the Product Information link.

- **Autodesk, Inc.**—Autodesk makes CAD, 3-D, animation, and other products used in architecture, engineering, and movie and game design. Visit **http://www.autodesk.com/** and click the Products and Solutions link.

- **Macromedia, Inc.**—Macromedia makes the Shockwave and Flash plug-ins and tools for creating content that use them. The company produces various design tools for graphics, multimedia, and the Web. Visit **http://www.macromedia.com/** and click the Products link.

2. **Find Some Clip Art.** There are many sources of clip art on the Web. Much of the clip art is free, but some requires a fee. You can find good clip art from reputable sources by checking these Web sites:

- Clipart.com—**http://www.clipart.com/**

- Shareware.com—**http://www.shareware.com/** (Use the Search tool to search for *clip art*.)

- Download.com—**http://www.download.com/** (Use the Search tool to search for *clip art*.)

IBE Labs

If you have the Interactive Browser Edition (IBE) CD-ROM for this textbook, you may complete the following interactive exercises using the instructions provided in the IBE.

1. **Matching.** Determine which scenarios call for graphics.

2. **Labeling.** This exercise focuses on types of graphics software.

3. **Scavenger Hunt.** Answer questions to find a clue toward solving the puzzle.

4. **Pixel by Pixel.** Learn about the impact of computers on graphics and design.

UNIT 12

The New Media

UNIT OBJECTIVES

Explain the basic concepts of multimedia and new media.

Describe how different media types are used together to create multimedia events.

List four distinct uses for multimedia products.

Name three ways multimedia content is distributed.

UNIT CONTENTS

This unit contains the following lessons:

Understanding Multimedia

OVERVIEW:
Bringing Content to Life

As technology improves, consumers become more and more demanding. In an era of high-speed communications, we want to receive information immediately and in many ways simultaneously. This demand explains why television news channels commonly feature text that crawls across the bottom of the screen while an announcer talks and videotaped images roll. It explains why Web sites now feature graphics, animation, and sound in addition to text and hyperlinks.

These demands extend to the way we work, learn, and entertain ourselves. Simple, one-dimensional content is no longer acceptable to most of us. Information, lessons, games, and shopping are more appealing and hold our attention longer if we can approach and arrange them in different ways, even on a whim. These demands and technological advances have worked hand in hand to propel the art and science of multimedia to new levels, resulting in products that weave together text, graphics, animation, audio, and video.

When we use these products—whether a Web-based encyclopedia or a CD-ROM video game—we are doing more than working with a computer program. We are experiencing a multimedia event. Today's multimedia products appeal to multiple senses at one time and respond to our changing needs with ever-increasing speed.

This lesson introduces you to basic multimedia concepts and explains how multimedia works. You will learn about some of the applications of multimedia technologies and how new media are changing the way we work and play.

OBJECTIVES

- Define the terms *multimedia, interactivity,* and *new media.*
- Explain how different types of media are used to create multimedia events.
- List three essential hardware components for a multimedia-capable PC.
- Describe one way in which multimedia products can be used in homes, schools, and businesses.

MULTIMEDIA, INTERACTIVITY, AND NEW MEDIA DEFINED

Figure 23.1
Speech is the most basic and universal medium for communicating thoughts and ideas. After centuries of practice, people find speech a natural and effective way to communicate.

For much of history, information was presented via a single, unique medium. In this context, a medium is simply a way of conveying information. Sound, such as the human voice, is one type of medium, and for centuries before written language came into widespread use, speech was the primary way of exchanging information (see Figure 23.1). Eventually, people began telling stories (and leaving a record of their lives) through drawings and paintings, such as the famous cave paintings found in the Ardèche region of France. The creation of written language gave people yet another medium for expressing their thoughts. Today, people commonly use speech, sounds, music, text, graphics, animation, and video to convey information. These are all different types of media (the term *media* is the plural of *medium*), and each has traditionally been used to present certain types of information.

Multiple Media = Multimedia

People long ago discovered that messages are more effective (that is, the audience understands and remembers them more easily) when they are presented through a combination of different media. This combination is what is meant by the term **multimedia**—using more than one type of medium at the same time.

In practice, you can say that even the simplest speech-and-text presentation is a multimedia event because it uses more than one unique medium to deliver a message (see Figure 23.2). As an example, consider teachers who use a chalkboard in the classroom so they can use written text to support a spoken lecture. At a more advanced level, people use movies and television to combine multiple types of media (sound, video, animation, still graphics, and text) to create different kinds of messages that inform or entertain in unique and meaningful ways.

Interactivity: Just Add Users

The computer, however, has taken multimedia to an even higher level by enabling us to use many different media simultaneously. A printed encyclopedia, for example, is basically pages of text and pictures. In a multimedia version, however, the encyclopedia's pictures can move, a narrator's recorded voice can provide the text, and the user can move around at will by clicking hypertext links and using navigational tools. By combining different types of media to present the message, the encyclopedia's developer improves the chances that users will understand and remember the information.

Of course, the same point can be made about television programming because it uses various media at the same time. Computer technologies, however, enable PC-based multimedia products to go one step further. Because the computer can accept input from the user, it can host **interactive** multimedia events, involving the user unlike any book, movie, or television program.

Interactivity has been defined in many ways, but in the realm of multimedia the term means that the user and program respond to one another; the program continually provides the user with a range of choices, which the user selects to direct the flow of

Figure 23.2

It does not take much to create a basic multimedia event. Simply by using text to underscore the important points of a spoken message, you incorporate two unique media. The number of media types used is not important, as long as the author has complete control of each and the presenter delivers the message in a clear and engaging way.

the program. This level of interactivity is the primary difference between computer-based multimedia programs and other kinds of multimedia events. Most television programs, for example, require the viewer only to sit and observe (see Figure 23.3). Computers, however, make it possible to create **interactive media,** which enable people to respond to—and even control—what they see and hear. By using the PC to control the program, the user can make choices, move freely from one part of the content to another, and in some cases customize the content to suit a specific purpose.

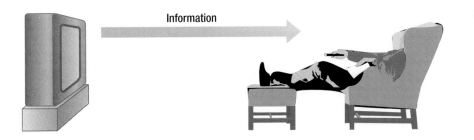

Information

Figure 23.3

Traditional medium with one-way communication. Although the viewer can select different programs to watch, television does not yet provide the level of interactivity currently available in computer-based interactive media products.

By accepting input from the user, interactive media create a **feedback loop,** which generally works as follows:

1. To start the loop, the user launches the interactive media program and chooses the content.

2. The program responds by displaying the content with choices (navigation tools, links to other topics, controls for displaying different types of content, and so on) for the user.

3. The user responds by making a choice, such as moving to a different place in the program or selecting different content.

NORTON
ONLINE

Visit **www.glencoe.com/norton/online/** for more information on **interactivity.**

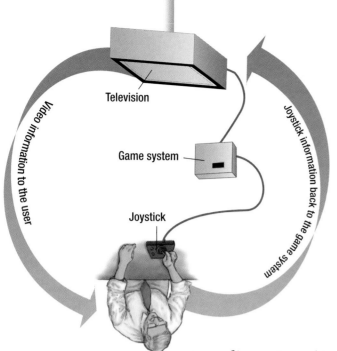

Television

Game system

Joystick

Video information to the user

Joystick information back to the game system

4. The program responds to the user's selection and usually presents a new set of options for the user.

5. The process continues—sometimes at a rapid and complex pace, as in the case of many computer games—until the user stops the program (see Figure 23.4).

Interactive media programs are effective (and successful) because they provide this give-and-take with the user. You will find this level of interactivity in practically any popular multimedia product, whether the program is a video game, a CD-based reference tool, an electronic test bank, or a shopping site on the Web (see Figure 23.5).

The New Media

Interactivity involves more than just a computer and a mouse. The **new media** (a term encompassing all types of interactive multimedia technologies) bring together different communication technologies, such as cable TV, telephone lines, private networks, the Internet, and others. As you will see throughout this unit, the new media are created by a convergence of many types of technology, enabling individuals and large groups to communicate and convey information using computers and communications systems.

At the core of new media is a concept known as **digital convergence.** Computers are used to create all kinds of digital content, from plain text to video. All these types of digital information can travel to the consumer along the same path—perhaps via a CD-ROM disk, a cable TV wire, or a satellite transmission. Rather than delivering movies on film or videotape, music on tapes or compact disks, and books on the printed page, different kinds of content can now reach the computer or cable TV box in the same way. Thus, a variety of content comes together, converging into one digital stream.

Figure 23.4

Interactive media with feedback loop. By choosing options continually and using the joystick to guide the action on-screen, the user can control the flow of the program's content.

NORTON

ONLINE

Visit **www.glencoe.com/norton/online/** for more information on **new media** and **digital convergence.**

Figure 23.5

Because they provide the user with different types of content and options for navigating and displaying that content, computer-based games and reference banks are highly interactive.

To the user, this technology means that multimedia content can be stored and delivered in several ways. As you use your PC, multimedia content may come from a compact disk, a DVD, your hard disk, the Internet, or an online service. If you use the television reception features of Windows 98 or Windows 2000, you may also receive such content in the form of television broadcasts delivered to your desktop. If you use a service such as WebTV, you can enjoy broadcast programming and Internet content simultaneously.

Depending on the technologies used, some multimedia events are strictly stand-alone, single-user applications, such as a reference book or training program on CD-ROM. Others can involve more than one user. Examples are multiplayer games that can be accessed over a local area network or the Internet, video conferences that enable participants to see one another and share data in real time over a telephone line or satellite connection, or interactive television shows that accept viewer input through a Web site or chatroom.

INFORMATION IN LAYERS AND DIMENSIONS

Multimedia developers continually struggle to find ways to make their products more appealing to users, whether the product is a fast-paced action game, a tutorial on disk, or an e-commerce Web site. A basic strategy in multimedia development is to provide information that is layered and multidimensional. This requirement may mean giving the user multiple pieces of information simultaneously—such as a rotating 3-D image of a motor, an audio description of its function, and pop-up text boxes that provide more information when the user points at certain parts of the graphic. In a multidimensional presentation, the user has the option of experiencing the information from different perspectives; for example, one user may prefer to see only an animated demonstration of a landscaping project, while another may prefer to read a text description.

One way to make plain text and pictures inviting to an audience is to add time-based content, such as audio, cartoon animation, and video. It is important, however, that the added media do more than merely mimic the static text and graphics content. It would be boring indeed to watch a video of someone reading a passage of text that appears on the screen. But if the text is a scene from Hamlet and the video displays that same scene with Sir Laurence Olivier's film portrayal, then the video enlivens the printed text.

More and more educational materials, including textbooks and encyclopedias, are being developed into multimedia products (see Figure 23.6). These products use sound, animation, and video clips to make the content "come alive."

A focus on the content of a multimedia program or presentation is essential. The content is what the consumer pays for or what the audience comes to see. For example, the first feature-length computer-animated film, *Toy Story,* would have had limited appeal for just its technical wizardry. Because it also had an appealing story and strong character development, the film attracted children and adults alike. Likewise, live-action

Figure 23.6
Interactive textbooks on compact disk or Web sites can offer multimedia content to enhance the learning process.

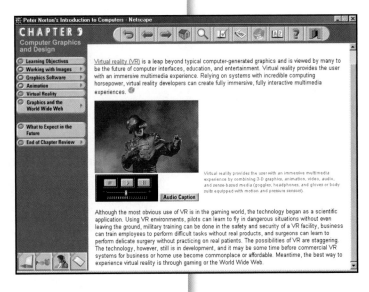

REWIND BACK 1 STOP PAUSE ADV.1 PLAY F-FWRD

Figure 23.7
This product displays a popular method of navigation in multimedia programs. By clicking the appropriate button, you can move forward or backward through the product's content.

films using computer animation and graphics to enhance or create objects or environments on the screen, such as the dream sequences in *The Matrix*, would have limited appeal if the story were flat.

Hypermedia: User-Directed Navigation

A major challenge accompanies the large volume of multimedia content that arrives via a compact disk, DVD, Web site, or online service: finding your way through the text, pictures, and other media available in the presentation. This challenge is where the interactivity component comes into play. The user is responsible for deciding where and when to go to a particular place within the collection of data.

Wending your way through electronic information is commonly called **navigation.** The content's developer is responsible for providing the user with on-screen aids to navigate. In software that mimics the old format of books, the navigation aid might be a simple palette of left- and right-facing arrow icons to navigate backward or forward one page. Because authors of digital content are not bound by the physical constraints of pages, they can also provide buttons that allow you to jump to locations outside the normal, linear sequence (see Figure 23.7).

The term **hypermedia** has been coined to describe the environment that allows users to click on one type of media to navigate to the same or other type of media. You have probably encountered various types of hypermedia tools if you have spent any time surfing the Web or using disk-based multimedia products. In a Web page devoted to The Beatles, for example, clicking on a photo of the band might bring up a page containing biographies of the band members. A click on such a link may automatically connect you to a related item on a computer in

Figure 23.8
In any Web page, clicking a hyper-linked word or image opens a new Web page in your browser window. The first and second page may be on the same Web server, or they may be on different servers many miles apart. The purpose of hypermedia links is to make information of all kinds, and in all locations, appear as a seamless whole so that accessing different types of information becomes as simple as flipping through the pages of a magazine.

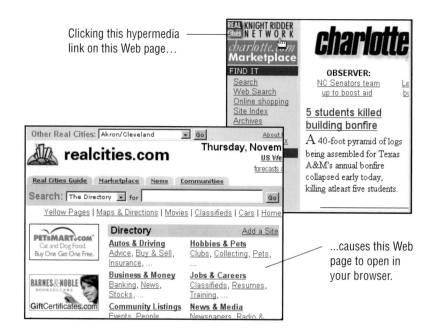

Clicking this hypermedia link on this Web page…

…causes this Web page to open in your browser.

another country—and it appears on your screen as if it were coming from your own hard disk (see Figure 23.8).

Hypermedia can also exist on a smaller scale. For example, Figure 23.9 shows a screen from the Help system in Microsoft Word that utilizes hypermedia. In this Help window, notice that some words are highlighted, indicating that they are hyperlinks. Clicking a link may display a pop-up window, which provides a definition of a term or a list of additional links. Other links may open separate Help windows, providing helpful information on a different topic.

Even though hypermedia links can often be helpful, sometimes it is undesirable to let the user wander off to other locations, perhaps never to return. Some content must continue to exist in a linear fashion, at least for part of the time. Steps in a tutorial or a carefully crafted story, for example, must be told in an unalterable sequence for accuracy or the most dramatic impact.

Figure 23.9
The Help system in Microsoft Word contains many hypertext links. Clicking a highlighted term displays the definition for that word. Clicking an underlined term opens a new help window, with information about that term.

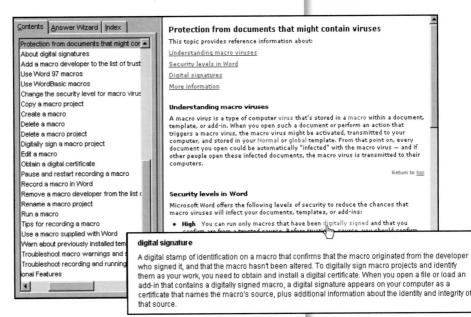

HARDWARE CONSIDERATIONS FOR MULTIMEDIA

Because of the intensive amount of digital information that goes into building every second of a program, multimedia publishers must always consider the user's equipment—the hardware on which the content will be displayed.

Modern PCs typically come with all the necessary multimedia components already installed (see Figure 23.10 on page 427). These computers ease the startup time for computer novices and home computer users because the users are not faced with complicated hardware issues, such as configuring a new CD-ROM player or installing a sound card. For older computers, it may be necessary to add one or more of the following components to turn the PC into a multimedia PC:

◆ Sound card

◆ Speakers

◆ CD-ROM or DVD-ROM drive

A multimedia computer also requires enough processing power (a fast CPU) and memory (RAM) to accommodate multimedia programs, which make great demands of the computer's processing components.

To help PC makers build computers capable of running newer generations of multimedia products, industry groups have defined minimum standards for multimedia PCs. As the capabilities of computers have increased and costs to the consumer have come down, the standards have become more rigorous.

NORTON
ONLINE

Visit **www.glencoe.com/norton/online/** for more information on **hypermedia**.

PRODUCTIVITY Tip

Throw Out Those Reference Books

Being a student once meant owning a shelf filled with reference books. Today, however, even in many homes where you cannot find a dictionary, you can find at least one PC and an Internet connection. And thus ends the need for many kinds of printed reference manuals. Reference books have gone online.

Although using an online encyclopedia or dictionary is not always as convenient as grabbing a book from a shelf, the online version offers two distinct advantages:

◆ **Up-to-Date Information.** Online references can be updated quickly and frequently, and the best ones are kept up-to-date by their owners.

◆ **Depth and Variety.** Printed reference books suffer from page-count and page-size limitations, so they can provide only so much information on a given topic. This limitation is not true of online references.

Here is an overview of some references you can find on the Internet:

◆ **Encyclopedias.** In recent years, several popular printed encyclopedias have become available on CD-ROM. These products provide a lot of value and most are filled with links to the Web (so you can find more and updated information), but they still have their limitations. Web-based encyclopedias, however, are rapidly gaining popularity. Sites such as Microsoft's Encarta and Encarta Deluxe (**www.encarta.com/**), Britannica Online (**www .britannica.com/**), and Compton's Encyclopedia Online (**www.comptons.com/**) provide all the articles you would expect to find, along with graphics, audio and video, links to relevant sites, search tools, and more. Other online encyclopedias include Encyberpedia (**www.encyberpedia.com/**), Funk and Wagnalls (**www.funkandwagnalls.com/**), and Encyclopedia.com (**www.encyclopedia.com/**).

◆ **Dictionaries.** Online dictionaries are better illustrated, are more detailed, and offer a variety of tools compared to their printed counterparts. You can find online editions of standard printed dictionaries, such as Webster's (**www.m-w.com/**) and the Cambridge International Dictionaries

Once almost every family wanted an encyclopedia but few could afford one. Now anyone with an Internet connection can access an encyclopedia online.

(**www.cup.cam.ac.uk/elt/dictionary/**), as well as lexicons available only online, such as OneLook Dictionaries (**www.onelook.com/**) and The Alternative Dictionaries (**www.notam.uio.no /~hcholm/altlang/**).

◆ **Thesauri.** The Internet is a great place to check your word choices. Online thesauri provide synonyms, antonyms, and homonyms in addition to definitions and pronunciations. Some allow you to look up phrases as well as single words. The king of the thesaurus world, Roget's, is available at **www .thesaurus.com/**, but others are also worth a look including The Wordsmyth Dictionary/Thesaurus (**www.wordsmyth.net/**), Lexical FreeNet (**www.link.cs.cmu.edu/lexfn/**), and Phrase Finder (**www.shu.ac.uk/web-admin/phrases/go.html**).

Of course, plenty of specialized reference guides are also on the Web, covering subjects from computer technology to law, economics to particle physics. If you need to find a specialty reference online, visit your favorite search engine (such as Yahoo!, Lycos, Northern Light, etc.) and look for a Reference link, which should lead to more information about online reference materials. Otherwise, you can search on the term that describes your field of study (such as particle physics). If you do not get the results you need, search on multiple terms, such as law AND reference guide.

In the early 1990s, a consortium of hardware and software companies began developing the Multimedia Personal Computer (MPC) standard, which specifies the minimum hardware requirements for personal computers to be fully multimedia-capable. The last version of the MPC standard, called MPC Level 3, was released in 1995. It stated that full-featured multimedia computers at that time should have at least 8 MB of RAM, a 540 MB hard drive, a 75 MHz Pentium processor, a 4x CD-ROM drive, and support for MPEG-format files. (MPEG is discussed later in this unit.) Today, all new PCs far exceed this configuration, making the MPC Level 3 standard out of date.

Figure 23.10
Today, nearly any new PC includes enough memory and the right hardware components to be fully multimedia-capable. Standard PCs typically include a fast CD-ROM or DVD-ROM drive, sound card with speakers and a microphone, a fast graphics card, and special ports for one or more game controllers.

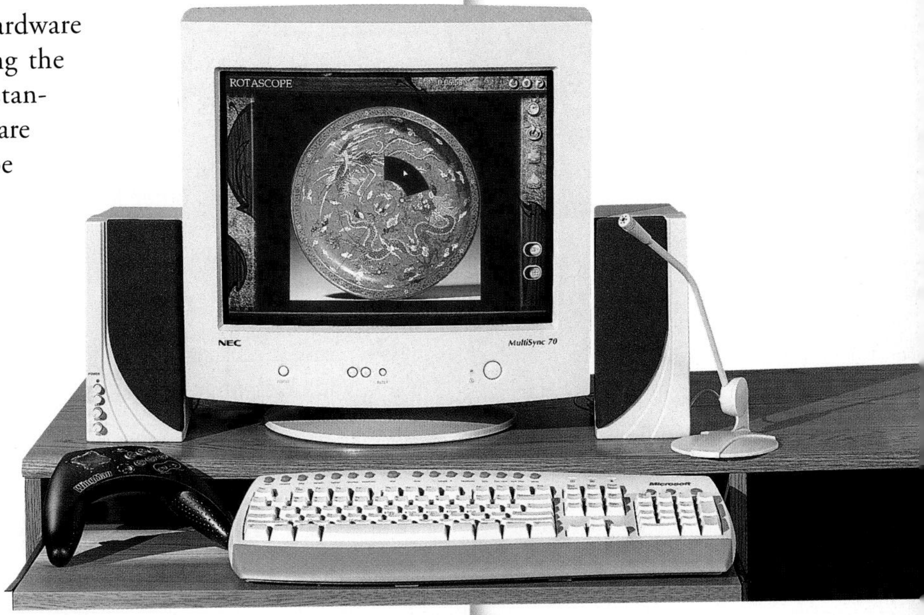

More recently, a group of hardware and software makers led by Microsoft and Intel began the ongoing development of hardware standards for personal computers of various types. Starting with the **PC 97 standard,** the group published sets of minimum configuration requirements for new PCs. Configuration requirements vary according to the PC's use; for example, the standard configuration for a "basic PC" is different from an "entertainment PC" or a "workstation PC" under the standard. The PC 97 requirements for a basic PC are higher than the old MPC Level 3 requirements and include at least 16 MB of RAM, a 120 MHz Pentium processor, and a USB port.

A newer version of the standard—called the PC 99 standard—raises the bar for new computers even higher, as shown in Table 23.1. While there will not be a PC 2000 standard, a PC 2001 standard will affect new PCs made in the latter half of 2001.

Table 23.1 Basic PC 99 Requirements and Recommendations

Feature	Basic PC	Entertainment PC
Clock speed	300 MHz	300 MHz
RAM	32 MB	64 MB (with 128 L2 cache)
USB ports	2 (minimum)	2 (minimum)
CD or DVD drive	Required	Required
Modem or other support for public network communications	Required	Required
Smart Card support	Required	Required
Television output	Recommended	Recommended
Network adapter	Recommended	Recommended
Analog television tuner	Recommended	Recommended
Support for IEEE 1394	Recommended	Recommended

NORTON ONLINE

Visit www.glencoe.com/norton/online/ for more information on the **PC 97/99/2001 hardware standards.**

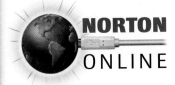

Answer the following questions by filling in the blank(s).

1. The level of _____ differentiates computer-based multimedia programs and other kinds of multimedia events.

2. New media are created by a(n) _____ of many types of technology.

3. _____ is the concept behind the hyperlinks found in World Wide Web pages.

APPLICATIONS FOR MULTIMEDIA

Despite the fact that PC-based multimedia technologies have been around a relatively short time, they have found many different applications. In the home, school, workplace, and elsewhere, multimedia programs are an integral part of the way we teach and learn, communicate, run businesses, and entertain ourselves. The following sections examine just a few uses of multimedia technologies.

In the School

Education has embraced new media technologies and is one of the first and best consumers of multimedia products. In today's schools, multimedia computers are an integral part of many classrooms and bring a new level of interactivity to learning.

One major reform movement in education promotes active and cooperative learning. Computers and multimedia help students and teachers make the transition to this new mode of learning. In the classroom, visual presentations that include animation, video, and sound motivate students to become active participants in the learning process. Interactive multimedia programs bring concepts to life and help students integrate critical-thinking and problem-solving skills.

The CD-ROM-based encyclopedia is probably the most obvious example of an interactive multimedia application for education. If students must write a report on a region of Africa, they can read about the history and geography and, with the click of the mouse button, can see video clips of the hustle and bustle of a city and hear audio clips of African languages or regional music. As a result, the information comes to life, and students may even have the software tools to produce their reports in the form of a multimedia presentation.

Even young children can engage in serious learning while having fun, and CD- and Internet-based multimedia products are at the forefront of this movement (see Figure 23.11). Using animated characters to lead the way, multimedia games such as Reader Rabbit, MathBlaster, JumpStart, and other programs help young students master basic skills in an enjoyable interactive environment that provides personalized feedback.

Figure 23.11
Multimedia learning products prove that children can have fun and master basic skills while working in a game environment.

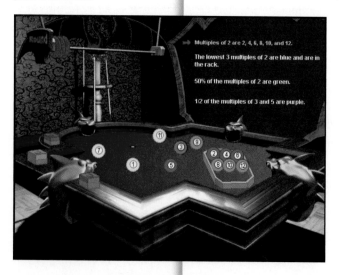

Multiples of 2 are 2, 4, 6, 8, 10, and 12.

The lowest 3 multiples of 2 are blue and are in the rack.

50% of the multiples of 2 are green.

1/2 of the multiples of 3 and 5 are purple.

The Internet provides a useful learning tool outside the classroom also. Hundreds of learning-oriented Web sites allow children to participate in interactive projects, puzzles, and games. Sites like **www.MaMaMedia.com/** enable kids to create stories and puzzles, participate in problem-solving activities, and share their creations with one another (see Figure 23.12).

Virtual universities are also appearing on the Web and offering **distance learning (DL).** These sites enable students to take classes, interact with instructors, send in homework and projects, and complete exams while online. Some DL sites provide Web-based learning, CD-ROM instruction, and live classroom instruction available over television broadcast. Some offer full degrees over the Internet, although the best solution for using DL is combining DL techniques with conventional classroom experiences.

Figure 23.12
The MaMaMedia Gallery enables children to post their artistic projects for others to see.

In the Workplace

It may seem odd that media such as animation, sound, and video would play a role in business, but there is an unstoppable trend toward enlisting these media in many business activities. Companies use new media technologies in many ways, to perform internal tasks more efficiently and to reach customers more effectively.

For example, training is a never-ending task in large corporations, especially as companies expect their employees to master the latest computer technologies. As a replacement for—or supplement to—classroom training, many companies have developed customized interactive training materials. These materials fall into a category of products called **computer-based training (CBT).** Corporations invest millions of dollars to develop custom CBT courses dealing with various issues, such as company policies, customized computer systems, and customer relations. Many companies use custom CBT products to keep sales representatives up-to-date about constantly changing products, services, and price structures—information that is essential to successful sales and account management.

CBT courseware is provided most commonly on compact disk, which is convenient for workers in the field or remote offices. These products can include audio and video content as well as text and can even provide real-time testing and evaluation to ensure that the user has mastered the concepts or skills being taught. In the example shown in Figure 23.13, an animated narrator leads the user through the course, one topic at a time. The user can follow the course linearly or skip from topic to topic at will. The product also features links to Web sites that provide more detailed information and updates on many topics. This type of content can be provided entirely over the Internet or a corporate intranet, using streaming audio and video technologies at the server end, and browser and plug-in technologies at the user's PC.

NORTON ONLINE

Visit **www.glencoe.com/norton/online/** for more information on the **new media in education, distance learning,** and **CBT.**

Figure 23.13
CBT products are popular training methods in corporations used to teach employees about products, company policies, and more.

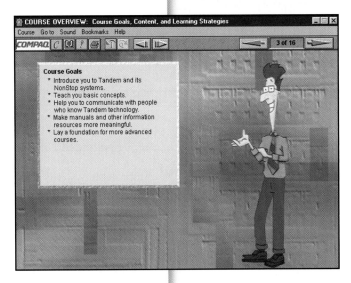

Sales and marketing are taking on new meaning in the age of multimedia. Information that used to be distributed only in printed catalogs may now be available in an interactive electronic catalog, mailed to customers in CD-ROM format, or presented on a company's Web site, as shown in Figure 23.14.

In the Home

Home users are probably the biggest consumers of multimedia products. The advent of the Internet, the accessibility of interactive television programming, and the proliferation of low-priced multimedia PCs have enabled even novice computer users to take advantage of powerful multimedia products. In the home, multimedia is typically used for the following purposes:

◆ Reference materials

◆ Self-help and instruction

◆ Entertainment

Figure 23.14
Companies that have traditionally served customers from "brick-and-mortar" buildings are increasingly setting up virtual stores on the Web. These sites provide interactive catalogs, shopping carts, and secure payment technologies to ensure that the customer's credit card and personal information is kept confidential.

Multimedia self-help and instructional products are many and varied in nature. For example, families can use the Internet or one of several disk-based products to connect to an investment firm (Fidelity Investments, Charles Schwab & Co., and Prudential are just a few) to get guidance about setting up a retirement portfolio. As shown in Figure 23.15, these interactive tools ask questions about earnings, spending, long-term financial goals, and willingness to take risks. The program then displays a report that recommends the right mix of investments to meet the customer's requirements. Many products can help families invest online, manage portfolios, and evaluate investments at any time.

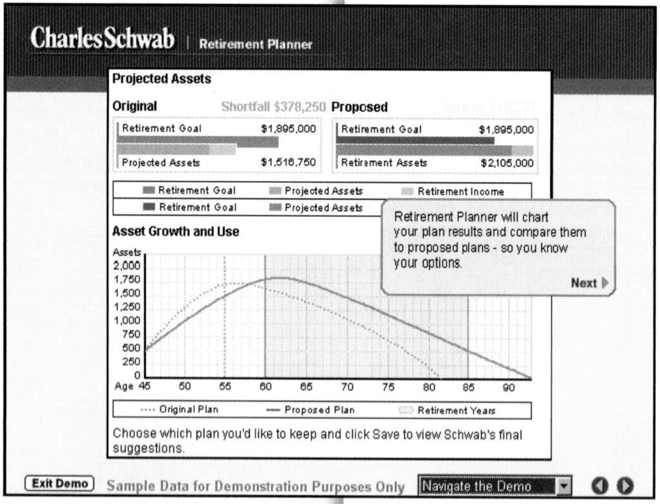

By far, the largest application for commercial multimedia is in the entertainment field. Video games sold on cartridges and CD-ROMs for dedicated game machines or for desktop computers are popular. The large storage capacity of CD-ROMs often allows higher quality animation, embedded video, digital-quality sound, and a broader variety of gaming techniques.

As convenient as these products may be, consumers still seem to be waiting for the ultimate multimedia experience: interactive television. In recent years, steps have been taken to make television a two-way experience rather than the one-way experience that has satisfied legions of couch potatoes for years. A basic form of interactive television is pay-per-view.

Figure 23.15
This interactive retirement planning program, available from the Charles Schwab & Co. Web site, can help you determine how much you need to save for retirement and create a plan for investing.

Some cable systems provide pay-per-view services by telephone only (for instance, you can call and order a recently released movie), which is not exactly interactive. Others such as satellite systems, hotel systems, and an increasing number of home systems, let you order a pay-per-view movie or event by using your remote control or special set-top box. (Television's role as a multimedia distribution channel is discussed in Lesson 24.)

Techview

VIRTUAL REALITY

Virtual reality (VR)—the computer-generated simulation of a real or imagined physical space—is probably the ultimate multimedia experience because it immerses you in a completely artificial environment. VR environments typically produce one of three possible image types:

◆ **Simulations of Real Places.** You might find yourself in a virtual room, car, or cave.

◆ **Simulations of Imaginary Places.** In this kind of simulation, you could be riding alongside King Arthur or battling aliens.

◆ **Simulations of Real Things That Do Not Exist.** In this kind of simulation, you could walk through a building that has not been built yet.

Uses for Virtual Reality

People use these VR simulations in many situations:

◆ **Training.** VR simulations of air combat, space shuttle flights, or nuclear reactor meltdowns provide excellent low-cost training areas.

◆ **Document and Facilities Management.** Virtual reality allows you to file electronic documents visually. Using such a system, you can create a virtual model of a factory and then attach maintenance records to each item within the factory.

◆ **Design.** By building a prototype in VR, a designer can work out design and construction flaws before the product leaves the drawing board.

◆ **Entertainment.** VR games and adventures are the ultimate fantasy experience.

VR Hardware and Software

VR technology appears in the following formats:

◆ **On-Screen.** Images are displayed on a computer screen. The user is outside the environment, which limits the "reality" effect.

◆ **Head-Mounted Displays.** Developers have created helmets and goggles that display stereoscopic images close to the user's eyes. The images block the outside world and create the illusion of a world that wraps around the wearer. As the wearer turns his or her head, tracking devices tell the computer

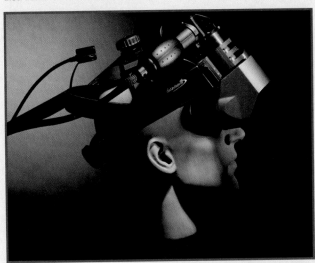

There are many different head-mounted VR displays. Using such a device, the wearer feels immersed in the virtual environment, without distractions from outside.

to change the image, allowing the wearer to look around the virtual environment rather than stare straight ahead.

◆ **Rooms.** These rooms, called Cave Automatic Virtual Environments (CAVEs), contain complex projection and stereo equipment that create a complete virtual world. The user can move around the room and move objects with the aid of a wand.

◆ **Clothing.** Developers are working on VR clothing, like chest pads and gloves, that provide tactile feedback when you touch a virtual object.

The most impressive VR equipment costs hundreds of thousands of dollars. Nevertheless, home users can experience convincing VR using low-end equipment and a home PC. Of course, even low-end VR hardware is not cheap. While you can spend as little as $99 on a pair of goggles, a top-of-the-line home-user helmet can easily cost more than $500.

NORTON ONLINE

Visit **www.glencoe.com/norton/online/** for more information on **virtual reality**.

LESSON QUIZ

True/False

Answer the following questions by circling True or False.

True   False   **1.** A medium is simply a means of conveying information.

True   False   **2.** PC-based multimedia events are said to be interactive because they can accept input from the user, unlike a book, movie, or television program.

True   False   **3.** Digital convergence is the practice of using individual technologies in distinct, separate ways.

True   False   **4.** A computer program's help system may provide examples of hypermedia.

True   False   **5.** Today, nearly every new computer is fully multimedia-capable.

Multiple Choice

Circle the word or phrase that best completes each sentence.

1. The practice of using more than one type of medium at the same time is called _____ .
   A. interactivity   **B.** multimedia   **C.** a computer game

2. In a _____ , the user and program respond to one another.
   A. feedback loop   **B.** head-mounted display   **C.** new media

3. Wending your way through electronic information is called _____ .
   A. interactivity   **B.** multimedia   **C.** navigation

4. New PCs should follow the guidelines for hardware configurations spelled out by the _____ standard.
   A. PC 97/99/2001   **B.** MPEG   **C.** MPC Level 3

5. _____ use multimedia technologies to enable students to take classes online.
   A. E-commerce Web sites   **B.** Virtual universities   **C.** CD-ROM encyclopedias

LESSON LABS

Complete the following exercises as directed by your instructor.

1. Determine whether your PC is multimedia-capable by taking stock of its hardware features. How fast is the processor, and how much RAM is available? Does the computer have a color monitor, sound card and speakers, and a CD-ROM (or DVD-ROM) drive? Does your computer lack any components that would enable it to support multimedia programs better?

2. If your school's computer lab or library has multimedia products on CD-ROM, check one out and use it. What type of application did you select? Determine what types of media it uses. What sorts of navigational tools does it provide? How easy is the product to use? Does it serve its purpose? Write a one-page report on the product and summarize its strengths and flaws.

Creating and Distributing New Media Content

OVERVIEW: How Is Multimedia Done?

Whether you are playing a video game, looking up information in an online encyclopedia, or learning a new language from a CD-ROM tutorial, you may be amazed at what you see on the screen. Newcomers to PC-based multimedia commonly ask aloud: "How do they *do* that?"

Simply stated, the process of creating multimedia is complex and can take months or even years of effort by many people. A full-featured multimedia event may include still images, animation, full-motion video, speech and music, and more. In addition, any program must include a command system to allow the user to control its function. The more elaborate the command system, the more interactivity the program can offer.

Another important aspect of multimedia development is distribution—that is, the means by which the product gets to the consumer. This factor can have a significant impact on the way a product behaves or the features it can offer. But as technology develops, various distribution methods promise to become more similar so that someday, any product will look and behave the same, regardless of how it reaches the end user.

OBJECTIVES

- Describe the six phases of the multimedia design process.
- List three technologies that support full-motion video in multimedia products.
- Identify one technology that supports streaming audio and video on the Web.
- Name three ways in which multimedia content is commonly distributed.

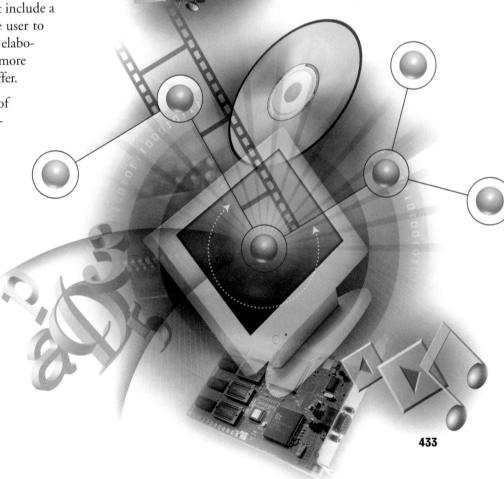

CREATING NEW MEDIA CONTENT

To capture and hold the user's attention and to remain competitive with other products, a multimedia program must provide three features:

◆ Information, action, or a story line that compels the user to interact with the program.

◆ A wide assortment of cleverly and seamlessly interwoven media types.

◆ Flexibility in navigation, thus enabling the user to move around at will or even redirect the flow of content.

As a result, creating effective multimedia can be a challenging process.

To cover all the bases, a multimedia development team usually includes people with various skills who adhere to a complex but well-defined development process. Figure 24.1 shows an overview of the multimedia development process. The following sections discuss each step of this process in greater detail.

Figure 24.1
The multimedia development process involves several distinct steps for achieving a final product.

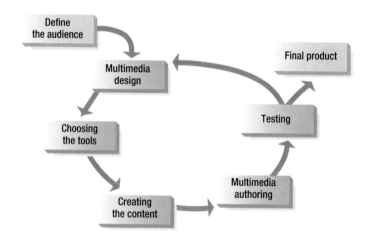

Defining the Audience

Because a multimedia program can offer so much in the way of content and can be developed in so many different ways, its creators must understand the audience. In other words, who will use the product? This issue is the most essential that developers must tackle, and it is discussed in detail long before actual development work begins. To define the audience for their product, developers ask questions such as these:

◆ **What specific interest will the product fulfill, and what type of person displays this interest?** For example, if you plan to develop a multimedia tutorial on the topic of deck building, you should identify the type of person who is interested in building a deck. If you must develop a Web site for the purpose of selling automotive parts, you should decide who would be interested in buying them.

◆ **What assumptions can be made about the audience?** For example, what skill level or experience should the user have before using the program? This skill level includes both experience with computers (or the specific technology on which the product will be delivered) and with the product's core subject matter.

♦ **What do users expect to gain by using the program?** For certain types of products, the user's goal is to learn something. In other cases, the user may want only to be entertained.

♦ **How much time will users want to spend exploring this content?** In the case of an interactive game, the user may expect to encounter plot twists or to be challenged repeatedly before reaching a final goal. In the case of a CBT, however, the user may want to go directly to the essential information.

♦ **What media will best deliver the message to this user?** The answer may depend on the user's goals and expectations. In the case of a tutorial, spoken narration, text-based instructions, and animated graphics may be the key. In a game, however, full-motion video, stereo sound, and human characters may be essential.

♦ **What method or methods (floppy disk, CD-ROM, DVD, dial-up Internet, broadband Internet, intranet) will be used to distribute the product?** The method of distribution determines the maximum size of the product. The speed of the delivery system determines how media-rich the product can be. Disk-based media require that the user's operating system (OS) be considered, and the Web requires that the user's browser and hardware/software configuration be considered. When a product is distributed across OS platforms (for example, for both Windows and Macintosh systems), the developer must choose cross-platform file types and authoring tools.

NORTON ONLINE

Visit **www.glencoe.com/norton/online/** for more information on **multimedia design.**

In reality, the preceding list is short. Development teams may spend weeks or months trying to define their product's users, getting to know the consumer's every want, need, and wish. Marketers may be recruited to interview prospective customers or meet with focus groups to seek consumer reactions to competing products (see Figure 24.2).

This part of the development process is common to the development of many, many types of products—from potato chips to self-help books, from automobiles to video games. "Know the customer" is the first rule of product development and is key to any product's long-term success. For this reason, the answers to audience-related questions are the most important factors in shaping a final product.

Figure 24.2
Developers seldom work in isolation when creating a new product. They frequently enlist the help of marketers, who may use focus groups to determine what consumers want from a specific type of product or to get reviews about competing products.

Design and Storyboarding

Planning the overall design is often the longest part of the development process. Much of this work goes on without any computers. A common way to start is by composing an outline of the sequences and blocks of information that will appear on the screen. Such an outline can take many forms, depending on the type of product to be developed. For example, suppose you are developing a multimedia dictionary. Your outline may resemble an outline for a book, including a list of terms to be defined, but with the addition of lines and arrows to indicate important links that must be provided within the information. If you are developing a CBT product, on the other hand, the outline may be considerably more complex, with placeholders for text, narration or animation that plays on cue, quizzes, links to other parts of the program or to Web sites, and much more.

Figure 24.3
Creating a storyboard.

Design and storyboarding is the time to determine how much information—text, graphics, links—will be presented on each screen. It is also the time to establish a navigation method for the user. Will there be a navigation bar with arrows leading from scene to scene, or will there be text or graphic objects that the user will click on to jump around the entire program? Can the user always return to a single starting point? Will the content ever change without input from the user?

When a program includes a great deal of animation or many different scenes, the best design aid is the storyboard. Used by film directors for productions ranging from thirty-second television commercials to feature-length motion pictures, the **storyboard** consists of sketches of the scenes and action. Mapping out a storyboard helps the author to recognize gaps in logic or flaws in the flow of the content. Some multimedia authoring programs provide facilities for drawing and organizing the frames of a storyboard, and stand-alone storyboard programs are available (see Figure 24.3). Many experienced multimedia designers create storyboards simply by using a word processor or drawing program.

Choosing Tools, Creating Content, and Authoring

Because multimedia includes different kinds of content, creating it involves many types of software. Creating text often requires a word processor; working with digital images requires graphics software; using video requires a video-capture program and editing software; sound often requires its own editing software. HTML is commonly used in interactive multimedia programs as well as Web pages, so HTML editors are important tools in the developer's arsenal (see Figure 24.4).

Figure 24.4
Many interactive multimedia products are based on Web technologies, including HTML, Java, and others. For this reason, multimedia developers commonly use tools once reserved for use by Web designers, such as HTML editing programs. This image shows the complex HTML code used for an interactive, frame-based tutorial on mainframe computer systems.

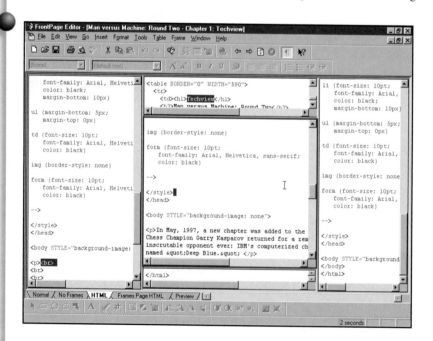

Similarly, products such as Macromedia's Shockwave, which helps developers incorporate interactive animation into multimedia products and Web pages, are increasingly common in content development. All this software is used to generate the content.

When the content is ready, it must be assembled in a process called **multimedia authoring.** This process requires still another type of software that can understand all the different types of media, combine them, control the sequences in which they appear, and create navigational tools and an interface for the user.

Macromedia Director is one of the most popular programs for combining all the elements of a multimedia presentation (see Figure 24.5). In it, the multimedia author assembles each element—text, graphics, sound, and video—into separate "tracks." The program helps the author to synchronize all the elements so that, for example, a crash sound effect is heard precisely when two animated objects collide. Macromedia Director is a powerful program for creating sophisticated presentations. These presentations are versatile enough to be distributed through various media. The file that Macromedia Director generates is the one that contains the entire multimedia presentation, ready for distribution on disk or CD-ROM.

NORTON ONLINE

Visit www.glencoe.com/norton/online/ for more information on **multimedia authoring tools.**

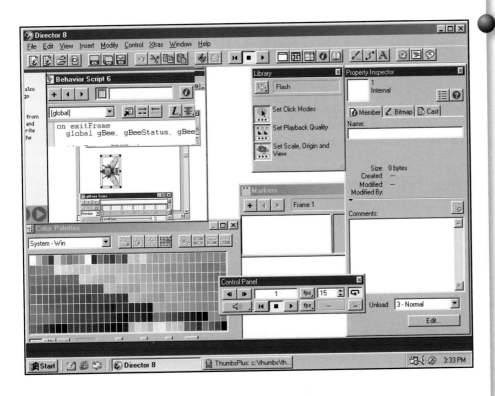

Figure 24.5
The most powerful multimedia products incorporate media such as full-motion video, narration, and powerful navigational aids. Developers use multiple tools to create the individual components of a multimedia program, then rely on a multimedia authoring application such as Macromedia Director to incorporate everything into a seamless whole for the user.

Testing

It is vital that the program be tested by the people who will be using it (see Figure 24.6 on page 438). With this testing, the programmer can locate any flaws and repair them before unleashing the finished product on the world.

Like the testing of any software product, it is helpful for the program's author(s) to watch users navigate through the product. The kinds of problems to watch for are any locations in the product where the user does not know what to do next. Is the user struggling to read a font size too small for descriptive text? Are there sufficient controls to stop a video or audio clip if the user wants to continue without going through the entire clip? Is the user following navigational paths that lead quickly to the desired information, or is the user sometimes lost in the maze?

Figure 24.6

Testing is an important final phase of any product's development. If the product does not perform as expected during testing, it may be returned to an earlier phase in the development cycle for repairs or improvements.

Before a program is ready for release, it may need to go through several testing-and-revision cycles so that everyone is comfortable with the finished product. As part of the planning process, sufficient time must be built into the schedule for the testing cycles. Most software developers and programmers employ firms to test the software or they have their own in-house testing departments.

A program's author and the final user often have different points of view. What the author believes to be simple to use—having designed the interface and used it for weeks or months during development—might be totally bewildering to someone seeing the interface for the first time. The author must learn to regard any problems the user detects with the program as constructive criticism. Testing is so valuable because it is easy to lose sight of the audience after the heavy-duty authoring starts.

TECHNOLOGIES THAT SUPPORT NEW MEDIA

Since the first PC-based multimedia products appeared, developers and programmers have worked ceaselessly to create new technologies that will allow graphics, audio, video, and user feedback to work more seamlessly. As a result, dozens of specialized file formats, audio/video platforms, and programming techniques have become available.

Today's most sophisticated multimedia products incorporate any number of these technologies, resulting in smoother animation, audio and video streams that flow without interruption, and a heightened level of interactivity. These technologies are used in products of all kinds, from games to Web sites, and are found in both CD-ROM-based and Web-based multimedia events.

The following sections provide a brief introduction to a few of the technologies commonly used to support multimedia products. It is not important to understand the details or operation of these technologies. However, you should be aware of their existence and the impact they can have on your multimedia experience, and that some of them require special software to function properly on your system.

MPEG and JPEG

Even though a modern multimedia PC is capable of displaying multimedia content, other factors must be considered by the multimedia developer. Perhaps the most important is the issue of data compression.

High-quality digital video requires that millions of bits be transmitted to the monitor every second. Remember, the monitor is attached to a video controller, which assigns 24 bits to each pixel on a full-color monitor. Monitors display a grid of pixels that measures at least 640 × 480, and video requires at least fifteen image frames per second. If you multiply all these numbers, you get the number of bits it takes to display digital video.

It does not matter whether the information comes from a CD-ROM and is being displayed on a monitor, or whether it comes through a cable box and is being

NORTON ONLINE

Visit www.glencoe.com/norton/online/ for more information on **MPEG** and **JPEG**.

COMPUTERS
in your career

Careers in Multimedia

Careers in multimedia are as varied and as numerous as multimedia products. The sheer variety and range of what can be done in multimedia is astonishing. These options can be both invigorating and overwhelming to the multimedia professional. How is the volume of work involved in a multimedia product accomplished? Multimedia work is usually done by teams.

At the helm of a multimedia project is the creative director, who is responsible for developing and refining the overall design process from start to finish. The creative director is also responsible for integrating that design process into the developmental process of the company. The team members of a multimedia project usually include some or all of the following:

◆ **Art Director.** He or she directs the creation of all art for the project. This work involves a variety of original media, which are changed to digital form for manipulation on the modern artist's "canvas," the computer.

◆ **Technical Lead.** He or she ensures that the technological process of a project works and that it accommodates all project components and media.

◆ **Interface Designer.** The interface designer directs the development of the user interface for a product, which includes not only what users see but also what they hear and touch.

◆ **Instructional Designer.** This team member designs the pedagogy, or instructional system, for how material is taught, if the product is educational.

◆ **Visual Designer.** He or she creates the various art forms, usually within a specialized area such as graphic design, calligraphy, illustration, photography, image manipulation, packaging, or typesetting.

◆ **Interactive Scriptwriter.** The scriptwriter weaves the project content among various media and forms of interactivity. A multimedia scriptwriter is part writer and part interactive designer.

◆ **Animator.** Animators used to create their finished work by photographing models and sculptures or hand-drawn and painted pictures. Today, animators have a wealth of specialized 2-D and 3-D software at their disposal that not only enables them to create animation more quickly but also produce effects that could not be created manually.

◆ **Sound Producer.** Part manager, part creative artist, and part programmer, a sound producer designs and produces all sounds within a product, including musical scores, vocals, voice-overs, and sound effects, and makes sure that each sound interacts correctly with all the other media.

◆ **Videographer.** He or she creates the video footage that interfaces with the interactive technology of the product. Video is often the most complex, time-consuming, and resource-demanding medium to create.

◆ **Programmer/Software Designer.** He or she designs and creates the underlying software that runs a multimedia program and carries out the user's commands.

Multimedia products are typically the result of a team effort.

displayed by the television. The components of the system usually are not capable of transmitting, processing, and displaying the digital information fast enough. The capacity for data transmission is known as bandwidth. Somewhere in a computer system, there is almost always a bottleneck in the bandwidth. When it comes to video, one potential solution is data compression.

Data compression typically uses mathematical analyses of digital source material to strip away unnecessary bits of data prior to sending it across the wire. This process is called **encoding** and results in much smaller image files than would be possible if they were not encoded. At the receiving end (for example, inside a modern cable TV converter or direct-broadcast satellite receiver), the compressed file undergoes a **decoding** process, and the missing bits are quickly reinserted to produce a copy that is extremely close to the original in quality and detail. Special hardware or software may be required to decode compressed files of certain types.

Among the most common multimedia compression schemes currently being used are JPEG (as you saw in Lesson 21, "Working With Images"), which is commonly used for high-resolution still images, and **MPEG** (pronounced EM-peg, for Motion Picture Experts Group), which is used for full-motion video files (see Figure 24.7). Each scheme is sponsored by an industry consortium whose goal is to achieve high rates of compression and industrywide agreement on standards.

The push for standards is important because it means that multimedia-equipped cable TV boxes and other hardware will have the requisite decompression facilities built in (usually requiring special integrated circuit chips and software—all of which work behind the scenes). The standards also allow multimedia developers to choose the right compression scheme for the target audience.

To play MPEG-format audio or video files, you need an MPEG-compliant player. Other MPEG-compliant players are also available, many of which can be downloaded from various sources on the Internet.

Figure 24.7

Many of the most colorful, high-resolution images on Web pages are JPEG-format graphics. MPEG compression allows high-quality video and audio to be viewed on the computer screen, whether the source is a compact disk or the Internet.

QuickTime and QuickTime VR

The **QuickTime** multimedia file format was developed for use on Apple computers and allows users to play high-quality audio and video files on the desktop. To play QuickTime-format files on your desktop, you need either the Apple QuickTime Player or a QuickTime plug-in that will work with your browser. (The plug-in will enable the browser to play QuickTime content directly in the browser window.) The QuickTime Player supports a wide variety of multimedia file formats, including MPEG, AVI, and others (see Figure 24.8).

An adaptation of the QuickTime format, called **QuickTime VR,** enables developers to create virtual reality-like environments from flat, two-dimensional images. By stitching together a series of images (such as a series of photographs creating a panoramic view of an entire room or the interior of a car), QuickTime VR can be used to create immersive environments that look and feel a lot like artificial 3-D environments created by expensive VR workstations. You can view QuickTime VR movies in the QuickTime Player or in a Web browser that includes the QuickTime plug-in, as shown in Figure 24.9.

Video for Windows (AVI Format)

The **Video for Windows** format was developed by Microsoft as a way to store compressed audio and video information. Video for Windows files use the file-name extension **AVI,** which stands for audio-video interleave. AVI-format files do not provide the resolution or speed available from MPEG, QuickTime, and other audio-video formats. Because AVI files require no special hardware or software, they can be played on any Windows computer. AVI is seldom used in high-quality multimedia products but is commonly found on Web sites and low-end products where video is not as important.

RealAudio and RealVideo

RealNetworks first released the RealAudio Player in 1995, and the program quickly became the standard for playing streaming audio over the Internet. Now called the **RealPlayer,** the product incorporates **RealVideo** and **RealAudio** technologies and can play streaming audio and video broadcast from a Web site.

As you learned in Unit 10, "The Internet and Online Resources," the terms *streaming audio* and *streaming video* refer to technologies that enable high-quality audio and video data to be transmitted over an Internet connection. Streaming capabilities are essential to many types

Figure 24.8
Apple's QuickTime Player is commonly used on the Internet for playing music videos, movie trailers, and other streaming video or audio files.

NORTON ONLINE

Visit www.glencoe.com/norton/online/ for more information on QuickTime, AVI, RealAudio, and RealVideo.

Figure 24.9
Using QuickTime VR movies, the Virtually VancouVR Web site enables you to navigate up and down any street of Vancouver, British Columbia.

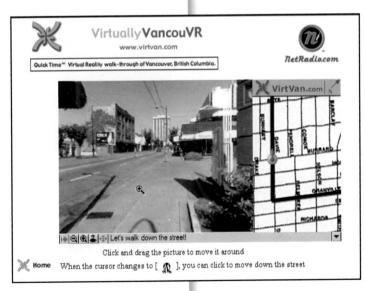

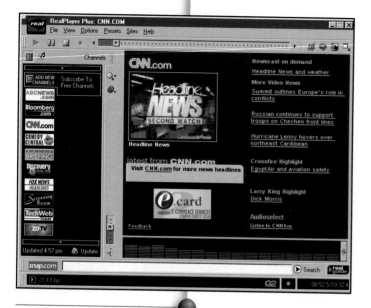

Figure 24.10
Using RealPlayer technology, Web sites such as CNN Headline News Online can broadcast its television programming over the World Wide Web.

NORTON ONLINE

Visit www.glencoe.com/norton/online/ for more information on **Shockwave**.

of multimedia Web sites, such as the CNN and Weather Channel sites, which broadcast their programming live over the Internet (see Figure 24.10). By using RealNetworks' technologies, artists such as Jimmy Buffet, the Rolling Stones, and others provide music and videos over the Web and can broadcast live concerts online. (The quality of the streaming audio and video depends on the speed of your Internet connection and the processing power of your PC.)

Several versions of the RealPlayer are available. You can use it as a stand-alone application for viewing television programming and listening to radio broadcasts over the Web and for viewing music videos, movies, and other forms of entertainment. A RealPlayer plug-in is also available. It allows RealAudio and RealVideo content to play directly in a browser window.

Shockwave

Macromedia Corp. created a stir in 1997 with the release of its Shockwave plug-in. **Shockwave** is part of a suite of products that allows developers to add multimedia content (such as audio, video, and animation) to Web pages. Web designers can create multimedia content and compress it into a Shockwave-format file that can be displayed directly in a Web page. Even though the Shockwave plug-in is required to view "Shocked" Web sites, the Shockwave material appears in the browser window, not in a separate window.

One advantage that Shockwave offers to Web designers is its ability to accept user input. For instance, you may be able to click on or roll your mouse pointer over a Shockwave animation to redirect the animation, cause a different event to occur, or initiate a hypertext jump. Because Shockwave supports user interaction, it can be used to develop online games, puzzles, and other types of fun interactive content (see Figure 24.11).

Figure 24.11
Using Shockwave content, developers can create interactive games, like this online football game, which can be played live on the Web.

Answer the following questions by filling in the blank(s).

1. The first step in creating a multimedia product is defining the product's _____ .

2. The process of combining different media files into a single product is called _____ .

3. The process of compressing audio or video files by removing unnecessary data is called _____ .

DISTRIBUTING NEW MEDIA CONTENT

An important part of the multimedia development process is understanding how a product will be distributed to its users. Currently, multimedia content is typically delivered to users by one of three means: CD-ROM (or DVD-ROM), the Internet or some sort of network connection, or television. Of course, each delivery technology has its own set of unique strengths and weaknesses. Each delivery method affects the product's ability to use certain technologies or the user's ability to interact with and direct the content.

As delivery technologies improve over the coming years, and as bandwidth becomes less of an issue for users (due to faster networks and Internet connections, improved CD-ROM/DVD-ROM technologies, and the integration of these technologies with television), many existing limitations will disappear. Ultimately (but not by the time you read this) many multimedia products will behave identically regardless of the way they come to the user.

CD-ROM

Perhaps the most obvious way to deliver multimedia content is on a compact disk. Because of their large storage capacities, low cost, and ease of use, compact disks were the obvious early choice of multimedia developers who needed a way to put their products in the hands of consumers. Early CD-ROM titles such as *Myst* and *Encarta* were successful and proved that PCs and gaming consoles could support a wide range of audio and video technologies, hypermedia, and other important types of multimedia content.

By incorporating new technologies such as MPEG, Java, Shockwave, and other formats that allow tightly compressed streaming media, the performance of CD-based products continues to improve. By correlation, the number of products available on CD-ROM continues to grow at a tremendous pace (see Figure 24.12).

Another strength of the compact disk format is its ability to interact with other technologies. For instance, it is possible

Figure 24.12
Despite advances in other delivery technologies, compact disks remain the leading delivery mechanism for multimedia products. Because nearly all new PCs include a CD-ROM drive and other multimedia components, the user base for disk-based products is huge and growing.

to use many CD-based products in multi-user environments, across networks, and even in tandem with separate Web sites or other Internet resources. Many disk-based encyclopedias, for example, are filled with links to Web pages, allowing the user to shift easily from one source to the other.

One drawback to CD technology is the relative slowness of CD-ROM drives. Although drive speeds are constantly increasing, they are still much slower than typical hard disks. Storage capacity has also become a concern as consumers demand more features and capabilities from their multimedia products. For this reason, some new products have been published on multiple disks, which can mean an interruption in use when disks must be swapped. However, as more multimedia products are published on DVD (and as more consumers purchase computers with DVD drives), the storage issue promises to fade in importance.

Visit www.glencoe.com/norton/online/ for more information on **multimedia on the Internet.**

The Internet

For several years, experts have envisioned the Internet (and, by extension, the individual networks that tie into the Internet) as the ultimate vehicle for multimedia delivery. Consumers have heard endless promises that, because it supports two-way interaction between users and servers, the Internet will someday become *the* place to go for online gaming, shopping, education, and other multimedia experiences—even interactive virtual reality. This dream, however, has been hampered by two problems: limited bandwidth and a lack of technologies that support streaming multimedia content. Fortunately, both problems are decreasing in importance with time.

As you read earlier, several technologies have recently been developed to support multimedia on the Web and enable developers to compress audio, video, and graphical content to a fraction of its original size, break it into packets, and deliver it in small, manageable chunks that can be put back together and played on the user's PC. Using plug-in technologies that are powerful but small in size, developers can customize the browser interface to display almost any type of content (see Figure 24.13). Many of these technologies also allow two-way interaction.

Figure 24.13
Streaming technologies and faster Internet connections enable Web sites to offer various interactive, multimedia products such as music videos on demand.

Bandwidth is becoming less of an issue for two reasons. First, Web designers are using compression technologies to ensure that Web pages (especially multimedia components) download and function faster than ever. Web sites are also shifting more processing functions away from the server and onto the user's computer, requiring less downloading and uploading time, and freeing the server from certain tasks. These advances make better use of existing bandwidth.

Also, more Internet users are adopting high-speed connections. The 56 Kbps modem is now considered a minimum data-transfer standard, and consumers are rapidly switching to ISDN, DSL, and cable-modem connections that provide much higher bandwidth and data-transmission speeds. By making these changes, consumers are opening a much larger pipeline for content to travel, making online multimedia events more accessible than ever.

As a result, the availability of online multimedia has exploded. Internet users can easily find games (including multiplayer games involving thousands of participants), music videos, radio and television broadcasts, reference materials, and distance learning resources. These multimedia products perform online with nearly the same speed and responsiveness provided by CD-ROM-based products.

Television

Television has long been the king of multimedia delivery vehicles. If you have a television in your home, you know how easy it is to choose from different programs, each providing its own blend of live action, spoken or musical audio, text, graphics, animation, and video. From this perspective, it is hard to beat television for the amount and variety of content it can deliver to an audience.

Television, however, is not interactive. It is limited in the types and amount of feedback it can accept from the audience because television has traditionally been a one-way medium. Content travels from the broadcaster to the user, but not vice versa (changing channels does not count). Until recently, it has been difficult or impossible for the viewer to respond in any meaningful way to a television program.

Currently, interactive television is possible to a limited extent and only because additional technologies have been incorporated into television. You can use your television for playing interactive video games, for example, but only with the addition of a game console and control devices (see Figure 24.14). The games themselves are separate from the television programming you receive through an aerial, cable, or satellite transmission.

One of the latest advancements toward making television interactive is the integration of Internet connectivity with broadcast programming. As mentioned earlier in this unit, Microsoft's WebTV service provides a set of special devices that connect to the user's television, converting it into an Internet appliance. Thus, the user can view normal television programming as well as content from the Internet, such as Web pages, e-mail, and more. By working with WebTV, some networks have begun to integrate their programs with special content exclusively for WebTV users, enabling the audience to participate in the programming.

Figure 24.14
Television is slowly becoming more interactive, but only through the addition of technologies such as game devices and Internet connections.

Other satellite-based services, such as DirecTV and DirecPC, are moving in the same direction as WebTV but promise much higher bandwidth through their dedicated satellite channels. DirecDuo, a combination of the DirecTV and DirecPC services, enables users to connect their home televisions and personal computers to the service, and thus enjoy broadcast programming and high-speed, high-bandwidth Internet service. Unlike WebTV, however, DirectPC users do not have to use their television to view Internet content.

Ultimately, services such as WebTV and satellite broadcast services may make television totally interactive, and users will be able to order programs and movies on demand, customize their programming schedules, participate in multi-user games and contests on television, and even direct the content of individual programs in progress (changing the plot of a movie, for example).

NORTON
ONLINE

Visit **www.glencoe.com/norton/online/** for more information on **interactive television services.**

Norton Notebook

ARE YOUR AUDIO CDs ANTIQUES?

MP3 (MPEG Layer 3) is an audio-compression standard that can compress digitized music to one-tenth its original size. Thus, a song that requires 10 MB of uncompressed storage space can be reduced to 1 MB or less. MP3 also handles the compression with almost no loss in sound quality. To compress a song in MP3 format, you need a special program called a ripper. After copying digitized music (from your computer's CD-ROM drive, for example) onto your hard drive, you can use the ripper to compress the music. The compressed MP3 file can be copied to another medium, such as CD-R or a special hardware player that stores MP3 files.

To play an MP3-format file from your computer, you need MP3 playback software, and there are hundreds. Some players act as a plug-in to your Web browser; others run as stand-alone programs. The newest versions of Windows Media Player and RealPlayer support MP3 files, but WinAmp (available from **www.winamp.com/**) is one of the most popular freeware players.

You can also carry your MP3 recordings with you and play them on a ViaPC or Rio player. These tiny devices cost around $200 and can store about an hour's worth of MP3-format music. Various small-format players are starting to become available for personal use or use in a car.

Using a handheld MP3 player, you can carry an hour's worth (or more) of compressed MP3-format music with you.

Uncopyrighted music is also being distributed on the Internet, and this practice is perfectly legal. Several Web sites allow you to download copyrighted music legally. These distributors have obtained permission to reproduce music in MP3 format and make it available on their Web sites, and even resell some music. Such "online outlets" provide a service to the music industry by making free samples available and advertising the work of new and established artists.

And Now, the Bad News

The problem with MP3 is that it makes it too easy to compress and distribute music. As a result, many copyrighted songs have been recorded in MP3 format and distributed illegally on the Internet. Music pirates set up Web sites (some of which stay active for only a few days before disappearing) where visitors can find and download all types of music.

Why is the practice illegal? Simply put, if a song has been published, then it is copyrighted and a person or company owns the rights to it. Technically, copying the song and distributing the copy is illegal unless the copier has permission from—and pays a fee to—the music's owner. Of course, record companies don't waste much effort hunting down the home copier who dubs a song from the radio or a CD and listens to it in the car. When someone reproduces a copyrighted song in MP3 format and puts it on the Web for anyone to copy, that's a different matter.

The Future of MP3

The future of MP3 is both bright and cloudy. The public likes the format and will buy MP3 files and hardware. With enough public dollars and enthusiasm behind the technology, MP3 may be valuable enough for all parties concerned to develop the standards and security necessary to make MP3 permanent.

On the other hand, MP3 has limitations and could be surpassed at any time by new and improved technology. In particular, Microsoft is developing MS Audio 4.0, which could improve upon both compressed file size and copyright security.

NORTON ONLINE

Visit **www.glencoe.com/norton/online/** for more information on **MP3** and **MS Audio.**

LESSON QUIZ

True/False

Answer the following questions by circling True or False.

True   False   **1.** Users of multimedia products are generally more interested in multimedia features than the information, action, or story line offered by the product.

True   False   **2.** The multimedia development process usually involves the efforts of a group of people.

True   False   **3.** Multimedia products are generally tested before being released.

True   False   **4.** Video files generally are not compressed before inclusion in a multimedia product.

True   False   **5.** A special feature of animation created in Shockwave is that it can accept user input.

Multiple Choice

Circle the word or phrase that best completes each sentence.

1. In defining the audience for a multimedia product, the developer must determine the user's _____ .
   A. interest   **B.** expectations   **C.** both A and B

2. Multimedia developers often use a(n) _____ to organize the product.
   A. storyboard   **B.** encoder   **C.** map

3. The _____ file format is commonly used for full-motion video files.
   A. JPEG   **B.** MPEG   **C.** neither A nor B

4. The term _____ refers to high-quality audio and video data transferred over an Internet connection.
   A. streaming   **B.** compression   **C.** multimedia

5. A problem with television as a distribution method for multimedia content is its lack of _____ capabilities.
   A. interactive   **B.** streaming   **C.** decoding

LESSON LABS

Complete the following exercises as directed by your instructor.

1. Find out if your PC is ready to play a game. Many multimedia games are available on CD-ROM and online, and you can thus play them on your PC instead of using a dedicated video game system and a television. But you may need to connect a special controller to your PC before playing certain games, which may require a joystick, steering wheel, or multi-function game pad. Check your PC for either a dedicated game port or a USB port. If you find one, note where it is located.

2. Is any multimedia software installed on your system? Click the Start button, point to Programs, and inspect the Programs menu. Look for programs like Windows Media Player, QuickTime Player, RealPlayer, and others. Are there any games or reference products installed?

LESSON 23: Understanding Multimedia

Multimedia, Interactivity, and New Media Defined

■ A medium is a way of communicating information, such as speech or text. Multimedia is the use of more than one unique medium at a time.

■ Multimedia programs are described as interactive if they accept input from the user and enable the user to direct the flow of information or action in the program.

■ The term *new media* is used to describe the combination of multimedia programming and communications technologies that enable multimedia to be distributed in different ways (such as on disk, via the Internet, or over television).

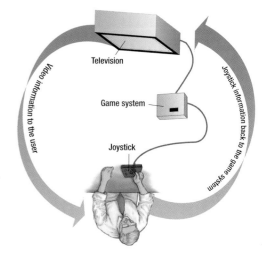

Information in Layers and Dimensions

■ Effective multimedia programming provides information that is layered and multidimensional.

■ In layered multimedia, multiple types of information may be presented simultaneously. In multidimensional programming, the user can approach information in different ways, such as a text-only description or an animated demonstration.

■ Navigation is the act of moving through electronic information. Multimedia products typically provide the user with a set of navigation tools.

■ Hypermedia is commonly used in multimedia products. When the user chooses a hypermedia link, the program moves to a different piece of information, possibly represented by a different type of media.

Hardware Considerations for Multimedia

■ In creating multimedia products, developers must be aware of the capabilities and features of the user's computer.

■ Hardware and software manufacturers have developed sets of standards for computer systems that will be used with multimedia products. An older set of standards, called MPC, was recently replaced by the more current PC 99 standards.

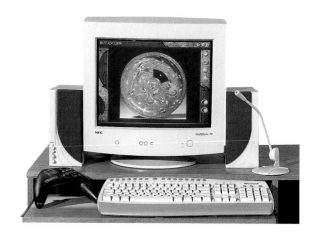

Applications for Multimedia

■ Multimedia programs are used in a wide variety of ways.

■ Multimedia is commonly used in schools, where students use CD-ROM-based reference materials and tutorials and use the Internet to collaborate with students in other locations.

■ By using multimedia programs and delivery mechanisms like the Internet and television, schools can support distance learning, which allows students to take classes without actually traveling to school. Online courses are typically called virtual universities.

■ In the workplace, companies commonly use multimedia programs to train employees. These training programs (called computer-based training, or CBT) are sometimes done online but can also be provided on disk.

■ Multimedia is frequently used in the home, whether on a PC, television, or the Internet. Home users consume a wide variety of multimedia products for entertainment and learning.

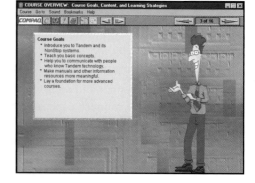

LESSON 24: Creating and Distributing New Media Content

Creating New Media Content

- The process of creating a multimedia product usually results from the effort of a group of professionals who follow a multistep process.

- The development process involves defining the audience, designing the product, choosing development tools, creating content, multimedia authoring, and testing.

- Multimedia developers must gain a detailed understanding of the audience who will use the final product to make sure it will succeed.

- Using basic tools such as outlines and storyboards, designers lay out and organize the content and flow of the information for their products.

- Because a multimedia product can use so many types of media, designers use a wide variety of tools to create individual components, ranging from text editors to video editors.

- After the individual components of a multimedia product are created, the developer uses sophisticated multimedia authoring tools to assemble them into a single working program.

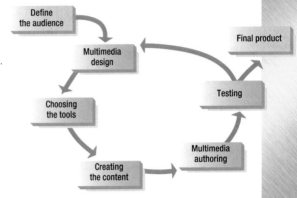

Technologies That Support New Media

- A wide range of new technologies has been created to support multimedia on CD-ROM and the Internet. These technologies enable developers to create sophisticated content using almost any type of medium and allow the end user to play the content in a seamless manner.

- The MPEG, AVI, and QuickTime formats are just a few technologies that allow full-motion video files to be compressed and played back on a PC, whether from a CD or an Internet connection.

- The RealAudio and RealVideo formats are the current standard for streaming audio and video played over an Internet connection.

- Formats such as Macromedia's Shockwave allow developers to create entertaining, colorful animation that not only displays directly within a browser but also accepts input from the user.

Distributing New Media Content

- The three primary means of distributing new media content are CD-ROM (or DVD-ROM), the Internet, and television.

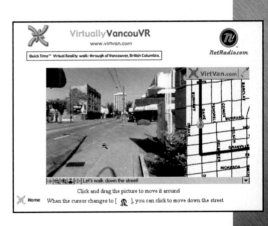

- CD-ROM is the most widely used vehicle for distributing multimedia programs. Because of its storage capacity and ease of use, CD-ROM is used for games, references, CBTs, and many other types of multimedia products.

- The Internet is rapidly becoming an effective way to distribute new media content as new technologies emerge to enhance interactivity and performance.

- Television is seen as the ultimate multimedia delivery vehicle, but its interactive capabilities are limited. This limitation may change, however, as two-way Internet and satellite connections are integrated into television programming.

UNIT REVIEW

KEY TERMS

After completing this unit, you should be able to define the following terms.

AVI, *441*
computer-based training (CBT), *429*
decode, *440*
digital convergence, *422*
distance learning (DL), *429*
encode, *440*
feedback loop, *421*
hypermedia, *424*
interactive, *420*
interactive media, *421*
interactivity, *421*
MPEG, *440*
multimedia, *420*

multimedia authoring, *437*
navigation, *424*
new media, *422*
PC 97 standard, *427*
QuickTime, *441*
QuickTime VR, *441*
RealAudio, *441*
RealPlayer, *441*
RealVideo, *441*
Shockwave, *442*
storyboard, *436*
Video for Windows, *441*
virtual university, *429*

KEY TERMS QUIZ

Fill in each blank with one of the terms listed under Key Terms.

1. The term _____ refers to the use of more than one type of medium at the same time.

2. By accepting input from the user, interactive media create a(n) _____ .

3. According to the concept of _____ , when various technologies are used, a variety of content can converge into a single digital stream.

4. Wending your way through electronic information is commonly called _____ .

5. The _____ standard replaces MPC Level 3 for stating the minimum configuration requirements for new PCs.

6. _____ enable students to take classes while online.

7. A(n) _____ consists of sketches of the scenes and action that will be organized into a multimedia program.

8. The _____ format is commonly used for high-resolution, moving images on multimedia products and Web sites.

9. Because they require no special hardware or software, _____ files can be played on any Windows computer.

10. The _____ and _____ standards are used to support streaming audio and video on the World Wide Web.

REVIEW QUESTIONS

In your own words, briefly answer the following questions.

1. What does the term *interactive media* mean?
2. What benefits can interactive multimedia bring to education?
3. Describe one contribution that new media technologies have brought to business.
4. What is the biggest single application of multimedia technology?
5. Briefly describe what is meant by digital convergence.
6. List the basic steps involved in developing a multimedia product.
7. What are the three key hardware components in a multimedia-capable PC?
8. Why is data compression such an important issue for multimedia developers?
9. Explain how hypermedia allows a user to navigate through digital content without necessarily following a linear sequence.
10. Why is it so important that a multimedia developer understand the audience before developing a multimedia product?

DISCUSSION QUESTIONS

As directed by your instructor, discuss the following questions in class or in groups.

1. Think about the issues that must be addressed by television, cable, and satellite companies as interactivity becomes a more integral part of television programming. What types of interactive programming can you envision? Will television programs and movies as we know them still be produced in thirty years?

2. You probably have been exposed to some examples of multimedia educational software. Describe the examples you have seen. What were the strengths and weaknesses of this software? What suggestions can you make for improving educational multimedia?

 ETHICAL ISSUES

Multimedia development and delivery technologies enable people to create and distribute digital content of all types to millions of consumers, but is all of it beneficial? With this thought in mind, discuss the following questions in class.

1. One of the biggest growth areas of multimedia is pornography. CD-ROM disks and Web sites are produced by the thousands each year, enabling users to view graphic adult-oriented content on their PCs. What is your opinion of this use of multimedia? Do you believe the government should restrict this type of material, as it does printed materials?

2. MP3 technology enables people to share recorded music like never before. What is your view of "ripping" songs from a popular CD and e-mailing them to a friend so she or he can play them on a PC? What if the friend lived in a country that does not protect copyright rules like the United States does?

UNIT LABS

You and the Computer

Complete the following exercises using a computer in your classroom, lab, or home. No other materials are needed.

1. **Check Your Multimedia Setup.** Windows lets you quickly check and configure your computer's multimedia settings. Take the following steps:

   A. Click the Start button, point to Settings, and then click Control Panel. The Control Panel window opens.

   B. Double-click the Multimedia icon. The Multimedia Properties dialog box opens, displaying Audio, Video, MIDI, CD Music, and Devices tabs.

   C. Click each tab in turn. Check the settings in each tab and write them down. Do not change any settings.

   D. Click Cancel to close the Multimedia Properties dialog box; then close the Control Panel window.

2. **Set Your Volume.** If your computer has a set of speakers, you can use Windows' volume control to set the volume, mute the speakers, and possibly configure special effects, such as a 3-D spatializer (if any such effects are installed). Take the following steps:

   A. On the Windows taskbar, double-click the speaker icon. The Volume Control dialog box opens.

   B. Use the slider controls to set the volume and balance for your PC's speakers. If you are not sure which setting to use, simply set them in the middle.

   C. Click the Advanced button to view any other options that may be available on your system. Check these settings but do not change them.

   D. Close all open dialog boxes. Now test your speaker volume by opening the Control Panel window and double-clicking the Sounds icon. When the Sounds Properties dialog box opens, select a sound from the Events list. Then click the play button under Preview. Close the dialog box and the Control Panel window.

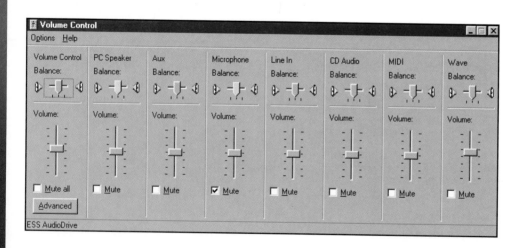

Internet Labs

To complete the following exercises, you need a computer with an Internet connection and a Web browser. (For more information on using these tools, see "Prerequisites" at the front of this textbook.)

1. **Check Out Some Audio-Video Players.** As you learned in this unit, several audio and video players are available for use on a PC, and each provides a unique set of features in addition to supporting various multimedia file types. Visit these Web sites for information on a few players, but do not download any software without your instructor's permission:

   - RealNetworks, Inc.—For information about RealPlayer, visit **http://www.real.com/**

   - Microsoft Corp.—For information about Windows Media Player, visit **http://www.microsoft.com/windows/mediaplayer/default.asp**

   - Apple Computer, Inc.—For information on QuickTime and QuickTime VR, visit **http://www.apple.com/quicktime/**

2. **Visit a "Shocked" Web Site.** To experience the fun and interactivity available through Shockwave technology, visit some "Shocked" Web sites. You can find a collection of links to such sites at **www.shockwave.com/**. Visit this URL, and then follow links to a few of the suggested sites. Your computer must have the appropriate Shockwave plug-in installed to use the Shockwave components at these sites. If your system does not have a Shockwave plug-in installed, ask your instructor for help.

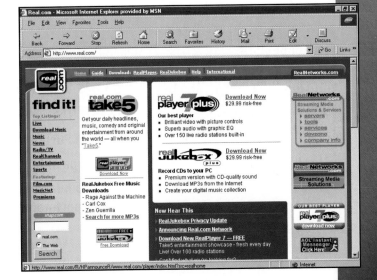

IBE Labs

If you have the Interactive Browser Edition (IBE) CD-ROM for this textbook, you may complete the following interactive exercises using the instructions provided in the IBE.

1. **Multimedia or New Media?** Classify the examples provided.

2. **Labeling.** Create a chart to show the distribution of multimedia content.

3. **Ask an Expert.** Compare how your recommendations for the use of multimedia match up with the expert's.

4. **Build a Multimedia Presentation.** Based on the design rules presented in this unit, combine media to create multimedia events.

Development of Information Systems

UNIT OBJECTIVES

List the major categories of information systems.

Explain the role of the information systems department in an organization.

Describe the function of key IS team members.

Identify the key phases of the systems development life cycle.

UNIT CONTENTS

This unit contains the following lessons:

The Basics of Information Systems

OVERVIEW: What Is an Information System?

In its most basic form, an **information system** is a mechanism that helps people collect, store, organize, and use information. Ultimately, the information system is the computer's reason for being.

Because there are so many types of information—and uses for it—many kinds of information systems have been developed. For example, if you think of a bank's database of customers and accounts as an information system, you are correct. But would you think of a factory's computer-controlled machining system, or NASA's system for launching and controlling the space shuttle? If so, you would be correct again.

As you study information systems, remember that they do much more than store and retrieve data. They help people *use* information in countless ways, whether that involves sorting lists, printing reports, matching a single fingerprint against a national database of millions of prints, or tracking the locations of planes in the night sky.

OBJECTIVES

- Define the term *information system*.
- Name five types of information systems.
- Explain the purpose of each major type of information system.
- List at least six jobs that are part of an IS department.

THE PURPOSE OF INFORMATION SYSTEMS

Information systems consist of three basic components:

◆ **The Physical Means for Storing Information Such as a File Cabinet or Hard Disk.** Depending on the organization's needs, storage requirements can be tiny (met by a day-planning notebook) or enormous (involving a mainframe system with terabytes of disk space).

◆ **The Procedures for Handling Information That Ensure Its Integrity.** In any information system, regardless of size, it is important to follow data-management procedures to eliminate duplicate entries, validate the accuracy or format of data, and avoid the loss of important information.

◆ **The Rules Regarding Information's Use and Distribution.** In any organization, data is meant to be used for specific purposes, to achieve a desired result. For example, a sales organization will use its data to make decisions about prices, inventory, and account management. By establishing rules governing the use of its information, an organization preserves its resources rather than wasting them on manipulating data in useless ways. To ensure the security of their mission-critical data, many organizations set rules that limit the information that can be made available to certain workers, enabling workers to access only the most appropriate types of information for their jobs. Different people require different information to perform their jobs. The rules of the system govern what information should be distributed to whom, at what time, and in what format.

Although these three basic components are simple, a complex information system can be very complicated. In addition to the three basic components listed above, you might add the means of distributing information to different users, whether it is a system of desk trays or a modern local area network. Most of today's information systems also include tools for sorting, categorizing, and analyzing information.

Imagine that you have agreed to maintain a list of 200 clients for a local flower shop. You start by buying 200 index cards. On each card, you write the name, address, and favorite flower of a client. When finished, you sort the cards alphabetically by the clients' last names. When a customer calls to order flowers, you write the type and quantity of flowers on that person's card.

Figure 25.1

For generations, card files have been a widely used (if somewhat inefficient) system for managing information. Most have been replaced by computerized systems.

Your choice of a card system (see Figure 25.1) is understandable. For generations, card-based systems have been a popular type of database system. Commonly found in public libraries, card files also were widely used in many kinds of businesses. Despite the fact that they can be slow to set up and use, card catalogs provide a relatively intuitive way to organize information.

However arduous, this initial step of creating the card database is not nearly as difficult as maintaining it. To provide timely and accurate information to the store's owner, you must update the list continually. Clients move away, and others change names or addresses. New clients are added, and clients' preferences change. As a result, your cards quickly become covered with crossed-out information. You need to replace outdated cards, create new ones, and then sort them again. And this effort is required simply to keep track of customers!

Suppose, too, that you want to use the information on the cards to control inventory. Each day, you must order fresh flowers to make sure that the florist has the right amount and types of flowers in stock. To determine what kinds of flowers to order (and how many), you thumb through all the index cards, every day, to see which flowers are selling the most and the least.

Now consider the following scenario. The store manager agrees to invest in a computer system for the store. Creating a database of information about the store's activities, you set up tables to store information about customers, products, suppliers, purchases orders, and more (see Figure 25.2). You enter relevant information, such as name, address, and every floral arrangement purchased, for each customer. When customers call for flowers, you can tell them instantly what they sent to their parents last year for their anniversary or what kind of flowers their aunt in Colorado likes.

Using the information on sales and inventory, you run a weekly report to determine which flowers sold well that week. Eventually, you have enough information to predict how many flowers of each type to buy each month. Due to the improved service, the customer base increases until the store expands into three locations. The employees of the other stores enter data regarding the flowers sold, so you can continue to improve your trends analysis on flower preferences at different times of the year. In addition, you set up a system so that you can check on the availability of flowers at the different stores by checking the database.

Figure 25.2
A simple database can serve as the basis for a company's entire information system by providing information about customers, products, sales, inventory, revenues, and much more.

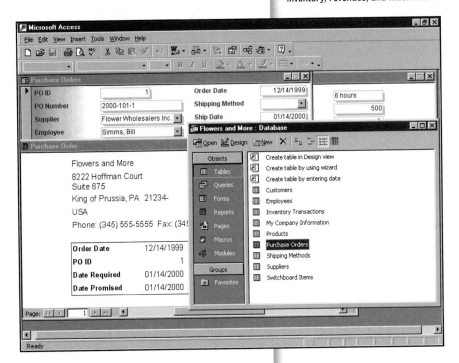

TYPES OF INFORMATION SYSTEMS

As more and more business functions have been automated, information systems have become increasingly specialized. One of a company's systems, for example, may be designed to help users gather and store sales orders. Another system may be designed to help managers analyze data. These specialized systems can operate alone or can be combined to create a larger system that provides different functions to different people.

Office Automation Systems

An **office automation system** uses computers and/or networks to carry out various operations, such as word processing, accounting, document management, or communications. The purposes of an office automation system are to manage information and, even more important, to help users handle certain information-related tasks more efficiently. In large organizations, simple tasks such as project scheduling, recordkeeping, and correspondence can become extremely time-consuming

NORTON
ONLINE

Visit **www.glencoe.com/norton/online/** for more information on **office automation software.**

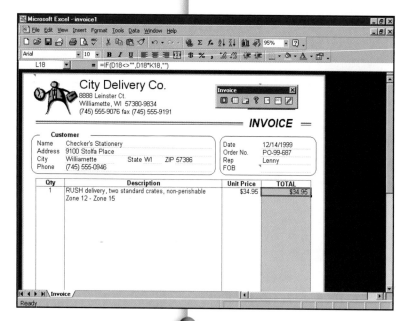

and labor-intensive. By using office automation tools, workers at all levels can reduce the amount of time and effort they spend on such mundane tasks, freeing them to handle more mission-critical jobs such as planning, designing, and selling. For this reason, nearly any complete information system has an office automation component.

Office automation systems can be built from **off-the-shelf applications.** Examples include applications such as WordPerfect, Paradox, and Excel (see Figure 25.3). Commercial software products typically provide all the functions required for automating standard office tasks and are far less expensive than building a system from customized software applications.

Figure 25.3
To streamline operations and improve productivity, companies often automate standard tasks, such as the generation of correspondence or the creation of invoices. Here, a worker is using Microsoft Excel to create an invoice based on an existing template and information from a customer database.

Transaction Processing Systems

A **transaction** is a complete event, which may occur as a series of many steps, such as taking an order from a customer. You conduct business transactions all the time but may have never considered the steps that make up a typical transaction—all of which can be processed through an information system. A system that handles the processing and tracking of transactions is called a **transaction processing system.**

For example, consider ordering a product from a catalog by telephone. The transaction typically begins when a customer service representative collects information about you, such as your name, address, credit card number, and the list of items you want to purchase. In the scenario described here, the customer service representative may enter the data into a database through an on-screen form, which ensures that the data is saved in the appropriate data tables. On the other hand, if you order or purchase a product in person, a sales clerk might "swipe" your credit card through a card reader and enter other information about you into a point-of-sales (POS) system. Either way, the critical data must be entered into the transaction system before the transaction's steps can be completed.

After taking your order, the company verifies your credit card information, checks its inventory to determine whether the items are available, "picks" the items from inventory, ships them to you, and bills your credit card. At each step, the order must be passed to the appropriate department (see Figure 25.4). It is essential that the right people review the data at the appropriate times. Suppose, for example, that an item is out of stock after you place your order. In a well-designed system, this information is made known to a customer service representative, who notifies you of the issue, gives you the option of placing the item on back-order, and ensures that your credit card will not be billed until the item is actually shipped to you. If you receive a product and want to return it, the information from your order is also used to process the return so you do not need to restart the process with the vendor.

Visit **www.glencoe.com/norton/online/** for more information on transaction processing systems and decision support systems.

Decision Support Systems

A **decision support system** is a specialized application used to collect and report certain types of business data, which can be used to aid managers in the decision-making

Figure 25.4
A simple example of a transaction processing system. In this case, your order information is used to manage the processes of inventory control, shipping, billing and payment, and more.

The seller takes your order and enters it in the information system . . .

. . . then checks its inventory.

IN STOCK?

YES!

If the item is in stock, it is taken from inventory and sent to you . . .

NO!

If not, it is placed on backorder.

BACK-ORDER

. . . and the order is billed to your credit card.

OK!

OK?

The company checks your credit.

CREDIT CARD CO.

Figure 25.5
A simple example of a decision support system.

process (see Figure 25.5). Business managers frequently use decision support systems to access the data in the company's transaction processing system. In addition, these systems can include or access other types of data, such as stock market reports or data about competitors. By compiling this kind of data, the decision support system can generate specific reports that managers can use in making mission-critical decisions. (This feature is where the application tools get their name: they assist people in making important decisions by providing information that supports a specific decision.)

Decision support systems are useful tools because they provide management with highly tailored, highly structured data about relevant issues. Many decision support systems are spreadsheet or database applications that have been customized for specific businesses. These powerful systems can import and analyze data in various formats, such as flat database tables or spreadsheets, two-dimensional charts, or multidimensional "cubes." They can generate reports quickly, based on existing data, and update those reports instantly as data changes.

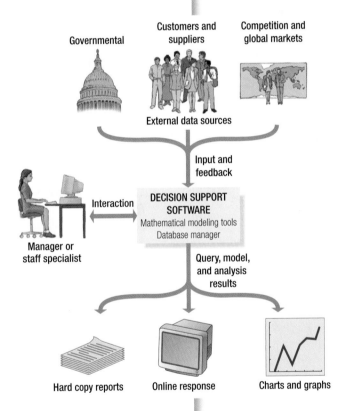

Governmental

Customers and suppliers

Competition and global markets

External data sources

Input and feedback

Interaction

DECISION SUPPORT SOFTWARE
Mathematical modeling tools
Database manager

Manager or staff specialist

Query, model, and analysis results

Hard copy reports

Online response

Charts and graphs

Management Information Systems

Within any business, workers at different levels need access to the same type of information, but they may need to view the information in different ways. At a call center, for example, a supervisor may need to see a daily report detailing the number of calls received, the types of requests made, and the production levels of

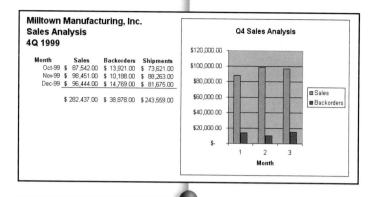

Milltown Manufacturing, Inc. Sales Analysis 4Q 1999			
Month	Sales	Backorders	Shipments
Oct-99	$ 87,542.00	$ 13,921.00	$ 73,621.00
Nov-99	$ 98,451.00	$ 10,188.00	$ 88,263.00
Dec-99	$ 96,444.00	$ 14,769.00	$ 81,675.00
	$ 282,437.00	$ 38,878.00	$ 243,559.00

Figure 25.6

Management information systems generate reports for managers at different levels.

individual staff members. A midlevel manager, such as a branch manager, may need to see only a monthly summary of this data shown in comparison to previous months, with a running total or average.

Managers at different levels may also need very different types of data. A senior manager, such as a vice president of finance or chief financial officer could be responsible for a company's financial performance and will view the company's financial information (usually in detail) regularly. A front-line manager who oversees daily production may receive little or no financial data, except when it specifically affects his or her area of responsibility.

A **management information system (MIS)** is a set of software tools that enables managers to gather, organize, and evaluate information about a workgroup, department, or an entire organization. These systems meet the needs of three different categories of managers—executives, middle managers, and front-line managers—by producing a range of standardized reports drawn from the organization's database. An efficient management information system summarizes vast amounts of business data into information that is useful to each type of manager (see Figure 25.6).

Expert Systems

An **expert system** is a specialized application that performs tasks that would normally be done by a human, such as medical diagnoses or review of credit histories for loan approvals. After analyzing the pertinent data, some expert systems produce a recommendation for a course of action. Some systems are empowered to make decisions and initiate actions, such as ordering a new shipment of a given product from a supplier when the current inventory falls below a given level.

Figure 25.7

The basic structure of an expert system.

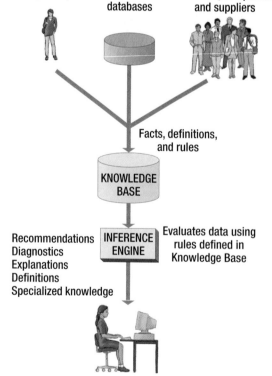

Expert systems are increasingly being used in the medical profession by enabling a physician to enter a patient's symptoms and then providing the most likely diagnosis of a patient's condition, along with treatment options. A financial expert system might recommend that a particular client be given a requested raise on his or her credit limit.

An expert system requires a large collection of human expertise in a specific area, as shown in Figure 25.7. This information is entered into a

highly detailed database, called a **knowledge base,** that is refined as new information becomes available. A piece of software, called an **inference engine,** then examines the user's request in light of that knowledge base and selects the most appropriate response or range of possible responses.

You might think that expert systems are used only by high-level managers or decision makers. However, such systems are commonly used by people who need to make quick decisions based on currently available data. In the bookselling industry, for example, a purchasing agent may use an expert system to determine which books to buy from publishers each month based on stocking levels and the sales of certain types of books. Such a system can help the agent establish a routine for replenishing stock, identifying poor-performance titles, and adjusting inventories among various stores.

If you have ever used the World Wide Web to get technical support with a computer product, then you may have used an expert system. In the example shown in Figure 25.8, you can specify the problem, and the system quickly finds one or more possible solutions. This type of Web-based system raises customer satisfaction by providing fast, accurate help at any time. It also helps the company manage costs by reducing the number of telephone inquiries from customers.

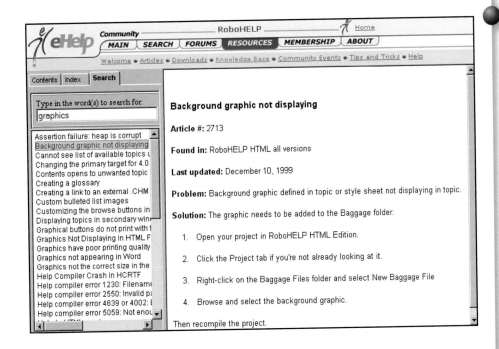

Figure 25.8
Online knowledge bases enable users to find specific answers to questions about using the company's products.

Self Check

Answer the following questions by filling in the blank(s).

1. In an information system, the procedures for handling information help ensure its _____ .

2. By using _____ tools, workers reduce the time and effort spent on some tasks.

3. A(n) _____ system provides different types of information for different types of managers.

Norton Notebook

THE KNOWLEDGE WORKER

As you will see in this lesson, a broad array of career opportunities exists for people who want to work directly in an information systems department. Beyond those specialized careers, however, many other professions have been changed because of information systems. People in these jobs (many of which are not technical in nature) now work differently using various tools and leveraging a different type of professional collateral. These people are the knowledge workers, and their ranks have increased by untold numbers in the past decade.

What Is a Knowledge Worker?

The term *knowledge worker* dates back to the mid-1990s when, thanks to the proliferation of the Internet, corporate networks, and computerized information systems, people began sharing information on an unprecedented scale. As more people and organizations became connected and exchanged data electronically, many experts saw a great societal shift occurring. We were moving, they said, from the "information age" to the "knowledge age."

The knowledge worker, therefore, was any person whose work involved the use or development of knowledge of any kind. The knowledge worker's tasks might include looking up, verifying, analyzing, organizing, storing, distributing, or selling knowledge. Although this may sound like a specialized field of endeavor, it really is not when you consider that any type of information may be considered knowledge, especially if it can be used in any way within a business.

As a result, *knowledge worker* has become a catch-all term, referring to any worker whose job involves the processing of information. A knowledge worker can be anyone who handles information in an organization, whether it includes mission-critical reports or involves a simple appointment book.

Even though the term *knowledge worker* has been diluted by overuse, it does not diminish the knowledge worker's role in the enterprise, especially when the knowledge at hand has real value. For example, consider the demographic data used by companies to market their products or services or the financial information crucial to helping a business overcome its accumulated debt. When analyzed and used properly, such knowledge can mean the difference between success and failure. For this reason, knowledge workers of all types should recognize the potential value of the information they handle and treat it accordingly.

Becoming an Effective Knowledge Worker

Regardless of your actual job title, your employability increases if you can prove your skills as an effective knowledge worker. Here are some tips:

◆ **Master Your Organization's Knowledge Management Tools.** The actual tools vary from one organization to another, but they often include file management, word processing, database, spreadsheet, data mining, and analytical tools.

◆ **Develop Your Information-Finding Skills.** An employer will not expect you to know everything but will respect your ability to find information quickly and effectively. Practice using information-finding tools such as Internet search engines, reference books, and others that apply to your profession.

◆ **Prove Your Trustworthiness.** Knowledge can include trade secrets, market feedback, contracts and licenses, and other types of proprietary information. Employers expect that such information will not be shared with anyone who should not see it. Learn to recognize private information and keep it confidential.

Programs such as FerretSoft's information-finding tools can be valuable for any knowledge worker who needs to find information quickly from various sources on the Internet.

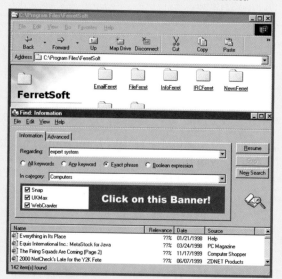

462

THE INFORMATION SYSTEMS DEPARTMENT

In large companies, the automation of business tasks encouraged the development of separate departments to service the emerging computer systems. Initially, these departments—and the people who worked in them—were isolated from the rest of a company's operations. These departments were in charge of creating the systems (typically using the corporate mainframe or minicomputer) that collected data from the operations level and turned it into information for managers.

Eventually, however, the rise of the PC and PC-based networks changed these departments and the systems they serviced. As people other than managers became information workers, the information systems departments started serving entire organizations and became integral parts of the business operation.

The size of a company's information systems department typically correlates with the size of the company it supports. In very large companies, these departments may employ hundreds or even thousands of people. The names of these departments vary as well as their size. The organization chart of one company may include an **Information Systems (IS) department,** while another company may use the name Management Information Systems (MIS), Information Technology (IT), or even Data Processing (DP). In this discussion, the department responsible for creating and maintaining information systems in a company is called the IS department.

The Role of the IS Department

You might imagine that the IS department's role is mainly technical—installing software, troubleshooting PCs, and so on. This description is true but only to an extent. Modern IS departments are actually involved in a much broader way in many businesses because they are responsible for providing technical resources and generating the information that the business needs to run effectively and efficiently.

In fact, IS personnel can be found in almost every part of an organization, from the production floor—where technicians install and maintain hardware and software—to the boardroom—where IS managers work with executives to plan enterprisewide systems. The IS department's role, therefore, has many facets and affects almost everyone in an organization. Here are some of the primary responsibilities of a typical IS department:

◆ **System Design and Planning.** As you will see in Lesson 26, "Building Information Systems," IS experts follow a set of procedures when creating a new information system or modifying an existing one. As part of the process, the IS team considers current and future information needs, methods in which a system can support the organization's basic mission, and ways the system can be used to benefit workers.

◆ **Information Generation.** To ensure that workers and managers get the exact information they need (and can input information easily), the IS team carefully plans and develops the types of forms and reports that must be generated from the system. These reports sift through the body of data, generate specific types of information, then present them in a predetermined way. For example, a company may provide sales managers with a range of reports on unit sales, revenue by product, territory sales figures, and the performance of individual account managers.

◆ **Custom Reporting.** Occasionally, special information needs arise in an organization, such as when a company decides to go public (by offering

Visit **www.glencoe.com/norton/online/** for more information on the **role of IS departments in business.**

shares of its stock for sale to the public) or when expansion is imminent. At these times, the IS staff may be called on to create unique, highly customized reports from the data in the company's transaction processing system.

◆ **Hardware and Software Installation and Maintenance.** As you would expect, the IS department provides hardware and software to any worker who needs them, and it also maintains the systems to ensure good performance. This part of the job includes installing and upgrading, troubleshooting, fixing problems, and even training workers in the use of their computerized systems.

◆ **Cost Control.** In most companies, the IS department is considered a cost center—that is, a portion of the business that costs money to run but generates little or no direct revenues. Even so, the IS department plays an important role in an organization's financial picture by providing essential information to management, assisting in important decisions, and ensuring that systems run as efficiently as possible. IS departments are also charged with running in the most cost-effective manner possible and thus avoiding a drain on the organization's overall budget.

A well-structured IS department also understands the mission of the organization and works to support that mission in the most direct manner possible, which is the key reason why IS departments are no longer isolated from the rest of the company and are becoming increasingly integrated in the day-to-day operations of organizations (see Figure 25.9). Seasoned IS professionals know that they are not simply working with computers. Rather, like the sales representative and production worker, they help the organization achieve its goals by providing the information and technical resources that each worker needs to accomplish his or her individual objectives.

The Roles of an IS Department's Members

Building and supporting computer systems is complex work and requires a wide range of skilled professionals. For this reason, and because IS workers can be involved in many areas of an organization, a well-staffed IS department may

Figure 25.9
Today's IS professionals are integrated throughout the organization, from the production line to the boardroom. IS workers are involved in a company's daily operations and in its long-term decision making.

include many different people working in various roles. The following sections identify a few of the professionals that may work in a large IS department and examines the skills and responsibilities of each.

Note that IS departments may not employ individuals in all these different roles. Large companies often hire other companies or individuals to provide specialized skills, such as the development of a help system. This approach, in which freelance workers or outside companies are hired as contractors to do specific jobs, is called **outsourcing.** In addition, a single IS employee may provide more than one skill set, especially in a small company. A technical writer, for example, may be able to develop the help system for a program, and a systems analyst may undertake a programming role in a project.

Visit **www.glencoe.com/norton/online/** for more information on **careers in information systems.**

IS Managers

Many IS departments are large enough to require their own management team, which may extend all the way to the senior level. A departmental management structure may be required for the same reasons it is required for other departments in a company: to screen and hire new workers, promote and reassign workers, oversee schedules and budgets, and perform other supervisory tasks.

IS managers, however, may also be involved in the running of a business and hold a status similar to that of a director, vice president, or another executive. In large companies, the IS department is often led by a **chief information officer (CIO),** who works at the same level as the chief operating officer (COO) and chief financial officer (CFO) in making large-scale decisions and plans. Such managers typically have a broad background in IS technology, networking, and computer systems. Many also have a business background or at least have a detailed understanding of the organization's mission and operations.

Computer Scientists

Computer scientists study the theory of computers by undertaking research, developing new computer designs, and attempting to achieve the next technological leap in the industry. They apply their high level of theoretical expertise to complex problems. Within academia, computer scientists undertake projects such as designing new hardware or developing new languages. They also work on multidisciplinary projects such as artificial intelligence. In private industry (most frequently, in companies that engage in a great deal of computer-related research and development), computer scientists apply theory, develop specialized languages, and design knowledge-based systems, such as the expert systems you read about earlier.

Figure 25.10
Systems analysts spend much of their time interviewing and listening to users.

Systems Analysts

Systems analysts are responsible for thinking of possible solutions when an information system needs to be updated, modified, or revamped. After users or managers identify a need, systems analysts discuss the business, scientific, or engineering problem with them. Systems analysts spend a significant amount of time at the beginning of projects defining the goals and issues of a new information system (see Figure 25.10). With the goals and issues

defined, the systems analysts, sometimes working with computer scientists, start designing solutions. They must provide enough detail in the design so that other members of the project team can perform the work. For example, systems analysts typically are responsible for specifying the exact files and records that must be accessed by the system and the format of the information produced by the system.

Programmers

Programmers create computer programs, either as commercial products or as part of a company's information system. In some information system projects, programmers are asked to modify or expand existing programs. In these situations, the programmers must analyze the existing code before making any modifications. In other projects, programmers create an entire system from scratch. Due to the complexity of information systems, this work is usually performed in teams, with each team responsible for specific components. You will learn more about programming and the programmer's job in Unit 14, "Software Programming and Development."

User Assistance Architects and Technical Writers

User assistance architects determine the organization of documentation and its structure, designing the instructional materials before the technical writers write the content. In the past, documentation was distributed on paper. Now, much of the information on systems is provided online, in help systems or tutorials (see Figure 25.11). The challenge in developing a help system is ensuring that users can find the information they seek with minimal effort. Meeting that challenge requires an understanding of how users look for information online. User assistance architects also decide how material should be presented: in class as part of a short presentation or in the online help system.

Figure 25.11
User assistance architects use products such as RoboHelp to develop complete online help systems. The resulting system enables the end user to search for information on specific topics, view demonstrations, link to information on the Web or an intranet, and more.

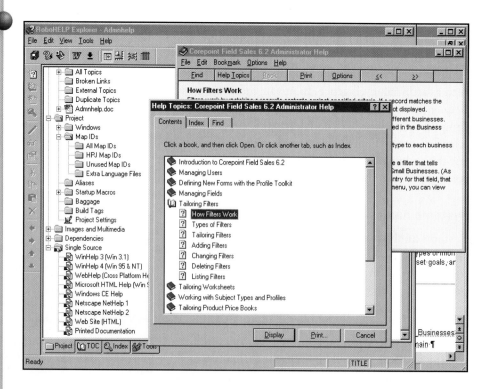

Technical writers explain in writing how an information system works. Typically, technical writers produce a set of manuals, called **documentation,** for a system. The documentation can be available in printed form or as part of an online help system. This documentation includes materials intended for the different audiences who use or support the information system, including end users, network managers, and system administrators.

Purchasing Agents

Hardware or software **purchasing agents** choose suppliers for system components and negotiate the terms for purchasing or leasing those items. Companies rely on agents because information systems are created from various components, including hardware and software. Because some percentage of these components will be bought rather than built from scratch, IS departments need purchasing agents to bring all the pieces together within a certain time frame.

Security Managers

Security is a sensitive issue in many organizations, especially those with networks that are connected to the Internet and that may be susceptible to infiltration. These organizations may hire one or more specialized **security managers** charged with ensuring the security of the information system. A security manager may oversee the design, installation, and maintenance of the organization's firewall. These specialists may also implement the organization's strategy for password protection, remote user access to the network, user access rights to specific disks or files, and so on.

Trainers

Trainers prepare users to accept a new information system even before it is put in place. Users should be comfortable with a system before they start working with it. Through classes and one-to-one teaching sessions, trainers give users the opportunity to explore the new system, ask questions, and practice common tasks (see Figure 25.12). Because users may forget a procedure they learned in a training class or encounter a problem they do not know how to solve, IS personnel also provide day-to-day ongoing support to a system's users.

Figure 25.12
Trainers teach corporate users in computer-equipped classrooms or labs similar to those found on college campuses.

System or Network Managers

System managers or **network managers** (sometimes called system administrators or network administrators) are responsible for keeping an information system up and running. Companies maintain their own internal networks, with links to outside networks such as the Internet. Today, practically every business and organization, from Fortune 500 corporations to very small companies, relies heavily on LANs. Although most PC-based

LANs do not require full-time attention, they do need occasional maintenance. Any problems that arise must be solved by someone who knows how to solve the problem. In organizations with multiple LANs, wide area networks (WANs), bridges, and gateways to other systems, the system or network manager typically has a staff of full-time technicians, analysts, and programmers. Some of the key concerns of network managers include controlling unauthorized access, protecting the integrity of data on the network, maintaining backups of critical data, and recovering data after computer disasters.

Database Specialists

Because many information systems are built around a central database, IS departments typically have at least one person who understands the database at a detailed level. **Database specialists**—sometimes called database administrators (DBAs)—may perform various essential functions, such as designing and building data tables, forms, queries, and reports used throughout the organization. Ultimately, the information system can provide information to its users only if a database specialist has created the appropriate data structures, queries, and reports. For this reason, database specialists are highly valued in their organizations. Database specialists have mastered the query language used by the organization's system (such as SQL) and often possess programming skills in addition to database-management expertise.

Hardware Maintenance Technicians

Hardware maintenance technicians maintain the hardware components of an information system. One of the most common problems for which technicians are called is a paper jam in a printer. Other problems, however, can be far more serious. Often, technicians are required for upgrading PCs with new peripherals, diagnosing problems with PCs and servers, scanning PCs for viruses, and maintaining the network (see Figure 25.13).

Figure 25.13
Hardware maintenance technicians install new devices and locate and solve problems in electronic equipment. Their offices are often full of circuit boards, computer parts, and testing devices.

COMPUTERS
in your career

So You Want to Be an IS Professional

As you have seen in this lesson, there are many different careers in information systems technology. If you are interested in pursuing such a career, you will be happy to know that there is a stable demand for IS professionals, and the need for certain IS specialists will continue to grow in the foreseeable future. However, a thorough knowledge of computers may not be enough to land a dream job in an IS department, although it is a good start. To improve your prospects, you should consider getting some specialized training in the area of technology that most interests you.

◆ **Network Administration Certification.** The network is an essential part of any information system, and many companies prefer to hire networking professionals who have earned certification in specific network technologies. For example, Novell and Microsoft offer certification programs for their network operating systems and other network-related products. Certification is also available for a range of hardware products, such as cabling, bridges, routers, and gateways. There are various certification levels available, from basic LAN administration to enterprisewide development and management.

◆ **Software Programming.** Software is a key component in any information system, and the demand for programmers continues to rise. Qualified programmers have training in current development languages such as C++, VisualBasic, and others. Because so many organizations depend on customized database systems, database-related skills (such as a knowledge of SQL and database structure) are considered essential to any programmer's résumé.

◆ **Database Administration.** A database management system is at the heart of any corporate IS department, and database programmers and developers are constantly in demand. If database management appeals to you, industry experts recommend that you study as many different DBMS applications as you can (such as Oracle, Sybase, Microsoft SQL Server, and others) and master the use of database querying tools, as well as the creation of forms and reports. Exposure to standard programming languages—such as C++, VisualBasic, and Java—can also help ensure your success in database development.

◆ **PC Hardware and Electronics.** Hardware maintenance technicians are always in demand, and their value increases as they learn more about new technologies. If a career in hardware maintenance appeals to you, consider studying electronics as well as PC technologies. A counterpart of the hardware maintenance technician is the configuration specialist, who focuses on customizing hardware to meet special needs and is essential in keeping businesses on the cutting edge of technology. These professionals have expertise not just in PC and electronics, but also in telecommunications and networking.

To ensure your long-term success in IS, remember that information systems are part of a complete business and not simply an entity unto themselves. Successful IS managers often study business in addition to technology, earning advanced degrees such as a master of business administration (MBA). With business expertise, the IS professional can better understand the relation of the IS department to the company and work more intelligently toward building information systems that help the company achieve its all-important business goals.

469

LESSON QUIZ

True/False

Answer the following questions by circling True or False.

True   False   **1.** A factory's computer-controlled machining system would not be an example of an information system.

True   False   **2.** Although old-fashioned, a card-based system (like a library card catalog) provides a natural and relatively intuitive way to organize information.

True   False   **3.** Most office automation systems must be built from customized software applications.

True   False   **4.** As their name implies, decision support systems are designed to help managers in the decision-making process.

True   False   **5.** IS departments are typically isolated from other parts of an organization, focusing exclusively on technical issues.

Multiple Choice

Circle the word or phrase that best completes each sentence.

1. Many organizations set _____ that limit the information available to certain workers.

   A. rules   **B.** help systems   **C.** information systems

2. A(n) _____ is a complete event, such as taking an order from a customer.

   A. inference   **B.** transaction   **C.** neither A nor B

3. Management information systems typically produce standardized _____ drawn from an organization's database.

   A. information   **B.** reports   **C.** queries

4. A well structured IS department understands and supports its organization's _____ .

   A. managers   **B.** cost centers   **C.** mission

5. _____ think of possible solutions when an information system needs to be updated, modified, or revamped.

   A. Systems analysts   **B.** User assistance architects   **C.** CIOs

LESSON LABS

Complete the following exercises as directed by your instructor.

1. Determine what types of information systems are in place at your school. You may need to interview members of the school's IS department. What types of services do the IS staff and information system itself provide, and to whom? Your instructor may break your class into teams to complete this exercise.

2. Find out which types of IS employees work in your school. Does your school's IS staff include a manager, systems analyst, database specialist, or other IS professionals? Interview each person on the staff and find out exactly what functions he or she performs. Your instructor may break your class into teams to complete this exercise.

Building Information Systems

OVERVIEW:
The Importance of
Well-Built Information Systems

As you learned in Lesson 25, "The Basics of Information Systems," a well designed information system can be an important factor in an organization's success. The system not only provides mission-critical information to its users but enables users to input information quickly and efficiently.

In any organization, crucial decisions may be based on the reports derived from an information system. For this reason, developers must ensure that the system works accurately and leaves out no details as it sorts, queries, and analyzes its data. Customer satisfaction may also rely on the performance of an information system, as is the case when support technicians use an expert system to help customers solve problems.

To create effective information systems, corpora-
tions will spend millions
of dollars on develop-
ment, in a process that
can take months and
involve input from dozens
of people. Along the way,
IS professionals analyze the
organization, its internal
processes, the needs of its
employees and customers,
technologies already in place,
and much more. All these
factors are crucial to understanding the business and
how an information system
will help it achieve its goals.
This lesson is a brief introduction to the process that IS
professionals follow in developing information systems—
a process called the systems
development life cycle.

OBJECTIVES

- Define the term *systems development life cycle (SDLC)*.

- Identify the five phases in the SDLC.

- Name the IS professionals involved in each phase of the SDLC.

- Describe four ways an organization can convert from an old information system to a new one.

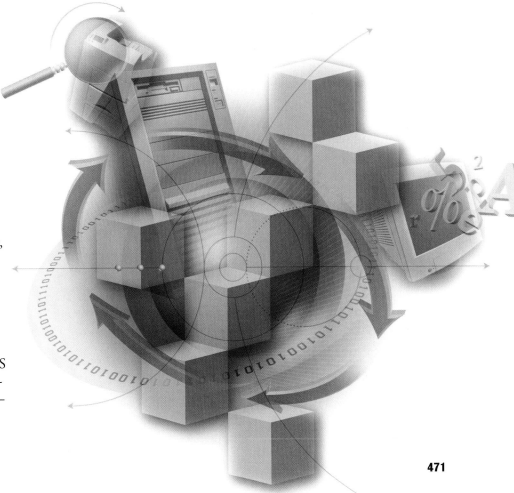

THE SYSTEMS DEVELOPMENT LIFE CYCLE

Creating an information system can be a complex task. It involves several distinct phases, each of which often must be completed before a subsequent task can begin. To help create successful information systems, the **systems development life cycle (SDLC)** was developed. SDLC is an organized way to build an information system. As you can see from Figure 26.1, the SDLC is composed of a series of five phases:

1. Needs analysis
2. Systems design
3. Development
4. Implementation
5. Maintenance

Together, the phases are called a life cycle because they cover the entire "life" of an information system.

PHASE 1: NEEDS ANALYSIS

During the **needs analysis phase,** the first phase of the SDLC, the development team focuses on completing three tasks:

1. Defining the problem and deciding whether to proceed
2. Analyzing the current system in depth and developing possible solutions to the problem
3. Selecting the best solution and defining its function

Phase 1 begins when a need is identified for a new or modified information system. Users may complain, for example, that the current system is too difficult to use or does not meet some business requirement. Simple procedures require too many steps, or the system crashes repeatedly, resulting in a loss of data. A manager may approach the IS department and request a report that is not currently produced by the system.

Systems analysts then begin a preliminary investigation, talking with users and the managers of the departments that are to be affected. The first challenge is to define the problem accurately. With the problem accurately defined, the IS department can decide whether to undertake the project (the "go/no go" decision). When a decision to proceed is made, systems analysts undertake a thorough investigation of the current system and its limitations. They work with the people directly involved with the problem to document how it can be solved.

The knowledge gathered regarding the current system is documented in several different ways. Some analysts use **data flow diagrams,** which show the flow of data through a system, as shown in Figure 26.2. Analysts may

Figure 26.1

The systems development life cycle.

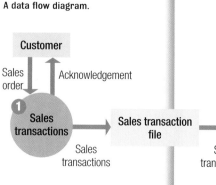

Figure 26.2

A data flow diagram.

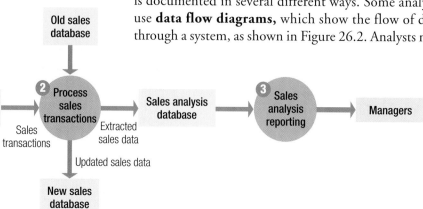

also use **structured English**—a method that uses plain English terms and phrases to describe events, actions, and alternative actions that can occur within the system, as shown in Figure 26.3. Another option is to present the actions taken under different conditions in a **decision tree,** which graphically illustrates the events and actions that can occur in the system, as shown in Figure 26.4.

> If item is received and
> > the invoice date is over 30 days old
> > > If supplier is on payment hold status
> > > > indicate status on invoice
> > > > issue pending/future payment transaction
> >
> > > Else issue payment voucher transaction
> >
> > Else calculate payment date
> > > issue pending/future payment transaction
>
> Else issue invoiced/not received transaction

Figure 26.3
Structured English.

At the end of phase 1, the team recommends a solution to be adopted. The analysts use information they have already gathered from system users to determine which features must be included in the solution (what reports should be generated, in what form they will be output, and what special tools are needed). Throughout the needs analysis phase, they remain focused on *what* the system must do, not on *how* the features will be implemented.

PHASE 2: SYSTEMS DESIGN

During the **systems design phase,** the project team tackles the "how" of the selected solution. For example, a database application must be able to accept data from users and store it in a database. These are general functions, but how will the team implement them? How many input screens are necessary, for example, and what will they look like? What kind of menu options must be available? What kind of database will the system use?

Figure 26.4
A decision tree.

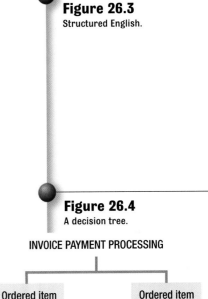

The analysts and programmers involved at this point often use a combination of top-down and bottom-up designs to answer these questions. In **top-down design,** team members start with the large picture and move to the details. They look at major functions that the system must provide and break these down into smaller and smaller activities. Each of these activities will then be programmed in the next phase of the SDLC.

In **bottom-up design,** the team starts with the details (for example, the reports to be produced by the system) and then moves to the big picture (the major functions or processes). This approach is particularly appropriate when users have specific requirements for output—for example, payroll checks, which must contain certain pieces of information.

Throughout phase 2, the manager of the project team reviews progress on the design of different system components. At the end of the phase, a larger review is conducted that typically involves the department that will be affected and top management. If the design passes inspection, development begins. In some instances, the review highlights problems with the overall solution, and the team must return to analysis or terminate the project.

Many tools are available to help teams through the steps of system design. Most of these tools can also be used during the development phase (phase 3) or even during analysis (phase 1). Many teams, for example, use working models called **prototypes** to explore the look and feel of screens with users. They also use special software applications for creating these prototypes quickly as well as for building diagrams, writing code, and managing the development effort. These applications fall into the category of **computer-aided software engineering (CASE)** tools. In other words, computer software is used to develop other computer software more quickly and reliably.

PHASE 3: DEVELOPMENT

NORTON ONLINE

Visit **www.glencoe.com/norton/online/** for more information on **CASE tools** and **documentation** and its creation.

During the **development phase,** programmers play the key role, creating or customizing the software for all the various parts of the system. Typically, the programmers on the team are assigned to specific components of the overall system. If a component is being built, the programmers write the necessary code or use CASE tools (if possible) to speed the development process. For purchased components, the programmers must customize the code as necessary to make the component fit into the new system.

There are two alternative paths through phase 3: the acquisition path or the local development path. As early as phase 1, needs analysis, the team may determine that some or all of the necessary system components are available as off-the-shelf hardware or software and may decide to acquire, rather than develop, these components. Acquiring off-the-shelf components means that the system can be built faster and cheaper than if every component is developed from scratch. Another advantage of acquired components is that they have already been tested and proven reliable, although they may need to be customized to fit into the overall information system. In many cases, project teams buy (or acquire) some components and build (or develop) others. Thus, they follow both acquisition and local development paths at the same time through the SDLC (see Figure 26.5).

Figure 26.5
These parts are created or acquired during phase 3.

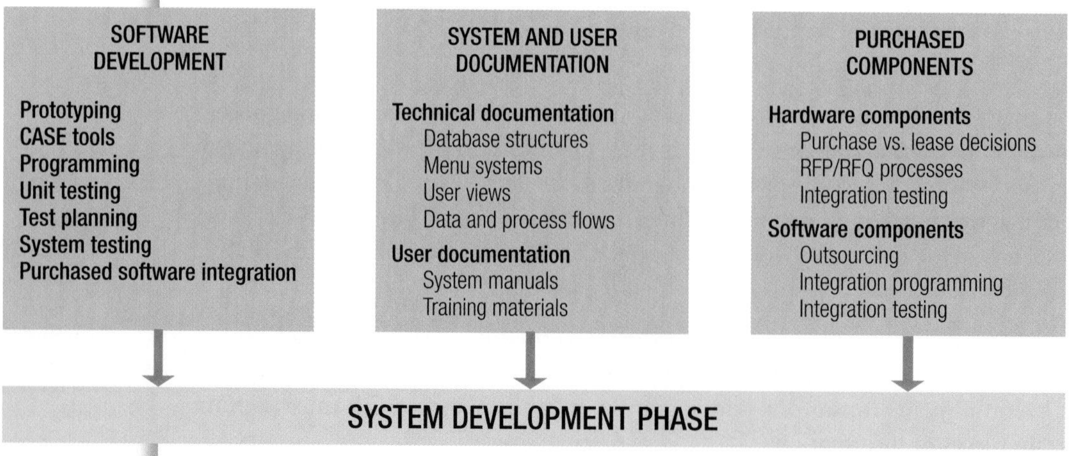

SOFTWARE DEVELOPMENT
Prototyping
CASE tools
Programming
Unit testing
Test planning
System testing
Purchased software integration
SYSTEM AND USER DOCUMENTATION
Technical documentation
Database structures
Menu systems
User views
Data and process flows
User documentation
System manuals
Training materials
PURCHASED COMPONENTS
Hardware components
Purchase vs. lease decisions
RFP/RFQ processes
Integration testing
Software components
Outsourcing
Integration programming
Integration testing
SYSTEM DEVELOPMENT PHASE

Techview

TECHNICAL DOCUMENTATION

Whether you are using an off-the-shelf software application at home or your employer's proprietary data-mining tools, you should find that both programs (and almost any other piece of software or hardware you use) are accompanied by documentation. Documentation can take several forms, but complete and useful documentation should always be part of any well-developed product—whether you buy the product from a store or your company developed it from scratch as part of the corporate information system.

Types of Documentation

Technical documentation takes two basic forms:

◆ **Printed Manuals.** Most software and hardware products feature some sort of printed documentation, although printed manuals are used less frequently now than in the past. At the least, most commercial products include a short "getting started" manual, which offers guidance on installation or basic use. More complex products, like those developed for use in corporate information systems, may include multiple printed manuals with hundreds of pages.

◆ **Online Documents and Help Systems.** In recent years, manufacturers have begun providing users with online documentation rather than printed manuals because electronic documents are less expensive to produce. This point is especially important for companies that develop their own software tools for in-house use. For these businesses, printing documentation can be a time-consuming and expensive process. (For more information on online help, see this lesson's Productivity Tip on page 478.)

Depending on the product, documentation may be developed for different types of users, based on the expertise or experience:

◆ **User Guides.** These are designed for end users—people who use the product simply to perform specific tasks. Generally, user documentation is tutorial in nature, providing step-by-step instructions, lots of illustrations, and little or no explanatory text.

◆ **Reference Manuals.** These manuals may be developed for various users. Instead of providing step-by-step instructions, reference manuals include detailed descriptions of commands, features, and capabilities as well as glossaries of special terms.

◆ **Technical Reference Guides.** Intended for high-level users or developers who will customize the product or develop other applications to work with the product, these guides are filled with technical details and are generally of little interest to end users.

◆ **Installation Guides.** These are designed to lead the user or administrator through the installation process. For many products, installation is a simple matter requiring little or no documentation. For complex products, however, especially those designed to work with corporate networks and database management systems, installation is filled with potential pitfalls. In these cases, detailed installation guides attempt to describe and resolve any problems the user may encounter.

◆ **Configuration Guides.** These guides are important references for high-level users or administrators who must change system settings to make the product work as desired.

◆ **Administration Guides.** These guides are written for system administrators who must ensure that the product works in tandem with all the other products in the information system, such as the operating system, network operating system, and DBMS.

Other specialized types of documentation include troubleshooting guides, technical specifications, and performance-assessment guides.

Printed documentation is less common in commercial software products, but with products used in corporate information systems, printed documentation can require many volumes.

Technical writers work with the programmers to produce the technical documentation for the system. Technical documentation is vastly different from the user documentation, which describes to end users how to use the system. The technical documentation includes information about software features and programming, the flow of data and processing through the system, and the design and layout of the necessary hardware. These materials provide an overall view of the system and thus serve as a reference for team members focused on individual components. In addition, the technical documentation is vital for support personnel and programmers in charge of the system during the maintenance phase.

Writers begin work on the user documentation, and user assistance architects start to lay out the architecture of the online help system. These efforts are usually not finished until the early stages of the implementation phase.

Testing is an integral part of phases 3 and 4 (development and implementation). The typical approach to testing is to move from the individual component to the system as a whole. The team tests each component separately (unit testing) and then tests the components of the system with each other (system testing). Errors are corrected, the necessary changes made, and the tests are then run again. Next comes installation testing, when the system is installed in a test environment and tested with other applications used by the business. Finally, acceptance testing is carried out, when the end users test the installed system to make sure that it meets their criteria.

Self Check

Answer the following questions by filling in the blank(s).

1. The _____ is an organized way to build an information system.

2. _____ begins when a need is identified for a new or modified information system.

3. During the systems design phase, the project team may take either the _____ or _____ approach to design.

PHASE 4: IMPLEMENTATION

In the **implementation phase,** the project team finishes buying any necessary hardware for the system and then installs the hardware and software in the user environment. The users start using the system to perform work, not just to provide feedback on the system's development.

The process of moving from the old system to the new is called **conversion.** IS professionals must handle this process carefully to avoid losing or corrupting data or frustrating users trying to perform their work. As shown in Figure 26.6, there are several different ways to convert a department or an organization, including the following:

◆ **Direct Conversion.** All users stop using the old system at the same time and then begin using the new. This option is fast but it can be disruptive; pressure on support personnel can be excessive.

◆ **Parallel Conversion.** Users continue to use the old system while an increasing amount of data is processed through the new system. The outputs from the two systems are compared; if they agree, the switch is made. This option is useful for additional live testing of the new system, but it is fairly time-intensive because both systems are operating at the same time.

◆ **Phased Conversion.** Users start using the new system, component by component. This option works only for systems that can be compartmentalized.

◆ **Pilot Conversion.** Personnel in a single pilot site use the new system, and then the entire organization makes the switch. Although this approach may take more time than the other three, it gives support personnel the opportunity to test user response to the system thoroughly, and they will be better prepared when many people make the conversion.

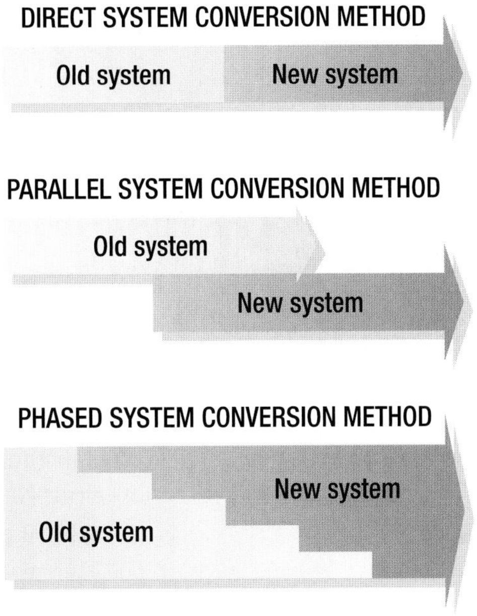

DIRECT SYSTEM CONVERSION METHOD

Old system | New system

PARALLEL SYSTEM CONVERSION METHOD

Old system

New system

PHASED SYSTEM CONVERSION METHOD

New system

Old system

Figure 26.6
Implementation methods.

Trainers and support personnel play a significant role during the conversion. Training courses usually involve classroom-style lectures, hands-on sessions with sample data, and computer-based training, which users can work with on their own time.

PHASE 5: MAINTENANCE

After the information systems are implemented, IS professionals continue to provide support during the **maintenance phase.** They monitor various indices of system performance, such as response time, to ensure that the system is performing as intended. They also respond to changes in users' requirements. These changes occur for various reasons. As users work with the system on a daily basis, they may recognize instances where a small change in the system would allow them to work more efficiently. Or management may request changes due to a change in state or federal regulations of the industry.

Errors in the system are also corrected during phase 5. Systems are often installed in a user environment with known programming or design errors. Typically, these errors have been identified as noncritical or not important enough to delay installation. Programmers have lists of such errors to correct during the maintenance phase. In addition, daily use of the system may highlight more serious errors for the programmers to fix.

Changes, or upgrades, to the system are made regularly during the remaining life of the system. At some point, however, patch repairs to the system no longer meet user requirements, which may have changed radically since the system was installed. IS professionals or managers in a user department start calling for a major modification or new system. At this point, the SDLC has come full circle, and the analysis phase begins again.

PRODUCTIVITY Tip

Understanding Online Help Systems

Online help systems have almost completely replaced printed manuals for many types of computer products for several reasons. First, they are cheaper to produce than printed materials. Second, they can be updated and distributed much more quickly. Third, they can be interactive and intuitive, making them far more instructive and easier to use than any printed manual.

Online help can take several forms that can be used in any combination:

◆ **Electronic Documents.** An electronic document is a computer-based version of a printed manual. (It may be included with software even when no printed manuals are provided.) Such documents look like printed books but are used on-screen, as seen in utilities such as Adobe's Acrobat Reader. Electronic documents may feature hyperlinked index and contents entries, as well as hyperlinked cross-references. You can click a heading, page number, or reference and jump to the appropriate section. Electronic documents also may feature search tools, bookmarking tools, and other helpful resources.

◆ **Application Help Systems.** Most software applications feature an online help system installed with the product. Windows-based application help systems use a standard interface, so after you learn how to use one of them, you can use another with ease. Application help systems can include audio, animation, video-based demonstrations, links to Internet resources, and much more.

◆ **Web Help.** Newer-generation help systems can be used over the World Wide Web or a corporate intranet through a standard Web browser. The advantage of Web help is that it is centralized—located on a single server—instead of being stored on each user's system. This centralization enables administrators to update the information quickly and frees customers from making duplicate copies on individual user machines.

◆ **FAQs.** Many companies post electronic documents containing frequently asked questions (FAQs) on their Web or intranet sites, on newsgroups, and on bulletin boards. As their name implies, FAQs provide answers to the most commonly asked questions about a product, and an FAQ may be the first place to look when you have a problem with a product.

◆ **Knowledge Bases.** As described elsewhere in this unit, knowledge bases can help you find information and technical support online. You can find many knowledge bases at the Web sites of companies that produce software and hardware products. To use a knowledge base, type a question or a term into the site's search box. The knowledge base will then provide you with one or more possible solutions to your problem.

◆ **E-Mail Support.** Some software companies provide technical support via e-mail. You compose an e-mail message describing your question or problem and submit it to the manufacturer. You receive a response within twenty-four hours in most cases. Depending on the nature of your problem, you may receive a standard document or a customized response from a technical support person.

This screen shows three types of online help in three windows: an electronic, read-only document viewed in Acrobat Reader; a typical Windows-based help system; and an FAQ at a Web site.

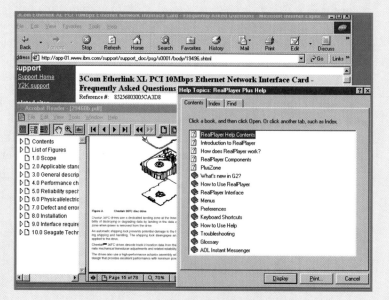

LESSON QUIZ

True/False

Answer the following questions by circling True or False.

True   False   **1.** In the needs analysis phase, the first challenge is to define accurately any problems that might exist in the information system.

True   False   **2.** In the systems design phase, designers decide what the system must do.

True   False   **3.** If off-the-shelf products can be used, the development phase of the SDLC can be skipped.

True   False   **4.** Testing takes place during the development and implementation phases of the SDLC.

True   False   **5.** In a pilot conversion, users start using the new information system component by component.

Multiple Choice

Circle the word or phrase that best completes each sentence.

1. During needs analysis, the development team must _____ .
   A. define the problem and decide whether to proceed
   B. determine how the new information system will work
   C. neither A nor B

2. By using _____ , developers can verbally describe the events, actions, and alternative actions that can occur within the system.
   A. data flow diagrams   **B.** structured English   **C.** decision trees

3. In _____ , developers look at major system functions and break them down into smaller and smaller activities.
   A. top-down design   **B.** bottom-up design   **C.** both A and B

4. When programmers take the _____ path, they elect to create system components.
   A. acquisition   **B.** maintenance   **C.** local development

5. The process of moving from an old system to a new one is called _____ .
   A. implementation   **B.** conversion   **C.** system design

LESSON LABS

Complete the following exercises as directed by your instructor.

1. Using a sheet of paper, draw a decision tree that shows the actions and alternatives (such as order input, customer support, billing, and so on) that can occur in one portion of a transaction processing system.

2. Create some user documentation. Open a word processor, write a single paragraph of text, and then format the text. Now create a one-page document that explains the process of creating and formatting that paragraph. Write the documentation for someone who has never used a word processor. Be sure to include numbered steps and explain the procedure in detail.

LESSON 25: The Basics of Information Systems

The Purpose of Information Systems

■ An information system includes a means of storing information, a set of procedures for handling information, and rules that govern the delivery of information to people in an organization.

■ Traditionally, information systems were manual and required users to manage each detail of information methodically. One popular type of manual information system is the card-based system, such as a card catalog in a library.

■ All information systems, regardless of their type, serve the same purpose, which is to help users get a certain type of value from their information.

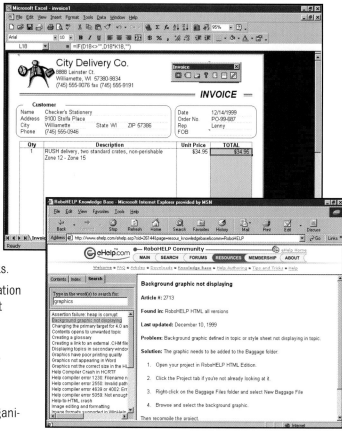

Types of Information Systems

■ Office automation systems automate routine office tasks.

■ Transaction processing systems not only store information about individual events but also provide information that is useful in running an organization, such as inventory status, billing, and more.

■ Management information systems produce reports for different types of managers.

■ Decision support systems can produce highly detailed, customized reports based on the information in an organization's transaction processing system and based on information from other sources. These systems are used to assist managers in making mission-critical decisions.

■ Expert systems include the knowledge of human experts in a particular subject area (such as medicine or technology) in a knowledge base. They analyze requests from users and assist the users in developing a course of action.

The Information Systems Department

■ A well-structured IS department not only supports an organization's information systems but is also involved in supporting the organization's overall mission.

■ A large IS department can include many people in a wide variety of positions, including IS managers, computer scientists, systems analysts, programmers, database specialists, user assistance architects, technical writers, purchasing agents, system or network managers, trainers, and hardware maintenance technicians.

■ The IS department not only provides technical support for hardware and software, but may be involved in the design and implementation of an organization's entire information system. IS professionals also ensure that systems generate all the appropriate types of information and reports required by the organization's managers and workers.

LESSON 26: Building Information Systems

The Systems Development Life Cycle

- The systems development life cycle (SDLC) is an organized method for building an information system.

- The SDLC includes five phases: needs analysis, systems design, development, implementation, and maintenance.

Phase 1: Needs Analysis

- During the needs analysis phase, the development team focuses on completing three tasks: (1) defining the problem and whether to proceed, (2) analyzing the current system in depth and developing possible solutions to the problem, and (3) selecting the best solution and defining its function.

Phase 2: Systems Design

- During the systems design phase, the project team decides how the selected solution will work. Each system activity is identified.

Phase 3: Development

- During the development phase, programmers play the key role: creating or customizing the software for the various parts of the system.

- There are two alternative paths through phase 3: the acquisition path or the local development path. In other words, project teams may decide to buy and then customize some components for an information system. Or, they may choose to develop the needed components themselves.

- Technical and user documentation is written during the development phase. Testing is also an integral part of this phase.

Phase 4: Implementation

- In the implementation phase, the hardware and software are installed in the user environment.

- The process of moving from an old system to a new one is called conversion. The project team may follow four different conversion methods: direct, parallel, phased, and pilot.

Phase 5: Maintenance

- During the maintenance phase, IS professionals provide ongoing training and support to the system's users. Fixes or improvements to the system are made regularly during the remaining life of the system.

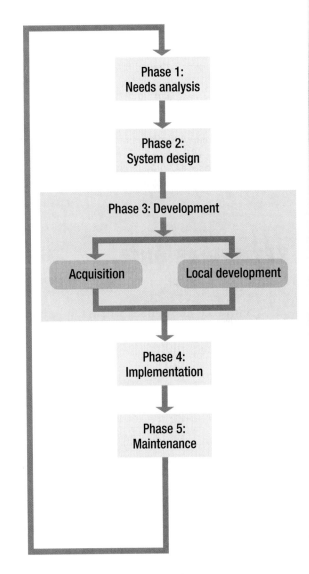

UNIT REVIEW

KEY TERMS

After completing this unit, you should be able to define the following terms.

bottom-up design, *473*
chief information officer (CIO), *465*
computer-aided software engineering (CASE), *474*
computer scientist, *465*
conversion, *476*
database specialist, *468*
data flow diagram, *472*
decision support system, *458*
decision tree, *473*
development phase, *474*
documentation, *467*
expert system, *460*
hardware maintenance technician, *468*
implementation phase, *476*
inference engine, *461*
information system, *455*
information systems (IS) department, *463*
knowledge base, *461*
maintenance phase, *477*
management information system (MIS), *460*

needs analysis phase, *472*
network manager, *467*
office automation system, *457*
off-the-shelf application, *458*
outsourcing, *465*
programmer, *466*
prototype, *474*
purchasing agent, *467*
security manager, *467*
structured English, *473*
system manager, *467*
systems analyst, *465*
systems design phase, *473*
systems development life cycle (SDLC), *472*
technical writer, *467*
top-down design, *473*
trainer, *467*
transaction, *458*
transaction processing system, *458*
user assistance architect, *466*

KEY TERMS QUIZ

Fill in each blank with one of the terms listed under Key Terms.

1. Many office automation systems can be built from _____ , like those found in any computer store.

2. Managers commonly use _____ systems to assist in the decision-making process.

3. A(n) _____ analyzes data and produces a recommended course of action.

4. In many organizations, the _____ is responsible for creating and maintaining information systems.

5. _____ study the theory of computers.

6. _____ (also called _____) are responsible for keeping an information system up and running.

7. The abbreviation SDLC stands for _____ .

8. During the _____ phase of the SDLC, the project team determines "how" a solution will work.

9. Programmers play the key role in the _____ phase of the SDLC.

10. The final phase of the SDLC is called the _____ phase.

REVIEW QUESTIONS

In your own words, briefly answer the following questions.

1. What is an information system?

2. What are the three basic components of an information system?

3. What is the basic purpose of any information system?

4. Why do organizations use office automation systems?

5. What is a transaction?

6. How does a management information system work?

7. How does an expert system work?

8. Why is it so important that information systems be well designed and well structured?

9. Describe the differences between top-down design and bottom-up design as each applies to the systems development life cycle for information systems.

10. What are the four types of conversion methods that may be used in the implementation phase of the SDLC?

DISCUSSION QUESTIONS

As directed by your instructor, discuss the following questions in class or in groups.

1. Suppose that you run a manufacturing facility that produces automotive parts. Discuss the types of information that would be important to the operation of the facility. What information system or systems should be designed for such a plant?

2. Discuss the issues addressed during the needs analysis phase of an SDLC for a new hospital. What are the biggest challenges during this phase?

 ETHICAL ISSUES
Information systems can make it easier for workers at many levels to access information within an organization. With this thought in mind, discuss the following questions in class.

1. In some organizations, managers insist that certain classes of employees be prevented from accessing some types of information, such as financial records. In your view, is this fair? Why? What business reasons would managers have for hiding such information from some employees?

2. You have become tired of your job so while at work, you use a PC and printer to create a new résumé and cover letter and store the files on the network. They are discovered by a manager, who threatens to fire you for your actions. Is the manager correct in following this course of action? Why?

You and the Computer

Complete the following exercises using a computer in your classroom, lab, or home. No other materials are needed.

1. **Create Your Own IS Department.** Suppose that your city has just been granted an NFL expansion team. The team's owner is in the process of building a new stadium and hiring office staff and has hired you to be the first CIO. Your first task is to determine the types of information systems the team will need, and then you must hire IS professionals to build and maintain these systems. Follow these steps:

   A. Using two pieces of paper, map the information systems you think will be needed.

   B. List the IS department positions you will want to fill.

   C. Describe the role you want each IS staff member to play.

2. **Chart the Flow.** Using a data flow diagram, map the flow of data for a transaction processing system for a large retail store.

Internet Labs

To complete the following exercises, you need a computer with an Internet connection and a Web browser. (For more information on using these tools, see "Prerequisites" at the front of this textbook.)

1. **Get a Job.** Visit the following Web sites and see if you can find job listings for IS professionals, such as systems analysts, network managers, or technical writers:

   - NationJob Network—
     http://www.nationjob.com/

   - Digital Station—
     http://www.digitalstation.com/

   - EDP Professionals—
     http://www.misjobs.com/

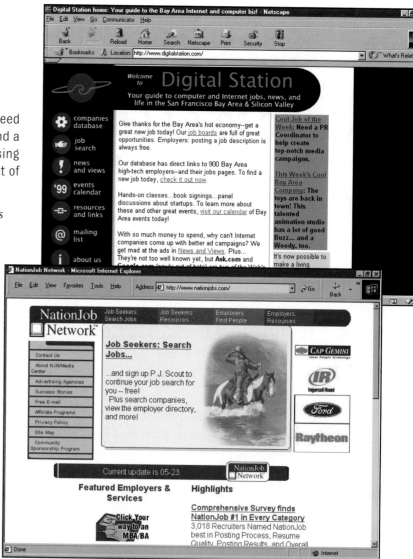

2. **Search for Knowledge.** The Microsoft Knowledge Base is an excellent example of an online expert system. You can use it to obtain technical support and answer questions about any Microsoft product. Access the Microsoft Knowledge Base:

A. Visit the Microsoft Web site at **http://www.microsoft.com/**

B. Click the Support option and then click Knowledge Base. You may need to register to use the Knowledge Base; if so, the process takes only a few minutes, requires only a user name and password, and is also free.

C. Select a Microsoft product (such as Windows 98 or Microsoft Excel), select a method for searching the knowledge base (by keywords, for example), and specify a keyword (such as *printing*) or type a free-text question (such as *How do I print charts in landscape mode?*). What type of response did you get from the system?

D. Search for information on two more Microsoft products.

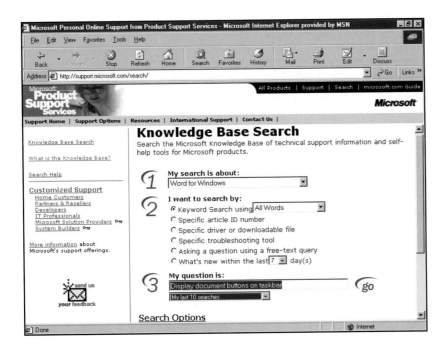

IBE Labs

If you have the Interactive Browser Edition (IBE) CD-ROM for this textbook, you may complete the following interactive exercises using the instructions provided in the IBE.

1. **Trivia.** Choose a category; then test your knowledge.

2. **Labeling.** Identify the key phases in systems development.

3. **Association Game.** Challenge your understanding of computer information systems by arranging information correctly in a table.

4. **Build a Development Team.** Mix and match the talents of individuals to put together a project team.

UNIT 14

Software Programming & Development

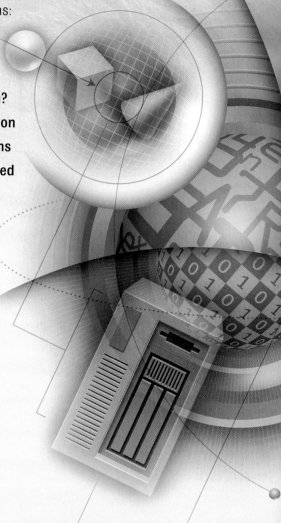

Creating Computer Programs

OVERVIEW:
Getting to Know Computer Software

Software, as you learned in Unit 1, is the intelligence that runs the hardware in a computer. Without software, the modern electronic digital computer is nothing more than a clever arrangement of electrical components—it can do nothing. Some software commands may be built into select pieces of hardware (like CPUs and ROM chips), but even in these cases the programming is simply a "hard-coded" version of software: the code is built directly into the hardware. Because software is such an integral part of any computer system, it is important to understand exactly what software is and where it comes from.

The term *software* can be used in a generic sense to refer to all of the variable parts of a computer. You can say, "Software tells the computer what to do." But you can also use the term more specifically to describe an operating system or application. For example, you might say, "Windows 2000 is a piece of software," or "Lotus 1-2-3 is a piece of software." On any one computer, the software usually consists of the operating system, various utilities (sometimes considered part of the operating system), applications, and documents. Figure 27.1 on page 488 shows the various divisions of software and some examples of that software.

All of the various types of software include one or more files, which contain commands that tell the computer what to do. These files are called programs. Because the term *software* may be used to refer to a specific application and because an application may consist of nothing more than a program file, the two terms are often used interchangeably. The following sections explain what programs are and how they function and describe some of the processes and tools that software developers use when creating computer programs.

OBJECTIVES

- Define the term *computer program.*
- Describe the use of flow-charts and pseudocode in programming.
- Identify two ways in which a program can work toward a solution.
- Differentiate the two main approaches to computer programming.
- List and describe three elements of object-oriented programming.

WHAT IS A COMPUTER PROGRAM?

A computer program is a set of instructions or statements (also called code) that is carried out by the computer's CPU. A program is typically composed of a main module and submodules. These modules are stored as a collection of files; large programs can contain thousands of individual files, each serving a specific purpose. Some of these files are program files that contain instructions for the computer, whereas other files contain data. For Windows-based PCs, some common extensions for program files are listed below:

Figure 27.1
Types of software: operating systems, utilities, and applications.

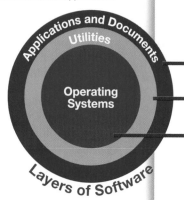

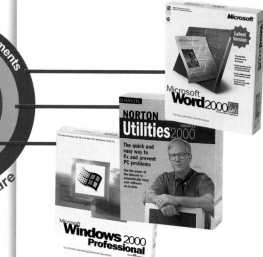

◆ **Executable (EXE) Files.** An **executable file** is the part of a program that actually sends commands to the processor. In fact, when you run a program, you are running the executable file. The processor executes the commands in the file—thus the name *executable file.* Executable files typically (but not necessarily) have the file-name extension EXE.

◆ **Dynamic Link Library (DLL) Files.** A **dynamic link library** is a partial EXE file. A DLL file will not run on its own; rather, its commands are accessed by another running program. Because a DLL file can contain part of an executable program, these files provide programmers with an effective way of breaking large programs into small, replaceable components. This feature makes the entire program easier to upgrade. In addition, DLL files can also be shared by several programs at one time, making DLL files especially powerful for upgrades and efficient for program storage.

Visit **www.glencoe.com/norton/online/** for more information on **program file extensions.**

◆ **Initialization (INI) Files.** An **initialization file** contains configuration information, such as the size and starting point of a window, the color of the background, the user's name, and so on. Initialization files help programs start running or contain information that programs can use as they run. Although initialization files are still in use, many newer programs now store user preferences and other program variables in the Windows Registry.

◆ **Help (HLP) Files.** A **help file** contains information in an indexed and cross-linked format. By including a help file, programmers can provide the user with PC-based help.

By default, most program files are stored in a folder that bears the application's name or an abbreviation of it. However, some of the program's files may be placed in other folders. For example, the INI file may be stored in the Windows folder. To view a list of most of the files needed to run an application, you can open that application's folder. Figure 27.2 shows a typical software directory, in this case, for a hypothetical program called CoolToys version 1.3.

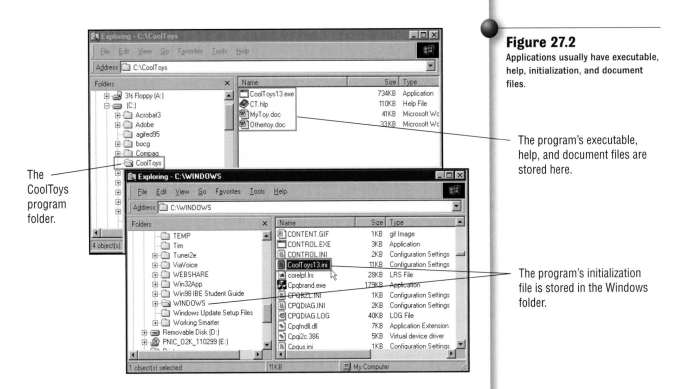

Figure 27.2
Applications usually have executable, help, initialization, and document files.

The CoolToys program folder.

The program's executable, help, and document files are stored here.

The program's initialization file is stored in the Windows folder.

HARDWARE/SOFTWARE INTERACTION

In telling the CPU what to do, programs operate at the hardware level; that is, the program tells the CPU to retrieve a specific piece of information from memory and to execute a specific interrupt. An **interrupt** is a preprogrammed set of steps that the CPU follows, such as adding or comparing two numbers. The results are returned to the computer's memory and the program tells the CPU what to do next.

An oversimplified example of hardware/software interaction might look like the following example, which loads a few numbers into memory and then performs an add-and-compare operation on the numbers:

Program	CPU	RAM
Reserve memory locations for 4 numbers	Reserve RAM at A, B, C, D	A[ ] B[ ] C[ ] D[ ]
Place the number 1 in memory location A	Get input, place it in A	A[1] B[ ] C[ ] D[ ]
3 in memory location B	Get input, place it in B	A[1] B[3] C[ ] D[ ]
4 in memory location D	Get input, place it in D	A[1] B[3] C[ ] D[4]
Get the number in memory location A	Get A, A is 1	A[1] B[3] C[ ] D[4]
location B	Get B, B is 3	A[1] B[3] C[ ] D[4]
Add A and B	1 + 3 is 4	A[1] B[3] C[ ] D[4]
Put the sum of A and B in memory location C	Place 4 in C	A[1] B[3] C[4] D[4]
Get the number in memory location C	Get C, C is 4	A[1] B[3] C[4] D[4]
location D	Get D, D is 4	A[1] B[3] C[4] D[4]
Compare C and D	Compare C and D 4 and 4 are equal	A[1] B[3] C[4] D[4]

Obviously, the previous example shows a small sample of software controlling hardware. In real-life, programs are much bigger and usually perform more complex tasks. For example, in a word processor, the software would tell the CPU to set aside memory for storing the words of a document. As the user types the document, the word processor instructs the CPU to accept and store each letter. If the user runs a spell check, the software instructs the CPU to load another set of words, this time from a spelling dictionary. Then the software directs the CPU to access each word in the document and compare that word against the words in the spelling dictionary.

Before a program can tell a computer to do anything, the program must speak the computer's language. Similarly, programmers must use tools that convert their human-language instructions into code that computers can understand. Machine language, programming languages, compilers, and interpreters play a role at this point in the process.

Machine Code

As you learned in Unit 1, the computer's memory and processing switches all operate on a binary number system consisting of 1s and 0s. Any software commands that directly affect hardware must be written in the binary number system. Because these 1s and 0s form the language of computer hardware, this code is often called **machine code** or **machine language.** In fact, to be a precise example of hardware/software interaction, the previous example would have to consist entirely of 1s and 0s. While this format would not make sense to you, it would make perfect sense to the computer and could be explained as the lowest language level.

Programming Languages

Although a computer's code must consist of nothing but 1s and 0s, computer programmers do not program that way. Technically, a programmer could write a program directly as machine code, but it would take a tremendous understanding of the inner workings of a PC and an absurd amount of time. Because it is not practical for programmers to approach their job that way, they use **programming languages** instead of machine code. Programming languages are higher-level languages than machine code and enable the programmer to describe a program using a variation of basic English. The resulting description is saved in a file and called **source code.**

Compilers and Interpreters

Once a programmer has a piece of source code, he or she must convert it into machine code before the program can run on a computer. The job of converting the source code is handled by another program, called a compiler or an interpreter. A **compiler** converts all of the source code into machine code, creating an executable file. The content of this executable file is called **object code.** The programmer can copy the executable object code onto any similar system and run the program. In other words, once compiled, the program is a stand-alone executable file that no longer needs the compiler to run. Of course, each programming language requires its own compiler to translate the particular nuances of that language. For example, the programming language C requires a C compiler, while the language Pascal requires a Pascal compiler. (Specific programming languages are introduced later in this unit.)

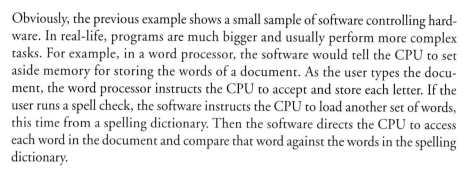

Visit **www.glencoe.com/norton/online/** for more information on **machine language.**

An **interpreter** also converts source code to machine code, but instead of creating an executable object code file, the interpreter simply executes each bit of machine code as it is converted. Because interpreters translate code on the fly, they have a certain flexibility that compilers lack. Because the code must be interpreted each time it is run, however, the interpreted code runs slower than compiled code, and a copy of the interpreter must accompany the code everywhere it goes. So every system that needs the program must have a copy of the interpreter as well as the source code. Some popular interpreted languages include LISP, BASIC, and PERL.

HOW PROGRAMS SOLVE PROBLEMS

You already know that a program is a set of steps for controlling a computer. But what do the steps look like? Their appearance or structure depends a little on the programming language, but the overall concept is the same regardless of the language. Each step in the code is an instruction that performs a single task in a sequence of steps that perform a more complex task.

Program Control Flow

When you launch a program, the computer begins reading and carrying out statements at the executable file's main entry point. Typically, this entry point is the first line (or statement) in the file, although it may be located elsewhere. After execution of the first statement, program control passes (or flows) to another statement, and so on, until the last statement of the program has been executed. Then the program ends. The order in which program statements are executed is called **program control flow.** When mapping a program, a programmer creates a **flowchart.** Also, a programmer will often create a rough text version of the code, which looks similar to programming code but does not have all of the precise syntax and details necessary for real code. This simplified text version of the program is called **pseudocode.**

Flowcharts and pseudocode are helpful in many tasks besides programming computers. Certainly, for example, more than one programmer has taped a flowchart to the side of the office coffee pot with the hope of encouraging other employees to make more coffee when they take the last cup. The example in Figure 27.3 shows such a flowchart.

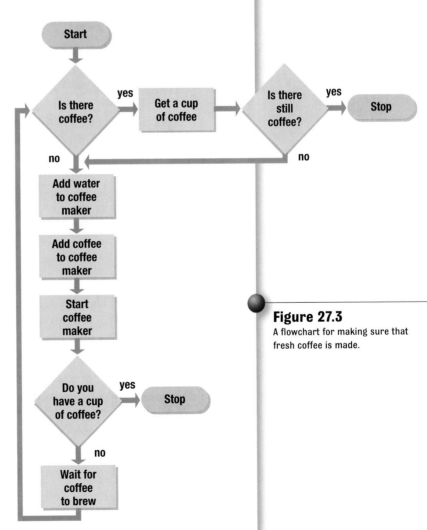

Figure 27.3
A flowchart for making sure that fresh coffee is made.

The program directs the person at the coffee pot to see if coffee is in the pot. If so, the person takes a cup of coffee; if not, the person follows the steps for making coffee. Regardless of whether or not coffee was in the pot originally, once the person has coffee, the program instructs the person to loop back to the beginning and check to see if coffee is still in the pot. If coffee is in the pot, the program ends and the person leaves. If not, the person is directed to the steps on how to make more coffee. In this way, the person will never leave an empty coffee pot for the next person.

Notice that the flowchart uses different shapes for different tasks. Each specific direction is in a rectangle, while each question is in a diamond. These different shapes help a programmer to follow the flow of a program. When creating a flowchart, programmers use a template to help create a readable chart. Figure 27.4 shows a flowchart template. It provides several different shapes, one for each of the basic types of steps a program might need.

Figure 27.4
A template for creating flowcharts.

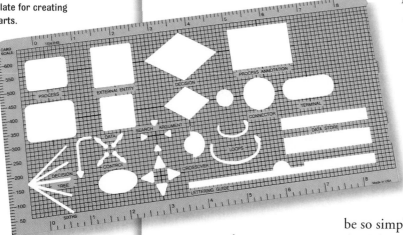

Flowcharts can depict almost any step-by-step process, regardless of the desired result. When describing flowcharts and program control flow, computer instructors often use the age-old example of a house thermostat. In such a flowchart, the thermostat continuously monitors the desired temperature and current temperature and turns the furnace on or off accordingly. The process and the associated steps need not be so simple, however. Far more complex flowcharts exist in everyday life, including those in a car's computer. Among these programs are those that monitor the current air temperature, engine temperature, throttle position, vehicle speed, engine speed, spark timing, and oxygen sensors—all to determine exactly how much air and fuel to put in a single cylinder for one stroke of the engine.

Algorithms

The steps represented in a flowchart usually lead to some desired result. Collectively, these steps are called an **algorithm.** Specifically, an algorithm is a set of steps that always lead to a solution. The steps to finding a solution remain the same, whether you are working out the solution by computer or by hand—which is why you can have both a hand-drawn flowchart and compiled object code that complete the same task.

Great thinkers have already worked out algorithms for solving a wide range of mathematical problems, such as adding numbers or finding a square root. In fact, the word *algorithm* comes from the name of an Arab mathematician, al-Khwarizmi, who compiled a vast collection of algorithms over one thousand years ago.

Figure 27.5 shows an algorithm for finding the highest peak on a topographical map. The algorithm simply samples each square on the grid, one square at a time, and compares the results with the current highest peak. The process is slow but it always finds the highest point.

Visit **www.glencoe.com/norton/online/** for more information on **algorithms** and their use.

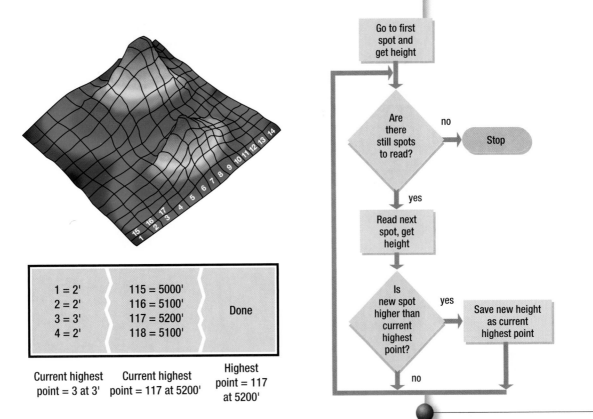

1 = 2'	115 = 5000'	
2 = 2'	116 = 5100'	Done
3 = 3'	117 = 5200'	
4 = 2'	118 = 5100'	

Current highest
point = 3 at 3'

Current highest
point = 117 at 5200'

Highest
point = 117
at 5200'

Figure 27.5
An algorithm always finds the best
possible solution.

Algorithms have many other uses. A spreadsheet program, for instance, might contain an algorithm to display the sum of cells highlighted by the user. Such an algorithm would allow the user to highlight cells, read the numbers in those cells, total the numbers, and display them on the screen. Another algorithm within the spreadsheet program might look for the longest word in a column and then adjust the width of the column to fit the text.

Heuristics

Sometimes, no possible algorithm exists to solve a given problem, or the algorithm is so complex or time-consuming that it cannot be coded or run. In these cases, programmers rely on heuristics to help solve problems or perform tasks. **Heuristics** are like algorithms because they are a set of steps for finding the solution to a problem, but unlike an algorithm, a heuristic does not come with a guarantee of finding the best possible solution. Heuristics provide a good chance of finding a solution, although not necessarily the best one.

Figure 27.6 on page 494 shows a heuristic for finding the highest peak on a topographical map. The heuristic works under the assumption that mountains build up from foothills and that the peak cannot be standing in a square by itself in the middle of a valley. Following this heuristic, the program samples ten random spots on the map and compares them to see which is the highest.

The heuristic assumes that, because you have to go up to reach the peak, the current highest point must lead up to the peak. To find the next step to the peak, the program samples a few spots immediately around the current highest point and compares them. Once the program has found a new highest point, it repeats the process of sampling around the current high point and looking for a new highest point. In this way, the heuristic climbs the mountain to

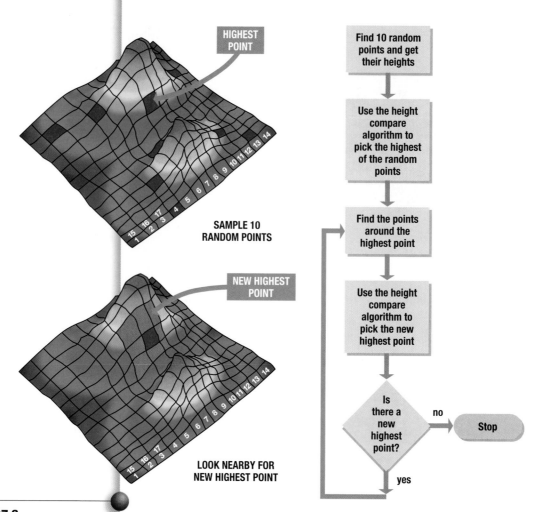

Figure 27.6
Heuristics provide a best-guess approach to problem solving.

the peak. As you can see, the heuristic always climbs up—and only up. It is possible that, based on the original starting points, the heuristic may climb the shorter mountain. While the heuristic supplies a solution, it may not supply the best one every time. Figure 27.7 shows the heuristic climbing the wrong peak.

Heuristics are less likely to appear in ordinary applications (such as a spreadsheet or word processor) because these applications rarely require a task to be performed for which there is no definite solution. Heuristics are extremely common in more advanced programs that track vast quantities of data in complex ways. For example, software that helps forecasters predict the weather cannot possibly process every possible iteration of every piece of data available. Even if the program could process all of the data, it still could not hope to predict accurately something as complex as the weather. By using heuristics, however, the programs can cull the data to find most of the more useful information. Then the program can create a reasonably accurate guess at the weather based on that data.

Common Flow Patterns

As you can imagine from seeing the sample flowchart earlier, the flow of a program falls into discrete sections. One section of code may repeat a task (such as prompting the user for input) while another performs some calculation and another

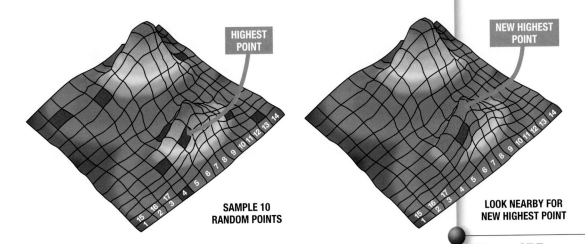

HIGHEST POINT

SAMPLE 10
RANDOM POINTS

NEW HIGHEST POINT

LOOK NEARBY FOR
NEW HIGHEST POINT

Figure 27.7
Heuristics are not always guaranteed to find the best possible answer.

makes a decision. These flow patterns have names, and some variation on them is built into most programming languages. These patterns include conditional statements and loops. In Figure 27.8, diagram A shows a conditional statement and diagram B shows a loop.

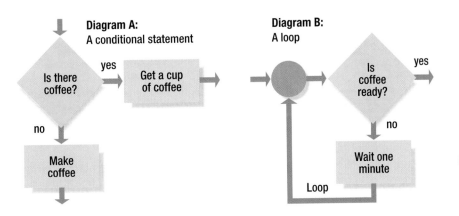

Diagram A:
A conditional statement

Is there coffee? — yes → Get a cup of coffee →

no ↓

Make coffee

Diagram B:
A loop

Is coffee ready? — yes →

no ↓

Wait one minute

Loop

Figure 27.8
Common flow patterns include the conditional statement and the loop.

Conditional Statements

A **conditional statement** is simply a test to determine what the program should do next. Conditional statements often come in the form of an If-Then statement, although there are other versions of the conditional statement, including Case statements and various embellishments of the If-Then statement that include Else and ElseIf commands.

The exact appearance of the conditional statements depends on the programming language used, but they all follow roughly the same logic. The following example shows a simple If-Then statement for walking through a doorway:

```
if door = open, then walk through
```

Of course, this conditional statement will not get you through a closed door, so you can add an Else statement to deal with that possible problem:

```
if door = open
then walk through
else
open door and walk through
```

NORTON
ONLINE

Visit **www.glencoe.com/norton/online/** for more information on **conditional statements**.

PRODUCTIVITY Tip

Finding Faster Algorithms

At first, the study of algorithm complexity might not seem important—especially with today's fast computers. Nevertheless, programmers and mathematicians have developed an entire field of study dedicated to understanding algorithm complexity and its effects on computer performance. A simple demonstration called The Traveling Salesman shows how a complex algorithm can get out of control.

In this problem, a salesman wants to visit all the cities in his route following the shortest possible path. With just a few cities, the problem seems quite simple; there are few possible combinations and the salesman can compare the distances easily. If another city is added, however, the number of steps to compare all of the possible different routes grows exponentially. After a few more cities are added, the number of comparisons makes the problem too time-consuming to attempt to solve.

How Is Complexity Determined?

Determining complexity is relatively simple in theory, although math skills are required if you want exact numbers. Roughly speaking, you can determine the complexity of an algorithm by creating a run-time equation that is a function of the input into the algorithm. The equation looks at the size of the algorithm's input—such as the size of a list to be sorted or the number of digits in a number to be factored—and determines the number of steps needed to reach a solution. In effect, you are creating an artificial run-time based on input size. In real life, the algorithm may not have to perform every step every time, so the equation represents a worst-case input. Once you have the run-time equation, you can test various input sizes and see how the run-time grows. If the run-time grows dramatically faster than the input size, you have a problem.

Categorizing Algorithms

To discuss algorithm complexity, mathematicians categorize algorithms as either tractable or intractable:

◆ **Tractable Problems.** These problems (which are also called fast, efficient, or easy) have a run-time that grows at a slow rate when compared to the input size. Technically, a tractable problem is one where the time equation is a polynomial function of the input size. You can solve a tractable problem in a reasonable amount of time or with a reasonable amount of computer resources.

◆ **Intractable Problems.** These problems (which are also called slow, inefficient, or hard) have a run-time that grows rapidly when compared to the input size. To be exact, an intractable problem has a time equation that is an exponential function of the input size. Occasionally you cannot solve these problems, but more often, they simply take lots of time or huge computer resources to reach a solution.

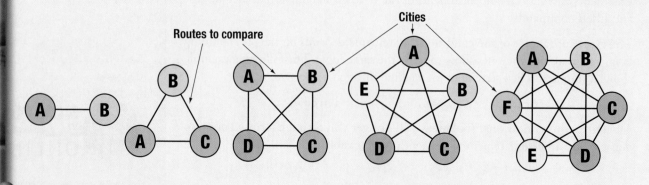

The addition of each city increases the number of route comparisons exponentially for The Traveling Salesman.

Sometimes you may run into a situation where the door may be in one of several states. In that case, you need an ElseIf statement to handle each state of the door and a final Else to deal with all other possible outcomes:

```
if door = wide open,
then walk through
elseif door = cracked
then open door by pushing hard and walk through
elseif door = half open
then open door by pushing lightly and walk through
else
open door by turning the knob and pushing hard and walk through
```

Case statements are used just like the last If/Then/ElseIf/Else example but with different commands:

```
case door = open—walk through
case door = cracked—push hard and walk through
case door = half open—push lightly and walk through
default—turn knob and push hard and walk through
```

It is possible that you would need a piece of code for opening doors, especially if you were programming robots or the machines that control elevator doors. However, a more PC-based example of a conditional statement might be found in a word processor. For instance, when you highlight a piece of text and click the Bold icon, the word processor must decide if the highlighted text is already in boldface or not. If the text is boldface, then the word processor removes the boldface; if the text is not boldface, the word processor adds boldface. The algorithm would look like this:

```
if text = bold
        remove bold
else
        add bold
```

Loops

A **loop** is a piece of code that repeats again and again until some condition, called an **exit condition**, is met. Each programming language has its own way of expressing these loops, and the precise details of how they behave varies with each language. Some common loops are as follows:

Figure 27.9
A For loop.

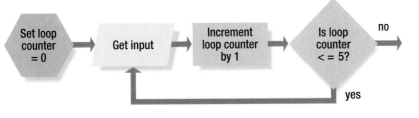

```
For Loop Counter = 1 to 5
   Prompt User "Enter Input"
   Get Input
   Loop Counter = Loop Counter + 1
Next Loop
```

Flowchart of a For loop

Pseudocode of a For loop

◆ **For.** Typically a For loop (also called a For-Next loop) repeats a process a specific number of times. You might use a For loop if you want to prompt a user to enter five numbers. No matter what the numbers are, the user is prompted five times. Figure 27.9 shows a typical For loop.

◆ **While.** In a While loop, the program determines first whether the exit condition has already been met. If the exit condition is not met, the program runs the code inside the loop again and again until the exit condition is met (that is, the loop runs while the condition is not met).

You might use a While loop if you want a user to enter his or her age and then additional numbers until the sum of the age and the numbers exceeds 30. In this example, the user might enter 25 for the age; in that case, the loop will run and prompt the user for additional numbers. If the user enters 32, the age exceeds 30 and the loop does not run. When it does run, the loop repeats as many times as necessary to meet the exit condition. So the user might enter 25 for an age and then the numbers 1, 1, 1, and 3. Or the user might enter 25 for an age and then the number 6.

Another more real-world example of a While loop occurs in spreadsheets. For example, if you highlight ten spreadsheet cells and then click the SUM button, the spreadsheet program loops through the highlighted cells, adding each number to a running total until there are no more highlighted cells. Figure 27.10 shows a typical While loop.

Figure 27.10
A While loop.

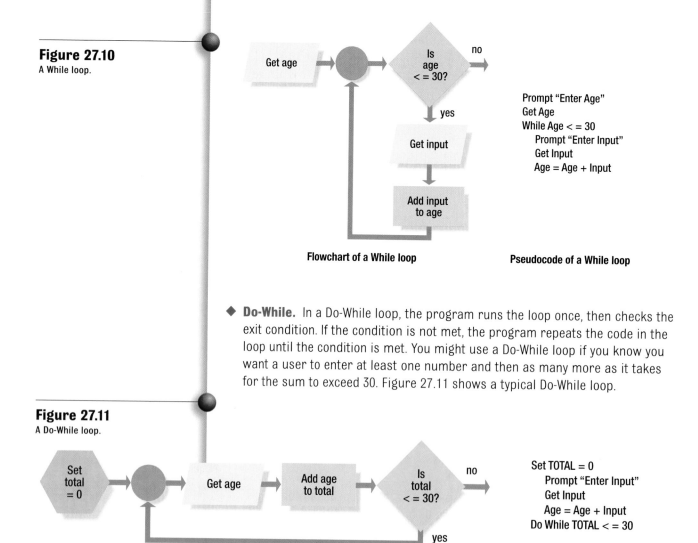

Flowchart of a While loop   Pseudocode of a While loop

◆ **Do-While.** In a Do-While loop, the program runs the loop once, then checks the exit condition. If the condition is not met, the program repeats the code in the loop until the condition is met. You might use a Do-While loop if you know you want a user to enter at least one number and then as many more as it takes for the sum to exceed 30. Figure 27.11 shows a typical Do-While loop.

Figure 27.11
A Do-While loop.

Flowchart of a Do-While loop   Pseudocode of a Do-While loop

Variables and Functions

So far, the flowcharts you have seen have all been somewhat vague. These examples are in basic English and do not account for the fact that computers require highly specific directions for each task they perform. For a program to store a number, you must tell the computer to reserve a spot in memory large enough to hold the number. If you want the computer to make a decision based on that number, you must tell the computer precisely what to compare and how to act. To perform these tasks, the actual programming process uses variables and functions.

Variables

A **variable** is a label and placeholder for data being processed. For example, imagine that you are writing a program that prompts users to enter their ages. You need a placeholder, or variable, to represent the data (different ages) they enter. In this case, you might choose to name the variable "Age" (see Figure 27.12). When a user enters a number at the prompt, this data becomes the value of the variable *Age*. You can also use variables in programs to perform actions on data. For example, consider the instruction:

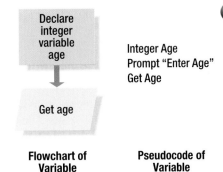

Flowchart of Variable

Declare integer variable age → Get age

Pseudocode of Variable

Integer Age
Prompt "Enter Age"
Get Age

Figure 27.12
Variables are used to store values.

```
Age + 2
```

If the value of Age is 20, the result of this instruction is 22; if the value is 30, the result is 32; and so on.

Procedures, Functions, and Subroutines

A **function** is a prewritten or user-created set of steps to perform one specific task. Essentially, a function is a mini-algorithm for performing a single task like finding the average of a set of numbers or the square root of a number. Most programming languages come with a built-in set of functions to perform a lot of the more common mathematical processes. Other functions are also included for handling jobs like parsing text or reading and writing to files. Most programming languages also allow the programmer to create his or her own functions for more unusual tasks, such as prompting the user for input.

By using built-in functions and creating new ones as necessary, programmers can develop a set of building blocks from which they can assemble more complete code. Programmers reuse functions as needed, thereby avoiding unnecessary typing and making it easy to edit the code later. For example, programming languages usually have a built-in function for finding an average that looks something like this:

```
avg(x, y, z)
```

Avg is the name of the function. The *(x, y, z)* after the name of the function is the called the function's **argument** or **parameters.** Arguments are used to pass input to functions as the program runs. In this example, *x*, *y*, and *z* are variables representing the numbers to be averaged. If *x* is 2, *y* is 4, and *z* is 6, then the function will find the average to be 4. After the function finds the average, it **returns** this value to the program (that is, it reports the results of the function to the program

NORTON ONLINE

Visit **www.glencoe.com/norton/online/** for more information on **variables** and **functions.**

so it can be used as needed). Figure 27.13 shows an expansion of the previous flowchart and pseudocode to include variables for storing three separate ages, a user-defined function for getting the ages, and a built-in function for calculating the average age.

Different computer languages use different names, such as **subroutines, procedures,** and **routines,** for these blocks of reusable code. There are subtle differences between these terms, but for now, the term *function* will be used for all of them.

Figure 27.13

Variables are used in decisions and calculations; functions carry out a predetermined process.

Flowchart of Age1, Age2, Age3

| Declare integer variable Age1 |
| Declare integer variable Age2 |
| Declare integer variable Age3 |
| Run user defined function Age1 = GetAge |
| Run user defined function Age2 = GetAge |
| Run user defined function Age3 = GetAge |
| Use built in function AVG (Age1, Age2, Age3) |

Flowchart of GetAge

| Declare integer variable TempAge |
| Get TempAge |
| Return TempAge |

Integer Age1
Integer Age2
Integer Age3
Age1 = GetAge
Age2 = GetAge
Age3 = GetAge
AVG (Age1, Age2, Age3)

GetAge
Integer TempAge
Prompt "Enter Age"
Get TempAge
Return TempAge

Pseudocode

Self Check

Answer the following questions by filling in the blank(s).

1. A(n) _____ is the part of a program that sends commands to the processor.

2. A compiler is used to convert source code into _____ a computer can use.

3. _____ are like algorithms, but they are not guaranteed to find the best solution to a problem.

STRUCTURED AND OBJECT-ORIENTED PROGRAMMING

When writing a program, a programmer first creates a flowchart of the algorithm or heuristic to be followed. Then the programmer translates the flowchart into pseudocode to get an idea of how the code will look. Once the programmer is ready, he or she uses a programming language to create a set of variables and functions that can be combined in a specific flow to produce the desired result. Once the source code is written, the programmer compiles or interprets the source code to create the machine code that controls the computer.

Until the 1960s, relatively little structure was imposed on the way programmers wrote code. As a result, following control flow through hundreds or thousands of lines of code was almost impossible. Programmers often used goto statements to jump to other parts of a program. A **goto statement** does exactly what the name implies. It identifies a different line of the program to which control jumps (it goes to). The issue with goto statements is identifying how program control flow proceeds after the jump. Does control return to the starting point, or does it continue at the new location? This tangled mess of code is often referred to as "spaghetti code," and it was a major problem in diagnosing the impact of Y2K problems. Many of these programs are still running and had to be evaluated by programmers for possible Y2K problems. Following this code is difficult and one program could take weeks to follow because of its many paths. Figure 27.14 shows a flowchart with a goto statement.

Figure 27.14
Goto statements can make it difficult to follow program control flow.

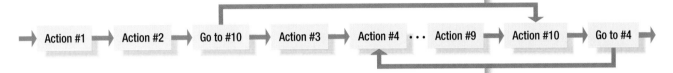

Structured programming evolved in the 1960s and 1970s. The name refers to the practice of building programs using a set of well-defined structures. One goal of structured programming is the elimination of goto statements. Software developers have found that using structured programming results in improved efficiency, but they continue to struggle with the process of building software quickly and correctly.

Reuse is recognized as the best solution to these software development problems. Reusing code allows programs to be built quickly and correctly. Functions, which are the building blocks of structured programming, are steps along this path. In the 1980s, computing took another leap forward with the development of **object-oriented programming (OOP).** The building blocks of OOP, called **objects,** are reusable, modular components (which are explained in detail later).

OOP builds on and enhances structured programming. You do not leave structured programming behind when you work with an object-oriented language. Objects are composed of structured program pieces, and the logic of manipulating objects is also structured.

Structured Programming

Researchers in the 1960s demonstrated that programs could be written with three control structures:

Visit **www.glencoe.com/norton/online/** for more information on **structured programming.**

◆ **Sequence structure** defines the default control flow in a program. Typically, this structure is built into programming languages. Unless directed otherwise, a computer executes lines of code in the order in which they are written. It is possible, as a result of a condition statement or a function call, that the flow may have the option of going in one of several different directions. Each direction is its own sequence, called a **branch.**

◆ **Selection structures** are built around the conditional statements you have already learned about. If the condition statement is true, certain lines of code are executed. If the condition statement is false, those lines of code are not executed.

◆ **Repetition structures** (or **looping structures**) use the loops discussed earlier in this lesson. In a repetitive structure, the program checks a condition statement and executes a loop based on the condition. If the condition is true, then a block of one or more commands is repeated until the condition is false.

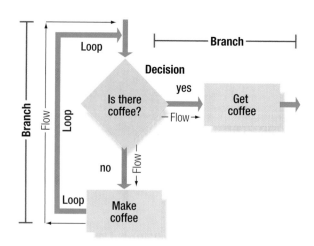

Figure 27.15 shows a flowchart with selection structure and a repetition structure. The entire flowchart represents a sequence structure because each step is executed in order from the beginning to the end of a branch—or from the beginning of a loop to the end of a loop.

Object-Oriented Programming

Concepts of object-oriented programming, such as objects and classes, can seem abstract at first, but many programmers claim that an object orientation is a natural way of thinking about the world. Because OOP gives them an intuitive way to model the world, they say, programs become simpler, programming becomes faster, and the burden of program maintenance is lessened.

Objects

Look around you—you are surrounded by objects. Right now, the list of objects around you might include a book, a computer, a light, walls, plants, pictures, and so forth.

Think for a moment about what you perceive when you look at a car on the street. Your first impression is probably of the car as a whole. You do not focus on the steel, chrome, and plastic elements that make up the car. The entire unit, or object, is what registers in your mind.

Now, how would you describe that car to someone sitting next to you? You might start with its **attributes,** such as the car's color, size, shape, top speed, and so on. An attribute is simply a component of the overall description. You might then talk about what the car can do; that is, you describe its functions. For example, the car moves forward, moves backward, opens its windows, and so on. Together, the attributes and the functions define the object. In the language of OOP, every object has attributes and functions that may **encapsulate** (contain) other objects.

When you look more closely at the car, you may begin to notice many smaller component objects. For example, the car has a chassis, a drive train, a body, and an interior. Each component is, in turn, composed of other objects. The drive train includes an engine, transmission, rear end, and axle. So an object can be either a whole unit or a component of other objects. Objects can include other objects. Figure 27.16 shows a car replete with attributes, functions, and encapsulated objects.

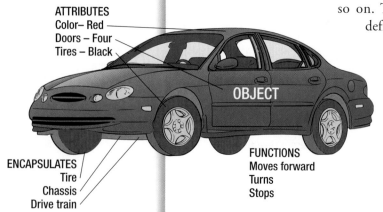

ATTRIBUTES
Color– Red
Doors – Four
Tires – Black

OBJECT

ENCAPSULATES
Tire
Chassis
Drive train

FUNCTIONS
Moves forward
Turns
Stops

Classes and Class Inheritance

Most people naturally place objects in abstract categories, or classes, with similar objects. For example, the Porsches and Saturns you see on the road are all cars, while the GMCs and Land Rovers are all trucks. In OOP, you would group the Porsche and Saturn into a car class and the GMC and Land Rover into a truck class.

A **class** consists of attributes and functions shared by more than one object. All cars, for example, have a steering wheel and four tires. All cars can drive forward, reverse, park, and accelerate. Class attributes are called **data members,** and class functions are represented as **member functions** or methods.

Classes can be divided into **subclasses.** The car class, for example, could have a luxury sedan class, a sports car class, and an economy car class (see Figure 27.17). Subclasses typically have all the attributes and methods of the parent class. Every sports car, for example, has a steering wheel and can drive forward. This phenomenon is called **class inheritance.** In addition to inherited characteristics, subclasses have unique characteristics of their own.

All objects belong to classes. When an object is created, it automatically has all the attributes and methods associated with that class. In the language of OOP, objects are **instantiated** (created).

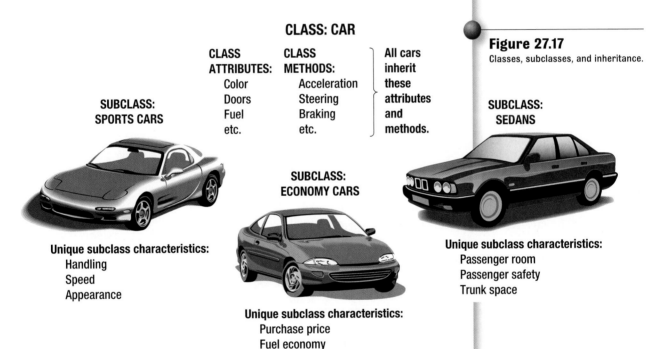

Figure 27.17
Classes, subclasses, and inheritance.

Messages

Objects do not typically perform behaviors spontaneously. After all, many of these behaviors may be contradictory. A car, for example, cannot move forward and backward at the same time. You also expect that the car will not drive forward spontaneously!

You send a signal to the car to move forward by pressing on the accelerator. Likewise, in OOP, **messages** are sent to objects, requesting them to perform a specific function. Part of designing a program is to identify the flow of sending and receiving messages among the objects.

Techview

ARTIFICIAL INTELLIGENCE

Artificial intelligence (AI) can be defined as a program or machine that can solve problems or recognize patterns. A more "pure" definition of AI might be a computer or program that can fool a human into thinking he or she is dealing with another human. Such a computer could both learn and reason, so yet another definition of artificial intelligence might be a computer that can learn and reason.

Artificial intelligence software is used in many real-world applications, from determining if banks should grant loans, to voice recognition and terrain-following missile guidance systems. Even applications like word processors and e-mail make use of AI concepts. For example, a word processor's grammar checker attempts to understand and correct a language concept that most users cannot fully explain themselves. Regardless of the actual task, artificial intelligence is used in two basic areas:

◆ **Problem Solving.** In problem solving, the artificial intelligence program must look at a problem or collection of data and determine what to do next. For example, a bank may use an artificial intelligence system to look at your credit history and life style before deciding whether or not to lend you money. This type of system is called an expert system.

◆ **Pattern Recognition.** In pattern recognition, the artificial intelligence program must look for repeated or known occurrences of data. Examples include artificial vision and speech recognition.

Of course, many artificial intelligence programs combine elements of both areas to solve a problem. For example, a data compression utility must look for repeated patterns in the data and then decide how to rewrite the data to eliminate the duplications.

Some Examples of AI Techniques

Artificial intelligence may be applied in many different ways depending on the problem to be solved and the resources available. Some common techniques include the following:

◆ **Decision Trees.** These software guides are simply maps that tell the computer what to do next based on each decision it makes. Each decision leads to a new branch with new decisions and consequences.

◆ **Rules-Based Systems.** These systems work by following a set of rules given by the programmer. So long as the programmer has anticipated every possible circumstance that the program may encounter, it can solve any problem.

◆ **Feedback.** This technique is used to modify programs. Basically, a feedback system monitors the results of a solution to see if the solution worked or in what areas it failed.

◆ **Knowledge-Based Systems.** These systems are similar to a rules-based system, but they use feedback to learn from their mistakes. As a result, knowledge-based systems can actually learn to solve new problems.

◆ **Heuristics.** This software technique is something like a recipe for a problem-solving approach rather than an algorithm that solves a specific problem.

Building an Artificial Brain

To create a true artificial intelligence, scientists could try building an artificial brain called a neural network. The human brain consists of billions and even trillions of neurons, each with as many as a million connections to other neurons. Scientists have identified hundreds of different types of neurons and more than fifty different patterns of neuron connections. This level of complexity is simply beyond any computer currently in existence. Even the most powerful parallel computers with tens of thousands of processors don't come close to equaling the number or variety of connections in a human brain.

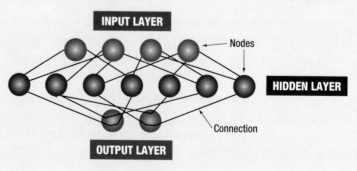

Neural networks are modeled after real neural connections in the human brain.

INPUT LAYER
Nodes
HIDDEN LAYER
Connection
OUTPUT LAYER

LESSON QUIZ

True/False

Answer the following questions by circling True or False.

True   False   **1.** All types of software include one or more files that contain commands telling the computer what to do.

True   False   **2.** New computers understand human language, so machine language is not necessary.

True   False   **3.** The order in which program statements are executed is called program logic.

True   False   **4.** A conditional statement is a test that determines what a program should do next.

True   False   **5.** An object is a placeholder for data being processed.

Multiple Choice

Circle the word or phrase that best completes each sentence.

1. A computer program is a collection of _____ , which are carried out by the computer's CPU.

    A. instructions   **B.** loops   **C.** neither A or B

2. Programming languages enable programmers to describe programs. This description is called _____ .

    A. a class   **B.** source code   **C.** an object

3. _____ is a simplified text version of a program.

    A. Pseudocode   **B.** Control flow   **C.** Neither A nor B

4. A loop repeats until a(n) _____ is met.

    A. function   **B.** statement   **C.** exit condition

5. One goal of _____ is the elimination of goto statements.

    A. programming languages   **B.** interpreters   **C.** structured programming

LESSON LABS

Complete the following exercise as directed by your instructor.

Take the following steps to see how many executable files are in your Windows folder:

A. Click the Start button; then click Programs, Windows Explorer.

B. In the left pane of the Exploring window, find and click the Windows folder. The folder's contents appear in the right pane of the window.

C. In the right pane, click the Type column heading. This action arranges the pane's contents by file or folder types.

D. List all the executable (.exe) files in the Windows folder (the exact number of executable files may vary from system to system).

E. Find the Notepad.exe file in the Windows folder and double-click the file. The Notepad text editing program will open on your screen.

F. Close Notepad; then close the Exploring window.

Programming Languages and the Programming Process

OBJECTIVES

- Identify the three main categories of programming languages.
- Describe the five generations of programming languages.
- Name at least five major programming languages.
- Describe a visual programming environment and how it is used.
- List the five phases of the systems development life cycle for programming.

OVERVIEW:
The Keys to Successful Programming

Programming can be a fairly complex process and requires training, planning, and some specialized tools. If you think this process sounds a bit like any other construction process, you are right because programming is actually like building a commercial property. You have to study the market, create a site plan, hire a crew, get special tools, build the building, and then continually update the structure to meet the changing needs of the tenants.

Successful programmers are knowledgeable in two key areas: programming tools (the software and languages they use to develop applications) and the programming process (the step-by-step procedures that they follow to ensure consistent, well-developed products). Software developers of all backgrounds—and in many different working environments—adhere to a fairly uniform set of procedures in their work. Thus, programmers can collaborate more easily on large development projects and can predict more accurately how their programs will work. You will learn more about the development process later, but for now, you'll learn about the programmer's special tools— programming languages.

THE EVOLUTION OF PROGRAMMING LANGUAGES

Visit **www.glencoe.com/norton/online/** for more information on the **history of programming**.

As you learned in Lesson 27, programming is a way of sending instructions to the computer. To create these instructions, programmers use rigidly defined programming languages to create source code, and the source code is then converted into machine (or object) code for the computer.

Machine code is the only language that a computer understands. People, however, have difficulty understanding machine code. As a result, researchers first developed assembly languages and then higher-level languages. This evolution represents a transition from strings of numbers (the machine code you learned about earlier) to command sequences that you can read like any other language. Higher-level languages focus on what the programmer wants the computer to do, not on how the computer will execute those commands.

As you will see in the following sections, programmers can choose from many development tools, each of which differs greatly in its capability, flexibility, and ease of use. Despite their differences, however, most programming languages share one characteristic: each requires the programmer to follow rules of syntax.

Programming languages follow many of the same types of rules as do the languages people use to communicate with each other. Programming languages require, for example, that information be provided in a certain order and structure, that symbols be used, and sometimes even that punctuation be used. These rules are called the **syntax** of the programming language, and they vary a great deal from one language to another. Figure 28.1 shows a piece of source code written in a programming language called C.

Notice that in Figure 28.1, each line of code includes special abbreviations, spacing, or punctuation. This special writing style is the syntax of C. If the code were written in a different language, you would see differences in spacing, phrasing, punctuation, and so on. Regardless of which language the programmer uses, however, he or she must follow the correct syntax for that language. If the syntax is not correct, the compiler or interpreter cannot understand the source code and will either fail or create incorrect object code.

Figure 28.1

The syntax of each programming language dictates the exact spacing, symbols, words, and punctuation used in the code.

```
SyntaxSample.c - Notepad
File  Edit  Search  Help

#include <stdio.h>

/* main excepts arguments from user */
main(argc, argv)
int argc;
char *argc[];
{
        int a, b;          /* a and b are counters */
        for (a=0;a<argc;a++)    /* loop through each word of main's arguments */
        {
                b=0;
                while (argv[a][b])       /* loop through each word */
                {
                        printf("%c", argv[a][b]);
                        b++;
                }
        }
}
```

Categories of Languages

Hundreds of programming languages are currently in use around the world. Some are highly specialized and are used in only one branch of science or industry, while others are well-known and are used almost everywhere. Some languages are obsolete and are used only to maintain older systems, while others are so new that many programmers do not even know that they exist or how to use them.

You can group programming languages in several different ways. For example, you might group them into those that use structured programming and those that do not. Or you might group them by those used in business versus those used in scientific circles. Programming languages are usually grouped first and foremost, however, by their place in the evolution of programming languages. Based on evolutionary history, programming languages fall into one of the following three broad categories:

◆ **Machine Languages.** Machine languages are the most basic of languages. They consist of strings of numbers and are defined by hardware design. In other words, the machine language for a Macintosh is not the same as the machine language for an IBM-compatible PC. A computer understands only its native machine language—the commands in its instruction set. These commands instruct the computer to perform elementary operations such as loading, storing, adding, and subtracting. Ultimately, machine code consists entirely of the 0s and 1s of the binary number system.

◆ **Assembly Languages.** These languages were developed by using English-like mnemonics for commonly used strings of machine language. Programmers worked in text editors (simple word processors) to create their source files. To convert the source files into object code, researchers created translator programs called **assemblers** to perform the conversion—thus the name **assembly language.** Assembly languages are highly detailed and cryptic but are still much easier to use than machine language. Programmers seldom write programs of any significant size in an assembly language. (One exception to this rule is action games, where the program's speed is critical.) Instead, they use assembly languages to fine-tune important parts of programs written in a higher-level language.

◆ **Higher-Level Languages.** Higher-level languages were developed to make programming easier. These languages are called **higher-level languages** because their syntax is closer to human language than it is to assembly or machine language code. They use familiar words instead of communicating in the detailed quagmire of digits that comprise the machine instructions. To express computer operations, these languages use operators, such as the plus or minus sign, that are the familiar components of mathematics. As a result, reading, writing, and understanding computer programs is easier with a higher-level language—although the instructions must still be translated into machine language before the computer can understand and carry them out.

Machine and Assembly-Level Languages

There is not much you can tell by looking at machine code (1s and 0s), and you would have to know a huge amount of specialized information before you could write it. Assembly code, however, is a bit less cryptic (but only a bit). As you can see in Figure 28.2, assembly code uses specialized English-like phrases as well as a considerable amount of hardware-specific numbers.

Assembly Code

```
;CLEAR SCREEN USING BIOS
CLR: MOV AX,0600H       ;SCROLL SCREEN
     MOV BH,30          ;COLOUR
     MOV CX,0000        ;FROM
     MOV DX,184FH       ;TO 24,79
     INT 10H            ;CALL BIOS;
;INPUTING OF A STRING
KEY: MOV AH,0AH         ;INPUT REQUEST
     LEA DX,BUFFER      ;POINT TO BUFFER WHERE STRING STORED
     INT 21H            ;CALL DOS
     RET                ;RETURN FROM SUBROUTINE TO MAIN PROGRAM;
; DISPLAY STRING TO SCREEN
SCR: MOV AH,09          ;DISPLAY REQUEST
     LEA DX,STRING      ;POINT TO STRING
     INT 21H            ;CALL DOS
     RET                ;RETURN FROM THIS SUBROUTINE;
```

Machine Code

```
0001010010110101010101010101
1110110101010101010101011100
0010100101010100101111010111
1001010010110101010101010101
0110100100110010111101011
0001000101011101010101010001
1010100101010010101011010111
0001010010110101010101010101
```

Figure 28.2
Machine code is just 1s and 0s, but assembler code is a step closer to English.

Higher-Level Languages

Programming languages are sometimes discussed in terms of generations, although these categories are somewhat arbitrary. Each successive generation is thought to contain languages that are easier to use and are more powerful than those in the previous generation. Machine languages are considered **first-generation languages,** and assembly languages are considered **second-generation languages.** The higher-level languages began with the third generation.

Third-Generation Languages

Third-generation languages (3GLs) can support structured programming, which means that they provide explicit structures for branches and loops. Because they are the first languages to use true English-like phrasing, they also make it easier for programmers to share in the development of programs. Team members can read each other's source code and understand the logic and program control flow. Figure 28.3 shows two pieces of source code, one written in BASIC, the other in C. Notice that while these third-generation languages are different from one another in their syntax, they are both fairly English-like and not too hard to follow.

Another important point to remember about third-generation languages is that these languages are **portable.** You can put the source code and a compiler or interpreter on practically any computer and create working object code (this procedure is called **porting** the code to another system). You might have to modify the source code a little when porting, especially if you are porting to a completely different kind of computer, for example, from a PC to a mainframe. As long as you have a compiler or interpreter for a given type of system, you can usually convert your source code to object code for that machine. In contrast, machine code and assembly code are highly processor-specific and must be specially written for each type of computer on which they run.

There are many higher-level languages and there is no reason why you should have to know the details of each. However, it is always helpful to know a little about the more common languages you may hear about in programming circles. Some of the fading third-generation languages include the following:

◆ **FORTRAN (FORmula TRANslator).** FORTRAN was designed specifically for mathematical and engineering programs. FORTRAN has not been widely used with personal computers. Instead, FORTRAN remains a common language on mainframe systems, especially those used for research and education.

Visit www.glencoe.com/norton/online/ for more information on third-generation languages.

Figure 28.3
Despite their special syntax, 3GLs use English-like words and phrases.

BASIC code

```
IF D& > 15 THEN
   DO WHILE D& > 1
      D& = D& - 1
   LOOP
END IF
```

C code

```
if (d > 15)
{
   do
   {
      d--;
   } while ();
}
```

- ◆ **COBOL (COmmon Business Oriented Language).** COBOL was developed in 1960 by a government-appointed committee to help solve the problem of incompatibilities among computer manufacturers. Although COBOL was once popular, especially on mainframe systems, it has lost some of its following over the past ten years. The Year 2000 Problem, however, drew many COBOL programmers out of "retirement" to help reprogram old COBOL programs to work after the year 2000.

- ◆ **BASIC (Beginner's All-Purpose Symbolic Instruction Code).** BASIC was developed in the mid-1960s, mainly as a tool for teaching programming to students. Because of its simplicity, BASIC quickly became popular. When the use of personal computers became widespread, it was the first high-level language to be implemented on these new machines. One early version of BASIC shipped on the newly popular PCs was GWBASIC. As you might have guessed, GW stands for "Gates, William" so you can see how influential Bill Gates was in the early development of PC software. Today, popular examples of BASIC include Microsoft's Visual Basic, Visual Basic for Applications (the scripting language behind Microsoft Office), and VBScript (which is common in many Web pages).

- ◆ **Pascal.** Named after the seventeenth-century French inventor Blaise Pascal, Pascal was intended in the early 1970s to overcome the limitations of other programming languages and to demonstrate the benefits of structured programming. More recently, developers have taken Pascal a step further, and it is now well-known for its implementation of object-oriented principles of programming.

Unlike the previous third-generation languages, the following languages still have a thriving following and a bright future:

- ◆ **C.** Often regarded as the thoroughbred of programming languages, C produces programs with fast and efficient executable code. C is also a powerful language. With it, you can make a computer do just about anything it is possible for a computer to do. Because of this programming freedom, C is extremely popular with professional developers, although it is now being replaced by C++.

- ◆ **C++.** C++ is the object-oriented implementation of C. Like C, C++ is an extremely powerful and efficient language. Learning C++ means learning everything about C and then learning about object-oriented programming and its implementation with C++. Nevertheless, more C programmers move to C++ every year, and the newer language has replaced C as the language of choice among software development companies.

- ◆ **Java.** Java is an object-oriented programming environment for creating cross-platform programs. When the Internet became popular in the mid-1990s, Java's developer, Sun Microsystems, redeveloped Java to become a programming environment for the Web. With Java, Web designers can create interactive and dynamic programs (called applets) for Web pages. Essentially, a Java program is a self-contained, semicompiled function that makes no reference to outside code or operating system functions. Thus, Java code is fully compatible with most any computer and operating system. To create Java code, a developer writes the applet and then compiles it into **bytecode.** To run the Java applet, a user accesses the bytecode, perhaps over the Internet. Then, using a Java virtual machine, the client PC converts the bytecode into machine code appropriate to that particular computer.

NORTON
ONLINE

Visit **www.glencoe.com/norton/online/** for more information on **Java, ActiveX,** and **other languages used in Web** development.

◆ **ActiveX.** Microsoft's answer to Java is ActiveX. ActiveX code creates self-contained functions similar to Java applets that may be accessed and executed by any other ActiveX-compatible program on any ActiveX system or network. At present, ActiveX is implemented on Windows 9*x*, Windows NT, and Macintosh systems, and there are plans for supporting UNIX also.

Of the third-generation languages, Java is probably the most important for the future development of PCs and the Internet. In fact, some developers see Java as a way of redefining the PC itself. By replacing the current expensive and platform-defining CPU with a cheap Java-decoding microchip, developers can create a machine that gets all of its software from Java servers on the Internet. To use such a machine, you would load a Web browser (also written in Java), connect to the Internet, and access Java programs for all of your software needs. If this prediction comes true, then all PCs will be both inexpensive and fully compatible.

Answer the following questions by filling in the blank(s).

1. All programming languages require users to follow certain rules of

   _____ .

2. The process of making object code from one system work on another type of system is called _____ .

3. Java applets are compiled into _____ .

Fourth-Generation Languages

Fourth-generation languages (4GLs) are programming languages that are easier to use than third-generation languages. Generally, a 4GL uses either a text environment, much like a 3GL, or a visual environment.

In the text environment, the programmer uses English-like words when generating source code. Typically, a single statement in a 4GL may perform the same tasks as many lines of a 3GL. For instance, a single 4GL line to create a database table might say:

```
Create table Customer, fields:
first_name, last_name, address, city, state, zip
```

To create a data entry form for the table, another line might say:

```
Create form Customer-Address from customer
```

In a 4GL visual environment, the programmer uses a toolbar to drag and drop various items like buttons, labels, and text boxes to create a visual definition of an application. Once the programmer has designed the appearance of the application, the programmer assigns various actions to objects on the screen. For example, a programmer may place a button on the screen and assign an action like "Open Customer table." Figure 28.4 on page 512 shows a visual development environment, in this case, Visual Basic.

As you may have guessed from the previous 4GL description, many 4GLs are database-aware; that is, you can build programs with a 4GL that work as front ends to databases. A **front end** is an interface to a program that hides much of the program from the user. Front ends are commonly used in large database applications.

NORTON ONLINE

Visit **www.glencoe.com/norton/online/** for more information on **fourth-generation languages.**

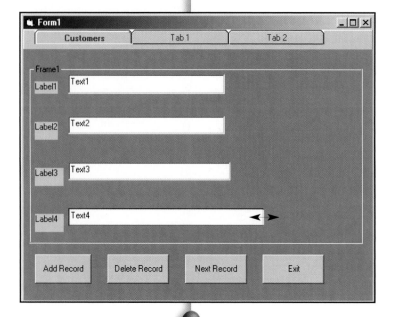

Figure 28.4

Creating a form using visual tools. For example, to place a box on a form, Visual Basic programmers simply drag the box from a toolbox onto the form. They can adjust the length of the box by dragging its borders.

Figure 28.5

The Visual Basic editor allows the programmer to design code visually or by typing code.

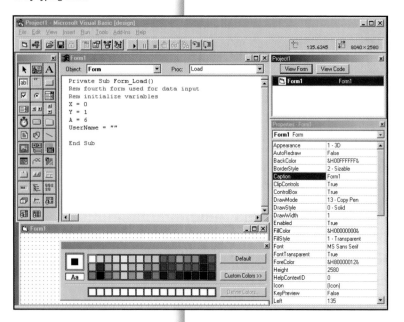

A front end typically provides users with only the tools and information they need to input data or find certain types of information from the database. These programs can include forms and dialog boxes for inputting data into databases, querying the database for information, and reporting information. Typically, much of the code required to "hook up" these dialog boxes and forms is generated automatically. A similar process in a 3GL can take pages and pages of code. Two of the more popular and robust of these developing environments are Borland's Delphi and Oracle's Developer/Designer series. With these tools, you can create huge client/server database systems with front ends that do not look like databases.

As part of the software-development process, programmers can also use 4GLs to develop prototypes of an application quickly. A **prototype** is a sample of an application that gives development teams and their clients an idea of how the finished application will look and operate before the code is finished. As a result, everyone involved in the development of the application can provide feedback on design and structural issues early in the process.

Fourth-generation languages include the following:

◆ **Visual Basic (VB).** Visual Basic is the newest incarnation of BASIC from Microsoft. VB supports object-oriented features and methods. With this language, programmers can build programs in a visual environment. Figure 28.5 shows the Visual Basic editor and a small part of the code used to create a database form similar to the one in Figure 28.4. Notice that Visual Basic offers several toolbars with lots of tools to assist the programmer in designing the code visually, as well as a window for editing code directly.

◆ **VisualAge.** VisualAge is a family of IBM development tools that allows the user to create entire Java- and Web-based systems using drag-and-drop development techniques.

◆ **Authoring Environments.** Authoring environments are special-purpose programming tools for creating multimedia, computer-based training, Web pages, and so forth. One example of an authoring environment is Macromedia Director (which uses the Lingo scripting language). You can use it to create multimedia titles combining music clips, text, animation, graphics, and so forth. As with other visual development environments, much of the code is written automatically. However, most of the robust authoring environments also include their own languages, called scripting languages, that provide tools for added control over the final product. The programs used to create World Wide Web pages fall into another category of tools that are often lumped together with authoring environments. Some of these programs include Microsoft FrontPage, Netscape Visual JavaScript, and NetObjects Fusion.

Fifth-Generation Languages

Fifth generation languages (5GLs) are actually something of a mystery. Depending on which expert you ask, they may or may not even agree that 5GLs exist. Some experts consider the more advanced development environments to be 5GLs, while others do not. In principle, a 5GL would use artificial intelligence to create software based on your description of what the software should do. This type of system is proving more difficult to invent than the code it was designed to create. Attempts at a true 5GL have been made, and a well-publicized effort by Japanese developers caused some panic among American programmers who saw their jobs threatened.

THE SYSTEMS DEVELOPMENT LIFE CYCLE FOR PROGRAMMING

Programs are the building blocks of information systems. Thus, programmers use a development process, or life cycle, that is similar to the life cycle for entire information systems. The systems development life cycle (SDLC) is detailed in Unit 13. The similar software development life cycle is discussed here.

Phase 1: Needs Analysis

Needs analysis is the stage when a need or problem is identified and understood. At this early stage, the programmer looks at the system design to see what the user needs for an interface and starting point and what the user needs the program to do. Once the programmer knows what the program's starting and stopping points are, he or she can begin to design the code.

Phase 2: Program Design

Program design is the stage at which programmers begin roughing out the logic they will use when the actual coding begins.

Many tools are used in the program design process, although programmers often rely on whiteboards and the backs of napkins. Three of these design tools are flowcharting (for structured programming), circles and message pipes (object-oriented programming), and pseudocode. Figure 28.6 shows a simple set of objects and message pipes, like those a programmer might develop when designing an object-oriented program.

Visit **www.glencoe.com/norton/online/** for more information on the **software development process, software bugs,** and **debugging.**

Figure 28.6
In the design phase, object-oriented programmers use objects and message pipes to design their programs.

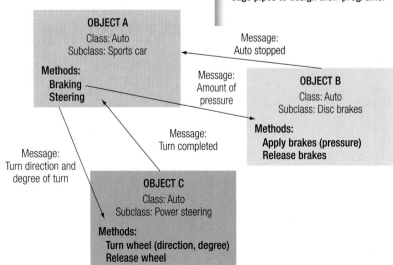

Norton Notebook

VISUAL PROGRAMMING

The object-oriented, event-driven environment of modern programming has changed how information flows through a program. It has given the control of a program's actions to the user.

In the past, programmers created program-centered processing, in which the flow of action was dictated totally by the program. Even in an interactive program, where information flowed in two directions, the central focus was always the program with its preset logic and processing path.

Object-oriented, event-driven programming has changed the programming environment by putting the user in control. The user now chooses which actions are used, chooses how each action is started, and directs the flow of the entire activity. As a result, the programmer cannot presume which objects the user will choose or the order in which they will be chosen.

Event-driven programs are designed around the interface options available to the user. An event is initiated by the user. When the user clicks an icon with the mouse, presses the Enter key, or moves the pointer on the screen, an event occurs. Each event causes an object to gather its data, structure it, and process it.

Event-driven programs are created in a visual WYSI-WYG environment that uses a visual programming language (VPL). A VPL allows the programmer to create visually the graphical images the user will see and use. The programmer combines graphical icons, forms,

The Visual Basic toolbox.

diagrams, and expressions to create two- or three-dimensional programs to run in a graphical user environment.

Some of the most commonly used visual languages are Prograph CPX for the Apple Macintosh, Microsoft's Visual Basic, and Visual C++ for the Windows environment. Visual programs for Java and scripting environments—JavaScript and VBScript—have recently emerged. These languages use graphical objects, such as icons, forms, or diagrams, to create programs that run in a visual environment. Programming in a visual language involves placing controls in the graphical presentation so that users can interact with them. Controls are the various tools through which the user can enter data, begin a process, or indicate a choice.

The Open dialog box (found in nearly all Windows-based programs), for example, is filled with various types of controls, such as buttons, lists, text boxes, and more. Placing controls on a graphical environment typically is done using the drag-and-drop technique. The programmer chooses the control to be made available to the user for an event and places it on the window form. Usually, the available controls are contained in a menu, list, or dialog box for the programmer's ease of access and use, as in the Visual Basic toolbox.

Visual programming is much easier for the programmer because it is based on how a programmer (and the user) sees items on the screen rather than on the structure of the program. As in many other areas of computer software, the visual interface is making highly complex functions accessible to the everyday user.

The Windows Open dialog box.

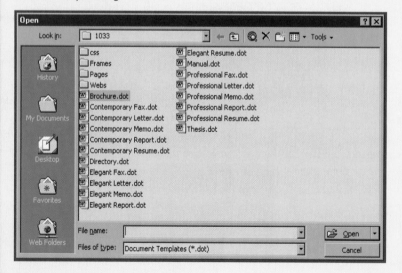

514

Figure 28.7 shows a flowchart used for developing a structured program.

Phase 3: Development

Development (also called coding) involves writing and testing source code. The software development phase is similar to the system life cycle's development phase, but instead of determining the system's overall layout, the programmer writes the code that implements the system's needs. The programmer might write source code in a text editor and then compile the code, or he or she may use a visual editor and create a picture of the application before compiling the code. Most of the time required to complete a program is spent in this phase using the programming languages you've been learning about.

Despite their best efforts, programmers inevitably create errors, or **bugs,** in their programs. There are two main types of errors, syntax errors and logic errors. **Syntax errors** violate the rules of the programming language. A compiler will locate and identify most syntax errors automatically. **Logic errors** are mistakes that cause the program to run in unexpected or incorrect ways. The process of identifying and eliminating these errors is called **debugging.** Figure 28.8 shows a list of syntax errors found by a C compiler. You can see by their cryptic nature that the programmer has to have some special knowledge to understand the errors and fix them.

Phase 4: Implementation

Implementation involves installing software and allowing users to test it. This step often includes a lot of documenting, both inside the code and in the form of manuals for the users. More than one programmer will also tell you that they do most of their debugging at this stage. Certainly it is the stage where any misconceptions the programmer had about the code are found and fixed.

Phase 5: Maintenance

Maintenance starts as soon as the program is installed. Work continues on products for several reasons. Some minor bugs may not have been fixed at the time the program was released. The programmers may also add major new functioning, in response to either market demands or user requests.

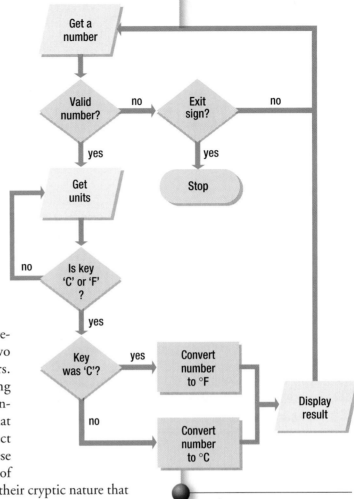

Figure 28.7
Structured programmers use flowcharts, like this one that converts degrees Celsius and Fahrenheit, to design their programs.

Figure 28.8
Compilers help programmers locate and fix syntax errors.

COMPUTERS
in your career

Careers in Programming

The growth in the economy and the popularity of graphics games and the Internet are driving a programming boom. And, not only are programming jobs available, they are getting more and more interesting. Programming jobs tend to be grouped into the following broad categories:

◆ **Scientific Programmer.** These programmers use a specialized knowledge of science and engineering to develop high-tech programs. Scientific programmers work in fields like aerospace engineering, meteorology, oceanography, and astronomy. They help program the space shuttle, the National Weather Service computers, deep-sea robotic submersibles, and deep-space probes.

◆ **Business Programmer.** Almost every business has a need for computers and every one of those computers needs programs. So there is a strong demand for programmers who combine a knowledge of programming with a knowledge of business operations. Among other tasks, these programmers develop databases, spreadsheets, accounting packages, and billing systems. In addition to the programmers that create these applications, other programmers create custom programs that work within the applications.

◆ **Operating System Programmer.** Of course, every computer and computer-controlled machine needs an operating system and some kind of programmed control. In some cases, like PCs, the programmers develop operating systems like DOS, Windows, or UNIX. The current success of the UNIX-based Linux operating system is creating a lot of excitement in the operating system industry. In the case of industrial machines, programmers develop special-purpose languages to control the equipment. For example, computer-controlled milling machines and robotic welders all need programming.

◆ **Entertainment Programmer.** Few programming environments are booming quite like the gaming industry. Game programmers develop everything from educational software to video games. In every case, the programmers must combine a strong knowledge of game theory with graphics and multimedia programming.

◆ **Web Programmer.** The World Wide Web has created a whole new programming field. Naturally, the existence of the Web has created a demand for HTML and Java programmers. However, the Web also fuels a demand for programmers who can develop tools that allow the Web to provide multimedia content. Because the Web is still in its infancy, no one can predict what Web content is likely to develop or what will be popular and what will fail.

NORTON ONLINE

Visit **www.glencoe.com/norton/online/** for more information on **careers in programming**.

LESSON QUIZ

True/False

Answer the following questions by circling True or False.

True False **1.** Machine languages are the most advanced of all programming languages.

True False **2.** BASIC stands for Beginner's All-Purpose Symbolic Instruction Code.

True False **3.** A major drawback of 4GLs is that they are not database-aware.

True False **4.** The systems development life cycle for programming is similar to the SDLC used for creating information systems.

True False **5.** The two primary software bugs are syntax errors and arithmetic errors.

Multiple Choice

Circle the word or phrase that best completes each sentence.

1. The syntax of a programming language may require that specific _____ be used.
 A. structures   **B.** symbols   **C.** both A and B

2. _____ are seldom used except to fine-tune important parts of programs written in a higher-level language.
 A. Compilers   **B.** Assembly languages **C.** Neither A nor B

3. FORTRAN and COBOL are examples of _____ languages.
 A. third-generation **B.** fourth-generation **C.** fifth-generation

4. A _____ is an interface to a program that hides much of the program from the user.
 A. report   **B.** database   **C.** front end

5. Programmers begin roughing out the logic they will use in the _____ stage of the software SDLC.
 A. program design **B.** development **C.** implementation

LESSON LABS

Complete the following exercises as directed by your instructor.

1. Using a text editor like Notepad and the following commands, write a pseudocode algorithm that goes through a finite list of numbers and places all of the even numbers into one list and all of the odd numbers in another list. Use these commands: While, get number, if/then/else, put number in even list, put number in odd list. Leave the editor open for the next exercise.

2. Using the same editor from Lesson Lab 1, review your pseudocode and add documentation to explain what the pseudocode does. Remember, the more documentation you add, the easier it is for others to understand your logic.

LESSON 27: Creating Computer Programs

What Is a Computer Program?

- Software is the intelligence that runs the hardware in a computer.

- A computer program is a set of commands that tell the CPU what to do. Software may contain only an executable program file, or it may have several other supporting files such as dynamic link libraries, initialization files, and help files.

Hardware/Software Interaction

- To create a program, a programmer creates source code, which is compiled or interpreted to create object code. Object code, also known as machine code, is the binary language file that tells the CPU what to do.

How Programs Solve Problems

- The order in which program statements are executed is called program flow control.

- Programmers use algorithms and heuristics to solve problems.

- Variables are placeholders for data being processed.

- Functions are discrete sets of code used to perform one task.

Structured and Object-Oriented Programming

- Structured programming uses functions built up along a logical program flow to perform each task in the algorithm or heuristic.

- Object-oriented programming allows a programmer to think modularly because programs are assembled into components called objects.

- An object is a self-contained unit containing functions and attributes. Every object falls into a class, and each class may contain several subclasses of objects.

- Objects talk to one another using messages.

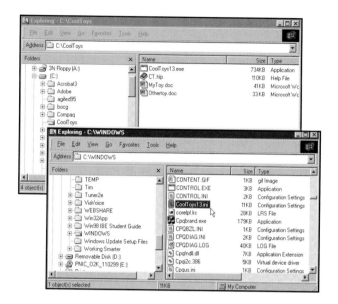

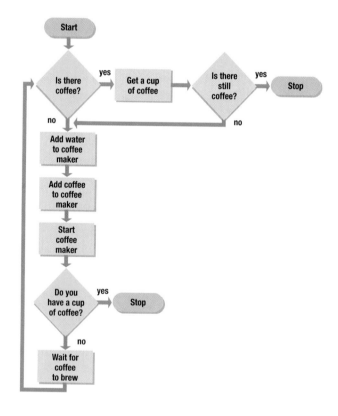

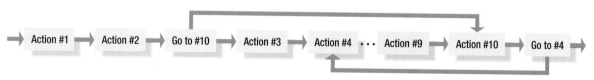

LESSON 28: Programming Languages and the Programming Process

The Evolution of Programming Languages

- The only real computer language is machine language, a series of binary digits that is meaningless to people but understood by computers.

- Programming languages can be placed into one of three basic categories: machine language, assembly language, and higher-level languages.

- Higher-level languages allow the programmer to create programs using English-like words and phrases. Some fourth-generation languages include visual environments that allow the programmer to draw the final outcome of his or her program.

```
SyntaxSample.c - Notepad
File  Edit  Search  Help

#include <stdio.h>

/* main excepts arguments from user */
main(argc, argv)
int argc;
char *argc[];
{
        int a, b;        /* a and b are counters */
        for (a=0;a<argc;a++)    /* loop through each word of main's arguments */
        {
                b=0;
                while (argv[a][b])      /* loop through each word */
                {
                        printf("%c", argv[a][b]);
                        b++;
                }
        }
}
```

The Systems Development Life Cycle for Programming

- Needs analysis is the stage when a need or problem is identified and understood.

- During program design, programmers use flowcharts, pseudocode, and message pipes to plan the programming process.

- Program development includes coding, compiling or interpreting, and debugging.

- Implementation involves installing software and allowing users to test it.

- After implementation, programs must be maintained with bug fixes and updated versions.

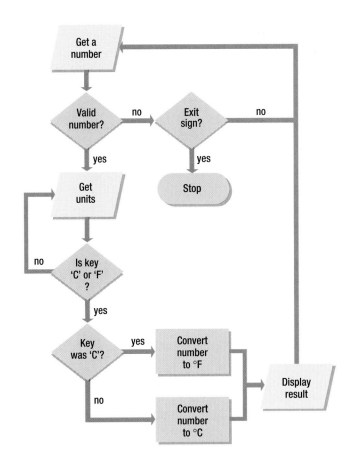

KEY TERMS

After completing this unit, you should be able to define the following terms.

algorithm, *492*
argument, *499*
assembler, *508*
assembly language, *508*
attribute, *502*
branch, *501*
bug, *515*
bytecode, *510*
class, *503*
class inheritance, *503*
compiler, *490*
conditional statement, *495*
data member, *503*
debug, *515*
dynamic link library (.dll) file, *488*
encapsulate, *502*
executable (.exe) file, *488*
exit condition, *497*
fifth-generation language (5GL), *513*
first-generation language, *509*
flowchart, *491*
fourth-generation language (4GL), *511*

front end, *511*
function, *499*
goto statement, *501*
help (.hlp) file, *488*
heuristics, *493*
higher-level language, *508*
initialization (.ini) file, *488*
instantiate, *503*
interpreter, *491*
interrupt, *489*
logic error, *515*
loop, *497*
looping structure, *501*
machine code, *490*
machine language, *490*
member function, *503*
message, *503*
object, *501*
object code, *490*
object-oriented programming (OOP), *501*
parameter, *499*

porting, *509*
portable, *509*
procedure, *500*
program control flow, *491*
programming language, *490*
prototype, *512*
pseudocode, *491*
repetition structure, *501*
return, *499*
routine, *500*
second-generation language, *509*
selection structure, *501*
sequence structure, *501*
source code, *490*
structured programming, *501*
subclass, *503*
subroutine, *500*
syntax, *507*
syntax error, *515*
third-generation language (3GL), *509*
variable, *499*

KEY TERMS QUIZ

Fill in each blank with one of the terms listed under Key Terms.

1. A(n) _____ file contains configuration information that helps a program start running.

2. Programmers use _____ to convert all of the source code for a program into machine code, thus creating an executable file.

3. The order in which program statements are executed is called _____ .

4. A(n) _____ is a set of steps that always leads to a solution.

5. A loop will repeat itself until a(n) _____ is met.

6. A(n) _____ identifies a different line of the program to which control jumps.

7. In object-oriented programming, any object may _____ other objects.

8. _____ languages are so named because their syntax is closer to human language than assembly or machine language code.

9. A(n) _____ is a sample of an application and gives an idea of how the finished application will look and operate.

10. Programmers debate whether _____ languages actually exist.

REVIEW QUESTIONS

In your own words, briefly answer the following questions.

1. What is an executable file?
2. Describe the difference between a compiler and an interpreter.
3. What is an algorithm?
4. Conditional statements and loops are examples of what?
5. Different computer languages call a "function" by a different name. What names may be used?
6. What is meant by "porting" code from one system to another?
7. What is a prototype?
8. What are the five phases of the systems development life cycle as applied to software development?
9. In the systems development life cycle for software, during what phase do programmers begin roughing out the logic they will use when the actual coding begins?
10. What are the two most common types of bugs found in software programs?

DISCUSSION QUESTIONS

As directed by your instructor, discuss the following questions in class or in groups.

1. Do you think it would be easier to write programs with a structured or an object-oriented programming language? Why?
2. When building their information systems, many organizations choose to create their own proprietary software from scratch instead of buying off-the-shelf software. Why do you think they choose this option? Can you think of an example where this approach would be necessary?

 ETHICAL ISSUES
Programming is a powerful tool that represents considerable processing and economic power. With this thought in mind, discuss the following questions in class:

1. Assume a programmer is attempting to develop a true artificial intelligence. If the programmer is successful, what are the ethical implications? Should the program be considered alive? If so, does the program have basic human rights? Is it ethical to turn the program off? Should the program be allowed to interact with other artificially intelligent computers? Can the program be guilty of a crime or the victim of a crime? What responsibility does the programmer bear in this scenario?

2. Discuss the implications of computer piracy. What happens to the economy when users pirate software and why? What happens to software innovation and why? What other problems may arise due to software piracy? What role should the government play in combating piracy?

You and the Computer

Other than a PC with a text editor and Web browser, you do not need any other materials to do the following exercise:

1. **Creating a JavaScript.** As you learned in the section on 4GLs, some authoring environments include their own programming languages, for example, the Web page programming languages HTML and JavaScript. HTML is the code used to format Web pages; JavaScript is sort of a mini-Java used to control specific actions and appearances within a Web page. In this exercise, you will create a small HTML page that displays the word *Hello!* You will also create a JavaScript to perform a "mouseover." In a mouseover, the text in the Web page changes appearance as the mouse cursor rolls over the text. Once your code is written, you will test it in your Web browser. (*Note:* This JavaScript works only in Microsoft Internet Explorer.)

   A. Open Notepad and type in the following HTML code, exactly as shown here, including blank spaces:

   ```
   <HTML>
   <HEAD>
   <TITLE>Mouse Rollover</TITLE>
   <style>
   <!—
   a:link {
   background: #088;
   color: #fff;
   font-family: arial, sans-serif;
   text-decoration: none;
   font-weight: bold;
   }
   a:hover {
   background: #403;
   color: #fff;
   font-family: arial, sans-serif;
   text-decoration: none; font-weight: bold;
   }
   —>
   </style>
   </HEAD>
   <body>
   <P><CENTER><font face="Arial"><A HREF="yourlink.htm">HELLO!</A></font></p>
   </BODY>
   </HTML>
   ```

   B. Save the HTML file as Test.html and close Notepad.

   C. Open Internet Explorer and then, within the browser, open Test.html. You should see the word *Hello!*

   D. Move your mouse cursor over the word *Hello!* Notice that the text's background changes to a different color. The change is caused by the "mouseover" code. When you are finished demonstrating your code, close your Web browser.

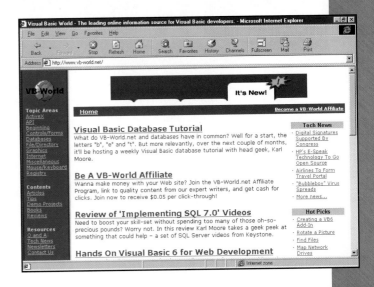

UNIT LABS

Internet Labs

To complete the following exercises, you need a computer with an Internet connection and a Web browser. (For more information on using these tools, see "Prerequisites" at the front of this textbook.)

1. Programmers are responsible for creating much of the Internet, so there is plenty of programming information available on the Internet. To find more basic information about programming, visit the following Web sites:

   • Introduction to Object-Oriented Programming Using C++—**http://www.zib.de/Visual /people/mueller/Course/Tutorial/tutorial.html**

   • Internet Resource Center— **http://www.itmweb.com/ooprogram.htm**

   • VB-World—**http://www.vb-world.net/**

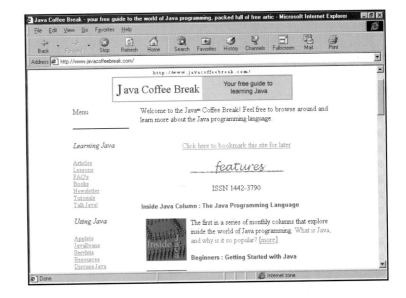

2. When you surf the Web, the pages you see are written using HTML and Java code. As you can imagine, more and more programmers are learning HTML and Java to further their careers. To learn more about HTML and Java, visit the following Web sites:

   • CNET's Builder.com— **http://www.cnet.com /webbuilding/0-3880.html**

   • Java Coffee Break, online tutorial—**http://www .javacoffeebreak.com/**

   • JavaSoft, news and reviews— **http://www.javasoft.com/**

IBE Labs

If you have the Interactive Browser Edition (IBE) CD-ROM for this textbook, you may complete the following interactive exercises using the instructions provided in the IBE.

1. **Crossword Puzzle.** Use the clues provided to complete the puzzle.

2. **Labeling.** The focus of this exercise is on the key phases of systems development.

3. **What's Your Recommendation?** Based on the scenarios provided, you must suggest the best programming approach.

4. **Dissect a Software Program.** Identify the programming structure used.

UNIT 15

Living With Computers

UNIT CONTENTS

This unit contains the following lessons:

LESSON 29

Computers and the Individual

OVERVIEW:
The Computer's Impact on You

As you have learned throughout this book, computers are wonderful tools. They help us work more productively, they provide new opportunities for communication and education, and they can be entertaining. For these reasons and others, many people find themselves spending increasing amounts of time using their computer and the Internet.

Despite all the advantages of computer use, however, there are also disadvantages. Although it may be hard to believe that a PC can pose a threat to its user, consider the caution we exercise when using any other appliance or tool. We carefully choose the television programs that children watch to ensure that they do not view inappropriate material. When operating a vehicle or a power tool, we are cautious to protect not only ourselves but also those around us.

It also makes sense to be cautious when using a computer, especially if you use the Internet regularly. Careless use of computers can result in physical injuries. Careless use of the Internet can result in a loss of privacy. These issues affect individual computer users every day—and may affect you directly or indirectly—whether they work with computers in business or use them at home or school.

OBJECTIVES

- Define the term *ergonomics* and list three health risks related to computer use.
- Define the terms *spamming* and *spoofing* and explain how they affect computer users.
- Name two normal activities that result in a threat to personal privacy.
- List four reasons why a business may monitor employees' use of its systems.

ERGONOMICS AND HEALTH ISSUES

Any office worker will tell you that sitting at a desk all day can become extremely uncomfortable. Sitting all day and using a computer can be even worse. Not only does the user's body ache from being in a chair too long, but hand and wrist injuries can result from keyboarding or from using a mouse for long periods, and eyes can become strained by staring at a monitor. Such injuries can be extreme, threatening the victim's general health and ability to work.

Much is being done to make computers easier, safer, and more comfortable to use. **Ergonomics,** the study of the physical relationship between people and their tools—such as their computers—addresses these issues. Thanks to the publicity that computer-related injuries have received over the past decade, most people now recognize the importance of ergonomically correct computer furniture and proper techniques for using the computer. (The term *ergonomically correct* means that a product is designed to work properly with the human body, reducing the risk of strain, stress, or other types of injuries.)

Repetitive Stress Injuries

The field of ergonomics did not receive much attention until **repetitive stress injuries (RSIs)**—a group of ailments caused by continuously using the body in ways it was not designed to work—began appearing among clerical workers who spend most of their time entering data on computer keyboards. One injury that is especially well documented among these workers is **carpal tunnel syndrome,** a wrist or hand injury caused by extended periods of keyboarding.

The carpal tunnel is a passageway in the wrist through which a bundle of nerves passes. In carpal tunnel syndrome, the tunnel becomes misshapen because the victim has held the wrists stiffly for long periods, as people tend to do at a keyboard. When the tunnel becomes distorted, it can pinch the nerves that run through it, causing tingling, numbness, pain, or an inability to use the hands. Carpal tunnel syndrome is the best-known repetitive stress injury. It can become so debilitating that employees suffering from it have to take weeks or even months off work. In some extreme cases, surgery is required.

If you routinely use a computer, you can avoid fatigue and strain by choosing the proper furniture for your workspace. Perhaps the most important piece of computer furniture is a comfortable, ergonomically designed chair, like those shown in Figure 29.1. Look for three characteristics in any office chair:

- ◆ Adjustable height
- ◆ Lower-back support
- ◆ Armrests (preferably adjustable)

Your desk should also be well-suited to computer use, like the one shown in Figure 29.2. Your desk should hold your keyboard and mouse at the proper height. Ideally, your hands should be at the same height as your elbows, or a few inches lower, when they hover above the keyboard.

Another important factor in avoiding keyboard-related RSIs is the keyboard itself. A few years ago, keyboard designers realized that a flat keyboard is

Figure 29.1
Ergonomically designed chairs.

not well-suited to the shape of our hands. If you relax your arms, your thumbs tend to point up. Logically, then, keyboards should be designed with two sides, one for each hand. Ergonomic keyboards allow the user's hands to rest in a more natural position than traditional flat keyboards.

If you type a great deal, a padded wrist support can also help. The support can be built onto the keyboard (see Figure 29.3) or placed in front of it. A wrist support allows you to rest your hands comfortably when you are not actually typing. Remember, however, that you should never rest your wrists on anything—even a comfortable wrist support—while you type. Use the support only when your fingers are not moving over the keyboard.

Figure 29.2
A properly designed computer desk features a built-in shelf or tray to hold the keyboard and mouse.

Figure 29.3
Ergonomically designed keyboards are available in several shapes and sizes. On this model, the keyboard is divided into two sections, allowing the hands to remain in a more natural position. It also features a built-in wrist pad.

Eyestrain

Eyestrain is the most frequently reported health problem associated with computers. Here are some ways to protect your vision and reduce eyestrain:

◆ Avoid staring at the screen for long stretches of time.

◆ Remember to blink. Lack of blinking causes dryness of the eye and eyestrain.

◆ Position your monitor between 2 and 2½ feet away from your eyes.

◆ Position your monitor so that no light reflects off the screen. If you cannot avoid reflections, purchase an antiglare screen like the one shown in Figure 29.4.

◆ Keep your screen clean.

◆ Look for a monitor that holds a steady image without appearing to pulsate or flicker. Make sure that the dot pitch is no greater than .28 mm and the refresh rate is at least 72 Hz.

Figure 29.4
An antiglare screen cuts down reflections on a monitor's surface. It is useful in bright offices or in cases where a window faces the monitor.

Electromagnetic Fields

Electromagnetic fields (EMFs) are created during the generation, transmission, and use of low-frequency electrical power. These fields exist near power lines, electrical appliances, and any piece of equipment that has an electric motor. A debate has continued for years whether EMFs can be linked to cancer. There is enough data, however, to raise suspicion.

EMFs are composed of an electrical and a magnetic component. Of the two, the magnetic field is the one that raises the health concern. Electrical fields lose strength when they come in contact with barriers such as clothing and skin. A magnetic field, however, will penetrate most materials, even concrete or lead. Magnetic fields attenuate—lose strength rapidly—with distance. Options to reduce your risk from EMFs include the following:

◆ Take frequent breaks away from the computer.

◆ Sit at arm's length away from the system unit and monitor.

◆ Use a flat-panel display, which does not radiate EMFs.

Answer the following questions by filling in the blank(s).

1. If a product is _____ , it has been designed to work properly with the human body to reduce strain or injuries.

2. Carpal tunnel syndrome is an example of a(n) _____ .

3. To reduce eyestrain, a monitor's _____ should be no greater than .28 mm.

PRIVACY ISSUES

As people use their computers, they generally assume that their activities are private and their personal information is safe. Unfortunately, this is not always true, especially when people use the Internet. For example, commercial Web sites often collect information from visitors. Many companies then sell this information, sometimes against the wishes of the individual. Privacy advocates view this practice as an invasion of the individual's privacy because it involves trading a person's private information such as address, phone number, social security number, and so on.

The collection and use of information is an important issue for many individuals. Consider the many ways in which electronic databases are used. Information provided for items such as magazine subscriptions and warranty or registration cards is often sold to national marketing organizations. In addition to data about your purchasing or subscription habits, there are also electronic records about your credit history, which many companies check before opening a new account for you. Before they accept you as a patient, doctors can find out whether you have ever filed a malpractice suit. Before accepting you as a tenant, landlords can see whether you have ever filed a complaint against another landlord. Are all these databases legal? They are. Are people using the information in these databases in morally acceptable ways,

NORTON
ONLINE

Visit **www.glencoe.com/norton/online/** for more information on **checking your credit report online.**

PRODUCTIVITY Tip

Tips for Healthy Computing

Although they may sound like minor ailments, RSIs can be serious—even crippling. Severe cases of carpal tunnel syndrome, for example, have been known to end their victims' careers. If you use a computer frequently, you can avoid RSIs by adopting good habits, such as the following:

◆ **Choose a Good Chair and Computer Desk.** Look for a chair that provides back support, armrests, and adjustable height. Your computer desk should hold the keyboard level with or slightly below your hands, and your forearms should be held parallel to the floor. The desk should allow you to change the keyboard's height. You should not have to reach up, forward, or down to touch the keyboard.

◆ **Position Your Monitor Correctly.** Place your monitor directly in front of you, about 2 to 2½ feet away, and a little below eye level. Tilt the monitor's face upward about 10 degrees. This angle will enable you to view the monitor comfortably without bending your neck. If you have vision problems that require corrective lenses, however, consult an optometrist about the best way to position your monitor.

◆ **Sit Up Straight.** Do not slouch as you type, and keep your feet flat on the floor in front of you. Do not cross your legs in front of you or under your chair for long periods.

◆ **Keep Your Wrists Straight.** Your hands should be in a straight line with your forearms as you type and when viewed either from above or from the side. If you keep your wrists bent in either direction, you can cause muscle fatigue and increase your risk of injuries.

An example of an ergonomically correct computer setup. The forearms and thighs are parallel to the floor, the keyboard is within easy reach to avoid bending or flexing the wrists, and the monitor is positioned to reduce eye and neck strain.

◆ **Do Not Rest Your Wrists on Anything as You Type.** If you have a wrist support, use it only when you are resting your hands, not when you are actually typing. Resting the wrist while typing disables the forearms from moving the hands and puts undue strain on the hands and fingers. Think of pianists, who do not rest their wrists on anything as they play, and they keep their wrists straight.

◆ **Learn to Type.** You will use the keyboard more efficiently and naturally if you learn how to type. If you hunt and peck, you probably slouch and keep your head down while looking at the keyboard. This technique not only hurts productivity but leads to fatigue and stiffness.

◆ **Rest Your Eyes Occasionally.** Eyestrain develops from staring at a fixed distance for too long. Even if you cannot get up, look around you and focus on different objects at various distances.

◆ **Set Your Monitor for Healthy Viewing.** Even if your monitor can operate at high resolution, it is not necessarily the best setting for your eyes. At higher resolutions, text and icons appear smaller on the screen, which can lead to squinting and eyestrain.

◆ **Take Frequent Breaks.** Get up and move around, and stretch occasionally during the day.

When typing, your hands should be in a straight line with your forearms at all times and when viewed from any angle. A split keyboard layout can help maintain the proper position.

Figure 29.5

Although it is now illegal to send unsolicited junk faxes without the sender's identification, junk fax messages are still common. These messages waste time, money, and resources.

Visit **www.glencoe.com/norton/online/** for more information on the anti-junk fax law.

and should people be allowed to sell or exchange such information? That question is more difficult.

Many computer users also see the distribution of junk faxes and junk e-mail as another form of privacy invasion. When your e-mail inbox or fax machine is clogged with unsolicited commercial messages as shown in Figure 29.5, time and energy must be spent reviewing and removing the uninvited messages. This activity equates to lost productivity for many individuals and businesses.

Junk Faxes and E-Mail

As fax machines gained popularity in homes and offices during the mid-1980s, people found their machines printing **junk faxes**—unsolicited and unwanted messages received from unnamed senders. Junk faxes, like junk mail, usually invite the recipient to purchase a product or service, to call a salesperson, or to consider a get-rich-quick scheme.

Congress passed an "anti-junk fax" law in 1991, which prohibits anyone from sending a fax without including an identifier and return phone number. Efforts are also under way in most states to toughen state and local anti-junk fax laws.

Junk e-mail is a lot like old-fashioned junk mail; that is, you open your electronic mailbox and find that it contains unwanted messages from various senders (see Figure 29.6). Like traditional junk mail, junk e-mail usually includes solicitations to purchase a product or service or invitations to participate in get-rich-quick schemes. Some junk e-mail messages, however, are filled with lewd—even obscene—material.

The two most popular tricks used by junk e-mailers are spamming and spoofing. In **spamming**, the sender (called a **spammer**) sends hundreds, thousands, or even tens of thousands of messages (called **spam**) at the same time to recipients across a wide geographic area. Spammers are very creative when it comes to procuring the

Figure 29.6

Any user of an Internet or online e-mail service runs the risk of receiving junk e-mail, or spam.

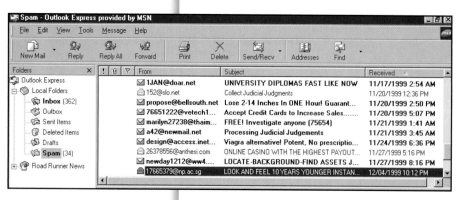

e-mail addresses of their recipients. Some rely on mailing lists purchased or hacked from the databases of legitimate marketers or service providers. Others simply use programs that generate addresses randomly based on the domain names of known Internet Service Providers (ISPs).

Regardless of how they obtain addresses, spammers are notorious for sending messages repeatedly, operating under the age-old marketing premise that if only a handful of recipients respond to the message, then the effort has shown a positive result.

Therefore, spammers frequently sell their services to both legitimate and illegitimate organizations, which hope the huge mailings will generate sales or responses.

A more difficult technique, called **spoofing,** enables the junk e-mailer to hide his or her identity from the recipient. In spoofing, the sender places a false return address on the junk message. When spoofed, the recipient has no idea who sent the message and has no way of responding or stopping the problem. Spoofing can even fool e-mail service providers when they attempt to help customers stem the flow of junk e-mail.

Currently, there is no comprehensive national law regulating spam (a few state laws are now in effect, and their effectiveness is being tested), but experts agree that federal laws should be in place within the next few years. While lawmakers discuss the issue, many ISPs have taken actions of their own to minimize junk e-mail, ranging from the use of filtering software to massive lawsuits. In one case, America Online (whose servers process an estimated 30 million pieces of e-mail daily, about 30 percent of which are spam) won a lawsuit against a spammer who relentlessly clogged the mailboxes of customers with junk e-mail.

Beating Spammers at Their Own Game

If you have an e-mail account and receive unwanted or unsolicited e-mail messages, you can try some strategies that may eliminate—or at least reduce—the junk mail in your inbox.

Start by working with your Internet Service Provider. Visit the ISP's Web site or call a customer service representative and check the company's policy regarding the use of its services, including e-mail. This policy is typically called an **appropriate use policy** (see Figure 29.7), and any reputable ISP should have one. An appropriate use policy should state how customers are permitted to use the ISP's resources and the penalties that can occur if a customer misuses any service. Most ISPs do not tolerate the use of their e-mail servers for the distribution of unsolicited e-mail messages, and they typically reserve the right to terminate service to anyone who knowingly violates the rules of the appropriate use policy. If your ISP does not have such a policy, encourage the provider to adopt one quickly or start looking for a new provider.

Some ISPs provide users with access to services such as Spaminator, a program that filters spam at the e-mail server. Using a database that consists of known spammers, the filtering service looks for incoming messages from known spammers and

Visit **www.glencoe.com/norton/online/** for more information on **spam** and **organizations combating spam.**

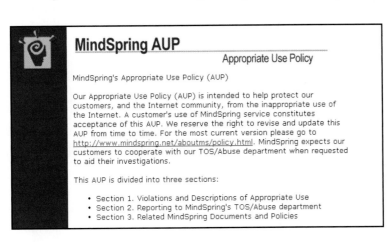

Figure 29.7
Your ISP should post its policies for appropriate use of its services. This document, found at MindSpring's Web site, explains MindSpring's policies regarding the use of e-mail, newsgroups, and other services.

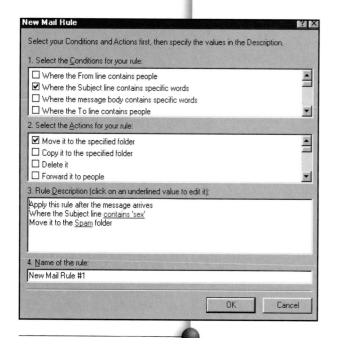

Figure 29.8
Setting a new mail filter (called a "rule") in Microsoft Outlook Express.

software programs that send bulk messages. These mailings—as well as messages with no originating address—are refused by the server and do not make it to the customer's mailbox.

As an added precaution, you may be able to use filters in your e-mail program to block out junk e-mail (see Figure 29.8). Microsoft Outlook, Netscape Messenger, Eudora Pro, and other e-mail clients provide simple filtering tools.

Several commercial Web-based services can also help you minimize junk e-mail. You can register your e-mail address with services such as NoThankYou (**www.nothankyou.com/**). For a fee, they will notify known junk e-mailers that you want to be removed from the mailing lists. Services such as Zero Junk Mail (**www.zerojunkmail.com/**) provide specialized filtering software to help you prevent spam from reaching your computer.

Privacy Issues Facing Corporate Computer Users

Another threat to privacy can occur between a company and its employees. Although some people contend that businesses have no right to monitor their employees' use of communications systems, the opposite is true. In a business setting, the computers, network, communications equipment, and software are usually the property of the company. By extension, all information contained on the system or carried by the system is also the property of the company (see Figure 29.9).

Many companies routinely monitor their employees' communications. Why would a company institute such a policy? There are several compelling reasons:

◆ To protect trade secrets

◆ To prevent the distribution of libelous or slanderous messages

◆ To prevent the system's users from downloading or copying data that is illegal, pornographic, or infected by computer viruses

◆ To ensure that organizational resources are not being wasted or abused

Figure 29.9
In the workplace, always remember that the computer systems—and the data stored on them, even your e-mail messages—is considered the company's property.

Norton Notebook

PROTECTING YOUR ONLINE PRIVACY

Information about our private lives is available to a degree unimaginable just a few years ago. With the Internet's explosion in popularity, people are revealing more about themselves than ever before. Some examples follow:

◆ If you purchase an item over the World Wide Web, you not only provide the seller with your e-mail address but you often include your credit card number. Many e-commerce Web sites also request other personal information, such as telephone numbers and mailing addresses.

◆ Many Web sites that offer special services—such as travel planning, job hunting, or car buying—require clients to complete forms that store vast amounts of information about them.

◆ If you post a message to an Internet newsgroup or participate in a chat room discussion, you reveal your e-mail address and interests to anyone who happens to be in the group at that time.

As an online consumer, you leave a trail of information about yourself wherever you go. This trail can be followed by marketers, spammers, hackers, and thieves right back to your PC—or even to your doorstep. There is not a lot you can do after your information has fallen into the wrong hands. You can take measures, however, to prevent too many people from getting that information,

especially if you use the Internet or an online service regularly. Here are some tips that can help:

◆ **Avoid Being Added to Mailing Lists.** When you fill out a warranty, subscription, or registration form—either on paper or online—make sure it includes an option that prevents your information from being added to a mailing list. If the option is available, check it; if it is not, do not return the form. If there is any doubt, contact the organization and learn its policies regarding mailing lists.

◆ **Make Online Purchases Only Through Secure Web Sites.** Before you purchase anything over the Internet, make sure that the transaction is secure. You can protect your privacy in two ways. First, if you use a current browser, such as Internet Explorer 5.0 or Netscape Navigator 5.0, the browser can tell you whether the server is secure. Check your browser's security settings before proceeding with a transaction. Second, check the vendor's Web site to see whether you have the option to switch to a secure server before making the transaction. If this option is available, take it.

◆ **Never Assume That Your E-Mail Is Private.** Watch what you say, especially when using your company's or school's e-mail system. Never respond to an unsolicited e-mail message, especially if you do not recognize the sender.

◆ **Be Careful When Posting to Newsgroups.** Many Internet newsgroups and chat rooms are unsupervised. If you post a message to a group, your e-mail address and interests can make you easy prey for spammers and pranksters. Before posting a message to any group, watch the group for a few days to determine whether its users are trustworthy. Try to find out if the group is supervised by a system operator and get that person's address, if possible.

◆ **Don't Flame.** An online argument can have disastrous results. There are many documented cases of ISPs being shut down by spam as a result of a flame—a critical or insulting message—posted by one of the ISP's users. This practice can result in a loss of online privacy and in your Internet service being cut off by the ISP. Resist the urge to be critical or argumentative online.

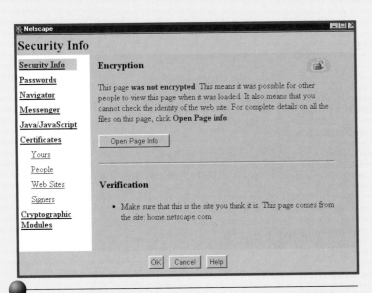

Current browsers can tell you whether a Web site is secure. In Netscape Navigator, for example, the security tool displays a window of information about the Web page that is currently open.

LESSON QUIZ

True/False

Answer the following questions by circling True or False.

True	False	**1.** Injuries to the hand or wrist can result from using a keyboard for long periods.
True	False	**2.** An ergonomic office chair should not have armrests.
True	False	**3.** When typing, you should set the chair and keyboard so that you must reach up to touch the keys.
True	False	**4.** It is illegal to send a fax without including an identifier and return telephone number.
True	False	**5.** Any reputable ISP should have an appropriate use policy.

Multiple Choice

Circle the word or phrase that best completes each sentence.

1. If a product is ergonomically correct, it is designed to _____ .
   A. work properly with the human body   **B.** reduce the risk of injuries   **C.** both A and B

2. To help reduce eyestrain, your monitor should be placed _____ away from your eyes.
   A. 1 to 1½ feet   **B.** 2 to 2½ feet   **C.** 3 to 3½ feet

3. Another term for sending junk e-mail messages is _____ .
   A. spamming   **B.** spoofing   **C.** either A or B

4. Your e-mail software should enable you to create _____ , which can block out some junk e-mail messages.
   A. filters   **B.** spaminators   **C.** trash

5. Spammers gather personal information from various sources, including _____ .
   A. mailing lists   **B.** credit reports   **C.** both A and B

LESSON LABS

Complete the following exercise as directed by your instructor.

Working with a classmate, sit at your computer as you normally do and place your hands at the keyboard as though you are typing in your usual way. Have your classmate answer the following questions:

Question	Answer
A. How far is the monitor from your face?	_____
B. When typing, are your hands and wrists in line with your arms?	_____
C. When typing, are your forearms parallel to the floor?	_____
D. Must you strain or squint to view text or icons on the screen?	_____
E. Are you sitting with your feet on the floor in front of you?	_____
F. Is the mouse next to the keyboard?	_____

Computing Issues That Affect Us All

OVERVIEW:
Computers, Society, and the Environment

As you learned in Lesson 29, privacy and health-related issues face individual computer users every day. On a larger scale, however, the entire computing community deals with more far-reaching problems. It is true that, like spamming, these concerns affect many individuals, but they have an impact on large segments of society and therefore are being addressed as societal problems.

Chief among these problems are computer-related crimes, such as hacking and the distribution of computer viruses, and environmental damage caused by the improper disposal of computer hardware and software. As society deals with these concerns, experts continue to discuss various ethical issues that relate to the impact of computers and networks on society. This lesson introduces you to some of the prevalent, far-reaching problems that stem from our reliance on and misuse of computer systems.

OBJECTIVES

- Define the term *software piracy* and explain why it is illegal.
- Name two ways in which computer viruses can be spread.
- Describe two methods used by organizations to limit access to their networks.

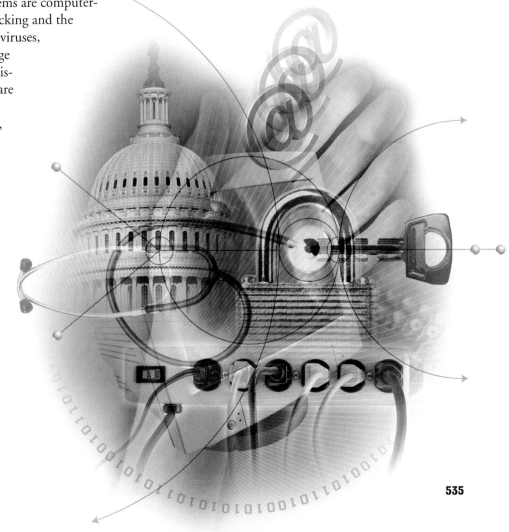

COMPUTER CRIME

Computers are used in all sorts of pursuits, including criminal. Since people began selling software and connecting computers with networks, criminals have found new and different ways to profit and destroy online. Although the types of computer-related crimes are numerous and widespread, a few categories of online criminal activity continue to attract the most attention and affect the most people. Those activities include the illegal copying of software, the spreading of computer viruses, and the stealing of hardware or data.

Although computer criminals can do a great deal of harm working with stand-alone PCs and LANs, the Internet has given them global reach. As it attracts more people to work and play, the Internet also attracts online predators. The profusion of online hooligans has led to myriad problems for typical computer users, including invasion of privacy, the spread of viruses, theft, e-mail abuse, and more. Even offline, computer users are threatened by the spread of viruses, and software companies lose millions each year because of software piracy.

Many events that occur in cyberspace are not addressed by the traditional body of law. For example, physical location has always been a fundamental concept in law; different laws govern according to the jurisdiction of community, state, or country. In cyberspace, however, physical location is not always relevant, so it is difficult to determine which laws govern certain transactions (see Figure 30.1). Suppose, for example, that someone in China downloads an interesting short story from a computer in New York. He then distributes copies of the story to several friends. Has that person broken the law if the material is protected by copyright in the United States?

Our legal system is currently developing or redefining the laws that govern trespassing, sabotage, and the ownership of software and data. However, government officials and legal professionals are finding it difficult to define laws that deal with the intangible issues most prevalent in computing today. An example is the question of **intellectual property**—that is, the ownership of ideas. As thousands of ideas are exchanged and spread over the Internet, governments are hard-pressed to find ways to protect (and in many cases, even to define) intellectual property rights. When you use a computer, whether alone, in an organization, or on the Internet, be aware that the programs, documents, images, and even ideas you encounter are probably the property of someone else.

Figure 30.1

Using the Internet, people can distribute documents around the world. These documents may be protected by copyright laws in some countries but not in others, raising questions about ownership and legal use.

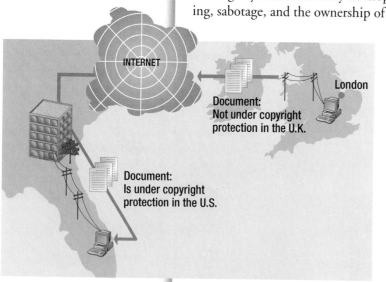

Software Piracy

The biggest legal issue affecting the computer industry is **software piracy,** which is the illegal copying of programs. Piracy is a huge problem because it is so easy to do. In most cases, it is no more difficult to steal a program than it is to copy a music CD that you have borrowed from a friend. Software pirates give up the right to receive upgrades and technical support, but they gain the use of the program without paying for it.

In May 1999, the Business Software Alliance and the Software and Information Industry Association reported that software publishers lost more than $11 billion worldwide because of software piracy in 1998. The report also estimates that in 1998, about 38 percent of all applications used by businesses were pirated copies.

Many **commercial software** programs—software you must purchase before using—cost as little as $20 to $50, but many of the most popular productivity applications cost between $100 and $500. Highly specialized or complex applications can cost several thousand dollars. When you consider the cost of commercial software, it is easy to see why illegal copying is so tempting for the pirate, and so expensive for software companies.

It is important to remember that, in most cases, when you purchase commercial software, you are not actually buying the software itself. Instead, you are paying for a license to use the software. Although software licensing agreements can vary in their terms, they usually place restrictions on the user, such as allowing the user to make only one archive (backup) copy of the program for safekeeping.

Visit **www.glencoe.com/norton/online/** for more information on **software piracy**.

Shareware also suffers from a high piracy rate; however, freeware does not. **Shareware** is software you can use for free on a trial basis, usually for a limited time. If you decide to keep and use the software, you are required to register your copy of the program and sometimes pay a small license fee to the developer. **Freeware** is software that is available free of charge and can be copied and distributed by anyone (see Figure 30.2).

Software is pirated in many ways. The simplest method is to copy the software from its original floppy disk or compact disk. Users on a network can copy certain types of software directly from the server or even exchange programs over their organization's e-mail system.

The Internet has become the biggest hotbed of piracy because pirates (sometimes called crackers, because they are able to "crack" the software's registration or copy protection system) distribute programs by e-mail, across rogue sites on the World Wide Web, on FTP servers, and in newsgroups. Certain Web sites and newsgroups—most notably the **Warez** (pronounced *wares*) sites and newsgroups—have become notorious for blatantly posting entire operating systems, **beta software** (software that is in the developmental stage and not ready for release to customers), upgrades, and commercial applications for anyone to download and use.

Figure 30.2
Piracy is not a significant problem for publishers of freeware.

Antipiracy

Part of the reason that piracy is so difficult to stop is that certain kinds of copying are legal, a fact that tempts some people to gloss over the distinctions. For example, it is generally legal to copy software that you own so that you have a backup copy in case your original is damaged. In fact, installing a new piece of software means copying the program to your computer's hard disk. After the program is installed, however, you are generally reminded of its copyrighted status each time you start it, as shown in Figure 30.3 on page 538.

In the past, software companies manufactured their programs with built-in **copy protection**—safeguards that prevented illegal copying but made installation and

Figure 30.3
Many programs display a splash screen when started, to remind the user of copyright and trademark information. In programs that have not been registered, this type of window may be called a "nag screen" or "beg screen" because it reminds the user that the software should be registered or paid for.

Visit www.glencoe.com/norton/online/ for more information on **organizations** that fight software piracy.

backup difficult. In the 1980s, for example, when nearly all programs were distributed on floppy disks, the disks were set up to be copied to the purchaser's hard disk only a specified number of times. This copy protection worked by recording the number of installation attempts on one of the diskettes. When the installation limit was reached, the software could not be installed again. Users found that they could circumvent this type of protection easily by making duplicates of the installation diskettes, then installing the program from the duplicates. Thus, the original diskettes were never actually used for installation and recorded no attempts.

Another early type of copy protection was the **hardware lock** (commonly called a dongle). This device had to be plugged into the user's PC, usually in the parallel port, and featured a built-in chip containing a code. When the user started the program, it would look for the hardware lock, find the code, and then launch. If no lock was found, the program would not run. Most companies, however, found that this kind of copy protection caused more problems than it solved, and hardware locks have almost completely disappeared.

Today, other antipiracy schemes are more common. One requires a password, serial number, or other code be entered when a program is installed. Most developers print a code or serial number on the packaging in which the installation disk is sold. Anyone who does not have the original packaging or who has not received the code from the original owner may not be able to install the software (see Figure 30.4). Some programs can be installed without the code but may have some features crippled or may "nag" the user to register the software or provide the code when the program is launched. This protection system worked well for years because individual users could not easily duplicate the contents of an entire compact disk. With the proliferation of CD-R and CD-RW systems, however, the illegal duplication of software from the original compact disk is becoming more common. As you can see from all these examples, no antipiracy scheme is foolproof.

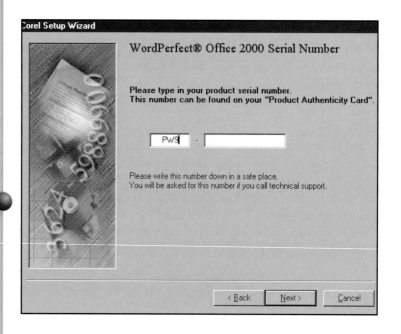

Figure 30.4
Many programs require you to provide a password, special code, or serial number during installation. This reduces piracy to a certain extent; would-be users who do not have the required information may not be able to install the software.

COMPUTER VIRUSES

In general, a **virus** is a parasitic program that infects another legitimate program, which is sometimes called the host. To infect the host program, the virus modifies the host so that it contains a copy of the virus. Some types of viruses are relatively harmless; their purpose is to annoy their victims rather than to cause specific damage. Such viruses are described as benign. Other viruses are indeed malicious, and can do great damage to a computer system if permitted to run.

Categories of Viruses

Depending on your source of information, different types of viruses may be described in slightly different ways. Some specific categories of viruses include the following:

◆ **Boot Sector Viruses.** Regarded as one of the most hostile types of virus, a boot sector virus infects the boot record of a hard or floppy disk. (A boot sector is a special area of a disk that stores essential files the computer accesses during start-up.) The virus moves the boot sector's data to a different part of the disk. When the computer is started, the virus copies itself into memory where it can hide and infect other disks. The virus allows the actual boot sector data to be read as though a normal start-up were occurring.

◆ **Cluster Viruses.** This type of virus makes changes to a disk's file system. If any program is run from the infected disk, the program causes the virus also to run. This technique creates the illusion that the virus has infected every program on the disk.

◆ **File-Infecting Viruses.** This type of virus infects program files on a disk (such as EXE or COM files). When an infected program is launched, the virus' code is also executed.

◆ **Worms.** A worm is a program whose purpose is to duplicate itself. An effective worm will fill entire disks with copies of itself, and it can spread to multiple computers on a network, essentially clogging the entire system with copies. Worms are commonly spread over the Internet via e-mail message attachments and Internet Relay Chat (IRC).

◆ **Bombs.** This type of virus hides on the user's disk and waits for a specific event to occur before running. Some bombs are activated by a date, a change to a file, or a particular action taken by a user or a program.

◆ **Trojan Horses.** A Trojan Horse is a malicious program that appears to be friendly. For example, some Trojan Horses appear to be games. Because Trojan Horses do not make duplicates of themselves on the victim's disk (or copy themselves to other disks), they are not technically viruses. But, because they can do harm, they are considered viruses.

◆ **Polymorphic, Self-Garbling, Self-Encrypting, or Self-Changing Viruses.** This type of virus can change itself each time it is copied, making it difficult to isolate.

◆ **Stealth Viruses.** These viruses take up residence in the computer's memory, making them hard to detect. They can also conceal changes they make to other files, hiding the damage from the user and the operating system.

◆ **Macro Viruses.** A macro virus is designed to infect a specific type of document file, such as Microsoft Word or Excel files. These types of documents can include macros, which are small programs that execute commands.

Visit **www.glencoe.com/norton/online/** for more information on **computer viruses**.

Techview

E-MAIL VIRUSES

Until recently, it was not considered possible to spread viruses within e-mail messages. Because e-mail messages are predominantly text, they could not carry viruses, which require executable code to run.

Newer-generation e-mail programs, however, support e-mail messages in various formats, including HTML. They also support attachments—you can attach a file (such as a DOC, EXE, or other binary file) to a message and send it to a recipient, who can open the file on receiving it. These features of e-mail programs have made them more convenient and useful. However, both features have also opened the door to new types of viruses—e-mail viruses—which can be devastating to anyone who receives them.

Macro Viruses

The more common type of e-mail virus—called a macro virus—relies on a file attached to the message. To create an e-mail virus, the programmer selects a popular application that has a macro language, such as Microsoft Word or Lotus 1-2-3. Then he or she creates a document in that application and places a macro within the document. The macro can contain commands that perform various tasks, including copying and deleting files, changing system settings, creating new e-mail messages, and more. Finally, the programmer attaches the document containing the macro code to an e-mail message and sends the file to one or more unsuspecting recipients. When a recipient downloads the attachment and opens it, the macro in the file runs automatically.

Once released, the virus looks for the recipient's e-mail address book and sends copies of the infected attachment to people in the address book. The virus may also remain on the first recipient's machine and do considerable damage, like a regular virus.

Viruses That Do Not Require Attachments

A newer and more frightening breed of e-mail virus does not require an attached file to inflict damage. This type of virus can reside directly within the text of an HTML-format e-mail message, in unseen code and written in a programming language such as Visual Basic Script (VBScript). The first known virus of this type—called "BubbleBoy"—was transmitted in November 1999. Although the virus did not become widespread, it aroused a new sense of urgency in development and

Web sites like Symantec's AntiVirus Research Center can give you the latest information on viruses.

antivirus communities. To become infected with the BubbleBoy virus, the recipient did not have to do anything; it was enough simply to receive the infected message. On restarting the computer, the user activates the virus code and the virus makes changes to the Windows Registry settings and sends copies of the infected e-mail message to everyone in the recipient's address book.

Protecting Yourself

Unlike other types of viruses, there may not be much you can do to protect yourself from e-mail viruses, but you should take the following precautions:

◆ Do not open e-mail attachments from people you do not know.

◆ Install a reputable antivirus program, run it frequently, and keep its virus definitions up to date. Some experts suggest using two different antivirus programs and running them on an alternating schedule.

◆ Check your Web browser, e-mail program, and newsreader and make sure that their security settings are set to the highest possible level. In addition, you may want to set your e-mail program not to accept messages delivered in HTML format.

◆ Be alert to new developments in viruses by periodically checking virus-related sites on the Web. These sites are hosted by the makers of antivirus programs, universities, and security experts.

(Macros are typically used to issue program-specific commands but can also issue certain OS-level commands.) A macro virus, disguised as a macro, is embedded in a document file and can do various levels of damage to data, from corrupting documents to deleting data.

◆ **Joke Programs.** Joke programs are not viruses and do not inflict any damage. Their purpose is to frighten their victims into thinking that a virus has infected and damaged their system. For example, a joke program may display a message that says the computer's hard disk is being reformatted.

◆ **Bimodal, Bipartite, or Multipartite Viruses.** This type of virus can infect both files and the boot record of a disk.

A new variety of viruses, called e-mail viruses, does not necessarily require a host program to infect a computer. While some e-mail viruses can be transmitted as an infected document file, others can be carried within the body of certain types of e-mail messages.

Viruses can be programmed to carry out many kinds of harm:

◆ Copy themselves to other programs or areas of a disk

◆ Display information on the screen

◆ Destroy data files

◆ Erase the contents of an entire disk

◆ Lie dormant for a specified time or until a given condition is met and then become active

Viruses may seem like major problems for individual computer users. For corporations, however, viruses can be devastating in terms of lost data and productivity. A report by the Federal Bureau of Investigation states that, in the first half of 1999, U.S. companies suffered more than $7 billion in losses attributable to viruses.

Preventing Infection

Safeguarding a system against viruses is not difficult if you have a little knowledge and some utility software. The first item you need to know is when your system is in danger of infection. Here are some common ways to pick up a virus:

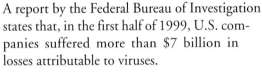

① Programmer creates boot sector virus and stores it on a hard disk. The virus is copied to any floppy disk that is inserted into the same computer.

② The programmer distributes infected floppies to other users.

③ The hard disks of other users are infected by the infected floppy. Every floppy that is placed in an infected computer also becomes infected, and the number of infected computers grows exponentially.

Figure 30.5
This diagram shows how a boot sector virus spreads from a single computer to many computers via an infected floppy disk. Viruses can also be spread from one machine to another across corporate computer networks or the Internet.

◆ Receiving an infected disk (a diskette, a CD created by someone with a CD-R system, a removable hard disk, and so on) from another user, as shown in Figure 30.5. In this case, the virus could be in the boot sector of the disk or in an executable file (a program) on the disk.

◆ Downloading an infected executable file to your computer across a network, an online service, or the Internet.

◆ Copying to your disk a document file that is infected with a macro virus. An infected document might be copied from another disk or received as an attachment to an e-mail message.

As mentioned earlier, e-mail viruses make it possible to pick up a virus from an infected message. Even programs purchased in shrink-wrapped packages from a reputable store have been known to harbor viruses. The best precaution is to treat all files attached to e-mail messages and all floppy disks as potential carriers of infection.

Checking for viruses requires antivirus software, which scans disks and programs for known viruses and eradicates them (see Figure 30.6). After it is installed on your system and activated, a good antivirus program checks for infected files automatically every time you insert any kind of disk or use your modem to retrieve a file. A few antivirus programs can even scan files as you download them from the Internet and can alert you instantly when you download or attempt to open an infected file. Some popular antivirus programs include the following:

◆ McAfee VirusScan

◆ IBM AntiVirus

◆ Symantec Antivirus for the Macintosh

◆ Dr. Solomon's Anti-Virus

◆ Norton AntiVirus

◆ Virex

New viruses are appearing all of the time so no program can offer absolute protection against them all. Virus utilities are constantly updated, however, to handle these new viruses. You can purchase subscriptions to receive the newest versions of the utilities automatically, or you can purchase the latest version every year or so. Some antivirus software vendors allow users to download updated **virus definitions** or **virus patterns** (databases of information about viruses and code that can eradicate them) to their programs over the Internet (see Figure 30.7).

Figure 30.6

Norton AntiVirus, one of several popular antivirus programs, at work. The program allows you to choose which disk, folders, or files to scan for viruses and then reports its findings. If a virus is detected, the program can walk you through the process of eradicating it from the disk and possibly recovering lost data.

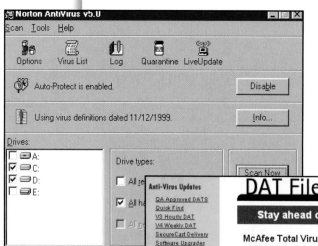

Figure 30.7

Many commercial antivirus programs allow users to download updated virus definitions from their Web sites. Here, the user is searching for the latest set of virus definitions from the Network Associates Web site for the company's antivirus product.

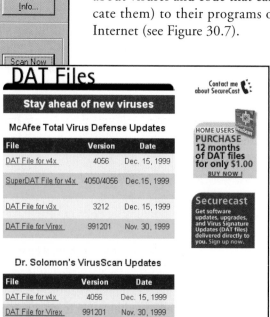

Answer the following questions by filling in the blank(s).

1. The illegal copying of software is called _____ .

2. _____ is software that is in development and not ready for release to the public.

3. A virus may be stored in a special area of a disk called the _____ .

THEFT

Although hardware theft has been going on for many years, the problem was not particularly serious until the introduction of the microcomputer in the 1970s made valuable equipment much easier to move. The problem has skyrocketed with the popularity of small portable computers. Many organizations now secure their computer equipment with steel cables (see Figure 30.8). Even relatively inexpensive items such as keyboards are often locked to the desk or to the rest of the computer.

In some facilities, especially businesses, expensive software can be found stored on bookshelves or in workers' cubicles or offices, within easy reach. When stored in the open, such software is easy to steal. Instead of taking an entire software package, a thief might simply remove the disks and a manual, leaving the box in place.

Organizations can protect against this type of software theft by forbidding employees to store software in the open. Many corporations maintain secure software "libraries," where valuable software is kept under lock and key. In these settings, if an employee needs to install a piece of software, he or she notifies the company's IS department. Then an IS worker installs the software on the employee's machine or gives the employee the user rights needed to access the software from the company's network server. Either way, the software cannot be duplicated from its original disks.

Figure 30.8
Steel cables, similar to those used to secure bicycles, are used to lock computers to desks at many schools, libraries, and businesses.

In businesses and government, the theft of data can be far more serious than the theft of hardware or software programs, which can be replaced fairly easily. **Hackers** are experts in computer technology who take great pleasure in solving software problems, frequently by circumventing established rules or security systems. Often, these experts are tempted by the power of their skills and become criminals. They can steal data (typically by gaining unauthorized access to corporate or government networks), transfer money from one account to another, or crash computer systems intentionally.

No one really knows the full extent of data theft by hackers. By some estimates, the losses are huge. In an October 1999 report to Congress, the Federal Bureau of Investigation reported that its hacking-related caseload had doubled since 1997. The

NORTON ONLINE

Visit **www.glencoe.com/norton/online/** for more information on all types of **computer theft.**

report also stated that, in a 1999 survey by the Computer Security Institute, 163 U.S. businesses disclosed losses of nearly $125 million associated with hacking and other types of computer security breaches.

Most companies and government agencies use security measures to limit access to their computer systems. One common method is to provide user identification codes and passwords to authorized employees. Before an employee can **log on,** or access a computer's files, the employee must enter a **user ID** or **user name** that identifies that person to the system. Usually, employees also need to enter a **password,** a word or symbol usually chosen by the user, that verifies the user's identity (see Figure 30.9). If a user's identification code or password does not match the records in the computer's security software, the user is locked out of the system.

Figure 30.9

A network log-on screen. Before accessing any disks or data on the network, the user must provide his or her identification and a password and specify the portion of the network to be accessed.

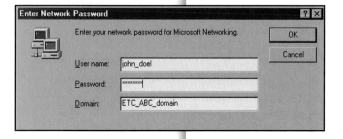

Perhaps the most effective form of security is encryption, which is a method of encoding and decoding data. Encryption is used most often in messaging systems such as electronic mail. One common encryption method, known as the DES (Data Encryption Standard), can encode a message in more than 72 quadrillion ways. Because a special software key is used to decode the message, unauthorized interception of the message is less of a threat. In many messaging systems, DES encryption takes place without users even knowing it.

COMPUTERS AND THE ENVIRONMENT

The sheer number of computers in homes and businesses today means that they must have a considerable impact on the environment.

Planned Obsolescence

A computer system bought today will be obsolete in, at most, two to three years. During that time, you may need to upgrade several parts of the machine. Hardware obsolescence is not the only computer-related threat to the environment. For example, software is typically packaged with one or more manuals, registration cards, sales brochures, and special offers. Every time that software is updated, the disks and other materials from the previous release are discarded.

Getting rid of old hardware is tricky. You should not throw old computers into the trash, because many of them contain nickel-cadmium (nicad) batteries, and cadmium is a toxic heavy metal. To address this problem, some hardware manufacturers have begun programs to collect and properly dispose of old computers. Some companies now donate their old computers to nonprofit organizations, which can use them because they often do not need the latest technological advances to stay competitive. Another option is to deposit the old computer at a local computer recycling center. These organizations reuse or recycle electronic parts and/or components. What remains is disposed of correctly.

Use of Power

Hardware and software manufacturers have taken steps to reduce the amount of power used by computer systems. Most newer computer systems feature energy-saving options (see Figure 30.10). For example, the user can set the system to "go to sleep" after a specified period of nonuse. In **sleep mode,** the computer's hard disk may stop spinning and the monitor may turn off. To "wake up" the system, the user needs only to move the mouse or press a key on the keyboard. PCs with such features are commonly called **green PCs** because they are more environmentally friendly than PCs without power-management options.

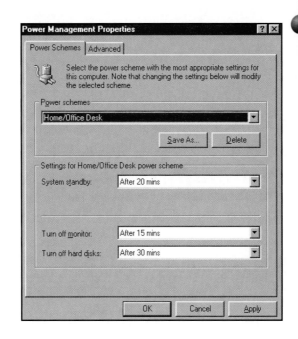

Many systems sport the Energy Star logo. The logo indicates that the equipment meets standards set by the U.S. Environmental Protection Agency's **Energy Star** program. To qualify for the logo, the hardware must meet federal standards for power consumption or approved methods for reducing power consumption.

Figure 30.10
Modern operating systems, such as Windows 98, provide users with some control over the power use of their systems.

Visit **www.glencoe.com/norton/online/** for more information on **computer recycling** and the **Energy Star program.**

ETHICAL ISSUES IN COMPUTING

Advances in computer and communications technologies have placed tremendous new capabilities in the hands of everyday people. We can use information, sounds, and images that once could be used only by specially trained professionals using highly sophisticated tools. With these new capabilities comes a set of responsibilities.

As our technology gives us wonderful new powers, we are faced with many ethical dilemmas. Lawmakers, activists, and everyday computer users will ponder these questions for some time. Laws will certainly be passed, challenged, enacted, and struck down. But until a set of laws is established for ethical computer use, personal ethics and common sense must guide us as we work and play with computers, both online and offline. A sample code of conduct suggested by the Computer Ethics Institute is listed below:

1. Do not use a computer to harm other people.

2. Do not interfere with other people's computer work.

3. Do not snoop around in other people's computer files.

4. Do not use a computer to steal.

5. Do not use a computer to bear false witness.

6. Do not copy or use proprietary software for which you have not paid.

7. Do not use other people's computer resources without authorization or proper compensation.

8. Do not appropriate other people's intellectual output.

9. Always think about the social consequences of the program you are writing or the system you are designing.

10. Always use a computer in ways that ensure consideration and respect for your fellow humans.

COMPUTERS
in your career

How Computer Technologies
Affect Some Professions

The topics discussed in this unit may not seem like obvious career opportunities, but a surprising number of people—in different professions and disciplines, with a wide range of computing skills and expertise—are working on these kinds of issues. Here are some examples:

◆ **Physicians, Medical Researchers, Insurance Professionals.** The health and safety of people in the workplace is receiving more attention than ever in the health-care community. If your career takes you into the medical or insurance industries, then you may become concerned with the prevention and cure of computer-related health issues, from RSIs to the effects of EMFs on pregnant women. Medical professionals are helping more people than ever to recover from RSIs, especially those involving the hands, wrists, and arms. Insurance professionals are actively working to verify the causes of workplace injuries and are helping government agencies and hardware manufacturers understand the importance of ergonomically correct hardware and equipment safety.

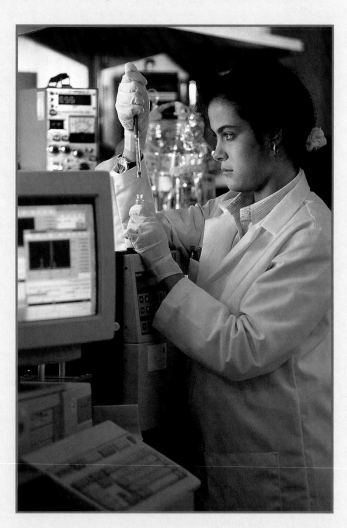

◆ **Environmentalists, Ecologists, Community Activists.** Either as a professional or volunteer, you may want to get involved with efforts in your area to reclaim and recycle old computer hardware and software. The benefits to the community are tremendous, from reducing waste in landfills to helping schools and nonprofit organizations find badly needed computer equipment. Most charitable organizations also maintain databases of their contributors. You may wish to consider volunteering your time to organize and update such files, gaining valuable experience in the process.

◆ **Law Enforcement Professionals, Security Specialists, Programmers.** If your professional goals involve a career in law enforcement, computer expertise is a valuable addition to your résumé. Law enforcement and government agencies are devoting more resources than ever to tracking down computer criminals of all kinds. Especially in demand are high-level computer users with skills in networking, programming, and security. This type of expertise is essential in tracking down computer criminals who ply their trade on the Internet.

LESSON QUIZ

True/False

Answer the following questions by circling True or False.

True   False   **1.** Because software pirates distribute copies of commercial software programs, the software developer benefits from additional sales.

True   False   **2.** The term *intellectual property* refers to the ownership of ideas.

True   False   **3.** No antipiracy scheme is foolproof.

True   False   **4.** If you use an effective antivirus product, you should never need to update its virus definitions.

True   False   **5.** Hardware locks are a popular copy-protection method.

Multiple Choice

Circle the word or phrase that best completes each sentence.

1. You must purchase a _____ software program before using it.
   A. commercial   **B.** shareware   **C.** beta

2. Viruses can be programmed to _____ .
   A. copy themselves   **B.** destroy data files   **C.** both A and B

3. A _____ is a database of information about viruses and codes that can eradicate them.
   A. definition   **B.** pattern   **C.** either A or B

4. In business and government, the theft of _____ can be the most serious type of computer-related theft.
   A. hardware   **B.** data   **C.** software

5. _____ is a method of encoding and decoding data.
   A. Copy protection   **B.** Encryption   **C.** Log-on

LESSON LABS

Complete the following exercises as directed by your instructor.

1. If your computer hardware or software is stolen, you can help authorities locate it if you have the serial numbers. Find and write down the brand name, model name or number, and serial numbers of your PC, monitor, printer, and other hardware devices attached to your computer. To find the serial numbers for your software products, check each program's help system or look in the documentation. Keep this list in a safe place, and be sure to update it whenever you add or change part of the system.

2. Determine whether you can set any power-management settings for your computer:
   A. Click the Start button to open the Start menu. Choose Settings; then click Control Panel. The Control Panel window appears.
   B. Look for an icon named Power Management. If you find such an icon, double-click it. The Power Management Properties dialog box appears. Check your current power-related settings and write them down. Change them, if you like. When you are finished, click Apply, then click OK.

LESSON 29: Computers and the Individual

Ergonomics and Health Issues

- Ergonomics is the study of the physical relationships between humans and their tools, including computers.

- By choosing ergonomically correct equipment and adopting proper computing habits, users can avoid potentially serious repetitive stress injuries such as carpal tunnel syndrome.

- Office chairs should be adjustable in height and should have lower-back support and armrests.

- Computer desks should allow you to adjust the height of the computer's keyboard.

- To prevent damage to your eyes, avoid staring at the screen for long periods, position the monitor between 2 and 2½ feet from your eyes, make sure no bright lights reflect off your screen, and use a monitor that has a relatively large screen without noticeable flicker.

Privacy Issues

- Computer databases have allowed corporations to collect and sift through massive amounts of data about individuals.

- Using information collected in various databases, both legitimate marketers and pranksters deluge people with junk mail, junk faxes, and junk e-mail (called spam).

- Junk e-mailers, known as spammers, often send out huge mailings to thousands of computer users over the Internet.

- Using a tactic known as spoofing, a spammer can conceal his or her own e-mail address from the persons being spammed.

- Two well-known types of databases that are kept about people are the mailing list and the credit history.

- Threats to privacy also occur between companies and their employees, especially with respect to company-owned channels of communication, such as e-mail.

LESSON 30: Computing Issues That Affect Us All

Computer Crime

- Our legal system is gradually developing a legal framework for working with computers and working on the Internet.

- The most prevalent breach of law in cyberspace is software piracy, or the illegal copying or use of a program.

- Several types of copy protection schemes can be used to stop or slow down pirates.

Computer Viruses

- A computer virus is a parasitic program that can replicate itself, infect computers, and destroy data.

- Viruses are most commonly spread by infected disks and when users download infected files over a network or from the Internet. A new breed of e-mail viruses is spread via files attached to e-mail messages or in the body of an e-mail message.

- Users can protect their data and software by using an antivirus program and by keeping the program's virus definitions up to date.

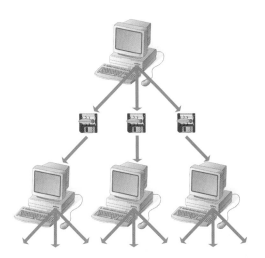

Theft

- Computer-related theft is a costly problem for organizations and individual users, especially those who use portable computers.

- Many companies literally lock their computer systems with anti-theft devices.

- Software theft is a common problem in organizations where software is left unattended. Companies can combat the problem by keeping software in a locked storage location and overseeing its installation on individual computers.

- Data theft is perhaps the greatest concern to organizations.

- Hackers steal data by accessing a computer's disks over a network. In addition to stealing data, hackers have been known to destroy data, crash computer networks, and steal funds electronically.

- Organizations can protect the data on their networks by taking appropriate security measures. Basic measures include requiring users to provide identification and passwords before accessing the network. More sophisticated measures include encrypting data to make it unusable to anyone without the proper decoding key.

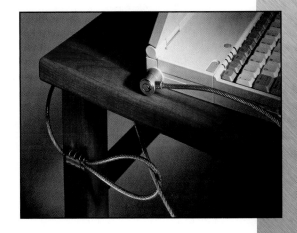

Computers and the Environment

- The computer industry has become known for planned obsolescence, with both hardware and software being replaced or upgraded every couple of years.

- When disposed of improperly, obsolete hardware and software contribute to pollution and negatively affect the environment.

- Many newer devices are designed under the Energy Star program, which sets power-consumption standards for computer equipment.

Ethical Issues in Computing

- Widespread access to computer technologies has created many ethical dilemmas.

- Government, legal, and computing professionals continue to debate computer-related ethical questions and attempt to develop laws that protect the freedoms of computer users while limiting immoral or illegal use of computers.

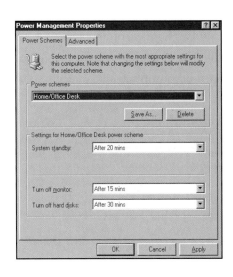

KEY TERMS

After completing this unit, you should be able to define the following terms.

appropriate use policy, *531*
beta software, *537*
carpal tunnel syndrome, *526*
commercial software, *537*
copy protection, *537*
electromagnetic field (EMF), *528*
Energy Star, *545*
ergonomics, *526*
freeware, *537*
green PC, *545*
hacker, *543*
hardware lock, *538*
intellectual property, *536*
junk e-mail, *530*
junk fax, *530*
log on, *544*

password, *544*
repetitive stress injury (RSI), *526*
shareware, *537*
sleep mode, *545*
software piracy, *536*
spam, *530*
spammer, *530*
spamming, *530*
spoofing, *531*
user ID, *544*
user name, *544*
virus, *539*
virus definition, *542*
virus pattern, *542*
Warez, *537*

KEY TERMS QUIZ

Fill in each blank with one of the terms listed under Key Terms.

1. The illegal copying or use of programs is called _____ .

2. The term _____ refers to pirated software that is distributed over the Internet, over certain Web sites and newsgroups.

3. Criminals who use their computer skills to steal data or crash computer systems are known as _____ .

4. The act of sending unsolicited e-mail messages is known as _____ .

5. The study of the physical relationship between people and their tools is called _____ .

6. Low-frequency power creates _____ .

7. _____ is a common injury among clerical personnel who spend a great deal of time using a computer keyboard or mouse.

8. Software developers can use one of several _____ schemes in an attempt to stop software piracy.

9. In many businesses, an employee must enter a(n) _____ to access a computer's files.

10. In _____ , the computer's hard disk may stop spinning and the monitor may turn off.

REVIEW QUESTIONS

In your own words, briefly answer the following questions.

1. Describe how your name and address might be included on more than one mailing list.

2. Describe the methods used to protect network systems from unauthorized access.

3. According to this unit, what is a hacker?

4. What is a "green PC"?

5. List three ways by which a virus can infect a computer system.

6. What are repetitive stress injuries?

7. What are the three characteristics you should look for in an office chair?

8. How can the average computer user protect him- or herself against junk e-mail?

9. What is a virus definition, and why should you update your virus definitions regularly?

10. How does computer obsolescence contribute to pollution and environmental problems?

DISCUSSION QUESTIONS

As directed by your instructor, discuss the following questions in class or in groups.

1. How do you feel about the use of the Internet for marketing products and services? Do you believe that unsolicited e-mail is ever warranted?

2. Suppose you are responsible for the acquisition and disposal of computer equipment for a large company. List and describe as many possibilities as you can for performing this function in an environmentally responsible manner.

ETHICAL ISSUES

Our daily use of computers gives us new abilities and responsibilities. With this thought in mind, discuss the following questions in class.

1. Many people feel that virus programmers and hackers provide a service by pointing out the weaknesses in computer programs and networks. How do you feel about this perspective? Do such benefits balance out the destruction that viruses and hackers cause? Do you think these people should be punished for their actions if they are caught? If you do, how should they be punished?

2. Some people do not agree with the concept of "intellectual property," saying that ideas cannot be owned or copyrighted by an individual. What do you think of the concept? Suppose you wrote a book (which is being sold in bookstores) and someone began distributing the text freely over the Internet. How would this type of activity affect your view of intellectual property?

UNIT LABS

You and the Computer

Complete the following exercises using a computer in your classroom, lab, or home. No other materials are needed.

1. Many new computers come with an antivirus program already installed. To find out if antivirus software is installed on your system, click the Start button, point to Programs, and study the contents of the Programs menu. Look for any program with the word "antivirus" in its name. If you find such a program, launch it; then open its help system to learn more about it. Can you determine how old the program's virus definitions are? Next, insert a diskette in the PC's diskette drive and use the antivirus software to scan the diskette. What results does it report? When you are finished, remove the diskette and close the antivirus program.

2. Windows enables you to set up a screen saver that includes password protection. If you leave your computer unused for a specified time and this feature is enabled, the screen saver activates. To turn off the screen saver and resume using the system, however, you must supply a password. This type of protection can discourage other people from using your PC when you are away but have left the system running. To configure a screen saver with password protection, take these steps:

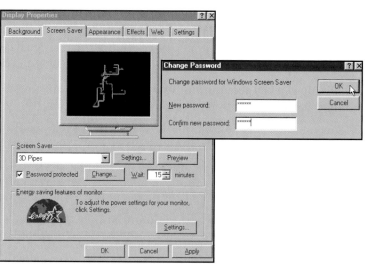

   A. Click the Start button to open the Start menu. Point to Settings, and then click Control Panel. The Control Panel window appears.

   B. Double-click the Display icon. The Display Properties dialog box appears. Click the Screen Saver tab.

   C. From the Screen Saver drop-down list, select a screen saver. You can use the Settings and Preview buttons to customize your screen saver and to see how it looks.

   D. In the Wait spin box, set the number of minutes the system should wait unused before the screen saver begins running. Fifteen minutes is a typical setting.

   E. To set up a password, click the Password Protected checkbox; then click the Change button. The Change Password dialog box appears.

   F. In the New password box, type a password. Make the password something that you can easily remember, but that other people cannot easily guess. Type the password again in the Confirm new password box; then click OK. (*Note:* Be sure to write the password down in case you forget it!)

   G. If you want to keep the password, click Apply. Then click OK to close the Display Properties dialog box. If you do not want to keep the password, click Cancel. (If you are using a school computer, your instructor may prefer that you click Cancel.)

Internet Labs

To complete the following exercises, you need a computer with an Internet connection and a Web browser. (For more information on using these tools, see "Prerequisites" at the front of this textbook.)

1. **Learn More About Viruses.** These sites not only teach you about viruses but can help you decide which antivirus program is right for you. Visit the following Web sites:

   - ICSA is a provider of network security services. Visit **http://www.icsa.net/** and click the Antivirus link.

   - Virus Bulletin is an online journal covering viruses and antivirus products. Visit **http://www.virusbtn.com/**

   - The Internet Society features a virus-related page on its Web site. Visit **http://www.isoc.org/internet/issues/viruses/**

2. **Computer Recycling.** Check these Web sites to learn more about computer recycling, look for a recycling center or agency in your area, and get involved yourself:

   - AnotheR BytE, Inc. is a nonprofit recycling group. Visit **http://www.recycles.org/**

   - PEP is a nationwide directory of computer recycling programs. Visit **http://www.microweb.com/pepsite/recycle/recycle_index.html**

   - Share the Technology is a nonprofit group whose Web site allows people to post requests for and offers of used computer equipment. Visit **http://www.sharetechnology.org/**

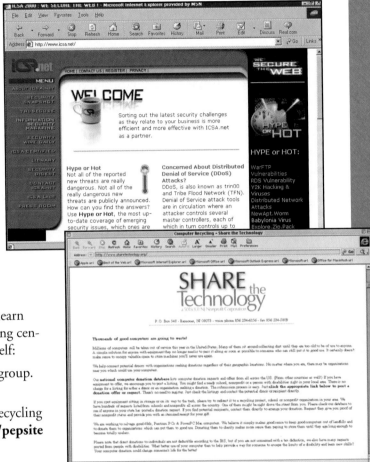

IBE Labs

If you have the Interactive Browser Edition (IBE) CD-ROM for this textbook, you may complete the following interactive exercises using the instructions provided in the IBE.

1. **Matching.** Determine if the situation is a threat to your privacy or not.

2. **Labeling.** The focus of this exercise is on ergonomics.

3. **Scavenger Hunt.** Answer questions to find a clue toward solving the puzzle.

4. **Computer Viruses.** Trace how a computer virus is spread, and how programs get rid of a bug after it is detected.

The History of Microcomputers

IN THE BEGINNING

In 1971, Dr. Ted Hoff puts together all the elements of a computer processor on a single silicon chip slightly larger than one square inch. The result of his efforts is the Intel 4004, the world's first commercially available micro-processor. The chip is a 4-bit computer containing 2,300 transistors (invented in 1948) that can perform 60,000 instructions per second. Designed for use in a calculator, it sells for $200. Intel sells more than 100,000 calculators based on the 4004 chip. Almost overnight, the chip finds thousands of applications, paving the way for today's computer-oriented world, and for the mass production of computer chips now containing millions of transistors.

1975

The first commercially available micro-computer, the Altair 880, is the first machine to be called a "personal computer." It has 64 KB of memory and an open 100-line bus structure. Selling for about $400, the Altair 880 comes in a kit to be assembled by the user.

Two young college students, Paul Allen and Bill Gates, unveil the BASIC language interpreter for the Altair computer. During summer vacation, the pair form a company called Microsoft, which eventually grows into the largest software company in the world.

At Bell Labs, Brian Kernighan and Dennis Ritchie develop the C pro-gramming language, which quickly becomes the most popular professional application development language.

1976

Steve Wozniak and Steve Jobs build the Apple I computer. It is less powerful than the Altair, but also less expensive and less complicated. Users must con-nect their own keyboard and video display, and have the option of mounting the

computer's motherboard in any container they choose—whether a metal case, a wooden box, or a briefcase. Jobs and Wozniak form the Apple Computer Company together on April Fool's Day, naming it after their favorite snack food.

1977

The Apple II computer is unveiled. It comes already assembled in a case, with a built-in keyboard. Users must plug in their own TVs for monitors. Fully assembled microcomputers hit the general market, with Radio Shack, Commodore, and Apple all selling models. Sales are slow because neither businesses nor the general public know exactly what to do with these new machines.

Datapoint Corporation announces Attached Resource Computing Network (ARCnet), the first

commercial LAN technology intended for use with micro-computer applications.

1978

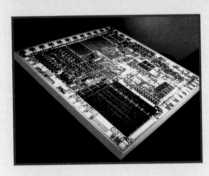

Intel releases the 8086 micro-processor, a 16-bit chip that sets a new standard for power, capacity, and speed in microprocessors.

Epson announces the MX-80 dot-matrix printer, coupling high performance with a relatively low price. (Epson from Japan sets up

operations in the U.S. in 1975 as Epson America, Inc. and becomes one of the first of many foreign companies to contribute to the growth of the PC industry. Up until this point, it has been U.S. companies only. According to Epson, they gain 60 percent of the dot printer market with the MX-80.)

1979

Intel introduces the 8088 microprocessor, featuring 16-bit internal architecture and an 8-bit external bus.

Motorola introduces the 68000 chip, used in early Macintosh computers.

Software Arts, Inc. releases VisiCalc, the first commercial spreadsheet program for personal computers. VisiCalc is generally credited as being the program that paved the way for the personal computer in the business world.

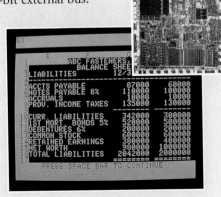

Bob Metcalf, the developer of Ethernet, forms 3Com Corp. to develop Ethernet-based net-working products. Ethernet eventually evolves into the world's most widely used network system.

MicroPro International intro-duces WordStar, the first com-mercially successful word processing program for IBM-compatible microcomputers.

1980

IBM chooses Microsoft (co-founded by Bill Gates and Paul Allen) to provide the operating system for its upcoming PC. Microsoft purchases a program developed by Seattle Computer Products called Q-DOS (for Quick and Dirty Operating System), and modifies it to run on IBM hardware.

Bell Laboratories invents the Bellmac-32, the first single-chip microprocessor with 32-bit internal architecture and a 32-bit data bus.

Lotus Development Corporation unveils the Lotus 1-2-3 integrated spreadsheet program combining

spreadsheet, graphics, and database features in one package.

1981

IBM introduces the IBM-PC, with a 4.77 MHz Intel 8088 CPU, 16 KB of memory, a keyboard, a monitor, one or two

5.25-inch floppy drives, and a price tag of $2,495.

Hayes Microcomputer Products, Inc., introduces the SmartModem 300, which quickly becomes the industry standard.

Xerox unveils the Xerox Star computer. Its high price eventually dooms the computer to commercial failure, but its features inspire a whole new direction in computer design. Its little box on

wheels (the first mouse) can execute commands on screen (the first graphical user interface).

1982

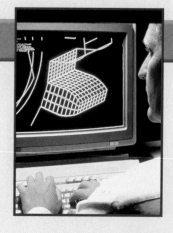

Intel releases the 80286, a 16-bit microprocessor.

AutoCAD, a program for designing 2-D and 3-D objects, is released. AutoCAD will go on to revolutionize the architecture and engineering industries.

Work begins on the development of TCP/IP. The term *Internet* is used for the first time to describe the worldwide network of networks that is emerging from the ARPANET.

1983

Time magazine features the computer as the 1982 "Machine of the Year," acknowledging the computer's new role in society.

Apple introduces the Lisa, the first commercial computer with a purely graphical operating system and a mouse. The industry is excited, but Lisa's $10,000 price tag discourages buyers.

IBM unveils the IBM-PC XT, essentially a PC with a hard disk

and more memory. The XT can store programs and data on its built-in 10 MB hard disk.

The first version of C++ programming language is developed, allowing programs to be written in reusable independent pieces, called objects.

The Compaq Portable is released, the first successful 100 percent PC-compatible clone. Despite its hefty 28 pounds, it becomes one

of the first computers to be lugged through airports.

1984

Adobe Systems releases its PostScript system, allowing printers to produce crisp print in a

number of typefaces, as well as elaborate graphic images.

Apple introduces the "user-friendly" Macintosh microcomputer.

IBM ships the IBM-PC AT, a 6 MHz computer using the Intel

80286 processor, which sets the standard for personal computers running DOS.

IBM introduces its Token Ring networking system. Reliable and redundant, it can send packets at 4 Mbps; several years later it speeds up to 16 Mbps.

Satellite Software International introduces the WordPerfect word processing program.

1985

Intel releases the 80386 processor (also called the 386), a 32-bit processor that can address more than 4 billion bytes of memory, and performs ten times faster than the 80286.

Aldus releases PageMaker for the Macintosh, the first desktop publishing software for microcomputers. Coupled with Apple's LaserWriter printer and Adobe's PostScript system, PageMaker ushers in the era of desktop publishing.

Microsoft announces the Windows 1.0 operating environment, featuring the first graphical user interface for PCs.

Hewlett-Packard introduces the Laser Jet laser printer, featuring 300 dpi resolution.

1986

IBM delivers the PC convertible, IBM's first laptop computer and the first Intel-based computer with a 3.5-inch floppy disk drive.

Microsoft sells its first public stock for $21 per share, raising $61 million in the initial public offering.

The First International Conference on CD-ROM technology is held in Seattle, hosted by Microsoft. Compact disks are seen as the storage medium of the future for computer users.

1987

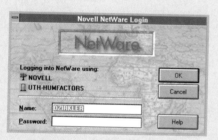

IBM unveils the new PS/2 line of computers, featuring a 20-MHz 80386 processor at its top end. This product line includes the MicroChannel bus, but is not a great success because consumers do not want to replace industry standard peripherals. To compete with IBM's MicroChannel architecture, a group of other computer makers introduces the EISA (Extended Industry Standard Architecture) bus.

IBM introduces its Video Graphics Array (VGA) monitor offering 256 colors at 320 × 200 resolution, and 16 colors at 640 × 480.

The Macintosh II computer, aimed at the desktop publishing market, is introduced by Apple Computer. It features an SVGA monitor.

Apple Computer introduced HyperCard, a programming language for the Macintosh, which used the metaphor of a stack of index cards to represent a program—a kind of visual programming language.

Motorola unveils its 68030 microprocessor.

Novell introduces its network operating system, called NetWare.

1988

IBM and Microsoft ship OS/2 1.0, the first multi-tasking desktop operating system. High price, a steep learning curve, and incompatibility with existing PCs contribute to its lack of market share.

Apple Computer files the single biggest lawsuit in the computer industry against Microsoft and Hewlett-Packard, claiming copyright infringement of its operating system and graphical user interface. Ashton-Tate sues Fox Software and The Santa Cruz Operation, alleging copyright infringement of dBase.

Hewlett-Packard introduces the first popular ink jet printer, the HP Deskjet.

Steve Jobs' new company, NeXT, Inc., unveils the NeXT computer featuring a 25-MHz Motorola 68030 processor. The NeXT is the first computer to use object-oriented programming in its operating system and an optical drive rather than a floppy drive.

Apple introduces the Apple CD SC, a CD-ROM storage device allowing access to up to 650 MB of data.

A virus called the "Internet Worm" is released on the Internet, disabling about ten percent of all Internet host computers.

1989

Intel releases the 80486 chip (also called the 486), the world's first one-million-transistor microprocessor. The 486 integrates a 386 CPU and math coprocessor onto the same chip.

Tim Berners-Lee develops software around the hypertext concept, enabling users to click on a word or phrase in a document and jump either to another location within the document or to another file. This software provides the foundation for the

development of the World Wide Web, and is the basis for the first Web browsers.

The World Wide Web is created at CERN, the European Particle Physics Laboratory in Geneva,

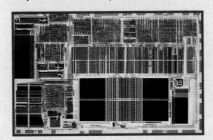

Switzerland for use by scientific researchers.

Microsoft's Word for Windows introduction begins the "Microsoft Office" suite adoption by millions of users. Word for DOS had been the second-highest-selling word processing package behind Word Perfect.

1990

Microsoft releases Windows 3.0, shipping 1 million copies in four months.

A multimedia PC specification setting the minimum hardware requirements for sound and graphics components of a PC is announced at the Microsoft Multimedia Developers' Conference.

The National Science Foundation Network (NSFNET) replaces ARPANET as the backbone of the Internet.

Motorola announces its 32-bit microprocessor, the 68040, incorporating 1.2 million transistors.

1991

Apple Computer launches the PowerBook series of battery-powered portable computers.

Apple, IBM, and Motorola sign a cooperative agreement to design and produce RISC-based chips, integrate the Mac OS into IBM's enterprise systems, produce a new object-oriented operating system, and develop common multimedia standards. The result is the PowerPC microprocessor.

1992

With an estimated 25 million users, the Internet becomes the world's largest electronic mail network.

In Apple Computer's five-year copyright infringement lawsuit, Judge Vaughn Walker rules in favor of defendants Microsoft and Hewlett-Packard, finding that the graphical user interface in dispute is not covered under Apple's copyrights.

Microsoft ships the Windows 3.1 operating environment, including improved memory management and TrueType fonts.

IBM introduces its ThinkPad laptop computer.

1993

Mosaic, a point-and-click graphical Web browser is developed at the National Center for Supercomputing Applications (NCSA), making the Internet accessible to those outside the scientific community.

Intel, mixing elements of its 486 design with new processes, features, and technology, delivers the long-awaited Pentium processor. It offers a 64-bit data path and more than 3.1 million transistors.

Apple Computer expands its entire product line, adding the Macintosh Color Classic, Macintosh LC III, Macintosh Centris 610 and 650, Macintosh Quadra 800, and the Powerbooks 165c and 180c.

Apple introduces the Newton MessagePad at the Macworld convention, selling 50,000 units in the first ten weeks.

Microsoft ships the Windows NT operating system.

IBM ships its first RISC-based RS/6000 workstation, featuring the PowerPC 601 chip developed jointly by Motorola, Apple, and IBM.

1994

Apple introduces the Power Macintosh line of microcomputers based on the PowerPC chip. This line introduces RISC to the desktop market. RISC was previously available only on high-end workstations.

Netscape Communications releases the Netscape Navigator program, a World Wide Web browser based on the Mosaic standard, but with more advanced features.

Online service providers Compu-Serve, America Online, and Prodigy add Internet access to their services.

After two million Pentium-based PCs hit the market, a flaw in the chip's floating-point unit is found by Dr. Thomas Nicely. His report is made public on CompuServe.

Linus Torvalds releases Linux, a freeware version of UNIX created by a worldwide collaboration of programmers who shared their work over the Internet.

1995

Intel releases the Pentium Pro microprocessor.

Motorola releases the PowerPC 604 chip, developed jointly with Apple and IBM.

Microsoft releases its Windows 95 operating system with a massive marketing campaign, including prime-time TV commercials. Seven million copies are sold the first month, with sales reaching 26 million by year's end.

Netscape Communications captures more than 80 percent of the World Wide Web browser market, going from a start-up company to a $2.9 billion company in one year.

A group of developers at Sun Microsystems create the Java development language. Because it enables programmers to develop applications that will run on any platform, Java is seen as the future of operating systems, applications, and the World Wide Web.

Power Computing ships the first-ever Macintosh clones, the Power 100 series with a PowerPC 601 processor.

1996

Intel announces the 200 MHz Pentium processor.

U.S. Robotics releases the PalmPilot, a personal digital assistant that quickly gains enormous popularity because of its rich features and ease of use.

Microsoft adds Internet connection capability to its Windows 95 operating system.

Several vendors introduce Virtual Reality Modeling Language (VRML) authoring tools that provide simple interfaces and drag-and-drop editing features to create three-dimensional worlds with color, texture, motion video, and sound on the Web.

The U.S. Congress enacts the Communications Decency Act as part of the Telecommunications Act of 1996. The act mandates fines of up to $100,000 and prison terms for transmission of any "comment, request, suggestion, proposal, image or other communication which is obscene, lewd, lascivious, filthy, or indecent" over the Internet. The day the law is passed, millions of Web page backgrounds turn black in protest. The law is immediately challenged on Constitutional grounds, ultimately deemed unconstitutional, and repealed.

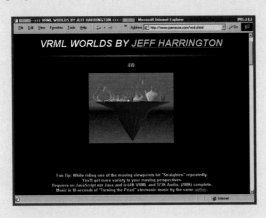

1997

Intel announces MMX technology, which increases the multimedia capabilities of a micro-processor. Also, Intel announces the Pentium II microprocessor. It has speeds of up to 333 MHz and introduces a new design in packaging, the Single Edge Contact (SEC) cartridge. It has more than 7.5 million transistors.

AMD and Cyrix step up efforts to compete with Intel for the

$1000-and-less PC market. Their competing processors are used by PC makers such as Dell, Compaq, Gateway, and even IBM.

The U.S. Justice Department charges Microsoft with an antitrust lawsuit, claiming Microsoft was practicing anticompetitive behavior by forcing PC makers to bundle its Internet Explorer Web browser with Windows 95.

Netscape Communications and Microsoft release new versions of their Web browser. Netscape's Communicator 4 and Microsoft's Internet Explorer 4 provide a full suite of Internet tools, including Web browser, newsreader, HTML editor, conferencing program, and e-mail application.

Digital Video/Versatile Disk (DVD) technology is introduced. Capable of storing computer, audio, and video data, a single DVD disk can hold an entire movie. DVD is seen as the storage technology for the future, ultimately replacing standard CD-ROM technology in PC and home entertainment systems.

1998

Microsoft releases the Windows 98 operating system. Seen mainly as an upgrade to Windows 95, Windows 98 is more reliable and less susceptible to crashes. It also offers improved Internet-related features, including a built-in copy of the Internet Explorer Web browser.

The Department of Justice expands its actions against Microsoft, attempting to block the release of Windows 98 unless Microsoft agrees to remove the Internet Explorer browser from the operating system. Microsoft fights back and a lengthy trial begins in federal court, as the government

attempts to prove that Microsoft is trying to hold back competitors such as Netscape.

Intel releases two new versions of its popular Pentium II chip. The Pentium II Celeron offers slower performance than the standard PII, but is aimed at the $1,000-and-less PC market, which quickly embraces this chip. At the high end, the Pentium II Xeon is designed for use in high-performance workstations and server systems, and is priced accordingly. Both chips boost Intel's market share, reaching deeper into more vertical markets.

Apple Computer releases the colorful iMac, an all-in-one system geared to a youthful market. The small, lightweight system features the new G3 processor, which outperforms Pentium II–based PCs in many respects. The iMac uses only USB connections, forcing many users to purchase adapters for system peripherals, and the computer does not include a floppy disk drive.

1999

Intel unveils the Pentium III processor, which features 9.5 million transistors. Although the Pentium III's performance is not vastly superior to the Pentium II, it features enhancements that take greater advantage of graphically rich applications and Web sites. A more powerful version of the chip (named Xeon) is also released, for use in higher-end workstations and network server systems.

With its Athlon microprocessor, Advanced Micro Devices finally releases a Pentium-class chip that outperforms the Pentium III processor. The advance is seen as a boon for the lower-price computer market, which relies heavily on chips from Intel's competitors.

Apple Computer introduces updated versions of its popular iMac computer, including a laptop version, as well as the new G4 system, with performance rated at 1 gigaflop, meaning the system can perform more than one billion floating point operations per second.

The world braces for January 1, 2000, as fears of the "Millenium Bug" come to a head. As airlines, government agencies, financial institutions, utilities, and PC owners scramble to make their systems "Y2K-compliant," some people panic, afraid that basic services will cease operation when the year changes from 1999 to 2000.

2000

Shortly after the New Year, computer experts and government officials around the world announce that no major damage resulted from the "millennium date change," when computer clocks rolled over from 1999 to 2000. Immediately, a global debate began to rage: had the entire "Y2K bug" been a hoax created by the computer industry, as a way to reap huge profits from people's fears? Industry leaders defended their approach to the Y2K issue, stating that years of planning and preventive measures had helped the world avoid a global computer-driven catastrophe, which could have brought the planet's economy to a stand-still.

Microsoft introduces Windows 2000 on Feb. 17. It is the biggest commercial software project ever attempted and one of the largest engineering projects of the century, involving 5345 full-time participants, over half of them engineers. The final product includes almost 30 million lines of code.

On March 6, Advanced Micro Devices (AMD) announces the shipment of a 1 GHz version of the Athlon processor, which will be used in PCs manufactured by Compaq and Gateway. It is the first 1 GHz processor to be commercially available to the consumer PC market. Within days, Intel Corp. announces the release of a 1 GHz version of the Pentium III processor.

In April, U.S. District Judge Thomas Penfield Jackson rules that Microsoft is guilty of taking advantage of its monopoly in operating systems to hurt competitors and leverage better deals with its business partners. Soon after the finding, the Department of Justice recommends that the judge break Microsoft into two separate companies: one focused solely on operating systems, the other focused solely on application development. Microsoft quickly counters by offering to change a number of its business practices. The judge rules to divide the software giant into two companies. As of this writing, Microsoft is appealing the ruling.

USING WEB-BASED SEARCH TOOLS

It is not always easy to find what you want on the Web. That is because there are tens of millions of unique Web sites, which include hundreds of millions of unique pages! This appendix explains the basics of Web search tools and their use. However, there are many more specific search tools available than can be listed here. To search the Web successfully, you should use this appendix as a starting point; then spend some time experimenting with a variety of search tools.

The exercises in this appendix assume your computer is connected to the Internet and you can launch and use a Web browser to navigate the World Wide Web. For more information, consult your instructor, or read "Prerequisites: What You Should Know Before Using This Book," and Unit 10, "The Internet and Online Resources."

SEARCH TOOLS

The two most basic and commonly used Web-based search tools are:

◆ **Directories.** A directory enables you to search for information by selecting categories of subject matter. The directory separates subjects into general categories (such as "companies"), which are broken into increasingly specific subcategories (such as "companies—construction—contractors—builders and designers"). After you select a category or subcategory, the directory displays a list of Web sites that provide content related to that subject.

◆ **Search Engines.** A search engine lets you search for information by typing one or more words. The engine then displays a list of Web pages that contain information related to your words. (This type of look-up is called a keyword search.) Any search engine lets you conduct a search based on a single word. Most also let you search for multiple words, such as "scanner AND printer." A growing number of engines also let you use "plain English" phrases or questions as the basis for your search, such as "movies starring Cary Grant" or "How do cells divide?" For a list of possible search engines, see Table 19.4 on page 353.

Note that both types of search tools are commonly called search engines. While this is not technically correct, the differences between the two are blurring. This is because most Web-based search tools provide both directories and keyword search engines.

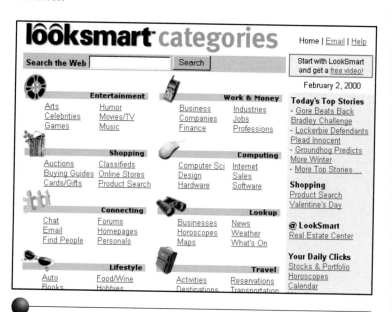

The LookSmart home page. You can use the site's directory to search for Web sites relating to many topics.

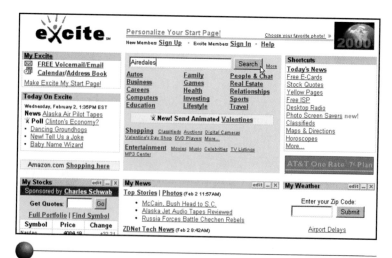

Excite is one of the older search engines on the Web, and keeps expanding its offerings. Using the Excite search engine, you can search for information by using one or more words, a phrase, or a question.

USING A DIRECTORY

Suppose you want to find some Web sites that provide information about the latest digital cameras. Perhaps you want to buy a camera, or just want to read about the technology before deciding whether to buy one. In the following exercise, you will use the LookSmart directory to find Web sites that provide "buyers guide" information.

1. Launch your Web browser.

2. In the Location/Address bar, type **www.looksmart.com/** and press Enter. The LookSmart home page opens in your browser window.

3. Under Computing, click the Hardware category. A new page appears, displaying a list of subcategories under the Hardware category.

4. Click the Peripherals subcategory; then click Digital Camera/Video; then click Buyers Guides. After you click the last subcategory (Buyers Guides), a new page appears listing sites that provide information about buying digital cameras.

5. Browse through the list of Web sites, and click one. The new site opens in your browser window. After reviewing it, you can use your browser's Back button to navigate back to the list of buyers guides to choose another.

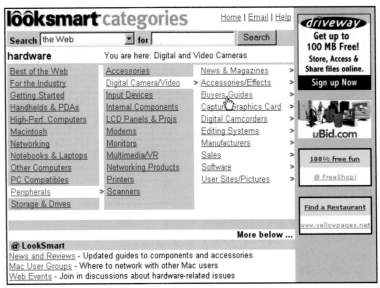

 Selecting categories and subcategories of topics in the LookSmart directory.

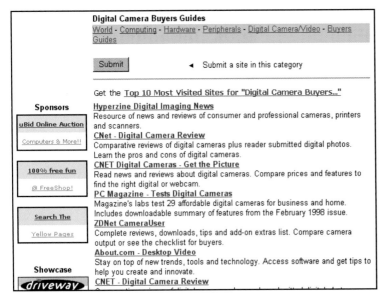

 After you select the final subcategory, LookSmart displays a list of Web sites that provide information related to your topic.

Sites listed in a directory will generally provide valuable, relevant information. This is because, before adding a site to its list, a directory reviews the site's content. Sites that offer poor content may not be included in the list. For this reason, Web sites listed in a directory are considered to be "pre-screened." Also, because the list of suggested sites has already been reviewed, you are unlikely to find a site listed multiple times within the same topic category. This is a big advantage over search engines, which are notorious for listing the same sites multiple times.

USING A SEARCH ENGINE

Suppose you want to find some information about ink jet printers. You know there are many different types of printers, available at a wide range of prices. You also know you are interested in a color printer rather than a black-and-white one. In the following exercise, you will use a search engine to help you find the information you need.

1. Launch your Web browser.

2. In the Location/Address bar, type **www.lycos.com/** and press Enter. The Lycos home page opens in your browser window.

3. In the Search For text box, type **"ink jet printer"** (include the quotation marks) and click the Go Get It! button. A new page appears, listing Web pages that contain information relating to ink jet printers. Note, however, that the list includes thousands of pages! Unlike most directories, search engines generally do not "screen" other Web sites for quality of content. Rather, they assume a Web site is relevant to your needs if it contains terms that match the keywords you provide.

4. To narrow the search results, you must provide more specific search criteria. Click in the Search For text box, and type **"color ink jet printer"** (again, including the quotation marks); then click the Go Get It! button. Another page appears, listing a new selection of Web sites that match your keywords. Note that this list is shorter than the original one, by several thousand matches. Still, you want to continue narrowing your search, so you decide to provide more criteria.

5. Click in the Search For text box, and type **"color ink jet printer reviews"** (with quotation marks); then click the Go Get It! button. The list of matching Web sites has shrunk even further, but is still quite long.

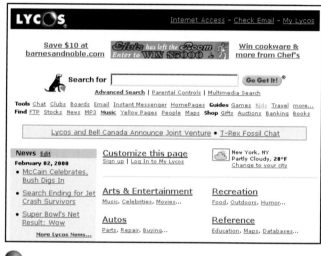

The Lycos home page.

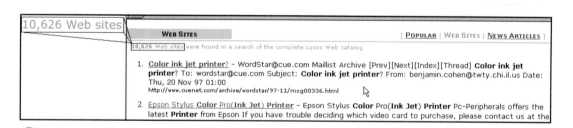

Search engines commonly produce thousands (even hundreds of thousands) of matches, depending on your search criteria. To narrow your list of results, you need to provide more specific keywords.

Scroll through the list, and notice if it contains any duplicate entries. How many of the suggested pages actually seem irrelevant to your search criteria? Duplicate and useless entries are two significant problems users encounter when working with search engines.

Further, in addition to listing Web pages, search engines frequently also list articles posted to Internet newsgroups and messages posted in chat rooms or in Web-based discussion groups. Sometimes you may find such results helpful, but other times they may only interfere with your search.

Fortunately, most search engines provide other tools to help you search more accurately, finding Web pages that are more relevant to your interests. These include Boolean operators and advanced search tools, which are discussed in the following sections.

Using Boolean Operators in Your Searches

Most search engines allow you to use special words, called Boolean operators, to modify your search criteria. Boolean operators are named after George Boole, a 19th century British mathematician.

There are three basic Boolean operators you can use in searching: AND, OR, and NOT. To use an operator, simply include it in the text box where you type your keywords. The following table shows simple examples of keyword searches that include the operators, and explains how the operator affects each search.

Operator	Search Criteria	Effect
AND	printer AND color	The search engine looks only for pages that include both terms, and ignores pages that include only one of them.
OR	printer OR color	The search engine looks for pages that include either or both of the terms.
NOT	printer NOT color	The search engine looks for pages that include the term *printer*, which do not also include the term *color*. The engine ignores any pages that include both terms.

Some search engines also support a fourth operator, NEAR. This operator determines the proximity, or closeness, of your specified keywords. For example, you may specify "printer NEAR color," with a closeness of 10 words. This tells the search engine to look for pages that include both terms, where the terms are no more than 10 words apart.

A good way to determine whether you need to use operators is to phrase your interest in the form of a sentence, and then use the important parts of the sentence as your keywords along with the appropriate operators. Here are some examples:

Interest	Search
I need information about cancer in children.	cancer AND children
I need information about dogs.	dog OR canine
I need information about acoustic guitars, but not electric guitars.	guitar NOT electric

A few (but not all) search engines will let you use multiple operators and set the order in which they are used. Suppose, for example, that you want to want to find information about cancer in dogs. You might set up your search criteria like this:

```
(dog OR canine) AND cancer
```

This tells the engine to look for pages that include either "dog," "canine," or both, and then to search those pages for ones that also include "cancer."

A few search engines accept symbols to represent operators. For example, you may be able to use a plus sign (+) to represent the AND operator, and a minus sign (−) to represent NOT.

Many search engines use implied Boolean logic by default, meaning you may not need to include an operator in some searches. For example, if you type this search criteria:

```
dog canine
```

Some search engines will assume that you want to find pages that include either term (using the OR operator by default), and others will assume you want pages that include both terms (using the AND operator by default).

When dealing with implied logic, remember that each search engine operates in a slightly different way. For example, in some engines, you should use quotation marks when searching for a phrase or when you want all words to be included, as in:

```
"ink jet printer"
```

Without the quotation marks, some engines will return pages that include the word "ink," others that include "jet," and others that include "printer," as well as pages that include all three.

The best way to determine how any search engine works is to study its Help-related pages. The Help section will tell you whether or how you can use operators with that particular engine.

Using Advanced Search Options

To overcome the problems of duplicate and irrelevant results, nearly all search engines provide a set of advanced search options, sometimes called advanced tools. It is important to remember that each engine's advanced tool set is somewhat different from the others', but they all have the same goal of helping you refine your search criteria to get the best results.

In some engines, advanced search options include support for phrase-based searching or Boolean operators, as already discussed. In other engines, an advanced search provides you with customized tools. At Excite, for example, if you select the Advanced Search link, you can work in a special form to structure your search criteria. The form lets you specify multiple words and phrases, and decide whether each one "must," "must not," or "should"

The Help links at the Google search engine site. This Help section provides a basic overview of Google and how it conducts searches. You also can find information about Google's support for Boolean operators, basic and advanced search techniques, and more. The Help section is the best place to start when working with a search engine for the first time.

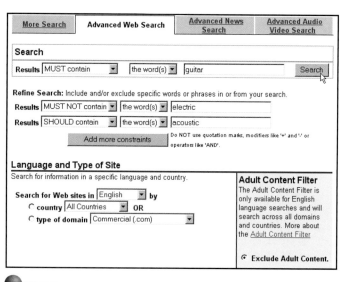

Setting up an advanced search in Excite.

be" included in the results. The form also provides tools that let you filter adult-oriented content (such as pornographic Web sites) from your results, and search for information in a different language or from a given country.

When using some advanced tool sets, such as those provided by Excite, you should not use operators in the text boxes. This is because the form itself is based on Boolean logic, and is designed to help you create complex Boolean-based searches without deciding which operators to use, or where to use them.

As mentioned earlier, the best way to learn about a specific search engine's advanced options is to study its Help section, and then to practice using the tools. After you learn to use an engine's advance options, you may never want to conduct a search without them.

METASEARCH ENGINES

In addition to the tools described in the preceding sections, a new breed of Web-based search engines is also gaining popularity. These sites, called metasearch engines, use multiple search engines simultaneously to look up sites that match your keywords, phrase, or question.

Examples of metasearch engines include Dogpile (**www.dogpile.com/**), Mamma (**www.mamma.com/**), and The BigHub (**www.thebighub.com/**). Metasearch engines are helpful if you are not certain which keywords to use, or if you want to get a very long list of Web sites that meet your search criteria.

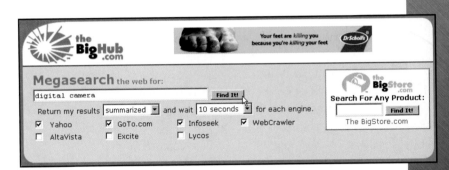

The BigHub is an example of a metasearch engine. This site enables you to specify terms for a keyword search, and to select the search engines you want to use. When you click the Find It! button, all the selected engines conduct simultaneous searches. The BigHub compiles all the results into a single list.

SITE-SPECIFIC SEARCH TOOLS

Many high-volume Web sites feature built-in search tools of their own, meaning you do not have to navigate to a different site in order to conduct a search. Sites such as Microsoft Corporation (**www.microsoft.com/**), CNN Interactive (**www.cnn.com/**), Netscape Communications (**www.netscape.com/**), and many others feature such tools. Generally, these site-specific search tools enable you to look for information on the Web site you are currently visiting.

Suppose, for example, you are visiting the Microsoft Web site and want to find information about Flight Simulator, a popular Microsoft game. Instead of jumping from one page to another looking for information, you can click in the Search box, type the words *Flight Simulator* and click the Go button. The site's search engine displays a list of pages on the Microsoft site that are related to Flight Simulator.

Some site-specific search tools also let you search outside that particular site. At ZDNet's site (**www.zdnet.com/**), for example, you can type one or more keywords in the Search box, then decide whether you want to search only the USA Today site or the entire Web for related information before clicking the Go button.

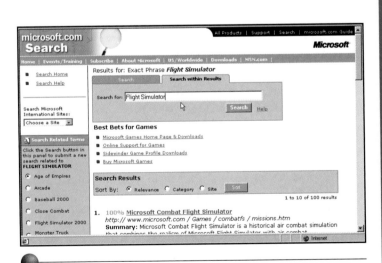

Searching for information about Flight Simulator at the Microsoft Web site.

Self Check Answers

Lesson 1, page 11
1. computer
2. memory
3. disk drive

Lesson 2, page 24
1. more than 1 trillion
2. terminal
3. midrange computers

Lesson 3, page 48
1. QWERTY, DVORAK
2. Shift
3. scan code

Lesson 4, page 60
1. Touch screen
2. game pads, joysticks
3. Optical character recognition (OCR) software

Lesson 5, page 80
1. Monochrome
2. magnetic coil
3. viewing angle

Lesson 6, page 92
1. print resolution
2. print head
3. Daisy wheel

Lesson 7, page 114
1. transistors
2. binary number system
3. Unicode

Lesson 8, page 134
1. architecture
2. multitasking
3. Athlon

Lesson 9, page 163
1. storage media
2. electromagnets
3. clusters

Lesson 10, page 173
1. milliseconds (ms)
2. File compression (or Data compression)
3. Data transfer rate

Lesson 11, page 193
1. user interface
2. Windows
3. task switching

Lesson 12, page 211
1. GUIs
2. Macintosh computer
3. operating environment

Lesson 13, page 235
1. Word processing software (or A word processor)
2. editing
3. Indents

Lesson 14, page 246
1. spreadsheet (or spreadsheet program)
2. cell pointer
3. value

Lesson 15, page 266
1. slide
2. template
3. handles

Lesson 16, page 285
1. database
2. flat-file database (or sequential file)
3. text

Lesson 17, page 308
1. network server
2. Electronic mail (e-mail)
3. peer-to-peer network

Lesson 18, page 322
1. modulator-demodulator
2. bits per second (bps)
3. uploading

Lesson 19, page 354
1. ARPANET
2. Internet protocol (IP) address
3. hyperlinks (or links)

Lesson 20, page 368
1. direct connection
2. digital subscriber line
3. cable modem

Lesson 21, page 389
1. workstation
2. pixels
3. file format

Lesson 22, page 401
1. bitmap
2. resolution-dependent
3. layers

Lesson 23, page 428
1. interactivity
2. convergence (or digital convergence)
3. Hypermedia

Lesson 24, page 443
1. audience
2. multimedia authoring
3. encoding

Lesson 25, page 461
1. integrity
2. office automation
3. management information

Lesson 26, page 476
1. systems development life cycle (SDLC)
2. Phase 1 (needs analysis)
3. top-down, bottom-up

Lesson 27, page 500
1. executable file
2. machine code
3. Heuristics

Lesson 28, page 511
1. syntax
2. porting
3. bytecode

Lesson 29, page 528
1. ergonomically correct
2. repetitive stress injury (RSI)
3. dot pitch

Lesson 30, page 543
1. piracy (or software piracy)
2. Beta software
3. boot sector

NUMERALS

3-D modeling software Graphics software used to create electronic models of three-dimensional objects. Types of 3-D modeling software include surface, solid, polygonal, and spline-based modelers.

3-D worksheet In a spreadsheet program, a workbook that contains multiple individual worksheets. The user can "layer" the sheets and perform calculations that include data from any or all sheets.

3GL See *third-generation language.*

4GL See *fourth-generation language.*

5GL See *fifth-generation language.*

A

absolute cell reference In a spreadsheet program, a cell reference that does not change when copied to a new cell.

Accelerated Graphics Port (AGP) A bus standard introduced in 1997, which incorporates a special architecture that allowed the video card to access the system's RAM directly, greatly speeding up graphics performance. The system must use a chip set that supports the AGP standard. Most new computers feature AGP graphics capabilities, in addition to a PCI system bus and an expansion bus.

accelerator card A circuit board that fits into an expansion slot and enhances the processing speed of the CPU.

activate (1) To initiate a command or load a program into memory and begin using it. (2) To choose; for example, you can activate a resource by choosing its icon, toolbar button, or file name.

active matrix LCD A liquid crystal display (LCD) technology that assigns a transistor to each pixel in a flat-panel monitor, improving display quality and eliminating the "submarining" effect produced by some types of flat-panel monitors. Also called a *thin-film transistor display.*

active window On the computer screen, the window in which the user's next action will occur. The active window's title bar is highlighted, while the title bars of inactive windows appear dimmed.

adapter See *expansion board.*

address bus A set of wires connecting the computer's CPU and RAM, across which memory addresses are transmitted. The number of wires in the bus determines the amount of memory that can be addressed at any one time.

Advanced Micro Devices (AMD) A chip manufacturer that makes processors for PC-compatible computers. AMD initially focused on chips for lower-price, lower-performance systems, but with the release of its K6 and Athlon processors, became a major manufacturer of high-performance processors for the PC market.

AGP See *Accelerated Graphics Port.*

algorithm A set of ordered steps or procedures necessary to solve a problem.

alignment The orientation of the lines of a paragraph with respect to the margins. In word processors, alignment options include left, right, center, and justified (also called *full justification*).

alphanumeric field See *text field.*

alphanumeric keys On a computer keyboard, the keys that include the letters of the alphabet, numerals, and commonly used symbols.

ALU See *arithmetic logic unit.*

AMD See *Advanced Micro Devices.*

American Standard Code for Information Interchange (ASCII) See *ASCII.*

animated GIF A special type of graphics file (in GIF format) that contains several slightly different versions of the same image. When viewed in a Web browser that supports animated GIFs, the images "play back" in rapid succession, creating a simple animation.

annotation In presentation programs, a feature that enables the user to embed notes in individual slides. The notes can be made visible only to the presenter, or they can be printed out for distribution to the audience.

anonymous FTP archives FTP sites with files available to the general public. So called because the user types the word "anonymous" as the account name.

antivirus program A program that scans a computer's disks and memory for viruses, detects them, and removes them. Some antivirus programs can help the user recover data and program files that have been damaged by a virus and can actively scan files as they are being copied from a disk or downloaded from the Internet.

application server A network server that hosts shared application files, enabling multiple users to use a network version of a software program. Generally, an application server also performs some or all of the processing tasks required by users of the application.

application software Any computer program used to create or process data, such as text documents, spreadsheets, graphics, and so on. Examples include database management software, desktop publishing programs, presentation programs, spreadsheet programs, and word processing programs.

appropriate use policy An ISP's statement to customers regarding the use of its services and the penalties that can occur if the service is misused.

Archie A catalog of file names maintained by McGill University in Montreal. Internet users can search and locate a file among thousands of directories listed on this service.

architecture The design of any part of a computer system, or of an entire system, including software and hardware. The design of a microprocessor's circuits, for example, is called its architecture.

archive file A file that stores one or more compressed files, which have been shrunk by a data-compression program.

argument (1) In a spreadsheet, the values or cell references within a formula on which the function performs its operation. (2) In programming, an item of information needed by a function or subroutine to carry out its instructions. Also called a *parameter.*

arithmetic logic unit (ALU) The component of the CPU that handles arithmetic and logic functions. Instructions are passed from memory to the ALU.

arithmetic operation One of two types of operations a computer can perform, which are handled by the arithmetic logic unit (ALU). Arithmetic operations include addition, subtraction, multiplication, and division. See also *logic operation*.

ARPANET Acronym for *Advanced Research Projects Agency Network*. An early network developed by the Department of Defense to connect computers at universities and defense contractors. This network eventually became part of the Internet.

article A message posted to an Internet newsgroup. A series of related articles and responses is called a *thread*.

ASCII A 7-bit binary code developed by the American National Standards Institute (ANSI) to represent symbolic, numeric, and alphanumeric characters. The ASCII character set is the most commonly used character set in PCs.

assembler A computer program that converts assembly language instructions into machine language.

assembly language A second-generation programming language that uses simple phrasing in place of the complex series of switches used in machine language.

Asynchronous Transfer Mode (ATM) A network protocol designed to send voice, video, and data transmissions over a single network. ATM provides different kinds of connections and bandwidth on demand, depending on the type of data being transmitted.

Athlon Released in 1999 by Advanced Micro Devices (AMD) a microprocessor for PC-compatible computers. At the time of its release the Athlon was the fastest microprocessor available, operating at speeds up to 650 MHz. The Athlon utilized a bus speed of 100 MHz at the time of its release and was designed to work with bus speeds of 200 MHz. The Athlon includes a 64 KB Level-1 cache and 512 KB of Level-2 cache. Capable of addressing 64 GB of memory, the Athlon also features 64-bit registers.

attribute (1) An enhancement or stylistic characteristic applied to text characters in a font, such as **bold** or *italic*. (2) In object-oriented programming, a component of the overall description of an object.

AutoCorrect In many types of productivity software (such as word processors or spreadsheet programs), a feature that recognizes certain types of mistakes and corrects them automatically. This feature can be configured to recognize many specific misspellings, to capitalize the first word of a sentence, and so on.

average access time The average amount of time a storage device requires to position its read/write heads over any spot on the medium; usually measured in milliseconds (ms). Also called *seek time*.

AVI Acronym for *audio-video interleave*. AVI is a file format supported by Microsoft's Video for Windows standard.

B

backbone The central structure of a network, which connects other elements of the network and handles the major traffic.

back up To create a duplicate set of program or data files in case the originals become damaged. (A duplicate file made for this purpose is called a *backup* file.) Files can be backed up individually, by entire folders, and by entire drives. Backups can be made to many types of storage media, such as diskettes, optical disks, or tape. The term is correctly used as two words as a verb ("I am going to *back up* the files on the server.") and as one word as a noun or adjective ("He used a *backup* utility to make a backup of that file.")

backup utility A program that enables the user to copy large groups of files from a hard disk to another storage medium (such as a floppy disk, tape, or compact disk) for safekeeping or use in case the original files become damaged.

bandwidth The amount of data that can be transmitted over a network at any given time. Bandwidth may be measured in bits per second (bps) or in hertz (Hz).

bar code A pattern of bars printed on a product or its packaging. A device called a *bar code reader* can scan a bar code and convert its pattern into numeric digits. After the bar code reader has converted a bar code image into a number, it transfers that number to a computer, just as though the number had been typed on a keyboard.

bar code reader An input device that converts a pattern of printed bars (called a *bar code*) into a number that a computer can read. A beam of light reflected off the bar code into a light-sensitive detector identifies the bar code and converts the bar patterns into numeric digits, which can be transferred to a computer. Bar code readers are commonly used in retail stores.

beta software Software that is in the developmental stage and is ready for large-scale testing but not for commercial sale or release to the public. Software publishers often provide copies of beta software to independent testers and other software developers, who work with the program to find bugs and test for compatibility with other products.

binary field A database field that stores binary objects (such as clip art, photographs, screen images, formatted text, sound objects, and video clips) or OLE objects (such as graphs or worksheets created with a spreadsheet or word processor).

binary large object (BLOB) (1) A graphic image file, such as clip art, a photograph, a screen image, formatted text, a sound object, or a video clip. (2) An OLE object, such as a graph or worksheet created with a spreadsheet or word processor; frequently used with object-oriented databases.

binary number system A system for representing the two possible states of electrical switches, which are on and off (also known as *base 2*). The binary number system gets its name from the fact that it includes only two numbers: 0 and 1. In computer storage and memory systems, the numeral 0 represents off, and a 1 represents on.

bit The smallest unit of data that can be used by a computer.

bitmap A binary representation of an image in which each part of the image, such as a pixel, is represented by one or more bits in a coordinate system. Also called a *raster*.

bits per second (bps) A measure of a modem's data transmission speed.

BLOB See *binary large object*.

block A contiguous series of characters, words, sentences, or paragraphs in a word processing document. This term is also sometimes used to describe a range of cells in a spreadsheet. Once a block of text or cells has been selected, the user can perform many different actions on it, such as moving, formatting, or deleting.

BMP Abbreviation for *bitmap*. BMP is a graphic-file format native to Windows and OS/2. BMP is widely used on PCs for icons and wallpaper. Some Macintosh programs also can read BMP files.

board See *expansion board*.

Boolean field See *logical field*.

booting Starting a computer. The term comes from the expression "pulling oneself up by one's own bootstraps."

boot sector The portion of a disk that contains the master boot record—a program that runs when the computer is first started, and which determines whether the disk has the basic operating system components required to run successfully.

border A paragraph format that displays a line on any side of a block. This type of formatting is often used to distinguish the block from regular text. Borders are generally applied to an entire paragraph or group of paragraphs.

bottom-up design A design method in which system details are developed first, followed by major functions or processes.

branch One of several directions that flows from a condition statement or function call within a sequence structure.

bps See *bits per second*.

bridge A device that connects two LANs and controls data flow between them.

browser See *Web browser*.

bug An error in a computer program.

bus The path between components of a computer or nodes of a network. The bus's width determines the speed at which data is transmitted. When used alone, the term commonly refers to a computer's data bus.

bus network A network topology in which all network nodes and peripheral devices are attached to a single conduit.

button In graphical user interfaces, a symbol that simulates a push button. The user clicks a button to initiate an action.

byte The amount of memory required to store a single character. A byte is comprised of eight bits.

bytecode The compiled code used for a Java-based applet. To run a Java applet, a user accesses the bytecode by downloading it over the Internet. Then, using a Java virtual machine, the user's PC converts the bytecode into machine code appropriate to that particular computer, allowing the applet to run.

C

cache memory High-speed memory that resides between the CPU and RAM in a computer. Cache memory stores data and instructions that the CPU is likely to need next. The CPU can retrieve data or instructions more quickly from cache than it can from RAM or a disk.

CAD See *computer-aided design*.

card See *expansion board*.

carpal tunnel syndrome A form of repetitive stress injury. Specifically, an injury of the wrist or hand commonly caused by repetitive motion, such as extended periods of keyboarding.

CASE See *computer-aided software engineering*.

cathode ray tube (CRT) A type of monitor or TV screen that uses a vacuum tube as a display screen. CRTs are most commonly used with desktop computers.

CBT See *computer-based training*.

CD See *compact disk*.

CD-Recordable (CD-R) drive A peripheral device that enables the user to create customized CD-ROM disks. Once data has been written to a CD-R disk, that data cannot be changed (overwritten). CD-R disks can be read by any CD-ROM drive. CD-R drives are commonly used to create backup copies of program or data files, or to create duplicates of existing compact disks.

CD-ReWritable (CD-RW) drive A peripheral device that enables the user to create customized CD-ROM disks. Unlike a CD-R disk, a CD-RW disk's data can be overwritten, meaning the data can be updated after it has been placed on the disk. CD-RW disks can be read by any CD-ROM drive.

CD-R See *CD-Recordable drive*.

CD-RW See *CD-ReWritable drive*.

CD-ROM See *compact disk, read-only memory*.

CD-ROM drive A specialized type of disk drive, which enables a computer to read data from a compact disk. Using a standard CD-ROM drive and compact disk, the computer can only read data from the disk and cannot write data to the disk.

Celeron A slower, less powerful version of Intel's Pentium II and Pentium III processors, designed for entry-level personal computers.

cell In a spreadsheet or database table, the intersection of a row and column, forming a box into which the user enters numbers, formulas, or text. The term also is used to refer to the individual blocks in a table created in a word processing program.

cell address In a spreadsheet, an identifier that indicates the location of a cell in a worksheet. The address is composed of the cell's row and column locations. For example, if the cell is located at the intersection of column B and row 3, then its cell address is B3.

cell pointer A square enclosing one cell of a spreadsheet, identifying that cell as the active cell. The user positions the cell pointer in a worksheet by clicking the mouse on the cell or by using the cursor movement keys on the keyboard.

cell reference The address of a spreadsheet cell used in a formula.

central processing unit (CPU) The computer's primary processing hardware, which interprets and executes program instructions and manages the functions of input, output, and storage devices. In personal computers, the CPU is composed of a control unit, an ALU, built-in memory, and supporting circuitry such as a dedicated math processor. The CPU may reside on a single chip on the computer's motherboard, or on a larger card inserted into a special slot on the motherboard. In larger computers, the CPU may reside on several circuit boards.

channel A discussion group where chat users convene to discuss a topic.

character animation The process of animating a character—such as a drawing of a person, animal, or some other organic or inorganic object—to create the illusion of movement.

character field See *text field*.

character formatting In a word processor, settings that control the attributes of individual text characters, such as font, type size, type style, and color.

characters per second (cps) A measure of the speed of impact printers, such as dot matrix printers.

chart A graphic representation of numbers created from spreadsheet data. Also called a *graph*.

chief information officer (CIO) In a large company, an executive manager who heads the IS department.

choose See *activate*.

CIO See *chief information officer*.

circuit board A rigid rectangular card—consisting of chips and electronic circuitry—that ties the processor to other hardware. In a personal computer, the primary circuit board (to which all components are attached) is called the *motherboard*.

circuit-switched Describes a type of communications line in which access to the connection is constant until broken by either party. This type of connection provides a specific amount of bandwidth to the users, which does not change during use. Circuit-switched lines are commonly used for telephone or modem transmissions.

CISC See *Complex Instruction Set Computing.*

class The attributes and functions that define an object in object-oriented program code.

class inheritance In object-oriented programming, the tendency for all subclasses to share the attributes and functions of the parent class.

clicking Selecting an object or command on the computer screen (for example, from a menu, toolbar, or dialog box) by pointing to the object and pressing and releasing the primary mouse button once.

client An application program on a user's computer that requests information from another computer, such as a network server or Web host, over a network or the Internet. The term may also be used to refer to the user's computer itself.

client/server A hierarchical network strategy in which the processing is shared by a server and numerous clients. In this type of network, clients provide the user interface, run applications, and request services from the server. The server contributes storage, printing, and some or all processing services.

clip art Predrawn or photographed graphic images, which are available for use by anyone. Some clip art is available through licensing, some through purchase, and some for free.

Clipboard A holding area maintained by the operating system in memory. The Clipboard is used for storing text, graphics, sound, video or other data that has been copied or cut from a document. After data has been placed in the Clipboard, it can be inserted from the Clipboard into other documents, in the same application or a different application.

clock cycle In a processor, the amount of time required to turn a transistor off and back on again. Also called a *tick.* A processor can execute an instruction in a given number of clock cycles, so as a computer's clock speed (the number of clock cycles in generates per second) increases, so does the number of instructions it can carry out each second.

clock speed A measure of a processor's operating speed, currently measured in megahertz (MHz), or millions of cycles per second. A computer's operating speed is based on the number of clock cycles, or *ticks*, it generates per second. For example, if a computer's clock speed is 300 MHz, it "ticks" 300 million times per second.

cluster On a magnetic disk (such as a hard disk) a group of sectors that are treated as a single data-storage unit. The number of sectors per disk can vary, depending on the type of disk and the manner in which it is formatted.

coaxial cable (coax) A cable composed of a single conductive wire wrapped in a conductive wire mesh shield with an insulator in between.

code The instructions or statements that are the basis of a computer program.

color monitor A computer monitor whose screen can display data in color. A color monitor's range and intensity are based on a variety of factors. Current high-resolution color monitors can display more than 16 million colors, but can also be set to display as few as 16 colors or varying shades of gray.

color separation A process used to prepare full-color pages for printing. This process creates a separate page for each color found in the image. During printing, the separations are combined to produce a single image that includes all the required colors.

column (1) A vertically arranged series of cells in a spreadsheet or database table, named with a letter or combination of letters. (2) In word processing, a document-formatting technique in which the page is divided into vertical sections, like a newspaper's columns.

command An instruction issued to the computer. The user can issue commands, usually by choosing from a menu, clicking an on-screen tool or icon, or pressing a combination of keys. Application programs and the operating system also issue commands to the computer.

command-line interface A user interface that enables the user to interact with the software by typing strings of characters at a prompt. MS-DOS is an example of a command-line interface.

command prompt See *prompt.*

commercial software Software that a manufacturer makes available for purchase. The consumer usually pays for a license to use the software, rather than the actual software itself.

communications device An input/output device used to connect one computer to another to share hardware and information. This family of devices includes modems and network interface cards.

compact disk (CD) A type of optical storage device, identical to audio CDs, which can store about 650 MB of data, or about 450 times as much as a diskette. The type of CD used in computers is called Compact Disk Read-Only Memory (CD-ROM). As the device's name implies, you cannot change the information on the disk, just as you cannot record over an audio CD.

compact disk read-only memory (CD-ROM) The most common type of optical storage medium. In CD-ROM, data is written in a series of lands and pits on the surface of a compact disk (CD), which can be read by a laser in a CD-ROM drive. A standard CD stores approximately 650 MB, but data on a standard compact disk cannot be altered.

compatible Describes the capability of one type of hardware, software, or data file to work with another.

compiler A program that translates a file of program source code into machine language.

Complex Instruction Set Computing (CISC) Describes a type of processor designed to handle large and comprehensive instruction sets. CISC processors are commonly used in IBM-compatible PCs and Macintosh computers.

compositing The process of combining separate images to create a new image, as is done when the image of an actor is placed in front of a background image.

computer An electronic device used to process data, converting the data into information that is useful to people.

computer-aided design (CAD) The use of computers to create complex two- or three-dimensional models of buildings and products, including architectural, engineering, and mechanical designs.

computer-aided software engineering (CASE) Software used to develop information systems. CASE automates the analysis, design, programming, and documentation tasks.

computer-based training (CBT) The use of customized, interactive computer tools (such as multimedia presentations displayed from CD-ROM or online) for training purposes.

computer-generated imagery (CGI) The process of using powerful computers and special graphics, animation, and compositing software to create digital special effects or unique images. CGI is frequently used in filmmaking, game design, animation, and multimedia design.

computer scientist A person who studies computer theory and researches and develops new techniques in computer design and programming.

computer system A four-part system that consists of hardware, software, data, and a user.

conditional statement A feature of selection structure programming that directs program flow by branching to one part of the program or another depending on the results of a comparison.

configure To adapt a computer to a specific need by selecting from a range of hardware or software options. Configuration may include installing new or replacement hardware or software, or changing settings in existing hardware or software.

context menu In the Windows 95 and Windows 98 operating systems, a brief menu that appears when the user right-clicks on certain items. The menu contains commands that apply specifically to the item that was right-clicked. Also called a *shortcut menu*.

continuous-feed paper A special type of paper for use with some types of impact printers. The individual sheets of paper are attached, end to end, forming a continuous chain of pages that can be pulled through the printer. Some types of continuous-feed paper feature holes along the long edges, which help guide it through the printer's sheet-feeding mechanism. Also called *tractor-feed paper*.

control unit The component of the CPU that contains the instruction set. The control unit directs the flow of data throughout the computer system.

conversion The process of replacing an existing system with an updated or improved version. Information systems (IS) professionals may use one or more different conversion methods when changing an organization's system.

cookie A special file that stores personal information, such as credit card data. Web sites create cookies and store them on the user's computer. Later visits to the site read the cookie to access your account.

cooperative multitasking A multitasking environment in which programs periodically check with the operating system to see whether other programs need the CPU and, if so, relinquish control of the CPU to the next program.

Copy An application command that makes a duplicate of data selected from a document and stores it in the Clipboard without removing the data from the original document. The data then can be used in other documents and other applications.

copy protection An antipiracy technique that prevents the illegal duplication of software.

counter field A database field that stores a unique incrementing numeric value (such as an invoice number) that the DBMS automatically assigns to each new record. Also called *autonumber field*.

cps See *characters per second*.

CPU See *central processing unit*.

CRT See *cathode ray tube*.

cursor A graphic symbol on screen that indicates where the next keystroke or command will appear when entered. Representations include a blinking vertical line or underline, a box, an arrow, and an I-beam pointer. Also called the *insertion point*.

cursor-movement keys On a computer keyboard, the keys that direct the movement of the on-screen cursor or insertion point, including the up, down, left, and right arrows, and the Home, End, Page Up, and Page Down keys.

Cut An application command that removes data selected from a document and stores it in the Clipboard. The data is no longer a part of the original document. While in the Clipboard, the data can be used in other documents or applications.

cylinder A vertical stack of tracks, one track on each side of each platter of a hard disk.

Cyrix One of several manufacturers that make processors that mimic the functionality of Intel's chips.

D

DAT See *digital audiotape*.

data Raw facts, numbers, letters, or symbols that the computer processes into meaningful information.

data area The part of the disk that remains free to store information after the logical formatting process has created the boot sector, FAT, and root folder.

data bus An electrical path composed of parallel wires that connect the CPU, memory, and other hardware on the motherboard. The number of wires determines the amount of data that can be transferred at one time.

data communications The electronic transfer of data between computers.

data compression The process of reducing data volume and increasing data-transfer rates by using mathematical algorithms to analyze groups of bits and encode repeating sequences of data.

data compression program A program that reduces the volume of data by manipulating the way the data is stored.

Data Exchange Format (DXF) A universal file format for use with vector graphics.

data flow diagram A method of documenting how data moves through a system, including input, processing, and output.

data member A class attribute in an object-oriented programming language.

data transfer rate The rate at which a data storage device can read or write data; expressed as either bits per second (bps) or bytes per second (Bps). Also called *throughput*.

database A collection of related data organized with a specific structure.

database management system (DBMS) A computer program used to manage the storage, organization, processing, and retrieval of data in a database; also called *data management software*.

database specialist In an information systems (IS) department, the person responsible for designing and building tables, forms, queries, and reports in the database. Also known as a *database administrator*.

date field A database field that stores a date.

debugging The process of tracking down and correcting errors (called *bugs*) in a software program.

decimal number system The system that uses 10 digits to represent numbers; also called *base 10*.

decision support system A specialized application used to collect and report certain types of business data, which can be used to aid managers in the decision-making process.

decision tree A graphical representation of the events and actions that can occur in a program or information system under different conditions.

decoding The process of reinserting bits stripped away during encoding, performed at the receiving end.

density A measure of the quality of a magnetic disk's surface. The higher a disk's density, the more closely the iron oxide particles are packed and the more data the disk can store.

description field See *memo field*.

deselect The opposite of *select*. In many applications, the user can select, or highlight, blocks of text or objects for editing. By clicking the mouse in a different location or pressing a cursor-movement key, the user removes the highlighting and the text or objects are no longer selected.

desktop In a computer operating system, a graphical workspace in which all of the computer's available resources (such as files, programs, printers, Internet tools, and utilities) can be easily accessed by the user. In such systems, the desktop is a colored background on which the user sees small pictures, called icons. The user accesses various resources by choosing icons on the desktop.

desktop publishing (DTP) software A program used to enhance standard word processing documents. DTP software creates professional-quality documents and publications using design, typesetting, and paste-up features.

development phase Phase 3 of the systems development life cycle, in which programmers create or customize software to fit the needs of an organization, technical documentation is prepared, and software testing is begun.

device Any electronic component attached to or part of a computer; hardware.

dialog box A special-purpose window that appears when the user issues certain commands in a program or graphical operating system. A dialog box gets its name from the "dialog" it conducts with the user as the program seeks the information it needs to perform a task.

digital The use of the numerals 1 and 0 (digits) to express data in a computer. The computer recognizes the numeral 1 as an "on" state of a transistor, whereas a 0 represents an "off" state.

digital audiotape (DAT) A magnetic storage medium that can store data at a very high density. Read by a DAT drive that has two write heads that write data with opposite magnetic polarities on overlapping areas of the tape, and two read heads that each read only one polarity or the other.

digital camera A video camera that converts light intensities into digital data. Digital cameras are used to record images that can be viewed and edited on a computer.

digital cash See *electronic cash*.

digital convergence The process of combining multiple digital media types (such as text, graphics, video, and sound) into a single multimedia product.

digital light processing (DLP) A technology used in some types of PC projectors, to project bright, crisp images. DLP devices use a special microchip, called a *digital micromirror device*, which uses mirrors to control the image display. DLP projectors can display clear images in normal lighting conditions.

Digital Subscriber Line (DSL) A form of digital telephone service used to transmit voice and data signals. There are several varieties of DSL technology, which include Asymmetrical DSL, Highbit-rate DSL, and others. DSL can achieve theoretical data-transmission rates of 52 Mbps.

digital video disk or **digital versatile disk (DVD)** A high-density optical medium capable of storing a full-length movie on a single disk the size of a standard compact disk (CD). Unlike

a standard CD, which stores data on only one side, a DVD-format disk stores data on both sides. Using compression technologies and very fine data areas on the disk's surface, newer-generation DVDs can store several gigabytes of data.

digitizing Converting an image or a sound into a series of binary numbers (1s and 0s), which can be stored in a computer.

dimension In a CAD program, a notation showing the measurements of an object.

DIMM See *Dual In-Line Memory Module*.

direct connection A permanent connection between your computer system and the Internet. Sometimes called a *dedicated line*.

direct conversion The complete transfer of all data and users from an existing system to a new system at one time.

directory A tool for organizing a disk. A directory contains a list of files and other directories stored on the disk. A disk can hold many directories, which can in turn store many files and other directories. Also called a *folder*.

disk A storage medium commonly used in computers. Two types of disks are used: magnetic disks, which store data as charged particles on the disk's surface; and optical disks, which use lasers to read data embossed on the disk in a series of lands and pits.

disk cartridge A removable magnetic storage medium that features a high-density disk enclosed in a plastic cartridge. Such cartridges generally provide greater storage capacities than standard floppy disks but less capacity than a hard disk.

disk controller A device that connects a disk drive to the computer's bus, enabling the drive to exchange data with other devices.

disk drive A storage device that holds, spins, reads data from, and writes data to disks.

diskette A removable magnetic disk, encased in a plastic sleeve. The most common diskette size is 3.5 inches; older 5.25-inches diskettes are less commonly used. Also called a *floppy disk* or a *floppy*.

diskette drive A device that holds a removable floppy disk when in use; read/write heads read and write data to the diskette.

display adapter See *video controller*.

distance learning (DL) The process of using communications and computer technologies to provide instruction over a long distance.

distributed computing A system configuration in which two or more computers in a network share applications, storage, and processing power. Also called *distributed processing*.

DL See *distance learning*.

DLL See *dynamic link library file*.

DLP See *digital light processing*.

DNS See *Domain Name System*.

docking station A base into which a portable computer can be inserted, essentially converting the portable computer into a desktop system. A docking station may provide connections to a full-size monitor, keyboard, and mouse, as well as additional devices like speakers or a digital video camera.

document A computer file consisting of a compilation of one or more kinds of data. There are many different types of documents, including text documents, spreadsheets, graphics files, and so on. A document, which a user can open and use, is different from a program file, which is required by a software program to operate.

document area In many software applications, the portion of the program's interface in which the active document appears. In this part of the interface, the user can work directly with the document and its contents. Also called the *document window*.

document formats In productivity applications, settings that affect the appearance of the entire document, such as page size, page orientation, and the presence of headers or footers.

document window See *document area*.

documentation Sets of printed or online manuals intended for people who use or support an information system.

domain A name given to a computer and its peripherals connected to the Internet, which identifies the type of organization using the computer. Examples of domain names are *.com* for commercial enterprises and *.edu* for schools. Also called a *top-level domain*.

domain name system (DNS) A naming system used for computers on the Internet. This system provides an individual name (representing the organization using the computer) and a domain name, which classifies the type of organization. DNS converts an e-mail address into a numeric Internet Protocol (IP) address for transmission.

dot matrix printer A type of impact printer that creates characters on a page by using small pins to strike an inked ribbon, pressing ink onto the paper. The arrangement of pins in the print head creates a matrix of dots—hence the device's name.

dot pitch The distance between phosphor dots on a monitor. The highest-resolution monitors have the smallest dot pitch.

dots per inch (dpi) A measure of resolution commonly applied to printers, scanners, and other devices that input or output text or images. The more dots per inch, the higher the resolution. For example, a printer with a resolution of 600 dpi, it can print 600 dots across and 600 down in a one-inch square, for a total of 360,000 dots in one square inch.

double-clicking Selecting an object or activating a command on the screen by pointing to an object (such as an icon) and pressing and releasing the mouse button twice in quick succession.

downloading Retrieving a file from a remote computer. The opposite of *uploading*.

dragging Moving an object on the screen by pointing to the object, pressing the primary mouse button, and holding down the button while dragging the object to a new location.

drag and drop Moving text or graphics from one part of the document to another by selecting the desired information, pressing and holding down the primary mouse button, dragging the selection to a new location, and releasing the mouse button. Also called *drag-and-drop editing*.

DRAM See *dynamic RAM*.

draw program A graphics program that uses vectors to create an image. Mathematical equations describe each line, shape, and pattern, allowing the user to manipulate all elements of the graphic separately.

driver A small program that accepts requests for action from the operating system and causes a device, such as a printer, to execute the requests.

dpi See *dots per inch*.

DSL See *Digital Subscriber Line*.

DTP See *desktop publishing software*.

Dual In-Line Memory Module (DIMM) One type of circuit board containing RAM chips.

dual-scan LCD An improved passive matrix technology for flat-panel monitors in which pixels are scanned twice as often, reducing the effects of submarining and blurry graphics.

DVD See *digital video disk* or *digital versatile disk*.

DXF See *Data Exchange Format*.

dye-sub (dye-sublimation) printer A printer that produces photographic-quality images by using a heat source to evaporate colored inks from a ribbon, transferring the color to specially coated paper. Also called a *thermal dye transfer printer* or *thermal dye diffusion printer*.

dynamic link library (DLL) file A partial executable file. A .dll file will not run all on its own; rather, its commands are accessed by another running program.

dynamic RAM (DRAM) The most common type of random access memory (RAM) used in personal computers. While dynamic RAM is less expensive than static RAM (SRAM), it must be recharged with electricity many times each second in order to retain its contents. Dynamic RAM supports access times of about 60 nanoseconds.

E

EBCDIC Acronym for *Extended Binary Coded Decimal Interchange Code*. An 8-bit binary code developed by IBM to represent symbols and numeric and alphanumeric characters; most commonly used on IBM mainframe computers.

e-commerce See *electronic commerce*.

edit To make modifications to an existing document file.

electromagnet A magnet made by wrapping a wire coil around an iron bar and sending an electric current through the coil. Reversing the direction of the current's flow reverses the polarity of the magnetic field. Electromagnets are part of the read/write heads used in magnetic storage devices.

electromagnetic field (EMF) A field of magnetic and electrical forces created during the generation, transmission, and use of low-frequency electrical power. EMFs are produced by computers.

electronic cash A redeemable electronic certificate, which the consumer purchased from a bank that provides electronic cash services. Also called *digital cash*.

electronic commerce The practice of conducting business transactions online, such as selling products from a World Wide Web site. The process often involves the customer's providing personal or credit card information online, presenting special security concerns. Also called *e-commerce*.

electronic mail A system for exchanging written, voice, and video messages through a computer network. Also called *e-mail*.

electronic pen An input device that allows the user to write directly on or point at a special pad or the screen of a pen-based computer, such as a PDA.

electronic wallet A program that stores on the user's computer credit card information, a digital certificate that verifies the user's identity, and shipping information.

EMF See *electromagnetic field*.

e-mail address An address that identifies an individual user of an electronic mail system, enabling the person to send and receive e-mail messages. The e-mail address consists of a user name, the "at" symbol (@), and the DNS.

e-mail program (or e-mail client) Software that lets you create, send, and receive e-mail.

encapsulate To include characteristics or other objects within an object in an object-oriented program.

encoding The process of stripping away unneeded bits of digital source material, resulting in the transmission of smaller files.

encryption The process of encoding and decoding data, making it useless to any system that cannot decode (decrypt) it.

Enhanced Integrated Drive Electronics (EIDE) An enhanced version of IDE, a drive-interface standard that was developed in 1983 by Maxtor Corporation as an improvement on the ST-506 interface.

Energy Star A program of the United States Environmental Protection Agency (EPA), which sets standards for many types of electrical appliances. To qualify to bear the program's seal of approval, an applicance (such as a computer monitor) must meet certain standards for energy savings.

enterprise A term that typically refers to an organization with large hardware and software applications, used by hundreds or thousands of people.

enterprise software A large-scale software application designed for use in a large organization, possibly by hundreds or thousands of users.

ergonomics The study of the physical relationship between people and their tools. In the world of computing, ergonomics seeks to help people use computers correctly to avoid physical problems such as fatigue, eyestrain, and repetitive stress injuries.

error-correction protocol A standard for correcting errors that occur when static interferes with data transmitted via modems over telephone lines.

Ethernet The most common network protocol.

executable (EXE) file The core program file responsible for launching software.

execute To load and carry out a program or a specific set of instructions. Executing is also called *running.*

execution cycle The second portion of the *machine cycle,* which is the series of steps a CPU takes when executing an instruction. During the execution cycle, the CPU actually carries out the instruction by converting it into microcode. In some cases, the CPU may be required to store the results of an instruction in memory; if so, this occurs during the execution cycle.

exit condition In programming, a condition that must be met in order for a loop to stop repeating.

expansion board A device that enables the user to configure or customize a computer to perform specific tasks or to enhance performance. An expansion board—also called a *card, adapter,* or *board*—contains a special set of chips and circuitry that add functionality to the computer. An expansion board may be installed to add fax/modem capabilities to the computer, for example, or to provide sound or video-editing capabilities.

expansion slot The area of the motherboard into which *expansion boards* are inserted, connecting them to the PC's bus.

expert system An information system in which decision-making processes are automated. A highly detailed database is accessed by an inference engine, which is capable of forming an intelligent response to a query.

Extended Data Output (EDO) RAM A type of RAM, which is faster than FPM RAM and commonly found on the fastest computers.

external modem A communications device used to modulate data signals. This type of device is described as "external"

because it is housed outside the computer and connected to the computer through a serial port and to the telephone system with a standard telephone jack.

extract To uncompress one or more compressed files that have been stored together in an archive file.

extranet A network connection that enables external users to access a portion of an organization's internal network, usually via an Internet connection. External users have access to specific parts of the internal network but are forbidden to access other areas, which are protected by firewalls.

F

FAQ See *frequently asked questions.*

Fast Ethernet A networking technology, also known as *100Base-T,* that uses the same network cabling scheme as Ethernet but uses different network interface cards to achieve data transfer speeds of up to 100 Mbps.

FAT See *file allocation table.*

fax modem A modem that can emulate a fax machine.

feedback loop In interactive multimedia products, the interaction that occurs between the user and the program. As the user responds to the program by making choices and the program responds to the user by changing its behavior, a two-way "loop" of interaction takes place.

fetching The first step of the CPU's instruction cycle, during which the control unit retrieves (or fetches) a command or data from the computer's memory.

fiber-optic cable A thin strand of glass wrapped in a protective coating. Fiber-optic cable transfers data by means of pulsating beams of light.

field The smallest unit of data in a database, used to group each piece or item of data into a specific category. Fields are arranged in a column and titled by the user.

field format See *mask.*

fiery print server A color laser printer typically used to produce high-quality graphics; used by print shops and publishing firms.

fifth-generation language (5GL) A high-level programming language that theoretically would use artificial intelligence techniques to create software, based on the programmer's description of the program. Some experts contend that 5GL programming languages do not yet exist.

file A set of related computer data (used by a person) or program instructions (used by an application or operating system) that has been given a name.

file-allocation table (FAT) In a diskette or hard disk, a log created during the logical formatting process that records the location of each file and the status of each sector on the disk.

file compression See *data compression.*

file defragmentation utility A program that locates the pieces of fragmented files saved in noncontiguous sectors on a disk and rearranges them so they are stored in contiguous sectors.

file format A standardized method of encoding data for storage.

file server The central computer of a network, used for shared storage. A server may store software applications, databases, and data files for the network's users. Depending on the way a server is used, it may also be called a *network server, application server,* or just *server.*

file server network A hierarchical network strategy in which the server is used to store and forward files to the nodes. Each node runs its own applications.

file transfer The process of sending a file from one computer to another by modem or across a network.

file transfer protocol (FTP) A set of rules that dictates the format in which data is sent from one computer to another.

filter A DBMS tool that enables the user to establish conditions for selecting and displaying a subset of records that meet those criteria.

firewall An antipiracy method for protecting networks. A network node acts as a gateway, permitting access to public sections of the network while protecting proprietary areas.

FireWire The version of the IEEE 1394 expansion bus standard used in Macintosh computers.

first-generation language A term applied to machine languages, which were the earliest and crudest programming languages used with personal computers.

flash memory A type of nonvolatile memory, like ROM, which stores data even when the system's power is off. Flash memory is commonly used in digital cameras.

flat-file database A database file consisting of a single data table, which is not linked to any other tables.

flat-panel display A thin, lightweight monitor used in laptop and notebook computers. Most flat-panel displays use LCD technology.

floppy See *diskette.*

floppy disk See *diskette.*

flowchart A diagram of the program control flow.

fly-by A specially rendered animation, created in a CAD or 3-D graphics program, that creates the illusion that the viewer is moving past, around, or over an object such as a building.

folder See *directory.*

font A family of alphanumeric characters, symbols, and punctuation marks that share the same design. Modern applications provide many different fonts and enable users to use different fonts in the same document. Also called a *typeface.*

footer A recurring line or paragraph of text appearing at the bottom of each page in a document. Footers often include page numbers, the document's title, the name of the current chapter, or other information.

form A custom screen created in a database management system (DBMS) for displaying and entering data related to a single database record.

format (1) As relating to magnetic storage devices, the layout of tracks and sectors in which data is stored. (2) In productivity applications, a setting that affects the appearance of a document or part of a document.

formatting (1) The process of magnetically mapping a disk with a series of tracks and sectors where data will be stored. Also called *initializing.* (2) The process of applying formatting options (such as character or paragraph formats) to a document.

formula A mathematical equation within a cell of a spreadsheet. To identify it and distinguish it from other spreadsheet entries, a formula begins with a special symbol, such as a plus sign or an equal sign.

formula bar In spreadsheet programs, a special text box that displays the active cell's address and the formula or data

entered in that cell. The user may be able to enter or edit data or formulas in this box.

fourth-generation language (4GL) An advanced programming language used to create an application, such as a report writer.

fragmented Describes a file that has been broken into sections, which are stored on noncontiguous sectors of a disk.

frame (1) In networking, a small block of data to be transmitted over a network. A frame includes an identifying header and the actual data to be sent. Also called a *packet.* (2) In animation, a single still image that, when viewed with many other images in rapid succession, creates the illusion of motion. (3) In many software applications, a special tool that enables the user to place an object—such as a text box or an image from a separate file—in a document. The frame surrounds the object in the document, enabling the user to position and resize the object as needed.

freeware Software that is made freely available to the public by the publisher. Freeware publishers usually allow users to distribute their software to others, as long as the software's source files are not modified, and as long as the distributor charges no fees or does not profit from the distribution.

frequently asked questions (FAQ) A document routinely developed by a news group, which lists questions most commonly asked in the news group, along with their answers. FAQs help a news group's members avoid the repeated posting of the same information to the group.

front end An interface to a program that hides much of the program from the user. Front ends are commonly used in large database applications.

FTP client software Programs that enable users to download files from an FTP site.

FTP server A computer used to store FTP sites, many containing thousands of individual programs and files.

FTP site A collection of files stored on an FTP server from which users can copy files from and to their own computer.

full-duplex The ability to send and receive data simultaneously over a common data path or communications link.

function (1) In a spreadsheet, a part of a formula used to perform complex operations, such as adding the contents of a range or finding the absolute value of a cell's contents. (2) In programming, a block of statements designed to perform a specific routine or task.

function keys The part of the keyboard that can be used to quickly activate commands, designated F1, F2, and so on.

G

G-3 The basis of the iMac and Power Mac computers, giving lower cost, better speed, and higher performance than the Intel Pentium IIs.

G-4 Described as having the heart of a supercomputer, the G4 operates at 500 MHz and more, is 128 bits, and uses Level 2 cache and a bus speed of 100 MHz.

game controller A specialized type of input device, which enables the user to interact with computer games. Two popular types of game controllers are *game pads* and *joysticks.*

game pad A type of game controller that usually provides two sets of controls—one for each hand. These devices are extremely flexible and are used to control a wide variety of game systems.

gateway A computer system that can translate one network protocol into another so that data can be transmitted between two dissimilar networks.

GB See *gigabyte*.

GIF Acronym for graphics interchange format. A graphics file format supported by many graphics programs. GIF files are commonly used in Web pages.

gigabyte (GB) Equivalent to approximately one billion bytes; a typical measurement of data storage.

gigaflops A measure of processor performance, equivalent to approximately one billion floating point operations per second.

goal seeking A data-analysis process that begins with a conclusion and calculates the values that will lead to the desired outcome, such as figuring a mortgage amount based on an affordable monthly payment.

Gopher An Internet service that organizes resources into multilevel menus to make finding information easier; first created by the University of Minnesota to provide easy access to computers campus-wide.

goto statement In programming, a statement that tells the program to move to a specific line of code, which may or may not be the next line in sequence.

gradient fill In presentation or graphics software, an option in which the color changes as you go from one side of the object to another.

grammar checker A language tool built into many productivity applications, especially word processors. The program checks the grammar in a document by comparing its wording to a dictionary of accepted grammatical rules. The program reports any phrases or sentences that violate a rule and may suggest improvements or allow the user to ignore the rule.

graph See *chart*.

graphical user interface (GUI) A user interface in which actions are initiated when the user selects an icon, a toolbar button, or an option from a pull-down menu with the mouse or other pointing device. GUIs also represent documents, programs, and devices on screen as graphical elements, which the user can use by clicking or dragging.

graphics program Software used to create and manipulate original images or to edit images created in another application.

grayscale monitor A monitor that displays up to 256 shades of gray, ranging from white to black.

green PC A category of personal computers that provide certain energy-saving features.

groupware Application software that enables multiple users on a network to cooperate on projects. Groupware suites usually include scheduling and calendar software, e-mail, and document-management tools.

GUI See *graphical user interface*.

H/PC See *handheld personal computer*.

H/PC Pro Handheld computer larger than a PDA but smaller than a typical notebook. H/PC Pro computers have longer battery life, instant-on access, larger monitors, and small keyboards, and they run more applications than most PDAs. However, they do not use disks, have little RAM, and are relatively slow.

hacker An expert in computer technology who uses skill and innovative techniques to solve complex computing problems. Hackers are more notorious, however, for creating problems such as invading private or governmental computer networks, accessing data from corporate databases, online extortion, and other activities.

half-duplex The ability to send or receive data—but not both simultaneously—over a common data path or communications link.

handheld personal computer (H/PC) (or **palmtop**) A personal computer that is small enough to be held in one hand.

handle In many productivity applications, a specialized portion of a *frame*, which enables the user to drag the frame to resize it.

hard disk A nonremovable magnetic storage device included in most PCs. A stack of aluminum or glass platters, each coated with iron oxide, enclosed in a hard disk drive.

hard disk drive (or **hard drive**) A device that consists of the hard disk platters, a spindle on which the platters spin, a read/write head for each side of each platter, and a sealed chamber that encloses the disks and spindle. Many hard disk drives also include the drive controller, although the controller is a separate unit on some hard disk drives.

hardware The physical components of a computer, including processor and memory chips, input/output devices, tapes, disks, modems, and cables.

hardware lock An early form of copy protection in which a device featuring a built-in chip that contained a code was plugged into the computer. When the software was launched, it looked for the device and would run only if the code matched. Now obsolete. Also called a *dongle*.

hardware maintenance technician In an IS department, a worker responsible for maintaining and repairing hardware components used in the information system.

head crash Describes the results when a read/write head makes contact with the surface of a spinning hard disk. The contact can damage the disk's surface and even destroy the read/write head.

header (1) The initial part of a data packet being transmitted across a network. The header contains information about the type of data in the payload, the source and destination of the data, and a sequence number so that data from multiple packets can be reassembled at the receiving computer in the proper order. See *frame*. (2) A recurring line or paragraph of text appearing at the top of each page in a document. Headers often include page numbers, the document's title, the name of the current chapter, or other information.

help (HLP) file A file included with most software programs, that provides information for the user, such as instructions for using the program's features.

helper application (or **plug-in application**) A program that must be added to your browser in order to play special content files, especially those with multimedia content, in real time.

hertz (Hz) The frequency of electrical vibrations, or cycles, per second.

heuristics A programming technique for solving a problem or performing a task, which does not involve the use of algorithms and which does not always find the best possible solution.

hierarchical database A database structure in which records are organized in parent-child relationships; each child type is related to only one parent type.

hierarchical file system A structured file organization system in which the root directory (also called a *folder*) may contain other directories, which in turn contain files.

high-capacity floppy disk A small, removable disk that resembles a standard diskette, but provides much higher data storage capacity. Typically, high-capacity floppy disks have data densities of 100 MB or greater.

higher-level language A language designed to make programming easier through the use of familiar English words and symbols.

highlight To select a block of text or cells for editing. Selected text is highlighted—displayed in a different color from the remaining text in a document.

hit A visit to a Web site. Also called a *page view*.

HLP See *help file*.

home page An organization's principal Web page, which provides pointers to other Web pages with additional information.

host A computer that provides services to other computers that connect to it. Host computers provide file transfer, communications services, and access to the Internet's high-speed data lines.

hot-swappable hard disk A magnetic storage device similar to a removable hard disk. A removable box encloses the disk, drive, and read/write heads in a sealed container. This type of hard disk can be added to or removed from a server without shutting down the server.

HTML See *Hypertext Markup Language*.

HTML tag A code used to format documents in Hypertext Markup Language (HTML) format.

HTTP See *Hypertext Transfer Protocol*.

hub In a network, a device that connects nodes and servers together at a central point.

hyperlink See *hypertext link*.

hypermedia Text, graphics, video, and sound linked and accessible in a hypertext format.

hypertext A software technology that provides fast and flexible access to information. The user can jump to a topic by selecting it on screen; used to create Web pages and help screens.

hypertext link (**hyperlink** or **link**) A word, icon, or other object that when clicked jumps to another location on the document or another Web page.

hypertext markup language (HTML) A page-description language used on the World Wide Web that defines the hypertext links between documents.

hypertext transfer protocol (HTTP) A set of file transfer rules used on the World Wide Web that control the way information is shared.

Hz See *hertz*.

I/O See *input/output*.

icon A graphical screen element that executes one or more commands when chosen with a mouse or other pointing device.

IEEE 1394 A new expansion bus technology that supports data-transfer rates of up to 400 Mbps. Called *FireWire* in Macintosh computers.

IGES See *Initial Graphics Exchange Specifications*.

image scanner An input device that digitizes printed images. Sensors determine the intensity of light reflected from the page, and the light intensities are converted to digital data that can be viewed and manipulated by the computer. Sometimes called simply a *scanner*.

impact printer A type of printer that creates images by striking an inked ribbon, pressing ink from the ribbon onto a piece of paper. Examples of impact printers are dot-matrix printers and line printers.

implementation phase Phase 4 of the software development life cycle, in which new software and hardware are installed in the user environment, training is offered, and system testing is completed.

incompatible The opposite of *compatible*. Describes the inability of one type of hardware, software, or data file to work with another.

indent The distance between the beginning or end of a line of text and the left or right margin, whichever is closer.

Industry Standard Architecture (ISA) A PC bus standard developed by IBM, extending the bus to 16 bits. An ISA bus can access 8-bit and 16-bit devices.

inference engine Software used with an expert system to examine data with respect to the knowledge base and to select an appropriate response.

information system A mechanism that helps people collect, store, organize, and use information. An information system does not necessarily include computers, but computers' primary reason for being is as part of an information system.

Information Systems (IS) department The people in an organization responsible for designing, developing, implementing, and maintaining the systems necessary to manage information for all levels of the organization.

initialization (INI) file A file containing configuration information, such as the size and starting point of a window, the color of the background, the user's name, and so on. Initialization files help programs start running or contain information that programs can use as they run.

initializing See *formatting*.

Initial Graphics Exchange Specifications (IGES) One of a few universal file formats for vector graphics.

ink jet printer A type of nonimpact printer that produces images by spraying ink onto the page.

input device Computer hardware that accepts data and instructions from the user. Input devices include the keyboard, mouse, joystick, pen, trackball, scanner, bar code reader, microphone, and touch screen, as well as other types of hardware.

input/output (I/O) Communications between the user and the computer or between hardware components that result in the transfer of data.

input/output device A device that performs both input and output functions. Modems and network interface cards are examples of input/output devices.

insertion mode In word processing, a text-entry mode. In this mode, when the user types characters, they are inserted into the document. If necessary, the computer forces existing characters apart to make room for the new text; existing text is not overwritten by new text.

insertion point See *cursor*.

instant messenger Chat software that enables users to set up buddy lists and open a window when anyone on the list is online.

instantiate In object-oriented programming, to create an object with all the attributes and methods associated with a specific class.

instruction A command, which the computer must execute so that a specific action can be carried out.

instruction cycle The first portion of the *machine cycle*, which is the series of steps a CPU takes when executing an instruction. During the instruction cycle, the CPU's control unit fetches a command or data from the computer's memory, enabling the CPU to execute an instruction. The control unit then decodes the command so it can be executed.

instruction set Machine language instructions that define all the operations a CPU can perform.

integrated pointing device A pointing device built into the computer's keyboard, consisting of a small joystick positioned near the middle of the keyboard, typically between the *g* and *h* keys. The joystick is controlled with either forefinger. Two buttons that perform the same function as mouse buttons are just beneath the spacebar and are pressed with the thumb. Also called a *TrackPoint*.

integrated services digital network (ISDN) A digital telecommunications standard that replaces analog transmissions and transmits voice, video, and data.

Intel One of the world's leading manufacturer of microprocessors. Intel invented the first microprocessor, which was used in electronic calculators. Intel's product line includes the *x*86 processors and the Pentium processor family.

intellectual property Ideas, statements, processes, and other intangible items that a person can claim to own or have originated.

interactive Refers to software products that can react and respond to commands issued by the user or choices the user makes.

interactivity In multimedia, a system in which the user and program respond to one another. The program gives the user choices, which the user selects to direct the program.

interface See *user interface*.

internal modem A communications device used to modulate data signals. This type of modem is described as "internal" because it is a circuit board that is plugged into one of the computer's expansion slots.

Internet Originally, a link between ARPANET, NSFnet, and other networks. Today, a worldwide network of networks.

Internet protocol (IP) address A unique four-part numeric address assigned to each computer on the Internet, containing routing information to identify its location. Each of the four parts is a number between 0 and 255.

Internet relay chat (IRC) A multiuser system made up of channels, which people join to exchange messages either publicly or privately. Messages are exchanged in real-time, meaning they are transmitted to other users on the channel as they are typed in.

Internet service provider (ISP) An intermediary service between the Internet backbone and the user, providing easy and relatively inexpensive access to shell accounts, direct TCP/IP connections, and high-speed access through dedicated data circuits.

internetworking The process of connecting separate networks together.

interpreter In programming, a software tool that converts source code to machine code. Instead of creating an executable file (as a *compiler* does), however, an interpreter executes each

bit of machine code as it is converted. Interpreters, therefore, are said to translate code on the fly.

interrupt A preprogrammed set of steps that a CPU follows.

interrupt request (IRQ) A signal sent by the operating system to the CPU, requesting processing time for a specific task.

intranet An internal network whose interface and accessibility are modeled after an Internet-based Web site. Only internal users are allowed to access information or resources on the intranet; if connected to an external network or the Internet, the intranet's resources are protected from outside access by firewalls.

IP address See *Internet Protocol address*.

IRC See *Internet Relay Chat*.

IRIS printer A type of ink jet printer that sprays the ink on paper mounted on a spinning drum. Such printers can produce images with a resolution of 1,800 dots per inch.

IRQ See *interrupt request*.

IS See *Information Systems department*.

ISA See *Industry Standard Architecture*.

ISDN See *Integrated Services Digital Network*.

ISP See *Internet service provider*.

J

Java A programming language, used for creating cross-platform programs. Java enables Web page designers to include small applications (called *applets*) in Web pages.

Java applet A Java-based program included in a Web page.

Joint Photographic Experts Group (JPEG) format A bitmap file format commonly used to display photographic images.

joystick An input device used to control the movement of on-screen components; typically used in video games.

JPEG See *Joint Photographic Experts Group format*.

junk e-mail Like regular paper junk mail. Unsolicited ads, offers, or lewd messages that appear in your inbox. Also called *spam*.

junk faxes Unsolicited and unwanted messages received on your fax machine from unnamed senders.

K

K6 A line of Pentium-class processors made by AMD.

KB See *kilobyte*.

kerning A text-editing feature that adjusts the distance between individual letters in a word to make that word easier to read.

keyboard The most common input device, used to enter letters, numbers, symbols, punctuation, and commands into the computer. Computer keyboards typically include numeric, alphanumeric, cursor-movement, modifier, and function keys, as well as other special keys.

keyboard buffer A part of memory that receives and stores the scan codes from the keyboard controller until the program can accept them.

keyboard controller A chip within the keyboard or the computer that receives the keystroke and generates the scan code.

keyboarding Touch typing using a computer keyboard.

keyframe In animation, the primary frame in a motion sequence, such as the starting or stopping point in a walk cycle.

kilobyte (KB) Equivalent to 1,024 bytes; a common measure of data storage.

knowledge base A highly specialized database used with an expert system to intelligently produce solutions.

L

label Descriptive text used in a spreadsheet cell to describe the data in a column or row.

LAN See *local area network*.

land A flat area on the metal surface of a CD-ROM that reflects the laser light into the sensor of an optical disk drive.

landscape orientation A document format in which the text is printed parallel to the widest page edge; the opposite of portrait orientation.

laptop computer See *notebook PC*.

laser printer A quiet, fast printer that produces high-quality output. A laser beam focused on an electrostatic drum creates an image to which powdered toner adheres, and that image is transferred to paper.

layer A portion of a drawing that can be placed on top of another layer while retaining all of its properties.

LCD monitor See *liquid crystal display monitor*.

leading In desktop publishing, the amount of space between lines in a document. DTP software enables the user to adjust this spacing precisely, to make text easier to read. (Pronounced LED-ding.)

Level-1 (L1) cache A type of cache memory built directly into the microprocessor. Also called *on-board cache*.

Level-2 (L2) cache A type of of cache memory that is external to the microprocessor, but is positioned between the CPU and RAM. Also called *external cache*.

line spacing The distance between lines of text in a document. The most common examples include single-spaced and double-spaced. See also *kerning*.

link See *hypertext link*.

Linux A freely available version of the UNIX operating system. Developed by a worldwide cooperative of programmers in the 1990s, Linux is a feature-rich, 32-bit, multi-user, multiprocessor operating system that runs on virtually any hardware platform.

liquid crystal display (LCD) monitor A flat-panel monitor on which an image is created when the liquid crystal becomes charged; used primarily in notebook and laptop computers.

listserv An e-mail server that contains a list name and enables users to communicate with others on the list in an ongoing discussion.

local area network (LAN) A system of PCs located relatively near to one another and connected by wire or a wireless link. A LAN permits simultaneous access to data and resources, enhances personal communication, and simplifies backup procedures.

local bus An internal system bus that runs between components on the motherboard.

logic error A bug in which the code directs the computer to perform a task incorrectly.

logical field A database field that stores only one of two values: yes or no, true or false, on or off, and so on. Also called a *Boolean field*.

logical formatting An operating system function in which tracks and sectors are mapped on the surface of a disk. This mapping creates the master boot record, FAT, root folder (also called the root directory), and the data area. Also called *soft formatting* and *low-level formatting*.

logical operation One of the two types of operations a computer can perform. Logical operations usually involve making a comparison, such as determining whether two values are equal. See also *arithmetic operation*.

log on To access a computer system. The process of logging on often requires the user to provide a user identification code and/or a password before the computer system will allow access.

loop A program or routine that executes a set of instructions repeatedly while a specific condition is true, or until a new event (called an *exit condition*) occurs.

looping structure See *repetition structure*.

M

MII A Pentium II-class microprocessor made by Cyrix that runs at speeds of 433 MHz.

machine code See *machine language*.

machine cycle The complete series of steps a CPU takes in executing an instruction. A machine cycle itself can be broken down into two smaller cycles: the *instruction cycle* and the *execution cycle*.

machine language The lowest level of computer language. Machine code includes the strings of 1s and 0s that the computer can understand. Although programs can be written in many different higher-level languages, they all must be converted to machine code before the computer can understand and use them. Also called *machine code*.

Macintosh operating system (Mac OS) The operating system that runs on PCs built by Apple Computer. The Mac OS was the first commercially available operating system to use a graphical user interface, to utilize Plug and Play hardware compatibility, to feature built-in networking, and to support common user access.

macro A simple programming tool, provided by most productivity applications, which allows the user to store and then automatically issue a sequence of commands or keystrokes.

magnetic disk A round, flat disk covered with a magnetic material (such as iron oxide), the most commonly used storage medium. Data is written magnetically on the disk and can be recorded over and over. The magnetic disk is the basic component of the diskette and hard disk.

magnetic storage A storage technology in which data is recorded when iron particles are polarized on a magnetic storage medium.

mail merge The process of combining a text document, such as a letter, with the contents of a database, such as an address list; commonly used to produce form letters.

mail server In an e-mail system, the server on which messages received from the post office server are stored until the recipients access their mailbox and retrieve the messages.

mainframe computer A large, multiuser computer system designed to handle massive amounts of input, output, and storage. A mainframe is usually composed of one or more powerful CPUs connected to many input/output devices, called *terminals*, or to personal computers. Mainframe systems are typically used in businesses requiring the maintenance of huge databases or simultaneous processing of multiple complex tasks.

maintenance phase Phase 5 of the software development life cycle, in which the new system is monitored, errors are corrected, and minor adjustments are made to improve system performance.

management information system (MIS) A set of software tools that enables managers to gather, organize, and evaluate information about a workgroup, department, or an entire organization. These systems meet the needs of three different categories of managers: executives, middle managers, and front-line managers, by producing a range of standardized reports drawn from the organization's database. A good management information system summarizes vast amounts of business data into information that is useful to each type of manager.

many-to-many relationship In a relational database, the ability of a table to have a relationship with any number of other tables.

margin The space between the edge of a page and the main body of the document. Text cannot be entered within the margin.

mask In a database management system (DBMS), a technique for controlling data entry, which ensures that data entered into any field adheres to a specific format. For example, in a database that contains a Telephone Number field, a field format can be set to ensure that each number is entered in the format (555) 555-5555. Also called a *field format* or *picture*.

massively parallel processors (MPP) A processing architecture that uses hundreds or thousands of microprocessors in one computer to perform complex processes quickly.

master boot record A small program that runs when a computer is started. This program determines whether the disk contains the basic components of an operating system necessary to run successfully. If the boot record determines that the required files are present and the disk has a valid format, it transfers control to one of the operating system programs, which continues the process of starting up.

master page A special page created in desktop publishing software that contains elements common to all the pages in the document, such as page numbers, headers and footers, ruling lines, margin features, special graphics, and layout guides.

maximum access time The maximum amount of time it takes a drive to access data.

mb See *megabit*.

mbps See *megabits per second*.

MB See *megabyte*.

MBps See *megabytes per second*.

media The plural form of the word *medium*. See *medium*.

MediaGX A microprocessor, made by Cyrix, that integrates audio and graphics functions.

medium (1) In storage technology, a medium is material used to store data, such as the magnetic coating on a disk or tape, or the metallic platter in a compact disk. (2) In networking, a medium is a means of conveying a signal across the network, such as a cable. (3) In multimedia, a medium is a single means of conveying a message, such as text or video.

megabit (mb) Equivalent to approximately one million bits. A common measure of data transfer speeds.

megabits per second (mbps) Equivalent to one million bits of data per second.

megabyte (MB) Equivalent to approximately one million bytes. A common measure of data storage capacity.

megabytes per second (MBps) Equivalent to one million bytes of data per second.

megahertz (MHz) Equivalent to millions of cycles per second; a common measure of clock speed.

member function A function of a class in object-oriented programming. Also called a *method*.

memo field A database field that stores text information of variable length. Also called *description field*.

memory A collection of chips on the motherboard or on a circuit board attached to the motherboard, where all computer processing and program instructions are stored while in use. The computer's memory enables the CPU to retrieve data quickly for processing.

memory address A number used by the CPU to locate each piece of data in memory.

menu A list of commands or functions displayed on screen for selection by the user.

menu bar A graphical screen element—located above the document area of an application window—displaying a list of the types of commands available to the user. When the user selects an option from the menu bar, a list appears, displaying the commands related to that menu option.

mesh topology An expensive, redundant cabling scheme for local area networks, in which each node is connected to every other node by a unique cable.

message A signal in an object-oriented program that is sent to an object, requesting it to perform a specific function.

method See *member function*.

Mhz See *megahertz*.

microcode Code that details the individual tasks the computer must perform to complete each instruction in the instruction set.

microcomputer See *personal computer (PC)*.

microphone An input device used to digitally record audio data, such as the human voice. Many productivity applications also can accept input via a microphone, enabling the user to dictate text or issue commands orally.

microprocessor An integrated circuit on a single chip that makes up the computer's CPU. Microprocessors are composed of silicon or other material etched with many tiny electronic circuits.

MIDI See *Musical Instrument Digital Interface*.

millisecond (ms) Equivalent to one thousandth of a second; used to measure access time.

minicomputer A midsize, multiuser computer capable of handling more input and output than a PC but with less processing power and storage than a mainframe. Also called a *midrange computer*.

MIS See *management information system*.

MMX A microprocessor technology incorporated by Intel in the Pentium Pro and later processors, which increases the multimedia capabilities of a computer chip. MMX processors process audio, video, and graphical data more efficiently than non-MMX processors, enabling one instruction to perform the same function on multiple pieces of data, reducing the number of loops required to handle video, audio, animation, and graphical data.

model A three-dimensional image that represents a real or imagined object or character; created using special computer software programs, including surface modelers, solid modelers, spline-based modelers, and others.

modem Abbreviation for *modulator/demodulator*. An input/output device that allows computers to communicate through telephone lines. A modem converts outgoing digital data into analog signals that can be transmitted over phone lines and converts incoming audio signals into digital data that can be processed by the computer.

moderator An overseer of a newsgroup, who sorts through articles before posting them and removes inappropriate ones.

modifier keys Keyboard keys that are used in conjunction with other keys to execute a command. The IBM-PC keyboard includes Shift, Ctrl, and Alt keys; the Macintosh keyboard also has the Command and Option keys.

monitor A display screen used to provide computer output to the user. Examples include the cathode ray tube (CRT) monitor, color monitor, monochrome monitor, flat-panel monitor, and liquid crystal display (LCD).

monochrome monitor A monitor that displays only one color (such as green or amber) against a contrasting background.

monospace font A font in which each character uses exactly the same amount of horizontal space.

Moore's Law A commonly held (and so far accurate) axiom, which states that computing power doubles every 18 months. Named after Intel founder Gordon Moore, this "law" is expected to hold true well into the 21st century.

motherboard The main circuit board of the computer, which contains the CPU, memory, expansion slots, bus, and video controller. Also called the *system board*.

Motorola A manufacturer of computer chips, most notably microprocessors and communications chips; the maker of processors used in Macintosh computers.

mouse An input device operated by rolling across a flat surface. The mouse is used to control the on-screen pointer by pointing and clicking, double-clicking, or dragging objects on the screen.

MP See *multiprocessing*.

MPP See *massively parallel processors*.

MPEG A multimedia data compression standard used to compress full-motion video. Stands for *Moving Pictures Experts Group*.

ms See *millisecond*.

MS-DOS Acronym for *Microsoft-Disk Operating System*. The command-line interface operating system developed by Microsoft for PCs. IBM selected DOS as the standard for early IBM and IBM-compatible machines.

multimedia Elements of text, graphics, animation, video, and sound combined for presentation to the consumer.

multimedia authoring An application that enables the user to combine text, graphics, animation, video, and sound documents developed with other software packages to create a multimedia product.

multimedia PC A PC capable of producing high-quality text, graphics, animation, video, and sound. A multimedia PC may include a CD-ROM or DVD drive, a microphone, speakers, a high-quality video controller, and a sound card.

multiprocessing (MP) See *parallel processing*.

multitasking The capability of an operating system to load multiple programs into memory at one time and to perform two or more processes concurrently, such as printing a document while editing another.

Musical Instrument Digital Interface (MIDI) A specialized category of input/output devices used in the creation, recording, editing, and performance of music.

N

nanosecond (ns) One-billionth of a second. A common unit of measure for the average access time of memory devices.

navigation The process of moving through a software program, a multimedia product, or a Web site.

needs analysis phase Phase 1 of the software development life cycle, in which needs are defined, the current system is analyzed, alternative solutions are developed, and the best solution and its functions are selected.

network (1) A system of interconnected computers that communicate with one another and share applications, data, and hardware components. (2) To connect computers together, in order to permit the transfer of data and programs between users.

network computer (NC) A specialized computer that provides basic input/output capabilities to a user on a network. Some types of NCs provide storage and processing capabilities, but other types include only a keyboard, mouse, and monitor. The latter category of network computer utilizes the network server for processing and storage.

network database A database structure in which any record type can relate to any number of other record types in a many-to-many relationship.

network interface card (NIC) A circuit board that controls the exchange of data over a network.

network manager See *system manager*.

network news transfer protocol A set of rules that enable news servers to exchange articles with other news servers.

network operating system (NOS) A group of programs that manage the resources on a network.

network protocol A set of standards used for network communications.

network server See *file server*.

network version An application program especially designed to work within a network environment. Users access the software from a shared storage device.

new media A term encompassing all types of interactive multimedia technologies.

news A public bulletin board service on the Internet, organized into discussion groups representing specific topics of interest.

news server A host computer that exchanges articles with other Internet servers.

newsgroup An electronic storage space where users can post messages to other users, carry on extended conversations, and trade information.

newsreader A software program that enables the user to post and read articles in an Internet news group.

NIC See *network interface card*.

node An individual computer that is connected to a network.

non-impact printer A type of printer that creates images on paper without striking the page in any way. Two common examples are ink jet printers, which spray tiny droplets of ink onto the page, and laser printers, which use heat to adhere particles of toner to specific points on the page.

nonvolatile The tendency for memory to retain data even when the computer is turned off (as is the case with ROM).

NNTP server Another name for news servers using the network news transfer protocol.

NOS See *network operating system.*

notebook computer A small, portable computer with an attached flat screen, typically battery or AC powered and weighing less than 10 pounds. Notebook computers commonly provide most of the same features found in full-size desktop computers, including a color monitor, a fast processor, a modem, and adequate RAM and storage for business-class software applications. Also called a *laptop computer.*

ns See *nanosecond.*

NSFnet Acronym for *National Science Foundation Network.* A network developed by the National Science Foundation (NSF) to accommodate the many users attempting to access the five academic research centers created by the NSF.

numeric field A database field that stores numeric characters.

numeric keypad The part of a keyboard that looks and works like a calculator keypad, with 10 digits and mathematical operators.

O

object In object-oriented programming, a data item and its associated characteristics, attributes, and procedures. An object's *characteristics* define the type of object—for example, whether it is text, a sound, a graphic, or video. *Attributes* might be color, size, style, and so on. A *procedure* refers to the processing or handling associated with the object.

object code The executable file in machine language that is the output of a compiler.

object embedding The process of integrating a copy of data from one application into another, as from a spreadsheet to a word processor. The data retains the formatting applied to it in the original application, but its relationship with the original file is destroyed.

object linking The process of integrating a copy of data from one application into another so that the data retains a link to the original document. Thereafter, a change in the original document also appears in the linked data in the second application.

Object Linking and Embedding (OLE) A Windows feature that combines object embedding and linking functions. OLE allows the user to construct a document containing data from a single point in time or one in which the data is constantly updated.

object-oriented database (OODB) A database structure in which data items, their characteristics, attributes, and procedures are grouped into units called *objects.*

object-oriented programming (OOP) A programming technology that makes use of reusable, modular components, called *objects.*

OCR See *optical character recognition.*

office automation system A system designed to manage information efficiently, in areas such as word processing, accounting, document management, or communications.

off-the-shelf application A software product that is packaged and available for sale; installed as-is in some system designs.

OLE See *Object Linking and Embedding.*

one-to-many relationship In a hierarchical database structure, the ability of a field in one table to have a relationship to another table. The fields in the second table may have relationships with other tables, and so on, forming a tree-like structure. Also called a *parent-child relationship.*

online (1) The state of being connected to, served by, or available through a networked computer system or the Internet. For example, when a user is browsing the World Wide Web, that person's computer is said to be online. (2) Describes any computer-related device that is turned on and connected, such as a printer or modem that is in use or ready for use.

online service A telecommunications service that supplies e-mail and information search tools.

OODB See *object-oriented database.*

OOP See *object-oriented programming.*

operating environment An intuitive graphical user interface that overlays the operating system but does not replace it. Microsoft Windows 3.*x* is an example.

operating system (OS) The master control program that provides an interface for a user to communicate with the computer, manages hardware devices, manages and maintains disk file systems, and supports application programs.

operator In a spreadsheet, the component of a formula that specifies the operation being performed on other parts of the formula; includes arithmetic, comparison, and text operators.

optical character recognition (OCR) Technology that enables a computer to translate optically scanned data into character codes, which can then be edited.

optical drive A storage device that writes data to and reads data from an optical storage medium, such as a compact disk.

optical storage Refers to storage systems that use light beams to read data from the surface of an optical disk. Data is stored as a series of lands and pits on the disk's reflective surface. Generally speaking, optical storage systems provide higher storage capacities than typical magnetic storage systems, but they operate at slower speeds.

OS See *operating system.*

OS/2 Warp A single-user, multitasking operating system with a point-and-click interface developed by IBM and Microsoft to take advantage of the multitasking capabilities of post-8086 computers.

output device A hardware component, such as a monitor or printer, that returns processed data to the user.

outsourcing Using outside expertise to accomplish a task, such as hiring a freelance writer to produce user documentation.

overtype mode A text entry mode. In overtype mode, when the user types characters, they overwrite (and erase) existing text that appears to the right of the insertion point.

P

packet A small block of data transmitted over a network, which includes an identifying header and the actual data to be sent. Also called a *frame.*

packet-switched Describes a type of communications line in which data is broken into distinct, addressed packets that can be transferred separately. Access to the connection can be intermittent; commonly used for networks.

page view See *hit.*

pages per minute (ppm) A common measure for printer output speed. Consumer-grade laser printers, for example, typically can print from 6 to 10 pages per minute depending on whether text or graphics are being printed.

paint program A graphics program that creates images as bitmaps, or a mosaic of pixels.

paragraph A series of letters, words, or sentences followed by a hard return.

paragraph format A setting that affects the appearance of one or more entire paragraphs, such as line spacing, paragraph spacing, indents, alignment, tab stops, borders, and shading.

paragraph spacing The amount of blank space between two paragraphs in a document. Typically, this spacing is equivalent to one line of text.

parallel conversion A conversion process that continues the use of an existing system while a new system is being implemented.

parallel interface A channel through which eight or more data bits can flow simultaneously, such as a computer bus. A parallel interface is commonly used to connect printers to the computer; also called a *parallel port*.

parallel processing The use of multiple processors to run a program. By harnessing multiple processors, which share the processing workload, the system can handle a much greater flow of data, complete more tasks in a shorter period of time, and deal with the demands of many input and output devices. Also called *multiprocessing (MP)* or *symmetric multiprocessing (SMP)*.

parameter See *argument*.

parent-child relationship See *one-to-many relationship*.

passive matrix LCD Liquid crystal display technology, used for flat-panel monitors, that relies on a grid of transistors arranged by rows and columns. In a passive matrix LCD, the color displayed by each pixel is determined by the electricity coming from the transistors at the end of the row and the top of the column.

password A word or code used as a security checkpoint by an individual computer system or a network, to verify the user's identity.

Paste An application command that copies data from the Clipboard and places it in the document at the position of the insertion point. Data in the Clipboard can be pasted into multiple places in one document, multiple documents, and documents in different applications.

payload In a packet, the actual data being transmitted across a network or over telephone lines. Also refers to the executable portion of a computer virus, or the output produced by a virus.

PC See *personal computer*.

PC 97/99 A set of standards for personal computers, set by a group of hardware and software manufacturers. The PC 97/99 standards establish minimum hardware and performance requirements for varying types of computers, based on the system's intended use.

PC Card A specialized expansion card the size of a credit card, which fits into a computer and is used to connect new components.

PCI See *Peripheral Component Interconnect*.

PC projector A light-projecting device that can display images directly from a computer's disk onto a projection screen, in much the same manner as an old-fashioned slide or overhead projector. A PC projector usually connects to the computer via a port (such as the parallel port).

PC video camera A small video camera, which connects to a special video card on a PC. When used with videoconferencing software, a PC video camera enables users to capture full-motion video images, save them to disk, edit them, and transmit them to other users across a network or the Internet.

PC-to-TV converter A hardware device that converts a computer's digital video signals into analog signals for display on a standard television screen.

PDA See *personal digital assistant*.

peer-to-peer network A network environment in which all nodes on the network have equal access to at least some of the resources on all other nodes.

pen-based organizer A handheld personal computer that enables the user to input data and issue commands by using an electronic pen. Some organizers allow the user to tap onscreen options with the pen, while some models also accept handwritten input, enabling the user to create text documents with the pen.

Pentium A family of microprocessors developed by Intel, including the Pentium, Pentium II, Pentium III, Pentium Pro, Celeron, and Xeon processors.

Pentium II An Intel processor based on a 32-bit microprocessor and holding 7.5 million transistors. The Pentium II supports MMX technology and dynamic execution, uses Slot One technology, and operates at speeds up to 450 MHz.

Pentium III An Intel processor with speeds up to 600 MHz, utilizing a Slot 2 connection to the motherboard and improved multimedia-handling features.

Pentium Pro An Intel processor utilizing a 32-bit microprocessor and capable of processing three program instructions in a single clock cycle. The Pentium Pro utilizes dynamic execution, which is the ability to execute program instructions in the most efficient order.

Peripheral Component Interconnect (PCI) A PC bus standard developed by Intel that supplies a high-speed data path between the CPU and peripheral devices.

personal computer (PC) The most common type of computer found in an office, classroom, or home. The PC is designed to fit on a desk and be used by one person at a time; also called a *microcomputer*.

personal digital assistant (PDA) A very small portable computer designed to be held in one hand; used to perform specific tasks, such as creating limited spreadsheets or storing phone numbers.

personalized start page A customized Web page, which a user can configure as the first page to open when the browser is launched.

phased conversion A conversion process in which components of the replacement system are introduced gradually.

photo-manipulation program A multimedia software tool used to modify scanned photographic images, including adjusting contrast and sharpness.

photorealistic Describes computer-generated images that are lifelike in appearance and not obviously models.

PICT Abbreviation for *picture*. A graphics file format developed for and commonly used on the Macintosh platform, and seldom used on the PC platform.

picture See *field format*.

pilot conversion A conversion process in which a new system is tested and run by a selected group before it is fully installed throughout the organization.

pipelining A technique that enables a processor to execute more instructions in a given time. In pipelining, the control unit begins executing a new instruction before the current instruction is completed.

pit A depressed area on the metal surface of a compact disk or digital video disk that scatters laser light. Also see *land*.

pixel Contraction of *picture element*. One or more dots that express a portion of an image on a computer screen.

plain old telephone system (POTS) Refers to the standard, existing system of telephone lines that has been in use for decades in the United States. The system includes millions of miles of copper wiring and thousands of switching stations, which ensure that analog telephone signals are routed to their intended destination. This system is now also commonly used to transmit digital data between computers; however, the data must be converted from digital form to analog form before entering the telephone line, then reconverted back to digital form when it reaches the destination computer. This conversion is handled at the computer by a device called a *modem*.

plotter An output device used to create large-format hard copy; generally used with CAD and design systems.

Plug and Play An operating system feature that enables the user to add hardware devices to the computer without performing technically difficult connection procedures.

plug-in application See *helper application*.

PNG Acronym for *portable network graphics*. A graphics file format developed as an alternative to GIF and JPEG. The PNG format was designed mainly for use in World Wide Web pages.

point (1) A standard unit used in measuring fonts. One point equals .02 inch in height. (2) To move the mouse pointer around the screen, by manipulating the mouse or another type of pointing device.

pointer An on-screen object, usually an arrow, used to select text; access menus; move files; and interact with programs, files, or data represented graphically on the screen.

point-to-point protocol (PPP) A communications protocol used for linking a computer directly to the Internet. PPP features include the ability to establish or terminate a session, to hang up and redial, and to use password protection.

pointing device A device that enables the user to freely move an on-screen pointer and to select text, menu options, icons, and other on-screen objects. Two popular types of pointing devices are mice and trackballs.

polarized The condition of a magnetic bar with ends having opposite magnetic polarity.

polygonal modeler A 3-D modeling program that builds images using an array of miniature polygons.

POP See *Post Office Protocol*.

POP server A server computer on an e-mail system that manages the flow of e-mail messages and attachments, using the *post office protocol*.

port (1) A socket on the back of the computer used to connect external devices to the computer. (2) To transfer a software application from one platform to another.

portable Describes software applications that are easily transferred from one platform to another, or hardware that can be easily moved.

portrait orientation A document format in which the text is printed parallel to the narrowest page edge; the opposite of landscape orientation.

posting Publishing a document on the Internet, using one of its services, such as news, FTP, or the World Wide Web.

post office protocol (POP) A networking protocol used by e-mail servers to manage the sending and receiving of e-mail messages and attachments.

PostScript A printing language created by Adobe Systems that produces high-quality images ready for the printing press.

POST See *power-on self-test*.

POTS See *plain old telephone system*.

power-on self-test (POST) A test run by the computer when it is first started, using instructions provided by the computer's Basic Input Output System (BIOS) and stored in the system's ROM. During start-up this test determines whether key components are attached and running properly.

PowerPC Created through a joint venture by IBM, Apple, and Motorola, a microprocessor designed to run both DOS and Macintosh-based software. Although the PowerPC never really gained market share, it set records for microprocessor performance.

PPP See *Point to Point Protocol*.

preemptive multitasking A multitasking environment in which the OS prioritizes system and application processes and performs them in the most efficient order. The OS can preempt a low-priority task with a more critical one.

prepress control A specialized feature provided by desktop publishing (DTP) programs, which give the user fine control over certain document elements, such as the placement of graphics and the attributes of text. This type of feature is called a prepress control because it helps the user prepare high-quality documents to be sent to a professional printer.

presentation program Software that enables the user to create professional-quality images, called *slides*, which can be shown as part of a presentation. Slides can be presented in any number of ways, but are typically displayed on a large screen or video monitor while the presenter speaks to the audience.

printer An output device that produces a hard copy on paper.

print head In impact printers, a device that strikes an inked ribbon, pressing ink onto the paper to create characters or graphics.

print job A single request for printing services, made by a user on a network, to be printed on a networked printer. A print job can include one or multiple documents.

procedure In programming, a term referring to blocks of reusable code. Also called a *subroutine* or a *routine*.

processing A complex procedure by which a computer transforms raw data into useful information.

processor See *central processing unit (CPU)*.

productivity software An application designed to help individuals complete tasks more efficiently. Examples include word processing programs, spreadsheets, graphics programs, and presentation software.

program (1) A set of instructions or code executed by the CPU, designed to help users solve problems or perform tasks. Also called *software*. (2) To create a computer program. The process of computer programming is also called *software development*.

program control flow The order in which a program's statements are executed when the program is run.

programmer The person responsible for creating a computer program, including writing new code and analyzing and modifying existing code.

programming language A higher-level language than machine code for writing programs. Programming languages use a variation of basic English.

prompt In a command-line interface, the onscreen location where the user types commands. A prompt usually provides a blinking cursor to indicate where commands can be typed. Also called a *command prompt*.

proportional font A font in which the characters use varying amounts of horizontal space.

protocol A set of rules and procedures that determine how a computer system receives and transmits data.

prototype A working system model used to clarify and refine system requirements.

pseudocode "Fake" code; a text version of the program control flow, similar to the program code but lacking the exact syntax and details.

purchasing agent In an IS department, the person responsible for purchasing hardware and software products.

Q

QBE See *Query by Example.*

query In a database management system (DBMS), a search question that instructs the program to locate records that meet specific criteria.

Query by Example (QBE) In a database management system (DBMS), a tool that accepts a query from a user and then creates the SQL code to locate data requested by the query. QBE enables the user to query a database without understanding SQL.

QWERTY A standard keyboard arrangement; refers to the first six letters on the top row of letters in the alphanumeric keyboard.

QuickTime A multimedia playback standard, developed for use with Macintosh computers, which enables the user to play high-quality audio and video content on the desktop.

QuickTime VR A "virtual reality" version of the QuickTime file format, which enables multimedia developers to create virtual-reality-like environments from flat, two-dimensional images.

R

random access memory (RAM) A computer's volatile or temporary memory, which exists as chips on the motherboard near the CPU. RAM stores data and programs while they are being used and requires a power source to maintain its integrity.

range In a spreadsheet, a rectangular group of contiguous cells.

raster See *bitmap.*

read-only access A type of security right, which a network administrator can assign to a user of the network. If a user has read-only access to a given file on the network server, the user can open and view the file but is not permitted to make changes to the file or save the file back to its original location. Depending on the right's configuration, the user may be able to make a copy of the file.

read-only memory (ROM) A permanent, or nonvolatile, memory chip used to store instructions and data, including the computer's startup instructions.

read/write access A type of security right, which a network administrator can assign to a user of the network. If a user has read/write access to a given file on the network server, the user can not only open and view the file but is also permitted to make changes to the file and save the file back to its original location.

read/write head The magnetic device within the disk drive that reads, records, and erases data on the disk's surface. A read/write head contains an electromagnet that alters the polarity of magnetic particles on the storage medium. Most disk drives have one read/write head for each side of each disk in the drive.

RealAudio A program that plays streaming audio broadcast over the Internet.

RealPlayer The standard for playing streaming audio and video content downloaded from Web servers.

RealVideo A program that plays streaming video broadcast over the Internet.

real-time processing The ability to process information as it is received, providing an immediate response to user input.

record A database row composed of related fields; a collection of records makes up the database.

Redo A software command that reverses the previous Undo command.

Reduced Instruction Set Computing (RISC) Refers to a type of microprocessor design that uses a simplified instruction set, using fewer instructions of constant size, each of which can be executed in one machine cycle.

refresh rate The number of times per second that each pixel on the computer screen is scanned; measured in hertz (Hz).

register High-speed memory locations built directly into the ALU and used to hold instructions and data currently being processed.

relational database A database structure capable of linking tables; a collection of files that share at least one common field.

relative cell reference A spreadsheet cell reference that changes with respect to its relative position on the spreadsheet when copied to a new location.

remote terminal connection An Internet connection in which the TCP/IP programs and protocols run on a UNIX host computer. The local computer exchanges data and commands in ASCII format.

removable hard drive A magnetic storage device that combines the speed and capacity of a hard disk with the portability of a diskette. A removable box encloses the disk, drive, and read/write heads in a sealed container that can be moved from computer to computer.

render To create an image of an object as it actually appears.

repeat rate A keyboard setting that determines how long an alphanumeric key must be held down until the character will be repeated and how rapidly the character is typed.

repetition structure (or **looping structure**) A control structure in which a condition is checked and a loop is executed based on the result of the condition.

repetitive stress injury (RSI) An injury to some part of the body caused by continuous movement. Computer-related injuries include wrist, neck, and back strain.

report A database product designed by the user that displays data satisfying a specific set of search criteria presented in a predefined layout.

resolution The degree of sharpness of an image, determined by the number of pixels on a screen, expressed as a matrix.

resolution-dependent Describes an image whose appearance may change, depending on the resolution at which it is displayed.

resolution-independent Describes an image whose appearance will not change, regardless of the resolution at which it is displayed.

return To report the results of a function to its program so the result can be used as needed.

right-click When using a two-button mouse, to use the right mouse button to select an object or command on the screen.

ring topology A network topology in which network nodes are connected in a circular configuration. Each node examines the data sent through the ring and passes on data not addressed to it.

RISC See *Reduced Instruction Set Computing.*

ROM See *read-only memory.*

root folder The top-level folder on a disk. This primary folder contains all other folders and subfolders stored on the disk. Also called a root *directory*, or sometimes just the *root.*

router A computer device that stores the addressing information of each computer on each LAN or WAN and uses this information to transfer data along the most efficient path between nodes of a LAN or WAN.

routine See *procedure.*

rule See *border.*

ruler An on-screen tool in a word processor's document window. The ruler shows the position of lines, tab stops, margins, and other parts of the document.

run See *execute.*

S

sans serif A typeface without decorative finishing strokes on the tips of the characters; commonly used in headings.

scan code A code—generated by the keyboard controller— that tells the keyboard buffer which key has been pressed.

scanner An input device used to copy a printed page into the computer's memory and transform the image into digital data. Various scanners can read text, images, or bar codes. Sometimes called an *image scanner.*

screen saver A utility program that displays moving images on the screen if no input is received for several minutes; originally developed to prevent an image from being burned into the screen.

scroll To move an entire document in relation to the document window, in order to see parts of the document not currently visible on screen.

scroll bar A vertical or horizontal bar displayed along the side or bottom of a document window, which enables the user to scroll horizontally or vertically through a document by clicking an arrow or dragging a box within the scroll bar.

SCSI See *Small Computer System Interface.*

SDLC See *systems development life cycle.*

search engine A Web site that uses powerful data-searching techniques to help the user locate Web sites containing specific types of content or information.

second-generation language Refers to *assembly language,* which is slightly more advanced and English-like than machine languages (which are considered first-generation languages).

section A user-defined portion of a document, which can have its own unique formatting.

sector A segment or division of a track on a disk.

Secure HTTP (S-HTTP) An Internet protocol used to encrypt individual pieces of data transmitted between a user's computer and a Web server, making the data unusable to anyone who does not have a key to the encryption method.

secure sockets layer (SSL) An Internet protocol that can be used to encrypt any amount of data sent over the Internet between a client computer and a host computer.

secure Web page A Web page that uses one or more encyption technologies to encode data received from and sent to the user.

security manager In an information systems (IS) department, a manager charged with overseeing the security of the network and data stored on it. A security manager may oversee the the organization's firewall, password strategies, and the handling of other security-related issues.

seek time See *average access time.*

select (1) To highlight a block of text (in a word processor) or range (in a spreadsheet), so the user can perform one or more editing operations on it. (2) To click once on an icon.

selection structure A control structure built around a conditional statement.

sequence structure A type of control structure in which a computer executes lines of code in the order in which they are written.

serial interface A channel through which a single data bit can flow at one time. Serial interfaces are used primarily to connect a mouse or a communications device to the computer. Also called a *serial port.*

serial line interface protocol (SLIP) A method for linking a computer directly to the Internet by using a phone line connected to a serial communications port.

serif A decorative finishing strokes on the tips of the characters in a font. Serif fonts are commonly used in the main body of text.

server See *file server.*

shading A paragraph format that displays a pattern or color as a background to the text. Shading may be used to emphasize a block of text.

shadow mask In a cathode ray tube (CRT) monitor, a fine mesh made of metal, fitted to the shape and size of the screen. The holes in the shadow mask's mesh are used to align the electron beams, to ensure that they strike precisely the correct phosphor dot. In most shadow masks, these holes are arranged in triangles.

shareware Software that can be used for free for a specified time period. After that time, the user is obligated to purchase and/or register the product.

shell account A type of Internet access used by remote terminal connections, which operates from a host computer running UNIX or a similar operating system.

Shockwave A plug-in application that allows interactive animations and audio to play directly in a Web browser window.

shortcut menu See *context menu.*

S-HTTP See *Secure HTTP.*

SIMD See *Single Instruction Multiple Data process.*

SIMM See *Single In-Line Memory Module.*

single edge connector A specialized motherboard slot, required by the Pentium II processor. Because the Pentium II requires this type of connector (also called a *Slot One connector*), new motherboard designs were required to accommodate the Pentium II chip.

Single In-Line Memory Module (SIMM) One type of circuit board containing memory chips.

Single Instruction Multiple Data (SIMD) process An architectural design enhancement on the Pentium Pro processor, the SIMD process enables one instruction to perform the same function on multiple pieces of data, reducing the number of loops required to handle video, audio, animation, and graphical data.

site license An agreement in which an organization purchases the right to use a program on a limited number of machines. The total cost is less than would be required if individual copies of the software were purchased for all users.

sleep mode A power-saving feature of many newer-model computers, which automatically turns off the monitor and stops the hard drive from spinning after a specified period of inactivity.

slide An individual graphic that is part of a presentation. Slides are created and edited in presentation programs.

SLIP See *serial line interface protocol.*

Small Computer System Interface (SCSI) A high-speed interface that extends the bus outside the computer, permitting the addition of more peripheral devices than normally could be connected using the available expansion slots.

SMP See *symmetric multiprocessing.*

snapshot printer A color printer for printing photo-quality images. These printers are typically used to print images captured with a digital camera or an image scanner.

soft formatting See *logical formatting.*

software See *program.*

software development Another term for computer programming. See *program.*

software piracy The illegal duplication and/or use of software.

solid model A 3-D model created in a solid modeling program, and which appears to be a solid object rather than a frame or polygon-based object.

solid modeler A 3-D modeling program that depicts an object as a solid block of material (such as steel or wood), which the user shapes by adding and subtracting material or joining with other objects.

sort To arrange database records in a particular order—such as alphabetical, numerical, or chronological order—according to the contents of one or more fields.

sort order The order in which database records are sorted, either ascending or descending.

sound card An expansion card that records and plays back sound by translating the analog signal from a microphone into a digitized form that the computer can store and process and then translating the modified data back into analog signals or sound.

source code Program statements created with a programming language.

spam (1) Another term for *junk e-mail.* (2) To distribute unrequested messages across the Internet or an online service. Spammers often flood news groups with messages and send e-mail messages to thousands of individuals. Spam messages often attempt to sell a product or service (like regular junk mail) but frequently carry negative, indecent, or obscene material.

spammer A person who distributes spam, or junk e-mail messages.

spawn To launch a program from within another program. For example, to allow the user to view streaming multimedia content, a Web browser may spawn a second application, such as the QuickTime Player.

speech recognition An input technology that can translate human speech into text. Some speech-recognition systems enable the user to navigate application programs and issue commands by voice control, as well as creating documents by dictating text. Also called *voice recognition.*

spell checker A language tool built into many types of productivity applications. A spelling checker can review any or all words in a document and compare each one to a dictionary of accepted spellings. If the checker encounters a word that appears to be misspelled, it notifies the user and provides alternative spellings, allows the user to add the word to the dictionary, or ignore the spelling.

spline-based modeler A 3-D modeling program that builds objects using mathematically defined curves.

spoof To distribute unrequested e-mail messages that conceal the sender's identity. In spoofing, the spoofer's message identifies the sender as someone else or shows no sender's identity at all. This method protects the spoofer from retaliation from those who receive unwanted messages. See also *spam.*

spooling The process of queuing multiple print jobs that have been sent to a networked printer. Print jobs are temporarily stored—usually on a hard drive in the network server, network print server, or a special print spooler—while they await their turn to be printed.

spreadsheet A grid of columns and rows used for recording and evaluating numbers. Spreadsheets are used primarily for financial analysis, record keeping, and management, and to create reports and presentations.

SQL See *Structured Query Language.*

SRAM See *static RAM.*

SSE See *Streaming SIMD Extensions.*

SSL See *Secure Sockets Layer.*

star network A network topology in which network nodes connect to a central hub through which all data is routed.

Start button A Windows 95/98/2000/NT screen element, found on the taskbar, that displays the Start menu when selected.

Start menu A menu in the Windows 95/98/2000/NT operating systems, which the user can open by clicking the Start button. The Start menu provides tools to locate documents, find help, change system settings, and run programs.

static RAM (SRAM) A type of random access memory (RAM) sometimes used in personal computers. Static RAM chips do not need to be refreshed (recharged with electricity) as often as dynamic RAM, another commonly used type of memory. As a result, SRAM can hold its contents longer than dynamic RAM. SRAM is also very fast, supporting access times of around 10 nanoseconds.

status bar An on-screen element that appears at the bottom of an application window and displays the current status of various parts of the current document or application, such as page number, text entry mode, and so on.

storage The portion of the computer that holds data or programs while they are not being used. Storage media include magnetic or optical disks, tape, and cartridges.

storage device The hardware components that write data to and read data from storage media. For example, a diskette is a type of storage medium, whereas a diskette drive is a storage device.

storage media The physical components or materials on which data is stored. Diskettes and compact disks are examples of storage media.

storing The second step of the CPU's execution cycle.

storyboard A production tool that consists of sketches of scenes and actions that map a sequence of events; helps the author to edit and improve the presentation.

streaming audio/video Multimedia content that is sent to the user's desktop in a continuous "stream" from a Web server. Because audio and video files are large, streaming content is sent to the user's disk in pieces; the first piece is temporarily buffered (stored on disk), then played as the next piece is stored and buffered.

streaming SIMD Extensions (SSE) An improved version of MMX technology, which debuted with the Pentium III processor. SSE technology allows for faster video and graphics handling within the processor.

structured English A programming design tool and a method of documenting a system using plain English terms and phrases to describe events, actions, and alternative actions that can occur.

structured programming A programming process that uses a set of well-defined structures, such as condition statements and loops.

Structured Query Language (SQL) The standard query language used for searching and selecting records and fields in a relational database.

subclass A subset of a class in object-oriented programming.

subdomain A division of a domain name system (DNS) address that specifies a particular level or area of an organization, such as a department or a branch office.

subroutine See *procedure*.

subscribe To select a news group so the user can regularly participate in its discussions. After subscribing to a news group in a newsreader program, the program automatically downloads an updated list of articles when it is launched.

supercomputer The largest, fastest, and most powerful type of computer. Supercomputers are often used for scientific and engineering applications and processing complex models using very large data sets.

superscalar A microprocessor architecture that allows more than one instruction to be processed in each clock cycle.

surface modeler A 3-D modeling program that depicts an object as an outer layer (a surface) stretched over a wire frame.

Super VGA (SVGA) An IBM video display standard capable of displaying resolutions up to 1024 × 768 pixels, with 16 million colors.

swap in To load essential parts of a program into memory as required for use.

swap out To unload, or remove, nonessential parts of a program from memory to make room for needed functions.

Synchronous Dynamic RAM (SDRAM) A type of RAM that delivers bursts of data at very high speeds (up to 100 MHz), providing more data to the CPU at a given time than older RAM technologies.

symmetric multiprocessing (SMP) See *parallel processing*.

syntax The precise sequence of characters required in a spreadsheet formula or in a programming language.

syntax error A bug in which the code is not entered correctly, so that the computer cannot understand its instructions.

system board See *motherboard*.

system call A feature built into an application program that requests a service from the operating system, as when a word processing program requests the use of the printer to print a document.

system clock The computer's internal clock, used to time processing operations. The clock's time intervals are based on the constant, unchanging vibrations of molecules in a quartz crystal, and currently measured in megahertz (MHz).

system manager In an information systems (IS) department, the person responsible for ensuring that a system is secure, protecting data integrity, performing routine maintenance, and recovering lost data. Also called a *network manager*.

system operator (sysop) In an online discussion group, the person who monitors the discussion.

system software A computer program that controls the system hardware and interacts with application software. The designation includes the operating system and the network operating system.

systems analyst In an information systems (IS) department, the individual who analyzes and designs software systems and provides maintenance and support functions for the users.

systems design phase Phase 2 of the systems development life cycle, in which the project team researches and develops alternative ways to meet an organization's computing needs.

systems development life cycle (SDLC) A formal methodology and process for the needs analysis, system design, development, implementation, and maintenance of a computer system.

T

T1 A communications line that represents a higher level of the ISDN standard service and supplies a bandwidth of 1.544 Mbps.

T3 A communications line capable of transmitting a total of 44.736 Mbps.

tab stop A preset position in a document to which the cursor moves when the Tab key is pressed.

table A grid of data, set up in rows and columns.

tape drive A magnetic storage device that reads and writes data to the surface of a magnetic tape. Tape drives are generally used for backing up data or restoring the data of a hard disk.

task switching The process of moving from one open window to another.

taskbar A Windows 95/98/2000/NT screen element, displayed on the desktop, which includes the Start button and lists the programs currently running on the computer.

TB See *terabyte*.

TCO See *total cost of ownership*.

TCP/IP See *Transmission Control Protocol/Internet Protocol*.

technical writer In an information systems (IS) department, the person who documents the system, from the technical details needed by system managers to the procedural instructions designed for the end users.

telecommuting Working at home or on the road and having access to a work computer via telecommunications equipment, such as modems and fax machines.

telecommuter A person who works at home or on the road and requires access to a work computer via telecommunications equipment, such as modems and fax machines.

teleconference A live, real-time communications session involving two or more people in different locations, using computers and telecommunications equipment.

Telnet An Internet service that provides a transparent window between the user's computer and a distant host system.

template A preformatted document used to quickly create a standard document, such as a memo or report.

terabyte Equivalent to one trillion bytes of data. A measure of storage capacity.

terminal An input/output device connected to a multiuser computer, such as a mainframe.

text box In word processing and desktop publishing software, a special frame that enables the user to contain text in a rectangular area. The user can size and position the text box like a frame, by dragging the box or one of its handles. Also see *frame*.

text code A standard system in which numbers represent the letters of the alphabet, punctuation marks, and other symbols. A text code enables programmers to use combinations of numbers to represent individual pieces of data. EBCDIC, ASCII, and Unicode are examples of text code systems.

text field A database field that stores a string of alphanumeric characters. Also called *alphanumeric field* or *character field*.

TFT See *thin-film transistor*.

thermal-wax printer A printer that produces high-quality images by using a heat source to evaporate colored wax from a ribbon, which adheres to the paper.

thesaurus A text editing tool that lists alternative words with similar meanings.

thin client See *network computer*.

thin wallet A type of electronic wallet, in which the information is stored on a server owned by the credit card company rather than on the user's computer.

thin-film transistor (TFT) See *active matrix LCD*.

third-generation language (3GL) A category of programming languages that supports structured programming and enables programmers to use true English-like phrasing when writing program code.

thread A series of related articles and responses about a specific subject, posted in a newsgroup.

throughput See *data-transfer rate*.

TIFF Acronym for *tagged image file format*. A graphics-file format widely used on both PCs and Macintosh computers. Commonly used when exchanging bitmap files that will be printed or edited, the TIFF format can faithfully store images that contain up to 16.7 million colors without any loss of image quality.

time field A database field that stores a time.

title bar An on-screen element displayed at the top of every window that identifies the window contents. Dragging the title bar changes the position of the window on the screen.

token In a network using ring topology, any piece of data that is being transferred across the network. Each node examines the data and passes it along until it reaches its destination.

Token Ring IBM's network protocol, based on a ring topology in which linked computers pass an electronic token containing addressing information to facilitate data transfer.

toner A substance composed of tiny particles of charged ink, used in laser printers. The ink particles stick to charged areas of a drum and are transferred to paper with pressure and heat.

toolbar In application software, an on-screen element appearing just below the menu bar. The toolbar contains multiple tools, which are graphic icons (called *buttons*) representing specific actions the user can perform. To initiate an action, the user clicks the appropriate button.

top-down design A systems design method in which the major functions or processes are developed first, followed by the details.

top-level domain See *domain*.

topology The physical layout of wires that connect the computers in a network; includes bus, star, ring, and mesh.

total cost of ownership (TCO) The total amount an organization pays to own a computer. This cost includes not only the purchase price, but expenses related to installation, configuration, maintenance, software, training, and so on.

touch screen An input/output device that accepts input directly from the monitor. The user touches words, graphical icons, or symbols displayed on screen to activate commands.

track An area used for storing data on a formatted disk. During the disk-formatting process, the operating system creates a set of magnetic concentric circles on the disk: these are the tracks. These tracks are then divided into sectors, with each sector able to hold a given amount of data. By using this system to store data, the operating system can quickly determine where data is located on the disk. Different types of disks can hold different numbers of tracks.

trackball An input device that functions like an upside-down mouse, consisting of a stationary casing containing a movable ball that is operated by hand. Trackballs are used frequently with laptop computers.

tracking The letter spacing within blocks of text. Adjusting this spacing can make text easier to read.

trackpad A stationary pointing device that the user operates by moving a finger across a small, touch-sensitive surface. Trackpads are often built into portable computers. Also called a *touchpad*.

TrackPoint See *integrated pointing device*.

tractor-feed paper See *continuous-feed paper*.

trainer In an IS department, the person responsible for teaching users how to use a new system, whether hardware, software, procedures, or a combination thereof.

transaction A series of steps required to complete an event, such as taking an order or preparing a time sheet.

transaction processing system A type of information system that handles the processing and tracking of transactions.

transistor An electronic switch within the CPU that exists in two states, conductive (on) or nonconductive (off). The resulting combinations are used to create the binary code that is the basis for machine language.

transition In a presentation program, an animation-like effect applied when switching from one slide to the next in a presentation.

Transmission Control Protocol/Internet Protocol (TCP/IP) The set of commands and timing specifications used by the Internet to connect dissimilar systems and control the flow of information.

tween Abbreviation for "in-between." In animation, tweens are the frames that depict a character's or object's motion between keyframes.

twisted-pair cable Cable used in network connections. Twisted-pair cable consists of copper strands, individually shrouded in plastic, twisted around each other in pairs and bound together in a layer of plastic insulation; also called *unshielded twisted-pair (UTP)* wire. Twisted-pair wire encased in a metal sheath is called *shielded twisted-pair (STP) wire*.

typeface See *font*.

type style An attribute applied to a text character, such as underlining, italic, and bold, among others. Most application programs provide a wide variety of type styles, which the user can freely apply to text anywhere in a document.

U

UART See *Universal Asynchronous Receiver Transmitter*.

Undo An application command that enables the user to reverse a previous action.

Unicode Worldwide Character Standard A character set that provides 16 bits to represent each symbol, resulting in 65,536 different characters or symbols, enough for all the languages of the world. The Unicode character set includes all the characters from the ASCII character set.

Uniform Resource Locator (URL) An Internet address used with HTTP in the format type://address/path.

Universal Asynchronous Receiver Transmitter (UART) A chip that converts parallel data from the bus into serial data that can flow through a serial cable, and vice versa.

Universal Serial Bus (USB) A new expansion bus technology that currently enables the user to connect 127 different devices into a single port. USB is relatively fast, supporting data-transfer rates of 12 Mbps.

UNIX A 32-bit, fully multitasking, multithreading operating system developed by Bell Labs in the 1970s. A powerful, highly scalable operating system, UNIX (and variants of it) is used to operate supercomputers, mainframes, minicomputers, and powerful PCs and workstations. UNIX generally features a command-line interface, although some variants of UNIX feature a graphical operating environment, as well.

uploading Sending a file to a remote computer. The opposite of *downloading*.

URL See *Uniform Resource Locator*.

USB See *Universal Serial Bus*.

Usenet A popular system of news groups accessible on the Internet and maintained by volunteers.

user The person who inputs and analyzes data using a computer.

user assistance architect In an information systems (IS) department, the individual who develops the organization and structure of online documentation, such as Help systems or tutorials.

user ID See *user name*.

user interface The on-screen elements that enable the user to interact with the software.

user name A code that identifies the user to the system; often the user's full name, a shortened version of the user's name, or the user's e-mail name. Also called a *user ID*.

utility A software program that may be used to enhance the functionality of an operating system. Examples of utility software are disk defragmenters and screen savers.

V

value A numerical entry in a spreadsheet—representing currency, a percentage, a date, a time, a fraction, and so on—which can be used in formulas.

variable In a program, a labeled placeholder that represents data that must be entered and processed.

vector A mathematical equation that describes the position of a line.

Veronica Acronym for *Very Easy Rodent-Oriented Net-wide Index to Computer Archives*. A keyword search tool that finds and displays items from Gopher menus.

Video Graphics Array (VGA) An IBM video display standard capable of displaying resolutions of 640 × 480, with 16 colors.

video capture card A specialized expansion board that enables the user to connect video devices—such as VCRs and camcorders—to the PC. This enables the user to transfer images from the video equipment to the PC, and vice versa. Many video cards enable the user to edit digitized video and record the edited images on videotape.

videoconference A live, real-time video communications session involving two or more people using computers, video cameras, telecommunications and videoconferencing software.

video controller A circuit board attached to the motherboard that contains the memory and other circuitry necessary to send information to the monitor for display on screen. This controller determines the refresh rate, resolution, and number of colors that can be displayed. Also called the *display adapter*.

Video for Windows An audio/visual standard developed by Microsoft as a way to store and display compressed audio and video information.

video RAM (VRAM) Memory on the video controller (sometimes called *dual-ported memory*), which can send a screen of data to the monitor while receiving the next data set.

viewing angle The widest angle from which a display monitor's image can be seen clearly. Generally speaking, cathode ray tube (CRT) monitors provide a wider viewing angle than liquid crystal display (LCD) monitors do.

virtual 8086 mode An operating mode of the Intel 80386 processor, which enables the processor to emulate 16 separate 8086 processors, with each one running a separate copy of the operating system. This feature enabled *multitasking*, or the ability to run different programs at the same time.

virtual reality (VR) A computer navigation tool that projects the user into three-dimensional space using special devices designed to simulate movement and spatial dimension.

Virtual Reality Modeling Language (VRML) A special programming language that enables designers to create 3-D virtual environments (such as furnished rooms, shopping centers, and so on) for use in World Wide Web pages. Users with VRML-enabled browsers can navigate through these environments with a great deal of freedom, entering and exiting rooms, interacting with objects, looking through windows, and so on.

virtual university Web sites that offer courses of college credit online.

virus A parasitic program that infects another, legitimate program, which is sometimes called the *host*. To infect the host program, the virus modifies the host so that it contains a copy of the virus.

virus definition A database of information about specific viruses, which enables an antivirus program to detect and eradicate viruses. Also called a *virus pattern*.

voice recognition See *speech recognition*.

volatile The tendency for memory to lose data when the computer is turned off, as is the case with RAM.

VRAM See *video RAM*.

VRML See *Virtual Reality Modeling Language*.

W

walk-through A specially rendered animation, created in a CAD or 3-D graphics program, which creates the illusion that the viewer is moving through an object, such as a building.

WAN See *wide area network*.

Warez An Internet newsgroup where users share pirated copies of software.

Web browser A program that enables the user to view Web pages, navigate Web sites, and move from one Web site to another.

Web master A person or group responsible for designing and maintaining a Web site.

Web page A document developed using HTTP and found on the World Wide Web. Web pages contain information about a particular subject with links to related Web pages and other resources.

Web server An Internet host computer that may store thousands of Web sites.

Web site A collection of related Web pages.

what-if analysis A data analysis process used to test how alternative scenarios affect numeric results.

wide area network (WAN) A computer network that spans a wide geographical area.

window An area on the computer screen in which an application or document is viewed and accessed.

Windows A family of operating system products developed and produced by Microsoft Corp. The vast majority of personal computers run Windows, whose versions include Windows 3.*x*, 95, 98, NT, and 2000. Windows versions 3.*x* and earlier were actually operating environments—graphical interfaces that ran on top of the DOS operating system. In versions 95 and later, Windows is a full-fledged operating system.

Windows 2000 An operating system that provides the file system, networking, power, and stability of Windows NT with the user-friendly interface and features of Windows 98.

Windows 3.*x* A term used to refer to the Windows 3.0, 3.1, and 3.11 family.

Windows 95 A 32-bit operating system developed by Microsoft and released in 1995. Windows 95 features preemptive multitasking, plug and play capabilities, built-in networking, and the ability to access 16- and 32-bit applications.

Windows 98 An upgrade to Windows 95, Windows 98 includes a number of enhancements, including a built-in Web browser and Internet-related tools, online upgradability, and other features.

Windows NT A 32-bit operating system developed by Microsoft and released in 1993; designed for powerful workstations and restricted to running 32-bit applications; supports peer-to-peer networking, preemptive multitasking, and multiprocessing. The NT stands for "new technology."

Windows NT Server Version of Windows NT incorporating all of the features of Windows NT Workstation with additional functions to support network servers.

Windows NT Workstation A version of Windows NT designed to look like consumer versions of Windows with an underlying OS almost completely different. Windows NT Workstation runs a wide variety of CPUs, is designed for a stand-alone PC, has good security features, and is more fault-tolerant than other Microsoft operating systems.

Winsock *Windows Sockets*, a standard network interface that makes it possible to mix and match application programs from more than one developer to communicate across the Internet.

wireframe model A CAD tool that represents 3-D shapes by displaying their outlines and edges.

wireless communication Communication via computers that relies on infrared signals, microwaves, or radio waves to transmit data.

word processing software Software used to create and edit text documents such as letters, memos, reports, and publications. Also called a *word processor*.

word size The size of the registers in the CPU, which determines the amount of data the computer can work with at any given time. Larger word sizes lead to faster processing; common word sizes include 16 bits, 32 bits, and 64 bits.

word wrap A word processing feature that computes the length of each line of text as the text is entered.

workbook A data file created with spreadsheet software, containing multiple worksheets.

worksheet The data file created with spreadsheet software.

workstation A fast, powerful microcomputer used for scientific applications, graphics, CAD, CAE, and other complex applications. Workstations are usually based on RISC technology and operated by some version of UNIX, although an increasing number of Intel/Windows NT-based workstations are coming into popular use.

World Wide Web (the Web or WWW) An Internet service developed to incorporate footnotes, figures, and cross-references into online hypertext documents.

WYSIWYG Acronym for *What You See Is What You Get*. A display mode that shows a document as it will appear when printed.

X, Y, Z

Xbase A generic database language used to construct queries. Xbase is similar to SQL, but more complex because its commands cover the full range of database activities beyond querying.

Xeon An enhanced version of Intel's Pentium II and Pentium III processors. Xeon processors feature enhanced multiprocessing capabilities, and are designed for use in high-power workstations and network servers.

INDEX

infected with viruses, 539
operating system management of, 195–196
programs as, 487
transferring, 320–321
types of, for programs, 488
film. *See* movies
filmmakers, 410
filter keys, 52
filters (in database management systems), 280–282
financial planners, 233
financial software, 250, 430
firewalls, 368
FireWire (IEEE 1394) bus, 118, 122
flaming, 361
flash memory, 114
flat-file databases, 275
flat-panel monitors (displays), 74, 76–77
CRT monitors versus, 81
floppy disks. *See* diskettes
flowcharts, 491–492
fly-bys, 404
folders (directories), 154, 196
fonts, 229
footers, in documents, 232
for loops, 497
formatting (initializing) magnetic disks, 151
logical (low-level), 153
when changing operating systems, 209
formatting slides, 262–263
formatting text, 252
character formats, 229–230
document formats, 232
HTML formatting, 237, 238
paragraph formats, 230–231
in slides, 262–263
formatting worksheets, 246–248
forms, 280
formula bars, 241
formulas, in worksheets, 244–245
FORTRAN (language), 509
four-color printing, 91
fourth-generation languages (4GLs), 511–513
fragmentation of files, 154
frames
in animation, 402
keyframes, 405
in slides, 261, 263
freeware, 537
frequently asked questions (FAQs), 199, 355, 478
front ends, 511–512
FTP (file transfer protocol), 321, 356–357
FTP client software, 356
FTP servers, 356
full-duplex communications, 321
function keys, 44, 47
functions
in programs, 499–500
in worksheets, 245

G

G3 Motorola processors, 136
G4 Motorola processors, 136
game controllers, 56–58
game designers, 57, 96, 410
game pads, 58
games
computer graphics in, 406
home-based networks for, 328
multimedia used for, 430
programmers for, 516
gas plasma displays, 78
gateways (for networks), 304, 341, 364
GIF file format, 409
goto statements, in programs, 501
gradient fills, 263
grammar checkers, 234
graphic artists, 57, 192
graphical user interfaces (GUIs), 186
command-line interfaces compared with, 191
desktop in, 187
dialog boxes in, 190
for Linux, 213
Macintosh operating system as, 206–207
menus in, 190
OS/2 Warp as, 208
running programs in windows in, 188–189
taskbar and start button in, 187–188
for UNIX, 204
Web browsers as, 347
Windows 3.*x* operating environments as, 207
graphics, 383
adding to documents, 235
careers in, 410
charts, generated by spreadsheet software, 248
computer platforms used for, 384–385
copyright issues in, 391
desktop publishing software controls for, 236
digital photography, 390
dye-sub printers for, 94
file types for, 386–389
image scanners for, 59
inputting images, 389–391
Internet piracy of, 392
IRIS printers for, 95
laser printing of, 92
World Wide Web and, 406–409
graphics software, 383, 394
3-D modeling programs, 401–402
for animation, 402–406
Computer-Aided Design (CAD) programs, 399–401
draw programs, 398
paint programs, 395–396
photo-manipulation programs, 396–397
presentation programs, 259–268
grayscale monitors, 75
grocery store managers, 18
groupware, 300

H

hackers, 543–544
half-duplex communications, 321
hand input devices, 55–58
game controllers, 56–58
mouse devices, 48–50, 64
pens, 55
pointers, 51
touch screens, 8, 55–56
trackballs, 50–51
handheld personal computers (H/PCs), 30, 32
hard disks (hard drives), 9, 157–159
backing up data on, 162
data compression utilities for, 172–173
data transfer rates on, 173
diskettes distinguished from, 151
formatting (initializing) of, 151
removable high-capacity magnetic disks, 159–161
tape drives for backing up, 161
hardware, 4
accessibility features for, 52
commands built into, 487
I/O (input/output) devices, 7–8
interactions between software and, 489–491
Linux support for, 216
magnetic storage devices, 148–161
memory, 6–7
modems, 318–321, 365
monitors, 74–81
for multimedia, 425–427
for networks, 310–313, 332–333
operating system management of, 196–198
optical storage devices, 163–167
PC projectors, 83
planned obsolescence of, 544
printers, 87–96
processors, 5–6
scanners, 389
shared over networks, 300–301
storage, 8–10
storage devices, 147, 178
theft of, 543–544
video controllers, 82–83
for virtual reality, 431
hardware configuration personnel, 135
hardware locks (dongles), 538
hardware maintenance technicians, 468, 469
hardware technicians, 192
Hayes Microcomputers Products, Inc., 318
HDTV (high definition television), 269
head crashes, 159
headers, in documents, 232
health issues, 526–528
electromagnetic fields, 528
eyestrain, 527
repetitive stress injuries, 526–527
help desk operators, 168, 288
help facilities, 199
online help systems, 478
help (.hlp) files, 488
Hertz (Hz), 116

structure of, 342–345
TCP/IP protocol for, 304
Telnet connections on, 355–356
UNIX operating system for, 204
Windows 98 and, 212
working on, 368–371
World Wide Web on, 345–352
See also World Wide Web
Internet Assigned Numbers Authority (IANA), 344
Internet Explorer (Web browser, Microsoft), 212, 347
Internet protocol addresses (IP addresses), 344
Internet relay chat (IRC), 357–358, 369
Internet service providers (ISPs), 345
appropriate-use policies of, 361, 531
free personal Web pages offered by, 369
Linux used by, 214
online services as, 358
Internet Society, 341, 344
internetworking, 340
interpreters, 491
interrupt requests (IRQs), 46, 48, 197
interrupts, 489
intranets, 370
Iomega Corporation, 160
IP addresses (Internet protocol addresses), 344
iPic (tiny computer), 25
IPX/SPX protocol, 304
IRC (Internet relay chat), 357–358, 369
IRIS printers, 95
ISA (Industry Standard Architecture) buses, 118
ISDN (integrated services digital network) telephone lines, 323, 365

J

Java (language), 510, 511, 514
joke programs, 541
journalists, 233
joysticks, 8
JPEG compression, 388, 440
junk e-mail and faxes, 530–532

K

K6 AMD processors, 133
kerning type, 236
keyboard buffers, 46, 48
keyboard controllers, 46
keyboard shortcuts, 47
keyboarding (typing), 42
carpal tunnel syndrome caused by, 526
health tips for, 529
keyboards, 8, 42, 66
accessibility features of, 52
ergonomic and specialty, 46
input sent to computer from, 46–48
repetitive stress injuries and, 526–527
standard layout of, 42–45

keyframes, 405
Khwarizmi, al-, 492
knowledge workers, 462
knowledge-based systems, 504
knowledgebases, 199, 461, 478

L

labels, in worksheets, 243, 248
lands (on CD-ROM disks), 164
landscape orientation, 232
languages. *See* programming languages
LANs (local area networks), 303–304
Internet connections through, 364–365
topologies for, 308–310
laptop (notebook) computers, 28, 32
flat-panel monitors for, 76–77
PC Cards (PCMCIA cards) for, 126
laser printers, 88, 91–92
law enforcement professionals, 546
layers, 400
information in, 423–425
LCDs (liquid crystal displays), 76–77
letters. *See* characters
Level-1 (L1) cache, 119
Level-2 (L2) cache, 119
LEXIS-NEXIS, 358
libel, 371
line printers, 90
Linux (operating system), 213–214, 216, 314
liquid crystal displays (LCDs), 76–77
listservs (list servers), 353–354
local area networks (LANs), 303–304
Internet connections through, 364–365
topologies for, 308–310
local buses, 118
logic errors, 515
logical (Boolean) fields, 279
logical (low-level; soft) formatting of disks, 153
logical operations, 111
loops, in programs, 497–498
Lotus SmartSuite, 359
LotusScript (macro language), 247
low-level (logical; soft) formatting of disks, 153

M

MII Cyrix processors, 134
machine code (machine language), 490, 507, 508
machine cycles, 112
Macintosh computers. *See* Apple Macintosh computers
Macintosh operating system, 206–207
MacPaint (program), 384
macro viruses, 539–541
Macromedia, Inc., 350
Shockwave by, 409, 437, 442
macros, 247

magnetic disks, 9, 149–151
average access time for, 171
data found by operating systems on, 153–154
diskettes (floppy disks), 154–157
hard disks, 157–159
organization of data of, 151–153
removable high-capacity magnetic disks, 159–161
magnetic media. *See* magnetic disks
magnetic storage devices, 148–149, 178
diskettes (floppy disks), 154–157
hard disks, 157–159
magnetic disks, 149–154
removable high-capacity magnetic disks, 159–161
tape drives, 161
mail merge feature, 234
mail server, 353
mainframe computers, 21–23
personal computers compared with, 26
maintenance phase of systems development life cycle, 477, 515
management information systems (MISs) departments, 459–460, 463
margins, 230–231
marketing professionals, 96
masks (in data entry forms), 280
massively parallel processors (MPP), 137, 174
master boot record, 153
master pages, 236
Matrix, The (film), 424
maximum access time (seek time), 155
McKinley Intel processors, 138
media, 420
See also multimedia
MediaGX Cyrix processors, 134
medical researchers, 546
megahertz (MHz), 116
member functions, 503
memo fields, 279
memory, 6–7
cache memory, 119
in laser printers, 92
processing speed and, 114–115
read-only memory (ROM), 12
storage distinguished from, 9
types of, 112–114
memory addresses, 113
address buses for, 117
menu bars, 190
menus, 190
Merced Intel processors, 138
mesh network topology, 310
messages, in programs, 503
microcode, 110
microcomputers, 26–27
miniaturized, 25
types of, 27–31
microphones, 8, 60–61
microprocessors, 5–6, 130
Microsoft Certification, 305

All Table of Contents and lesson opener illustrations created by Tom White.

Abbreviation Key: IBM = Courtesy International Business Machines Corporation. Unauthorized use not permitted.

Feature Article Headers: *Computers in Your Career* Comstock; *Productivity Tip* PhotoDisc; *Techview* Richard Laird/FPG.

Cover: Guy Crittenden; **iv** Aaron Haupt; **v** (tl)Aaron Haupt, (tc)J. Arbogast/SuperStock, (tr)Dan Abrams, (cl)SuperStock, (c)US Department of Defense Camera Combat Center, (cr)Dan Nelken/Liaison Agency, (bl)Liaison Agency, (br)NASA/Roger Ressmeyer/CORBIS; **xxiii xxiv** Aaron Haupt; **xxvi** Amanita Pictures; **5 6 7** Kreber Studios; **8** IBM; **9** Amanita Pictures; **10** Tom McCarthy/SKA; **11** (l r)Mark Burnett, (c)Gary Gladstone/The Image Bank; **13** Henry Sims/The Image Bank; **18** Joe Baraban/The Stock Market; **21** SGI; **22** IBM; **23** Hewlett Packard; **24** Sun Microsystems; **25** H. Shrikumar; **26** Aaron Haupt; **27** IBM; **28** (t)Sony, (b)Compaq; **29** Amanita Pictures; **30** Sun Microsystems; **31** (t)Hewlett Packard, (b)Nokia; **32** Mark Romanelli/The Image Bank; **34** Kreber Studios; **35** (t)SGI, (c)IBM, (bl)Sun Microsystems, (br)Aaron Haupt; **44 45** Aaron Haupt; **46** Amanita Pictures; **48** IBM; **50** Aaron Haupt; **51** (t)Logitech, (c)Compaq, (b)IBM; **55** (t)Aaron Haupt, (b)United Parcel Service; **56** Bob Daemmrich/The Image Works, (b)Jose L. Peleaz/The Stock Market; **57** (b)Telegraph Color Library/FPG; **58** (t)IBM, (b)Federal Express; **60** (t)Jon Feingersh/The Stock Market, (b)The Stock Market; **61** Mark Burnett; **62** B. Busco/The Image Bank; **63** Sony; **64** The Bootstrap Institute; **66** Aaron Haupt; **67** (t)Aaron Haupt, (c)Federal Express, (bl)The Stock Market, (br)B. Busco/The Image Bank; **74** (l)SGI, (r)IBM; **76 77** IBM; **78** Applied Optical Company; **81** (l)Compaq, (r)SGI; **83** Mark Burnett; **84** Kreber Studios; **88** (l)Amanita Pictures, (r)Hewlett Packard; **90** IBM; **91 92** Hewlett Packard; **93** SuperStock; **94 95** Hewlett Packard; **96** Kreber Studios; **98** (tl)IBM, (tr)SGI, (c)Mark Burnett, (b)Amanita Pictures; **99** Hewlett Packard; **113** ©Kingston Technology Company. All rights reserved; **116** Newer Technology; **120** Aaron Haupt; **123 124** Mark Burnett; **125** (tr)Aaron Haupt, (others)Mark Burnett **126** 3Com; **127** Dan Nelken/Liaison Agency; **130 131 132** Intel Corporation; **133** (t)Intel Corporation, (others)Advanced Micro Devices; **134** Cyrix; **136** Aaron Haupt; **137** Compaq; **141** (t)Mark Burnett, (c)Intel Corporation, (b)Cyrix; **144** Mark Burnett; **150** (tl)Amanita Pictures, (tr)Mark Burnett, (cl)IBM, (c)Aaron Haupt, (cr)Hewlett Packard, (bl)Seagate Technology, (br)Sony; **160** Sony; **161** (t)Iomega, (b)Sony; **165** Mark Burnett; **166** (t)Amanita Pictures, (bl)Sony, (br)Mark Burnett; **167** (t)Mark Burnett, (b)IBM; **168** Mark Burnett; **175** Sun Microsystems; **176** Compaq; **179** (t)Mark Burnett, (c)Aaron Haupt, (b)Sony; **192** Sun Microsystems; **233** Richard Price/FPG; **265** Everybook; **268** Telegraph Color Library/FPG; **269** Mark Burnett; **288** Charles Gupton/The Stock Market; **290** Mark Burnett; **298** Chuck Keeler/Stone; **310** Tom McCarthy/SKA; **311** (t)Property of AT&T Archives. Reprinted with permission of AT&T, (b)D. Sarraute/The Image Bank; **315** CORBIS; **320** Diamond Multimedia Systems, (b)Doug Martin; **321** Hewlett Packard; **324** IBM; **329** Intel Corporation; **330** Kreber Studios; **333** Diamond Multimedia Systems; **339** Glencoe photo; **365** 3Com; **367** Courtesy Motorola; **374** Kreber Studios; **384** Mark Burnett; **385** (tl)Universal photo/MPTV, (tc)1998 Touchstone/MPTV, (tr)1997 Disney/MPTV, (others)Larry Hamill; **387** Walt Disney/Kobel; **389** Amanita Pictures; **390** Hewlett Packard; **391** Courtesy Noritsu Koki, Ltd.; **396** (tl)Fractal, (tr)Corel, (b)Larry Hamill; **397** Glencoe photo;

404 (t)1997 Universal photo by David James/MPTV, (others)Glencoe photo; **406** (l)Larry Hamill, (r)2000 Touchstone, photo by Rob McEwan/MPTV; **410** Mark Burnett; **412** (t)Mark Burnett, (b)Amanita Pictures; **413** Larry Hamill; **420** Aaron Haupt; **421** (l)Aaron Haupt, (r)LWA/The Stock Market; **427** Kreber Studios; **431** Used with permission from n-vision, inc; **435** Larry Hamill; **438** Charles Gupton/The Stock Market; **439** Adamsmith Productions/CORBIS; **443** Amanita Pictures; **445 446** Mark Burnett; **448** Kreber Studios; **456** Michael S. Yamashita/CORBIS; **464** (l)Sun Microsystems, (r)Aaron Haupt; **465** Sun Microsystems; **467** SuperStock; **468** Mark Burnett; **469** Lee White/CORBIS; **475** Amanita Pictures; **480** Aaron Haupt; **488** Amanita Pictures; **492 516** Aaron Haupt; **526** BodyBilt Seating; **527** (t)Aaron Haupt, (c)Doug Martin, (b)Fellowes; **530** Amanita Pictures; **532** Kit Kittle/CORBIS; **543** Kensington Microware; **546** Roger Tully/Stone; **548** (t)BodyBilt Seating, (b)Amanita Pictures; **549** Kensington Microware; **554** (t)Intel Corporation, (others)The Computer Museum, Boston; **555** (tl)Datapoint Corporation, (tr)Apple Corporation, (c br)Intel Corporation, (bl)VisiCalc; **556** (tl)Microsoft Corporation, (tc)used with permission of Lotus Development Corporation, (tr)Bell Laboratories, (cl)IBM, (cr)Apple Corporation, (bl)Hewlett Packard, (br)Intel Corporation; **557** (t)Compaq, (cl)Apple Corporation, (cr)IBM, (bl)Microsoft Corporation, (lc)Intel Corporation, (rc)Adobe, (br)Hewlett Packard; **558** (tl)IBM, (tr)PhotoDisc, all rights reserved, (cl)IBM, (cr)Apple Corporation, (bl)Shahn Kermani/Liaison Agency, (br)courtesy Motorola; **559** (tl)Intel Corporation, (tr)Donna Coveny/MIT News Office, (c)IBM, (b)Apple Corporation; **560** (tl)Microsoft Corporation, (tr)IBM, (cl)Intel Corporation, (cr)courtesy Motorola, (b)Apple Corporation; **561** (tl)Microsoft Corporation, (tc)Intel Corporation, (tr)courtesy Motorola, (c)Power Computing, (b)Amanita Pictures; **562** (t)Intel Corporation, (cr bl)Amanita Pictures, (br)Aaron Haupt; **563** (tl)Intel Corporation, (tr)Aaron Haupt, (c)Amanita Pictures, (b)Advanced Micro Devices.

Abbreviation Key: AV = Reproduced with the permission of AltaVista. Alta Vista and the AltaVista logo are trademarks of AltaVista Company. **COREL** = Screen shots are copyright ©Corel Corporation and Corel Corporation Limited. All rights reserved. Corel, WordPerfect, Quattro, Presentations, and Paradox are trademarks or registered trademarks of Corel Corporation or Corel Corporation Limited. Reprinted by permission. **IBM** = Courtesy International Business Machines Corporation. Unauthorized use not permitted. **LOTUS** = Screen Captures ©2001 Lotus Development Corporation. Used with permission of Lotus Development Corporation. **MS** = Screen shot reprinted by permission from Microsoft Corporation. **NET** = Netscape Communicator browser window ©1999 Netscape Communications Corporation. Used with permission. **REAL** = ©RealNetworks and/or its licensors, 1995–1999, All rights reserved. RealNetworks, RealAudio, RealPlayer, WebActive, and the RN logo are registered trademarks of RealNetworks.

Cover Guy Crittenden; **xxiv** MS; **xxvii** (t)MS, (c b)NET; **xxviii** (t)MS & ©2000 USA TODAY, a division of Gannett Co., (b)NET & ©2000 sgi; **xxix xxx** NET; **15** (t)COREL, (c)LOTUS, (b)MS; **16** (t)©2000 Adobe, (b)MS; **17** (t)NET, (b)REAL; **38** MS; **39** NET & AV; **45** ©200_ Adobe; **47** MS; **52** NET; **61 70** MS; **71** NET & ©2000 footmouse.c_ All rights reserved; **74** (t)MS, (b)MS & ©2000 Cartoon Netw_ A Time Warner Company. All rights reserved; **85** REAL; **102_ 103** NET & ©1999 NEC Technologies. All rights reserved; **145** (t)MS & ©1991–2000 Unicode. All rights reserved, (_